A DICTIONARY OF CANADIAN ECONOMICS

A DICTIONARY OF CANADIAN ECONOMICS

David Crane

Hurtig Publishers
Edmonton

Hurtig Publishers
10560-105 Street
Edmonton, Alberta

Canadian Cataloguing in Publication Data

Crane, David.
A dictionary of Canadian economics

ISBN 0-88830-173-1 paper
ISBN 0-88830-174-X cloth

1. Economics — Dictionaries. 2. Canada — Economic conditions — 1945- — Dictionaries. I. Title

HC112.C73 330'.03 C79-091195-7

Design/David Shaw
Cover/Jacket/Michael van Elsen

Printed and bound in Canada by
D.W. Friesen & Sons Ltd.

Preface

This dictionary is quite straightforward in purpose. It has been written to answer a clear need, to provide Canadians with a convenient source of information about our own economic institutions, about traditional economic and business terms, and about the ideas of major economists and schools of economic thought.

There are many dictionaries of economics already available in our bookstores. Unfortunately, none of them deals with Canadian terms and institutions; nor has any of our economists found the time to write such a dictionary. Yet it is surely frustrating for a student or an ordinary citizen to have to rely on dictionaries that talk about the U.S. Federal Reserve and the British Treasury instead of our own Bank of Canada and Department of Finance, to read about U.S. farm policy or British securities laws instead of Canadian farm marketing boards or the Toronto Stock Exchange. And while it is interesting to know how fiscal policy works in the United States or how monetary policy is implemented in Britain, it is more useful for Canadians to know how these policies operate in their own country.

This dictionary has not been written for experts. It is intended to help the interested non-expert who wants to understand what is going on in the news or who is puzzled by a reference in a school book or a magazine article. It should serve as a handy reference rather than as a definitive textbook; however, it should also tell the reader enough so that he or she will have a basic idea of the subject and will perhaps even be spurred on to dig further.

In preparing this dictionary I have concentrated on certain key areas. These include: traditional economic and business terms; common words found in labour relations, agriculture, the manufacturing and service industries, banking and investment, telecommunications, and resources; words used in public finance and economic policy-making; Canada's principal financial and economic institutions, and constitutional arrangements; leading economists and economic schools of thought; international economic institutions and terms, especially those that are relevant to Canada; the findings of major royal commissions; some basic references to Canadian economic history; and terms relating to Canadian-American economic relations and foreign direct investment in Canada. Wherever possible, I have tried to put the terms in the dictionary in a Canadian context.

To help readers to use the dictionary, I have included cross-references to related words or terms that should yield additional information; these references appear within the entries in small-capital letters.

No doubt someone is going to find a word that he or she considers critical to be missing from this dictionary; for that, I can only apologize in advance. With the best will in the world it is still possible to leave out something important. Moreover, some people are undoubtedly going to differ with the definitions of particular words; in reply, all I can say is that a dictionary is not intended to be a restrictive work that presumes to outlaw other ways of defining the same word. A dictionary is simply a tool to help people. Feedback and comments from readers would be welcomed.

This dictionary could not have been written without help from countless people, including *The Toronto Star*'s hardworking librarians. I am grateful to all of them for their help, but I take full responsibility for all errors and omissions. I am also grateful to *The Toronto Star* for bearing with me while I worked on the book. Four individuals deserve special mention as well. The first is Sigrid McFarland, my tireless and always cheerful secretary, who was enormously helpful in getting the dictionary organized and ready for my publisher. Mel Hurtig, in turn, patiently accepted delays in completing the book, while my editor, Susan Kent, did much to improve its readability and accuracy. And particular credit must go to Françoise Hébert, who not only put up with a grumpy, neophyte author, but also helped to research and write the dictionary. Without her encouragement, it could not have been written.

DAVID CRANE

Toronto
November 1979

Abbreviations

ADC Atlantic Development Council
AEC Alberta Energy Company
AECB Atomic Energy Control Board
AECL Atomic Energy of Canada Limited
AFL-CIO American Federation of Labor–Congress of Industrial Organizations
AIB Anti-Inflation Board
APEC Atlantic Provinces Economic Council
ARDA Agricultural Rehabilitation and Development Act
ASE Alberta Stock Exchange

BIS Bank for International Settlements
BNA Act British North America Act

CA chartered accountant
CAC Consumers' Association of Canada
CACM Central American Common Market
CALURA Corporations and Labour Unions Returns Act
CAP Canada Assistance Plan
CARC Canadian Arctic Resources Committee
CBA Canadian Bankers' Association
CCA Consumer and Corporate Affairs, Department of
CCU Confederation of Canadian Unions
CD certificate of deposit
CDC Canada Development Corporation
CDIC Canada Deposit Insurance Corporation
CEIC Canada Employment and Immigration Commission
CEO chief executive officer
CFA Canadian Federation of Agriculture
CGA certified general accountant
CIC Committee for an Independent Canada
CIDA Canadian International Development Agency
CIEC Conference on International Economic Co-operation
CIEP Canadian Institute for Economic Policy
CIPEC International Council of Copper Exporting Countries
CLC Canadian Labour Congress
CLRB Canada Labour Relations Board
CMA Canadian Manufacturers' Association
CMHC Canada Mortgage and Housing Corporation
CNTU Confederation of National Trade Unions
COCOM Co-ordinating Committee
COMECON Council for Mutual Economic Assistance
CPA Canadian Petroleum Association
CPI consumer price index
CPM critical-path method
CPP Canada Pension Plan
CRTC Canadian Radio-television and Telecommunications Commission
CSA Canadian Standards Association
CSB Canada Savings Bond
CSI Canadian Securities Institute
CTC Canadian Transport Commission
CWB Canadian Wheat Board

DAC Development Assistance Committee
DOC Communications, Department of
DPW Public Works, Department of
DRB Defence Research Board
DREE Regional Economic Expansion, Department of

ECC Economic Council of Canada
ECU European Currency Unit
EDC Export Development Corporation
EEC European Economic Community
EMR Energy, Mines and Resources, Department of
EMS European Monetary System

FAO Food and Agriculture Organization
FBDB Federal Business Development Bank
FCC Farm Credit Corporation
FDI foreign direct investment
FIFO first in, first out
FIRA Foreign Investment Review Agency
FRED Fund for Rural Economic Development

G-10 Group of Ten
GATT General Agreement on Tariffs and Trade
GDP gross domestic product

GNE gross national expenditure
GNP gross national product
GPP gross provincial product

HRI Howe Research Institute

IAEA International Atomic Energy Agency
IBRD International Bank for Reconstruction and Development
ICAO International Civil Aviation Organization
ICFTU International Confederation of Free Trade Unions
IDA International Development Association
IDA Investment Dealers Association
IDRC International Development Research Centre
IEA International Energy Agency
IFC International Finance Corporation
IJC International Joint Commission
ILO International Labour Organization
IMF International Monetary Fund
ITC Industry, Trade and Commerce, Department of
ITU International Telecommunications Union
IWC International Wheat Council

LAFTA Latin American Free Trade Association
LDC less-developed country
LIBOR London inter-bank offer rate
LIFO last in, first out
LME London Metal Exchange

MBA Master of Business Administration
MEC Maritime Energy Corporation
MFN most-favoured nation
MLS multiple-listing service
MOSST Science and Technology, Ministry of State for
MOT Transport, Ministry of
MSE Montreal Stock Exchange

NAFO Northwest Atlantic Fisheries Organization
NATO North Atlantic Treaty Organization
NCI National Commission on Inflation
NEB National Energy Board
NFU National Farmers Union
NHA National Housing Act
NHB National Harbours Board
NIC newly industrialized country
NIEO new international economic order
NRC National Research Council
NSF not sufficient funds
NTB non-tariff barrier
NYSE New York Stock Exchange

OAPEC Organization of Arab Petroleum Exporting Countries
ODA official development assistance
OEC Ontario Economic Council
OECD Organization for Economic Co-operation and Development
OMB Ontario Municipal Board
OPEC Organization of Petroleum Exporting Countries
OSC Ontario Securities Commission
OTC over the counter

P/E ratio price-earnings ratio
PCO Privy Council Office
PERT program-evaluation and -review technique
PFRA Prairie Farm Rehabilitation Administration
PIC Prices and Incomes Commission
PMO Prime Minister's Office
PPBS planning-programming-budgeting system
PQLI physical quality-of-life index
PSC Public Service Commission

QPP Quebec Pension Plan

REIT real-estate investment trust
RHSOP registered home-ownership savings plan
RIA registered industrial accountant
RRSP registered retirement savings plan

SDR Special Drawing Rights
SIN social-insurance number

TCTS TransCanada Telephone System
TSE Toronto Stock Exchange

UIC Unemployment Insurance Commission
UNCLOS United Nations Conference on the Law of the Sea

UNCTAD United Nations Conference on Trade and Development
UNDP United Nations Development Program
UNEP United Nations Environment Program
UNRRA United Nations Relief and Rehabilitation Administration
UPU Universal Postal Union

VAT value-added tax
VSE Vancouver Stock Exchange

WCE Winnipeg Commodity Exchange
WEOC Western Economic Opportunities Conference
WFC World Food Council
WHO World Health Organization
WIPO World Intellectual Property Organization
WP-3 Working Party Three

ZBBS zero-base budgeting system
ZPG zero population growth

A DICTIONARY OF CANADIAN ECONOMICS

ability-to-pay principle of taxation The principle that taxes collected from individual taxpayers should be related to their actual wealth and income, and hence their ability to pay after meeting the basic cost of supporting themselves and their families. This is the tax philosophy of most modern countries, including Canada. It assumes that one of the roles of the tax system is to redistribute income by making those with more income or wealth pay a proportionately greater share of the costs of government. Hence, INCOME-TAX rates rise in line with income. This was the philosophy of the Carter Commission, or ROYAL COMMISSION ON TAXATION, which re-examined Canada's entire tax system in the mid-1960s. "Taxes are equitable when they are levied according to a defined tax capacity, or ability to pay, of individuals or groups," the commission said. See also BENEFITS-RECEIVED PRINCIPLE OF TAXATION.

absenteeism Improper absence from work by an employee. The employee's absence is not due to a labour dispute, holiday, illness, family death, or any other legitimate cause; it may simply be due to a desire to take a long weekend, or to spend a workday shopping or visiting friends. Absenteeism so defined can be a cause for dismissal from employment.

absolute advantage The ability of a country or firm to set the price of a particular good or service without fear of competition, because it possesses a unique resource or technology. See also COMPARATIVE ADVANTAGE.

abstinence from consumption The decision by an individual to save instead of spend. The saver foregoes consumption now in order to enjoy greater consumption in the future, made possible by the interest or capital gain resulting from his saving and investment of money.

accelerated depreciation A tax incentive to encourage business investment. Such an incentive, which is for a limited period, allows a business to depreciate a new investment against its tax liabilities at a faster rate than normal, although it does not permit a larger amount of depreciation over the life of the asset. By deducting larger amounts of depreciation in the early years of the asset, a business reduces its immediate tax liabilities and, in effect, gets an interest-free loan. This incentive has been used a number of times by the federal government—in the 1963, 1965, 1972, and 1973 budgets, for example.

accelerator principle The process by which changes in consumer demand cause accentuated changes in the rate of capital investment by business in new productive facilities. These changes in investment spending, working through the MULTIPLIER, in turn affect the rate of change in total income in the economy.

The accelerator helps to explain the BUSINESS CYCLE, and is a factor in assessments of the outlook for the economy. For example, as the level of output rises during the recovery period of the cycle and business approaches the limits of its capacity to produce goods, further small increases in demand will generate significant new spending on plant, machinery, and equipment, so that business can meet rising demand. This additional capital spending will, through the multiplier, add to total income and thus to the rising level of consumer demand. Similarly, as consumer spending levels off and even stops growing, business will cease to add to its productive capacity. The absence of new capital spending, again working through the multiplier, will slow the economy down further by reducing the demand for machinery and equipment and new factories. Hence, a recession may occur even though consumer demand remains high, because the economy has less business investment. At some point, though, the productive capacity of business will decline as machinery is removed from production through wear and tear, to the point where companies must begin to replace their machinery and equipment. When this happens, the economy begins to recover from the recession. As investment rises, the multiplier effect helps to boost consumer demand, thus generating new growth and the need for even greater capital investment. The accelerator, then, reinforces economic growth as the business cycle moves from the recession through recovery, but has the opposite effect during the downswing into recession.

acceptance company A SALES-FINANCE COMPANY.

acceptance paper Promissory notes issued by SALES-FINANCE COMPANIES, in denominations ranging from five thousand to five million dollars, to cover their financing of consumer and other credit services. The big automobile companies, for example, operate acceptance companies to finance car purchases by consumers through their franchised dealers, and raise part of their financial needs through the sale of acceptance paper on the MONEY MARKET.

account **1.** In bookkeeping, the record of expenses on the left side of the ledger and of income or revenue on the right side. **2.** In banks, credit unions, caisses populaires, and trust companies, the record of deposits and withdrawals of a customer. **3.** In a department store or other sales organization, a statement of purchases and payments. **4.** In advertising, the term used to describe the ongoing work for a client's particular product or service.

accountant Person who carries out bookkeeping, auditing, and other financial reporting and analysis. This is a generic term referring to a wide range of skills, from semi-clerical to highly trained professional work. See also AUDITOR, CERTIFIED GENERAL ACCOUNTANT, CHARTERED ACCOUNTANT, and REGISTERED INDUSTRIAL ACCOUNTANT.

accounting The profession of preparing and auditing reports on financial transactions of firms, government agencies, charitable institutions, and other organizations.

accounting period The fiscal year of a corporation or other organization; or the period between the dates of two consecutive financial reports, as in a quarterly report.

accounts payable The outstanding bills of a firm; money that a firm owes to its suppliers for goods and services purchased for the normal operations of the business. Accounts payable are included on the balance sheet under CURRENT LIABILITIES.

accounts receivable The money that is owed to a firm by its customers for goods or services they have purchased from it. Accounts receivable are included on the balance sheet under CURRENT ASSETS.

accrual-basis accounting The standard method of business accounting, with revenues and expenses recorded at the time that transactions occur, rather than when payment is actually received or made. Thus, in a company annual report, the net earnings shown represent the profit or loss on the transactions that occurred during the accounting period, rather than actual cash transactions. See also CASH-BASIS ACCOUNTING.

accrued interest The interest that has built up on a loan since the last interest payment was made. When someone buys a bond, the accrued interest will be taken into account in the price.

accumulated dividend A dividend that is due on a preferred share but has not been paid. It becomes an obligation of the corporation; until it is paid, no dividend can be paid to common shareholders.

Achnacarry Agreement An agreement made by the world's three largest oil companies, Royal Dutch Shell, the Anglo-Persian Oil Company (later British Petroleum), and Standard Oil of New Jersey (later Exxon), at Achnacarry Castle in Scotland on 17 September 1928, to fix world oil prices and end the existing international price war in oil. Under the so-called As-Is Agreement, the oil companies agreed to accept the status quo with regard to the share each had in the world market, and to take other steps to preserve price stability and restrain oil production. Between 1928 and 1932, a number of other oil companies, including Texaco, Gulf, and Mobil, signed the agreement. By 1932, a number of other agreements had been reached to control prices and production in regional oil markets and to allow the bigger oil companies to acquire control of smaller companies and thus prevent competition. In 1938, Standard of New Jersey gave notice of its plan to withdraw from the agreement, and the following year the agreement was ended.

acid-test ratio A measure of a company's ability to pay its bills and other obligations; also known as the liquid or quick ratio. The ratio is calculated by dividing the company's quick assets (current assets minus inventories) by its current liabilities. A ratio of, say, 1.5:1, means that there is $1.50 of quick assets to meet every $1 of current liabilities. If it were, say, .75:1, there would be 75¢ of quick assets to meet every $1 of current liabilities. There is no general rule to say what the ratio should be, but if it is 1:1 or more than 1:1, then the company concerned is in a good financial position. However, financial analysts say that, if a company has a fast turnover of inventory, a ratio of less than 1:1 might be acceptable. See also CURRENT RATIO.

acquisition See TAKEOVER.

across the board **1.** In a collective agreement, the same wage increase for all employees covered by the agreement. **2.** In pricing policy, a uniform price increase or reduction for all products in a producer's line or for all products on shelves. **3.** In trade policy, a uniform tariff reduction or increase on all items imported.

act of God A natural disaster; the damage caused by a flood, earthquake, hurricane, or tornado, for instance. Insurance companies will often exclude acts of God from coverage in insurance policies.

active market A stock, commodity, or bond market in which there is a high volume of turnover generally, or for a particular share, commodity future, or bond. The existence of an active market for an investment will make it more appealing, since the investor knows that he can always resell his investment without having to take a big discount or loss.

active shares A daily listing compiled by a STOCK EXCHANGE and published on the financial pages of a newspaper, showing the shares traded that day or the previous day by price and volume, along with their high and low prices during the past twelve months.

actuary A person trained in mathematics and statistics who calculates the risks of insuring people for insurance companies. These calculations, depending on age, sex, occupation, and other considerations, help to determine the premiums charged to particular individuals for insurance coverage.

ad valorem tax An indirect tax such as a tariff, excise tax or duty, or manufacturer's sales tax, which is levied as a per cent of the value of the item taxed. The term is from the Latin, meaning "on the value of the item."

adjuster A person whose job it is to assess damage resulting from a fire, accident, theft, vandalism, or other cause of damage or loss against which someone is insured, and to arrive at an agreement with the insured person on the amount of compensation to be paid. The adjuster acts on behalf of an insurance company or broker.

adjustment assistance Programs to help workers and firms affected by reductions in tariffs and by other trade-liberalization policies. For workers, the policies may include retraining or additional payments to encourage early retirement. For firms, assistance may consist of grants to modernize facilities or to develop new product lines.

administered price A price that is set, usually in a monopolistic or oligopolistic industry, without great regard for the LAW OF SUPPLY AND DEMAND. Although prices in a competitive market would be expected to decline during a recession, when demand is weak, administered prices are unlikely to fall and may even be increased. Manufacturers calculate their costs and add on a mark-up designed to yield a profit target regardless of short-term market conditions.

administrative law The law that governs the conduct of government regulatory agencies, tribunals, and other bodies, to make sure that the rights of those who fall under their jurisdiction are protected. The FEDERAL COURT OF CANADA hears appeals from those who believe that their legal rights have been overridden by such government bodies.

advance A payment to a business firm or crown corporation to tide it over until arrangements for long-term financing have been made. An advance is, in effect, a short-term loan.

advertising Methods of informing the public of the availability, quality, and distinctive features of goods and services, and of persuading consumers to buy particular brands of goods or services. Most advertising is placed in newspapers and magazines, on radio, television, or billboards, or in direct mail.

Economists are divided over the role of advertising. Some argue that it is a vital means of informing consumers about the existence of and changes in goods and services. Without such information, consumers would not benefit from the lower prices achieved through ECONOMIES OF SCALE in industry, which are made possible by mass markets. Critical economists argue that much advertising spending is wasted, or leads people to buy things they don't need or really want, and hence represents a waste of resources. They also argue that a large investment in advertising by a company is a form of product differentiation that acts as a barrier to the entry of would-be competitors into the market. See also ADVERTISING AGENCY, MISLEADING ADVERTISING.

advertising agency A firm that performs services for advertisers, including the creation and production of advertising campaigns, MARKET RESEARCH, and purchase and placement of advertising in different media. The agency is either paid a commission of, say, 15 per cent of the value of the advertising it places in the various media for the client, or it bills the advertiser for the work actually done.

Advisory Council on the Status of Women A federal advisory body created in 1976 to advise the government on changes needed in laws and government practices and in private-sector practices to improve the status of women, including their opportunities for employment, promotion, equal pay, and adequate pensions.

Aeronautics Act Federal legislation that gives the federal government the authority to regulate civil aviation in Canada, including the operation of airports and air-traffic control, and that delegates to the CANADIAN TRANSPORT COMMISSION responsibility for approving air-fare changes, the introduction of new types of air fares, and changes in air routes.

affiliated company A subsidiary company, or one that is related through common ownership by the same parent company. The parent company may own less than 50 per cent of the voting shares of the subsidiary.

affluent society The term made famous by economist JOHN KENNETH GALBRAITH in his 1958 book of the same name. In it, he argued that scarcity was no longer a problem in the private sector, and economists should therefore encourage the allocation of additional resources to the public sector, where scarcity in the form of inadequate health care, schools, parks, and other facilities and services still existed. An affluent society, Galbraith contended, produced more cars and trucks but neglected the construction of roads, highways, and transit. As he defined the problem, business was able, through advertising, to maintain the idea of scarcity or unfilled needs for consumer goods; but no equivalent pressure existed for the production of more public goods and services, even though the need for them was much more urgent. This imbalance, in Galbraith's view, was a sign that the market economy could not effectively allocate resources to meet the real needs of society. Increases in the general welfare and increases in gross national product, he argued, were not necessarily the same thing.

agency shop A bargaining unit where workers who are covered by the collective agreement do not have to belong to the union, but where the employer deducts an amount equal to union dues from non-members and turns over the money to the union.

agent Someone who acts for another person or group of persons in dealings with a third party. For example, a union officer will act on behalf of employees in dealing with their employer: similarly, a real-estate agent acts on behalf of a person trying to sell a property. See also BROKER.

aggregate demand The total demand for goods and services in the economy. It determines the overall level of activity in the economy, including the level of production and employment. Hence, policies to change the level of production or employment are known as DEMAND-MANAGEMENT policies. The level of aggregate demand is the total of GROSS NATIONAL EXPENDITURE, published quarterly by Statistics Canada. Its main components are: consumer spending on goods and services; government spending on goods and services; capital-investment spending by business and government; changes in inventories; and exports of goods and services. The importance of aggregate demand in determining levels of output and employment, and hence the need for policies to stimulate or restrain the level of aggregate demand, was first identified by JOHN MAYNARD KEYNES.

agribusiness A term originally used to describe the agricultural economy, ranging from the production of farm supplies such as tractors, fertilizers, and pesticides, to the production, transportation, and distribution of farm products to food processors and foodstores. Today, it is used to describe the major farm corporations and food-processing companies that farmers fear will take over much of the country's farmland and squeeze out the family farm as an important supplier of food.

Agricultural Economics Research Council A national agricultural-research institute created in 1962 with federal, provincial, and agricultural-industry financial assistance. It is now fully funded by the agricultural industry. It conducts studies and publishes reports on a wide range of agricultural questions, ranging from farm financing and agricultural tariffs to better methods of farm production and rural development. It is based in Ottawa.

Agricultural Products Co-operative Marketing Act A 1939 law passed by Parliament to help farmers establish marketing pools so that they could get better prices for their products. The passage of the act was an important step in the development of FARM MARKETING BOARDS in Canada. The federal government had first tried in the early 1930s to give farmers the power to establish marketing boards to control the sale of their products, with the Natural Products Marketing Act of 1934. But this legislation was ruled unconstitutional by the courts. In 1936, British Columbia passed its Natural Products Marketing Act, which the courts found to be within provincial jurisdiction; the other provinces modelled their legislation after that of British Columbia. Under its 1939 legalization, the federal government guaranteed farmers an initial payment for their products at the time of delivery to the pool, usually a percentage of the estimated market price. The law thus made it easier for farmers to form national marketing organizations, which could get them better prices by bargaining from a position of strength with food processors and foodstore chains. The act did not cover wheat and other grains, which came within the jurisdiction of the CANADIAN WHEAT BOARD.

Agricultural Products Marketing Act A federal law, passed in 1949, that allowed the federal government to delegate powers to provincial farm marketing boards so that they could engage in interprovincial or export trade. Without such enabling legislation, provincial marketing boards would be restricted to activities within their own boundaries. See also FARM PRODUCTS MARKETING AGENCIES ACT.

Agricultural Rehabilitation and Development Act (ARDA) A regional-development program launched in 1961 to alleviate rural poverty and to finance water and land-use projects. In cost-sharing projects with the provinces, it worked initially to keep farmers on the land through programs of farm consolidation and land reclamation. Its emphasis later shifted to land-use projects, including the conversion of low-productivity farmland for other purposes, such as recreation, woodlot, and timber, and for soil- and water-conservation programs. The program came to an end on 31 March 1979. See also REGIONAL ECONOMIC EXPANSION, DEPARTMENT OF.

Agricultural Stabilization Board A federal crown corporation established in 1958 to stabilize or support farm prices. The initial commodities it was set up to help were slaughter cattle, hogs, sheep, industrial milk, industrial cream, corn, soybeans, oats, and barley. Since then other commodities have been added, such as apples, tomatoes, potatoes, and wool. The board determines a prescribed price for a commodity, usually 90 per cent of the five-year average of the market price, adjusted for inflation of the costs of production. It makes deficiency payments when prices are below the prescribed price and purchases quantities of the surplus commodity so as to push the price up. The agency assures farmers of a minimum price for their products.

Agricultural Supplies Board A federal board established during the Second World War to ensure that agricultural production was high enough to meet Canadian and British food and fibre needs. The board allocated fertilizer and pesticide supplies and arranged the production of seeds normally imported from Europe. Working with the federal board were provincial production committees. Independent of the board but working with it were three other boards that purchased Canadian farm products for shipment to Britain. These were the Bacon Board (later the Meat Board), the Dairy Products Board, and the Special Products Board. This apparatus was dismantled at the end of the Second World War.

Agriculture, Department of The federal government department responsible for the well-being of Canadian agriculture. Its first responsibility is the economic health of Canadian farming: the department supervises national FARM MARKETING BOARDS, farm credit, compensation in the event of crop failure, emergency farm relief due to flooding or other natural disasters, and crop insurance. Its second responsibility is the provision of technical and other services to improve farm productivity and the inspection and grading of farm products: it promotes the most effective ways to use fertilizers and pesticides and the use of improved crop- and livestock-production techniques. Its third responsibility is agricultural research: it operates agricultural laboratories and experimental farms to conduct crop, livestock, soil, and other research. The department dates back to 1867. See also AGRICULTURAL STABILIZATION BOARD, AGRICULTURAL PRODUCTS MARKETING ACT, CROP INSURANCE, CANADIAN DAIRY COMMISSION, CANADIAN LIVESTOCK FEED BOARD, FARM CREDIT CORPORATION, FARM PRODUCTS MARKETING AGENCIES ACT, FARM IMPROVEMENT LOANS ACT, FARM MARKETING BOARDS, PRAIRIE FARM REHABILITATION ADMINISTRATION, CANADIAN GRAIN COMMISSION.

airport tax A USER-PAY tax levied by the federal government since 1 December 1974 to help pay for the operating and construction costs of Canadian airports. It is a percentage of the air fare up to a specified maximum.

Alberta Energy Company (AEC) A corporation created by the Alberta government in 1973 to develop the industrial resource base of Canada, mainly with investments in Alberta. Shares were sold to residents of Alberta in 1975; the Alberta government's goal is to reduce its ownership to 50 per cent of the voting shares. Shares can only be owned by Canadian citizens or residents of Canada and are traded on stock exchanges across the country. The investments of AEC include lease rights for oil and gas on major parcels of land at Suffield and Primrose, participation in coal-mining, petrochemicals, forest-products and tar-sands projects, ownership of an electronics firm, and a major interest in western Canada's principal steel company, IPSCO.

Alberta Energy Resources Conservation Board. See ENERGY RESOURCES CONSERVATION BOARD.

Alberta Heritage Savings Trust Fund A special fund created by the Alberta government in 1976 to invest 30 per cent of the public revenue from the sale of Alberta's oil, natural gas, and other non-renewable resources for the future benefit of Albertans. The fund is divided into three sections: **1.** The capital division, which can invest up to 20 percent of the money in the fund in capital projects within the province, such as medical-research centres, homes for the aged, or other projects that yield social or economic benefits. **2.** The Canada investment division, which can use up to 15 per cent of the money in the fund to make loans to other provincial governments or to crown corporations. **3.** The Alberta investment division, which can use up to 65 per cent of the money in the fund to invest in projects to strengthen or diversify the Albertan economy. The fund is required by law to produce a quarterly report on its investment activities and a more detailed annual report that is reviewed by a special committee of the Alberta legislature.

Alberta Petroleum Marketing Commission A provincial agency created under the Petroleum Marketing Act of 1973 to sell the petroleum that is produced from Alberta crown leases. The commission sells its royalties, in the form of oil, within the province, and acts as the agent for the sale of the oil companies' oil outside the province at the best price it can negotiate. So far, pricing is a matter of federal-provincial negotiation. The commission also sells the Alberta government's share of oil production from the Syncrude TAR-SANDS project and is responsible for the marketing of pentanes plus. Profits go to the provincial treasurer. The commission is further responsible for the sale of Alberta natural gas under the Natural Gas Pricing Agreement Act of 1975; pricing of natural gas is, again, a matter of federal-provincial negotiation.

Alberta Stock Exchange (ASE) The stock exchange founded as the Calgary Stock Exchange in 1913, which became important the following year when oil was discovered in Alberta's Turner Valley. Since then its growth has been closely allied to the performance of the oil and gas industry, although the diversification of the Alberta economy in recent years has benefitted the exchange. Still located in Calgary, it changed its name to the Alberta Stock Exchange in 1974.

allocation of resources The use of society's resources—its FACTORS OF PRODUCTION—to achieve the most efficient or lowest-cost output of goods and services. In a world of PERFECT COMPETITION this is assumed to be accomplished through the workings of the LAW OF SUPPLY AND DEMAND and the INVISIBLE HAND. However, in the real world of IMPERFECT COMPETITION, the efficient allocation of resources is much more difficult to accomplish; MONOPOLY or OLIGOPOLY leads to a misallocation of resources, the cost being the extra profit earned by monopoly or oligopoly producers. But there are many other barriers to the efficient allocation of resources, including poorly functioning labour markets, in which it is hard to match workers seeking jobs with job vacancies, low levels of skills and knowledge, resistance to change, laws, regulations, and red tape, emphasis on non-economic goals, or excessive protection for owners of copyright and patents.

alloy A metal, such as stainless steel, brass, or bronze, formed by the fusion of other metals.

amalgamation The creation of a new corporation to take over the assets and liabilities of other existing businesses. Se also MERGER, TAKEOVER, CONSOLIDATION.

American Federation of Labor–Congress of Industrial Organizations (AFL-CIO). A federation of the American Federation of Labor and the Congress of Industrial Organizations formed in 1955, which is financed by per capita dues from member unions in Canada and the United States. Approximately 40 per cent of Canadian union members belong to unions affiliated with both the AFL-CIO and the CANADIAN LABOUR CONGRESS. There is, however, no formal connection between the

AFL-CIO and the CLC, and the CLC has a strongly worded policy to support the autonomy of Canadian locals of international unions headquartered in the United States. See also CANADIAN STANDARDS OF SELF-GOVERNMENT.

amortization The reduction and retirement of a debt over a period of time by setting aside funds for regular payment of interest and part of the principal with each payment. Often a corporation will establish a SINKING FUND in which it sets aside money on a regular and predetermined basis for the repayment of the debt. A mortgage is an example of an amortized debt, since each payment includes interest and principal so that the loan may be paid off in a specified period of time. Similarly, a corporation may amortize the costs of INTANGIBLE ASSETS, such as COPYRIGHT, PATENTS, TRADEMARKS, and GOODWILL, over a number of years instead of lumping them together in one year; each year a portion of the cost of the investment will be charged off as an expense. See also DEPRECIATION, DEPLETION.

amusement tax A tax on admission to places of entertainment, such as movie theatres. Most provinces have such a tax, although a number of them, including Quebec, Manitoba, and Saskatchewan, have delegated the collection or imposition of such a tax to their municipalities.

Andean Pact A common market formed by Ecuador, Colombia, Peru, and Chile in 1969; Chile subsequently left, while Bolivia and Venezuela later became members. The purpose of the pact was to establish a common external tariff and, through an industrial strategy, to integrate the manufacturing sector of the member-countries. For example, the Andean Pact members have sought to develop a single automobile and truck industry, instead of competing with one another for plants and investment. But there have been disagreements on who gets which shares of which industries. The Andean Pact countries are part of the LATIN AMERICA FREE TRADE AREA.

annual meeting The annual meeting for shareholders of a company, at which they elect directors, approve the reappointment of auditors along with the auditors' report for the past year, approve other company business, and question management on the company's affairs. Shareholders must receive adequate notice of annual meetings, according to federal or provincial laws.

annual rate The attempt to calculate an annual rate from a monthly statistic, by multiplying the monthly figure by twelve. This approach is criticized by statisticians because the figure for a particular month may contain special or seasonal factors, an unusual development such as the effects of a strike, or other irregularities. A much more reliable measure is the year-over-year increase: for example, the percentage increase in the CONSUMER PRICE INDEX in November, from November of the preceding year. To get a picture of the inflation trend, statisticians can chart, for example, the July, August, September, October, and November year-over-year increases, to see whether the inflation rate is moving up or down.

annual report The annual financial statement of a corporation, government department, or agency or non-profit institution, which contains an account of the past year's financial activities. All publicly traded corporations are required to produce an annual report that contains a BALANCE SHEET, EARNINGS STATEMENT, RETAINED-EARNINGS STATEMENT, and STATEMENT OF CHANGES IN FINANCIAL POSITION, verified in an independent AUDITOR'S REPORT, along with comparable financial information for the previous financial year. Such reports have to meet acceptable accounting standards, must contain information required under provincial securities legislation or federal or provincial corporation laws, and must be made available to shareholders within a specified period of time. Annual reports also contain the names of directors, details of remuneration for officers and directors, details of employees' and officers' share-purchase plans, a list of investments in other corporations wholly or partly owned by the company, details of long-term debts, and information on any lawsuits facing the company that could affect its profits, along with a statement on the company's prospects and plans by the chief executive officer and an outline of the company's performance and activities during the past year. A copy of the annual report must be sent to all shareholders of record at a specified date in advance of the company's annual meeting.

Annual reports of government departments do not contain the same type of financial information; they include, for example, no balance sheet. A government-department annual report details how the department spent its money in the past fiscal year, program by program, and gives some information on the effectiveness and use of such programs.

annual return Financial information that must be filed with a government department each year. Non-profit charitable institutions must file a financial return each year with the Department of NATIONAL REVENUE if they wish to maintain their tax-exempt status and their right to issue tax-deductible receipts to financial supporters. Unions and corporations in Canada above a certain size are required to file information annually under the CORPORATIONS AND LABOUR UNIONS RETURNS ACT. Federally incorporated companies have to file an annual return on their financial activities for deposit with the Department of CONSUMER AND CORPORATE AFFAIRS. Provincially incorporated companies are also required to file an annual return with the provincial government if they wish to maintain the privileges of incorporation.

annuity The payment of a regular pension or similar benefit for a specified number of years or for the lifetime of the beneficiary, paid out of an invested sum of capital. The proceeds of REGISTERED RETIREMENT SAVINGS PLANS are usually converted into an annuity known as a registered retirement income fund. The federal government stopped selling annuities in 1975; when it began selling them in 1908, before there were government pensions, annuities provided an important way for ordinary Canadians to put aside money for their old age. Now they are sold only by insurance companies.

anti-combines See COMPETITION POLICY, COMBINES INVESTIGATION ACT.

Anti-Dumping Tribunal A five-member federal tribunal set up under the Anti-Dumping Act of 1968 to investigate charges of DUMPING in Canada by foreign producers. The deputy minister of NATIONAL REVENUE determines whether the export price set by a foreign producer is less than the price the same producer charges in his domestic market. If it is, then the tribunal must also determine whether this dumping is causing or is likely to cause material injury to the producer of similar goods in Canada, or has materially retarded or is materially retarding the production of similar goods in Canada. If so, the tribunal has the power to impose an anti-dumping duty equal to the difference between the dumped price and what should have been the price in Canada. The minister of FINANCE, who is responsible to Parliament for the activities of the tribunal, can also request the tribunal to carry out special studies on imports causing problems for Canadian producers. The tribunal conducts public hearings and publishes its reports; it is a court of record and has full powers to order the production of papers and appearance of witnesses. Appeals on the way it has conducted a hearing or on its interpretation of its powers, but not of its actual decisions, can be made to the FEDERAL COURT OF CANADA.

Anti-Inflation Board (AIB) A federal board established by order-in-council on 14 October 1975 to administer wage and price controls; the AIB was confirmed by legislation on 15 December 1975. The controls were phased out between 14 April and 31 December 1978.

The role of the AIB was: **1.** To monitor price, pay, profit, and dividend changes, to see that they stayed within government guidelines. **2.** To identify changes in prices, profits, pay, or dividends that contravened the guidelines in fact or in spirit. **3.** To identify wage or price behaviour that was likely to have an inflationary impact in the economy, and to attempt to negotiate a rollback. **4.** Where a negotiated rollback was impossible, to negotiate a reduction in prices, profits, pay, or dividends, or to ask the anti-inflation administrator to order a rollback or take other action. **5.** To educate Canadians to the dangers of continued inflation, its causes, and to action that individual citizens could take to help reduce inflation.

The legislation established an anti-inflation administrator, whose job it was to enforce the AIB guidelines with binding rollback orders and other measures. In cases of excessive price increases or profit levels, the administrator could order the excess revenues to be returned to consumers, to the market in the form of price reductions, or to the Crown. Excess pay increases could be recovered from employees, the employer, or both. An anti-inflation-appeal tribunal was also created to hear appeals from businesses, unions, and other groups against the decisions of the anti-inflation administrator.

The controls applied to about 1,500 firms with about 2.3 million employees in the private sector, and to federal, provincial, and municipal governments and their agencies, with about 2 million employees. The basic wage guideline was 10 per cent in the first year, 8 per cent in the second year, and 6 per cent in the third year. Businesses were required to hold prices to levels producing pre-tax profit margins no higher than average profit margins of the previous five years. Price increases were restricted to cost increases and were expected to be cut if costs declined. Farmers or fishermen were exempt from the price guidelines, but the government said that it would try to have farm marketing boards respect the guidelines. Regulated industries were also exempt from the guidelines. At the same time that the AIB came into being, rent controls or guidelines were introduced by the provinces.

The AIB controls were only one element of the government's anti-inflation program. Other measures promised included tighter monetary and fiscal policies, and limits on the growth of government spending and structural policies to increase the supply of energy, food, and housing, increase the competitiveness of the economy, and improve the climate of labour-management relations. At the time the AIB controls were introduced, a white paper on anti-inflation policies was also tabled in Parliament.

anti-trust See COMPETITION POLICY, COMBINES INVESTIGATION ACT.

appraisal The valuation of real estate, antiques, jewellery, and other assets for insurance, sale, or collateral purposes by qualified experts recognized by the insurance industry, banks, and antique, jewellery, and other dealers.

appreciation An increase in the market value of an asset or security such as real estate, shares, antiques, or foreign exchange.

apprenticeship A formal program of job training to teach a person a trade or skill. The training takes place on the job and under the direction of a skilled worker. In some trades, apprenticeship training is necessary if a person wants to join the union and get work—as an electrician, plumber, auto mechanic, barber, or sheetmetal worker, for example. Apprenticeship training is also available in many other trades or crafts, such as carpentry, bricklaying, cooking, or television repair. Apprentices usually work for relatively low pay and have to work for a specified number of years in their trade before qualifying for a certificate showing that they have completed their apprenticeship training successfully.

appropriate technology Technology developed from local skills to meet the needs of a LESS-DEVELOPED COUNTRY, according to its own culture and requirements. Proponents of "appropriate technology" argue that it doesn't make sense for less-developed countries to import capital-intensive, costly, and energy-consuming technologies when those countries have high unemployment and lack the capital to pay for sophisticated technology that was not designed to meet their needs in the first place.

appropriation act An act of Parliament authorizing the spending of money for a specific purpose. Such an act must be passed each fiscal year for all government spending out of the CONSOLIDATED REVENUE FUND that is not covered by some other act of Parliament.

Generally speaking, there are four such acts in a fiscal year, but there could be fewer or more. Shortly after the government presents the spending ESTIMATES—say, in February

—for the fiscal year that begins on 1 April, it will introduce an interim supply bill, which is an appropriation act, to allow spending to take place while Parliament considers the estimates. In June a second appropriation act is debated by Parliament after consideration of the estimates is complete; this second act approves spending plans for the balance of the fiscal year, up to 31 March of the following year. Later in the year, when the SUPPLEMENTARY ESTIMATES "A" and a later "B" are presented, each must be accompanied by an appropriation act. Once each act has been passed by Parliament, an ORDER-IN-COUNCIL is sent to the governor general asking him to sign a warrant that authorizes spending out of the consolidated revenue fund. See also SPECIAL GOVERNOR GENERAL'S WARRANTS.

arbitrage A sophisticated form of investment in which shares, commodity futures, foreign exchange, or other securities are simultaneously purchased on one market and sold in another, with the investor realizing a profit on the difference in price between the two markets. For example, the price of a share listed on the Toronto and American stock exchanges is not always identical; a fast investor can take advantage of the difference, if it is big enough, to make a quick profit by buying on one market and selling on the other. The same is true with foreign-exchange quotations in different financial centres, commodity futures traded in different commodity markets, bonds sold in several different markets, or gold and other precious metals sold in different centres.

arbitration Third-party efforts to resolve labour-management differences in the negotiation of a new collective agreement, thus to avoid a strike or lockout; or third-party efforts to resolve labour or management grievances over the way an existing collective agreement is being interpreted or implemented by management or labour. An arbitration board may consist of a single individual not connected with either party, or it may be a three-man body with representatives of both labour and management and an independent third party. Federal and provincial labour departments can supply arbitration assistance and help in the selection of arbitrators.

Arbitrators spend a great deal of time dealing with labour-management disagreements over the interpretation of existing collective agreements—on the rights of management to reassign workers or to change work procedures, for example. In compulsory or binding arbitration, the federal or provincial government will order striking or locked-out employees back to work and appoint an arbitrator to resolve the dispute by awarding a settlement that both parties have to live with. Compulsory arbitration may be used to resolve public-sector disputes—strikes by teachers or municipal transit workers, for example—or disputes that may cause public hardship, in industries such as the railways, grain handling, or the airlines.

Sometimes labour and management will agree to voluntary arbitration to settle outstanding issues in the negotiation of a new collective agreement. Arbitrators may also be used to settle unresolved issues in negotiating a new collective agreement through a process known as final-offer selection. Each side makes a final offer dealing with all the unresolved issues in a dispute, leaving it to the arbitrator to decide which one should be accepted.

arm's length A transaction conducted between parties that have no corporate or other direct connections with each other, and thus act each in its own self-interest. A foreign multinational corporation and its Canadian subsidiary do not have an arm's-length relationship with each other when the parent firm supplies parts, or charges for research or management services. Tax authorities in the Department of NATIONAL REVENUE are supposed to make sure that charges by the foreign parent for head-office services, or TRANSFER PRICES in intercorporate sale and purchase of parts or finished products, are set as if an arm's-length relationship did exist, so that real market prices are charged on these transactions and the proper amount of corporate income tax and WITHHOLDING TAX may be collected.

arrears Accounts payable that are overdue. The term also refers to overdue and unpaid INTEREST and PREFERRED-SHARE dividends.

articles of incorporation See INCORPORATION.

Asian Development Bank (ADB) A regional-development bank created in 1966 to stimulate economic growth and trade in Asia and the Far East, modelled along the lines of the INTERNATIONAL BANK FOR RECONSTRUCTION AND DEVELOPMENT (World Bank). About 60 per cent of the capital of the bank has come from countries within the region, including Japan and Australia; Canada is one of the non-regional providers of capital to the bank, along with the United States, Britain, West Germany, and Switzerland. Canada is also a contributor to the Asian Development Fund, a part of the bank that provides low-interest assistance to the poorest members of the region.

ask-price The price sought by a would-be seller of a share, bond, or commodity contract. See also BID.

assay The test carried out to determine the mineral content of samples of rock obtained from a mineral-exploration site. Mining companies that sell their shares to the public are required to get an independent assay report before making any comment on the mineral potential of a new mineral site.

assembly line A method of industrial production in which the job of each worker has been reduced to its simplest routine, and various standardized parts are assembled by workers in a series of isolated steps into a finished product. In the auto industry, for example, a car will start on the assembly line as a bare frame and, step by step, have all of its parts, ranging from motor, transmission, and body to wheels, windows, seats, hubcaps, and headlights, added to it by different workers, each doing one job as the car moves along a conveyor system.

assessment The value placed on land and buildings for the purpose of levying a property tax. Property may be assessed on the basis of FAIR MARKET VALUE, but many municipalities still employ arbitrary methods of assessment based on historical cost or use of property. As a result, properties of the same market value in the same community may be assessed quite differently for property-tax purposes, depending on when they were built and how they are used. See also MILL RATE.

assessment work The exploration and development work that a mining company is required to do on a property if it wishes to retain its rights to minerals that may exist on the land, and obtain a lease to extract those minerals.

asset Anything that can be sold, on which a money value hence can be placed. In a BALANCE SHEET, everything that a company or other organization owns that can be expressed as a dollar value is listed. Assets include land, buildings, machinery, inventories, oil and gas reserves, mineral or timber rights, patents, trademarks, copyright, cash, securities, investments in other companies and affiliates, money loaned to affiliated companies, and money owed by customers. Assets are usually divided into CURRENT ASSETS and FIXED ASSETS. Current assets consist of cash and assets that are readily turned into cash within a normal operating year, such as inventories, accounts receivable, and short-term securities. Fixed assets include property, plant and equipment, long-term investments in other companies, and INTANGIBLE ASSETS such as patents and copyright.

assignment The transfer of a property or specified rights by the owner to another person in writing. A debtor may assign his property to a trustee, who will dispose of it at the best possible price and use the proceeds to pay off creditors. The owner of a copyright or patent may assign the rights generally, or for a specified market or use, to a manufacturer, film-maker, or other party in return for a royalty or other payment. Similarly, a retailer who sells a product to a customer on credit may assign the debt to a sales-finance company, which pays off the retailer and assumes the rights to the interest and principal.

assurance See INSURANCE.

Atlantic Acceptance affair The 1965 bankruptcy of a major Toronto-based sales-finance company, which, when it was put into receivership, had debts of $115 million and assets $32 million short of that. The company's shares fell from close to $21 to about $1 when it went into receivership; its collapse led to the disappearance of the British Mortgage and Trust Company of Stratford, Ontario, which lost more than $1 million in Atlantic shares and $4 million in Atlantic notes. British Mortgage was merged with Victoria and Grey Trust Company.

The Ontario government appointed Mr. Justice Samuel Hughes of the Supreme Court of Ontario to head an inquiry into the collapse. He found a serious lack of supervision over the operations of NEAR BANKS in Ontario in his royal commission report, published four years later in 1969. It led, in 1970, to sweeping changes in the Loan and Trust Companies Act that gave the provincial government important new regulatory powers and the authority to intervene in the affairs of companies in difficulty, including taking over the administration of such companies. The amendments also increased the obligations of companies to act responsibly.

Atlantic Development Council (ADC) An eleven-person advisory board created in 1969 to advise the minister of Regional Economic Expansion on policies that might strengthen the economy of the four Atlantic provinces and ease social adjustment in the region, and on the merits of particular projects or programs. Its headquarters are in St. John's, Newfoundland, and it has a small research staff there. The council replaced the Atlantic Development Board, which had been created in 1962 to advise the federal government on capital projects and general policies to accelerate economic growth, and which, in 1963, was given a $100-million fund to stimulate growth in the region.

Atlantic provinces The provinces of New Brunswick, Nova Scotia, Prince Edward Island, and Newfoundland. See also MARITIME PROVINCES.

Atlantic Provinces Economic Council (APEC) An economic-research organization founded in 1954 to develop policies to improve the economy of the Atlantic region. It has advocated a number of important measures to narrow the gap between the region's per capita income and output and that of the rest of Canada, including regional-development programs and a regional-growth strategy based on the identification of five principal growth centres in the four Atlantic provinces. It has also been a strong advocate of Maritime union. APEC is financed mainly by business, but has some provincial-government support. It is located in Halifax.

Atomic Energy Control Board (AECB) A federal regulatory agency created under the Atomic Energy Control Act of 1946 to regulate the construction and operation of nuclear reactors, the transportation and disposal of nuclear wastes, the operation of uranium mines, and the export of uranium to countries that accept nuclear safeguards.

Atomic Energy of Canada Limited (AECL) A crown corporation established under the Atomic Energy Control Act of 1946 to develop Canada's capacity to build its own nuclear-power and heavy-water production systems, to engage in nuclear research and development, to identify and develop other uses of nuclear technology in medicine and other areas, to develop an export market for Canadian nuclear technology, and to devise methods of disposing of nuclear wastes. The crown corporation came into being in 1952 when it took over the Chalk River nuclear-research station from the NATIONAL RESEARCH COUNCIL. The crown corporation does most of the research and development and advanced engineering work on nuclear-power and heavy-water systems in Canada, but does not have its own manufacturing capacity; instead, it contracts out actual manufacturing to a number of different manufacturing firms in Canada. It reports to Parliament through the minister of ENERGY, MINES AND RESOURCES.

atomistic economy An economy made up of many small, independent producers; the type of economy that predated the Industrial Revolution and the shift to large producers and capital-intensive production facilities.

attrition A method of reducing the number of employees of an organization by failing to fill vacancies when employees leave for another job or retire. It is one way of dealing with the elimination of jobs caused by technological change, or of handling the problem of overstaffing in an organization without having to lay off employees.

auction A sale in which goods are offered to competing buyers and in which the goods offered go to the highest bidders. The auctioneer attempts to get the best possible price for the seller and is paid a commission on the money he gets for the seller. In some instances, the seller may set a reserve price below which he will not sell particular goods. Auctions are often used to dispose of the assets of bankrupt firms or of individuals or firms that have not paid their taxes. Similarly, auctions are used by governments to dispose of unclaimed stolen or lost property or goods seized by customs officers. Livestock, oil and gas leases, and used cars at the wholesale level are sold by auction. The assets of an estate, such as furniture, jewellery, or works of art, are often sold for cash at an auction. See also DUTCH AUCTION.

audit A review of the financial records of a corporation or other organization to verify their accuracy and to ensure that proper accounting procedures are being followed. All companies in Canada are required to maintain proper financial records and to have them verified by independent, professional accountants. These accountants are required to check the actual financial records of the company, to run whatever tests they feel are necessary to verify the accuracy of the records, to review the accounting system and internal audit controls, and to ensure that the current year's financial figures are fully comparable with those of earlier years. See also AUDITOR'S REPORT.

auditor 1. An accountant in public practice who is retained to examine and report on the accuracy and soundness of the financial statements of a corporation or other organization. He is an independent scrutineer whose verification and signature attach credibility to the organization's financial statements, and thus reassure investors, shareholders, and creditors. **2.** Employees within an organization who may or may not be trained accountants, who report to management on whether or not its policies, including financial controls, are being carried out by employees.

auditor general An officer of Parliament who, along with his staff, conducts an annual audit of government spending to see whether proper accounts are being maintained, whether money is being spent for the purposes stipulated by Parliament, whether effective spending controls are being maintained, that money designated for one purpose is not being diverted to another, that all money collected from the public is properly accounted for, that proper records are being kept on public property, and that generally accepted accounting procedures are being followed by government departments and agencies. The auditor general makes an annual report to Parliament that is then reviewed by the PUBLIC ACCOUNTS COMMITTEE of Parliament. The report itemizes instances of misspending or lack of adequate financial controls, and may contain recommendations on ways to improve financial procedures within the government. The office of auditor general, which dates back to 1878, is one of the important checks or controls on the spending and accounting practices of government departments, agencies, and crown corporations. The minister of FINANCE reports to Parliament for the auditor general.

auditor's report The annual examination of the financial records of a corporation or other organization by outside, independent accountants, to verify the accuracy of those financial records. Every PUBLIC COMPANY is required to appoint outside auditors to represent the shareholders and to verify, once a year, the accuracy and consistency of the company's financial statements. These outside auditors will usually state in their own report to shareholders that: "Our examination was made in accordance with generally accepted auditing standards, and accordingly included such tests and other procedures as we considered necessary in the circumstances. In our opinion, these consolidated financial statements present fairly the financial position of the company at

31 December 1979, and the results of its operations and the changes in the financial position for the year then ended, in accordance with GENERALLY ACCEPTED ACCOUNTING PRINCIPLES applied on a basis consistent with that of the preceding year.''

Since the auditors are bound by their own professional code of ethics, their certification of a company's financial records is an assurance to shareholders that a company's annual report gives a true picture of its financial health, bearing in mind the qualifications contained in the NOTES TO FINANCIAL STATEMENTS. In principle, the outside auditors are there to look after the interests of the shareholders, not those of the management of the company. However, management usually has enough power at shareholders' meetings to replace troublesome auditors, although such a move may raise public suspicions and lower the value of company shares; it may also draw the attention of a provincial securities commission.

austerity program Government policies that deliberately restrain the purchasing power of consumers, or restrict other economic activities in order to solve balance-of-payments problems, to allocate more of a country's resources to new investment, to reduce significantly a large government deficit, or to finance a war. Canada embarked on a temporary austerity program in 1962 to improve its balance of payments. Import surcharges were imposed on about half of Canada's imports; duty-free exemptions for Canadians returning from foreign holidays were sharply reduced; interest rates were raised; government spending was reduced, and the exchange rate of the Canadian dollar was reduced to 92.5 U.S. cents. In the fall of 1962, the government began to remove some of the import surcharges; they were all lifted by the end of 1963.

autarky An economic and political system whose goal is economic self-sufficiency, in spite of the high costs that result from such a policy. To achieve self-sufficiency in food, machinery, technology, energy, and other basics of political and economic life, a country may impose import barriers or exchange controls, or may heavily subsidize local industry and adopt regimented national planning. Nazi Germany and the pre–Second World War Japan and Greater East Asia Co-Prosperity Sphere adopted such policies in the 1930s, while the Soviet Union and its East European satellites did the same after the war. Autarky is sometimes spelled autarchy, although the latter term properly refers to the rule of an absolute sovereign.

authorized capital The maximum number of shares and their par value, if any, that a corporation is permitted to issue under its articles of incorporation. The number of issued shares is the number the company has sold, while the outstanding shares are those that remain in public hands; PREFERRED SHARES may have been redeemed while COMMON SHARES may have been bought back by the company, thus reducing the number of outstanding shares. A company does not usually issue all of its authorized shares, because it wants to have some left to sell in the future when they are worth more. But if it has issued all of its authorized shares, it can amend its articles of incorporation or charter by SUPPLEMENTARY LETTERS PATENT and increase its authorized capital.

auto pact See CANADA–UNITED STATES AUTOMOTIVE PRODUCTS AGREEMENT.

automatic stabilizer See BUILT-IN STABILIZER.

automation The automatic and self-regulating control of all or part of a production process by machines. In the late 1940s, automation was applied mainly to the development of machines in the automotive industry that could, without human intervention, handle parts between successive stages of production. But since then, with the rapid development of computer and communications systems, automatic switching, and process-control systems, automation has led to much more sophisticated control and operation of industrial production, business administration, and other tasks.

Computerized systems can direct the operation of machinery and control entire processes, such as the workings of refineries and nuclear-power stations. With the development of silicon chips, automation will become even more advanced. Process-control systems allow computers to adjust or correct the production process if feedback from the production process indicates that something is out of line; if, for example, a boiler overheats, the system will activate changes in valve pressures or whatever else is needed to bring the boiler temperature down to its desired level. In an automated inventory-control system in a supermarket chain, coded prices record sales at the check-out counters, automatically adjusting inventory records. When inventories of particular products reach pre-determined levels, the computer system will automatically re-order the products; no human intervention is needed.

Automation has contributed significantly to postwar growth in productivity and to a general improvement in the standard of living. So long as society is able to retrain workers and sustain a rate of economic growth that generates new job opportunities, automation should not generate massive unemployment. None the less, unions are seeking greater say in the introduction of automation, in the form of improved contract rights and more protection against layoffs through changes in labour laws.

average A single number that is intended to be typical of series of numbers. For example, the average weekly wage is a figure that is representative of a wide range of individual weekly wages; the average selling price of a new home is representative of the different prices being charged for new homes.

Averages are useful because they give a more accurate picture of performance over periods of time, a picture that can be used as a standard in assessing short-term performance. For example, current inflation, unemployment, and gross-national-product growth rates are better understood if they are measured against the average of the past five or ten years. Averages also give a truer picture, in the sense that they smooth out the effects of short-term fluctuations such as bad weather or an industrial dispute.

There are different methods of calculating average figures. The most commonly used average is the simple average, which is produced by taking a series of numbers, adding them together, and dividing the total by the number of numbers; for example, if a country had, in a five-year period, inflation rates of 6.7, 7.4, 8.9, 9.3, and 8.2, its average annual inflation rate would be 8.1 per cent. A weighted average is calculated in a similar fashion, except that the relative importance of different components of the average are taken into account. For example, in calculating the CONSUMER PRICE INDEX, which represents an average of a typical bundle of consumer purchases in a month, more weight is given to food costs, which represent a large element of a family's budget, while a relatively small weight is attached to recreational spending. See also MOVING AVERAGE, MODE, MEDIAN, MEAN AVERAGE.

B

baby budget A supplementary BUDGET brought down by the minister of FINANCE to deal with unexpected economic conditions, or to strengthen the direction of policy set out in his original budget if its measures have had less effect than expected.

backlog A build-up of orders that have yet to be filled; goods ordered by customers but not yet delivered. The volume of unfilled orders is an important business indicator for economic analysts trying to determine the short-term outlook for the economy. If the backlog of orders is on the rise, then factories will have plenty of work to keep them busy for some time, perhaps so much that they will need to hire more workers and expand their facilities. If the backlog is declining, factories will have a declining amount of work ahead, so they may lay off workers and delay expansion plans. Statistics Canada publishes regular figures on the volume of unfilled orders.

bad debt A debt that is not expected to be repaid. Businesses make a provision in their accounts for such debts, while banks and other financial institutions set aside reserves to cover such debts. In their annual reports, for example, banks will show an appropriation for losses in their EARNINGS STATEMENTS; this figure is deducted from pre-tax profits. Interest rates charged by financial institutions also take into account the fact that not all debts will be repaid, just as retail prices take into account losses due to shoplifting and spoilage.

bad faith Negotiation of a collective agreement or contract when one of the parties either is not intent on reaching agreement or does not intend to honour the agreement when it is signed.

bait-and-switch selling The technique, illegal under the COMBINES INVESTIGATION ACT, of luring potential customers into a store by advertising or promoting big-discount bargains without having the merchandise available, then trying to persuade the customers to buy other, more expensive goods.

balance of payments A summary of all the transactions between Canadians and residents of the rest of the world over a given period of time. The net inflow and outflow of money arising from Canada's economic dealings with other countries is a good indicator of its ability to earn enough to pay for the goods and services it needs, and thus pay its way in the world.

The balance of payments is divided into two accounts: current and capital. The current account records the flow of goods and services between Canada and the rest of the world: merchandise imports and exports and non-merchandise transactions such as travel and tourist spending, for example, or payments and receipts for shipping, freight, banking, insurance, and other business services, interest and dividend payments, and payments to corporate head offices for management services, research and development, and copyrights, patents, trademarks, and industrial-design royalties. Canada usually has a surplus on merchandise trade and a deficit on non-merchandise trade, and an overall current-account deficit.

The capital account consists of long- and short-term capital flows between Canada and other countries. These flows include DIRECT and PORTFOLIO INVESTMENTS, short-term investments such as those in finance and commercial paper, bank term deposits and certificates of deposit for terms of one year or less, Canadian foreign aid and export credit financing, immigrants' remittances to relatives in their native countries and funds brought by immigrants to Canada, and movements of insurance funds. Canada usually imports more capital than it exports. Since the balance of payments must balance out at zero, the balancing item consists of a reduction in Canada's foreign-exchange reserves—or, if Canada has a surplus on its current and capital accounts, an increase in its foreign-exchange reserves.

If a country runs a persistent deficit on its balance of payments, it must reduce its imports, increase its exports, increase foreign investment in its economy, increase its foreign indebtedness, reduce its foreign-exchange reserves, or seek assistance from the INTERNATIONAL MONETARY FUND or foreign commercial and central banks. Statistics Canada publishes quarterly reports on Canada's balance of payments as part of the system of NATIONAL ACCOUNTS.

balance of trade The difference between the dollar or money value of a country's exports and imports of merchandise or of goods and services. If a country exports more than it imports, it has a trade surplus; if it imports more than it exports, it has a trade deficit. The balance of trade is an important part of a country's overall BALANCE OF PAYMENTS.

balance sheet One of four basic financial statements in an annual report, the others being the EARNINGS STATEMENT, the RETAINED-EARNINGS STATEMENT, and the STATEMENT OF CHANGES IN FINANCIAL POSITION. The balance sheet shows the assets, liabilities, and shareholders' equity of a corporation on the last day of the financial year. Assets are what the company owns or is owed. They include current assets, such as cash, short-term securities, accounts receivable, inventories, and prepaid taxes; and fixed assets, such as buildings, factories, machinery, and equipment, minus DEPRECIATION. Liabilities are what the company owes others, and include current liabilities, such as accounts payable, income tax payable, and the portion of long-term debt paid off that year; and long-term debt. Shareholders' equity, which is calculated by deducting total liabilities from total assets, consists of equity capital invested by shareholders in the corporation, accumulated retained earnings, and the CONTRIBUTED SURPLUS if any. A balance sheet must always balance: assets must equal liabilities plus shareholders' equity.

bank A financial institution whose principal business is to accept deposits, pay interest on the deposits, honour cheques drawn on the deposits, and make loans using a proportion of the deposits not needed for chequing purposes and other daily transactions. In Canada, a bank must be recognized as such under the BANK ACT and by the BANK OF CANADA. There is no legal definition of a bank in Canada. See also CHARTERED BANK.

bank account Money deposited in a bank by an individual, corporation, or other depositor. There are three basic types: **1.** A chequing account, in which money is deposited and on which cheques are drawn, but on which no interest is earned. **2.** A chequing-savings account, in which money is deposited, on which cheques are drawn, and in which interest is paid on a minimum credit balance. **3.** A non-chequing–savings account, in which money is deposited and interest paid on the minimum credit balance, but on which no cheques can be written. This type of account pays a higher rate of interest. In law, a bank can refuse to release funds from a chequing-savings or from a non-chequing–savings account unless it has been given prior notice of withdrawal. No such notice is required on a chequing account; funds can be withdrawn on demand.

Bank Act The federal law, dating back to 1870, that regulates the chartered banks; it is revised approximately every ten years to take into account changes in the economy and changes in the BANKING SYSTEM. It defines who may own and operate a bank and how a bank may be established, what types of activities a bank may engage in, the types of reserves that a bank must retain, the types of investments that a bank may make, a bank's relationship with the government, the public, and the Bank of Canada, the types of directorships that a bank officer may hold, the qualifications for bank directors, the way banks maintain their books of account, procedures for banks to follow in reporting to the INSPECTOR GENERAL OF BANKS, the issuing of bank shares, and other matters affecting banks and the functioning of the banking system.

bank deposit Money in banks that belongs to depositors but can be used by the banks to make loans and other investments; bank deposits are liabilities of the banks and assets of the depositors or customers. There are many different types of bank deposits; they include chequing accounts that pay no interest, chequing-savings accounts on which cheques can be written and on which interest is paid, non-chequing–savings accounts on which a higher rate of interest is paid, and term deposits, which are sums of money left with a bank for a fixed term in return for a higher rate of interest. Bank deposits are an important part of the MONEY SUPPLY.

bank draft A cheque issued by a bank in its own name rather than the name of the customer who has actually provided the funds for the cheque. It is used when a creditor does not want to accept a cheque from the bank customer himself, usually after previous cheques have been returned because insufficient funds were in the bank-customer's account. A bank draft, on the other hand, bears the name of the bank itself and is equivalent to cash.

Bank for International Settlements (BIS) An international financial body serving as a central bank for the central banks of individual nations. It was formed in 1930, following the 1929 collapse of several European central banks, on the initiative of France, Germany,

Britain, and Italy. Since then it has been expanded to include all the central banks of Western Europe, along with those of Canada and Japan; the United States participates, but on an informal basis. Although many of its earlier functions have been taken over by the INTERNATIONAL MONETARY FUND, the bank remains important because it provides an extremely valuable forum for monetary authorities from the Western world, and enables members to make unofficial arrangements to deal with currency speculations and other problems. The bank holds a monthly meeting at its headquarters in Basle, Switzerland. It also publishes its own assessment of world economic problems, and monitors international lending through EUROCURRENCY and other international financial markets.

bank loan A loan made by a bank to a borrower. The loan may be SECURED OR UNSECURED; if it is secured, the interest charged is lower. Banks may make consumer loans, which are used to finance consumer purchases, MORTGAGE LOANS to finance the purchase of real estate, DEMAND LOANS, which can be called in at any time, TERM LOANS, which are for a fixed term, CALL LOANS to INVESTMENT DEALERS, and various specialized forms of loans to finance exports and fluctuations in the WORKING CAPITAL of firms, to farmers, and to SALES-FINANCE and ACCEPTANCE COMPANIES.

Bank of Canada The federal agency that plays a vital role in determining the overall rate of economic growth in the country by influencing the level of interest rates, the availability of credit, and the external value of the Canadian dollar. Its other responsibilities include the printing of money, the management of the national debt, the investment of funds for government agencies such as the Unemployment Insurance Fund, and advising the minister of FINANCE on appropriate economic policies. Under the Bank of Canada Act, it is charged with the responsibility to regulate "credit and currency in the best interest of the economic life of the nation."

The implementation of MONETARY POLICY is the most important role of the central bank. By influencing the level of short-term interest rates, the Bank of Canada controls the growth of the MONEY SUPPLY (narrowly defined to include currency and the public's holdings of chartered-bank demand deposits). The basic principle underlying Canadian monetary policy today is that the money supply should grow at a rate capable of accommodating a satisfactory rate of real economic growth, while continuously moving towards the goal of price stability. The Bank of Canada influences the level of short-term interest rates through its CASH-RESERVE MANAGEMENT policies (OPEN-MARKET OPERATIONS), by which it buys and sells government securities, and through the transfer of government cash balances between the chartered banks and the Bank of Canada. The Bank of Canada can also shape monetary policy by changing the SECONDARY RESERVE RATIO of the chartered banks, by changing the BANK RATE, and by using moral suasion to influence the behaviour of the banking system. It also makes loans of up to six months to the chartered banks and to MONEY-MARKET DEALERS to help them meet reserve requirements and cash needs.

The bank regulates the external value of the Canadian dollar by managing the foreign-exchange reserves in the EXCHANGE-FUND ACCOUNT and by intervening in international foreign-exchange markets. As fiscal agent for the federal government, the Bank of Canada is directly concerned with the management of the national debt; it advises the government on the method of financing and the terms of new issues of bonds and treasury bills. The bank also plays an important role in the money market through its weekly auction of TREASURY BILLS, as well as its sale and purchase of government securities.

The Bank of Canada was established as a privately owned corporation in 1934 and began operation in March 1935; but the Bank of Canada Act was amended so that, by 1938, it was a government-owned operation. It is managed by a fourteen-person board of directors, including a governor and deputy-governor who each serve for seven-year terms. The deputy minister of FINANCE serves as an *ex officio* but non-voting member of the board, thus providing a link between the bank and the government. At the same time, the Bank of Canada Act requires the governor of the bank to meet regularly with the minister of Finance to discuss both monetary policy and its relationship to overall economic policy. While the Bank of Canada has considerable independence in pursuing its monetary-policy objectives, the government can overrule the bank. To do so, the minister of Finance must issue written instructions to the bank; the instructions must be specific, for a specified period of time, and must be made public. Thus, the government has the ultimate responsibility for monetary policy.

bank rate The rate of interest the BANK OF CANADA charges to the CHARTERED BANKS and to MONEY-MARKET DEALERS for their infrequent loans. The chartered banks can borrow from the Bank of Canada as a last resort, usually for just a few days. A bank, for example, may need a one-million-dollar loan for a day or two to maintain its minimum cash balance until its cash position has improved. The bank rate is more important, though, as a signal to the banking system on the direction of MONETARY POLICY. An increase in the bank rate is normally a sign that the Bank of Canada plans to tighten the MONEY SUPPLY. This in turn will lead to an increase in interest rates charged by the chartered banks and other financial institutions to their customers. A drop in the bank rate is normally a signal that the Bank of Canada intends to relax monetary policy, and the banking system will respond by lowering interest rates. The Bank of Canada will follow up changes in the bank rate with other actions to increase or decrease money supply.

The speed with which the banking system responds to changes in the bank rate depends on the state of financial markets. For example, increases in the bank rate may not be followed by immediate increases in MORTGAGE interest rates if there is an abundant supply of mortgage funds and a shortage of customers for mortgages. But if higher interest rates were to continue for some time, mortgage lenders would have to raise their rates as well. Increases in the bank rate, and hence in lending rates in the banking system, also mean that banks and other financial institutions have to pay higher interest rates to their depositors.

The U.S. equivalent to the bank rate, set by the Federal Reserve Board in Washington, is the discount rate.

bank reserves See PRIMARY RESERVE RATIO, SECONDARY RESERVE RATIO.

banking group A group of investment firms that together manage and assume financial responsibility for a new issue of shares, bonds, or other securities. Each firm assumes part of the financial responsibility. See also UNDERWRITER.

banking system The activities of the CHARTERED BANKS, carried out in conjunction with the BANK OF CANADA, in accepting deposits and making loans.

bankruptcy The condition of a corporation or individual unable to repay creditors; the corporation or individual is therefore placed under the supervision of a trustee, under the terms of the federal Bankruptcy Act. The bankrupt debtor turns control of his assets over to the trustee, who disposes of them to the creditors according to the creditors' various claims. The Bankruptcy Act is administered by the superintendent of Bankruptcy, an official of the Department of CONSUMER AND CORPORATE AFFAIRS. Usually, if a firm is bankrupt, it not only lacks the funds to pay its bills but is also so heavily in debt that its liabilities exceed its assets and it has no additional collateral against which to borrow more money to pay its bills. Under part X of the Bankruptcy Act, an individual heavily in debt may go to the courts and make an arrangement for the orderly repayment of his debts. The debtor pays an agreed-on amount to the court on a regular basis, and the court allocates the money among the various creditors. This part of the act is in effect only in those provinces whose provincial governments have given their concurrence.

bargaining agent A union that has been chosen by a majority of employees in a BARGAINING UNIT and has been recognized by a federal or provincial LABOUR-RELATIONS BOARD as the legal representative of the employees in negotiating and implementing a COLLECTIVE AGREEMENT.

bargaining theory of wages The theory that wage levels depend on the bargaining strength of unions and employers, and not simply on the supply of and demand for labour.

bargaining unit A group of employees in a firm, government agency, or in a trade or occupation, and recognized as a unit for collective-bargaining purposes by a federal or provincial LABOUR-RELATIONS BOARD. A bargaining unit may consist of all the employees of a firm, a particular group of employees in a firm, or of a particular trade or skill in all firms in an industry.

barriers to entry Market obstacles that inhibit or prevent the entry of new firms into an industry and thus restrict competition. Economies of scale in capital-intensive industries restrict entry; there are high start-up costs and a new competitor will have to have a high level of production to be price-competitive. Unless he thinks he can justify those huge start-up costs, a would-be competitor in a capital-intensive industry will be reluctant to make the investment. But deliberate anti-competitive policies by existing producers—such as PRODUCT DIFFERENTIATION based on a large investment in advertising, EXCLUSIVE-DEALING CONTRACTS with retailers, and patent restrictions—also make it extremely difficult for a new firm to enter an industry. Similarly, government regulation can be a barrier to entry; for example, farm marketing boards make it difficult for new agricultural producers to enter the market, while government licensing requirements restrict the entry of new radio, television, and airline services.

Where there are significant barriers to entry, existing producers may be able to earn excess profits; but if there is relative ease of entry, then profit margins are likely to be lower. The barriers to entry represent the costs that would-be producers must overcome; their existence usually means, unless there is relative ease of entry, that new producers have higher costs, at least on first entering the industry, than do existing producers. A country that wants to increase competition has to find ways to reduce barriers to entry in many industries, by changing patent laws, for example, or by outlawing exclusive dealing and other such arrangements.

barter A transaction in which goods or services are exchanged for other goods or services rather than money. Barter was common in primitive economies, where trading took place for the most part in a single community and there were few goods or services exchanged. But in any economy where goods or services are traded over wide distances and where there is a large number of goods and services available, it is extremely difficult to bring buyers and sellers together or to determine fair exchanges.

Today, barter is sometimes used as a form of TAX EVASION. A dentist, for example, may provide braces for a carpenter's child, in exchange for the construction of new cupboards in his home; the dentist avoids taxes and the carpenter's dentistry bill is lower than it might have been. Barter is also used in trade between nations, with a country rich in resources but poor in manufacturing, for example, exchanging a fixed amount of a commodity for a TURN-KEY factory or major machinery and equipment. In 1969, the government of Saskatchewan traded wheat for electrical machinery needed by the Saskatchewan Power Corporation.

base period A selected month, year, or set of years used in calculating an index number or growth rate. Statistics Canada uses 1971 as its base year for most indexes and in calculating changes in CONSTANT DOLLARS or in real terms. If 1971 is the base year (1971=100) and the consumer price index is 193.8, then consumer prices have risen 93.8 per cent since 1971. Similarly, if 1971 is the base year and the gross national product has risen by 49 per cent in 1971 dollars (after inflation has been deducted for the period), then real growth or growth in physical output has been 49 per cent.

base rate The lowest rate of pay in a collective agreement. It is the pay that the lowest-paid class of worker would get. See also BASIC RATE.

basic rate The rate of pay for doing a job during a normal shift; it does not include MERIT PAY, OVERTIME, bonuses, or night or other differentials or premiums.

basis point One one-hundredth of a percentage point. If the prevailing short-term interest rate falls from 9.255 per cent to 9.125 per cent in the course of a week, for example, it is said to have fallen by 125 basis points, or one-eighth of a percentage point.

basis-point pricing A method of pricing in which a producer sets his price by calculating the transportation costs from some fixed location to his customer and adding this to a fixed price; the fixed location may not be the location of the producer's plant, so the price arrived at may be higher than the fixed price plus the cost of transporting the product from the producer to the customer. It is as if a group of producers in Canada decided that the price of a product would be a fixed price plus a delivery transportation charge using Windsor as the fixed location; a buyer obtaining the product from a plant in Cornwall would still pay the same price as if the product had come from Windsor.

Bay Street The heart of Canada's financial markets, in downtown Toronto, where the TORONTO STOCK EXCHANGE and Canada's MONEY MARKET, CAPITAL MARKET, and FOREIGN-EXCHANGE MARKET are based. The major banks, investment dealers, stockbrokers, and institutional investors are all located in this financial district.

bear An investor who believes that the prices of shares, bonds, and commodities are about to decline. Thus, he may sell his existing investments and also try to make a profit by selling, for future delivery, shares he doesn't own, in the hope that he can buy them on the market at a lower price when he has to make delivery. This form of speculation is known as SELLING SHORT. See also BULL.

bear market A market for shares, bonds, or commodities in which the trend of prices is down. See also BULL MARKET.

bearer bond A bond that is presumed to be legally owned by the person who possesses it; it is not registered in anyone's name in the books of the company issuing it or on the security. Interest is paid through coupons attached to the bond, each bearing the date on which it can be redeemed at a bank or elsewhere for cash. A bearer bond is as negotiable as cash at a bank or other financial institution.

beggar-thy-neighbour policies Protectionist policies to reduce imports and increase exports, usually motivated by a country's desire to export its unemployment problems to its neighbours. Such policies include increased tariffs or other import barriers, export subsidies, and currency devaluations. These policies were employed by many different nations during the depression of the 1930s as they scrambled to shift their unemployment to other countries by reducing imports and increasing exports. But such policies were self-defeating, since they led to retaliation; in the end, everyone was worse off because everyone's exports were reduced.

beneficial owner The person who is the true owner of a business, shares in a company, or other asset. In some businesses the beneficial owner may be unknown, since he or she chooses to operate through an agent, trust officer, lawyer, or business partner. In other cases, shares and other securities may be registered in the name of a stockbroker or trust company simply to facilitate the sale of the securities. See also SILENT PARTNER.

beneficiary A person who is left something in a will or who is named to receive the proceeds of an insurance policy.

benefits-received principle of taxation The principle that the taxes levied on a person or corporation should be related to the benefits that that person or corporation receives from public services. While this approach can be used in some very selective instances, in such forms as an airport tax to cover the costs of building and operating airports, a gasoline tax to help pay for road construction and maintenance, or a charge for postal services or entry to public parks, museums, and the like, it is difficult to apportion the costs of police, public health, scientific research, and other such public services. See also ABILITY-TO-PAY PRINCIPLE OF TAXATION.

Bennett New Deal A series of measures by which Prime Minister R. B. Bennett in 1935 attempted to reinvigorate the economy, crack down on unfair business practices, provide better pay and working conditions, improve social assistance, and create jobs. The measures were first outlined in a series of five radio talks to the country, starting on 2 January, and were subsequently spelled out in the government's SPEECH FROM THE THRONE. A number of measures were passed in mid-1935, but many were later declared to be unconstitutional.

The principle items of legislation were: **1.** The Employment and Insurance Act, which provided UNEMPLOYMENT INSURANCE, a national employment service, and other measures to assist the jobless. It was later declared unconstitutional. **2.** The Dominion Trade and Industry Commission Act, establishing a commission to enforce the COMBINES INVESTIGATION ACT, investigate unfair business practices, recommend other measures to outlaw unfair business practices, and apply the national trademark "Canada Standard" to products meeting government specifications for quality. It was declared constitutional. **3.** The Minimum Wages Act, which allowed the government to set MINIMUM WAGES in different industries across the country. It was declared unconstitutional. **4.** The Weekly Day of Rest Act, which provided for one compulsory day of rest for workers each week, preferably Sunday. It was declared unconstitutional. **5.** The Limitation of Hours of Work Act, which set out an eight-hour day and a forty-eight-hour work week. It was declared unconstitutional. **6.** Amendments to the Natural Products Marketing Act of 1934, which already permitted the establishment of MARKETING BOARDS for farm products such as milk and cheese. It was extended to include pulp and paper and other forest products. The act and its amendments were declared unconstitutional. **7.** Amendments to the Criminal Code imposing criminal penalties for MISLEADING ADVERTISING, failing to pay the minimum wage, or engaging in unfair business practices such as trade discrimination and price cutting to eliminate competition or a competitor. The amendments were upheld, except for the minimum-wage provision.

In all of these cases, the Supreme Court delivered its judgements on 17 June 1936. The decisions on appeals to the Judicial Committee of the Privy Council were made on 28 January 1937. Other New Deal measures proposed by Bennett included establishment of an Economic Council of Canada, tax reform to make the tax system more closely related to ability to pay, public works and monetary expansion to create jobs, health and sickness insurance, and other measures to protect the public and investors against unfair business practices. In spite of these measures, Bennett was defeated in the general election of 1935. Many Canadians believed that he had done far too little to fight the Depression in earlier years and that his New Deal was a last-minute election gimmick.

bequest A gift of money, securities, real estate, works of art, and personal property left to relatives, friends, and other beneficiaries in the will of a deceased person.

beyond-economic-reach reserves Proven oil or natural-gas reserves that cannot be included in the calculation of reserves because they are too far away from markets, or too small to be connected by pipeline or removed by tanker or liquefaction and tanker. For example, oil and natural-gas reserves in the far North cannot be included in NATIONAL ENERGY BOARD estimates of what may be surplus to Canada's needs until a pipeline or other transportation link has been established.

bid The price a would-be buyer is willing to pay for a share, bond, or other security or asset; see also ASK-PRICE. A bid is also an offer to purchase at a stated price made by a prospective buyer at an auction or by a person making an offer to purchase on a property.

bid and asked quotations The bid is the highest price a buyer is willing to pay, while the asked price is the lowest a seller will accept; together they represent a quotation, for a share on a stock market, for example.

bid-rigging See RIGGED BID.

big business The biggest corporations and financial institutions in a country; the top one hundred corporations in Canada. *The Financial Post*, a weekly business newspaper, compiles an annual list of the country's top five hundred corporations. *Canadian Business* magazine compiles a similar annual list. These corporations account for a disproportionately large share of economic activity in Canada and include the principal banking, transportation, energy, steel, forest-products, mining, automotive, telecommunications, electrical, chemical, food-processing, and other corporations.

bilateral agreement An agreement on trade, investment, or other economic relations negotiated between just two countries; as opposed to a multilateral agreement, which applies the same treatment to all of a country's normal trading partners. Prior to the Second World War many of the economic dealings among nations were based on bilateral agreements. But since 1945, non-discriminatory multilateral agreements have come to dominate trade, monetary, and other economic relations, although nations still negotiate bilateral arrangements. A recent example of a bilateral agreement is the 1965 CANADA–UNITED STATES AUTOMOTIVE PRODUCTS AGREEMENT. See also MULTILATERALISM.

bilateral monopoly A double MONOPOLY, in which there is one producer or supplier and one buyer or consumer of a particular good or service. Such situations are rare but can exist; for example, the government may be the only buyer for a sophisticated weapon, while there may be only one manufacturer of the weapon.

bill 1. A statement to a buyer from a seller stating the amount owed for itemized goods or services. **2.** A financial document indicating a debt or payment, that can be accepted as equivalent to cash in settling a business transaction.

bimetallism A monetary system in which the value of the monetary unit of a country is defined in terms of two different metals, usually gold and silver. The two metals are made legal tender, each being defined in the weight of the other. The system had some appeal in the nineteenth century, since an increase in the supply of either metal could be used to justify an increase in total money supply; it also made for easier trade and other transactions between gold-standard and silver-standard countries, such as Britain and India. But fluctuations in gold and silver prices made the system unstable. A number of countries, led by France, had adopted bimetallism but dropped it when Germany moved to the gold standard in the nineteenth century. The United States also abandoned bimetallism. Prior to Confederation, Canada's dollar was valued in terms of gold only.

birth rate See CRUDE BIRTH RATE.

black market An illegal market established during conditions of war, military occupation, or economic crisis. Its purpose is to circumvent rationing and other restrictions, such as price controls. Consumers making purchases in a black market pay excessive prices, reflecting the monopoly power of the sellers and the high risk of operating such a market.

blanket policy An insurance policy covering damages or loss—resulting from theft, fire, accident, or other cause of harm—of all the possessions of a homeowner or tenant, without requiring an inventory of the possessions for the insurance company.

blind trust A trust established to manage the assets of an individual, such as a cabinet minister or senior government official, so as to enable him to carry out his responsibilities without fear of a potential conflict of interest. While the trustee keeps the person informed of the value of his trust, he keeps confidential the actual securities bought and sold.

block trade The sale or purchase of an unusually large number of shares in a public company on a stock exchange, with the sale and purchase being made by a single seller, and often, a single buyer.

blocked currency Foreign-exchange controls to prevent non-residents from acquiring, using, or repatriating a country's currency. Such controls may be invoked during a balance-of-payments crisis or during a war or political crisis.

blue chip The common share of a large, reputable, low-risk company that has a long record of regular dividend payments. In Canada, such companies would include Bell Canada, Imperial Oil, the five major banks, and the largest steel companies.

blue-collar workers Workers who, generally speaking, are employed in an industrial plant where conditions are dirty and where workers may change their clothes before leaving the plant. They are production and maintenance workers and may be unskilled, semi-skilled, or skilled workers; they either work with their hands or operate machines. See also WHITE-COLLAR WORKERS.

board lot The regular trading block of shares in a stock exchange, usually one hundred shares.

board of directors The managerial board of a company, made up of duly elected or appointed DIRECTORS. The board supervises the activities of the company and its senior officers and sets or approves company policies and objectives. The work of the board of directors usually includes the appointment and supervision of senior executives, the approval of budgets, financing plans, new products, takeovers and other business plans, the payment of dividends, and the approval of major contracts, including collective agreements.

boiler room The place from which highly dubious stocks are sold by telephone. Promoters usually work with so-called sucker lists of individuals likely to have investment capital available, frequently doctors, lawyers, dentists, and people operating their own businesses. High-pressure sales tactics are applied, promising would-be investors fast profits if they purchase the stocks immediately. In the U.S., securities legislation in the 1930s made such swindles much harder to pull off, but such operations were relatively easy to run from Canada until the 1950s. Canadian promoters frequently applied boiler-room tactics to lists of U.S. investors, especially in the sale of dubious mining stocks. Such operations are now illegal in Canada.

bonanza Discovery of an extremely rich orebody.

bond A debt security in the form of a promissory note or certificate of indebtedness, issued usually for a term running from at least five to seven years up to twenty years or longer. The bond certificate shows the name of the government or corporation issuing it, its face value, the annual rate of interest that will be paid and when, and the date on which the bond matures and the principal must be repaid in full. Although CANADA SAVINGS BONDS may be issued in denominations as small as one hundred dollars, most bonds are issued in denominations of at least one thousand.

Bonds are issued by federal, provincial, and municipal governments, school boards, crown corporations, business corporations, and financial institutions, to raise long-term capital. Bond issues are subject to the regulations of the securities commission of the province in which they are issued. Their appeal to investors, especially INSTITUTIONAL INVESTORS, is that they have an assured return and usually low risk. There is also a secondary market, the BOND MARKET, in which traders deal in already-issued bonds, hoping to earn capital gains on changes in the market value of bonds due to changes in interest rates.

Sometimes a bond is registered in the name of its owner, so that if it is stolen it is harder to dispose of. Coupon bonds have interest coupons attached, which can be cashed each year as they become payable. A first-mortgage bond is one that is secured by a mortgage against the corporation's assets. A DEBENTURE is a bond against which no assets of the corporation are pledged, and that represents a general claim against the corporation. A sinking-fund bond is one against which the corporation is setting aside funds each year for eventual repayment. A serial-bond issue is one in which a certain number of the bonds mature each year. A callable bond is one that can be redeemed at any time. A convertible bond is one that the owner may convert into common or preferred shares. See also PERPETUAL BOND, PRIVATE PLACEMENT.

bond market. The network of bond traders working in the banks, insurance companies, investment-dealer firms, and other financial institutions, who trade in bonds either on their own account or on behalf of their clients. There is no bond exchange, as there is a stock exchange with its own building, but there is a telecommunications network of bond traders. Investors buy and sell corporate, government, and hydro bonds for profit, as interest rates —and hence, the market value of the bonds —change; a $10,000 bond with an interest rate of 8.875 per cent, for example, would be worth more than $10,000 if average bond rates fell to 8.125 per cent, and less if the average bond rate rose to 9.125 per cent. The bond market consists of the primary market for new bond issues and the secondary market for the resale and purchase of bonds already in public hands. The bond market is regulated by the INVESTMENT DEALERS ASSOCIATION of Canada, along with the Toronto Bond Traders' Association and the Montreal Bond Traders' Association.

bond rating The grading by an independent professional analyst of a corporate or government bond indicating the quality of the bond. The rating indicates the borrower's ability to pay the interest and repay the principal of the bond. The two top bond-rating firms, based in New York, are Moody's and Standard and Poor. The two principal Canadian firms are Dominion Bond Rating Service and Canadian Bond Rating Service. The top rating is Aaa.

bonded carrier A carrier that has posted a bond with the Department of NATIONAL REVENUE and is permitted to bring goods across Canada's borders to a final or other destination without having to complete the importing paperwork or to pay duties and taxes at the border. The paperwork is completed and the duties and taxes are paid at the carrier's destination. The bond required ranges from five thousand dollars for a truck to eighty thousand for a plane, depending on size.

bonus bid The successful bid in a government auction of oil or natural-gas PERMITS or LEASES. The bonus bid is the highest bid.

book value The net value of a corporation or its individual assets, based on the value appearing in its balance sheet. Book value may or may not be market value; it may, for example, be the acquisition cost minus the depreciation to date, or it may simply be the purchase price. Hence, book value is not always a reliable guide to what a corporation or an asset is worth. It could significantly understate the value of land, mineral reserves, or patents, for example.

bookkeeping Accounting records that show all transactions—that is, all expenses and all income. See also DOUBLE-ENTRY BOOKKEEPING.

boom A high and unsustainable level of business activity. It is usually characterized by high profits, soaring stock and commodity markets, full employment, and business operating at its full productive capacity; it is the high point in the BUSINESS CYCLE. But as that peak is reached, shortages in labour and goods develop, forcing up wages and prices. The ensuing inflation undermines the boom. A RECESSION normally follows. A boom is characterized not only by strong growth but by rapid growth. Its upper limit is reached when all the resources in the economy are fully utilized.

bootlegger A person who sells goods illegally; for example, someone who sells liquor to minors or during hours or on days when provincially operated stores are closed: this is a contravention of provincial laws that forbid customers to resell liquor to others. The bootlegger makes his profit by charging a higher price per bottle than the price he has paid. Sometimes a bootlegger may sell an illegally made product—that is, one on which taxes have not been paid: privately distilled liquor, for example.

bottom line A widely used term that means "what really counts." In accounting, the bottom line is the net profit remaining to the business and its shareholders after all expenses, taxes, and loan interest have been paid.

boycott The refusal by an individual, organization, or nation to deal with a firm or nation until it changes its policies or behaviour. It is a form of economic or political pressure. A union and its members may boycott the products of a firm if they or another union are engaged in a labour dispute with it. Similarly, consumers may boycott a firm's products if they feel that it is overcharging, or they may boycott a particular store if they object to some of the merchandise it is selling. An example of a trade boycott is that of the Arab nations on economic dealings with Israel; it consists of a primary boycott by the Arab nations themselves against direct dealing with Israel, and a secondary boycott in which the Arab nations also refuse to have economic dealings with firms from non-Arab countries that have dealings with Israel.

branch banking A banking system in which there are only a few banks, with each one operating branches throughout the country. This enables each bank to acquire significant financial strength and to avoid being dependent on the economic health of a single region or community. This is the kind of banking system Canada has, as opposed to the regional banking system in the United States, where there are thousands of banks, most of them serving a relatively small area, perhaps a single community. Thus, while U.S. residents may benefit from a more competitive banking system in their biggest cities, Canadian residents are more likely to have a choice of banks if they live in smaller communities. Without the development of large national banks operating throughout the country, it is hard to see how Canada could have developed a banking system that is effectively Canadian owned and controlled.

branchplant economy An economy in which a large share of business activity is carried out by subsidiaries of foreign corporations. This means that important decisions on investment, jobs, research and development, new products, export markets, and financing are made in another country and not in the country where the activity may take place. Canada is an example. See also TRUNCATION, FOREIGN DIRECT INVESTMENT.

brand name The name used by a firm to identify to consumers a product, line of products, or the firm itself, and thus to differentiate its goods and services from those of its competitors. Since the value of a brand name normally increases as a result of long-term investment in advertising and promotion to build customer loyalty, brand names can be worth a lot of money. Since they are also a form of product differentiation, brand names can become a powerful barrier to entry into an industry by would-be competitors. Brand names include those of manufacturers whose products are sold throughout the country; private brands are products that bear the name of the retailer or a name owned by the retailer, even though they may be manufactured by the same company that manufactures the national brand. Brand names are intangible assets—they are worth money and are registered.

Brandt Commission An international commission of sixteen persons appointed in September 1977 by World Bank President Robert McNamara to seek out solutions to North-South problems and to demands for a NEW INTERNATIONAL ECONOMIC ORDER. It was headed by former West German Chancellor Willy Brandt, and its members included one Canadian, former Canadian Labour Congress President Joe Morris. It was to report in 1980. See also NORTH-SOUTH DIALOGUE.

bread A slang term meaning money.

break-even point The level of sales or other income needed to recover the costs of a firm. When income exceeds expenses, the firm makes a profit; when income fails to cover expenses, the firm suffers a loss.

break-up value What the owners of a business would get if it were wound up and after its creditors had been paid.

Bretton Woods Agreement An agreement reached among the governments of the United States, Britain, and Canada at a New Hampshire resort in 1944, to establish a multilateral and non-discriminatory monetary, trading, and investment order as the basis for postwar economic recovery. They wanted to prevent a return to the BEGGAR-THY-NEIGHBOUR POLICIES of the 1930s. The agreement was based on the deep-rooted belief that the citizens of individual nations would fare best in a global economy based on international specialization and comparative advantage, and non-discriminatory policies among nations. The agreement led to the creation of the INTERNATIONAL MONETARY FUND (IMF), the INTERNATIONAL BANK FOR RECONSTRUCTION AND DEVELOPMENT (IBRD), or World Bank, and the GENERAL AGREEMENT ON TARIFFS AND TRADE (GATT). At the heart of the postwar economic framework was a system of FIXED EXCHANGE RATES and convertible currencies, to be regulated by the strict rules of the IMF.

bridge financing Short-term financing, particularly applicable to construction financing, until a mortgage or other long-term financing can be arranged.

British North America Act (BNA Act) An act of the British Parliament that brought Canada into being as a nation on 1 July 1867, by joining together in a federation Ontario, Quebec, New Brunswick, and Nova Scotia. Since then, six other provinces have been created or have joined, the most recent being Newfoundland in 1949. The BNA Act is, in effect, Canada's constitution. It sets out the federal and provincial spending and taxing powers, including concurrent powers, states the desire of the Fathers of Confederation that Canada be a single or common market, and spells out other details of the new nation, including the organization of political institutions. The act has been amended a number of times since Confederation; any changes must be made by the British Parliament since the BNA Act is an act of the British Parliament. Attempts to make it an act of the Canadian Parliament have foundered so far on the inability of the federal and provincial governments to agree on an amending formula. See also FEDERAL SPENDING POWER, FEDERAL TAXING POWER, PROVINCIAL SPENDING POWER, PROVINCIAL TAXING POWER, DISTRIBUTION OF POWERS.

British preferential tariff A tariff scheme that levies a lower or preferential tariff on goods traded among Commonwealth or former Commonwealth countries. The system dates back to 1919, but took on greater importance with the Ottawa Conference of 1932, at which Britain, Canada, and other Commonwealth members signed reciprocal agreements instituting preferential tariff rates for each other's products. The Canada–United Kingdom reciprocal agreement was phased out after 1973, when Britain entered the EUROPEAN ECONOMIC COMMUNITY. But Canada still has reciprocal agreements with Australia and New Zealand and non-reciprocal agreements with other members of the Commonwealth. In July 1979, Canada gave South Africa six months' notice that it was planning to withdraw from the Canada–South Africa Trade Agreement of 1932.

The tariff rate under the British preferential tariff is less than the MOST-FAVOURED-NATION rate. But it is of declining importance and, for many less-developed Commonwealth countries, the GENERALIZED SYSTEM OF PREFERENCES results in lower tariffs than the so-called British preferential rate. The existence of the British preferential tariff was an important factor for a time in encouraging U.S.-owned companies to establish subsidiaries in Canada or to take over established Canadian firms. These Canadian branchplants gave the U.S. firms access to British and Commonwealth markets at the British preferential tariff, which for a time was much lower than the rate charged on goods shipped directly from the U.S. See also OTTAWA AGREEMENTS.

British Thermal Unit The amount of heat necessary to raise one pint of water one degree Fahrenheit. The measure is frequently used to compare the relative energy content of different sources of energy, such as oil, coal, natural gas, and uranium.

broker An independent agent who brings together a buyer and a seller so that a sale can be made. There are many different kinds of brokers, each with specialized knowledge of his market: in shares traded on a stock exchange, the stockbroker; in property (such as houses or commercial buildings), the real-estate broker; in commodities (such as wheat and porkbellies), the commodities broker; and in insurance, the insurance broker. For their services, brokers are paid a commission (BROKERAGE), which is usually related to the value of the transaction.

brokerage The fee or commission charged to a customer by a stockbroker, commodity dealer, real-estate agent, or other kind of broker.

bubble A speculative commercial venture, common in the eighteenth and early nineteenth centuries, in which the value of shares would rise so high that they would bear no relationship whatever to the asset value or future earning power of the enterprise. Most such ventures were created to defraud investors; often, they succeeded. The psychological fever, usually for a company with land or mineral investments in another part of the world, would reach such a pitch that even normally rational investors would come to feel that they couldn't afford to stay out. At some point the bubble would burst; share prices would plummet, and investors would be left with worthless pieces of paper. Frequently their entire fortunes would be wiped out. The Bubble Act was passed in Britain in 1720 after the infamous South Sea Bubble, to control the sale of shares to the public. It was one of the first acts anywhere to protect investors.

bucket shop An illegal act by a stockbroker, which consists of accepting an order to buy or sell a share without the intention of carrying out the transaction. The broker delays carrying out the transaction in the hope that the price of the share will change, thus enabling him to make a personal profit.

budget **1.** The annual statement, usually in the spring, by the federal minister of FINANCE, setting out the government's expected revenues, spending, and resulting surplus or deficit. The budget speech contains a review of the economy and an indication of expected economic performance for the year ahead, along with any proposed tax or tariff changes. It follows the presentation of the spending ESTIMATES and sets out the country's fiscal policy for the ensuing year. Similar annual statements are made by each of the provincial Finance ministers or treasurers.

The federal government presents its budget in three different forms: the BUDGETARY-ACCOUNTS BUDGET, the CASH-NEEDS BUDGET, and the NATIONAL-ACCOUNTS BUDGET; at the end of the FISCAL YEAR, Statistics Canada presents the budget data in a fourth form, the FINANCIAL-MANAGEMENT BUDGET. The budgetary-accounts budget gives the best picture of department-by-department spending. The cash-needs budget shows the activities of the federal government in capital markets, and hence helps to analyze the impact of the budget on MONETARY POLICY and the availability of funds for private borrowers. The national-accounts budget measures the impact of government activity on the economy. And the financial-management budget shows government spending by function, in areas such as health care, industrial development, and social welfare; it also details revenue by the type of tax and its base or by the kind of revenue from the sale of goods or services.

2. A financial plan for any business or other organization, showing expected sources of revenue, expected expenditures, and the resulting profit or loss. Budgets are usually drafted for the next fiscal year, but some organizations operate on five-year budgets, since this gives a better picture—and hence control—of revenue and expenditure trends and is more suited to strategic planning.

budget speech The speech made by the minister of FINANCE, reviewing the state of the economy and setting out the FISCAL POLICY the government intends to follow in the ensuing twelve months. At the end of the speech setting out the budget, the Finance minister tables budget papers, containing detailed information on the economy and the government's accounts, and moves formal WAYS AND MEANS MOTIONS that allow him to introduce legislation implementing the precise tax and tariff measures contained in his budget. The House of Commons has a six-day debate on these motions in what is known as the budget debate. At the end of the debate, a vote is taken that the government has to win; if it doesn't, it has lost the confidence of the House of Commons, and either a new cabinet must be installed or, more likely, a general election held. If the ways and means motions are adopted, the exact budget measures, usually in the form of amendments to the Income Tax Act or other existing legislation, are presented to the House of Commons for debate, for clause-by-clause scrutiny and approval; the legislation must also be approved by the Senate. Although the budget measures must have the approval of Parliament, it is assumed that they will receive it, and the budget measures therefore usually come into effect the same evening the budget speech is read to the House of Commons. The speech is usually delivered after 8 P.M., when all financial markets are closed.

budgetary-accounts budget The revenue and spending program of the federal government, presented by the minister of FINANCE each year, usually in the spring, for the coming fiscal year. The spending program is set out in the ESTIMATES, published in advance of the BUDGET SPEECH, while the budget gives the government's projection of revenues from taxes and other sources for the coming year. These budgetary accounts set out spending on a department-by-department basis that is approved by Parliament and paid out of the CONSOLIDATED REVENUE FUND. The difference between spending and revenue is the budgetary deficit or surplus.

The budgetary-accounts figure is not the best guide to the impact of the government's FISCAL POLICY on the economy, in particular to whether that policy is stimulative, restrictive, or neutral. Economists use both the CASH-NEEDS BUDGET and the NATIONAL-ACCOUNTS BUDGET to assess the economic impact of government spending and taxing for the coming fiscal year. The budgetary-accounts budget is important as a system for Parliamentary control of actual government spending, since it presents spending by department, on the basis of which MPs can vote approval. It also shows the amount by which the federal net debt is raised or reduced. Its weakness for economic analysis is that it excludes a great deal of government spending and revenue, such as the operations of the Canada Pension Plan, unemployment insurance, and government-owned crown corporations. See also FINANCIAL-MANAGEMENT budget.

The PUBLIC ACCOUNTS, published at the end of the fiscal year, show the actual expenditures and revenues, and can be compared with the earlier estimates and budget-speech projection of revenues. The Department of Finance publishes monthly statistics on the budgetary accounts.

budgetary control A form of financial control in an organization in which senior and middle managers are expected to keep their costs and revenues in line with the budget that has been prepared for the financial year. If costs are out of line with those in the budget, then either new controls must be brought to bear to reduce them, or the budget itself must be revised to reflect those added costs. In most organizations, monthly and cumulative performance can be compared with budgetary projections for the same periods.

buffer stocks Stocks of commodities of international importance that are purchased when prices are low and supplies excessive, and sold when prices are high and supplies scarce, with the aim of stabilizing prices. The less-developed countries have proposed that buffer stocks be established for a wide range of commodities through the creation of a COMMON FUND to finance the acquisition of such stocks. Agreement in principle on such a fund was reached between developed and less-developed countries in 1979. A buffer-stock program currently in existence is the one operated under the INTERNATIONAL TIN AGREEMENTS.

building permit A permit issued by a municipality, granting permission for the construction of a particular type of building on a designated parcel of land. National and regional statistics on the value of building permits granted are a useful indicator of future economic activity, since such figures give an indication of the demand for construction labour, building materials, steel, and certain consumer durables such as furniture and appliances. Statistics Canada publishes monthly figures on the value of building permits granted, using figures supplied by about 1,700 municipalities. The statistics are broken down by province, municipality, and metropolitan area, and also indicate residential, industrial, commercial, government, and institutional spending. If the monthly value of building permits granted shows a series of increases, then construction activity, an important source of economic growth, is about to pick up. Conversely, a consistent decline in building permits issued indicates that economic activity may be heading for a decline or recession.

built-in stabilizer A government program that automatically offsets fluctuations in the BUSINESS CYCLE and hence helps the economy to adjust to new conditions. For example, in a recession, unemployment-insurance and social-welfare payments help to sustain the overall level of demand in the economy. In a period of inflation, the income-tax system takes a bigger bite of rising incomes, even with indexation for inflation, thus relieving the pressure on demand in the economy. The existence of such built-in stabilizers means that the economic system adjusts to some extent to changing economic conditions, without having to await government intervention. Normally, though, there is still a need for direct government intervention as well—through tax cuts or increases, for example, through changes in MONETARY POLICY, or perhaps through the adoption of an INCOMES POLICY.

bull In stock, bond, and commodity markets, a person who expects prices to go up and who backs up that belief by investing. The term itself dates back to the London Stock Exchange in the early part of the eighteenth century. See also BEAR.

bull market A market in which the prevailing mood is one of optimism and in which prices are rising. See also BEAR MARKET.

bullion Gold, silver, and other precious metals in the form of bars and ingots rather than coins, with a money value stamped on them. Part of Canada's foreign-exchange reserves are maintained in the form of bullion, and gold bullion is sometimes used, though less so now than in the past, by central banks to settle international payments. The price of gold bullion is determined in the GOLD MARKET. See also GOLD STANDARD.

Bureau of Competition Policy A branch of the Department of CONSUMER AND CORPORATE AFFAIRS that administers the COMBINES INVESTIGATION ACT. It is responsible for strengthening competition in the economy and halting unfair business practices that reduce competition or defraud the public. It deals with mergers, monopolies and combines, price-fixing and other restrictive business practices, and false or misleading advertising. The director of Investigation and Research conducts investigations or refers them to the RESTRICTIVE TRADE PRACTICES COMMISSION.

Bureau of Consumer Affairs A branch of the Department of CONSUMER AND CORPORATE AFFAIRS that administers federal laws designed to protect consumers against fraudulent weights and measures, deceptive packaging, and hazardous or unsafe products. It also plays a role in consumer education.

Bureau of Corporate Affairs A branch of the Department of CONSUMER AND CORPORATE AFFAIRS that administers federal laws governing the operating of a business in Canada. This includes the Canada Business Corporations Act, which sets out the procedure for incorporation and the filing of financial statements, as well as the various responsibilities of directors and officers of a corporation. The bureau also administers the Bankruptcy Act, and has a special division that is responsible for federal activities in the regulation of securities markets in Canada.

Bureau of Intellectual Property A branch of the Department of CONSUMER AND CORPORATE AFFAIRS that is responsible for the administration of PATENTS, COPYRIGHTS, industrial design, and TRADEMARK laws, and for Canada's participation in international INTELLECTUAL-PROPERTY organizations. The laws administered by the bureau include the Patent Act, the Copyright Act, the Industrial Design Act, and the Trade Marks Act.

business The production of goods or services for profit. Such activity can be carried out by an individual, a family, a partnership, or an incorporated company.

business agent An employee of a union or union local whose job it is to look after the business affairs of a local, to help negotiate collective agreements, and to help union officers see that a collective agreement is implemented in the best interests of the union membership.

business cycle The fluctuations in economic activity, alternating between recovery and fast growth towards FULL EMPLOYMENT, and contraction and slower growth down into RECESSION. While the sharp swings of the business cycle have been largely smoothed out since the introduction of KEYNESIAN ECONOMICS, many economists still believe that the business cycle is an important feature of economic life. The business cycle goes through five basic stages: **1.** Recovery from the trough of the cycle, with economic growth, stimulated by lower interest rates, a ready supply of investment capital and consumer credit, and government incentives such as a stimulative FISCAL POLICY, all working to make use of idle capacity in the economy. **2.** A period of gathering steam as the pace of recovery gains momentum, increased demand leads to new investment, and the economy moves towards full employment. **3.** Excess demand and the peak of the business cycle as growth pushes the economy beyond its full-employment potential, with shortages and inflation developing and government being forced to raise taxes and interest rates, reduce the growth rate of the money supply, and cut back on its own spending. **4.** Contraction of economic growth, with industry postponing new investment and cutting back production, employees being laid off, and tighter credit conditions taking effect. **5.** The recession or trough, with business activities cut back, unemployment much higher, inventories sharply reduced, and inflation and costs under control. This last stage is the turning point in the down cycle, with government using MONETARY and fiscal policies to get economic recovery, or stage one, underway again.

There is disagreement among economists on whether business cycles are an inevitable part of economic life or reflect the failure to refine economic policies to the point where EQUILIBRIUM can be maintained; economists also disagree on the causes of such business fluctuations, with some putting the blame on poor monetary management, others blaming fluctuations in investment in new productive facilities, others blaming under-consumption by consumers, and still others maintaining that fundamental changes are occurring, based on resources shortages, the decline of market forces, and other such factors. See also ACCELERATOR PRINCIPLE.

business failures Business firms that go out of business either by going bankrupt or by being wound up because they cannot continue in operation. An increase in the number of business failures is usually a sign of worsening business conditions since, in a recession, with money tighter and demand weaker, marginal businesses have a harder time getting credit or finding new customers and orders. Statistics Canada reports business failures coming under the federal Bankruptcy Act and the Winding-up Act. Failures are reported by province, industry, and by dollar amount.

business game See GAME THEORY.

bust A sharp and severe drop in economic activity resulting in high unemployment, a severe drop in prices, and a decline in investment. No major industrial country with a diversified economy and BUILT-IN STABILIZERS has experienced a bust since the depression of the 1930s. But less-developed countries, which depend on a single commodity for much of their economic activity and most of their foreign-exchange earnings, can still experience such dramatic declines in economic performance. So can individual industries in industrial countries, industries such as gold mining and agriculture, if world prices collapse in the face of oversupply or a sharp drop in demand. See also BOOM.

buyer's market A market in which supply is greater than demand, and hence one in which there are more sellers than buyers. This means that buyers have some market power that allows them to push down or hold down prices. See also SELLER'S MARKET.

buyers' strike See CONSUMER BOYCOTT.

by-laws **1.** The set of rules adopted by shareholders of a company, setting out the timing and date of shareholders' meetings, the role of directors' meetings, the election and qualification of directors, the number and duties of corporate officers to be appointed by the directors, the financial procedures of the company, and other such matters. Shareholders can amend their by-laws. **2.** Laws passed by municipalities, dealing with such matters as land use, shopping hours, licensing of local businesses, and traffic controls.

by-product A secondary product that is produced in the course of processing or manufacturing a principal product. It is not a waste because a use can be found for it. Sulphur, for example, is a by-product of the forest-products industry, produced during the processing of natural gas and wood chips to make wallboard.

Byrne Report See NEW BRUNSWICK ROYAL COMMISSION ON FINANCE AND MUNICIPAL TAXATION.

C

CANDIDE The econometric model of the Canadian economy developed by the ECONOMIC COUNCIL OF CANADA, with the help of a number of federal government departments, to calculate performance targets for the Canadian economy and to evaluate Canada's economic prospects under various sets of assumptions. Work on the model has been underway since 1970, with a revised model developed in 1976. CANDIDE is used by a number of government departments and agencies, such as the National Energy Board, in making calculations about future economic growth and other developments.

CANSIM (Canadian Socio-Economic Information Management System) A fully computerized data bank of STATISTICS CANADA's current and historical information from its most widely used series of statistics. In addition to a full range of economics statistics, the data bank contains a considerable amount of social information, including statistics on health, education, science, culture, and the judicial system.

COLA clause In a collective agreement, a cost-of-living-allowance clause that automatically raises pay rates at specified periods during the life of the contract, in line with increases in the CONSUMER PRICE INDEX. The clause may provide for complete indexation or put a limit on the percentage increase that will be paid.

COMECON See COUNCIL FOR MUTUAL ECONOMIC ASSISTANCE.

cabinet The prime minister and the various ministers who are appointed by him to head the different departments of government or to undertake special tasks. The cabinet meets together as a group to decide on government policy. There is also an inner cabinet, made up of a smaller number of key ministers, which determines the government's basic goals, makes major policy decisions, and is the long-term planning arm of the government. In matters of economic policy, the cabinet has the final say on the overall spending level, and sets out the government's spending priorities within that ceiling. There are also five cabinet committees: social and native affairs, external affairs and defence, federal-provincial relations, economy in government, and economic development. The committee on government economy is responsible for the effective management of government spending and for government organization. The committee on economic development deals with policies to promote the growth of the Canadian economy and with the setting and implementation of economic policy goals. Each committee consists of a small number of cabinet ministers.

cable address A word that stands for the name and address of a firm or government agency that regularly sends and receives telegrams and cables. The cable address is often indicated on the letterhead of a firm. Its value is that it saves both time and money, time because the full name and address don't have to be typed out, and money because cable or telegram charges are usually based on the number of words in a message.

cable television A communications system designed to improve the reception of local and regional television stations and other services to subscribers through their television sets. A central antenna system and amplifiers are linked to individual homes by coaxial cable. Cable television is part of the Canadian broadcasting system, and its activities are regulated by the CANADIAN RADIO-TELEVISION AND TELECOMMUNICATIONS COMMISSION, which grants licences, holds licence-renewal and change-of-ownership hearings, and considers applications to raise subscribers' fees and add new services. Once installed, a cable-television system can be used to provide many other services over unused channels, such as pay television, news, educational programming, service information, and specialized programming. New interactive or two-way cable will allow the system to be used for fire and burglar alarms, home shopping, education, and games and entertainment. Cable television was introduced in Canada largely to bring U.S.-border television stations to Canadian viewers.

caisses populaires CREDIT UNIONS operated in Quebec; they are important financial institutions, providing many banking and other services. They are co-operatively owned by their members and in many cases are tied to churches. The first caisse populaire or credit union in North America was started by Alphonse Desjardins, a House of Commons shorthand reporter, in 1900 in Lévis, Quebec. A network of caisses populaires, La Fédération du Québec des Unions Régionales des Caisses Populaires Desjardins, has a number of important investments, including a share of the Provincial Bank of Canada and ownership of La Société de Fiducie du Québec. Caisses populaires are regulated by the Quebec Ministry of Financial Institutions.

call A contract that gives the holder the right to buy from the existing owner of shares a specified number of shares in a particular company at a specified price during a specified period of time. The purchaser of this privilege pays the existing owner of the shares, the maker, a fee for this privilege. The purchaser is under no obligation actually to buy the shares; what he has purchased is the option of buying them if he decides he wants to.

The purchase of calls instead of the shares themselves is a form of stock-market speculation. The investor is speculating that the price of the shares will rise above the call price by a certain date and is willing to pay a fee to buy a block of shares at the specified call price. His profit is the difference between the actual market price and the call price, minus the fee he pays for the call. If the shares don't go up, his only loss is for the price of the call. The existing owner of the shares, the maker, gets money from the sale of the option and, if the option or call is exercised, still stands to make a profit, since the call price is higher than the existing market price. See also PUT, OPTION, STRADDLE.

call-back pay The extra pay due an employee who has completed his shift and is then called back to work before he is scheduled to return, either to fill in for an employee who has booked off sick, or because some emergency or special need has arisen. The amount and conditions under which he is paid are specified in a COLLECTIVE AGREEMENT.

call loan A loan that the lender may call in at any time or the borrower may repay at any time, without notice. This type of loan is used to finance the purchase of shares, bonds, and other securities.

Cambridge School See NEOCLASSICAL ECONOMICS.

Canada Assistance Plan (CAP) A federal program, introduced in 1966, to pay half the costs of provincial-municipal social assistance as defined under the program. It replaced a multitude of federal cost-sharing programs, and extended federal assistance into new areas, such as assistance to needy mothers with dependent children, health-care costs of welfare recipients, and welfare services aimed at reducing the causes and effects of poverty, such as special training for people unable to retain jobs or programs to reduce child abuse. Aid is based on an assessment of need rather than means. Assistance under the program includes aid to provide necessities such as food, shelter, clothing, fuel, and personal necessities; maintenance in a home for the aged, nursing home, or child-care institution; welfare services such as counselling, rehabilitation services, day-care, homemaker, and adoption services; and special needs for the rehabilitation, safety, and well-being of people in need. The provinces integrated their social-assistance programs under the Canada Assistance Plan. Quebec was the exception; it opted out and gets payments instead under the Established Programs (Interim Arrangements) Act.

Canada Deposit Insurance Corporation (CDIC) An insurer of deposits and lender of last resort for financial institutions. The corporation was established in 1967 to protect Canadian depositors against the loss of their savings, following the failure of several financial institutions. (See ATLANTIC ACCEPTANCE AFFAIR, PRUDENTIAL FINANCE CORPORATION AFFAIR.) Deposits of up to twenty thousand dollars of savings and checking accounts, deposit receipts, savings certificates, and debentures and other funds repayable on demand, or on a fixed date of five years or less, are protected. Protection only applies to deposits in Canadian financial institutions and denominated in Canadian dollars. Insurance is compulsory for the chartered banks, Quebec savings banks, federally incorporated trust and loan companies, and for provincially incorporated trust and loan companies and other institutions such as credit unions where the provincial government consents (except Quebec —see also QUEBEC DEPOSIT INSURANCE BOARD). Financial institutions are required to pay an annual premium (one-thirtieth of one per cent of insured deposits) and can borrow from the corporation, which acts as a lender of last resort.

Canada Development Corporation (CDC) A corporation created by the federal government in 1971 under the Canada Development Corporation Act. Its purposes are to help develop and maintain strong Canadian-controlled and Canadian-managed corporations in the private sector of the economy and to give Canadians greater opportunities to invest and participate in the economic development of their country. In introducing the act establishing the corporation, the minister of Finance said that it should emphasize support for industries in which there are opportunities for the development and application of new technologies or for the exploitation and upgrading of Canadian natural resources, or those that have special relevance to the development of the North and in which Canada now has or can develop significant comparative advantages by international standards. The CDC was also expected to play a role in the RATIONALIZATION and improvement of various sectors of industry in Canada. The CDC was not assigned the role of trying to buy back Canadian corporations from foreign owners, although it might do this in rationalization of an industry or in developing the base for an effective, Canadian-owned firm in an industry. The CDC was not to be a lender of last resort to firms in trouble; its investments were to meet the normal business test of profitability.

The CDC takes control positions in firms in which it makes investments. So far it has selected six industries for investment: petrochemicals, mining, oil and gas, health care, pipelines, and VENTURE CAPITAL. Its major assets include Polysar Limited, 60 per cent of Petrosar Limited, and 30 per cent of Texasgulf Incorporated. It has authorized capitalization of 200 million shares of NO PAR VALUE and $1 billion of PREFERRED SHARES. As the CDC increases in size and profitability, the government's share of voting stock may be reduced to 10 per cent. At present, the government holds about two-thirds of the voting shares, the others being owned by private investors. The CDC is not a crown corporation or an agent of the Crown.

Canada Employment and Immigration Commission (CEIC) A federal agency that administers federal manpower-training and assistance programs, unemployment insurance, and labour-market activities, including job-placement services in Canada Employment Centres. The agency also administers Canada's immigrant-recruiting and -processing services overseas and settlement in Canada. It was created in 1977, merging the former UNEMPLOYMENT INSURANCE COMMISSION and Canada Manpower Centre and taking over immigration recruiting. It reports to Parliament through the Department of EMPLOYMENT AND IMMIGRATION.

Canada Grains Council A federal body created in 1969 to improve grain production, processing, handling, transportation, and marketing, including export sales. Its members are non-government representatives of the grains industry, including farmers, flour-milling companies, railways, terminal operators, wheat pools, and grain companies. The council meets twice a year, while its board of directors meets ten times a year. It has two basic purposes: to improve co-operation within the grains industry, and to make recommendations on changes in government policy to aid the development of the grains industry.

Canada Labour Code The main body of federal labour law, which came into effect in July 1971. It covers about 10 per cent of the Canadian labour force, namely workers in industries that come under federal jurisdiction, such as railways, airlines, banks, and shipping companies. In addition, each province has its own labour laws. The Canada Labour Code was divided into five parts: part I dealt with fair-employment practices, such as a ban on job discrimination based on race, colour, religion, and national origin. Responsibility has since been transferred to the CANADIAN HUMAN RIGHTS COMMISSION. Part II has been consolidated with part III, which deals with labour standards such as the length of the work week, maximum hours of work, minimum wages, overtime, layoffs, dismissal, and maternity leave; part IV deals with job safety; part V deals with the conduct of industrial relations, and is administered by the Mediation and Conciliation Branch of the Department of LABOUR and the CANADA LABOUR RELATIONS BOARD.

The code deals with the organization of workers into unions, certification of bargaining units, and supervision of collective-bargaining procedures. It also gives unions a limited right to strike over technological change, even though a collective agreement is in effect. On any technological change likely to affect a significant number of employees, the employer must give ninety days' notice. The union may seek from the Canada Labour Relations Board the right to bargain or strike, but the board may grant permission only if there is no technological-change clause in a contract, or where the employer failed to give proper notice and the impact on the employees would be "substantial and adverse."

Canada Labour Relations Board (CLRB) A federal board that deals with complaints from unions and employees concerning unfair practices under part V of the CANADA LABOUR CODE. Matters coming under its jurisdiction include certification and decertification of BARGAINING UNITS, illegal strikes and lockouts, applications by unions to reopen collective bargaining in the event of technological change, and interference by employers with efforts of employees to organize and join unions.

Canada Labour Relations Council (CLRC) A tripartite business-labour-government advisory body created by the federal minister of LABOUR in 1975 to study ways of improving labour-management relations and thus to reduce the number of strikes and lockouts. The council, which is chaired by the minister of Labour, created an independent research group to provide data that labour and management both could accept as accurate during negotiations. The council has reviewed a number of questions, including the potential for industry-wide bargaining in industries under federal jurisdiction, such as grain handling. It has a wide enough mandate to allow it to review federal labour laws, the role of government in collective bargaining, and new services that could be introduced to improve collective bargaining. The council consists of nine representatives each for labour and management and four representatives from government. It has a permanent secretariat in the Department of Labour. In March 1976, labour withdrew its members in protest over the ANTI-INFLATION BOARD.

Canada Mortgage and Housing Corporation (CMHC) A federal crown corporation created in 1945 as part of the federal government's postwar reconstruction program. Its basic role is to administer the NATIONAL HOUSING ACT, and to help meet the housing needs of Canadians by insuring mortgage loans on new housing projects, to aid in the construction of sewage and water-supply systems, help service land, fund the construction of senior-citizen and student housing, aid urban redevelopment and finance neighbourhood-improvement projects, help needy Canadians to obtain homes, finance rental-housing projects for low-income Canadians, including non-profit and other co-operative housing, and administer other programs approved by Parliament to meet the housing needs of Canadians. It also carries out research on Canadian housing and mortgage markets and on building technology, and helps to determine the country's future housing needs. Its programs include mortgage loans, direct grants, and mortgage insurance and mortgage guarantees to mortgage lenders. Its headquarters are in Ottawa.

Canada Pension Plan (CPP) A national compulsory and contributory pension plan, introduced in 1965, which all working Canadians between the ages of eighteen and seventy must join. Quebec established its own parallel plan, the Quebec Pension Plan, which is fully integrated with the CPP, so that all Canadians get benefits under one or the other of the plans and carry their benefits with them if they move to or out of Quebec. Employers and employees each pay 50 per cent of the individual's premium, which, like the pension and other benefits, is related to the individual's wage or salary. There is an upper limit on premiums and benefits. The CPP pays retirement, disability, and survivor pensions, and orphan and death benefits, adjusted annually in line with the cost of living. Premiums paid to the CPP are lent to the provincial governments. The CPP is the single most important pension plan for most working Canadians; first pensions under the plan were paid in 1967.

Canada Savings Bond (CSB) A savings bond sold to the public, starting each October, every year since 1946. CSBs are a popular form of savings, with most major companies offering payroll-deduction schemes so that employees can purchase them over the course of a year. They can also be purchased for cash. CSBs are attractive to investors because they can always be cashed in at any branch of a bank for their face value plus accrued interest.

The annual sale is handled by the Bank of Canada, working through the chartered banks, investment dealers, and other authorized sales agents, after the government has decided what the rate of interest shall be and what special features, if any, should be attached to the bonds. CSBs are issued in denominations ranging from one hundred to five thousand dollars, and are of two types: regular interest bonds, which pay interest each year, and compound-interest bonds, which accumulate interest and pay it when the bond matures. There are restrictions on who can buy CSBs—only individuals, some types of REGISTERED RETIREMENT SAVINGS PLANS, and estates—and there is usually a limit on how many can be purchased. There is no limit on the size of each year's issue, but the minister of Finance can cut off sales at any time.

CSBs were launched at the end of the Second World War after Canadians had developed the habit of this type of saving through the purchase of Victory Bonds. Today, CSBs account for some 35 per cent of the national debt.

Canada–United Kingdom Loan Agreement A critical postwar loan by Canada to Britain of $1.25 billion, made in 1946 after the United States suddenly cut back its expected postwar assistance. The British had estimated that they needed $6 billion to avert a severe financial crisis, but the United States provided only $3.75 billion, and that under tough conditions. The Canadian loan to Britain, in relative terms, was a much greater level of assistance, as a percentage of the Canadian economy, than the Marshall Plan aid subsequently was as a percentage of the U.S. economy.

Canada–United States Automotive Products Agreement An agreement signed by Canada and the United States on 16 January

1965, to create a North American market for motor-vehicle production and, in the process, give Canadian workers more jobs and Canadian consumers lower prices for North American automobiles. The two countries hoped to create a broader market so that there would be greater specialization and hence greater efficiency, especially in Canada, and expected that conditional free trade in motor vehicles, original parts, and tires for original vehicles would make Canada more attractive as a location for motor-vehicle-industry plants.

Canada agreed to allow eligible motor-vehicle manufacturers and auto-parts firms to import parts and finished vehicles duty-free. To qualify, a motor-vehicle manufacturer in Canada had to meet three conditions. **1.** To continue to manufacture motor vehicles in the same ratio to his motor-vehicle sales as existed in the 1964-model year. **2.** To maintain Canadian VALUE-ADDED at least equal to that of the 1964-model year. **3.** To meet specific capital-investment targets set out in letters of commitment to the Canadian government from each of the vehicle manufacturers. Canada hoped to increase production and employment, to boost its share of North American production to roughly the same as its consumption of North American motor vehicles, to reduce the gap between U.S. and Canadian motor-vehicle prices, to reduce its balance-of-payments deficit in the Canada-U.S. motor-vehicle and parts trade, and to obtain a share of research and development spending in the industry.

For its part, the U.S. granted unconditional free entry of motor vehicles and original equipment parts from Canada. The agreement provided for a comprehensive review in 1968, and allowed either country to withdraw on one year's notice.

Canada–United States Defence Production Sharing Arrangement An agreement between Canada and the United States to maintain a long-term rough balance in defence trade between the two countries. In 1959, after Canada cancelled plans to build its own military plane, the Arrow, officials of Canada and the United States reached an agreement under which Canada would rely on the United States for its major defence technology, while, in return, the U.S. would facilitate the development of a defence industry in Canada by permitting the duty-free entry of most military products and by making an exception to the Buy America Act, which required the U.S. Defense Department to purchase U.S-made equipment. The agreement was reaffirmed in 1963, when the U.S. secretary of Defense, Robert McNamara, and the Canadian minister of Defence Production, C.M. Drury, signed a memorandum of understanding that the two countries would aim for a general balance in defence procurement from each other. Once a year, officials from the Department of INDUSTRY, TRADE AND COMMERCE and the U.S. Defense Department meet to review the level of procurement from each other's country.

Canada–United States trade agreements Trade agreements signed between the two countries in 1935 and 1938 to reverse protectionist trends in both countries, following the passage by the U.S. Congress of the Reciprocal Trade Agreements Act in 1934. In the 1935 treaty, the U.S. reduced its high tariffs to some extent, while Canada lifted some of its restrictions on the purchase of U.S. goods. The treaty made it easier for Canada to sell certain commodities, such as fish, lumber, cattle, dairy products, potatoes, and whisky, to the U.S., and improved access to the Canadian market for U.S. farm machinery, automobiles, electrical machinery and equipment, industrial machinery, and gasoline. However, the general level of tariffs remained higher than it had been at the start of the Depression. The 1938 treaty made much greater progress in reducing tariffs on both sides of the border, and remained in effect until the GENERAL AGREEMENT ON TARIFFS AND TRADE came into effect on 1 January 1948.

Canadian Arctic Resources Committee (CARC) A public-interest organization founded in 1971 to conduct research into questions of northern-development policy, publish its research and recommendations, and participate in public hearings, such as those of the National Energy Board and environmental-assessment panels. It is funded by private individuals, foundations, corporations, and government. Its headquarters are in Ottawa.

Canadian Bankers' Association (CBA) An association representing the Canadian banking industry to which all Canadian chartered banks are required by law to belong. The association was created by an act of Parliament in 1900 and consists of all the chartered banks, which are represented by their chief general managers on the CBA executive council. One of its early responsibilities was to supervise the printing and distribution of paper money by the banks. It was only after the creation of the BANK OF CANADA in 1934 that the role of the banks in printing money was reduced and eventually ended.

Today, the CBA supervises the operation of the bank CLEARING SYSTEM. It also operates an educational program for banking-industry employees through its Institute of Canadian Bankers, has an extensive research and development division that tries to improve the country's payments system—by developing improved use of computerized banking techniques, for example—runs a major public-information program, carries out research on the economics of banking and financial markets, and works with police departments and other groups to improve bank security and prevent crime. It makes representations to federal and provincial governments on behalf of the banking industry and helps the banks respond to government plans for new legislation affecting the banking industry. Its headquarters are in Toronto.

Canadian Chamber of Commerce A national association of corporations, boards of trade, local chambers of commerce, and trade associations, founded in 1929 to represent the interests of its members in national affairs. All provincial chambers of commerce, except that of Quebec, are affiliates. The chamber makes representations to the federal government and keeps its members informed on changes in federal policies and programs. Since 1945, it has been affiliated with the INTERNATIONAL CHAMBER OF COMMERCE.

Canadian Commercial Corporation A crown corporation that acts as agent of the federal government in dealing with foreign governments and state-owned companies, either to sell military and non-military goods and services or to purchase military and non-military goods and services. It helps Canadian firms to sell defence and non-defence goods and services to foreign governments and state-owned companies, as well as disposing of government surplus items, such as fighter aircraft, ships, and other used military hardware. It was created in 1946, originally for the purpose of procuring in Canada goods and services for U.N. relief agencies and foreign governments in need of food, motor vehicles, and other necessities.

Canadian Construction Association A national association of construction companies, created in 1918, that represents more than seventeen thousand firms in commercial, industrial, institutional, highway, and engineering construction. Provincial construction associations are affiliates. The association is a strong advocate of INDUSTRY-WIDE BARGAINING. It monitors and provides information to member firms on wage rates, collective agreements, arbitration awards, and working conditions in the construction industry. It also participates in the INTERNATIONAL LABOUR ORGANIZATION and provides the normal association services to members, such as representing their views to government and distributing information on tax and other government policy changes. The association's headquarters are located in Ottawa.

Canadian Consumer Council An advisory body of twenty-three persons concerned with consumer affairs that meets several times a year to discuss consumer matters. It was created in 1968 to advise the minister of CONSUMER AND CORPORATE AFFAIRS on ways to improve consumer protection.

Canadian content Government rules to ensure that a minimum level of Canadian goods and services are employed in particular activities or projects. Examples include specified hours of Canadian programming on radio and television, the proportion of Canadian investments that must be held by insurance companies and pension funds, and the required level of Canadian goods and services, including labour, that must be employed on major resource projects in the North or on pipeline and tar-sands projects.

Canadian Council on Social Development A research organization for social-policy issues. It was founded in 1920 as the Child Welfare Council, later became the Canadian Welfare Council, and adopted its present name in 1970. It has five research groups, staffed by economists and social-policy experts: housing, citizen participation and social planning, health care, income maintenance and security, and personal social services. Its membership includes individuals, social agencies, federal, provincial, and municipal governments, and corporations. Its headquarters are in Ottawa.

Canadian Dairy Commission A federal agency created in 1966, becoming operative in 1967, to regulate milk and cream production in Canada so that farmers might receive what the commission considered to be a fair return on their labour and investment. The chairman of the commission chairs the Canadian Milk Supply Management Committee, which includes representatives of the provincial milk-MARKETING BOARDS and the provincial governments. The job of the committee is to manage the Milk Share Quota System, which allocates milk- and cream-production shares to each of the provinces under a federal milk-marketing plan. The Dairy Commission may help to stabilize milk and cream prices by purchasing excess supplies, and can pay direct subsidies to dairy farmers to assure them of reasonable returns without pushing milk and cream prices up sharply. The commission also arranges export sales of skim-milk powder and other dairy products. It was the first national farm marketing agency to be created after the Canadian Wheat Board was set up in 1935.

Canadian dollar The official currency of the provinces of Canada, adopted in 1858 after Canadians indicated their preference for the decimal system over the British pound. The dollar was adopted in turn by the new nation of Canada with the passage of the Uniform Currency Act in 1871. Until 1910, the Canadian dollar was valued in terms of the British gold sovereign. But with the Currency Act of 1910, it was redefined in terms of fine gold.

From Confederation until the mid-1930s, the production of paper currency was largely in the hands of the chartered banks, with the government regulating the amount of dollars any bank could issue as legal tender. In 1934, the BANK OF CANADA was established as the country's central bank and it quickly took over the printing of Canadian dollars, although chartered-bank dollars were not fully withdrawn from circulation until about a decade later. The international value of the Canadian dollar is usually expressed either in terms of the U.S. dollar or of SPECIAL DRAWING RIGHTS.

Canadian Energy Research Institute An energy-research institute located at the University of Calgary, and funded by the federal and Alberta governments and private industry. It carries out independent economic research into Canadian energy needs and energy alternatives.

Canadian Export Association An association of Canadian manufacturers, agricultural producers, construction companies, consulting engineers, and others interested in export sales. Founded in 1943, the association provides information to members on changes in the trade policies and procedures of importing countries and of the Canadian government, occasionally makes representations to foreign governments on matters of concern, and represents the views of its members to the federal government. It is based in Ottawa.

Canadian Federation of Agriculture (CFA) A national federation of provincial farm organizations and national or regional commodity organizations, formed to promote the interests of farmers and other agricultural interests, and to represent Canadian farmers in the International Federation of Agricultural Producers. The Canadian federation was originally set up in 1935 as the Canadian Chamber of Agriculture. Its headquarters are in Ottawa. See also NATIONAL FARMERS UNION.

Canadian Grain Commission A federal agency created in 1971 to administer the Canada Grain Act. It licenses all grain elevators in Canada used to store western-produced grain, and sets maximum tariffs that elevators may charge for storage. The commission also is responsible for grain-grading standards, inspects the quality of grain being delivered to storage, conducts surveys on the quality of each year's grain crop through its Grain Research Laboratory, studies new grain varieties, and conducts research into cereal grains and oil seeds. The commission, which replaced the Board of Grain Commissioners that dated back to 1912, is based in Winnipeg.

Canadian Human Rights Commission A federal agency created in 1977 to enforce the Canadian Human Rights Act. Among other areas of responsibility, it provides protection for EQUAL PAY and against job discrimination based on age, physical handicap, race, sex, marital status, national or ethnic origin, religion, or colour. Part I of the CANADA LABOUR CODE has been transferred to its jurisdiction.

Canadian Importers Association An association of companies, including manufacturers, agents, distributors, customs brokers, carriers, brokers, and others, with an interest in Canada's import trade. Much of the work of the association, created in 1932, consists of helping importers to meet Canada's import requirements and paperwork, or making representations to the federal government to simplify import procedures and reduce import barriers. It also helps to promote exports of Canadian manufactured goods. Its headquarters are in Toronto.

Canadian Institute for Economic Policy An economic - policy research organization, formed in 1978 and funded by private citizens, that studies and recommends fiscal, industrial, and other related policies to strengthen Canada in a rapidly changing international environment. It sponsors economic research and publishes its findings, with an emphasis on measures to increase Canadian economic, political, and cultural independence. Its headquarters are in Ottawa.

Canadian International Development Agency (CIDA) A federal agency responsible for the administration of Canada's foreign-aid or official development-assistance program. It was originally established in 1960 as the External Aid Office, but in 1968 was reorganized as CIDA. It is headed by a president and its board includes the deputy ministers of the departments of External Affairs, Finance, Industry, Trade and Commerce, the governor of the Bank of Canada, and the secretary of the Treasury Board. In 1979 a cabinet minister, the minister for International Development, was appointed to represent the agency in cabinet and to report on its activities to Parliament.

Canada's aid programs are divided into three principal groupings: multilateral aid, bilateral aid, and food aid. Just over 40 per cent of Canada's aid goes to multilateral organizations, including the aid programs of the United Nations, the INTERNATIONAL BANK FOR RECONSTRUCTION AND DEVELOPMENT, various regional-development banks, and regional-development institutions. About 50 per cent goes into bilateral assistance, divided roughly 50:50 between grants and SOFT LOANS, which carry no interest rate, can be paid back over fifty years, and require no start to repayment for the first ten years. Bilateral aid may consist of technical assistance, economic assistance, or food aid. The remaining Canadian aid goes to emergency relief programs, scholarships, assistance to religious and other groups aiding the less-developed countries, and other means of aiding the less-developed countries.

Canadian International Grains Institute A federal organization created in 1972 to work with the CANADIAN WHEAT BOARD and the CANADIAN GRAIN COMMISSION to help develop new markets for Canadian grains. Its efforts include developing new uses for grains and oilseeds within Canada, and helping less-developed countries to adapt grains to their diet, expand their grain-handling and transportation systems, and improve their skills in flour milling, bread baking, and the manufacture of macaroni and other pastas. Its headquarters are in Winnipeg.

Canadian Labour Congress (CLC) A national labour federation representing just under 70 per cent of all union members in Canada through its roughly 115 affiliated unions. The CLC was formed in 1956 through a merger of two rival labour federations, the Trades and Labour Congress of Canada and the Canadian Congress of Labour. The CLC is a voluntary organization and exercises no legal authority over its affiliated unions, although it acts as the country's principal spokesman for union members. Its activities, through a thirty-member executive council and a national convention held every two years, include: pressing for union interests in federal government policies, including budgets, legislation, and social-security benefits; the establishment of codes of behaviour to prevent conflicts over jurisdiction between unions, raiding, and other damaging practices; strengthening union democracy and ethics; research for member unions into pay, fringe benefits, and other questions; and various educational and public-affairs programs to improve public understanding of the role of unions. The CLC also represents Canada in international labour organizations, works to increase the autonomy of Canadian locals of U.S.-based international unions, and speaks for union members on questions of human and civil rights. See also CANADIAN STANDARDS OF SELF-GOVERNMENT, CHARTER OF LABOUR RIGHTS, CODE OF ETHICAL PRACTICES, CONFEDERATION OF NATIONAL TRADE UNIONS, CONFEDERATION OF CANADIAN UNIONS.

Canadian Livestock Feed Board A federal agency created in 1967 under the Livestock Feed Assistance Act to make sure that adequate feed grain is available to meet the needs of farmers, adequate storage space is available in Eastern Canada, and the prices of feed grain in eastern Canada and British Columbia remain relatively stable and reasonably similar. Its headquarters are in Montreal and it reports to Parliament through the minister of Agriculture.

Canadian Manufacturers' Association (CMA) A national association of roughly 9,500 manufacturers of all sizes from big to small. It represents the interests of Canadian manufacturers before federal and provincial governments and their agencies, and provides a wide range of services, on industrial relations, exports, customs, and transportation, for example, for its members. It was founded in 1871 and its headquarters are in Toronto.

Canadian Patents and Development Limited A federal crown corporation created in 1947 as a subsidiary of the NATIONAL RESEARCH COUNCIL to own and sell the right to use the patented inventions of the council and other government-financed research and development. All inventions by government employees are, under the Public Servants' Inventions Act of 1954, the property of the Canadian government. The corporation also arranges foreign patents for Canadian government inventions and helps universities, provincial government agencies, and other research organizations that are publicly funded to patent and license their inventions.

Canadian Petroleum Association (CPA) An association of oil and natural-gas exploration, production, and pipeline companies and associated financing, engineering, geophysical, drilling, and other supplier industries, founded in 1952 and based in Calgary. Its members account for close to 80 per cent of oil and natural-gas production in Canada. The association publishes an annual report on changes in the country's established oil and natural-gas reserves, and an annual statistical handbook on drilling, exploration spending, oil and gas production, and other industry statistics. The association, which represents industry views to federal and provincial governments, has six committees: exploration, natural-gas policy matters, oil policy matters, production, resource economics, and public affairs and socio-economic matters.

Canadian Pulp and Paper Association An association of pulp, paper, and paperboard manufacturers, established in 1913 to carry out normal trade-association activities, such as presenting briefs to government and disseminating information to members on government policies and industry developments. It has two scientific groups, one dealing with pulp- and papermill technology and the other with woodlands. In addition, along with the federal government and McGill University, it funds the Pulp and Paper Research Institute. Its headquarters are in Montreal.

Canadian Radio-television and Telecommunications Commission (CRTC) A federal regulatory agency created in 1968 under the

Broadcasting Act to supervise and regulate the Canadian broadcasting system, including radio and television stations and cable television. It issues and renews broadcast licences if it is satisfied that radio and television stations meet Canadian-content and other programming requirements, regulates cable-television rates, and must approve changes of ownership of radio, television, and cable TV companies. It also has a responsibility to see that Canadian-ownership requirements are met, and advises the minister of COMMUNICATIONS on policies to deal with such questions as the introduction of pay TV or concentration of ownership in the broadcasting industry. In 1976, the CRTC was also given the responsibility of regulating rates, business practices, and services of federally incorporated telephone and TELECOMMUNICATIONS companies, a responsibility previously exercised by the CANADIAN TRANSPORT COMMISSION. The commission regulates the rates and tariffs of TELESAT CANADA and also regulates communications satellites through its jurisdiction over what may be carried by broadcasters and cable systems, including non-broadcast programming. The commission reports to Parliament through the minister of Communications.

Canadian Securities Institute (CSI) An organization established in 1970 by the Investment Dealers Association (IDA) and the Montreal, Toronto, Alberta, and Vancouver stock exchanges to improve the educational level of persons working in the securities industry, including financial analysts, securities salesmen, and mutual-fund salesmen. The CSI offers a number of courses on securities markets, and an advanced program, Canadian Investment Finance. Those who complete the advanced program become Fellows of the Canadian Securities Institute (FCSI). The CSI also administers qualifying examinations for candidates to become new partners, directors, or officers of IDA-member firms. It is based in Toronto.

Canadian standards of self-government A set of principles adopted by the CANADIAN LABOUR CONGRESS in 1974 and included in its constitution, to increase the autonomy of Canadian affiliates and locals of international unions. The standards support the election of Canadian officers in Canadian affiliates and locals, the principle that policies dealing with Canadian affairs are to be set by Canadian officers and members, and that Canadian elected representatives have the authority to speak for the union in Canada. In cases where an international union is affiliated with an international trade secretariat, the Canadian section of the union is supposed to be affiliated separately so that there is a separate Canadian presence and voice at the international level. The standards further state that international unions should do whatever is necessary so that constitutional requirements or policies of the international union do not prevent Canadian members "from participating in the social, cultural, economic, and political life of the Canadian community."

Canadian Standards Association (CSA) A non-profit association of manufacturers, government agencies, utilities, hospitals, retailers, consulting firms, and other groups, established to develop product safety, quality, and, in some cases, performance standards, and to test products to see whether they meet these standards. Those that do bear a CSA trademark indicating that they have been tested and approved. CSA standards themselves are not legal but they have, in many instances, been adopted by government agencies or departments. For example, under provincial laws, all household appliances sold in Canada must meet CSA standards and display a CSA trademark. The CSA has some four hundred product committees, staffed by volunteers, which write product standards. When the CSA was founded in 1919 it concentrated on the fields of electrical and civil engineering, but today it writes standards and carries out testing for a wide range of products and technologies, ranging from solar energy and health-care systems to hockey helmets and safety footwear. Its headquarters are in Toronto.

Canadian Tax Foundation A tax-research organization, supported by the Canadian Bar Association, the Canadian Institute of Chartered Accountants, business corporations, and individuals. It conducts research into problems of taxation and public finance, ranging from technical taxation issues to questions of tax efficiency or fairness, the division of federal and provincial taxing and spending powers, and the revenue implications of tax changes. The foundation publishes an annual analysis of the revenues and spending of the federal government for the current fiscal year, along with a similar publication on provincial and municipal finances. It also publishes special studies and a journal, the *Canadian Tax Journal*. Founded in 1945, its headquarters are in Toronto.

Canadian Transport Commission (CTC) A federal regulatory agency created in 1967 under the National Transportation Act to supervise and regulate the activities of Canada's airlines, railways, shipping companies, interprovincial motor-vehicle transport, and commodity (except oil or natural gas) pipelines. The commission, for example, rules on applications by railways to withdraw, reduce, or to increase services, and has limited regulatory power over railway rates. It regulates the classes of air service available in Canada and those that may be offered for sale to overseas destinations, regulates air fares, and licenses airlines. It licenses and supervises shipping on the Great Lakes and other inland waterways, such as the Mackenzie and Yukon Rivers, and has limited jurisdiction over international shipping operations out of Canadian ports. It also has a research role; it is responsible for carrying out studies into all forms of transportation in Canada. Its responsibility for telephone and telecommunications carriers was transferred to the CANADIAN RADIO-TELEVISION AND TELECOMMUNICATIONS COMMISSION in 1976. It reports to Parliament through the minister of TRANSPORT.

Canadian Wheat Board (CWB) A federal crown corporation, created in 1935, that has the overall responsibility for the sale of western-grown grains within Canada and in export markets. The board either sells grains directly or through grains companies acting as its agents. As well as controlling the sale of western grains, it also controls the amount of grains that farmers produce, the delivery of grains into elevators, the allocation of rail cars to move grain, and the shipping of grain by freighter to foreign markets.

Farmers deliver their grains to country elevators according to their quotas. From there, the board arranges shipment to large terminals in eastern Canada, to Thunder Bay, Churchill, and various west-coast ports. The board pays farmers in two stages. The first payment, the INITIAL PAYMENT, is set by the federal cabinet before the start of the CROP YEAR and is a guaranteed floor price to farmers when they deliver their grain to elevators. The second payment, the FINAL PAYMENT, is made at the end of the crop year and depends on the amount of money the board has left over from selling the grain after paying its costs. The final payment must be authorized by the cabinet.

The board also administers the PRAIRIE GRAIN ADVANCE PAYMENTS ACT, which provides interest-free cash advances to farmers for farm-stored grain, and the WESTERN GRAIN STABILIZATION PLAN, which assures farmers of a minimum net cash flow in any crop year.

Canfarm A national, computerized farm-management service established in 1969 by the federal DEPARTMENT OF AGRICULTURE. In 1979, the service was taken over by Canfarm Co-operative Services Limited, a co-operative consisting of the CANADIAN FEDERATION OF AGRICULTURE, provincial federations of agriculture, and other co-operatives, after the federal government decided to discontinue the service. The system provides detailed financial record-keeping and analysis for farmers and is a useful planning tool. It provides an income-expenditure report for each crop and kind of livestock, and allocates farm overhead expenses for each, thus helping a farmer to identify his most profitable and least profitable or unprofitable activities. It calculates crop yields per acre, machinery and fertilizer costs per acre, farm cash flow, states of loans, standard EARNINGS-STATEMENT and BALANCE-SHEET data, and other information that should help farmers to improve the efficiency and profitability of their operations.

capacity The normal amount that can be produced by a factory, refinery, smelter, pipeline, or other industrial facility over a sustained period of time.

capacity-utilization rate The actual output of an industry as a percentage of the output it can produce with its existing plant, equipment, and workforce. It is an important economic statistic, since it shows not only the level of activity in the industrial sector but also indicates whether or not new capital investment is likely to be needed. If industry is operating well below its capacity, it is unlikely that new capital investment will be made in the near future; conversely, if industry is operating at close to capacity and the economy is growing, then new investments to expand capacity are likely to be made. Statistics Canada publishes quarterly figures on manufacturing-capacity utilization rates and has statistics dating back to 1961.

Cape Breton Development Corporation An economic-development corporation created in 1967 by the federal government to take over and rehabilitate coal mines at Cape Breton, N.S., and to broaden the industrial base of the region. Working with the Department of REGIONAL ECONOMIC EXPANSION and the Nova Scotia government, it has broad powers to help develop, through funding and advice, new local industries to provide jobs outside the coal-mining industry. It is based in Sydney, N.S.

capital **1.** In economics, one of the FACTORS OF PRODUCTION that is essential to the functioning of the economy. It represents the mines, factories, machinery, railways, power stations, department stores, inventories, and all the other capital goods that are used to produce goods and services and on which income is earned. The capital in an economy increases as new investments are made from the profits earned on existing capital. **2.** In financial markets, the funds available for investment in financial assets, such as shares, bonds, CERTIFICATES OF DEPOSIT, or real property. See CAPITAL MARKET. **3.** In business, the total funds invested in the company to enable it to carry out its activities. These funds include long-term debt, COMMON and PREFERRED SHARES, and retained earnings.

capital account See BALANCE OF PAYMENTS.

capital asset An asset that is to be used over a long period of time, which therefore has a productive life of more than a year. Examples would include factories, machinery, and equipment, and might also include PATENTS and other forms of INTELLECTUAL PROPERTY.

capital budget A budget that sets out planned investment in new facilities such as buildings, machinery, and equipment, along with details on how these are to be financed.

capital-cost allowances **1.** The term used in the Income Tax Act for DEPRECIATION. **2.** An entry in the calculation of the gross national product and national income, representing the depreciation of business plant, machinery, and equipment, and the loss of such fixed capital due to fires, floods, train wrecks, and other accidents or natural disasters.

capital formation The increase in a country's capital assets, such as factories, mines, machinery and equipment, buildings, highways, railways, and other assets. It is calculated from gross-national-product statistics as follows: add together gross fixed-capital formation plus the value of change in physical inventories, and subtract depreciation or capital-consumption allowances, which represent replacement of existing capital assets. The resulting figure is the net investment in the economy or the net capital formation.

capital gain An increase in the money value of an asset such as a share, bond, parcel of land, house, antique, or other asset, which results in a profit if the asset is sold. For example, if a share is bought at $26 and sold at $31, there is a capital gain of $5. See also CAPITAL-GAINS TAX.

capital-gains tax A tax levied on the profits from the sale of assets or the deemed sale of assets. Canada introduced such a tax on 1 January 1972, treating one-half of the capital gains as ordinary income in the hands of the taxpayer and subjecting it to the taxpayer's top marginal income-tax rate. The capital-gains tax applies to profits from the sale of shares, bonds, land, recreational and investment properties, and personal-use assets, such as jewellery, antiques, works of art, stamps, and coin collections, if they are worth more than one thousand dollars. Capital losses may be deducted each year from capital gains. Capital-gains taxes are levied at the time of death, on certain gifts, and on the assets of Canadians who emigrate to other countries, although the assets themselves may not necessarily be sold; this provision was made in the Income Tax Act to replace the estate tax, which was abolished at the same time the capital-gains tax was introduced. Exemptions are allowed for personal residences and for property transfers to a spouse. See also VALUATION DAY.

capital good A good, such as a machine, building, or truck, that is used to produce other goods. An automobile is a capital good if it is used by a business. See also CONSUMER GOOD.

capital-intensive industry An industry that makes heavy use of capital equipment, such as machinery, relative to its labour force and level of output. Examples of capital-intensive industries include oil refining, petrochemicals, electric power, steel production, tar-sands oil production, and newsprint. Capital-intensive industries tend to show greater productivity gains than labour-intensive industries, and hence make a contribution to better rates of real or non-inflationary growth in the economy.

capital investment The amount of spending in the economy each year to replace worn-out and obsolete production facilities and to increase the productive capacity of the economy. Public capital investment consists of spending on new government buildings, highways, schools, hospitals, and the like; private capital investment consists of spending by private and crown corporations on new factories, mines, machines and equipment, housing, offices, hotels, refineries, power plants, railways, and the like. Capital investment is an important source of economic growth and improved PRODUCTIVITY. See also ACCELERATOR PRINCIPLE.

Every six months, Statistics Canada publishes a review of public and private investment intentions, while the Department of Industry, Trade and Commerce publishes a twice-yearly survey of capital-investment decisions by close to three hundred of the top corporations, accounting for about 70 per cent of business capital investment. CANADA MORTGAGE AND HOUSING CORPORATION also publishes statistics on new housing starts.

capital loss A decline in the money value of an asset such as a share, bond, parcel of land, house, antique, or other asset, which results in a loss if the asset is sold. For example, if a share is bought at $26 and sold at $21, there is a capital loss of $5. See also CAPITAL-GAINS TAX.

capital market Taken together, the various markets in which governments and corporations raise long-term capital. The sources of such capital include pension plans, insurance companies, trust companies, and individual investors. The agents through which these savers act include investment dealers, stockbrokers, bond traders, underwriters, trust companies, and banks, while the principal institutions include the bond market and various stock exchanges. The market not only provides new capital but also provides a means of trading in existing financial securities, thus improving their marketability.

capital movements Flows of long-term and short-term capital between Canada and other countries. The main factors affecting the flow of money back and forth across the border are differences in interest rates and exchange rates. Funds invested by corporations and individuals, especially short-term funds, tend to seek out the highest interest rates. See BALANCE OF PAYMENTS.

capital-output ratio The ratio between the capital employed in a business and the output of the business; it is also defined as the amount of capital needed to produce an additional unit of output. Capital-output ratios vary from industry to industry and from country to country. For example, the industrial countries have higher capital-output ratios, since many of their industries are modern and CAPITAL INTENSIVE, whereas the less-developed countries tend to have low capital-output ratios, since they have abundant labour, less-advanced technologies, and hence LABOUR-INTENSIVE INDUSTRIES.

capital spending See CAPITAL INVESTMENT.

capital stock The equity capital invested in a business through the purchase of various classes of COMMON and PREFERRED SHARES. This capital may be contributed by the founder of the business and by other investors at the time the business is started, or it may be raised by the sale of new issues of common or preferred shares, depending on the authorized capital of the business. Owners of common shares have a say in the running of the business and have the ultimate claim on the assets of the business if it is wound up after all creditors have been paid off. It is the money permanently invested in the business.

capital structure See INVESTED CAPITAL.

capital surplus See CONTRIBUTED SURPLUS.

capital tax A tax levied on wealth or assets rather than income. For example, Quebec, Ontario, Manitoba, and British Columbia levy a tax on the paid-up capital of corporations. See also WEALTH TAX.

capitalism An economic and political system in which the means of production are largely privately owned and the rights of private property are respected by the state according to the RULE OF LAW and due process. Individuals are free to enter into contracts, to engage in entrepreneurial activity, and to consume or save and earn profits, while the role of the government is to protect individuals against abuses of power, to protect the public interest, and to maintain an economic climate in which private entrepreneurs can make a profit. Such a system relies on the energies and imagination of individuals acting in their own best interests to achieve economic and social progress for the community. Most capitalist societies have evolved into MIXED ECONOMIES, with governments playing a larger role in redistributing income, setting priorities, and correcting some of the ill effects of unrestrained market forces. See also PRIVATE ENTERPRISE, MARKET ECONOMY.

capitalist A person who owns shares in a business enterprise.

capitalization See INVESTED CAPITAL.

captive market A market in which a firm faces little if any competition. It may be due to geographical location: for example, there may be only one cement manufacturer or sugar refinery in a particular region of the country, while transportation costs may discourage competition from outside producers. A firm may have a captive market because of vertical integration with another company: for example, a telephone-manufacturing company may be owned by a telephone company providing telephone service; it will have a captive market for its products if telephones made by other companies cannot be attached to its system. Or a firm may produce a unique product that other manufacturers use as a component in their products, or may be the sole source of a resource or commodity for which there are no readily available substitutes.

car loadings A weekly statistic published by Statistics Canada that shows the number of freight cars loaded in seven-day periods. The statistic is helpful in monitoring the general level of business activity in the country.

carat A method of weighing diamonds and other precious stones. One carat is equal to 0.200 grams.

Caribbean Development Facility A special foreign-aid program for the Caribbean countries established in mid-1978 by Canada, the United States, Britain, Venezuela, Colombia, France, the Netherlands, Norway, the OPEC Special Fund, and the World Bank. The fund is managed by the World Bank, or INTERNATIONAL BANK FOR RECONSTRUCTION AND DEVELOPMENT (IBRD).

carrying charges The interest, insurance, warehouse, and other costs involved in maintaining an inventory.

carry-over stocks The amount of a crop that is still unsold at the end of a CROP YEAR or season, which therefore becomes part of the following year's supply. In the grain trade, for example, the carry-over is the amount of wheat that remains in storage at the end of the crop year. While some carry-over may be desirable if inventories or BUFFER STOCKS are low, a large carry-over of a crop means that producers will have a harder time getting higher prices in the new crop year, since supplies will be high.

cartel An organization of producers—firms or nations—who band together in some kind of formal arrangement to set prices, determine production levels, and, sometimes, to allocate markets. The goal of such an organization is to get higher prices and earn bigger profits by curbing competition and restricting output. Cartels of business firms are illegal in Canada and most other countries, as are cartel-like arrangements such as RIGGED BIDS and other restrictive practices.

The best example of a cartel today is the ORGANIZATION OF PETROLEUM EXPORTING COUNTRIES, which has succeeded in sharply increasing the price of oil while restraining oil production among its members to prevent any significant weakening of the cartel price. Other efforts by producer nations to establish commodity cartels have been less successful. See also INTERNATIONAL BAUXITE ASSOCIATION, INTERNATIONAL COUNCIL OF COPPER EXPORTING COUNTRIES (CIPEC). For a cartel to be successful, there has to be a small number of producers, no ready substitute for the commodity, and a willingness by the cartel members to accept quotas on their own production.

cash Paper money and coins. In accounting, cash on a company's books also includes the money it has in its bank accounts, and other negotiable securities that are included in CURRENT ASSETS on a BALANCE SHEET.

cash-basis accounting A system of accounting in which revenues and expenditures are recorded as they are received or paid out; as opposed to ACCRUAL-BASIS ACCOUNTING, which records revenues and expenditures when transactions take place rather than when the money is received or paid out. Cash-basis accounting is rarely used in business.

cash flow The funds available to a company to pay dividends and finance expansion. It is calculated by adding together net earnings or after-tax profits (before extraordinary items), all deductions that do not require an actual cash outlay, such as DEPRECIATION, DEPLETION ALLOWANCES, or DEFERRED INCOME TAXES, and any minority interest in the earnings of another company. Since it includes tax deductions that do not require an actual cash outlay, the cash-flow figure gives a more useful picture of a company's financial position than net earnings or after-tax profits alone.

cash-needs budget An estimate of the federal government's cash needs for the ensuing fiscal year, and hence its impact on the capital market. The estimate is contained in the minister of Finance's annual BUDGET speech and is an important figure for economists. It indicates the probable level of government borrowing in the year ahead, and is used to assess the impact of the government's spending and taxing policies on financial markets, the availability of funds for private borrowers, monetary policy, money supply, changes in the national debt, and government balances in the chartered banks. Cash needs are financed by increasing the level of government debt in public hands or by running down government cash balances, or both. If there is a surplus, then funds can be used to retire part of the national debt, to build up government cash balances in the chartered banks, or both.

The cash-needs budget includes many elements of government activity excluded from the budgetary-accounts budget—the receipts and payments under the unemployment-insurance program and the Canada Pension Plan, for example, or loans and advances to government agencies such as CANADA MORTGAGE AND HOUSING CORPORATION, to provincial, municipal, and foreign governments, and to international agencies. The cash-needs budget also includes transactions of the EXCHANGE-FUND ACCOUNT, which can have an important impact on the government's cash needs. Excluded from the cash-needs budget are the operations of crown corporations, aside from transfers to or from the government.

cash-reserve management The manipulation

of the excess cash reserves of the banking system by the BANK OF CANADA to implement its monetary policy. The ability of the banking system to make loans and purchase securities depends on the level of its excess cash reserves. Through its OPEN-MARKET OPERATIONS and transfer of government deposits between the chartered banks and the Bank of Canada, the central bank adjusts the level of excess cash reserves available to finance economic activity.

cash squeeze A shortage of cash in a corporation. Causes may include too many overdue accounts payable, a decline in sales, rising costs, the withdrawal of normal short-term credit, overinvestment in non-liquid assets, and a large volume of long-term debt.

cash surrender value The value of a life-insurance policy should it be cancelled. It is the amount the owner of the policy would get, representing premiums paid and bonuses or interest earned on those premiums, minus administrative, sales, and other costs incurred by the insurance company.

casual workers Workers employed only on a seasonal basis during peak periods, as department-store salesclerks at Christmas, for example, or as food-processing workers in late summer. Casual workers do not have the same rights, such as severance pay and notice of layoff, as full-time employees.

casualty insurance A general term usually used to describe all forms of insurance other than accident and life insurance. Examples include liability insurance and fire and theft insurance.

catch-up bargaining Efforts by a union in collective bargaining to obtain wage increases that take into account past losses in purchasing power due to inflation or the existence of wage and price controls. There may also be an effort to regain a wage position relative to other workers or trades that have won a big gain and altered previously existing wage relationships or differentials.

caveat emptor Latin phrase that means "Let the buyer beware." In other words, it is up to the consumer to exercise caution when buying goods or services or signing a contract.

caveat venditor Latin phrase that means "Let the seller beware." This is the philosophy of modern consumer laws. The merchant or producer has to be careful to follow consumer-protection laws; if he doesn't, the consumer or government can take legal action against him.

census A nation-wide survey of the population of a country to determine the number of people in the country, where they live, their age and sex, education, occupational status, type of residence, income, spending habits, religion, place of birth, language, and other such details. In Canada, a census must be carried out every ten years so that the boundaries and number of seats in the House of Commons can be redistributed in line with shifts in population. The last census was taken in 1971 and the next will be taken in 1981.

Census data provides some of the most important information available to a country to determine such basic trends as aging of the population, population movements among regions, levels of work skills and education, housing needs, school population, and other information necessary in determining government policies and spending priorities. The census data is also vital to business planning in determining the size and location of future markets, the demand for new products, and other effects on national markets.

The first census in Canada was taken in 1665–66 by Jean Talon, in what was then New France. The first census after Confederation was taken in 1871. Statistics Canada, which is responsible for the census, now takes a second census every five years, the last being in 1976, to revise the decennial census. It uses a household-sample technique, similar to that used in the decennial census but with a shorter list of questions, restricting itself to such matters as place of residence five years earlier, education, school attendance, and labour-force activity. Statistics Canada can obtain other information on population from income-tax returns, changes of address for family-allowance cheques, and the number of pensioners applying for pension supplements.

census of manufactures A detailed annual census of manufacturing in Canada showing the number and size of establishments, the number of production employees, the wage bill for production employees, spending on energy, cost of materials and supplies used, value of shipments of own manufacture, production VALUE-ADDED, the total number of employees including those in non-production jobs, the total wage and salary bill, the total value-added, final value of shipments, and the location by province of manufacturing activity. An industry-wide series of statistics is published by Statistics Canada each year, along with separate reports on all major manufacturing industries, such as automobiles, steel, food processing, chemicals, electrical machinery, and many others.

Central American Common Market (CACM) A would-be common market that came into being in 1961, linking five Central American countries—El Salvador, Guatemala, Honduras, and Nicaragua, with Costa Rica joining the following year. Although CACM has had ambitious plans to develop an effective economic union with a common external tariff, it has been plagued by internal differences. Honduras withdrew in 1970, and in 1971 Costa Rica imposed new tariff restrictions on a number of sensitive products from other CACM members.

central bank A national bank, usually a government-owned bank with a defined level of independence, whose job it is to work with the government in deciding and implementing a country's MONETARY POLICY, by regulating the growth of the money supply, controlling interest rates, determining the currency's exchange rate in foreign markets, altering the reserve requirements of the chartered banks, printing paper currency, managing the national debt, and using moral suasion to influence the behaviour of the banking system. Thus, a central bank regulates money and credit and helps to achieve economic goals such as higher economic growth or less inflation. The central bank of a country usually manages the country's foreign-exchange reserves, carries out day-to-day activities in the foreign-exchange market, and acts as a fiscal agent for the government in managing the NATIONAL DEBT. Canada's central bank is the BANK OF CANADA. The U.S. central bank is the U.S. Federal Reserve Board, Britain's the Bank of England, France's the Banque de France, Germany's the Deutsche Bundesbank, and Japan's the Bank of Japan.

central Canada Ontario and Quebec.

centralization **1.** In business, the tendency for decision-making to be concentrated in the corporate head office instead of among subsidiaries, branches, and divisions. **2.** In Canada's federal system, the tendency for decision-making to be concentrated in the national government in Ottawa instead of among the provincial governments. The Canadian federal system is characterized by alternating centralizing and decentralizing pressures. See also DECENTRALIZATION.

Centre for the Study of Inflation and Productivity An agency formed within the ECONOMIC COUNCIL OF CANADA in 1978 to monitor individual wage and price developments and general inflation trends in the economy, to alert the federal government to particular wage and price trends that deserved further attention, and generally to educate Canadians on the problem of inflation and the need for restraint. The centre was set up as a successor to the ANTI-INFLATION BOARD. But it had no special powers to obtain information from employers or unions, and had to rely on published information. Nor did it have wage and price guidelines within which to work. It was replaced in March 1979 by the NATIONAL COMMISSION ON INFLATION.

certificate A document establishing legal ownership to shares in a corporation, a bond, or other security.

certificate of deposit An interest-bearing debt security of some multiple of one thousand dollars, issued by a bank to a depositor, the deposit to be paid back at a stipulated date in the future. These certificates are usually for large sums of money and for terms of one to six years; they are negotiable and allow a depositor to earn a higher rate of interest than he otherwise would. If he needs his money, the depositor can sell the certificate of deposit to someone else. This is an important form of investment, particularly for corporations, developed originally by the big New York banks in the mid-1960s but which has since spread to Canada.

certificate of origin A document showing the country of origin of an imported product, that must be shown to customs officials from the Department of NATIONAL REVENUE when the product arrives in Canada.

certificate of public convenience and necessity A licence issued by the NATIONAL ENERGY BOARD authorizing a company or group of companies to build an oil or natural-gas pipeline. The certificate gives the applicant the power to expropriate land along the route approved by the Energy Board and sets out the terms and conditions under which the pipeline shall be built.

certification Recognition by a federal or provincial labour-relations board of a particular union as the official bargaining agent for a recognized BARGAINING UNIT. Such recognition must be preceded by proof that a majority of employees in a bargaining unit have freely chosen to join the union.

certified cheque A cheque endorsed by a bank to certify that the funds have been set aside in the issuer's account to ensure payment.

certified general accountant (**CGA**) A person who has been trained in internal-management accounting and in public accounting in a program of training that meets the standards of the Canadian Certified General Accountants' Association and its provincial associates. CGAs are found more frequently in industry and government than in public practice.

ceteris paribus A Latin phrase frequently used by economists, meaning "all relevant facts being equal" or "other things remaining unchanged." For example, if an economist says that an increase in the price of French wine will lead to greater consumption of Italian, Spanish, and Californian wine, *ceteris paribus,* he means that there will be greater consumption of these wines provided their prices remain the same and there is no change in consumer desire for wine.

chain store One of many stores owned and operated by the same company, either in the same community, region, province, or across the nation. Chain stores usually specialize in some branch of retailing, such as food, clothing, shoes, automotive parts, books, hardware, drugs and cosmetics, or general merchandise, or operate as department stores. Chains usually operate under the general direction of a corporate head office and are able to achieve ECONOMIES OF SCALE through centralized advertising, purchasing, management training, and the use of computer facilities.

chairman of the board The senior officer in a company, who chairs the board of directors. He is not necessarily the most powerful single person in a company: if he is also the CHIEF EXECUTIVE OFFICER, then he is the most powerful person; but if the president is the chief executive officer, then the chairman may be holding only an honorary position, perhaps reflecting his past service in the company as president and chief executive.

charter The document of incorporation of a company, setting out its AUTHORIZED CAPITAL, business purpose, and other such information.

Charter of Economic Rights and Duties of States A set of guidelines adopted by the U.N. General Assembly in December 1974 for the conduct of international economic relations, similar to those adopted for a NEW INTERNATIONAL ECONOMIC ORDER by the United Nations in May 1974. The charter, proposed originally by Mexico, asserted the right of states to absolute sovereignty over their natural resources, with compensation for nationalization of foreign business only according to domestic laws, the right of states to form natural-resources cartels, the right of less-developed countries to preferential and non-reciprocal trade treatment, and the right of less-developed countries to peg their export prices to import costs.

charter of labour rights A charter added to the CANADIAN LABOUR CONGRESS constitution in 1972 setting out union goals. They include: the unfettered right to peaceful assembly and picketing; the right to bargain on technological changes and automation; the right to strike during the term of a collective agreement if bargaining cannot resolve a matter in dispute not covered by the agreement; the right to a "meaningful say" on all economic and social questions affecting the vital interests of workers, along with union representation on government boards administering social programs; the right to training and retraining at the expense of the employer or the government; the right to take whatever steps may be necessary to protect the on-the-job safety and health of workers; the right to leisure through extended vacations and paid holidays; and the right to "a complete, secure retirement" at the age of sixty, if so desired.

chartered accountant (CA) An accountant certified by a provincial institute of chartered accountants. CAs are trained to engage in public practice, which means setting up their own offices to act as AUDITORS and to provide tax, financial-management, and other such advice to clients, or to work in managerial positions in industry and government. Their national organization is the Canadian Institute of Chartered Accountants.

chartered bank A financial institution that accepts deposits and makes loans and that plays an important role in the implementation of MONETARY POLICY. Chartered banks are created by individual acts of Parliament under the BANK ACT, which specifies their powers and regulates their methods of operation. The chartered banks are supervised by the minister of FINANCE and the INSPECTOR GENERAL OF BANKS; they also work closely with the BANK OF CANADA, which influences the size of their excess reserves, and hence the volume of loans they can make or securities they can buy. This is how monetary policy is implemented.

The banks accept a wide range of Canadian-dollar and foreign-currency deposits from Canadians and non-residents, including those against which cheques can be written. They also make a wide variety of Canadian-dollar and foreign-currency loans, ranging from mortgage and consumer loans to business, farm, construction, and MONEY-MARKET loans. They are active in the money market, the bond market, the capital market, and the foreign-exchange market. The chartered banks are permitted to own up to 50 per cent of the voting shares of other corporations, provided that the value does not exceed five million dollars. They can only hold 10 per cent of the voting shares when the shares are valued at more than five million dollars. There is no limit on the percentage or dollar value of preferred shares they may own; nor do these restrictions apply to bank service corporations. The banks are also active in providing export financing and various financial services for their corporate customers, such as financial and corporate planning, corporate reorganization, takeover financing, and economic analysis. The banks provide some computer services for their corporate clients as well, including payroll management and cash-flow information. But the Bank Act limits their activities to the business of banking. The banks make their profits on the difference between the interest rates they pay depositors and the interest they charge on loans, and on the services they provide for their customers.

The Bank of Canada shapes monetary policy through the chartered banks by the sale and purchase of government securities, including TREASURY bills, manipulation of the level of the government's cash balances on deposit with the banks, changes in the BANK RATE, and changes in their SECONDARY RESERVE RATIO. The Bank of Canada also uses MORAL SUASION to try to direct bank lending to specific areas of the economy, such as small business or slow-growth areas, or away from specific areas, such as the financing of takeovers of Canadian companies by non-residents. The banks also act as agents for the government in the sale of CANADA SAVINGS BONDS. Because of their role in implementing monetary policy, the banks have the right to borrow funds from the Bank of Canada to maintain their reserve requirements and meet other needs.

Under the Bank Act, no individual or group of associated individuals is allowed to own more than 10 per cent of the voting shares of a bank, while non-residents collectively may not own more than 25 per cent of a bank's voting shares. For an exception, see MERCANTILE BANK AFFAIR. Proposed changes in the Bank Act in 1979 would allow foreign banks to operate, under certain restrictions, in Canada. The proposed amendments would also make it easier for Canadians to establish new banks: banks would be established on approval by the governor-in-council instead of a special act of Parliament, while CLOSELY HELD banks could be established with as few as four shareholders, each owning 25 per cent of the voting shares. Provincial governments would be permitted to own up to 25 per cent of the shares of closely held banks. But, like other shareholders, their position would have to be reduced to 10 per cent after ten years. The banks carry compulsory deposit insurance on all Canadian-dollar accounts of up to twenty thousand dollars.

chartist A financial analyst who attempts to determine the trend of future prices of individual shares by charting their past financial performance and volume of trading, and extrapolating into the future according to one of several patterns of movement of share prices said to exist.

chattel Personal property that is movable, such as an automobile, work of art, or coin collection.

chattel mortgage A loan that is secured by a chattel such as an automobile. If the borrower fails to repay the loan, then the lender can seize the chattel. Since chattel mortgages are registered in provincial registry offices, chattels being purchased by another party have to be checked to make sure that a chattel mortgage does not exist on the item being purchased; otherwise, the chattel could still be seized from the new owner if the earlier owner had failed to keep up his payments.

check-off A clause in a collective agreement requiring an employer to deduct union dues and assessments from employees in the bargaining unit who either belong to the union or have to pay dues even if they don't belong (see RAND FORMULA), and to turn these funds over to the union. This is the normal method of collecting union dues, and it relieves the union of the cost and time it would take to collect dues on its own. Although check-off is a standard clause in most collective agreements, it is still an arrangement that has to be negotiated in the first collective agreement between a union and an employer in most provinces.

cheque A written order, usually on a standard cheque form printed by a bank or other deposit-taking financial institution, instructing the bank or other institution to pay the bearer or person named on the order—either immediately or on some future date written on the cheque—a sum of money specified on the order, and to deduct the amount from the cheque-writer's account. The person receiving the cheque can endorse it over to another party by signing it on the back. See also CERTIFIED CHEQUE, POST-DATED CHEQUE.

Chicago School See MONETARISM.

chief executive officer (CEO) The member of the board of directors of a firm, and officer in a corporation, who exercises the highest level of authority over the day-to-day activities and policies of the firm. He or she may be either the president or the chairman of the corporation, and is responsible to the BOARD OF DIRECTORS and to the shareholders.

chip A piece of silicon so small it can almost be slipped through the eye of a needle; yet imprinted on it is a powerful semi-conductor called a large-scale integrated circuit, containing thousands of transistors. It has the capacity to do the work formerly done by great banks of transistors, adding enormously to the power of computer systems while dramatically reducing computer costs. Over the next few years, a so-called superchip is expected to be developed that will reduce the cost of computing even more significantly and put computing power in the hands of individuals.

City The square mile of London in which is based one of the world's most important financial and commercial centres. It is the location of the London Stock Exchange, the LONDON METALS EXCHANGE, major insurance firms, including Lloyd's, the institutions that are responsible for much of the EURO-CURRENCY investing and lending, the merchant banks, foreign-exchange and gold markets, and a major short-term money market. It is Europe's largest financial centre and, after New York, the world's second largest financial centre. See also BAY STREET, WALL STREET.

city-gate price The price for natural gas delivered by a pipeline company to the collection point for a local gas distributor. For example, the Toronto city-gate price is the price charged by the gas-pipeline company shipping it from western Canada to a delivery point at Toronto. It consists of the PLANT-GATE PRICE charged by the natural-gas producer, plus the transmission charge for delivering it to Toronto.

civil code The system of civil law used in Quebec. While the province has developed its own code, its system is based on the Napoleonic and Justinian codes. Under this system, cases are decided on the detailed principles set out in the code, unlike the COMMON-LAW system inherited from Britain that the other provinces use, which relies heavily on precedents set in earlier cases.

There are two elements of the civil code: **1.** The set of rules to be followed in all the different areas of civil law. **2.** The rules of procedure to be followed in civil actions. If the code itself is not clear enough to allow a judge to decide a case, he has three forms of clarification he can use. First, there are the Codifiers' Reports, documents prepared by the officials who drafted various sections of the code, which explain the intent of the relevant sections. Second, there is what is known as *la doctrine,* consisting of written opinions by legal experts specializing in various areas of law. And third, there is a body of written judgements, *la jurisprudence,* which shows how judges have interpreted various parts of the code in the past and which is similar to the use of precedents by common-law judges. While Quebec has its own civil code, it is governed by the same CRIMINAL CODE as the rest of the country; criminal law falls under federal jurisdiction.

claim A portion of land containing mineral prospects that have been staked out, under federal or provincial law, by a prospector or mining company. The claim gives the holder the right to continue exploration and, if commercially feasible, to exploit the resources.

class action A legal action launched on behalf of most or all of the consumers of a product or victims of someone else's negligence. The costs of launching an action to recover damages may be too high for each individual, but make sense if a large number of individuals file a joint suit and share the costs of the action. Class actions can be launched in Canadian courts, but their application is limited and they have not been widely used.

class struggle KARL MARX's economic interpretation of history; it is based on the theory that the different social classes—in particular, capitalists and workers—are locked in an inevitable conflict that will ultimately result in the revolution of the workers or proletariat, and the overthrow of the capitalists or bourgeoisie. The revolution will lead to the establishment of a socialist state, to be followed by its evolution into a COMMUNIST state.

classical economics The school of economic thought originating with ADAM SMITH (1723–90), and further developed by THOMAS ROBERT MALTHUS (1766–1834), DAVID RICARDO (1772–1823), JOHN STUART MILL (1806–73), and Jean Baptiste Say (1767–1832; see also SAY'S LAW). It contended that society and individuals were best served by an economy that enjoyed vigorous growth, and that such growth was best assured by a free market, unhindered by government regulation or policies of income redistribution.

Classical economists believed that the economy functioned through natural laws, much as the physical universe operates through the laws of nature; the LAW OF SUPPLY AND DEMAND in a free-market economy, for example, should yield full-employment conditions. In the classical model, each citizen pursued his own interests in a competitive market with the total of all those transactions and activities producing high levels of economic growth. The classical economists reacted against the earlier MERCANTILIST age, which emphasized a significant role for government in the economy. Classical economics provided the foundation for theories of FREE TRADE and COMPARATIVE ADVANTAGE, as well as the view that the least government is the best government. See also INVISIBLE HAND.

clearing system **1.** A network of centres across Canada operated by the CHARTERED BANKS and the CANADIAN BANKERS' ASSOCIATION to exchange cheques, money orders, traveller's cheques, and CANADA SAVINGS BONDS on a daily basis and to settle any outstanding balances with one another. Other financial institutions, such as trust companies, have access to the clearing system through a chartered bank. The clearing system handles well over one billion cheques a year. **2.** Centres operated by STOCK EXCHANGES and member firms through the INVESTMENT DEALERS ASSOCIATION, to exchange share certificates and cheques for the thousands of transactions they handle on the floor of stock exchanges each day in buying and selling shares for customers. A similar arrangement exists to exchange traded bonds.

closed economy An economy that has no external trade or virtually no external trade. Postwar examples have included China after the communist takeover in 1949, North Korea, and, for a time, Cambodia.

closed-end investment company An investment company that owns major interests in other operating companies and whose shares are traded on a stock exchange. A closed-end investment company issues a fixed number of shares that are bought and sold by investors on the market, unlike a mutual fund, which redeems outstanding shares held by investors and regularly issues new shares as fast as it can sell them. Examples of closed-end investment companies include Argus Corporation, Power Corporation, and Canadian Pacific Investments Limited.

closed shop A clause in a collective agreement that says that the only people who can be hired for jobs in a bargaining unit must be members of the union before being hired. This means that they will usually be hired through the union. Closed shops are most common in the construction industry and on the docks, where union hiring halls allocate jobs among members in good standing.

closely held corporation A corporation owned by a small number of individuals. Its shares are not traded on a stock exchange or in the OVER-THE-COUNTER MARKET. See also PRIVATE COMPANY.

closing prices The prices on a stock exchange, bond market, or commodities market at the end of the day's trading.

Club of Rome A private international association of about seventy-five businessmen, scientists, and scholars, founded in 1968 to study mankind's common problems, particularly problems of long-term resource supplies, environmental pressures, economic growth, and food supplies. The club has published several important studies that it financed. They include *The Limits to Growth* (1972), *Mankind at the Turning Point* (1974), and *RIO: Reshaping the International Order* (1976). While *The Limits to Growth* presented the stark and dramatic view that mankind would be doomed by environmental crises, a lack of natural resources, famine, and overpopulation, without a halt to economic and population growth, the RIO report said that economic growth should not be abandoned and that adoption of a NEW INTERNATIONAL ECONOMIC ORDER was a better approach to solve the problems of world poverty. The club was founded by Aurelio Peccei, an Italian industrialist, and is financed by the Agnelli Foundation of Italy and Volkswagen Foundation of Germany. See also LIMITS TO GROWTH, RIO PROJECT.

code of ethical practices A code adopted by the CANADIAN LABOUR CONGRESS in 1970 to strengthen union democracy, to encourage membership participation in union activities, and to prevent corrupt persons from holding union office. The code, which is part of the CLC constitution, gives the CLC and its affiliated unions the power to take disciplinary and corrective actions, including, if need be, the appointment of a TRUSTEE where union members have been deprived of their rights or union officers have been found to be corrupt.

The code calls on all union members to exercise their union citizenship by participating in union meetings and affairs, and states the right of union members to vote for union officers, to be assured of honest elections, to be eligible for union office, and to be free to voice their views on union affairs without fear of punishment. It adds that, while a member has the right to criticize union policies and union officers, this does not include the right to undermine the union as an institution, to advocate dual unionism, to destroy or weaken the union as a collective-bargaining agency, or to engage in slander and libel. It states that union disciplinary actions must be carried out according to due process, with adequate notice, a hearing, and judgement on the basis of evidence. It calls for regular union conventions to elect officers freely.

co-determination The participation by employees in the management of an enterprise —by having employee representatives sitting on the boards of directors of corporations, for example. The participation of workers on the boards of companies was made mandatory in West Germany in 1952, and has since been adopted as an objective for all countries within the EUROPEAN ECONOMIC COMMUNITY. It has been discussed in Canada, but with little enthusiasm from either employers or unions. Employers fear interference with the rights of management, while unions fear that they will be co-opted, and hence their bargaining power in collective bargaining will be reduced.

codicil A document altering a will.

coin Pieces of metal bearing the imprint of the Canadian government that are recognized as legal tender or a medium of exchange. The metal used in smaller coins is usually worth less than the value stamped on them; but they have the higher face value because they can be exchanged for paper money at their stated value. In Canada, coins are produced by the ROYAL CANADIAN MINT.

coincident indicator A statistical measure of economic performance showing current economic conditions. Examples include real gross national product, real domestic product, the index of industrial production, and the seasonally adjusted unemployment rate. See also LAGGING INDICATOR, LEADING INDICATOR.

collateral Various types of securities, such as shares, bonds, insurance policies, or other property, that are deposited by a borrower with a creditor to reduce the creditor's risk in case the loan is not repaid. If the borrower fails to repay the loan, the creditor can sell the collateral to recover his money.

collective agreement A contract for a stated period of time, usually one to three years, between a union or group of unions and an employer or group of employers, that sets out the rates of pay, hours of work, vacations, fringe benefits, pension rights, working conditions, rights of workers, methods of dealing with technological change, check-off of union dues, procedures to be followed in settling grievances, and other terms and conditions of employment.

collective bargaining The negotiation of a collective agreement between representatives of an employer or group of employers and representatives of a union or group of unions. Such bargaining is supposed to be conducted in good faith; that is, both sides are supposed to be sincere in their desire to reach an agreement. Collective bargaining is subject to rules and procedures set out in federal and provincial labour laws, which determine when and under what conditions a strike or lockout may occur, provide for conciliation and mediation, and may provide for compulsory arbitration.

collective ownership A synonym for PUBLIC OWNERSHIP.

Colombo Plan A program adopted in 1950 by a group of donor countries, including originally Canada, Britain, Australia, and New Zealand, and later the United States and Japan, to assist the economic development of the nations of South-East Asia, including India, Pakistan, Bangladesh, South Korea, Indonesia, Burma, Malaysia, the Philippines, Sri Lanka, Thailand, Afghanistan, and Singapore. Other countries that have received help under the plan include Iran, South Vietnam, and Cambodia. The Colombo Plan was one of Canada's first foreign-aid activities. It provides technical, educational, and economic assistance. Its consultative committee meets once a year. In 1974, it established a Colombo Plan Staff College for Technical Education, located in Singapore, which sends instructors to member countries and provides some training at its facilities in Singapore. The plan was originally intended to run for six years only, but it has been extended several times since and is now to run to 1981.

Columbia River Treaty A treaty between Canada and the United States, signed on 17 January 1961, under which Canada agreed to build dams on the Columbia River in British Columbia that would substantially increase hydro-electric-power capacity south of the border and achieve flood-control benefits for both countries. Dams were to be built at the Arrow Lakes and the Duncan River within five years, while the Mica Dam was to be completed by 1970, with Canada and British Columbia bearing the costs. In return, Canada was to get half the power generated in the United States, plus payment for the flood-control benefits.

combination Temporary or ongoing collusion by allegedly competing firms in an industry, to reduce competition and to obtain higher profits by charging excessive prices, restraining production, and dividing the market. Such collusion may be in the form of a written agreement, may result from secret meetings between representatives of the different members of the combination, or may be implicit, with firms in the industry following an acknowledged price leader. See also COMBINES INVESTIGATION ACT, COMPETITION POLICY.

Combines Investigation Act The principal federal law that deals with restrictive trade practices, mergers and monopolies, misleading advertising, or other practices that restrict competition. Its purpose is to curb restrictive trade practices and to protect consumers by encouraging competition. It is based on the belief that consumers will benefit from a competitive market, which leads to the most efficient allocation of resources to produce and distribute goods and services.

It is a criminal offence under the act to create and operate a combine, oligopoly, or monopoly that prevents or lessens unduly competition in the production, manufacture, purchase, barter, sale, storage, rental, transportation, or supply of any good or service. Companies are prohibited from exchanging statistics, working together to set standards, and meeting together, if their purpose is to reduce competition in the production, prices, quantity, quality of goods or services, to reduce competition in markets or distribution channels, to restrict the entry of new producers into an industry, or to prevent the expansion of a firm within the industry. Companies are allowed to act together without fear of penalty in seeking export sales.

A wide number of business practices are also prohibited. They include MISLEADING ADVERTISING, PRICE DISCRIMINATION, RESALE-PRICE MAINTENANCE, PREDATORY PRICING, DOUBLE TICKETING, and BAIT-AND-SWITCH SELLING. The act also regulates promotional contests to protect the consumer.

The act is administered by the Department of CONSUMER AND CORPORATE AFFAIRS, while the RESTRICTIVE TRADE PRACTICES COMMISSION has wide power to investigate complaints for the director of Investigation and Research in the BUREAU OF COMPETITION POLICY, and to make recommendations for legal action to the minister of Consumer and Corporate Affairs. See also COMPETITION POLICY, BARRIERS TO ENTRY.

commerce A term sometimes used to describe the buying, storing, selling, and distribution of goods; as opposed to industry, which deals with the production of goods, and finance, which deals with the financing of industry and commerce.

commercial An advertisement broadcast on radio or television. Privately owned radio and television stations rely on the income from commercials to pay their costs and earn their profits. The CANADIAN RADIO-TELEVISION AND TELECOMMUNICATIONS COMMISSION regulates the amount of broadcast time that may be taken up, in any consecutive sixty minutes, with commercials.

commercial paper Short-term promissory notes and other negotiable securities issued by major corporations and repayable on a specified date. Commercial paper is an important form of short-term investment for corporations and others with temporary cash surpluses.

commercial policy Government policy that deals with foreign trade and investment, and which includes tariff and other trade agreements, export-financing facilities, rules to prevent dumping and other unfair trading practices, the establishment of trade-promotion offices in other countries, and export incentives.

commission **1.** A government regulatory board or agency, such as the CANADIAN TRANSPORT COMMISSION and the CANADIAN RADIO-TELEVISION AND TELECOMMUNICATIONS COMMISSION. **2.** A fee paid to a stockbroker, real-estate agent, customs broker, or other salesman or agent in return for arranging a sale or purchase or carrying out some other service.

commission of inquiry The new name for a federal or provincial ROYAL COMMISSION.

Committee for an Independent Canada (CIC) A non-partisan committee of Canadians, formed in 1970, to campaign for greater Canadian ownership and control of the economy and to increase support for Canadian cultural expression. Its more precise goals include: **1.** Increased Canadian ownership of resources and industry, including efforts to regain ownership of foreign-owned enterprises in Canada. **2.** A national-development program that would allocate more resources to the under-developed parts of the country. **3.** Canadian control, Canadian content, and adequate financing of Canada's communications media. **4.** Greater autonomy for Canadian unions. **5.** The Canadian design of the country's urban environment. **6.** A greater Canadian orientation in education and foreign policy.

commodity Although it can be used to refer to any product or good, the term is normally used to describe raw materials, or semi-finished goods, such as wheat, coffee, pork bellies, copper, nickel, lumber, oil, cotton, rubber, or tin.

commodity agreement An agreement between producer and consumer nations to stabilize prices and, usually, to provide for higher prices of a specific commodity. Such agreements exist for sugar, tin, coffee, rubber, copper, and cocoa. The initiative for commodity agreements usually comes from producer nations, who seek protection against declining prices and excessive production, and who want to make sure that commodity prices at least stay even with inflation. Many less-developed countries rely heavily on a single commodity for a large share of their foreign-exchange earnings, and must sustain the income from commodity exports to pay for essential imports and the service costs of their foreign debt. With fluctuations in the business cycle of industrial nations, the price of basic commodities can also fluctuate widely, since most commodities are highly sensitive to the LAW OF SUPPLY AND DEMAND. Some commodity agreements provide for a BUFFER STOCK, built up through purchases of the commodity when there is excess supply and sold off when there are shortages; some operate with maximum and minimum prices, with a top price at which the commodity will be sold and a minimum price at which consumers buy. Other features may include production restrictions, marketing quotas, or export controls. See also COMMON FUND.

commodity broker A broker who buys and sells COMMODITY FUTURES, COMMODITY OPTIONS, and SPOT contracts on COMMODITY MARKETS for his customers. Like a stockbroker, he earns a commission that is a percentage of the value of the transaction.

commodity exchange A market in which commodities and FUTURES contracts for commodities are traded. The commodities themselves are not brought to the exchange; only contracts for immediate or spot delivery and future delivery are traded. There are commodity exchanges for grains, lumber, gold, silver, copper, nickel, soybeans, frozen orange juice, pork bellies, potatoes, coffee, tea, cotton, and other commodities. The WINNIPEG COMMODITY EXCHANGE is the principal commodity exchange in Canada. Other major commodity exchanges include the Chicago Board of Trade, the Chicago Mercantile Exchange, the London Metal Exchange, the New York Coffee and Sugar Exchange, and the New York Commodity Exchange, which includes the New York Cotton Exchange and the New York Mercantile Exchange. Contracts are purchased through COMMODITY BROKERS, who play a role similar to stockbrokers in arranging stock-exchange transactions.

commodity futures Contracts to deliver or to take delivery of a specified quantity of a commodity at a specified price on a specified date in the future. Such contracts are traded on COMMODITY EXCHANGES; their main role is to provide industries that trade in or use commodities with a means of HEDGING against sharp price fluctuations. See also FUTURES MARKET, COMMODITY EXCHANGE.

commodity market See FUTURES MARKET, COMMODITY EXCHANGE.

commodity money Commodities that can be used as a medium of exchange and a store of value—gold, silver, diamonds, cattle, wampum, and furs, for example.

commodity option An OPTION that an investor can purchase, giving him the right to purchase a futures contract at a specified price for a specified period of time. The investor pays a relatively low price for the option. If the futures contract does not rise above its value at the time the option was purchased plus the price of the option, then the option is not exercised. But if the futures contract is, say, $14.75 at the time the option is purchased, the option price is 50 cents, and the futures contract rises to $15.75, then the option will be exercised, since $15.75 is greater than $14.75 plus 50 cents.

commodity theory of money The theory that the value of money is set by the value of the metal, such as gold or silver, of which it is made or upon which it is based. In the nineteenth century, a close relationship was maintained between the supply of gold in a nation's reserves and the supply of paper money in circulation.

Common Agricultural Policy (CAP) An arrangement within the EUROPEAN ECONOMIC COMMUNITY (EEC), under which official target prices for individual farm products are set throughout the EEC each year, and which sets a common external tariff to be levied on imports, calculated by subtracting the world price from the CAP price. Thus, the EEC tariffs on farm products are automatically adjusted to prevent the entry of farm products below CAP prices from Canada and other countries.

In principle, the aim of CAP is to stabilize farm prices, to improve agricultural productivity, and to make sure that EEC food output is sufficient to meet the basic needs of the population. In practice, CAP is seen by Canada and other food-exporting nations as a protectionist trade policy. The EUROPEAN COMMISSION may buy surplus farm products and stockpile them to help bring prices up to the official target level; it either exports the surplus, or holds it to sell if prices get too high. The revenue from tariffs is used to subsidize EEC agricultural exports if world prices are below CAP prices. CAP also provides financial assistance to help modernize farms. Since different EEC members have different currencies, a common "green pound" is used to calculate common official target prices throughout the EEC.

common carrier A company or individual providing a service that must be available to everyone who wants to pay for it, and at the same price to all users. Examples include airlines, railways, trucking companies, bus and transit companies, taxicabs, telephone and telecommunications companies, and some pipelines. Common carriers are regulated by government at the federal, provincial, or municipal level, depending on the service. The federal government, for example, regulates airlines, pipelines, and telecommunications; the provincial governments regulate inter-city bus services, and municipal governments regulate taxicabs.

common fund An agreement in principle

reached in March 1979 among 101 developed and less-developed countries, including Canada, to establish a $750-million fund to be used to help finance BUFFER STOCKS of key commodities, and thus to help prevent sharp fluctuations in their prices. The fund was established following a concerted campaign by less-developed countries, many of whom depend heavily on foreign-exchange earnings from a single commodity whose price fluctuates sharply, and who thus face periodic exchange crises, since the manufactured goods they must import do not show similar fluctuations in price. The managers of buffer stocks of selected commodities—tin, cocoa, coffee, rubber, and sugar are possible candidates—would sell stocks when prices are high and buy stocks when prices are low. The fund is divided into two parts, $400 million put up by the participants, and a $350-million second window, or special fund, to help poorer nations increase their commodity revenue by developing new markets, improving crop yields, and using research and development to improve crop varieties.

common law A system of law in which the precedents and principles established in past judgements are incorporated into current decisions by the courts. The system dates back to feudal days in Britain and has been transported to Canada, where it is the basis for civil law in all provinces except Quebec (see also CIVIL CODE) and is an important part of the interpretation of criminal law. Parliament or a provincial legislature can overturn common law by passing a new statute.

common market An arrangement among sovereign nations to eliminate tariffs and other barriers among them and to permit the free movement of goods, services, people, and capital. A common market also implies a common external tariff on trade by all members of the common market with non-members. See also EUROPEAN ECONOMIC COMMUNITY.

common shares Shares that represent an ownership interest in a company and usually, but not always, entitle the owners to vote at company annual and special meetings. Owners of common shares are entitled to receive any dividends declared, but a company has no legal obligation to pay dividends to the owners of common shares. The owners of common shares are entitled to all of the assets of the company after outstanding debts and taxes have been paid. SHAREHOLDERS' EQUITY in a company BALANCE SHEET is the interest of the owners of common shares.

Commonwealth preference See BRITISH PREFERENTIAL TARIFF.

Commonwealth Trade and Economic Conference A meeting of Commonwealth nations, chaired by Canada and held in Montreal in September 1958, to foster "an expanding Commonwealth in an expanding world." Its purpose was to encourage trade and investment among Commonwealth members, to increase the flow of development assistance from the rich Commonwealth nations to poor Commonwealth nations, and to bring about the convertibility of British sterling and other currencies within the Commonwealth. Canada hoped that the conference would lead to a substantial reduction in its trade dependence on the United States by the rapid development of new markets in Britain and other Commonwealth members.

Communications, Department of A federal government department established in 1969 to encourage and set policy for telecommunications services in Canada, and to protect Canadian interests in the allocation of airwaves and communications-satellite channels and in the development of international standards. The department funds research and development in FIBRE OPTICS, COMMUNICATIONS SATELLITES, the application of new microelectronics and fibre-optics technology, and operates the Communications Research Centre. The department tries to ensure that Canadians develop their own technologies and industries in the new world of microelectronics and telecommunications, and that consumers have access to such services at reasonable prices. The department also co-ordinates federal-provincial relations in communications policy and is responsible to Parliament for TELESAT CANADA, a government-industry corporation that provides communications-satellite services in Canada.

communications satellite A satellite that receives and rebroadcasts microwave messages over long distances and at rapidly declining costs. A communications satellite is connected to senders and receivers by earth stations, and can carry voice, computer, facsimile, and television-broadcast messages; as the communications capacity and radiating power of satellites both increase, the size of earth stations can be sharply reduced, as can the cost of transmission.

Just as microelectronics is reducing the cost of computer services, so the communications satellite is reducing the cost of long-distance communications. This is expected to lead to many new applications, including the provision of a wide range of television-viewing and -service choices in areas too remote or sparsely populated to be served by cable television, and to electronic mail, by which corporations, government agencies, and other major users will be able to convert mail to short computer messages that can be sent from one point and received at another, where a computer terminal will reconvert the message to print or visual-display form.

Canada's first commercial communications satellite, Anik I, was launched by TELESAT CANADA in November 1972, with initial service available in January 1973.

communism An economic and political system in which all private property, aside from some consumer goods, is abolished, and the state not only owns all the means of production but relies on central planning rather than on market forces to determine the allocation of resources, prices, new investments, and output. Communism traces its modern roots to KARL MARX (1818-83), who saw it as the final and inevitable stage of social revolution, originating in slavery, moving from there through feudalism to CAPITALISM, and, with the collapse of capitalism, socialism. Communism would succeed socialism, with the withering away of the state, the elimination of all inequality and social classes, and the creation of a society based on the principle, "from each according to his ability, to each according to his needs." In such a society, there would be no limit to the development of human potential. In the countries that call themselves communist today, such as the Soviet Union, its Eastern European satellites, China, North Korea, Vietnam, Outer Mongolia, and Cambodia, the practical administration of the state bears little resemblance to the social and economic vision of Marx. See also MARXIST ECONOMICS.

company See CORPORATION.

company law See CORPORATION LAW.

company seal The official seal of a company, which has to be used on certain corporate documents as required by law.

company secretary A company officer whose responsibility it is to see that the company carries out its legal obligations, such as giving shareholders adequate notice of annual and special meetings, making sure that they get proxy documents and other corporate information, making sure that the share register of the company is kept up to date, filing corporate disclosure statements, and keeping proper minutes of meetings of the company's board of directors.

company town A town in which there is only one significant employer and in which much of the housing and land may also be owned by the company. Company towns may exist where there are big mining or pulp and paper operations; Ottawa has sometimes been called a company town, because most people who live there work for the federal government or its agencies.

company union An organization of employees, all of whom work for the same company, that is not affiliated with a union that also represents employees in other firms. Company unions tend to be employee associations; often, they are organized by management as a way of keeping out a national or international union. They rarely provide for the right to strike or the negotiation of a normal collective agreement.

comparative advantage An important principle in international trade, based on the assumption that each country is probably more efficient than others in producing some particular good or service and that each country should concentrate on producing what it can produce more efficiently. Even if two countries can produce the same goods with equal efficiency, it still pays for each to specialize in just some of those goods and import the others, since specialization will lead to greater total production and lower costs for both.

A country is said to have a comparative advantage in the goods that it can produce most efficiently. If every country concentrates on those goods in which it has a comparative advantage, then trade between nations will benefit everyone, with consumers in all countries concerned buying the goods they need at the lowest prices. Each country gets the largest possible market for what it produces more efficiently, and benefits from lower-cost products it can't produce efficiently itself, from countries that have a comparative advantage in those products. For example, it makes more sense for Canada to concentrate on growing wheat and raising livestock and to import citrus fruits and winter vegetables than to divert resources from wheat and livestock to produce, under costly hothouse conditions, much more expensive citrus fruits and winter vegetables.

The notion of comparative advantage, developed by ADAM SMITH (1723–90), DAVID RICARDO (1772–1823), and JOHN STUART MILL (1806–73), is the basis of the FREE-TRADE argument.

compensatory fiscal policy The use of FISCAL POLICY to offset fluctuations in the BUSINESS CYCLE. Thus, in a recession, the government would incur or increase its deficit by cutting taxes or increasing spending or both, to raise the level of demand in the economy. In a period of inflation caused by excess demand, it would raise taxes or reduce spending or both, in order to reduce the overall level of demand.

competition A market in which rival sellers are trying to gain extra business at one another's expense, and thus are forced both to be as efficient as possible and to hold their prices down as much as possible. Competition is thus a sophisticated yet unco-ordinated mechanism that sorts out the actions of millions of buyers and sellers, and uses the resulting pattern of supply and demand to determine what shall be produced, in what quantities, and at what price.

Insofar as competition exists, it is an effective way of achieving the efficient allocation of resources and the lowest cost for goods and services. Much of CLASSICAL and NEOCLASSICAL ECONOMICS is based on the notion of PERFECT COMPETITION, in which numerous firms sell identical goods and therefore have to hold down prices. But the real world of the modern MIXED ECONOMY is one of IMPERFECT COMPETITION, where large firms are able to exercise a significant control over prices and where the BARRIERS TO ENTRY prevent new firms from entering the industry and competing by selling at lower prices. See also COMPETITION POLICY, COMBINES INVESTIGATION ACT, RESTRICTIVE TRADE PRACTICES COMMISSION.

competition policy Legislation that protects the consumer against unfair business practices and the exploitation by OLIGOPOLIES and MONOPOLIES of their excessive market power to charge high prices and curb competition. Thus, the purpose of competition policy is to improve the efficiency of the marketplace and to promote COMPETITION. Among the specific practices covered by competition law are collusion among competitors to fix prices, to allocate markets, or to prevent the entry of new firms, or takeovers of competitors to reduce competition and achieve monopoly power, RESALE-PRICE MAINTENANCE to prevent lower prices, MISLEADING ADVERTISING, and other restrictive practices. See also COMBINES INVESTIGATION ACT.

complementary goods Products that are not substitutes for one another, but demand for which is linked: if the demand for one rises, the demand for the other will automatically rise; similarly, a decline in the demand for one will result in a decline in demand for the other. Examples include new housing and furniture and appliances, automobiles and snow tires, turkeys and bread used for stuffing.

composite demand The total demand for a particular good or service, originating with a great many different users who may require it for many different purposes. For example, the total demand for steel will come from the automobile, machinery, construction, railway, electric-utility, farm-equipment, typewriter, household-appliance, aircraft, pipeline, refinery, shipbuilding, and many other different industries. See also INPUT-OUTPUT ANALYSIS.

compound interest A rate of interest calculated by adding previous years' interest payments on to the original principal in calculating the current year's interest. For example, on a $100 bond paying 5 per cent compound interest for five years, the first year's interest would be 5 per cent of $100, or $5. The second years's interest would be 5 per cent of $105, or $5.25. The third year's interest would be 5 per cent of $110.25, or $5.51, and so forth, through to the fifth year. Compound interest can produce large increases; for example, a $1,000 bond at 6 per cent compound interest and a term of twelve years would pay out $2,012 at the end of twelve years. See also SIMPLE INTEREST.

comptroller See CONTROLLER.

compulsory arbitration The intervention by government in a strike or lockout, ordering the two sides to abide by the decision of an arbitrator appointed to settle their dispute. Compulsory arbitration is often used to resolve a strike that is hurting the economy or members of the public, such as a railway or dockworkers' strike, a strike by teachers, or by municipal or hospital workers.

compulsory check-off See RAND FORMULA.

computer An electronic machine that can store and process vast quantities of information, activate or adjust other machines through feedback, and carry out a huge array of functions for business firms and government. Technological advances are sharply reducing the costs of operating computers, while at the same time significantly increasing the ways computers can be used. Not only can they handle simple, routine tasks that would require a large number of people to perform otherwise, such as processing the payrolls and billings of large corporations and pension and family-allowance payments by government; computers can be used to control industrial processes, such as the workings of petrochemical refineries, steel furnaces, nuclear-power plants, and automated machinery and production lines. They can also be used to do things that man cannot do himself, or can do only with enormous, costly, and time-consuming effort; in this sense, computers are an extension of man's intellectual powers. They can be used to solve extremely complicated business, economic, military, scientific, and other problems, and can produce a series of alternative solutions, depending on the different sets of criteria that are given; they can also suggest the most important criteria. Thus, much of modern decision-making is the result of computerized analysis.

Computers have already had an enormous impact on society, including its culture. With growing miniaturization, increasing power, and declining cost, computers will bring even greater changes in society in the future. Along with the steam engine, electricity, medical discoveries, the internal-combustion engine, petrochemicals technology, jet propulsion, and nuclear power, the computer is one of the great inventions of man. Combined with modern TELECOMMUNICATIONS and computer networks, the computer is the basis for a new industrial revolution that is already underway.

computer program A series of instructions that tells a computer what to do. Although sophisticated programming languages are needed to run a computer system, individuals can operate a computer for simple functions using simple sets of instructions that are transmitted, for example, through the keyboard of a computer terminal. The keys on the keyboard will have human instructions on them, although they activate a computer system that follows programming languages.

computer science Research and development into new uses for computers, new computer technology, COMPUTER SOFTWARE, and the impact of computers on organizations. Many Canadian universities have computer-science departments.

computer software Computer programs, frequently designed and developed by independent software firms, to make possible the application of computer systems to a wide range of industrial, administrative, educational, health, and other uses. The software industry is one of the major new industries of the information or POST-INDUSTRIAL SOCIETY.

computer terminal Any device used to enter information into a computer system or to get information out of the system. Among the most widely used terminals are typewriter-like units, through which information is typed into the computer and received either by a print-out or by display on a video terminal; optical-character readers, which read information into a computer; and different types of gauges and other monitoring equipment, which, in process-control systems, feed the information they measure into the computer.

concentrate A semi-processed mineral ore, from which almost all of the waste material has been extracted and which is ready for final processing into a refined product. Many of Canada's minerals have been exported in the past in this form, with the final processing and manufacturing use of the mineral being carried out in the importing country.

concentration The extent to which a small number of firms or establishments account for the major proportion of output, assets, employment, and profits in a particular industry. An industry is said to be highly concentrated when a small number of firms account for a significant proportion of output, employment, assets, or profits. The Department of CONSUMER AND CORPORATE AFFAIRS, in a 1971 study, *Concentration in the Manufacturing Industries of Canada,* said: "Where an industry consists of a number of firms such that no single one or single small group can exert a dominant influence on pricing, then the structural basis for a reasonably competitive market mechanism exists. On the other hand, where a small group of firms, such as the largest four or the largest eight in the industry, account for a dominant share of output, then the possibility of serious restrictions on the competitive process must be taken into account." The study found the degree of concentration in Canada to be higher than that in the United States. See also MONOPOLY, OLIGOPOLY, PERFECT COMPETITION, IMPERFECT COMPETITION, CONCENTRATION RATIO.

concentration ratio The percentage of shipments, employment, assets, or profits accounted for by the four largest establishments or four largest enterprises within a group of competing firms. Three common measures are used: **1.** The inverse index, which shows the number of firms or establishments that account for 80 per cent of factory shipments or employment in a particular industry. **2.** Industry concentration ratios, which show the percentage of the value of shipments accounted for by the largest 4, 8, 12, 16, 20, and 50 enterprises or establishments in a particular industry. **3.** The Herfindahl Index, which measures concentration in terms of employment and shipments added together.

concentrator A mineral-processing plant that removes much of the waste material from a mineral ore and produces a CONCENTRATE or semi-processed metal. The concentrate must then be further processed, in a smelter, for example, to produce a fully refined metal.

concession The granting, usually by a government, of the right to do something—to search for and extract oil, gas, or other minerals, for example; to cut timber, build an access road, or construct a railway. In return, the government agency will normally levy a charge and, in the case of mineral and timber rights, impose various conditions, such as a minimum level of exploration spending per year, or replacement tree-planting.

conciliation The use of a third party, usually a federal or provincial labour-department official, to avert a strike or lockout or to end one during collective-bargaining negotiations. A conciliator attempts to come up with a compromise solution through intensive discussions with both sides in a dispute, but neither side is under any legal obligation to accept a conciliator's recommendations.

conciliation report A further stage in the conciliation process during collective-bargaining negotiations. It is the recommendation of a conciliation board, consisting of management and union representatives and a government official, for the settlement of a dispute over a new contract. A conciliation officer from a federal or provincial department of labour makes a preliminary effort at conciliation on his own and, depending on progress or lack of progress, recommends to the federal or provincial minister of labour that a conciliation board be appointed or not be appointed, depending on whether he thinks anything can be accomplished. The minister then decides whether or not to appoint such a board. If he does decide that there should be a further conciliation effort, the formal conciliation board is set up and given the task of hearing the arguments of both sides and trying to resolve their differences. The conciliation report that is produced is not binding on either side and may not be a unanimous report.

Generally speaking, a strike or lockout cannot occur until after a week-long cooling-off period following the presentation of the conciliation-board report, or two weeks after the decision by a federal or provincial labour minister that no conciliation board will be appointed. Failure of a conciliation board to reach unanimous agreement does not mean that there will be a strike or lockout. The employer and the union may decide to call in a mediator. See also MEDIATION.

concurrent powers Under the British North America Act, taxing or spending powers that may be exercised by either the federal or provincial governments, or both. For example, both levels of government can impose DIRECT TAXES, establish pension plans, legislate consumer protection and environmental standards, and implement agricultural development and assistance programs.

conditional discharge The freeing of a bankrupt firm or person from his liabilities, provided he carry out certain steps specified in the conditional-discharge order.

conditional grant The payment of a grant from one level of government to another for a specific purpose, as set out in law. Examples would be payments from the federal government to the provincial governments under the CANADA ASSISTANCE PLAN or other such programs, or payments by provincial governments to municipalities for transit, police, or other specified purposes. The money cannot be used by the receiving level of government for anything other than the purpose specified by the donor level of government. See also SHARED-COST PROGRAMS.

conditional sale A sale that is not completed (hence transfer of title is not made) until agreed-on conditions have been met. For example, the sale of a building may be conditional on the vendor making certain repairs or alterations, on his winding up an existing mortgage on the property, or on the purchaser being able to arrange a new mortgage.

condominium The ownership of a dwelling unit, an apartment or townhouse, for example, in a multi-unit building, along with a share of the ownership of the land and of the common areas of the building, such as the lobby, recreation and service areas, and hallways. The cost of maintenance and repair of the project is shared among all the owners. Individual owners are taxed separately by the municipality. See also CO-OPERATIVE, where owners have shares in the project instead of title to a specific dwelling unit.

Confederation of Canadian Unions (CCU) A small federation of Canadian unions, formed in 1969 as an alternative to the CANADIAN LABOUR CONGRESS, which represents both Canadian and INTERNATIONAL UNIONS. A number of locals of international unions have affiliated with the CCU, but it still represents no more than 1 per cent of Canadian union membership.

Confederation of National Trade Unions (CNTU) A labour federation based largely in Quebec that grew out of the Canadian Catholic Federation of Labour, established in 1921 with the active encouragement and support of the Roman Catholic Church. In 1960, the labour federation changed its name to the CNTU and eliminated all religious references or connections from its charter of organization. The

CNTU exercises significant power over its affiliated unions and has its own strike fund. It represents less than 10 per cent of Canadian union membership.

Conference Board in Canada A non-profit economic-research and -analysis organization, which is funded by business, government, labour, and universities. It has a large economic-research group that publishes quarterly reports on the national and provincial economic outlook, along with two quarterly surveys, one on business attitudes and investment-spending intentions, and the other on consumer spending intentions. Its compensation-research centre conducts research into pay scales, industrial relations, and fringe benefits, and publishes *Datafacts,* a statistical report on labour markets. It has a market-research division, which studies market-research applications, and a public-affairs division, which publishes reports on such issues as the responsibilities of corporate directors. The board was established in the United States in 1914. In 1954, a Canadian office was established in Montreal. The institute became much more of a Canadian organization after 1970, when its headquarters were moved to Ottawa.

conference of first ministers A meeting of the prime minister and the ten provincial premiers. Such conferences have become annual events and are held for basically three purposes: **1.** To deal with constitutional reform. **2.** To discuss economic and energy policies. **3.** To work out agreements on SHARED-COST PROGRAMS and changes in fiscal arrangements. A small secretariat exists in Ottawa to provide various ongoing services for such conferences. The first conference was held in 1906, but they did not become annual events until the late 1960s. See also FEDERAL-PROVINCIAL CONFERENCE, PREMIERS' CONFERENCE, FEDERAL-PROVINCIAL RELATIONS OFFICE.

conference of ministers of finance and provincial treasurers Regular meetings of the federal and provincial ministers and their senior advisers, which have been taking place at least once a year since 1964 to discuss economic and fiscal policies and to co-ordinate fiscal policies in the preparation of annual budgets. The ministers also meet to discuss tax-sharing and changes in fiscal arrangements, special economic problems such as inflation, and co-ordination of such matters as foreign borrowing. The federal minister of FINANCE chairs the meetings.

Conference on International Economic Co-operation (CIEC) A conference, co-chaired by Canada and Venezuela, held to negotiate agreement on a NEW INTERNATIONAL ECONOMIC ORDER; the conference was made up of eight developed countries, seven members of the ORGANIZATION OF PETROLEUM EXPORTING COUNTRIES, and twelve less-developed countries. The conference first met in Paris in December 1975 to deal with the work of four commissions that had been established beforehand to deal with energy, raw materials and commodity agreements, foreign aid, and the problem of foreign debts. Canada was a member of the commissions dealing with energy and foreign aid. During 1976, the four commissions attempted to work out specific recommendations, but the subsequent ministerial conference in Paris at the end of the year failed to reach agreement on major issues. The less-developed countries wanted relief from the burden of their foreign debts and a new system of pricing raw materials; the developed countries wanted OPEC members to agree to restrain energy-price increases. The conference was terminated in June 1977 without much progress. Since then, agreement has been reached on a COMMON FUND for certain commodities that are important to the LESS-DEVELOPED COUNTRIES.

confidence factor The level of optimism or pessimism among consumers, businessmen, and investors. While difficult to measure, the outlook of consumers, businessmen, and investors has an important effect on their decisions whether or not to spend and invest. Consumers will postpone purchases of homes or major consumer products if they think that economic conditions will worsen, for example. Similarly, businessmen will delay hiring workers or expanding their production capacity if the economic outlook is uncertain. The CONFERENCE BOARD IN CANADA publishes quarterly consumer- and business-confidence surveys.

conflict of interest The situation that can arise when a person in a position of trust, such as a director of a firm, can personally benefit from a decision he may help to make—the opportunity of a company director, for example, to steer a contract to a firm in which he has a sizable investment, even though this may not be the most economic decision for the company making the purchase. Provincial securities legislation imposes penalties on INSIDERS in publicly traded companies to prevent them from using corporate information not available to other shareholders to make a profit or avoid a loss.

conglomerate A corporation that grows by acquiring control of various companies in unrelated industries. The purpose is not to increase VERTICAL or HORIZONTAL INTEGRATION. Such acquisitions are usually financed in part by cash and in part by an exchange of shares, or by issuing new preferred or convertible shares. A conglomerate with a rapid acquisition record can show significant gains in earnings from year to year. But some investors, influenced by the experience of the 1960s, have cooled on conglomerates, because too high a price may be paid for acquisitions, the acquisitions may not have been carefully checked out, or the conglomerate itself may have built up a large debt obligation that depends on steadily rising earnings for repayment and maintenance of dividends. There are also benefits to diversification: it may represent the best way of investing excess funds; and such diversification may also be necessary to maintain the life of the firm.

Congress of Industrial Organizations (CIO) See AMERICAN FEDERATION OF LABOUR–CONGRESS OF INDUSTRIAL ORGANIZATIONS.

Conseil du Patronat A federation of more than 125 employer associations in Quebec; it also has some three hundred major corporations as members, along with small- and medium-sized businesses. Its principal role is to represent the views of private industry to the Quebec government. It is particularly active in the field of industrial relations, although it does not itself intervene in collective bargaining. The conseil was established in 1969 and is based in Montreal.

conservation The careful use of renewable and non-renewable natural resources to ensure their greatest long-term benefit to society and to prevent them from being wasted or damaged through environmental carelessness. Conservation of renewable resources includes policies to control the catch of species of fish or species of wildlife, programs to replace harvested trees, measures to protect the fertility of the soil, and laws to prevent the pollution of air and water. Conservation of non-renewable resources includes policies to prevent the waste of these resources by pricing them to reflect their real value, the use of technology to find more efficient uses or substitutes, and direct limits on production or end-use.

conserver society A term originating with the SCIENCE COUNCIL OF CANADA to describe an economic system that puts less emphasis on increases in per capita consumption and greater emphasis on the careful use of resources and technology. Such a system would be based on the assumption that the supply of natural resources is limited and that more attention should be paid to the needs of future generations; that the process of industrialization often leads to unanticipated results, such as pollution, so that growth is not an unmixed blessing; and that, too often, man seems to be an afterthought to technology, rather than the master of technology.

The conserver society does not mean a no-growth society; it anticipates new industries and new technologies, but with more emphasis on product durability and efficiency. It puts emphasis on much more careful use of energy and other resources, and on stronger efforts to anticipate and reduce waste and pollution. It emphasizes economy in design, doing more with less, and favours greater efforts at recycling. In a conserver society, the pricing mechanism would reflect not only the private production costs of a product but, as far as possible, the total cost to society, such as the ecological and social impact, so the market system would allocate resources more efficiently. The Science Council first used the term in 1973, and spelled out the concept of a conserver society in detail in a 1977 report entitled *Canada as a Conserver Society*.

consideration A payment or gift in return for something.

consignment The shipment of goods to another person or firm acting as the seller; until the goods are sold, the shipper remains the owner of the goods. For example, a manufacturer in Winnipeg, who sends goods on consignment to an agent in Toronto to sell to other firms or individuals, retains ownership of the unsold goods and pays the agent a fee or commission on the goods that have been sold. The seller or agent can return the goods to the manufacturer if he cannot sell them.

consolidated financial statement A financial statement, such as a company annual report, that presents the financial reports of a parent company and of its subsidiaries together. If the parent company has only a part-interest in one of the subsidiaries, say 60 per cent, then the financial statements are adjusted to reflect this; 40 per cent of the earnings would be deducted for this subsidiary and allocated to minority interests.

consolidated revenue fund The general pool of all income of the federal government, such as tax, tariff, and licence-fee income, and profits from crown corporations. All money received by the federal government must be credited to this fund and be properly accounted for. The RECEIVER GENERAL OF CANADA, normally the minister of SUPPLY AND SERVICES, is the official recipient. The money does not actually sit in one big bank account; it is divided among the chartered banks and their branches across Canada, or is on deposit to the receiver general at the BANK OF CANADA. Not only does the TREASURY BOARD strictly control the deposit of all government income, but none of the money can be spent unless there is a specific law passed by Parliament authorizing specific uses for the money. APPROPRIATION ACTS, for example, must be passed by Parliament each year authorizing the payment of civil-service salaries and other administrative costs. Other spending, such as interest on the public debt or family allowances, is authorized by individual acts of Parliament. Each provincial and municipal government has a similar fund.

consolidation The merger of two or more existing companies into an entirely new company; as opposed to a takeover or merger, where one of the firms becomes a subsidiary of another, or becomes a part of the other and loses its own identity.

consortium A group of companies that have joined together to undertake a specific project. The COMBINES INVESTIGATION ACT imposes restraints on such combinations in domestic projects, but permits groups of companies to join together for export sales. There are different types of consortia. One example is that of a group of companies in related industries banding together to bid on an export sale of, say, a nuclear reactor, an airport, or a transit system. Since the prospective customer wants to deal with one supplier and to have firm total-price bids, it makes more sense for a construction company, bidding to build an airport, to find a navigations-system supplier and other such suppliers or partners so that a complete bid can be made. Another type of consortium is that of a group of companies in the same industry —say, lumber products—banding together to promote and increase sales in another country, sharing the promotion costs. A domestic consortium may be formed by a group of oil companies to build a pipeline serving all of them, or a group of companies may band together to build a project that is too large for any one of them to undertake, such as a tar-sands oil plant.

conspicuous consumption The purchase of goods and services to impress other people; the pleasure of the purchase comes from the envy aroused in other people rather than from any intrinsic use of the good or service itself. The American economist and social thinker, Thorstein Veblen, explored the psychological dimensions of consumer spending in his book, *The Theory of the Leisure Class* (1899). He argued that all income groups spend at least part of their income for this purpose, and identified such spending by its contribution to the "comfort" or "fullness" of life.

constant costs Costs that remain unchanged in spite of increases in total output. An example would be custom-made jewellery or handmade clothes, which require the time and skills of highly specialized workers.

constant dollars A statistical term designed to show physical changes in output, income, profits, or sales by adjusting dollar values for a year, or a series of years, for inflation. For example, the gross national product for 1980 can be expressed either in current 1980 dollars or in constant dollars with, say, 1971 as the base year. The constant-dollar figure will deduct all the inflation of the period 1971–80 and show the GNP in terms of 1971 purchasing power, or as the real growth of the economy. Such an exercise is useful in showing the real changes taking place in output, income, and other economic measures, especially in times of high inflation; it shows the real changes that have occurred, as opposed to the changes that simply reflect inflation.

constitutional law The body of law that deals with the respective powers of each level of government and their agencies, and resolves conflicts among these different levels. In effect, this body of law interprets the BRITISH NORTH AMERICA ACT, various other British laws that have been passed by the British Parliament that apply to Canada, various Canadian laws, and the pattern of power-sharing that has evolved in Canada. The central issues include the respective SPENDING and TAXING POWERS of each level of government, and jurisdictional questions, such as which level of government has the power to issue oil- and gas-exploration permits in the offshore waters of Canada. One of the most recent constitutional issues was whether the federal government had the power under the BNA Act to impose, on its own, wage and price controls. The Supreme Court of Canada, in May 1976, ruled that rapidly rising inflation was a valid reason for the federal government to impose its ANTI-INFLATION BOARD controls under section 91 of the BNA Act, which allows the federal government to make laws for the "peace, order, and good government" of Canada. A number of provinces argued that controls fell under section 92, which allocates to them responsibilities for "property and civil rights."

constrained-share company Canadian companies that have restrictions or constraints on the sale of their shares to non-Canadians or non-residents. Bank, trust-company, broadcasting, telephone, and insurance-company shares are examples. Any company can impose restrictions on the sale of its shares to non-residents through its charter of incorporation or through company by-laws.

consumer The ultimate user of all goods and services. The gross national product, for example, measures national output as it reaches consumers, and does not count in its measure of output intermediate and semi-finished goods. According to classical economic theory, the consumer is king in the economy because he decides, through his purchases and the prices he is willing to pay, what goods and services shall be produced. See also CONSUMER SOVEREIGNTY.

Consumer and Corporate Affairs, Department of The federal government department whose job it is to protect the consumer and promote competition, thus ensuring fair treatment and achieving economic efficiency. The department enforces laws dealing with consumer packaging, labelling, product safety, advertising, weights and measures, and standards of performance for consumer products, including warranties. It deals with PATENTS, COPYRIGHT, TRADEMARKS, and industrial design. It enforces the COMBINES INVESTIGATION ACT and thus deals with mergers, takeovers, monopolies, and restraint of trade. It also administers federal business laws governing the incorporation and administration of business firms under the Canada Corporations Act and the Business Corporations Act. It thus protects consumers, investors, and business managers as participants in the marketplace.

consumer boycott A decision by consumers, often the result of organized efforts by consumer groups, to refrain from purchasing a product because of price increases or for other reasons.

consumer credit Credit available to consumers, in the form of cash loans, instalment buying, or credit cards, to purchase consumer goods and services. Consumer credit statistics produced by Statistics Canada exclude residential mortgages, home-improvement loans, and fully secured bank loans. The statistics include department-store credit, credit-card credit, personal loans, and instalment purchases. The main sources of consumer credit are banks, finance companies, trust companies, credit unions, caisses populaires, acceptance companies, and department stores.

Changes in the volume of outstanding consumer credit can be an indicator of consumer confidence, and hence of the economic outlook. If credit balances are rising, that may be a sign that consumers are feeling optimistic, and hence are confident of their ability to repay their increased debt; conversely, if balances decline, the decline may be a sign that consumers are getting worried about their jobs or the cost of living, and want to reduce their existing debts and build up their savings.

consumer demand The total volume of consumer purchases of goods and services. While consumer demand for necessities shows little fluctuation, consumer demand for durable goods such as cars, appliances, television sets, and the like can fluctuate considerably, depending on economic conditions. A decline in consumer demand for such durables can have an important impact on overall economic conditions, since such durables are an important segment of total industrial output and affect many ancillary industries, such as steel, plastics, rubber, aluminum, copper, nickel, forest products, and the like. Similarly, an upsurge in consumer demand can have a dramatic effect on employment and investment, as industries expand to meet the growth in consumer purchases. One of the most direct ways to stimulate economic activity during periods of economic sluggishness is to cut personal income taxes, and thus boost the purchasing power of consumers. The increased consumer spending should result in more jobs and investment, which also increases government tax revenues and reduces government spending on social assistance and unemployment insurance. Similarly, in periods of excess demand and rising inflation, a tax increase can cool off consumer spending and thus slow down the economy.

consumer good A good that is produced to satisfy the need of a person, as opposed to a CAPITAL GOOD, which is used to further the production and distribution of other goods or services. A washing machine purchased by an individual is a consumer good; if purchased by a hotel, it is a capital good. Consumer goods consist of durables, such as automobiles, appliances, or furniture, which have a fairly long life; semi-durables, such as clothing, which have a relatively short life; and non-durables, such as food and soap, which are consumed almost as soon as they are purchased.

consumer law Law that is designed to protect consumers against dangerous products, or deceptive or fraudulent business practices. Federal laws, for example, protect consumers against misleading advertising, false packaging and labelling, dangerous foods and drugs, hazardous products, and various forms of price manipulation. Provincial laws provide protection against unfair contracts, regulate door-to-door salesmen, and permit municipalities to inspect restaurants and other facilities for health infractions, to control taxicab rates, to license many forms of commercial activity, and to implement other measures to protect consumers.

consumer price index (CPI) A monthly measure of changes in the retail prices of goods and services purchased by Canadians living in all parts of the country in communities with a population of thirty thousand people or more. The index is based on the shopping basket of three hundred goods and services that, in 1967, families of from two to six people, with annual incomes of four to twelve thousand dollars, would normally buy. It is a weighted index, which attributes greater importance to price changes for food and housing, for example, than to price changes for bus tickets and movie-theatre admissions. The CPI is published monthly for Canada and for fourteen major cities, using 1971 as the base year (1971=100). Price changes can be broken down into sub-groups—as, for example, they affect goods and services, food and non-food prices, or any of the individual sectors measured. A seasonally adjusted monthly consumer price index is also produced, showing inflation trends. Generally, it is the CPI that is used in COLA CLAUSES and in INDEXATION of the income-tax system, or of social benefits such as the old-age pension.

consumer sovereignty The free-market assumption that it is the consumer who, through his power to choose how to spend his money, determines what shall be produced and in what quantity. The price a consumer is willing to pay and the changes in his tastes are said to make the consumer king. If a price is too high, he will signal the economic system that he's unwilling to pay—either prices will decline or production will decline. Similarly, if he no longer derives any satisfaction from a particular product, he will stop buying it and the producer may go out of business. While consumers undoubtedly can exercise enormous power in the economic system, economists also note that there are other forces shaping economic output, such as the exercise of monopoly power, the use of advertising to shape consumer wants and tastes, and the absence of full product and price information. See also POST-KEYNESIAN ECONOMICS.

consumer surplus The difference between the total satisfaction a consumer obtains from a good or service (and hence, the maximum price he would be willing to pay) and the actual price the consumer has to pay. ALFRED MARSHALL developed the concept; it assumes that consumers generally would be willing to pay more for many goods and services than they actually pay, the difference being the consumer surplus. Hence, the total utility of a good or service for a consumer is the price he pays plus the consumer surplus.

Consumers' Association of Canada (CAC) A voluntary organization formed in 1947 as the Canadian Association of Consumers by women who had served in the women's section of the WARTIME PRICES AND TRADE BOARD; its name was changed in 1961 to the Consumers' Association of Canada. The national association and its provincial counterparts are financed largely by government and act as a voice for consumers, making representations to government, industry, producers, and retailers. CAC campaigns for improvements in consumer-protection laws. Its headquarters are in Ottawa.

consumption Spending by consumers, individually or in the aggregate, on goods and services. Consumption consists of private spending on goods and services such as food, houses, furniture, and clothing, and public spending on such services as health, education, and welfare. Spending on investment goods and services, such as factories, machinery, engineering, and geological services, is not usually included. Between 80 and 85 per cent of the gross national product is spent on consumption, depending on the stage of the business cycle in any particular year and the bunching of major investment projects. The remaining portion of GNP is spent on capital investment.

continental shelf The offshore area, under water, marking the transition from the continent to the sharp drop to the ocean depths; it is believed to be rich in minerals, and oil and natural-gas reserves. Along the Nova Scotia coast, it varies from 60 to 100 nautical miles from shore, and from Newfoundland it varies from 100 to 280 nautical miles, before dropping to between 183 and 366 metres at the outer edge. On the Pacific coast, it extends 50 to 100 nautical miles from shore and drops to 366 metres below the water surface at its outer edge. In the Arctic it ranges through most of the region, with the Arctic Islands perched on top. It extends past Greenland on the east and 50 to 300 miles west from the outermost Arctic islands.

continentalist A political term sometimes used to describe those who advocate the closer integration of the Canadian and U.S. economies through free trade, energy-sharing, or other such policies.

contingency fund Money set aside in a corporation or other organization to meet an unforeseen expenditure.

contract An agreement between two or more parties to do something or not to do something, usually in exchange for money or some other consideration, which is enforceable under law. If one of the parties fails to live up to his obligations under a contract, he can be sued by the other party or parties. Usually a contract is in writing, but it does not have to be. For example, a sale of a good in which money changes hands, and hence a transaction takes place, is a contract in which the seller is assumed to have supplied a good or service that is what it was represented to be and can perform the service the seller claimed it would perform. A contract made under duress or undue influence, or made as a result of misrepresentation, can be overturned by the courts.

contract law The body of law that defines contracts and sets out the conditions under which contracts must be made if they are to be legally binding. For example, a contract must be entered into freely, must be made by parties legally competent to enter into contracts, and must not be made as a result of misrepresentation or force. Contracts must also represent an exchange between the parties.

contract proposals Proposals made by an employer or a union for a new collective agreement during collective bargaining. Such proposals are the subject of negotiation between representatives of the employer and the union.

contraction A stage in the BUSINESS CYCLE; it is the decline in economic activity that occurs after the peak in the cycle has been reached and before the trough of the recession has been reached.

contractual link See FRAMEWORK AGREEMENT FOR COMMERICAL AND ECONOMIC CO-OPERATION BETWEEN CANADA AND THE EUROPEAN COMMUNITIES.

contributed surplus That part of the SHAREHOLDERS' EQUITY in a firm that results from the firm being able to sell new shares for more than PAR VALUE or, if NO PAR VALUE, their stated price at the time they were offered to the public. The difference between the par value or stated price and the price obtained is the contributed surplus. Thus, if a company issues 100,000 new shares at $10 a share and is able to sell them at $12 a share, the extra $2 a share or $200,000 in total is listed as contributed surplus on the company's books.

contributory pension plan A pension plan whose costs are shared, usually equally, by the employees and the employer, with weekly premium deductions being made from the paycheques of employees. Under Canadian pension laws, an employee loses the share paid on his behalf by his employer if he changes jobs, unless he has paid into the plan for a long period of time, usually at least ten years, and has reached a certain age, usually forty-five.

controlled economy An economy in which government planning and ownership rather than private-sector decisions determine what is produced, what types of investments are made, and what proportion of national income will be invested rather than allocated to consumption. Examples include the Soviet Union, China, and most of the nations of Eastern Europe in the Soviet bloc.

controller An executive within a corporation or other organization who is responsible for designing the system of financial controls and financial reporting, and for seeing that these systems are carried out properly. The controller is usually an accountant. His functions should not be confused with those of the treasurer or the vice-president of finance of an organization, who are responsible for financial planning, budgeting, management of the organization's cash, arranging bank and other credit, and generally determining profit and other targets.

controlling interest The block of shares in a company that is sufficient to allow the holder to control the management and choose the directors. In a widely held company, a shareholder may need only, say, 10 per cent of the shares to have a dominant voice in the company; but usually, 51 per cent of the voting shares are needed to ensure control.

conventional areas Those parts of Canada that have a long history of oil or natural-gas production; essentially, Alberta, Saskatchewan, and British Columbia.

conventional mortgage A mortgage on a home that has been obtained from a financial institution or other investor without being insured under the National Housing Act or other government program.

conventional recovery The production of crude oil from oil reservoirs through traditional recovery techniques, including waterflooding and infill drilling.

conventional reserves Oil or natural-gas reserves that can be exploited with normal recovery technologies.

conversion loan of 1958 A major refinancing of government bonds in 1958. Holders of wartime Victory Loan Bonds of $6.4 billion that were to mature between 1959 and 1966 were offered a conversion-loan issue maturing in 1961 at 3 per cent, in 1965 at 3.75 per cent, in 1971 at 4.5 per cent; and in 1983 at 4.5 per cent. Victory Loan Bonds totalling $5.8 billion, or about 90 per cent of the outstanding bonds, were turned in for the new bonds. At the time, it was a major government financing exercise, since it equalled roughly half of the federal government's marketable debt. It had unforeseen results, however, since it decreased the liquidity of the Canadian financial markets and forced many borrowers, such as the provinces and corporations, to turn to the U.S. market. This, in turn, put upward pressure on the Canadian dollar and hurt Canadian efforts to recover from a recession.

convertibility The ability to convert one currency into another. The Canadian dollar is freely convertible into other major currencies. But some countries maintain foreign-exchange controls and restrict the convertibility of their currency to essential purposes, such as the financing of necessary imports. During the Second World War, Canada imposed strict controls on the convertibility of the Canadian dollar.

convertible bond A corporate BOND that can be exchanged for a stated number of common shares in the same corporation at the option of the purchaser of the bond. Convertible bonds are a device to attract bond buyers during periods of rising inflation rates. Would-be buyers who fear that future inflation will reduce the value of their bonds may be reassured by knowing that they can exchange them for common shares. The convertibility feature may also allow corporations to raise money at somewhat lower interest rates.

convertible preferred share A PREFERRED SHARE that can be exchanged for a stated number of common shares in the same corporation at the option of the purchaser. The option of convertibility is used as a device to increase the marketability of the preferred shares.

conveyance The transfer of the title of ownership from the seller of land or buildings to the purchaser, and the registration of this transfer in a registry office.

cooling-off period 1. In collective bargaining, the period of time after CONCILIATION before a strike or lockout can legally take place —usually one to two weeks. **2.** In consumer-protection law, the period of time a consumer has to change his or her mind after signing a contract with a door-to-door or similar salesman—in Ontario, it is two days.

co-operative A business organized for the mutual benefit of all its members. They own the enterprise, use its services, run it, and share in its profits or surplus at the end of the financial year. Co-operatives are common in many parts of Canada and include credit unions, caisses populaires, housing projects, farm marketing organizations, farm-supply organizations, and stores selling such consumer goods as food supplies. The greatest use of co-operatives is made in Quebec and Saskatchewan.

Co-ordinating Committee (COCOM) A committee of representatives of NORTH ATLANTIC TREATY ORGANIZATION (NATO) countries, including Canada, which compiles lists of strategic goods NATO members want to deny communist states and therefore will not sell to them. It surveys both military technology and civilian products, such as computers and telecommunications equipment, that may have military applications.

copyright Legal protection for writers, sculptors, architects, painters, movie producers, phonograph-record artists and companies, dance choreographers, and others, against the production, performance, publication, or conversion of their work into another form (for example, a book into a movie) without their express permission. The government, through the Copyright Act of 1921, confers on creative people the exclusive right to ownership of their works. Creative people are thus able to derive income from their intellectual property by selling rights of reproduction for royalty or other income. In Canada, the author of a book is assured copyright protection for his lifetime and for another fifty years after his death. In other cases, such as photographs or phonograph records, the protection is for a straight fifty years. It is not necessary to register ownership of copyright in Canada. Canadian copyrights are protected in other countries through international reciprocal arrangements.

Copyright and Industrial Design Office See BUREAU OF INTELLECTUAL PROPERTY.

core A sample of mineral rock obtained for ASSAY purposes, and generally to help determine the location of valuable minerals. A core is obtained by drilling and is usually about one inch in diameter.

corner the market The purchase by a single buyer, or a small group of buyers acting together, of a large part of the available supply of a particular commodity or shares in a particular company. The buyers are thus in a position to control the price and resell at a much higher price than they paid.

corporate bond A bond that has been issued by a corporation.

corporate income tax Tax levied on the income of a corporation after business expenses and other permitted deductions. Canadian corporations must pay tax on income earned anywhere in the world, while Canadian subsidiaries of foreign corporations must also pay tax on their Canadian income. Corporations are permitted to deduct all of their operating expenses, local property taxes, interest payments, and bad debts, along with DEPRECIATION and DEPLETION ALLOWANCES. Oil, gas, and mining companies are allowed to deduct exploration spending as it is made, and mining companies are permitted to write off capital equipment for new mines in the year the spending is done; but provincial oil and gas or mineral royalties, and provincial mining taxes, cannot be deducted as expenses in calculating federal taxable income.

Both the federal and provincial governments are allowed, under the British North America Act, to levy corporate income taxes. The basic federal rate is 46 per cent, with a 40 per cent rate on manufacturing and processing profits and a 25 per cent rate on Canadian-owned small business (20 per cent on manufacturing and processing profits), from profits of up to $150,000 a year, to a maximum claim of $750,000 after 1971. The provincial rates vary, but are about 12 per cent. Federal corporate income taxes were introduced in Canada in 1917 to help finance the costs of the First World War and to reduce the high profits of wartime industries; they had been levied by the provinces since the turn of the century, although the rates were quite low.

corporate state A form of political and economic system in which decision-making is in the hands of the major power groups, usually business, labour, and governments. In such a system, the role of democratically elected government is reduced, and power, perhaps even statutory power, is allocated to non-elected groups such as business and union leaders. While there is a need for co-operation among such groups—in the evolution of consensus policies, for example, to get agreement on fair-pay, profit, and price standards, or on economic priorities—there is the danger that such TRIPARTISM could lead to a diminution of the role of the ordinary citizen, who does not have a say through membership in a power group. The principle of government accountability to the voters may also be reduced.

corporate strategy The long-range plans of a corporation, say for five years but possibly longer, for new products, new markets, acquisitions, or takeovers, in order to diversify into new lines of business. Major corporations usually plan research and development projects, investment plans for new facilities, diversification, acquisitions (to increase their market share, or to extend the business backward into raw materials or forward into further processing or distribution), and profit targets several years in advance. Once overall corporate strategy has been devised, individual sectors of the business, such as corporate finance, engineering, marketing, or research, can then develop their own strategies to help reach corporate goals.

corporation A legal entity, under federal or provincial company law, with an existence or life of its own, quite separate from those who created it. It has the rights and obligations, under law, of a person, but differs from a person in that its life is infinite, unless it goes bankrupt or its owners decide to wind it up. The assets of a corporation belong to the corporation and not to the owners; the owners are entitled to a share of the assets if the corporation is wound up and to a share of the profits, in the form of dividends that are not reinvested in the corporation. If a corporation goes bankrupt, the owners are not liable for its debts; their loss is restricted to the investments they have made in the corporation. See also LIMITED LIABILITY, INCORPORATION, PRIVATE COMPANY, PUBLIC COMPANY. Some corporations have been created by an act of Parliament, such as Bell Canada and the chartered banks.

corporation law The body of federal and provincial law that governs the incorporation of companies, sets out the rules under which they will operate, controls takeovers and deals with restrictive trade practices, regulates the financial structure of corporations, and deals with the rights of shareholders and responsibilities of company directors and officers.

Corporations and Labour Unions Returns Act (CALURA) Legislation passed by Parliament in 1962, and effective 1 January 1963, to help document and assess the extent and relative importance of foreign-controlled corporations in the Canadian economy, and to provide information on the internal administrative practices and financial operations of unions whose headquarters are in the United States. The information on foreign-controlled corporations includes spending on research and development, charitable donations, tax payments to federal and provincial governments, as well as broader statistics on balance-sheet details and income and expense statements. Details are provided on Canadian-controlled corporations as well, so that the relative significance of foreign-controlled firms can be determined. Separate annual reports are published by Statistics Canada on corporations and unions.

correspondent bank A bank in another country that handles the affairs there on behalf of a Canadian bank. Canadian banks also act as correspondent banks for many foreign banks in Canada.

cost The total expense in producing a good or service. Economists talk of many different types of costs. For example: **1.** Total cost is the sum of all the expenses for all the factors of production used in producing a given level of goods or services. **2.** A fixed cost is the basic expense or overhead of an enterprise, and exists regardless of the level of production—the mortgage payments or rental costs for productive facilities, for example, or maintenance expenditures and management salaries. **3.** A variable cost is the expense for the parts and components, raw materials, energy, and production-worker wages in producing goods and services. **4.** A marginal cost is the cost of producing one extra unit of output. **5.** The average cost is the total cost of the enterprise's output divided by the number of units of output. See also OPPORTUNITY COST.

cost accounting A specialized system of accounting to help businesses identify and allocate the true costs of producing a given unit of output. Among other things, the enterprise is broken down into cost centres or departments where individual stages of production take place; a portion of the overhead or FIXED COSTS is allocated to each of the cost centres, depending on floor space, number of workers, energy use, or some other factor or set of factors. Cost accounting is an important technique, since it allows a business to analyze precisely its true costs and allocate them among different operations in the business. The company can then implement more effective cost controls, or consider alternative ways of undertaking a particular part of the production process.

cost-benefit analysis The technique used to determine the overall costs and benefits to the community of undertaking a particular project, such as a new highway, hospital, subway system, or airport. Business investment decisions are usually made on the basis of expected rate of return on capital, or DISCOUNTED CASH FLOW. But, in the absence of such a measurement for many public projects, with the requirement that net public welfare be a consideration in public projects, and with growing concern over external costs such as congestion and pollution, cost-benefit analysis is now widely used in public-project analysis and in government review of industrial projects such as pipelines and refineries.

Applying cost-benefit analysis, planners looking at a proposed new expressway would include among the benefits the reduced travelling time of motorists and the advantages this brings to individuals and businesses, the value of the construction work in the local economy, and the possibility that the new expressway would lead to the creation of new businesses along the route, hence, to new jobs and tax revenues. Among the costs would be included the permanent loss of the land for alternative purposes, the cost of the land, the cost of access roads, the possibility that the new expressway will bring extra traffic into the community and thus cause traffic congestion, and the possibility that the new expressway will lead to a reduction in use of transit systems. The technique is still in its early stages of development, since economists and accountants have yet to find ways to calculate many of these costs and attach meaningful weights to them.

cost centre A distinct department or production point in an enterprise, whose costs can be separately identified and to which a measurable part of the firm's overhead or FIXED COSTS can be allocated. It is an important part of COST ACCOUNTING, designed to help businesses allocate their total costs to the different stages of production and distribution.

cost of capital The average cost to a company of all of its forms of capital, such as the interest it must pay on its debt and the dividends it pays its common and preferred shareholders. The cost, expressed as a percentage, is weighted to reflect the relative shares of the different forms of debt. The cost of capital is one tool used by a company in making an investment decision; it is usually the minimum rate of return that a company will seek on a new investment.

cost-of-living allowance clause See COLA CLAUSE.

cost-of-service principle of taxation See USER-PAY PRINCIPLE OF TAXATION.

cost-plus contract A contract that allows the contractor to charge for his costs of completing the contract, and to add a percentage of the cost or a fixed fee as his profit; as opposed to a contract that sets a fixed amount of money the contractor may charge to supply goods and services or to complete a certain type of work, such as construction of a building. A cost-plus contract is sometimes used when it is difficult to calculate the total cost of a project. Its disadvantage is that it provides no incentive to the contractor to control his costs.

cost-push inflation Inflation said to be caused by excessive wage and price increases, reflecting the market power of particular unions and corporations, rather than by excess demand or spending in the economy. In such a situation, wage increases rise faster than productivity, thus raising business operating costs. Businesses grant such wage increases because they believe that they can pass them along to consumers though higher prices, without suffering a loss of sales or a drop in profits. Such cost-push inflation may also be caused by a sharp increase in commodity prices.

While business leaders put much of the blame on unions for rising costs, union leaders contend that they are merely responding to earlier price increases and argue that price increases are not related to wage increases. Whatever the cause, it would seem to be the case that, when the total of wage increases in the economy is higher than productivity gains in the economy, either profits will fall significantly, or the excess of additional wages over national output will have to represent inflation. During cost-push inflation, wages and prices may be moving up at a fast rate, even if there is considerable unemployment and slow economic growth. A growing number of economists argue that some form of INCOMES POLICY is necessary to deal with cost-push inflation. See also STAGFLATION, DEMAND-PULL INFLATION, WAGE-PRICE SPIRAL.

Council for Mutual Economic Assistance (COMECON) A council created in 1949 by the Soviet Union in response to the Marshall Plan in Western Europe. Its members include, in addition to the Soviet Union, Czechoslovakia, East Germany, Poland, Hungary, Romania, Bulgaria, Outer Mongolia, Cuba, and Vietnam. Albania has been a member, but withdrew in 1961. At its thirty-third annual conference, in June 1979, North Yemen, Afghanistan, Angola, Ethiopia, Finland, Iraq, Laos, Mexico, Mozambique, and Yugoslavia attended as official observers.

The council was originally established as a means of integrating the economies of Eastern Europe and Outer Mongolia with that of the Soviet Union. In its early days, the COMECON countries attempted to develop a self-sufficient economy and discouraged trade with the West. The Soviet Union, through COMECON, also attempted to make other members specialize in particular economic sectors, and thus integrate their economies into that of the Soviet Union; but most COMECON countries refused to cooperate. In recent years, the council has encouraged, up to a point, economic ties with the West.

Council of Maritime Premiers A cooperative arrangement among the three Maritime provinces of Nova Scotia, New Brunswick, and Prince Edward Island, signed in 1971 following the MARITIME UNION STUDY published the previous year. The three provinces agreed to meet quarterly to discuss common problems and to co-ordinate activities, to establish a secretariat to serve the council, to create a Maritime Provinces Commission for long-term planning, to examine the feasibility of a joint legislature, and to discuss ways to make legislation uniform throughout the region. The three provinces hoped to initiate studies on common economic, social, and cultural policies, to co-ordinate activities that affected all three provinces, and to make joint submissions to the federal government. The commission was not activated, and consideration of a joint legislature was quietly dropped.

counter-cyclical policies Government policies to offset the trend of the business cycle; for example, the use of monetary, fiscal, and other policies to create jobs during the contraction of the economy or in a recession, or the use of these same policies to curtail economic growth and check inflation pressures as the economy moves towards its peak in the business cycle.

countervailing duty A duty imposed to offset the effect of an export subsidy in the country of origin, or to offset the effect of dumping. The United States has imposed or threatened to impose countervailing duties on goods shipped by Canadian firms that have received regional-development grants or research and development assistance.

countervailing power Checks and balances in the economy to prevent powerful groups from freely exercising their power. Examples include the ability of strong unions to challenge large corporations, the bargaining power of big retail chains in negotiating prices with large manufacturers, and the use of government regulation and competition laws to check oligopolistic practices by labour, business, and the professions. The existence of such countervailing power is a characteristic feature of the MIXED ECONOMY. See also JOHN KENNETH GALBRAITH.

coupon rate The annual interest paid on the face value of a BOND.

craft union A union whose membership is restricted to workers with a particular skill. Examples include unions representing different types of construction workers, such as plumbers, electricians, bricklayers, carpenters, and labourers, or such workers as truck drivers. But as skills have changed, and even disappeared in the economy, craft unions have broadened their membership to include other types of workers. See also INDUSTRIAL UNION.

Crane's law There's no such thing as a free lunch.

crawling peg A modification of the fixed-exchange-rate system, which would allow a wider fluctuation up and down from the par value than the 1 per cent either way permitted in the fixed-exchange-rate system of the INTERNATIONAL MONETARY FUND. It would allow more movement in a country's exchange rate, before monetary authorities had to intervene to maintain its value, than the PAR-VALUE system did up until 1971, but less flexibility than the FLOATING-EXCHANGE-RATE system. The crawling peg was advocated by some economists, but not adopted, following the breakdown of the fixed-exchange-rate system in 1971. The floating-exchange-rate system was adopted instead.

credit **1.** Obtaining the use of goods or services now with a promise to pay for them later. Consumer credit permits a consumer, for example, to acquire goods immediately and to pay for them over several months or years; it also provides loans to consumers so that they can buy goods or services now. Similarly, trade credit allows retailers, wholesalers, and manufacturers to obtain goods and services without paying for them immediately. **2.** Loans by banks, trust companies, credit unions, caisses populaires, and other lenders, to enable individuals, corporations, and governments to buy goods and services now, on the promise of future repayment plus interest. **3.** In double-entry bookkeeping, an entry signifying an increase in liabilities or income or a decrease in assets or expenses. See also DEBIT.

credit bureau A company that keeps records of the credit history and personal habits of individuals, and supplies information for a fee to financial institutions that are considering making loans, giving a credit card, or granting a line of credit for an instalment-purchase account in a department store, to an individual. In recent years there has been growing concern over the accuracy of information in credit-bureau files and the injustice that can arise if a person is denied a loan because his credit-bureau file contains false information. This has been offset, to some extent, by laws permitting individuals to see their files in credit bureaus and to challenge their accuracy.

credit card A card issued by a department store, bank, credit-card company, airline, car-rental agency, gasoline company, or other business, which entitles the holder to credit. Billings are normally monthly, and interest is usually only charged on the balance outstanding at the end of thirty days. Credit-card companies and banks issuing credit cards usually charge stores, restaurants, airlines, and others a percentage of the bill as a handling charge. The profits from such credit cards come from such handling charges and from the interest earned on outstanding balances of card users.

credit control Policies of the Bank of Canada or the government to expand or reduce the availability of credit or to restrict credit to certain uses. Aside from the normal techniques used in setting MONETARY POLICY to determine the overall supply of credit, a government can be selective, and require high downpayments for consumer purchases on credit, require stock exchanges to increase the MARGIN requirements on the purchase of shares, or require higher downpayments on the purchase of houses if, for example, it wants to slow economic growth.

credit line Approval by a bank or other financial institution for a loan to a customer up to a specified amount, to be made if and when the customer needs the money.

credit rating An evaluation by a bank, other financial institution, or a CREDIT BUREAU, of the credit worthiness of an individual or firm.

It is usually based on a number of factors, such as NET WORTH, past credit record, and future earning ability and hence, ability to repay.

credit union A co-operative credit organization, which operates for the benefit of all its members by accepting savings deposits and making loans, including mortgage loans, and providing other services. Most credit unions are one-branch organizations associated with a place of employment; however, in Quebec, where they are known as CAISSES POPULAIRES, there are multi-branch systems. Credit unions date back to 1900 in Canada. They are subject to provincial regulation, Nova Scotia having introduced the first regulatory laws in 1932.

creditor A person, bank, supplier, or other business, to whom money is owed. For example, accounts payable listed under current liabilities on a firm's balance sheet are the claims of creditors against the firm. Other creditors would include the holders of long-term debt notes, such as banks or the owners of the firm's outstanding bonds, mortgages, and other such instruments.

creditor nation A nation that has a balance-of-payments surplus in its trade and other economic transactions with other countries, which is hence in a position to lend money or to make investments in other countries with its balance-of-payments surplus. According to some economists, a country should evolve, as its economy develops, from a DEBTOR NATION with infant industries to a mature creditor nation. Some economists worry that that has not happened in Canada's case, and that this country has moved from being a young debtor nation to the status of a mature debtor nation.

critical-path method (CPM) A technique to find the shortest and lowest-cost way to complete a major project, such as the construction of a nuclear-power station, a tar-sands or heavy-oil plant, a mining smelter, pipeline, or subway system. Using this technique, each sequence of activities that must be carried out consecutively is set down as a "path." In any project, there are many such paths. The "critical path" is the one that will take the longest to complete, and therefore determines the length of time it will take to complete the project. The other paths are scheduled around the critical path so that no time is lost in completing the project. At the same time, every effort is made to reduce the time needed to complete the critical path. The great benefit of this technique is that it identifies the various paths of the project and enables the most efficient scheduling of work to take place.

crop insurance A form of insurance to protect farmers against heavy financial losses due to the loss of crops caused by bad weather, floods, and other such threats. In 1959, Parliament passed the Crop Insurance Act, to permit the federal government, with the provinces, to make crop insurance available to farmers across the country. The initiative for such a program has to come from each provincial government; farmers pay half of the premiums, and the federal and provincial governments share the remaining costs.

crop year In the grain industry, the year that starts at 1 August with harvesting, and runs to 31 July of the following year. Hence the 1979–80 crop year began 1 August 1979 and ended 31 July 1980.

crop yield A measure of the productivity of the land: the amount of a crop produced per acre of land in production. It is calculated by dividing the total production of a crop for a farm, region, or country by the number of acres planted. In Canada in 1966–70, wheat yields averaged 24.3 bushels per acre; in 1971–75, wheat yields averaged 25.3 bushels per acre.

cross-elasticity of demand A measure of the impact of a price change in one good on the demand for another good. If the price of coffee goes up and leads to an increase in demand for tea, then the two are substitutes. But if the price of tea goes up and this leads to a fall in demand for lemons, then the two are COMPLEMENTARY GOODS. The cross-elasticity of demand is calculated by taking the percentage change in the demand for the second good and dividing it by the percentage change in the price of the first good. If there is a positive result, the goods are substitutes; if negative, they are complements.

Crow's Nest Pass Agreement An agreement between the federal government and the Canadian Pacific Railway Company, made in 1897, in which the railway agreed to maintain in perpetuity a fixed schedule of freight rates in western Canada for wheat and flour, in exchange for large land grants and a subsidy towards the construction of the railway. The railway has charged the maximum permitted since the end of the First World War and has tried repeatedly to end the agreement or to get a subsidy. Western farmers have vigorously resisted any change, arguing that the railway made a deal and should live with it.

crown corporation A federal or provincial, publicly owned enterprise, established to carry out a regulatory, advisory, administrative, financial, or other service for the government, or to provide goods or services, much as would a business corporation. Federal examples include Air Canada, PETRO-CANADA, the EXPORT DEVELOPMENT CORPORATION, ATOMIC ENERGY OF CANADA LIMITED, and the ECONOMIC COUNCIL OF CANADA. Provincial examples include Ontario Hydro, B.C. Hydro, and Hydro Quebec, the POTASH CORPORATION OF SASKATCHEWAN, Alberta Government Telephones, and Nova Scotia's Industrial Estates Limited. A joint federal-provincial crown corporation is the MARITIME ENERGY CORPORATION.

Crown corporations have played a dynamic role in the development of the Canadian economy and in meeting important public needs efficiently where private investors were unwilling or unable to meet Canadian needs at reasonable prices; they are a unique response to the needs of a country with a relatively small and spread-out population. Crown corporations pre-date Confederation. For example, in 1841 a crown corporation was established to build a canal system for the United Provinces of Canada. The oldest existing crown corporation is the National Battlefields Commission, established in 1908. The establishment of Canadian National Railways in 1919 represented a major step in the evolution of the crown corporation towards the operation of a public enterprise. Others that followed included the Canadian Broadcasting Corporation (1932) and the CANADIAN WHEAT BOARD (1935).

The federal government identifies four different types of national crown corporations: **1.** Departmental crown corporations, which exist as agents of the crown and are responsible for an administrative, supervisory, or regulatory activity; examples include the SCIENCE COUNCIL OF CANADA, the ATOMIC ENERGY CONTROL BOARD, the ECONOMIC COUNCIL OF CANADA, and the NATIONAL RESEARCH COUNCIL. **2.** Agency corporations, which are responsible for various trading or service activities of the government, or for the handling of various government procurement, construction, or disposal activities. Examples include ATOMIC ENERGY OF CANADA LIMITED, the CANADIAN COMMERCIAL CORPORATION, the CANADIAN DAIRY COMMISSION, and the ROYAL CANADIAN MINT. **3.** Proprietary corporations, which provide financial services or produce other goods or services for the public, and which operate on their own without annual funding from Parliament. Examples include Air Canada, the EXPORT DEVELOPMENT CORPORATION, ELDORADO NUCLEAR LIMITED, PETRO-CANADA, and TELEGLOBE CANADA. Some of these corporations pay corporate income taxes just as private corporations do. **4.** Unclassified corporations, which are created by special acts of Parliament and which do not fall under the rules and requirements of the FINANCIAL ADMINISTRATION ACT. Examples include the BANK OF CANADA and the CANADIAN WHEAT BOARD.

All crown corporations report to Parliament through a designated cabinet minister. The federal government participates in other businesses as a shareholder, but these businesses—for example, the CANADA DEVELOPMENT CORPORATION AND PANARCTIC OILS LIMITED—are not crown corporations, since they have other shareholders.

crown forest Forest lands owned by the federal government or a provincial government, and which may be harvested by lumber or pulp and paper companies operating under a federal or provincial timber licence or other such arrangement.

crown land All federally and provincially owned lands, including national and provincial parks, crown forests, historic sites, and undeveloped land not owned by a private individual or entity.

crude birth rate The number of live births, per year, for each thousand of population at the middle of that year. The rate of natural increase in population is the difference between the crude birth rate and the CRUDE DEATH RATE, and is usually expressed as a percentage rate of change. While the crude birth rate is useful in making international comparisons of population change, its weakness is that it depends very much on the age composition of the population, as well as on the number of children that women of child-bearing age are actually having. Hence, population experts also look at the FERTILITY RATE and the INFANT-MORTALITY RATE of different countries in analyzing population trends.

crude death rate The number of deaths per year for each thousand of population at the middle of that year. The rate of natural increase in population is the difference between the crude birth rate and the crude death rate, expressed as a percentage rate of change. The crude death rate depends on the age composition of the population, life expectancy, and the INFANT-MORTALITY RATE.

crude oil and equivalent A term used to describe total oil production from conventional oil reservoirs, synthetic-oil production from tar-sands plants, and pentanes plus, a by-product from natural-gas production.

Cultural Property Export and Import Act Federal legislation passed in June 1975, which came into force in September 1977, to control the export of national cultural treasures and to police the illegal importation of foreign cultural treasures. It is administered by the Department of the Secretary of State, through the Canadian Cultural Property Export Review Board.

cum dividend With dividend. The purchaser of a share *cum* dividend will receive the next dividend payable, because the transaction takes place before the date of record when the next dividend is declared. Shareholders on the company's books on the date of record are the ones who will receive the dividend. The price of a share sold just before the next dividend takes into account the fact that the new owner will get the dividend. See also EX DIVIDEND.

cumulative preferred share A PREFERRED SHARE whose owners are entitled to an annual dividend; if the dividend is not paid in a particular year, the unpaid dividend becomes a liability of the corporation and must be paid before any more dividends are paid to the owners of common shares.

currency The various notes and coins used in a country as a medium of exchange. In Canada, this consists of paper money issued by the Bank of Canada and coins produced by the Royal Canadian Mint. The Bank of Canada took over the responsibility for producing paper money when it was created in 1934. Until then, paper money was produced by the chartered banks; their role was phased out between 1935 and 1945. In 1950, the remaining chartered-bank notes became a liability of the Bank of Canada.

current account See BALANCE OF PAYMENTS.

current asset An asset that, during the course of the year, will either be used in the production of goods or services, or be converted into cash. Examples include cash and short-term securities, accounts receivable, inventories, and work in progress. These are the liquid assets of a firm and, after CURRENT LIABILITIES are deducted, represent its WORKING CAPITAL and hence its capacity to finance its ongoing operations. Current assets are listed in a firm's BALANCE SHEET.

current liability A liability of a firm that must be paid within the next twelve months. The most common examples are accounts payable to suppliers, the current year's interest on long-term debt, taxes, and dividends payable within the year. Current liabilities are listed on a firm's BALANCE SHEET. See also CURRENT ASSET.

current ratio The ratio of a firm's CURRENT ASSETS to its CURRENT LIABILITIES. It is one measure of a firm's liquidity, and hence its ability to meet current costs out of current income. It is calculated by dividing current assets by current liabilities. See also ACID-TEST RATIO, QUICK RATIO.

current return The annual return or yield on an investment as calculated at any point in time. In the case of a company share, it is the current annual dividend divided by the current market price. In the case of a corporate or government bond, it is the annual interest paid on the bond divided by its current market price.

curriculum vitae An outline of a person's age, education, work experience, awards, and other interests and hobbies. Such a résumé is frequently sought by employers screening applicants for jobs.

customs broker A broker or agent who does the paperwork and manages other steps in clearing imports through the Department of NATIONAL REVENUE on behalf of an importer.

customs union A free-trade agreement among two or more nations who also impose a common external tariff on imports from nations outside the customs union. The EUROPEAN ECONOMIC COMMUNITY, when it was created in 1957, was a customs union. Since then it has evolved into a COMMON MARKET, in which the free movement of workers, capital, and business operations are also permitted. A customs union differs from a FREE-TRADE AREA in that it has a common external tariff, whereas individual nations in a free-trade area each apply their own tariff schedule on imports from nations that do not belong to the free-trade area.

cutthroat competition Price-slashing by competitive firms to gain a larger share of market or to drive a competitor out of business. Since such price-slashing usually means operating at a loss, there must be an opportunity at some point in the future for a successful firm to recoup those losses by establishing a strong enough market position to raise prices to a higher level than existed before. Otherwise, in cases of excess supply, cutthroat competition may lead to losses for all the firms; if that were to appear the likely outcome, it would make more sense for competitors to reach an understanding on price restraint.

cybernetics The study of control and communications, developed in the mid 1940s, that attempted to duplicate the feedback functions of the human nervous system in computer-communications systems. The term originated with Norbert Wiener, a prominent mathematician at the Massachusetts Institute of Technology, and Dr. Arturo Rosenbleuth of the Harvard Medical School. Since then, there has been extensive study of the possibilities of developing computer systems that are "more human"—that is, computers that can "think" for themselves and do creative things on their own.

cyclical fluctuations Changes in the pace of economic activity, reflecting changes in the phase of the business cycle or changes in economic activity resulting from seasonal factors. Examples would be increased retail sales at Christmas on reduced construction activity in winter.

cyclical industry An industry whose sales and profits fluctuate with changes in the business cycle. A cyclical industry is thus unlike a stable industry, whose performance is largely unaffected by changes in the business cycle because its products or services are needed at roughly the same level, regardless of the state of the economy. Nor should a cyclical industry be confused with a seasonal industry, whose goods or services have a peak level of demand in a particular season or seasons each year; a seasonal industry may also be a stable industry. Examples of cyclical industries include the machinery, steel, and nickel industries; the demand for their products is directly related to the level of economic activity.

cyclical unemployment Changes in the unemployment rate resulting from changes in the pace of economic activity; increases in unemployment resulting from a downturn in the business cycle. COUNTER-CYCLICAL POLICIES, such as increased government spending, can be used to reduce such unemployment.

D

damages Money that must be paid to indemnify someone for a loss or an added cost resulting from some action or failure to act by the person required to make this payment.

data bank A large and organized body of information, stored in a computer, that can be readily obtained through a COMPUTER TERMINAL. Examples include economic statistics maintained by Statistics Canada in its CANSIM series, information on the financial performance of companies listed on stock exchanges maintained by *The Financial Post,* credit-rating records, future airline reservations, bank-account records, department store and bank credit-card records, and corporate financial records. As it becomes easier, with advancing technology, for individuals to have access to computers, many new types of data-bank library, news, and other services are expected to become available.

data communications The high-speed transmission of information, often over long distances, among computer systems or among a computer system and connected terminals that can enter information into the central computer and receive information from it. The data may be carried over telephone lines, by microwave systems, or by communications satellites. An airline-reservations system is a typical example of a data-communications system. The airline will have a central computer system along with connected computer terminals all over the country, the continent, or even the world. The central computer contains all the flight, reservations, and other information, while the terminals are used to obtain information on flights available, to make reservations, to supply such information as whether the ticket has been purchased or whether passenger assistance will be needed, and to cancel reservations.

days of grace Extra time that is normally allowed beyond the stated payment date, during which payment can usually still be made without penalty. The time is usually three days.

dead time Time when an employee is being paid but is not working because machinery is not functioning or needed parts or materials are not available. See also DOWN TIME.

deadheading The movement of empty freight cars or other railway rolling stock, trucks, aircraft, and buses. This may occur in the movement of grain and mineral ores, for example, where large shipments are made from grain elevators or mines to customer-delivery points such as ports or steel plants, but where there are no major shipments of products to be carried back to the grain-producing areas or mining communities.

death rate See CRUDE DEATH RATE.

debasement The reduction of the metallic value of a coin below its face value.

debenture A corporate or government bond or promissory note that is not secured by a mortgage or a claim on any specific asset of the borrower, but is based simply on the general credit-worthiness of the borrower. Because of this, holders of debentures have a lesser claim on a corporation's assets should it fail than holders of secured debt such as first-mortgage bonds. Sometimes debentures are CONVERTIBLE into common shares or carry WARRANTS permitting the owner to pay for common shares at some specified price that is expected to be below the future market price; the purpose is to increase the attractiveness of the issue to would-be investors. Sinking-fund debentures require the borrower to pay a fixed amount towards redemption to a trustee each year. A subordinated debenture is one that is designated as junior to the other securities or debts issued by the borrower.

debit An entry on the left side of the books of

account in double-entry bookkeeping. A debit is a payment to someone else, and represents a reduction in liabilities or income or an increase in expenses or assets. On the other side of the ledger, the debit is represented as an increase in assets, indicating the receipt of goods in return for the payment. A debit balance exists if total debits are greater than total credits.

debt Money or property that is owed to another person or corporate lender, and that must be repaid, normally with interest. It can take many forms, including bank loans, BONDS, DEBENTURES, and PROMISSORY NOTES.

debt capacity The ability of a borrower to take on a new debt. The upper limit is determined by the total volume of interest that the borrower can reasonably bear. As a firm's debt increases, the burden of debt costs may become too great, forcing the firm to pay even higher interest rates on new debt, to resort to EQUITY financing for new capital, or to curtail expansion plans and cut back on its existing operations.

debt capital Investment capital that consists of long-term bonds and, to some extent, preferred shares, which hence does not represent ownership. Many critics of Canada's high level of foreign ownership of industry argue that the country should have relied much more on debt capital than on EQUITY CAPITAL, which consists of common shares and, hence, ownership of industrial assets. Others argue that reliance on debt capital would have been more costly, since owners of debt capital must be paid interest each year, regardless of the performance of the business, whereas owners of the equity capital of a business may collect no dividends until many years after the business has been established.

debt-equity ratio A ratio used by financial analysts and lending institutions to determine whether a company's outstanding long-term debt can be further increased, or whether the company should raise additional capital through a new issue of common or preferred shares or an increase in retained earnings. There are two ways of determining the debt-equity ratio. One is by dividing the outstanding long-term debt by the market value of all outstanding preferred and common shares; the other is to divide all outstanding long-term debt by the book value of SHAREHOLDERS' EQUITY, as listed in the company's annual report. In either case, as a general rule, the total outstanding long-term debt should not be greater than the market value of outstanding common and preferred shares, or the book value of the shareholders' equity.

debt management The raising of funds by the BANK OF CANADA for the federal government to make sure it has sufficient money to pay its bills and meet its various obligations. This role also entails advising the government on the total level of debt, its composition, its term to maturity, cost, and its influence on overall credit conditions. The bank, acting as the federal government's banker, thus assists the government in carrying out its FISCAL POLICY by helping to finance its budget deficit. The bank, as fiscal agent for the government, issues new bonds on its behalf; depending on the government's needs, the issue could be sold to replace or roll over existing bonds, or to raise new money. The bank also discusses with the government the upper limits it believes are appropriate for the government's cash demands from money markets, and the dangers to the economy of an excessively large budget deficit. The bank may indicate to the government that it is not prepared to accommodate a rising deficit in time of high inflation, thus forcing the government to reduce spending, delay planned programs, increase taxes, or order the bank to meet its demands. A rising government deficit can always be accommodated in the market at rising interest rates; if the government deficit replaces other forms of borrowing, interest rates need not increase.

debt relief Measures to reduce the debt burden of the poorest less-developed countries. The debts of these countries have risen significantly since 1973–74, when the ORGANIZATION OF PETROLEUM EXPORTING COUNTRIES (OPEC) quadrupled the world price of oil. The GROUP OF SEVENTY-SEVEN in the UNITED NATIONS CONFERENCE ON TRADE AND DEVELOPMENT (UNCTAD), representing the less-developed countries, has sought the cancellation of debts owed by the poorest nations, a moratorium on the repayment of debts by those developing countries hit hardest by the increases in the price of oil, consolidation of outstanding debts through an international financial institution, and rescheduling of the repayment of outstanding debts over twenty-five years or longer. Debt relief is a major demand of the NEW INTERNATIONAL ECONOMIC ORDER. The subject was discussed at the CONFERENCE ON INTERNATIONAL ECONOMIC CO-OPERATION in 1975–77, and Canada, a participant, cancelled $232 million in debts owed by a number of the poorest countries in 1977.

debt service The interest and other costs of a debt.

debtor A person, company, government, or other institution, that owes money to someone else. See also CREDITOR.

debtor nation A nation that runs a recurring BALANCE-OF-PAYMENTS deficit. It must attract foreign capital—either DEBT CAPITAL or EQUITY CAPITAL—to meet its international obligations, since it cannot pay its way in the world through the export of goods and services or from its income from foreign investments and other sources.

In the early stages of development, a country is expected to run a chronic balance-of-payments deficit, since it is busy building up its industry and INFRASTRUCTURE, such as railways, power stations, universities, water and sewer systems, and highways. But it is expected to evolve, first into a mature debtor, with interest and dividend payments to foreigners still holding back a current-account surplus, then, as interest payments decline and exports of goods and services expand, into a CREDITOR NATION, exporting debt and equity capital and helping younger nations to build up their economies. Canada has not followed this pattern; it has a mature industrial economy in many respects, and yet still runs a chronic balance-of-payments deficit. One of the roles of the INTERNATIONAL MONETARY FUND is to help debtor nations to manage their external debt.

decentralization **1.** In corporate organization, a system that gives decision-making authority to individual divisions or subsidiaries of the firm, with head office setting only major policies and approving new expenditures above those required for the routine operation of the division or subsidiary. **2.** In production planning, the location of manufacturing plants and other facilities close to markets, instead of concentrating manufacturing in one or a few large, centralized plants. **3.** In a system of federalism, such as Canada's, the granting of considerable autonomy in taxing and spending to the provinces, as opposed to the central or national government. See also CENTRALIZATION.

decertification The loss of the right by a union to represent a group of workers in a BARGAINING UNIT in COLLECTIVE BARGAINING with their employer. This right is lost if the majority of members of the bargaining unit vote to apply to a federal or provincial LABOUR-RELATIONS BOARD to take away the union's right to be their representative.

decreasing costs The decrease in production costs per unit of output as production increases. See also ECONOMIES OF SCALE, MASS PRODUCTION.

decreasing term insurance A form of TERM INSURANCE in which the amount payable to beneficiaries in the event of death declines each year. This form of insurance is often used in conjunction with major debts, such as a mortgage on a house or a loan obtained by a partnership. Thus, payment of the debt is assured if the borrower dies, so that, in the case of the house, the family can pay off the mortgage or, in the case of the partnership, the remaining partner can continue the business without being burdened by repayment of the late partner's share of the debt.

deductible clause A clause in an insurance policy that requires the insured person to pay the first part of the cost of damages covered. For example, automobile-insurance policies require the automobile owner to pay the first, say, one hundred dollars of the repairs. This saves the insurance companies from having to handle thousands of claims where the administrative and handling costs would probably exceed the repair costs.

deed A document transferring ownership of land, buildings, or other property from one party to another.

deemed realization The assumption that an asset has been sold, even though it hasn't been, so that CAPITAL-GAINS TAX or other kinds of tax on capital or wealth can be levied. For example, there is deemed realization of the shares and other assets left in the estate of an individual when he dies, so that a capital-gains tax is collected from the estate, even though the assets themselves may not be sold. Similarly, a Canadian who gives up residence in this country pays a capital-gains tax on his assets; if they are not sold, there is deemed realization.

defalcation The misuse or theft of money by someone holding it in trust for others—a lawyer holding trust funds for his clients, for example.

default The failure by a person, corporation, or government to live up to obligations under a contract. The obligations may include completing work, delivering goods, making payments on a loan, or redeeming bonds or preferred shares by a certain date.

Defence Construction (1951) Limited A federal crown corporation that manages major national defence construction and maintenance programs, including the award of tenders, supervision of construction work, and certification that the work has been completed satisfactorily.

Defence Research Board (DRB) An advisory board, created in 1947, to give the minister of National Defence advice on how science and technology can be used to help national defence. The board has a full-time chairman and vice-chairman, and twelve appointed members. The president of the NATIONAL RESEARCH COUNCIL, the minister of National Defence, and three senior military officers also sit on the board.

deferred annuity An ANNUITY whose payments don't begin until some time in the future—say, on reaching the age of sixty-five—although the premiums have to be paid a number of years in advance. Such annuities are sold by life-insurance and trust companies.

deferred demand Demand for goods and services that can be postponed into the future if there are shortages. While the demand for food cannot be deferred, the demand for cars, appliances, furniture, and other consumer goods and services such as house-painting can be deferred.

deferred income taxes A method of reducing tax liabilities and hence increasing profits in the early life of a company's assets. The Income Tax Act permits a company to use the declining-balance method of calculating DEPRECIATION in its tax return, which results in larger depreciation deductions than those obtained through the straight-line method of calculating depreciation used in the company's annual report to shareholders. This extra depreciation in the early life of the asset is accounted for in the company's EARNINGS STATEMENT as deferred income taxes, and is added on the liability side of the BALANCE SHEET to the reserve for deferred income taxes. In later years, the tax deduction for depreciation of the asset will be less than that claimed in the company's annual report, and the extra payment will have to come from the reserve. But in the meantime, the company has the use of the money, interest free. An individual's tax liability may also be deferred by certain types of investments, by investments in, for example, REGISTERED RETIREMENT SAVINGS PLANS, CONTRIBUTORY PENSION PLANS, and various TAX SHELTERS.

deficiency payment A government subsidy to farmers for the difference between market prices and those guaranteed under an agricultural-support program.

deficit The situation that exists when spending exceeds revenues, or liabilities are greater than assets; the opposite is a SURPLUS. See also BUDGET.

deficit financing The decision of a government to spend more than it raises by taxation and other means, with the BUDGET deficit being financed by government borrowing. Deficit financing is common during periods of high unemployment and slow economic growth, and is a means of raising purchasing power or the overall level of DEMAND in the economy. In fact, since the late 1950s, deficit financing has been a regular feature of federal budgetary policy, although there has been a concern to see that the national debt does not represent a rapidly rising per cent of the gross national product. See also BUDGETARY-ACCOUNTS BUDGET, CASH-NEEDS BUDGET, NATIONAL-ACCOUNTS BUDGET.

deflation 1. The lowering of either the general level of prices in the economy or of the rate of inflation. The cause is usually a protracted slowdown in economic activity. Deflationary policies may be pursued to slow down the rate of inflation by tightening up MONETARY POLICY and FISCAL POLICY. Demand falls, interest rates rise, and credit is harder to obtain. **2.** The adjustment of the GROSS NATIONAL PRODUCT and its various components, expressed in current dollars, by the overall rate of inflation in the economy, to show the change in GNP or its components in real terms. The inflation index used is called the GNP deflator.

deflationary gap The gap between the level of spending, including investment, needed in an economy to maintain full employment, and the actual level of spending and investment taking place. Full employment can only be achieved if the level of investment in the economy consumes all available savings. If private investment is too low, full employment cannot be achieved or maintained unless government steps in and either uses the excess savings itself, through higher taxes or government borrowing, to boost demand, or adopts policies so that others will.

delisted stock A common or preferred share that is no longer traded on a stock exchange. The reasons for delisting include the repeated failure by a company to abide by stock-exchange rules, the bankruptcy of a business, the redemption of the share, usually a preferred share, and the withdrawal of so many shares from distribution that the number still outstanding for trading is far too low.

deliverability The maximum amount of natural gas that can be delivered from a natural-gas reservoir at any particular point in its life without jeopardizing the size or long-term production capability of the reservoir.

Delphi technique A method of technological and social forecasting developed in the early 1960s. A group of experts are asked, individually, to give their opinion on some future event. The responses are then assembled and circulated to the same group of experts, who thus have the chance to revise their own views or respond to other forecasts. These revised forecasts are again assembled and recirculated. The process may be repeated several more times, until some kind of group forecast or consensus is reached.

demand The combined desire, ability, and willingness on the part of consumers to buy a good or service. Aggregate demand or market demand is the total of the demands of all consumers in the economy. Demand is determined by income and by price, which is, in part, determined by SUPPLY. Government can raise the level of aggregate demand by lowering taxes or increasing its own spending, or both. See LAW OF SUPPLY AND DEMAND.

demand and supply curves The representation of the DEMAND SCHEDULE and SUPPLY SCHEDULE for a particular good or service. Their intersection is the meeting point of producers and consumers and, other things being equal, shows the likely price and volume of production, or the EQUILIBRIUM point, for the particular good or service.

demand deposit A bank deposit that can be withdrawn at any time without prior notice to the bank or other deposit-taking institution. Demand deposits include funds in checking–non-savings accounts, and do not earn interest; they are part of the most narrowly defined MONEY SUPPLY (M-1).

demand loan A loan that must be repaid

whenever the lender says; as opposed to an instalment loan, which has to be paid by a predetermined date, usually in monthly or weekly amounts. Because demand loans can be called at any time, they usually carry a lower rate of interest.

demand management The use of government spending, monetary, and taxing policies to control the level of demand in the economy, and hence the rate of economic growth and level of unemployment. See also KEYNESIAN ECONOMICS, FISCAL POLICY, MONETARY POLICY.

demand-pull inflation Inflation caused by too much demand or purchasing power in the economy; when there is excess purchasing power relative to the physical supply of goods and services, the only outcome can be rising prices. Too much money available for spending when there is a limited supply of goods and services, plus full employment, leads consumers to bid up the prices of available goods and services and firms to bid up available supplies of labour. The GROSS NATIONAL PRODUCT will go up because prices go up, but the real GNP cannot rise faster than a country's ability to produce goods and services at full-employment levels. Hence, demand-pull inflation is often described as too much money chasing too few goods.

Monetary and fiscal policies can be used to avoid demand-pull inflation, by cutting back on demand in the economy before the BUSINESS CYCLE hits its peak; the same policies can also be used to curb demand if demand-pull inflation already exists. Raising interest rates, reducing the growth rate of the money supply, raising taxes, and freezing government spending will all help to reduce demand and thus to cool off demand-pull inflation. See also COST-PUSH INFLATION.

demand schedule (curve) A curve that shows the quantity of a good or service that consumers will buy at different prices. As prices rise, demand tends to fall, while a decline in prices will tend to raise demand. Hence, there is always a relationship between the demand for a good and its price; a demand curve shows this relationship. Price is usually shown on the vertical axis and demand along the horizontal axis, so that the curve rises upward to the left and downward to the right.

demographic transition The changeover in the rate of population growth of a country, from a high rate of growth to a low rate of growth, with both the birth and death rates moving from a high rate of growth to a low rate of growth. Usually, the death rate of a population declines first, with birth rates continuing at a high level. The result is rapid population growth. Birth rates begin to decline until birth and death rates are about equal, and both are significantly lower than they were earlier.

demography The scientific study of human populations, including their size, composition by age and sex, distribution and growth, along with the factors determining population growth, such as birth and death rates and migration.

demurrage Extra charges made by railways, trucking and shipping companies, and airlines, to load, unload, or store goods if there is a delay or if extra time is required. For example, if a grain terminal is backed up, due to congestion in a port, the railways may charge a demurrage fee to compensate them for the extra time needed to unload their wheat, and ships will do likewise.

Dene nation A proposal presented to the federal government by the Indians of the Northwest Territories, in October 1976, for a form of self-rule. The Indians called themselves the Dene and argued that they had aboriginal rights that should be recognized by formal settlement, including the recognition of their property rights, and of rights to a form of self-determination and exclusive jurisdiction within a region of northern Canada. The Dene said that they wanted to replace Treaty Eight of 1899 and Treaty Eleven of 1921 with a new arrangement that would reduce their dependency on the non-Dene or white man's world and allow the Dene to make their own decisions about their educational system, political institutions, and other such matters, as well as to develop their own economic base.

The physical borders of the proposed Dene nation are largely undefined. According to the Dene, they want to "retain ownership of so much of their traditional lands, and under such terms, as to ensure their independence and self-reliance, traditionally, economically, and socially, and the maintenance of whatever other rights they have . . ." They also want compensation for past use of their land by the non-Dene. They reject the "last frontier" view of southern Canadians, who see the North as the country's last region to settle and develop.

density 1. The amount of building that can be done on a given parcel of land. It is usually expressed as the number of housing units or as the coverage or gross floor space permitted. If a piece of land is zoned at 3.2 times coverage, the gross floor area can be no greater than 3.2 times the area of the lot. Municipal zoning by-laws are usually expressed in terms of the type of building permitted in an area and the density of construction. Some municipalities also impose height restrictions. **2.** The number of people per acre or hectare.

departure tax A tax charged by some countries, including many of the less-developed countries, on travellers departing from an airport or port.

depletion allowance A tax deduction, similar to depreciation, that is granted to oil, natural-gas, mining, forest-products, and other natural-resource industries. The principal assets of these companies, known as wasting assets, consist of their natural resources, which are reduced over time as they are exploited. Companies are permitted a deduction for depletion, based on the cost of finding and developing the natural resource, so that they can recover these costs and find new natural resources. In Canada, depletion must be earned and is one-third of the expenditure in finding new natural resources. Like depreciation, depletion is not a cash outlay. It reduces a company's tax liability, and hence increases its after-tax profits.

deposit 1. A small downpayment on a product made by a would-be buyer, signifying his probable intention of purchasing it. **2.** Funds placed in a bank account.

deposit institution A bank, trust company, credit union, caisse populaire, or other financial institution that accepts deposits of money from the public, manages accounts on which cheques can be written, sells guaranteed-investment and other savings certificates, and makes loans. The activities of deposit institutions are regulated by federal or provincial legislation, depending on the type of financial institution and whether they are federally or provincially incorporated. See also FINANCIAL INTERMEDIARY.

deposit insurance Insurance to protect depositors against the complete loss of their savings deposited in a bank, trust company, major credit union, caisse populaire, or other deposit institution, if the financial institution fails. The CANADA DEPOSIT INSURANCE CORPORATION and the QUEBEC DEPOSIT INSURANCE BOARD provide protection for all Canadian-dollar deposits up to twenty thousand dollars at insured institutions, with the institutions legally required to obtain and pay for such insurance. The existence of deposit insurance adds to the stability of the financial system and makes it easier for a small and new deposit institution to compete in the market for savings dollars. Canada has had deposit insurance since 1967, following the failure of several financial institutions, including the ATLANTIC ACCEPTANCE Company, British Mortgage and Trust Corporation, and PRUDENTIAL FINANCE CORPORATION.

depreciation A method of calculating and writing off the costs to a firm of FIXED ASSETS, such as machinery, buildings, trucks, and equipment. Investment in such fixed assets, which wear out or become obsolete over time, is a normal expense of business. But since such assets have a reasonably long life—buildings usually longer than machinery and machinery longer than vehicles—it makes more sense, in determining the real costs of operating the business, to allocate a share of the total cost to each year of the normal life of the asset, rather than to deduct the total cost as an expense in the year of purchase. Hence, the cost of the asset is divided by the number of years of useful life as calculated for accounting or tax purposes, and the resulting amount is deducted for each of the years as an ordinary business expense. The amount claimed is not actually paid out as an expense each year when it is claimed for tax purposes, but it is deducted from taxable income and reduces the firm's tax liability. Hence, it increases profits and represents money available to the firm for the replacement of machinery and equipment, expansion, retirement of debt, diversification, or payment of a higher dividend to shareholders.

The depreciation claimed by a firm is included in the EARNINGS STATEMENT under expenses. Depreciation claimed by all Canadian businesses is identified in the GROSS-NATIONAL-PRODUCT statistics as capital-cost allowances. When the government wishes to encourage business investment, it can bring in ACCELERATED-DEPRECIATION provisions for a short period. If it wishes to encourage a particular form of activity, such as RESEARCH AND DEVELOPMENT, it may allow firms to claim, say, 150 per cent of the capital costs for depreciation purposes. Depreciation is thus an important contribution to a firm's cash flow.

There are two basic methods of calculating depreciation: **1.** Straight-line depreciation, where the cost of the asset is divided by the number of years of its useful life and the same amount is deducted each year. This is usually used in a company's annual report. **2.** Declining-balance depreciation, which provides a greater write-off in the early years of life of the asset. The depreciation each year is calculated as a per cent of the cost of the asset after the depreciation of the previous year is deducted. This is the usual method used in a company's tax return. See also DEFERRED INCOME TAXES.

depressed area See REGIONAL DEVELOPMENT, REGIONAL ECONOMIC EXPANSION.

depression An extended period of sharply reduced economic activity, with widespread unemployment, declining prices, little capital investment, and a large number of business failures. A depression is much more severe than a recession, lasts for a much longer period of time, and tends to be global in impact. Depressions hit the Canadian economy in 1873–79 and 1929–39.

deregulation A reduction in government regulation of business activities, including approval for new investment projects. The purpose is usually to reduce business operating costs created by complying with government regulations, and to speed up new investment. Deregulation should reduce the number of minor regulations, but may retain the most important regulatory activities governing a particular industry.

derived demand The demand for a factor of production, such as land, labour, or capital, or for another commodity, which results from the demand for a good or service that it helps to produce or that is used in association with the good or service being produced. Thus, the construction of a house or apartment leads to a demand for construction workers, land, mortgage money, and building materials, as well as a demand for appliances, furniture, and carpeting when it is finished.

deterrent fee An extra fee charged to discourage the unnecessary use of a service. For example, provincial governments may permit doctors to charge patients an extra fee, in addition to the payment they get from the provincial health service, to discourage people from making unnecessary visits to a doctor. The problem with the deterrent fee in such cases is that it is also levied on necessary visits, and is a burden for people with low incomes. Another example is the fee charged by a telephone company for personal directory assistance, if the desired number is already listed in the phone directory.

devaluation The reduction by a government of the par or official value of its currency in terms of the value of the currencies of other nations in a régime of fixed exchange rates. When exchange rates are floating, a large and chronic balance-of-payments deficit will have the same effect. On 2 May 1962, when exchange rates were fixed, Canada pegged its exchange rate at 92.5 U.S. cents; it had been floating at 95 U.S. cents shortly before. Devaluation can serve as an economic stimulus, since it reduces the price of exports and makes them easier to sell, while raising the price of imports, making it easier for domestic producers to compete against imports. It also has an inflationary impact, since it raises the price of essential imports, such as tea, coffee, oranges, and computers, in Canada's case. If Canada's foreign debt, including interest charges, is in U.S. dollars, for example, devaluation also raises the cost of servicing Canada's foreign debt.

developed country A country that has a per capita income of at least two thousand dollars, and fairly high standards of health care, education, housing, advanced industrial development, technology, and agricultural productivity. The developed countries include Canada, the members of the EUROPEAN ECONOMIC COMMUNITY, the United States, Japan, Australia, New Zealand, the Soviet Union, and its Eastern European satellites. The developed countries are also known as the North in the NORTH-SOUTH DIALOGUE. See also LESS-DEVELOPED COUNTRIES.

developing countries See LESS-DEVELOPED COUNTRIES.

development **1.** The modernization of a country's economy, including investment in INFRASTRUCTURE, such as power stations, schools, and railways, and in technologically advanced industries. **2.** The work that is carried out to bring an oil or natural-gas reservoir into production or to open up and extract a mineral-ore deposit. **3.** The refinery and design of a new invention to turn it into a commercially acceptable product.

development assistance See OFFICIAL DEVELOPMENT ASSISTANCE.

Development Assistance Committee (DAC) A special committee within the ORGANIZATION FOR ECONOMIC CO-OPERATION AND DEVELOPMENT, set up to monitor, co-ordinate, and assess OFFICIAL DEVELOPMENT ASSISTANCE of member countries, including Canada. DAC publishes an annual assessment of each member's aid activities and reports on the progress each member nation is making towards the PEARSON COMMISSION target of official development assistance equal to 0.7 per cent of each member's gross national product. DAC also assesses the needs and problems of the LESS-DEVELOPED COUNTRIES.

development decades Ten-year plans by the United Nations to strengthen the economies of the LESS-DEVELOPED COUNTRIES. The first development decade, proclaimed in 1961, set a goal of at least 5 per cent annual growth in national income in the less-developed countries by the end of the decade. Developed countries, such as Canada, were asked to provide 1 per cent of their gross national product as aid to the developing countries. The second development decade, adopted in 1970, called for an annual growth rate of 6 per cent for gross national product and 3.5 per cent for per capita income in the less-developed countries through the 1970s, and aid of at least 1 per cent of GNP from the developed countries, including 0.7 per cent of GNP as OFFICIAL DEVELOPMENT ASSISTANCE, by the end of the 1970s.

development economics The branch of economics concerned with how LESS-DEVELOPED COUNTRIES can evolve into more affluent industrial societies with higher per capita incomes. It deals with different types of development strategies open to poor countries.

dilution The reduction in a company's EARNINGS PER SHARE caused by an increase in the number of outstanding shares in the company. This can result from the conversion of CONVERTIBLE BONDS or CONVERTIBLE PREFERRED SHARES into COMMON SHARES, from the issue of new common shares, or from the exercising of WARRANTS to acquire new common shares.

diminishing marginal productivity An economic law stating that, the larger the quantity of one factor when it is combined with fixed quantities of the other FACTORS OF PRODUCTION, the lower the extra output achieved from using each extra unit of that factor. For example, in a factory with fixed space and fixed numbers of machines, the use of additional workers will increase output. But each extra worker will add less to the total output than the previous worker, so long as the factory space and number of machines remain unchanged.

diminishing marginal utility An economic law that states that each extra unit consumed yields less utility or satisfaction than the previous unit consumed. For example, while one chocolate bar may yield enormous satisfaction and a second one almost as much, the seventh, eighth, and ninth chocolate bars will yield less and less satisfaction. The same is true with rising money income.

diminishing returns See LAW OF DIMINISHING RETURNS.

direct cost A cost that is related directly to the volume of output—the raw materials or parts used to manufacture a product, for example, or the labour required to make the product. Such costs are also known as variable costs. See also INDIRECT COST.

direct investment Investment made for the purpose of exercising direct control over an operating company; as opposed to PORTFOLIO INVESTMENT, which is made simply for the yield in interest, dividends, and capital gains that can be obtained. Direct investment consists of investment made to expand an existing business by providing new EQUITY CAPITAL, to start up a new business, or to take over an existing business. FOREIGN DIRECT INVESTMENT consists of direct investments made by corporations or individuals from one country in the business sector of another country. Statistics Canada reports on foreign direct-investment flows in its BALANCE-OF-PAYMENTS statistics.

direct selling A sales campaign aimed directly at the final consumer of a good or service, organized usually by the producer. This type of sales effort thus bypasses retailers and other sales organizations; it includes, for example, door-to-door sales and direct-mail sales.

direct tax A tax that is paid directly by the person or firm on which it is levied and which, generally speaking, is hard to shift to another person. Examples include personal and corporate income tax, capital-gains tax, property tax, and the retail sales tax. Under the British North America Act, both the federal government and the provincial governments have the power to levy direct taxes. The federal power is in section 91 (3) and section 122, while the provincial power is in section 92 (2).

director A person who is elected by a company's shareholders or appointed by a company's owners to serve on the company's BOARD OF DIRECTORS. Directors supervise the work of the company's officers and set company policy. They must own at least one share in the company and are expected to act in the best interests of the shareholders. Under federal and provincial CORPORATION LAWS, directors are required to make it their business to know what is going on in the company on whose board they serve. They may be liable for illegal acts committed by the company if those acts are committed with their knowledge or consent, and they are liable for gross negligence if they are delinquent in their role as supervisors of the company's activities and policies. They are, under law, expected to exercise, as Ontario puts it, "the degree of care, diligence, and skill that a reasonably prudent person would exercise in comparable circumstances." Thus, the position of company director is no longer the honorary post it used to be. Today, the law imposes important responsibilities on directors to protect the interests of shareholders and the company. Compensation is paid in the form of directors' fees.

dirty float The situation that exists if a country says that it is letting its currency float freely in foreign-exchange markets, when in fact it is actively intervening, either to move its exchange rate up or down or to prevent its exchange rate from moving at all in the face of strong market pressures. This differs from modest intervention to smooth out day-to-day fluctuations in the rate, and thus to maintain an orderly market.

disability benefits Payments through WORKMEN'S COMPENSATION and various insurance programs to employees who are no longer able to work, or who can only work at a lesser job, as a result of injuries or ill health suffered on the job.

disclosure A requirement that information be made available to the public at large or to specific individuals who may be affected by a specific action. For example, publicly traded corporations are required to publish extensive financial information, verified by an AUDITOR according to GENERALLY ACCEPTED ACCOUNTING PRINCIPLES, each year. Similarly, a bank, finance company, credit union, or other financial institution lending money to someone must disclose the interest rate and the cost of the loan, while someone in a position of public trust—an elected representative, for example—must disclose whether he or she has a financial or other interest in the outcome of a decision, determining, for example, who should get a contract.

discomfort index An index designed by U.S. economist Arthur Okun to show the combined effect of inflation and unemployment at any point in time. It is obtained by adding the unemployment rate and the rate of increase in the consumer price index for the same period.

discount **1.** A reduction in the price of a good or service for prompt payment, a large-volume purchase, or other similar reason. **2.** The amount by which a preferred share or bond sells below its face or par value. **3.** The charge made for cashing in a promissory note, investment certificate, or other debt before it matures.

discount market See MONEY MARKET.

discounted When something that affects the price of a share or other security, such as a drop in profits or a market glut of its product, has already been taken into account in determining its price, it has been discounted by investors.

discounted cash flow An analytical tool that helps corporations to determine the true profitability of a project. Since money received in the future is worth less than money in hand today—due both to the erosion of its value from inflation and to the lost income that could be earned if it were available to invest—the profitability of a project cannot be determined by simply adding together the profits from each future year. Using the discounted-cash-flow method, the value of future earnings is discounted by an anticipated future rate of inflation and the number of years before the profit is earned. The discounted values of profits from each future year are added together to produce a true rate of return. A firm can then decide, based on its calculation of risk and its normal discounted-cash-flow rate of return, whether to make the investment. See also NET PRESENT VALUE, TIME VALUE OF MONEY.

discounted value In the process of making an investment decision, the value of the future profits that a producer expects to get from a new plant or piece of machinery or equipment, as opposed to what he would get if he lent the same money out at prevailing rates of interest.

discouraged worker An unemployed person who has given up looking for a new job and who therefore is unlikely to be counted as unemployed in the official LABOUR-FORCE SURVEY. He may be an older and unskilled worker in a declining industry or a resident of a slow-growth area.

discovery rate The rate at which net new additions are added to oil and natural-gas reserves in a twelve-month period. For a country's oil or natural-gas reserves to increase, the discovery of new reserves must be greater than the consumption of oil or natural gas in the same period.

discretionary income The after-tax income of individuals that is not needed to pay for essentials such as food, shelter, and clothing. Hence, it can either be saved or spent on alternative goods or services, depending on the tastes, interests, or wants of the consumer.

diseconomies of scale An increase in the average cost per unit of production, as production rises, because of the exceedingly large scale on which the producer operates. This can be due to internal factors: for example, the firm may become so big that it becomes increasingly costly and difficult to manage and operate. Or it can be due to external factors, such as higher wages resulting from increasing demands for labour by competing firms in the same industry, or increased pollution clean-up costs due to the concentration of major industries along the same river or lake system. See also ECONOMIES OF SCALE.

disguised unemployment Forms of unemployment that do not show up in official unemployment statistics. There are two principal types: **1.** Persons engaged in activities well below their skills or talents, or activities that provide little useful employment, such as subsistence farming. **2.** Persons who would like to work but see little opportunity, and decide not to seek employment. Examples include housewives who don't enter the labour force, or students who decide to continue their education because jobs aren't available.

disinvestment The lack of sufficient new investment to replace plant, machinery, and equipment that is wearing out. The result is a decline in the productive capacity of the economy.

disposable income The money available to individuals for spending and saving after taxes and social-insurance premiums, such as unemployment insurance and the Canada Pension Plan premiums, have been deducted. Total personal disposable income in the economy can be obtained from gross-national-product statistics by deducting current transfers to government from personal income. These transfers include income tax, succession duties and estate taxes, employer and employee contributions to social-insurance and government pension funds, and other transfers to government.

dissaving A level of consumer spending that is greater than disposable income for the same period. It means that an individual, or all individuals together, are either dipping into past savings or taking on debts that will have to be repaid from future earnings.

distribution **1.** In economics, the study of how the total income in the economy is shared among workers, landlords, investors, and others. The question of who gets what and how the total flow of goods and services is allocated is one of the principal concerns of modern economics. This branch of economics includes the study of market forces, competition, and the role of market forces and supply and demand in determining prices, wages, profits, rents, and interest rates. **2.** In the economic system, the physical and financial means of moving goods from factories, through wholesalers and retailers, to the ultimate consumers.

distribution costs The various costs of advertising, marketing, warehousing, selling, and delivering goods and services.

distribution of powers The division of spending, taxing, and regulatory powers between the federal and provincial governments under the BRITISH NORTH AMERICA ACT. See also FEDERAL SPENDING POWER, FEDERAL TAXING POWER, PROVINCIAL SPENDING POWER, PROVINCIAL TAXING POWER.

The federal government, through Parliament, has jurisdiction over: monetary policy and banking; interprovincial and international trade, tariffs, patents, copyright, weights and measures; interprovincial and international transport and communications, including railways, airlines, telephones, telecommunications, broadcasting, and pipelines; incorporation of companies with extra-provincial objectives, along with competition policies, bankruptcy, and laws dealing with business practices; labour relations in areas under federal jurisdiction, such as banking and transportation; and postal services and navigation. The federal government also has jurisdiction over lands, mines, and minerals in the Northwest Territories and the Yukon and, probably, in the offshore areas of Canada. It may also regulate the intraprovincial and international movement of resources and levy taxes on them. In an emergency, the federal government may set energy-resource prices and allocate supplies.

The provincial governments have jurisdiction over: economic matters having to do with "property and civil rights," such as contracts, regulation of selling securities, and insurance; intraprovincial production, trade, and marketing; intraprovincial transport and communications (except for aeronautics); labour relations covering all workers and employees under provincial jurisdiction, and regulation of the professions; and the incorporation and practice of businesses operating within the province.

The provinces own and regulate mineral, oil, and natural-gas and land and water rights, including timber and hydro-electric rights. Agriculture and consumer protection are both areas of concurrent jurisdiction. While in fisheries the federal government has clear jurisdiction over the negotiation of INTERNATIONAL FISHERIES CONVENTIONS, along with international and interprovincial trade, navigation, and pollution controls, the provinces control the catch and marketing of fish within their boundaries. In 1967 the Supreme Court of Canada ruled that the federal government had jurisdiction over offshore resources along the Pacific coast. In 1976, it ruled that the federal government could impose wage and price controls. And in 1978, it ruled that cable television also came under federal jurisdiction.

distributive justice The form of justice that is concerned with fairness in the distribution of wealth and income, economic opportunity, and political and civil rights.

disutility The opposite of utility or satisfaction; the ability of a good or service to cause inconvenience, discomfort, and even pain. Once a person has more of something than he can consume or store, the good stops providing even a diminishing marginal utility and yields disutility instead. The same is true of work. A person wants to work so that he can earn enough money to meet his various wants. But, after a certain number of hours of work, disutility or inconvenience replaces utility or satisfaction; this is one reason why additional or overtime hours of work command a higher rate of pay.

diversification **1.** As applied to the investment portfolio of an individual or institution, the spreading of risk by purchasing shares of various companies in different industries, or a variety of securities, such as bonds, preferred shares, and common shares. **2.** As applied to corporations, the entry into new types of businesses or product lines, so as to reduce the risk of becoming too dependent on a single or restricted product line that could become obsolete, or to expand opportunities for higher profits. A company may diversify into related or unrelated areas of business. For example, a sugar company could diversify into convenience foods, soft drinks, fast-food restaurants, and other related areas; or it could diversify into property development, cable television, and other unrelated areas. Diversification is often the most rapid means of business growth; in the case of the sugar company, for example, there is little it can do to increase sugar consumption directly once per capita consumption reaches a high level, so it uses its profits to diversify.

dividend Payments made out of profits by a corporation to its COMMON and PREFERRED shareholders. While the payment is usually in cash, it can also be made in the form of new shares. When the dividend is in the form of new shares, it is not treated as income but is taxed for capital gains when the shares are sold. The advantage to a company of issuing shares or stock dividends is that it retains more of its profits for reinvestment. Canadian companies tend to pay out about half of their after-tax profits as dividends, although this varies widely from company to company. The amount of dividend paid to owners of common shares usually depends a great deal on the level of profits. But preferred shareholders are entitled to a fixed annual dividend.

dividend tax credit A tax incentive to encourage Canadians to invest in Canadian corporations. Shareholders, in their tax returns, add together their dividends from Canadian corporations, gross this income up by 50 per cent, calculate the federal tax, then deduct a federal tax credit equal to 75 per cent of the gross-up. This results in a lower tax rate on dividend income for Canadian taxpayers who invest in Canadian shares. Corresponding reductions are also available for the provincial portion of the income tax. If a shareholder received $2,000 in dividends, he would gross this up by

50 per cent or $1,000, creating a taxable amount of $3,000. Federal tax would be calculated on this amount, but the taxpayer would also be able to deduct from the tax payable a federal tax credit of 75 per cent of the gross amount, in this case $1,000, yielding a tax credit of $750. Thus, the tax liability could be reduced to zero, depending on the taxpayer's income bracket.

dividend yield The annual rate of return on common shares, obtained by dividing the annual dividend by the current market price of the share.

division of labour Specialization in an economy, so that individual workers perform a single task in the production process and use their particular talents or skills to the best advantage. It is the key to increased output, higher productivity, and the application of ECONOMIES OF SCALE. ADAM SMITH was probably the first economist to write about the benefits accruing to everyone from the division of labour. He used the model of a pin factory, noting that one man could only make a few complete pins each day but, if each worker made only a part of each pin, then the same number of workers could produce thousands of pins in a day. Smith also emphasized that the opportunity to realize the greatest benefits from the division of labour depended on having access to a large market. Hence, just as a domestic economy could benefit up to a point from the division of labour, a world economy with free trade would lead to international specialization and even greater benefits from the international division of labour.

division of powers In the British North America Act, the division of spending and taxing power between the federal and provincial governments. See also FEDERAL SPENDING POWER, FEDERAL TAXING POWER, PROVINCIAL SPENDING POWER, PROVINCIAL TAXING POWER, DISTRIBUTION OF POWERS.

dole Social assistance in the form of cash, food, shelter, and clothing. Prime Minister R. B. Bennett, in the depths of the Depression in 1935, said that the dole "was a condemnation of our economic system. If we cannot abolish the dole, we should abolish the system."

Dominion Lands Policy The policy pursued by the federal government between 1870 and 1930 in settling the prairie provinces, following the transfer by the British government of Rupert's Land and the Northwest Territories from the Hudson's Bay Company to the new dominion. The federal government, under the Dominion Lands Acts of 1872 and 1908, disposed of crown lands and granted exploitation rights for natural resources, such as minerals, timber, and water, a power that, under the BRITISH NORTH AMERICA ACT, would normally have belonged to the provinces. These lands and their natural resources, known as Dominion Lands, were used to stimulate the construction of railways and the settlement of the region, in a race to prevent rapid U.S. westward expansion from spilling north into the prairies, and thus to prevent the region from becoming part of the United States. The federal government made railway land grants, including twenty-five million acres to the Canadian Pacific Railway Company, provided free homesteads for settlers, set aside land for schools and townsites, created the great Rocky Mountain national parks, granted mineral, water, and timber rights, and designated land for cattle grazing. The program of western settlement, lasting sixty years, was probably one of the most important activities of the federal government in the first hundred years of Confederation. In 1930, the federal government turned over remaining crown lands and mineral rights to Alberta, Saskatchewan, and Manitoba.

dormant company An incorporated company that is no longer active, but files annual returns and meets other obligations to retain its legal status.

double-entry bookkeeping The standard system of accounting or financial record-keeping. Every transaction results in a credit on one side of the ledger and a debit on the other side, so that total credits on one side of the ledger should equal total debits on the other side and the books will balance. Credits represent money owed the firm or assets owned by the firm, while debits represent debts of the firm owed to others. If, for example, a firm borrows one million dollars to buy new machinery, the borrowed funds represent a credit, while the machinery represents a debit.

double taxation The taxation of the taxable income more than once. This can happen in two different ways. First, the same taxable income may be taxed more than once within the same jurisdiction. For example, corporate profits are taxed as they are earned by a business enterprise and then taxed again when they are received by shareholders in the form of dividends. The Income Tax Act offsets this to some extent through a GROSS-UP AND CREDIT system; see also DIVIDEND TAX CREDIT. Second, double taxation can occur when competing tax authorities each tax the same tax base. For example, in the absence of federal-provincial agreements, Canadians could find the federal and provincial governments each trying to raise revenue by operating competing income-tax systems. Similarly, in the absence of TAX TREATIES, foreign-controlled corporations could find themselves taxed both by Canada and by the tax authorities of the parent firm's country on the profits earned by the Canadian subsidiary.

double ticketing Selling a product that has two different price stickers or tags on it at the higher of the two prices. This is illegal under the COMBINES INVESTIGATION ACT. The lower price must always prevail.

dough A slang term for money.

down time The period of time in which machinery and other equipment is not in operation, so that repairs, adjustments, and maintenance can be carried out. During this period of time, workers are idle.

downpayment A real-estate term for the amount of EQUITY CAPITAL a purchaser invests in a new house or other property. The difference between the price of the property and the downpayment is usually covered by a mortgage or mortgages.

draft A written order to pay, such as a cheque, but written by the person to whom money is owed, and addressed to the debtor, instructing him to pay the funds to the bank. The order is sent by the creditor to the bank, which presents it to the debtor for payment.

dumping The sale of a product in a foreign market at a price less than that charged in the country of origin. It is barred under the GENERAL AGREEMENT ON TARIFFS AND TRADE (GATT), which adopted an anti-dumping code in 1967. Canada implemented the code the following year, with the passage of legislation establishing the ANTI-DUMPING TRIBUNAL.

Dumping may take place to get rid of excess production; it means that the extra production can be sold without having to cut prices in normal markets. Or it may occur as part of a corporate strategy, either to discourage the entry of a new firm into the business, to enlarge a producer's share of the market, or to gain entry to a market. Sometimes dumping is assisted by the government of the producer's country, through hidden subsidies and other devices, to increase exports and thus to create jobs at home.

Dumping is difficult to identify. In Canada, not only must dumping be proven; it must also be shown that the dumping is causing injury or inhibiting industrial growth. Dumping by Communist-bloc countries is especially difficult to prove, since state trading corporations are government agencies and prices are set by government without a direct relationship, necessarily, to costs. Dumping is the international price equivalent of PRICE DISCRIMINATION by domestic producers. According to GATT, dumping can be subject to penalty if "it causes or threatens material injury to an established industry," or if it "materially retards the establishment of a domestic industry."

duopoly A market in which there are only two producers or suppliers of a particular good or service. Neither producer can behave as if he had a complete MONOPOLY, because he has to take the other's pricing and production policies into account. But the opportunity is there for an understanding between the two producers to limit production, divide markets, and charge monopoly prices. See also OLIGOPOLY.

duopsony A market in which there are only

two purchasers or consumers and many producers of a particular good or service. The market power of the two consumers may be such that they can force producers to sell at unprofitable or barely profitable prices.

durable goods Producer or consumer goods with a life expectancy of more than three years. Examples include production machinery, trucks, railway rolling stock, and consumer durables such as household appliances and automobiles. The purchase of durable goods can be postponed, so the demand for durable goods can be subject to wide swings, depending on the state of the economy.

dutch auction An auction in which the auctioneer sets a high opening price and then lowers the bids until a buyer is found.

duty A TAX or TARIFF levied on goods when they are imported, exported, or consumed.

dwelling unit A separate living quarter that has a private entrance from the outside or from a common hall or stairway inside the building. Thus, a dwelling unit can be a separate house, apartment, flat, townhouse, or other such premises. The term is used in census surveys. In the 1971 census, Statistics Canada found 6,034,510 dwelling units, 59.5 per cent of which were single-family residences. Some 60.3 per cent were owner-occupied and 39.7 per cent were rented.

earmarked tax A tax that is designated for a particular purpose. Education taxes are earmarked for the school system and gasoline taxes usually are designated for road and highway construction and maintenance. Tax experts dislike designating taxes for specific purposes, since this can lead to under- or overspending in particular public sectors; they prefer to see all tax revenues go into consolidated government funds, with spending based on demonstrated need.

earnings See PROFIT.

earnings per share The net earnings of a firm, before extraordinary items and minus preferred dividends, divided by the number of outstanding common shares. Financial analysts watch carefully to see the trend over time in earnings per share. A company with a rising earnings-per-share record will hold more appeal than one whose earnings per share, though perhaps higher, remain stagnant or are declining. The figure shows individual shareholders how well they are doing on their investment, since these earnings per share belong to them, regardless of whether they are paid out in dividends or reinvested in the business to build up SHAREHOLDERS' EQUITY. The earnings-per-share figure forms the denominator for the PRICE-EARNINGS RATIO, another important figure used by investors in trying to determine the future price of shares in a company.

earnings statement That part of an ANNUAL or QUARTERLY REPORT issued by a company that shows the sources of its revenues and how they have been spent. What is left over is the net earnings or profit of the company, the money that can be used to pay dividends to shareholders and to reinvest in the business.

An earnings statement is divided into four sections: **1.** The operating section outlines total income from the sale of the firm's goods or services, minus the cost of sales, which includes labour, parts, raw materials, and energy used to produce the firm's goods or services. This yields the gross operating profit. From this are deducted the selling and administrative costs of the firm, depreciation, and various other costs, such as contributions to employee pension plans or payments for directors' fees. All of these costs are deducted from the gross operating profit to give the net operating profit, or loss. **2.** The non-operating section of the earnings statement adds non-operating income, such as interest and dividends from company investments, royalty payments on its patents, and rents from surplus property the firm owns, to the net operating profit. To this is added something called extraordinary items. These are unusual additions to income or losses and can include a big profit on the sale of a piece of company land or subsidiary, an unusual loss from a bad investment, or loss of part of the business due to a flood or other disaster. The resulting figure is the company's remaining income from all sources. **3.** The creditors' section of the earnings statement shows payments to creditors, who have to get their money before the owners can get their profits. Payments to creditors include interest on bank loans or outstanding bonds or mortgages, and income taxes. These are deducted from the income of the company. **4.** The owners' section of the earnings statement shows the net earnings (profit) or deficit (loss). The net earnings are transferred to the RETAINED-EARNINGS STATEMENT, which shows how much of the profits is reinvested in the business and how much is paid out to shareholders in the form of dividends. See also BALANCE SHEET, STATEMENT OF CHANGES IN FINANCIAL POSITION.

easement The right of the owner of a particular piece of land in an adjoining piece of land. The right may be for access to his land through his neighbour's property—a right-of-way. Or it may be to prevent his neighbour from building in such a way as to interfere with his enjoyment of his own property—by interfering with light reaching his windows, for example.

Eastern Canada New Brunswick, Nova Scotia, Prince Edward Island, and Newfoundland.

easy money The condition in financial markets when interest rates are low and credit can be easily obtained. See also TIGHT MONEY.

ecology The study of the impact of man and his activities, including his economic activities, on the web of biological relationships that together constitute the environment.

econometrics The application of mathematics and statistics, usually with the aid of computers, to build models of the economy based on a large number of equations expressing relationships between different economic activities. The models are used to help understand economic behaviour and to measure the impact of various economic policies on future economic performance. Economic models try to bring together mathematically, through a series of equations, a picture of the way the economy—or a region, market, or industry—functions. The equations, for example, identify relationships, say between prices and wages, consumer spending, and investment or production, and the demand for capital.

Economic Council of Canada (ECC) An advisory body created in 1963 to develop a national consensus on medium- and long-term policy needs and to help the country to improve its economic performance. The council consists of a full-time chairman and two directors who are professional economists, along with twenty-five other members who are drawn from the business, labour, farm, academic, and other communities; they are appointed by the prime minister. The council is backed up by its own staff of professional economists. The council held its first meeting in January 1964. It publishes an annual review on the economy, special studies on economic issues, staff research reports, and special studies carried out at the request of the government.

The council's role, as defined in the legislation setting it up, is to suggest "how Canada can achieve the highest possible level of employment and efficient production, in order that the country may enjoy a high and consistent rate of economic growth and that all Candians share in rising living standards." Specifically, its role is: **1.** To assess regularly the medium- and long-term prospects of the economy and compare them with the country's potential for economic growth. **2.** To recommend government policies that would help Canada achieve its economic potential. **3.** To consider ways to strengthen and improve Canada's international financial and trade position. **4.** To study ways to increase Canadian ownership, control, and management of industries in Canada. **5.** To study how growth, technological change, automation, and changing international conditions may affect employment in Canada.

The council has had a number of special studies referred to it by the government, including studies on how to reform competition policy and laws dealing with intellectual property, including copyright and patent laws, and how to reduce both government regulation and instability in the construction industry. The council staff has also developed a highly sophisticated econometric model of the Canadian economy, known as CANDIDE. For a brief period in 1979, it was charged with the responsibility of monitoring wage and price changes in the economy, following the phasing out of the ANTI-INFLATION BOARD; it created the CENTRE FOR THE STUDY OF INFLATION AND PRODUCTIVITY to carry out this function. The council is the largest single economic-research body in Canada. See also ONTARIO ECONOMIC COUNCIL, ATLANTIC PROVINCES ECONOMIC COUNCIL, FRASER INSTITUTE, HOWE RESEARCH INSTITUTE, INSTITUTE FOR RESEARCH ON PUBLIC POLICY, and the CANADIAN INSTITUTE FOR ECONOMIC POLICY.

economic determinism In Marxist terms, the belief that our political, cultural, and social attitudes are determined by ownership of the means of production; attitudes will differ significantly among feudal, capitalist, and communist societies, because the economic relationships among people differ in each. Since KARL MARX and his followers also believed that economic systems evolved according to immutable laws of history, they took public attitudes to be predetermined and granted that capitalists couldn't be personally blamed for their behaviour. In a broader sense, the view that social, cultural, and political progress is shaped mainly by economic forces.

economic good Anything that is relatively scarce; unlike a FREE GOOD, it is only available at a cost or sacrifice of some other good. Anything that can be bought or sold is an economic good. Thus, the definition also includes the services of a person, as well as something a person produces.

economic growth The increase over a period of time in the production of goods and services and the capacity to produce goods and services. Economic growth is usually measured as the percentage increase in GROSS NATIONAL PRODUCT over a specified period of time, after adjusting for inflation; since population is constantly changing, a more precise measure is the rate of growth of real per capita income.

Economic growth is one of the principal goals of virtually all modern societies, since it is considered necessary to increase the size of the economic pie if the standard of living of most people in the world is to be raised. Even the CONSERVER SOCIETY allows for some economic growth. But economic growth does not reflect all the gains and losses in a modern economy. It does not show the leisure-time gains from the shorter work week made possible by improved productivity; nor does it adequately reflect the costs to society of dealing with pollution, industrial disease, and similar problems.

Many factors affect the rate of growth in a country, and not all countries need the same rate of economic growth to achieve full employment. Among the factors are: growth in the size of the labour force, the level of capital stock, the rate of innovation, the investment in research and development, the level of education of the work force, cultural attitudes towards business and growth, the possession of natural resources, the level of managerial know-how, and the sophistication of financial markets.

economic history An account of past events and forces that have influenced the growth of a nation, region, or institution, or the study of past events and institutions to develop a theory of economic growth or development in a particular society. HAROLD INNIS is Canada's best-known economic historian. See W. T. Easterbrook and M. H. Watkins, eds., *Approaches to Canadian Economic History* (Toronto, 1967). See also STAPLE THEORY.

economic imperialism The use of economic power by a nation or corporations to exploit another part of the world. Marxists argued that economic imperialism was the inevitable result of capitalism and represented its final stage before its collapse. The accumulation of capital at home would lead to declining profit rates, forcing capitalists to seek higher profits through investments abroad. Because of their control over governments, capitalists would use the power of the state, including its armies and navies, to help them to secure raw materials and markets. But, according to Marxists, such empire-building was bound to lead to international conflict among competing capitalist states, with the resulting wars bringing on revolution by the workers and the overthrow of capitalism. By this definition, only capitalists can be imperialists.

In today's world, many LESS-DEVELOPED COUNTRIES claim that they are the victims of economic imperialism by the industrial powers and their alleged agents, the multinational corporations. The less-developed nations contend that, while they have gained a measure of self-government, they remain economic colonies, supplying raw materials to and buying manufactured goods from the industrialized world. In such an economic arrangement, the less-developed countries contend, they are doomed to poverty. See NEW INTERNATIONAL ECONOMIC ORDER.

economic indicator Economic statistics that give important clues to changing economic conditions. There are three types: LEADING INDICATORS, COINCIDENT INDICATORS, and LAGGING INDICATORS.

economic law A proposition that expresses a precise relationship among different economic phenomena, and that may be used to predict the outcome of economic events. Two of the best-known economic laws are the LAW OF SUPPLY AND DEMAND and the LAW OF DIMINISHING RETURNS.

economic life The useful life of a machine, pipeline, building, smelter, or other asset. After a period of time, it makes more sense to replace an asset than to pay the rising costs of maintenance and repair.

economic man The theoretical view of man developed by CLASSICAL economists. According to this view, man possesses full knowledge of the market and is motivated solely by rational economic considerations. The classical school used this view of man to develop its model of PERFECT COMPETITION. The theory overlooked other motivations of man, such as family, religion, nation, envy, and revenge.

economic model A way to analyze economic problems, using a series of mathematical equations that define numerically the relationships among different sectors of the economy. Typical relationships include those between changes in personal income and consumer spending, between prices and the exchange rate, or between output and demand. Most econometric models, using computers, contain more than one thousand equations. The best-known economic models are those of the Bank of Canada, the Economic Council of Canada, and the University of Toronto.

Economic models depict the economy in several different ways. For example, a model will typically show a gross-national product statement, which explains all the sources of income in an economy, such as wages, dividends, profits, and how that income is used —on consumer spending, for example, capital investment, and public goods and services. An economic model will also include an input-output system that traces INTERMEDIATE GOODS through the economy—iron ore, for example, as a raw material for steel, steel as a raw material for semi-finished steel products, semi-finished steel products for use in the production of automobiles, and automobiles delivered to car dealers for sale to consumers. A third element of an economic model is the national balance sheet or flow of funds in the economy. This shows the volume of savings, financial investments, interest-rate and saving relationships, and other features of financial activity. Models are kept up to date with the latest statistical data, and are used to forecast economic performance and to test the effects of different policies or assumptions, such as budget plans, on future economic performance.

economic nationalism The desire to control one's own economic future. Economic nationalism can range from a concern over the high level of foreign control of the economy to a desire to be almost completely self-sufficient in everything one consumes. Moderate economic nationalism is not opposed to foreign ownership as such but to excessively high levels of foreign ownership, since this puts too much investment decision-making power into the hands of foreign boards of directors, leading to TRUNCATION in the economy—that is, to the absence of a reasonable level of research and development, managerial know-how, and highly skilled jobs. See COMMITTEE FOR AN INDEPENDENT CANADA.

economic planning Government intervention in investment and spending decisions. There are various types of economic planning: **1.** Consensus planning, where the government attempts to bring in business and labour as partners in an effort to reach agreement on economic goals and investment priorities. See also TRIPARTISM. **2.** INDICATIVE PLANNING, in which the government sets out investment and other targets for the economy and tries to get business and labour support. **3.** Social-democratic planning, in which the government nationalizes certain key industries or has a stake in them and directs their investment and other activities, influencing activity throughout the economy in the process. **4.** Total state planning, as practised in communist countries, where the government owns all the industries and sets economic targets that the managers of its own industries must meet.

In the MIXED ECONOMIES of most Western nations, the government engages in some kind of economic planning, however informal. Governments have many tools at their disposal to direct economic growth. These include not only the broad levers of fiscal and monetary policy, but a wide range of incentives and grants. One of the functions of the ECONOMIC COUNCIL OF CANADA is to set performance indicators for the country, indicating desired targets for economic growth, investment, unemployment, and inflation, for example. Economic planning is not confined to governments; most major corporations engage in long-term planning. See also CORPORATE STRATEGY.

economic rent In the case of natural resources, the surplus value that is generated from the sale of the resource, above and beyond the payment needed to satisfy the normal profit needs of the industry and the wage and salary demands of those who work in the industry. It is the surplus value of the resource itself. For example, when oil in Alberta and Saskatchewan was priced at two dollars a barrel in the early 1970s, this was sufficient to meet the needs of the industry and its workers and to produce a profit. The sudden increase in the price of oil after 1973 represented the economic rent of the oil. A key question when economic rent is produced, is who should get it; in the case of the oil, it is shared among the shareholders of the oil industry, the producing-province governments, and the federal government. See also RENT.

economic sanctions Measures to halt or restrict trade, investment, and other economic relations with a country or group of countries, as punishment for particular domestic or international behaviour, and thus to bring pressure, through the harmful effect of the sanctions, for a change in those policies. For example, in 1965 the United Nations adopted economic sanctions against Rhodesia, to force it to change its policies of racial discrimination. In 1935, the League of Nations voted sanctions against Italy after it invaded Ethiopia.

economic scarcity See SCARCITY.

economic self-sufficiency See SELF-SUFFICIENCY.

economic system The way in which economic life is organized; in particular, the way in which wealth and income are distributed, the means of production owned, and the way in which the public and private sectors influence consumption, investment, and savings. In a LAISSEZ-FAIRE economy the allocation of resources is left to market forces and the means of production are in private hands. In a MIXED ECONOMY, both government and private citizens determine the allocation of resources and own the means of production. In a totally planned economy, the government alone determines the allocation of resources and owns the means of production.

economic theory A descriptive statement about how the economic system or some part of it functions, and how economic performance, however defined, can be improved. Economic theories include both broad MACROECONOMIC theories, dealing with growth, consumption, investment, saving, prices, trade, money, and employment; and MICROECONOMIC theories, dealing with particular industries, labour markets, competition, and the firm. Many economic theories are identified with particular schools of economic thought, such as MERCANTILISM, CLASSICAL ECONOMICS, MARXIST ECONOMICS, NEOCLASSICAL ECONOMICS, KEYNESIAN ECONOMICS, POST-KEYNESIAN ECONOMICS, and MONETARISM.

economic warfare Actions to hinder the ability of an enemy to wage war. Methods can include the dumping of forged currency in the territory of an enemy to create confusion; the blockading of an enemy's ports to prevent the entry of vital materials; and the bombing or sabotage of the enemy's vital industrial, communications, and transportation centres, or reserves of essential supplies such as oil.

economics The study of choice in a world of scarcity. Economics examines how individuals, firms, and society decide what to produce, how it should be priced, how output should be distributed, and how all of these various activities are interrelated. It is concerned with finding ways to maximize welfare through the most efficient means of allocating scarce resources. Economists both develop economic principles or laws, and apply economic laws to achieve such goals as full employment and stable prices. See MACROECONOMICS, MICROECONOMICS, WELFARE ECONOMICS.

economies of scale Reductions in the average cost of production, achieved by increasing the volume of output and thus using the various factors of production more efficiently. By making use of advanced machinery, specialized labour, interchangeable parts, automation, large-scale distribution, and ongoing research and development, a firm should be able to produce a product much more efficiently. But these economies can only be achieved when the volume of production is high enough to justify the heavy capital investment and extensive division of labour; when production is high enough, the big, capital-intensive, highly specialized plant can produce at a much lower average cost than a similar but smaller plant.

This explains why, in many modern industries such as petrochemicals, mineral processing, computers, automobile assembly, and telecommunications, it is hard for small companies to survive, and why it is important to have access to large markets. In many instances, where the costs of innovation and of capital equipment are so high, access to large markets is essential if the benefits of economies of scale are to be achieved—or indeed, the investment in a new plant made. At some point, when MARGINAL COST equals AVERAGE COST, a plant will stop yielding economies of scale; it will then be at a point where DISECONOMIES OF SCALE begin, with each extra unit of output costing more than the average cost and thus being unprofitable. In other words, a plant can produce both too little and too much.

economist An individual who has been trained in economics and who makes his living by applying his economic knowledge to the problems of the real world, teaching economics or studying economics with the object of adding to human knowledge and understanding of how economic systems really work. An economist may work for a business, government, university, or other organization.

effective demand A term that means the actual consumption and investment that takes place in the economy as a result of existing purchasing power. It is the principal determinant of output and employment.

effective rate of interest The true rate of interest that is paid, at an annual rate, for a sum of money that is repaid in regular instalments of more than one per year. For example, $1,200 borrowed at an 18 per cent annual nominal rate of interest, and repaid in twelve monthly instalments, carries an effective rate of interest that is 19.86 per cent, since the borrower does not have the use of the entire

$1,200 for the full year but only of a declining unpaid balance.

effective rate of protection The real impact of a tariff on the price of a product, as opposed to the tariff rate listed in a customs schedule. Effective tariff rates are normally higher than the listed tariff schedule would suggest. For example, most countries charge lower tariffs on imported raw materials than on imported finished products; this means that the effective tariff on the VALUE-ADDED in the finished product is higher than the listed tariff for the product. Suppose you have a simple product that is half labour and half a raw material. If there is a 15 per cent tariff on the product itself and no tariff on the raw material, then the effective tariff rate on the labour half of the product is 30 per cent. This is the effective rate of protection.

effective tax rate The percentage of income paid out in tax. In the progressive-income-tax schedule, the marginal tax rate rises as taxable income rises; to determine the effective tax rate, the total income tax payable is divided by the total income on which it was paid. In a sales tax, the effective rate and the nominal tax rate are identical.

efficiency The most effective use or allocation of resources to yield the maximum benefits —for example, the lowest possible costs, or the satisfaction of the greatest number of people. Efficiency in the first sense—the effective use of resources—is often applied to individual firms in comparing how well they organize the productive process (labour, management, machinery, new technology) to achieve the lowest possible production cost for their products. But efficiency has a much broader meaning as well, referring to the way in which all of the various FACTORS OF PRODUCTION are used to achieve maximum output throughout the economy at the lowest cost, or to achieve a distribution of the output of society that results in the greatest degree of satisfaction. See PARETO OPTIMUM, WELFARE ECONOMICS, MONOPOLY, IMPERFECT COMPETITION.

An economy with a high level of monopoly power held by some factor or factors of production will have a low level of economic efficiency. PERFECT COMPETITION, in theory, should yield the highest level of economic efficiency.

egalitarianism The reduction or elimination of the great disparities between wealth and poverty in a society. Reducing such disparities is one of the basic aims of civilized societies, though there are great differences over how far they should be reduced. It is argued, for example, that near-equality of incomes would reduce the incentive to work hard, and thus lead to less innovation in society and a lower standard of living for everyone.

Some experts argue that the emphasis should be on equality of opportunity rather than on equality of result. Most societies aim for some kind of middle ground, with some emphasizing egalitarianism and others emphasizing incentives and opportunity. But experience shows that equality of opportunity by itself is insufficient to achieve a balanced distribution of wealth, since there are basic differences in the aptitudes of people. Moreover, those who inherit wealth start off in life well ahead of those who come from needy backgrounds; and even a person's earliest childhood can affect his ability to recognize and take advantage of opportunity in later life. Some techniques to achieve egalitarianism include free elementary and high-school education and subsidized university education, a PROGRESSIVE-TAX system, a CAPITAL-GAINS TAX, INCOME-MAINTENANCE PROGRAMS, and a WEALTH TAX. See John Porter, *The Vertical Mosaic* (Toronto, 1965); John Rawls, *A Theory of Justice* (Cambridge, Mass., 1971); and Arthur Okun, *Equality and Efficiency: The Big Tradeoff* (Washington, 1975).

elasticity The responsiveness in the supply or demand for a particular good or service to a change in its price. A particular good or service is said to be highly elastic if changes in price produce significant changes in its consumption or production; conversely, a product is said to be inelastic if its consumption or production shows little change, even with a significant price change. The consumption of French wines or chocolate bars may increase sharply if prices fall significantly, and vice versa. But, if the price of electricity or bread rises or falls, it may have only a modest impact on consumption. Elasticity is usually measured as the percentage change in supply or demand for each 1 per cent of change in price.

elasticity of demand The change in demand that results from a change in price. Usually, if the price of a good or service goes up, demand will fall. But the degree to which this happens varies widely among goods and services. Elasticity of demand attempts to measure the extent to which increases or decreases in price produce decreases or increases in consumption. Generally speaking, price changes for essentials will result in little change in demand; demand in such cases is said to be inelastic. Price changes for luxury goods, on the other hand, may have a large impact on demand; demand is then said to be highly elastic.

elasticity of supply The change in supply that results from a change in price. Usually, if the price of a good or service goes up, supply will increase and vice versa. But the degree to which this happens varies widely among goods and services and depends, among other things, on how fast producers can respond to price changes. For example, there may be a long delay between a sharp increase in the price of wheat or beef cattle and an increase in the supply of wheat or beef cattle. But if an industry is operating below capacity and there is an increase in demand for its product, it should be able to respond quickly. If producers are earning high profits, they can absorb lower prices; if they are producing at low profits, a lower price may lead to reduced production, and hence reduced supply.

Eldorado Nuclear Limited A federal crown corporation, formed in 1944, which mines and refines uranium and produces nuclear fuels. It reports to Parliament through the minister of ENERGY, MINES AND RESOURCES. In September 1979, the federal government said that it would be willing to sell the firm to private investors if they were willing to pay a fair price.

electric power Electricity generated principally from three sources: hydro-electric power, generated by installing dams and turbines on major rivers; thermal power, generated in power stations by burning oil, natural gas, or coal; and nuclear power, generated by using uranium in nuclear-power reactors. New sources of electricity include solar energy and the use of modern windmills.

electronic data-processing The use of computers and computer terminals to store and manipulate data according to programmed sequences. Typical applications include the maintenance of payroll records and production of paycheques, billing for credit-card systems, and inventory control.

electronic mail The transmission of letters over wire, radio, and communications-satellite systems to addresses with telex printers, facsimile receivers, and word-processing screens.

electronic payments system The use of advances in computers and telecommunications systems to eliminate largely the need for cash, cheques, and credit cards and to reduce substantially the paperwork in handling the payment of bills, mailing of pension and other cheques, and processing of customer accounts. Such a system would include point-of-sale terminals in stores, restaurants, airports, gasoline stations, and elsewhere, which would be connected to a master computer system that, in turn, would be connected to the computer systems of banks and other financial institutions. A sale would automatically be deducted from the customer's bank account and credited to the retailer's bank account, either immediately or on a specified date. Similarly, automated teller machines would, round-the-clock, handle withdrawals and deposits for individuals, accept instructions for the payment of utility and other bills, and carry out other such transactions. Paycheques, pensions, family allowances, and other such cheques could be automatically deposited, eliminating the need for a considerable volume of mail and reducing the risk of theft.

Although the electronic-payments system is not here yet, it is on the way. Some key questions have yet to be answered, though. Can the system be made secure against computer theft?

Can privacy be protected? Who should operate the system? And should there be one system, or competitive systems?

embargo A government-imposed ban on the import or export of certain goods for health, national-security, political, or other reasons. An embargo may be imposed on cattle and beef imports from a country where cattle disease has broken out; similarly, Canada may restrict the export of technologically advanced products to the Soviet Union or its satellites if the products have an important military application. See EXPORT AND IMPORT PERMITS ACT.

embezzlement A form of WHITE-COLLAR CRIME: an embezzler, through fraudulent accounting methods and other techniques, steals money or other assets from his employer. Embezzlement is an offence under the Criminal Code.

emergency power The power of the federal government to exercise, in times of emergency, powers that would normally belong to the provinces. This power—the "Peace, Order, and good Government" clause in section 91 of the BRITISH NORTH AMERICA ACT—has been used not only in wartime but, in 1975 for the first time, in peacetime. In 1975, the federal government established the ANTI-INFLATION BOARD to implement a nation-wide system of wage and price controls, although the power to control wages and prices to a large extent falls under provincial jurisdiction. In 1976, the SUPREME COURT OF CANADA ruled that this power could be invoked in "very exceptional" economic circumstances, such as sharply rising inflation during a period of high unemployment.

emigration Movement out of a particular country or part of a country.

eminent domain A government's right to expropriate private property for public use. In return, it is required to pay fair compensation. The government may exercise its right of eminent domain, for example, if it needs land for a highway, airport, public housing, or park. Usually, a government will try to buy the land it needs without having to resort to the exercise of its expropriating powers. However, in cases where a large number of properties have to be acquired or where property owners either refuse to sell or are demanding unreasonable prices, the right of eminent domain is exercised. It is an example of the limitations that exist on the rights of private property.

employed person As defined in the monthly LABOUR-FORCE SURVEY produced by Statistics Canada, a person who, during the survey week, did any work at all, full- or part-time, or who had a job but was not at work due to illness, disability, personal or family responsibilities, bad weather, a labour dispute, or vacation. Work, as defined in the survey, includes any kind of work for pay or profit, including unpaid family work that contributes directly to the operation of a farm, business, or professional practice owned or operated by a related member of the same household.

employer association An organization of employers formed mainly to engage in joint bargaining with labour unions, either in a metropolitan area or in a province. Without such organizations, industry-wide bargaining cannot take place. See, for example, CANADIAN CONSTRUCTION ASSOCIATION.

employer of last resort The idea that government should employ anyone who is able and willing to work but who cannot get a job in private industry due to an insufficient number of jobs. This could include payments by government to charitable agencies and similar groups to hire unemployed people to do socially useful tasks. The federal government's 1973 *Working Paper on Social Security in Canada* recommended that community employment programs be established to provide useful local jobs in areas of chronic unemployment, or for people who, due to handicaps or for other reasons, had a hard time finding jobs. See also GUARANTEED ANNUAL INCOME.

employment agency A middleman who recruits full- and part-time workers for employers and helps people to find jobs. Some deal exclusively in the placement of executive or professional staff and others specialize in providing temporary workers. The largest employment agency is the CANADA EMPLOYMENT AND IMMIGRATION COMMISSION, operated by the federal government. Most agencies are privately operated.

Employment and Immigration, Department of A federal government department created in 1976 to develop and evaluate manpower training, immigration, the labour market, unemployment assistance, and temporary job programs, and to project and analyze trends in labour markets. Its actual programs are implemented by the CANADA EMPLOYMENT AND IMMIGRATION COMMISSION.

employment index A monthly index published by Statistics Canada that measures changes in employment in different industries and regions. The publication is *Employment, Earnings and Hours*.

employment standards Laws governing basic conditions of work, such as minimum wages, overtime pay, public holidays, vacations with pay, pregnancy leave, and payment of wages.

end product A manufactured product ready for use by a consumer or by a producer of consumer goods and services.

endogenous change A change in economic activity resulting from another economic variable—inflation caused by excessive demand, for instance. See also EXOGENOUS CHANGE.

endorsement The signature on the back of a CHEQUE or other bill of exchange, which transfers ownership to another person.

endowment A gift of revenue-producing assets to a charitable, religious, or educational institution. Only the revenue is spent; the assets, which may consist of shares, bonds, mortgages, real estate, or even rights to a patent, are kept intact.

endowment insurance A form of life insurance under which the person insured receives the insurance benefit, provided he lives to a certain age. If he dies before then, his beneficiaries get the money.

energy-conversion efficiency A measure of how much energy is needed to convert a primary source of energy into energy for use by consumers—how much energy it takes, for example, to convert the bitumen from tar sands into crude oil, or how much coal has to be burned to create so much electricity.

energy efficiency The amount of energy required to operate an automobile, machine, appliance, or other product. One of the most important ways of conserving energy is to reduce the amount of energy needed to achieve a given level of output — to reduce the amount of gasoline needed to carry an automobile a mile or a kilometre, for example.

Energy, Mines and Resources, Department of The federal government department responsible for energy, mineral, and geological policies and programs. The department is divided into three major branches: **1.** The energy-policy branch, which formulates and administers federal energy programs, is responsible for energy pricing, offshore drilling, and other discussions with the provinces, carries out energy-supply and -demand analysis, funds research programs for new energy technologies such as solar energy, promotes energy conservation, undertakes energy negotiations with other countries, and represents Canada in the INTERNATIONAL ENERGY AGENCY. **2.** The mineral-policy branch, which monitors national mineral supply and demand, represents Canada in international negotiations on mineral policy, such as in commodity associations dealing with copper and other such minerals, deals with the provinces on mineral policies, administers federal aid to gold-mining communities, and is responsible for federal mineral-resource-development policies. **3.** The science and technology branch, which includes the GEOLOGICAL SURVEY OF CANADA, the Polar Continental Shelf Project, the Canada Centre for Remote Sensing, federal mapping and survey work, and the funding of mining and energy research. The minister of Energy, Mines and Resources reports to Parliament for ATOMIC ENERGY OF CANADA LIMITED, the ATOMIC ENERGY CONTROL BOARD, ELDORADO NUCLEAR LIMITED, the NATIONAL ENERGY BOARD, URANIUM CANADA LIMITED, and PETRO-CANADA.

Energy Resources Conservation Board Alberta's energy regulatory agency; it regulates the activities of the oil, gas, coal, and electric-power industries. Its specific functions include the determination of Alberta's natural-gas reserves and Alberta's own future needs, and hence the level of reserves available for export to other parts of Canada or the United States; the issuing of permits to drill oil and gas wells; the approval of construction plans for oil or gas pipelines to be built within the province; the administration of a system of prorationing, to determine the level of oil production; the approval of exploration and development plans for coal mining; the approval of new electricity-transmission lines in the province; and the responsibility for reviewing the need for new electric-power plants. The board was established in 1938 as the Oil and Gas Conservation Board; it was given new powers and its name was changed in 1971. It is based in Calgary.

Energy Supplies Emergency Act A law passed by Parliament in 1979 giving the federal government sweeping powers to allocate oil, natural gas, and coal in the event of shortages caused by international events, natural disasters, technical failures, strikes, embargoes or other emergencies. With the declaration of an emergency by the government, an Energy Supplies Allocation Board can be created to implement emergency plans, allocate supplies, set prices, and, on instruction from the government, introduce a system of rationing, including gasoline rationing. The law replaced a similar 1974 law that lapsed in 1976. Its passage in 1979 also implemented a Canadian promise to the INTERNATIONAL ENERGY AGENCY to put in place a law permitting the government to control the allocation of oil supplies in an emergency.

Engel's law As a family's income increases, it spends a declining proportion of that income on food and other necessities; in other words, poor families spend a much greater share of their income on food and necessities than do rich families. The law was formulated by Ernst Engel, a German statistician, in the nineteenth century. It led to the notion of DISCRETIONARY INCOME.

enhanced recovery The additional oil or natural gas recoverable, in addition to that which can be recovered through natural production processes. It is the total oil or natural gas that can be recovered through SECONDARY and TERTIARY RECOVERY.

Enterprise Development Program A federal program established in 1977, to provide last-resort loan guarantees for companies attempting to modernize or reorganize their facilities to meet import competition, and to provide grants to companies developing new technology in Canada. The program is administered by a sixteen-person Enterprise Development Board, half of whose members are from the public sector, half from the private sector; the board approves loan guarantees and grants. The minister of INDUSTRY, TRADE AND COMMERCE is responsible to Parliament for the program.

entrepreneur A person who either starts his own business or aggressively expands an existing one. An entrepreneur is normally identified with risk-taking and new ideas, as opposed to a businessman or corporate executive, who keeps an existing business going. The entrepreneur is considered vital in a dynamic economy, since he is often in the forefront of innovation, new technology, and new products and services. The entrepreneur frequently assumes all of the financial and other risks, and the failure rate among entrepreneurs is high. But the entrepreneurial spirit may be essential if new ideas and products are to be introduced; in fact, it is sometimes regarded as a FACTOR OF PRODUCTION.

entry and exit The ease with which firms are able to enter or leave an industry. In a world of PERFECT COMPETITION there should be no BARRIERS TO ENTRY for new firms; in a world of IMPERFECT COMPETITION, there are, by definition, barriers to entry.

Environment, Department of the The federal government department, created in 1971, that is responsible for the administration of Canada's environmental laws to protect air, water, and soil, the administration of laws for the protection of the country's renewable resources (such as forests, wildlife, and birds), the operation of Canada's weather services, the implementation of rules and regulations set down by the INTERNATIONAL JOINT COMMISSION, and the encouragement of land-use planning.

Renewable-resource programs include the Canadian Wildlife Service and the Canadian Forestry Service. In addition, an Inland Waters Directorate manages water-resources programs within Canada or with the United States and carries out river-basin studies under the Canada Water Act. The Lands Directorate carries out land-use planning and has completed a Canada Land Inventory. The Department's Environmental Protection Service deals with air and water pollution, under the Clean Air Act and the Canada Water Act, and with solid wastes and environmental contaminants, under the Environmental Hazards Act. The department operates a number of research facilities, including the Canada Centre for Inland Waters at Burlington, Ontario, and the Atmospheric Environment Service, which does research in addition to providing weather services.

environmental-impact statement A document that spells out the impact on the environment of a proposed project. It is a form of cost-benefit analysis, and, while such statements usually deal with the physical and ecological impact, they can also include the social or cultural impact—say, of a new airport on a small community. Most provinces and the federal government have an environmental-impact process. The NATIONAL ENERGY BOARD, for example, requires an environmental-impact statement for proposed pipelines. Alberta requires a statement on projects where the surface of the land is to be disturbed—for surface coal mines and tar-sands plants, for example. Ontario's Environmental Assessment Board has wide powers to hold hearings on most major projects with environmental implications, although the cabinet can grant exemptions from hearings and overturn the board's decisions.

equal pay As set out in the federal Human Rights Code, the principle that men and women should receive equal pay for work of equal value. The provinces have similar requirements, but none that go so far as the federal law. In Ontario, for example, it is illegal for an employer to pay male and female workers different rates of pay for substantially the same work performed in the same establishment, when performing the work requires substantially the same skills, effort, and responsibility, and when it is performed under similar working conditions. Ontario permits exemptions for seniority, merit, pay based on volume of output, or similar differentials. The federal law came into effect in 1978. Most provincial laws came into effect earlier; for example, the Ontario law came into effect in 1975. The federal law is enforced through the CANADIAN HUMAN RIGHTS COMMISSION; provincial laws tend to be enforced through the employment-standards branches of their labour departments.

equalization payments Unconditional transfer payments, through the federal government, from the rich provinces to the poorer provinces to help equalize per capita tax revenues from coast to coast. They are based on the principle that every Canadian, regardless of where he or she lives, is entitled to a basic level of public services, such as health care, education, and social assistance, and infrastructure, such as roads, sewer systems, and water supplies. Without equalization payments, Canadians living in the poorer provinces would either have to accept a much lower level of basic public services, or impose even higher levels of taxation on their residents, something that would only contribute to a more rapid exodus of people and even greater difficulties for those who remained.

Equalization payments are of great importance to some provinces; in Atlantic Canada, they account for about 25 per cent of provincial revenues, in Quebec and Manitoba about 10 per cent, and in Saskatchewan less. Equalization agreements are renewed every five years, and the current legislation, the Federal-Provincial Fiscal Arrangements and Established Programs Act 1977, expires in 1981.

Under the act, provincial taxing capacity is measured in twenty-nine different categories, such as income tax, sales tax, school tax, and resource royalties, and compared to the national average. In some cases—for example, in a province with low per capita income—the taxing capacity under the provincial income-tax system will be below the national average and the province will be entitled to equalization; in other areas—say, resource revenue—the same province may have taxing capacity in excess of the national average. The plusses and minuses of the twenty-nine categories are added together, and the net result constitutes the total equalization payment. A province that has a negative net result gets an amount equal to that total; a province that has a positive net result gets no money but does not have to contribute that amount to the federal government for redistribution. Instead, the federal government collects the money for equalization payments from its own tax base. Thus, if, for example, Alberta's oil and gas revenues lead to higher equalization payments for other provinces, the greatest share is raised in Ontario since Ontario taxpayers form the largest portion of the federal tax base.

In the 1977 amendments, a special formula was established to calculate resource revenues, because oil and gas royalties and sales of leases for oil and gas exploration were yielding such high revenues in Alberta and Saskatchewan that even Ontario would have qualified for equalization payments in the near future. In the new formula, only 50 per cent of resource revenues qualify in considered resource-tax capacity, but the definition of resource revenue was extended to include all renewable and non-renewable resources, forest-industry payments for timber licences and stumpage, for example. The 1977 amendments also included the transfer of 9.143 tax points from the federal to provincial governments to replace conditional payments for medicare, hospital insurance, and post-secondary education, with a provision for equalization for the poorer provinces.

Since then, further changes have been proposed, including the phase-out of equalization for revenue from the sale of oil and gas leases and the exclusion of Ontario, Alberta, and British Columbia from qualifying for equalization, through a formula that would deny equalization to any province whose per capita personal income was greater than the national average for three consecutive years, up to the year for which equalization might be sought.

Equalization payments date back to the tax-rental agreements between Ottawa and the provinces that commenced during the Second World War. But provinces did not then qualify for the modest equalization payments available unless they signed a rental agreement. After the Second World War, Quebec did not sign the 1947 and 1952 tax-rental agreements, and so did not get equalization payments. Under a new formula in 1957, Quebec again participated. The present system of equalization payments came into being in 1967.

equilibrium The state of the economy when supply and demand are equal. Equilibrium is rarely, if ever, achieved, because of constant changes in technology, products, prices, and tastes. But economic forces are assumed to be moving towards or away from equilibrium at any point in time. Until the time of JOHN MAYNARD KEYNES, economists believed that equilibrium would result in FULL EMPLOYMENT, but Keynes showed that it was possible to have both equilibrium and high unemployment. Equilibrium is assumed to represent a balance in which there is no tendency for economic variables to change.

equilibrium price The sustainable price in a competitive market; the intersection of the DEMAND AND SUPPLY CURVES; the point at which the amount that producers will readily supply and the amount that consumers will readily buy is equal. Higher prices will lead to a reduction in the amount that consumers will buy; lower prices will lead to a reduction in the amount that producers will supply. See also ALFRED MARSHALL.

equity **1.** Fairness, as in the tax system. The best way to achieve equity or fairness in the tax system is to base it on the ABILITY-TO-PAY PRINCIPLE OF TAXATION. **2.** See EQUITY CAPITAL.

equity capital The capital in a firm that represents ownership. The owners of the equity capital—the firm's common shares—are entitled to all the assets and income of the firm after all the claims of creditors have been paid.

SHAREHOLDERS' EQUITY consists of all assets minus all liabilities; it is represented on a firm's balance sheet, and consists of the original capital put into the firm by its backers, subsequent issues of common shares sold to the public, and RETAINED EARNINGS. While equity capital represents ownership and is only entitled to a return after creditors have been paid, DEBT CAPITAL consists of loans that must be repaid with interest but represent no permanent claim on the firm's assets. DIRECT INVESTMENT is equity investment; critics of the high level of foreign ownership in the economy argue that Canada should have encouraged more debt capital and less equity capital in financing the growth of the economy.

erosion The loss of land caused by the removal of rock and soil, through flooding or by the action of the wind, rain, or rivers and other bodies of water. During the 1930s, drought and strong winds combined to sweep away large areas of topsoil in the prairie provinces. The PRAIRIE FARM REHABILITATION ADMINISTRATION was established by the federal government in 1935 to restore prairie farmlands and to prevent a recurrence of the 1930s dustbowls.

escalation clause A clause in a contract providing for an increase in the price of goods or services if costs rise above a specified level. In a construction project, the contractor may require a clause that relates the final price of the project to changes in the cost of labour or building materials. Some union collective agreements give union members an automatic wage increase if the rate of inflation rises above a certain level. See also COLA CLAUSE.

escape clause A clause in a contract that permits one of the parties to withdraw or alter his obligations without penalty under certain specified circumstances. In a treaty granting preferential tariffs on imports from less-developed countries, there may be an escape clause that permits the importing country to suspend the preferential tariff on a particular product if imports of the product reach such a level that they cause severe problems for a domestic industry. See also FORCE MAJEURE.

escrowed shares Shares of a corporation that cannot be sold by the owner until certain conditions have been met, or without the approval of a regulatory authority, such as a stock exchange or provincial securities commission. In the meantime, the owner is entitled to receive dividends, if any, and to vote the shares at company annual meetings.

Escrow arrangements are often made when a small mining or oil and gas company buys exploration properties, paying the vendors with TREASURY SHARES. The vendors have to deposit their shares with a trustee until a specified amount of exploration work has been done or a specified length of time has passed. This is to prevent the sale of the shares on the market before exploration has been carried out. Similarly, the founders of a new company who have issued shares to the public may be required to hold their shares in escrow for a period of time to ensure that the founders do not abandon the business once they have sold shares to the public.

established reserves Oil or natural-gas reserves that can be recovered under current technology and present and anticipated economic conditions, and are already specifically proved by drilling, testing, or production; plus contiguous recoverable reserves that are interpreted to exist, based on geological, geophysical, or similar information, with reasonable certainty. See also ULTIMATE POTENTIAL RESERVES.

estate The real and personal property owned by an individual after debts have been deducted. The word is normally used to describe the net worth of an individual at the time of his or her death.

estate tax The tax imposed on an estate before its proceeds are distributed to the beneficiaries of the estate. The estate tax was abolished in Canada at the end of 1971. It was replaced by the CAPITAL-GAINS TAX, with deemed realization of capital gains included in the tax return of the individual in the year of his or her death. An exception is made for those assets in the estate transferred to the spouse. See also SUCCESSION DUTY, GIFT TAX.

estimates The document submitted to Parliament each year by the president of the TREASURY BOARD, spelling out in detail the spending plans of the government for the new fiscal year that begins on 1 April. The process of preparing the estimates is a long one, taking close to a year. The first stage is the preparation by individual departments and agencies of two spending budgets in March of the previous year. The "A" budget outlines the expected costs of continuing existing levels of service for the next three years. The "B" budget outlines proposals for new spending programs, along with their estimated costs. The Treasury Board reviews these in the context of overall spending guidelines set out by the cabinet —the so-called FISCAL FRAMEWORK—and the government's priorities as determined by the cabinet. By August, the Treasury Board has sent the "A" and "B" budgets back to individual departments and agencies, stating the resources that will, in fact, be allocated to each department or agency. By October, the individual departments and agencies are required to resubmit their spending plans in the context of the government's priorities. Departments and agencies then appear before a committee of cabinet, the Treasury Board committee, where they are questioned on their plans. This is where changes and cuts are negotiated or ordered. This work has to be completed by February, when the estimates document, the so-called Blue Book, is tabled in Parliament. The spending plans of different departments must then be referred, by 1 March, to individual committees of the House of Commons, where the spending plans are examined in detail and cabinet ministers and senior officials are called to explain their spending activities and answer questions from MPs.

The estimates must be reported back to the House of Commons by 31 May. If not, they are considered to have been approved by their respective committees. The House of Commons discusses the spending plans in the supply debate, which extends over several months. Actual spending is approved through votes on various APPROPRIATION ACTS. These authorize the payment of funds for specific purposes out of the government's CONSOLIDATED REVENUE FUND.

Some of the spending in the estimates does not require approval each year, since it is mandatory under other legislation passed by Parliament—for example, legislation setting up EQUALIZATION PAYMENTS to the provinces, or social benefits, such as old-age pensions and family allowances to individuals. However, such spending is included in the annual estimates to give a more complete picture of government spending. In addition to the main estimates presented to Parliament each February, there are supplementary estimates covering new spending programs introduced after the start of the fiscal year or additional spending under existing programs. The FINANCIAL ADMINISTRATION ACT permits the government to spend unauthorized money in an emergency through SPECIAL GOVERNOR GENERAL'S WARRANTS. These warrants must be published in the *Canada Gazette* within thirty days, so that the public has been given notice, and they must be reported to Parliament within fifteen days of the opening of the next session.

This would be the timetable for the estimates for the 1980–81 fiscal year that begins on 1 April 1980. 1 April 1979: Deadline for departmental "A" and "B" budgets, followed by review of the budgets by the Treasury Board in line with priorities and spending ceilings set down by the cabinet. August 1979: The Treasury Board returns spending plans to individual departments and agencies, setting out the allocation of spending resources and government priorities. October 1979: Departments and agencies resubmit spending plans to the Treasury Board; the Treasury Board committee of cabinet, over the next several months, reviews, changes, and approves spending plans. February 1980: Estimates are tabled in Parliament. 1 March 1980: Deadline for government to refer departmental and agency spending estimates to Parliamentary committees for scrutiny by MPs. 1 April 1980: Start of the 1980–81 fiscal year. 31 May 1980: Deadline for parliamentary committees to report back to the House of Commons on spending plans.

Eurobond market That part of the EUROCURRENCY MARKET that deals in government and corporation bonds. It started up in the mid-1960s when U.S. corporations began floating bond issues with overseas investors who held U.S. dollars. It is not the largest part of the Eurocurrency market; even in the area of medium-term securities (those running from five to ten years), Eurocurrency bank loans are much more significant. Some Canadian corporations, provincial utilities, and governments, including municipalities and school boards, have borrowed in the Eurobond market, but it is not a significant market for Canadian borrowers. Canadian banks and investment dealers are active in helping to place issues of Eurobonds. The Eurobond market also provides one-way surplus PETRODOLLARS from the oil-rich Arab nations, which can be recycled in the form of medium-term and long-term loans to other nations and to corporations.

Eurocurrency A vast pool of currencies held by banks and investors outside the jurisdiction of the national economies issuing the currencies, and hence outside any national currency controls and other regulations. Eurodollars are U.S. dollars loaned and borrowed in financial markets outside the United States; Euromarks are German marks loaned and borrowed outside Germany; Euroyen are Japanese yen loaned and borrowed outside Japan.

Eurocurrency market The financial market for a variety of national currencies loaned and borrowed outside the jurisdiction of the countries issuing the particular currencies. The substantial portion of Eurocurrency funds is loaned and borrowed in Europe, although there are smaller Eurocurrency markets in other parts of the world. The Eurocurrency market today is the largest and least regulated money market in the world. It includes Canadian dollars on deposit in banks in London and elsewhere outside Canada. The Eurocurrency markets are closely linked by telex connections among such centres as New York, London, Frankfurt, Brussels, Toronto, and Zurich. Funds flow into the Eurocurrency market, seeking short-term investments in banks and other financial institutions; these institutions in turn lend the money out, largely in the form of medium- and long-term loans, or in EUROBONDS. A large portion of PETRODOLLARS or surplus funds from oil-rich Arab nations are recycled through Eurocurrency markets.

There is concern on the part of some monetary authorities about the lack of regulation of Eurocurrency markets, which, according to some estimates, amount to more than $450 billion in financial assets, and there is talk of imposing some kind of regulatory régime. One cause for concern is the extent to which LESS-DEVELOPED COUNTRIES have borrowed in Eurocurrency markets; there is a fear that some countries will be unable to pay the interest they owe, let alone repay the principal. It is feared that if this were to happen, it would trigger a collapse of some financial institutions, much like the collapse of financial institutions in the depression of the 1930s, following the failure of the big Austrian bank, the Credit-Anstalt, in 1931. Another concern is that speculators in the Eurocurrency market exercise an excessive influence on the exchange rates of individual countries by their ability to buy and sell currencies, and thus make it much harder for central-bank authorities and international institutions to achieve stability in foreign-exchange markets.

While Eurocurrency markets today represent a pool of many different currencies, the market began with the pool of surplus U.S. dollars held outside the United States. Starting in the late 1950s, U.S. banks and corporations began borrowing U.S. dollars held by Europeans. The U.S. dollar remains the most significant currency traded in Eurocurrency markets.

Eurodollar U.S. dollars loaned and borrowed outside the United States, and hence outside the control of U.S. monetary and securities authorities. See EUROCURRENCY, EUROCURRENCY MARKET.

European Commission A body of thirteen members, representing the nine nations in the EUROPEAN ECONOMIC COMMUNITY, that implements the decisions of the member-state governments as reached by the EUROPEAN COUNCIL OF MINISTERS and advises EEC member-governments on policy options. It also administers the vast staff of the EEC headquarters in Brussels and other parts of the world, and prepares the annual EEC budget.

Each of the EEC commissioners heads a department of the EEC administration, such as energy, industrial policy, or foreign affairs. The commissioners are appointed by the member-governments (two each from France, Germany, Italy, and Britain, and one each from Luxembourg, the Netherlands, Belgium, Denmark, and Ireland) for renewable four-year terms. The president and five vice-presidents are appointed from among the commission members for renewable two-year terms. While appointed by member-state governments, the commission is supposed to think European and act on behalf of the community, rather than for the countries from which individual members come. The EUROPEAN PARLIAMENT has the power, by a two-thirds vote, to fire the commission, and also controls the spending budget of the commission.

European Council of Ministers The main decision-making body of the EUROPEAN ECONOMIC COMMUNITY, it consists of one cabinet minister from each of the EEC member-governments. The job of each minister is to represent the interests of his or her own country. The council meets several times a month, with the ministers attending depending on the subject under discussion. Topics can range, for example, from energy, agriculture, and trade, to monetary affairs, competition policy, consumer protection, or foreign relations; in each case, the appropriate cabinet minister for each of the member-countries attends.

Decisions are made by a majority vote, which must include the vote of at least six members. Germany, France, Italy, and Britain have ten votes each, Belgium and the Netherlands five votes each, Denmark and Ireland three votes each, and Luxembourg, two votes. A member can seek a unanimous vote on a matter that it considers to be of national interest; some broader questions, such as the admission of new members to the EEC, also need a unanimous vote. The council has an advisory committee of permanent representatives, which consists of the ambassadors accredited by the member-states to the EEC. All decisions by the council must be based on proposals of the EUROPEAN COMMISSION. See also EUROPEAN PARLIAMENT.

European Currency Unit (ECU) A central bankers' currency, based on a basket of EUROPEAN ECONOMIC COMMUNITY members' currencies, introduced in 1979 as part of the EUROPEAN MONETARY SYSTEM. The ECU is being used to settle debts among central banks of EEC members participating in the EMS, and also plays an important role in determining the need for currency intervention and in funding credit facilities in the EMS. It may become an important reserve asset, not only for EEC members but for other nations as well.

European Economic Community (EEC) A common market agreed to by six Western European countries (France, West Germany, Italy, the Netherlands, Belgium, and Luxembourg) in March 1957 under the Treaty of Rome, and which came into being on 1 January 1958. Since then, the EEC has been expanded to include, as of 1 January 1973, Britain, Ireland, and Denmark. New members scheduled to join in the early 1980s are Spain, Portugal, and Greece. Canada has a trade and investment treaty with the EEC, signed in 1976. See FRAMEWORK AGREEMENT FOR COMMERCIAL AND ECONOMIC CO-OPERATION BETWEEN CANADA AND THE EUROPEAN COMMUNITIES.

The original purpose of the EEC was to achieve free trade among its members, which was accomplished by 1 January 1968, with a common external tariff levied on all imports from outside the EEC. But the broader goal of the EEC is to achieve a high level of economic, social, and political integration, with widespread co-operation on industrial, scientific, and regional-development policies, the free movement of labour and capital within the EEC, and agreement on EEC-wide policies on agriculture, competition policy, transportation, communications, international economic policy, monetary arrangements, and foreign policy.

The EEC is managed by a EUROPEAN COMMISSION made up of appointed representatives of EEC members, plus a supporting bureaucracy, based in Brussels, which reports to a EUROPEAN COUNCIL OF MINISTERS, consisting of one cabinet minister from each EEC state. The EUROPEAN PARLIAMENT, whose members were directly elected for the first time in 1979, is expected to strengthen the evolution of political union within the EEC, although the powers of the parliament are strictly limited. It cannot initiate EEC-wide legislation, or even reject it, but it does control the EEC budget. EEC agricultural policy is administered through the COMMON AGRICULTURAL POLICY, which guarantees minimum prices to farmers and finances them through levies on member-states and agricultural imports. The EEC purchases surplus farm commodities at the support or intervention price; the common external tariff on farm products is the difference between the import price and the price just above the intervention or support price. A European Investment Bank was created within the EEC to assist regional development. The EUROPEAN MONETARY SYSTEM, which came into effect in 1979, is an attempt to provide more stable exchange rates among EEC members and to bring the monetary and other economic policies of EEC members into closer harmony. Labour has had greater freedom of movement within the EEC since 1969, when work permits and visas were no longer required; but residence permits are still needed. Workers and their families moving from one EEC state to another are assured of the same social-security rights.

In recent years, EEC commissioners in such areas as industrial policy have put greater emphasis on the development of high-technology European corporations, increased scientific effort, and greater energy co-operation. A number of former colonies of EEC members have associate membership in the EEC, which entitles them to preferential tariff treatment. While full economic, social, and political union are held out as long-term goals, the EEC is still many years away from becoming a United States of Europe. It still lacks a common currency, a common tax system, and a mechanism to harmonize effectively monetary and fiscal policy or political institutions that have effective power over the member-states.

European Free Trade Association (EFTA) A free-trade area established by seven European nations in 1959 under the Stockholm Agreement, as an alternative to the EUROPEAN ECONOMIC COMMUNITY. Its members were Britain, Sweden, Norway, Denmark, Switzerland, Portugal, and Austria. While the members agreed to the eventual elimination of tariffs on trade among themselves (this was achieved by the end of 1966), they did not establish a common external tariff, as the European Economic Community had, on trade with other countries. Each member of EFTA was left free to make whatever kind of commercial arrangements it wished with non-EFTA nations. Nor did EFTA members adopt other policies to integrate their economies, as the European Economic Community had. In 1961, Finland became a member, and in 1970 Iceland joined; membership of Finland and Austria in the European Economic Community was out of the question, due to conditions of neutrality imposed on them by the Soviets.

EFTA was shattered in 1973, when Britain and Denmark became members of the European Economic Community. In 1979, Portugal was accepted for membership in the European Economic Community, with the intent of becoming a full member in the early 1980s. The EEC has negotiated free-trade agreements with EFTA members who decided not to seek membership in the community. Thus, the sixteen nations of the EEC and EFTA are joined together in a free-trade arrangement.

European Monetary Agreement An arrangement made by the European members of the ORGANIZATION FOR ECONOMIC CO-OPERATION AND DEVELOPMENT to facilitate the settlement of outstanding payments balances among the European countries and to provide short-term balance-of-payments assistance, through a European Fund, to European nations participating in the agreement. It came into effect in December 1958, with the BANK FOR INTERNATIONAL SETTLEMENTS acting as its agent.

The European Monetary Agreement was a further step in the postwar restoration of currency convertibility and the establishment of common procedures for European countries in dealing with balance-of-payments problems. After the Second World War, when Europe was economically shattered and currency transactions rigidly controlled, the Intra-European Payments Agreement was set up under the EUROPEAN RECOVERY PROGRAM (Marshall Plan) to facilitate trade among European nations. This was replaced in 1950 by the European Payments Union, organized by the Organization for European Economic Co-operation (later the OECD). The purpose of the European Payments Union was to act as a clearinghouse to settle balances among members, to provide short-term balance-of-payments assistance to members, and to encourage the European nations to pursue a multilateral approach to balance-of-payments arrangements, rather than a network of bilateral arrangements. In 1958, the European Payments Union was replaced by the European Monetary Agreement.

European Monetary System (EMS) A system of FIXED EXCHANGE RATES within the EUROPEAN ECONOMIC COMMUNITY, agreed to in July 1978 and implemented in March 1979. Although it is an EEC initiative, Britain did not join and Italy entered only after it had negotiated special treatment. None the less, the EEC is committed to the creation of a European Monetary Fund by December 1980, which, combined with the EMS, is expected to move the EEC further towards monetary union, and perhaps, eventually, a common European currency.

The purpose of the EMS is to stabilize currency rates among EEC members and thus to encourage trade and investment within the community. Fluctuating international exchange rates in the 1970s caused constant changes in exchange rates between different EEC members and thus discouraged investment decisions, since businesses could never be sure of how different EEC-member exchange rates would relate to one another. Under the EMS, each nation set its exchange rate in relation to the others at a fixed level. Each currency could move up or down by 2.5 per cent against the others (in Italy's case, 6 per cent), and both the deficit and the surplus nations within the EEC are required to take steps to ensure that their currencies do not move away from those fixed exchange rates by more than 2.5 per cent. Intervention in exchange markets is to be with European currencies rather than U.S. dollars.

The EUROPEAN CURRENCY UNIT was created as a central-bank currency that could be used by the EMS central banks as a reserve asset to settle balance-of-payment deficits and to help define exchange rates, to determine the need for intervention, and to finance EMS credit facilities for deficit countries. EMS members deposited 20 per cent of their gold and U.S.-dollar reserves in exchange for credits denominated in ECUs, and agreed to a credit arrangement of about twenty-five billion ECUs or thirty-three billion U.S. dollars.

Countries within the EMS can alter their exchange rates, but only under specific conditions, much like the fixed-exchange-rate system operated by the INTERNATIONAL MONETARY FUND until the start of the 1970s. The EEC architects of the system hope that EMS will reduce currency instability among members, expand investment, force EEC members to deal with economic problems such as inflation, take pressure off the U.S. dollar by developing the ECU as an alternative reserve asset, and move the community towards monetary union.

European Parliament A consultative body of 410 elected representatives from the nine member states of the EUROPEAN ECONOMIC COMMUNITY. It has limited powers, but is of growing importance. In 1979, the members of the European Parliament were directly elected for the first time in the largest democratic elections in history. About 175 million people were qualified to vote. Prior to this, a smaller chamber of 198 members had been appointed from the parliaments of member countries.

Members of the European Parliament do not form a government and opposition, nor can they pass laws. But they review all EEC-wide laws drafted by the EUROPEAN COMMISSION for approval by the EUROPEAN COUNCIL OF MINISTERS, and they can pass resolutions concerning these laws. The commission frequently incorporates such resolutions into its revised draft laws. Similarly, the parliament can initiate new policies by passing resolutions calling for EEC action. The parliament also controls the EEC budget, mainly by setting the spending budget of the community; it has no say over the raising of revenue. It can also fire the European Commission, investigate some forms of spending, establish investigating committees that can summon EEC officials and commissioners, extract and publish information on the way the community is run, and take other EEC institutions to the European Court of Justice for an infringement of EEC treaties.

European Recovery Program The program named after the U.S. Secretary of State General George C. Marshall as the Marshall Plan. It followed a speech made by Marshall at Harvard University in June 1947, in which he proposed generous U.S. aid for the recovery of Europe, provided that the Europeans agreed to work together and developed specific plans for their economic recovery. The offer was extended to all European nations, including the Soviet Union and Eastern Europe, but was taken up only by the nations of Western Europe.

Sixteen European nations met in Paris in 1947 at a meeting that led to the formation of the Organization for European Economic Co-operation the following year. Its task was to co-ordinate the use of Marshall Plan assistance and to ensure that the aid was being employed properly. In 1948, the U.S. Congress passed the Economic Co-operation Act, authorizing the spending of money under the Marshall Plan. Between 1948 and 1951, when the program was terminated, the U.S. provided between eleven and twelve billion dollars of assistance to Europe.

The Marshall Plan was also important to Canada, which was experiencing severe balance-of-payments problems following the Second World War. Following lengthy negotiations with the United States, the U.S. government agreed that Marshall Plan funds could be used by European countries to purchase goods and services from Canada. As a result, more than one billion dollars was spent on Canadian goods and services by European nations using Marshall Plan funds; these purchases played an important role in improving Canada's balance-of-payments situation in the period before the Korean War.

ex dividend Without dividend. Dividends are payable to owners of common shares registered on a particular date. If the share is sold after that particular date and before the dividend is mailed out, the seller and not the new owner will receive the dividend cheque.

ex interest A calculation made in the sale and purchase of bonds. If a bond is sold, say, three months before the next annual interest payment is due, the seller's price will include a calculation for his share of the interest (three-quarters, in this case). The purchaser will get this back, since he will be entitled to the full year's interest when it is paid.

ex officio A position held by an individual by virtue of another post he holds, rather than because of his personal aptitudes. For example, the deputy minister of ENERGY, MINES AND RESOURCES is an *ex officio* member of the board of directors of PETRO-CANADA; the deputy minister of FINANCE is an *ex officio* member of the board of directors of both the BANK OF CANADA and CANADA DEVELOPMENT CORPORATION. The president of a corporation is usually an *ex officio* member of all senior corporate committees.

excess capacity The situation that exists when the actual output of a firm or industry is less than that needed to utilize fully all the resources or factors of production employed in the firm or industry. In economic terms, it means that a firm or industry is operating at a level from which it is still possible to decrease its average cost; its MARGINAL COST is still lower than its average cost. By producing more, it is possible to make marginal cost and average cost equal, the production level that achieves the lowest possible price for the consumer. Excess capacity may be caused by fluctuations in the business cycle or the existence of too many firms in an industry. It is the second situation that concerns economists, because the presence of too many firms means that ECONOMIES OF SCALE cannot be achieved, and the consumer must pay the cost of chronic excess capacity through higher prices. Statistics Canada publishes quarterly figures showing capacity utilization in the manufacturing industry.

excess cash reserves The surplus of deposits with, and notes of, the BANK OF CANADA held by the chartered banks above and beyond the primary reserves that must be maintained under the BANK ACT. By altering the level of excess cash reserves relative to what the chartered banks wish to hold, the Bank of Canada puts upward or downward pressure on interest rates, thereby affecting the growth of money and credit in the economy. Manipulation of the level of excess cash reserves is an important tool of MONETARY POLICY. See also PRIMARY RESERVE RATIO, SECONDARY RESERVE RATIO.

excess demand The situation that exists when the demand for goods and services in the economy is greater than the supply available to meet the demand. As a result, consumers bid up prices to pay for the same goods and services, and inflation results. See DEMAND-PULL INFLATION. The normal response of government authorities is to check the growth of demand by raising taxes, cutting back on money-supply expansion, and increasing interest rates.

excess-profits tax A tax to reduce profits arising from unusual and temporary business conditions. For example, countries usually impose such a tax during wartime, when demand is abnormally high and most industries are operating at full capacity. Canada imposed the Business Profits War Tax in 1916 and introduced an excess-profits tax in 1939, which was made much more severe in 1940. Such a tax is usually levied at an extremely high rate, up to 100 per cent, on profits in excess of a normal or base period.

excess supply The situation in which the quantity of goods or services available from suppliers at a particular price is greater than the demand from consumers. This should cause producers to reduce prices so that consumers will increase their purchases.

exchange 1. One of the principal activities studied in economics, the process in which one good or service is accepted for another. In a world of increased specialization, the need for an efficient means of exchange is vital. The use of money as a medium of exchange enables a wide variety of goods and services to be produced and the benefits of COMPARATIVE ADVANTAGE to be widely pursued. **2.** A place where trading occurs. For example, a stock exchange is a place where buyers and sellers of shares can negotiate prices and carry out transactions.

exchange control Any restriction by a government on the sale or purchase of foreign currencies by its own citizens. Such restrictions may range from a ban on the export of the country's currency or restrictions on the repatriation of profits from a subsidiary to its foreign parent, to restrictions on the convertibility of a currency into other currencies, and government regulation of the amounts of foreign exchange that can be obtained and the purposes for which it can be used. During the Second World War, for example, Canada limited the purchase of U.S. dollars by Canadians to essential imports and essential travel. See also FOREIGN EXCHANGE CONTROL BOARD. The purposes of foreign-exchange controls are to discourage imports and foreign travel, to prevent the outflow of capital or otherwise to solve balance-of-payments problems, to preserve scarce foreign-exchange reserves, and to boost domestic employment opportunities.

exchange-fund account Canada's FOREIGN-EXCHANGE RESERVES of U.S. dollars, gold, SPECIAL DRAWING RIGHTS, and other reserve assets, maintained by the BANK OF CANADA on behalf of the Canadian government. The bank's transactions in foreign-exchange markets are made from this account. The Department of FINANCE publishes monthly statistics showing changes in foreign-exchange reserves, thus enabling analysts to monitor the intervention activities of the bank, and hence its policy on Canada's exchange rate.

exchange rate The price of a national currency—the Canadian dollar, for example—in terms of another. It is a way of stating the number of Canadian dollars it will take to buy a unit of a foreign currency, or the number of units of a foreign currency it will take to buy a Canadian dollar. If the exchange rate of the Canadian dollar is 90 U.S. cents, this means that one Canadian dollar buys 90 U.S. cents, or that it takes $1.11 Canadian to buy a U.S. dollar. Changes in the exchange rate of a country's currency can make a difference in the price of its imports and exports and the cost of foreign travel. See also FIXED EX-

CHANGE RATE, FLOATING EXCHANGE RATE, VALUE OF THE CANADIAN DOLLAR, INTERNATIONAL MONETARY FUND.

excise tax A tax levied on a particular commodity or service; it is levied on the manufacturer in the case of domestically made goods, or on the duty-paid value of imported goods. The Excise Tax Act levies the tax on domestic and imported spirits, beer, wine, tobacco products, jewellery, slot machines, playing cards, matches, airline tickets, snuff, and gasoline. Exported goods are exempt. Although the tax is levied on manufacturers and importers, the tax itself is shifted on to the consumer, who pays it in the retail price of the product.

exclusive dealing An agreement between a supplier and a customer, under which the customer agrees not to handle the products sold by the supplier's competitors. Such agreements are common in FRANCHISE contracts.

exclusive economic zone The right of a coastal state to control the living resources, such as fisheries, and non-living resources, such as oil, natural gas, and seabed minerals, of the sea for two hundred miles off its coast, while allowing freedom of navigation to other states beyond twelve miles. The coastal state also has the responsibility to manage the conservation of all natural resources within the two-hundred-mile limit. This was the position adopted at the third session of the Third U.N. Conference on the Law of the Sea, in 1975. Canada declared its adoption of a two-hundred-mile fishing zone, but not an exclusive economic zone, effective 1 January 1977.

exclusive listing An agreement between a real-estate agent and the owner of a house or other property, that guarantees the real-estate agent a specified commission if the property is sold during a specified period (say, the next thirty days), whether or not the real-estate agent actually brings about the sale. See also MULTIPLE-LISTING SERVICE.

executive A person in a business corporation, government agency, or any other institution, who is responsible for setting or implementing assigned tasks or policies and who has the decision-making authority to carry out his or her responsibilities. The amount of authority is related to the responsibilities of the executive. As his or her responsibilities increase, so does the decision-making authority.

executor The person named in a WILL to see that its instructions are carried out. The most important responsibility of a executor is to see that the ESTATE of a deceased person is distributed to beneficiaries properly.

exogenous change A change in economic activity resulting from a non-economic cause —for instance, a sharp increase in food prices, resulting from widespread flooding. See also ENDOGENOUS CHANGE.

expectations Attitudes or beliefs about future economic activity. While expectations are hard to measure, they can have a significant impact on future trends. Consumers who expect interest rates to rise may delay the purchase of homes or major consumer products, thus slowing down business activity. Wage-earners who expect inflation to continue or to get worse may demand even bigger wage increases in collective bargaining, thus adding to inflation pressures. Businessmen who are gloomy about future profits because they expect costs to rise sharply or because they see few signs of future market growth will delay investment plans, thus slowing down economic growth. Economists now use business- and consumer-confidence surveys to help measure changes in expectations. But this remains a crude tool. Business- and consumer-confidence surveys are published quarterly by the CONFERENCE BOARD IN CANADA.

expense account Money spent by business, union, government or other officials for travel, entertainment, reading material, and other such items to help them carry out their jobs. Such expenses are tax deductible, but the organization claiming them must be able to show the Department of NATIONAL REVENUE that the expenses are related to business, and must be able to provide receipts if they are requested.

exponential growth A continuous, compound

rate of growth—compound interest in a bank account, for example, unrestrained population growth, or continuous economic growth. Exponential growth is often expressed in terms of doubling. For example, if savings, population, or the economy grow by 1 per cent a year, they will double in 70 years; but if they grow at 4 per cent a year, they will double in 18 years, and if they grow at 10 per cent a year they will double in 7 years. The doubling time is equal, roughly, to 70 divided by the growth rate.

Export and Import Permits Act The act giving the federal government the power to control the volume and destination of exports and to regulate imports. Its underlying purpose is to ensure sufficient essential commodities or products to meet essential Canadian needs, and to protect domestic industries against damaging imports, through the maintenance of an import-control list that sets limits on imports—for example, on textiles from different countries. Through export controls, the government can prevent the sale of strategic products where that sale might be detrimental to the security of Canada and its allies, restrict the sale of Canadian products or commodities at a time of international shortages by requiring that Canadian needs be met first, require the processing of natural resources before they are exported, and prevent the excessive export of Canadian natural resources during a period of depressed prices.

export consortium A group of companies submitting a common bid on a foreign project or acting together to promote the sale of a product, such as lumber, which they all make. Canada's COMBINES INVESTIGATION ACT inhibits companies in related industries from acting together for domestic sales, but permits them to work together on an export sale. Such a consortium may be formed to bid on an airport, power station, pulp and paper plant, and other such projects, or generally to promote the export sale of Canadian commodities.

export controls Any kind of limitation on exports, either by quantity, destination, or level of processing. Uranium exports can only be exported after Canada's own needs have been ensured, and after the importing nation has satisfied Canada that it will meet certain safeguard conditions to prevent the uranium from being used to make nuclear weapons. Nuclear reactors can only be exported to countries that agree to similar safeguard conditions. Militarily significant products cannot be exported to the Soviet bloc, Cuba, Vietnam, North Korea, or China. See also EXPORT AND IMPORT PERMITS ACT, TRADE EMBARGO.

Export Development Corporation (EDC) A crown corporation established to help expand Canada's export trade. It provides various kinds of assistance to Canadian corporations, such as: **1.** Export-credit insurance, which provides Canadian firms with payment of up to 90 per cent if foreign buyers fail to pay for purchases of Canadian goods and services, including fees to engineering companies, payments for patent rights and advertising, for auditors, design companies, and technological services. **2.** Long-term loans to foreign buyers, usually foreign governments, of Canadian capital equipment, such as nuclear-power stations or hydro-electric equipment, rail and transit systems, airports, hospitals, pulp and paper plants, or telecommunications systems, or for the purchase of Canadian services, such as engineering or feasibility studies. **3.** Guarantees to Canadian corporations investing abroad against up to 85 per cent of losses caused by nationalization or political upheaval. **4.** Guarantees to financial institutions against losses in financing a Canadian exporter or a foreign importer of Canadian goods and services.

The Export Development Corporation plays a significant role in the financing of Canadian trade, even though Canada has a large banking system. The corporation was established in 1969, replacing its predecessor, Export Credits Insurance Corporation, a crown corporation established at the end of the Second World War as part of Canada's postwar RECONSTRUCTION program. The EDC reports to Parliament through the minister of INDUSTRY, TRADE AND COMMERCE.

export incentive Any form of government assistance to increase exports. Incentives may range from government help in developing foreign markets to subsidized export financing, tax rebates or concessions, or special grants for export marketing, transportation, or other costs. The GENERAL AGREEMENT ON TARIFFS AND TRADE limits the kinds of incentives individual countries can offer, but individual countries still manage to find ways to provide export incentives. The ORGANIZATION FOR ECONOMIC CO-OPERATION AND DEVELOPMENT has set limits on the use of subsidized or concessional interest rates in export financing.

export licence Government approval to export a particular commodity or product to a particular country or to any country. An export licence is needed in Canada to export strategic goods of possible military value to the Soviet bloc, China, Cuba, or certain other countries. An export licence is also required in Canada to export uranium or nuclear-reactor systems or natural gas. In the event of a shortage of a particular commodity, the federal government may invoke the EXPORT AND IMPORT PERMITS ACT to ensure that exports do not deprive Canadians of a needed commodity because non-residents are willing to pay much higher prices.

export multiplier The total increase in a country's gross national product that results from an increase in exports. See also MULTIPLIER.

export-price index A monthly index of changes in the level of export prices, published by Statistics Canada. See also TERMS OF TRADE.

export quota A restriction on the level of exports from a producer country. A quota may be imposed by the exporting country to protect domestic consumers from shortages. But in international trade, importing countries sometimes negotiate export quotas with exporting countries to protect their own domestic industries—in the steel, television-set, and textile industries, for example. Canada has negotiated a number of such "voluntary" export-quota agreements with Asian countries to limit textile shipments. Within the GENERAL AGREEMENT ON TARIFFS AND TRADE, exporters and importers have negotiated the MULTI-FIBRE ARRANGEMENT, which provides for bilateral quotas on wool, synthetic, and cotton products.

export-restraint arrangement An agreement negotiated by Canada with countries that are exporting to Canada, in which the exporting countries agree to limit their exports of specified products to specified ceilings.

export subsidy See EXPORT INCENTIVE.

export tax A tax or duty on an exported commodity. Such taxes are unusual. But Canada has levied an export tax on oil, under the PETROLEUM ADMINISTRATION ACT, since 1974. The price of oil in Canada has been controlled and held below the world price since 1973. The purpose of the tax is to recover, on export sales, the difference between the price charged Canadians for oil and the world price U.S. refineries would pay to get the same grade and quantity of oil. Thus, the export tax includes not only a calculation of the world price for a comparable grade of Canadian oil, but other factors, such as the freight cost of delivering alternative oil to the U.S. refiner. The export tax is earmarked to subsidize the price paid for oil imports in eastern Canada.

exports Goods and services produced in one country that are sold and shipped to another. Merchandise exports—sometimes called visibles—consist of products or commodities. Service exports—sometimes called invisibles—consist of banking and insurance services, transportation, travel and tourism, technology and know-how, and the receipts from foreign investment, such as interest and dividends. Merchandise exports account for just over 20 per cent of the Canadian GROSS NATIONAL PRODUCT. Merchandise and service exports together account for just over 25 per cent of the GNP.

expropriation The forced sale of one's property. The power to expropriate may be exercised by government or its agencies and, where provided by law, by private companies, such as railways and pipeline companies. A government may expropriate a corporation: for example, Saskatchewan's expropriation of potash-mining companies, Quebec's proposed expropriation of a private asbestos-mining company, or the expropriation by Quebec and British Columbia of private power companies. Or it may expropriate land: for an airport, for public housing, for expansion of a university, for a right-of-way for a new highway, for a power-transmission line, or for a park.

The principal federal law is the 1970 Expropriation Act, which sets out the procedures that must be followed and provides certain protections to those whose property is being acquired. The act includes procedures for pre-expropriation notice and hearings to deal with objections to the planned acquisition, procedures for the actual expropriation and possession, and for compensation, including the arbitration of disputes over price. The compensation code is based on FAIR MARKET VALUE. Generally speaking, governments use expropriation as a last resort when property owners refuse to sell, or hold out for excessive prices. Sometimes governments resort to expropriation when they need to acquire a very large area of land that may be owned by several hundred property owners. There are also provincial laws dealing with expropriation.

External Affairs, Department of The federal government department responsible for looking after Canada's interests abroad and responding to foreign nations that have interests in Canada. While many aspects of Canada's foreign commercial relations and trade promotion are in the hands of the Department of FINANCE or the Department of INDUSTRY, TRADE AND COMMERCE, the Department of External Affairs also plays a role in setting trade, investment, and other such policies, and takes part in negotiations on energy, communications, transportation, and science. It is responsible for Canadian relations with the United States, the European Economic Community, Japan, the Soviet bloc, China, and other areas, along with Canada's participation in the United Nations. Canada's relations with the INTERNATIONAL MONETARY FUND, the GENERAL AGREEMENT ON TARIFFS AND TRADE, and the ORGANIZATION FOR ECONOMIC CO-OPERATION AND DEVELOPMENT are conducted through the departments of Finance or Industry, Trade and Commerce. But External Affairs deals with environmental questions, law-of-the-sea negotiations, and relations with the LESS-DEVELOPED COUNTRIES. The secretary of state for External Affairs is responsible to Parliament for the INTERNATIONAL JOINT COMMISSION and the CANADIAN INTERNATIONAL DEVELOPMENT AGENCY. The department was set up in 1909.

external diseconomies The harmful effect that one person's actions have on others. These damages can be widespread, or may affect some quite specific group. Examples of external diseconomies affecting the public at large are air and water pollution from factories, the radioactive fallout from aboveground nuclear testing, and emissions from automobiles; an example of an external diseconomy affecting a specific group would be the loss of livelihood by fishermen due to mercury poisoning in waters where fishing was once commercially successful.

In recent years, economists and policymakers have tried to find ways of identifying such external diseconomies and attributing them as much as possible to those who do the damage. For example, pollution-control requirements in the pulp and paper, mineral-smelting, and steelmaking industries are an attempt to make the polluter pay; in economic terms, the cost of an external diseconomy has thus been attributed to its source, so that it appears in the price system. But some examples cannot be costed in this way. For example, while it is possible to legislate fuel-efficient cars, with the car companies recovering the costs in the price they charge to consumers, it is more difficult to attribute other costs of the automobile. In street congestion, for example, it might be unfair to levy a charge against every user of the road, since this would impose a heavier burden on those with low incomes using a public facility.

external economies The beneficial effect that one person's actions can have on others. Research and development that results in inventions that help everyone is an example. The external economies resulting from the invention of electricity, the telephone, petrochemical fertilizers, modern pharmaceuticals, and the computer are enormous. Smaller but still important examples might include the decision by one farmer to plant a long line of trees to prevent soil erosion; his neighbours would also benefit. Or a firm may carry out a skill-training program for new workers; other firms can benefit, since they can hire workers away once they have been trained. Because of the external economies they produce for the public at large or for particular industries or groups, governments can justify spending on research and development, universities, and other such activities.

external public debt The proportion of the debt of all levels of government and their agencies that is owed to foreigners. In Canada's case, most such foreign debt is incurred in foreign currencies, making the future cost of repaying those obligations vulnerable to fluctuations in exchange rates.

externalities The direct impact that one person's action has on others. The impact can be harmful; see EXTERNAL DISECONOMIES. Or it can be beneficial; see EXTERNAL ECONOMIES. The study of externalities, or social costs and benefits, has become an increasingly important area of economics in recent years. In particular, there has been a strong effort to identify external diseconomies and recover their costs—through taxes or pollution-control laws, for example; at the same time, there has been much more effort to identify social benefits resulting from investments in research and development, health care, and education.

extractive industry A natural-resource industry that exploits oil, gas, and other minerals from the earth or from underneath bodies of water. Some economists also include the forest-products industry.

extraordinary item In a corporate annual report, an unusual gain or loss that affects net profits. It can be a one-time gain from the sale of an asset, or a write-off of the loss on an unsuccessful business venture; in a corporate EARNINGS STATEMENT, it is added to (a gain) or deducted from (a loss) net operating profit.

extrapolation A technique of economic forecasting that consists of projecting past trends forward in time. For example, if per capita consumption of refined-oil products has averaged 5 per cent a year for the past twenty-five years, a forecaster might calculate the demand in, say, 1990 by assuming that the same rate of growth will continue. The danger in this technique is that it does not take account of factors that could affect per capita consumption—in this case, a sharp rise in oil prices that might lead to significant energy-conservation measures, smaller and fuel-efficient cars, or a switch to electric power or natural gas.

extraterritoriality The attempt by one country to extend its laws to cover activities taking place in another country. This has been a major source of contention between Canada and the United States, because the United States has tried to apply its antitrust, securities, and international trade laws to the Canadian subsidiaries of U.S. corporations. For example, the United States has used its Trading with the Enemy Act to ban U.S. exports to Cuba and China; in the process, it has also tried to stop Canadian subsidiaries of U.S. firms from trading with Cuba, China, or other countries on its embargo list. Similarly, the United States has extended its antitrust laws to the activities of its firms abroad, including those in Canada, while the Securities and Exchange Commission has claimed the right to require registration of any corporation in which 30 per cent of the stock is owned by U.S. citizens. U.S. legislation countering the Arab world's anti-Israel boycott also applies to the foreign subsidiaries of U.S. firms.

Canada and the United States have had a long series of discussions on this issue. In January 1959, Canadian Justice Minister E. Davie Fulton and U.S. Attorney General William Rogers agreed that in future the two countries would consult with each other whenever it appeared that the interests of one would be affected by action taken under the other's anti-combines laws. In November 1969, Canadian Justice Minister Ron Basford and U.S. Attorney General John Mitchell extended the Fulton-Rogers understanding to Canada-U.S. co-operation in the prosecution of international restrictive business practices, such as cartel activities and restrictive practices of MULTINATIONAL CORPORATIONS. New efforts to improve Canada-U.S. co-operation and to avoid conflict over extraterritoriality were initiated with the visit to Canada, in January 1978, of U.S. Vice-President Walter Mondale. Thus, the United States has not given up the right to apply its laws beyond its borders but, in Canada's case, it has agreed to deal with the issue case by case, and to work through the Canadian government.

Canada is also an active member of the Committee of Experts on Restrictive Business Practices in the ORGANIZATION FOR ECONOMIC CO-OPERATION AND DEVELOPMENT. The committee works on international agreements dealing with restrictive business practices.

F

face value See PAR VALUE.

factor A financial institution that takes over the accounts receivable of a firm, at a discount, and collects the money owing. This saves small manufacturers, for example, the trouble of operating their own credit departments, and keeps them supplied with WORKING CAPITAL. The firm using the factor may have to get the factor's approval if credit passes a specified limit for certain customers or before granting credit to a new customer. Factors are usually equipped to run credit checks. The chartered banks are among the financial institutions offering factoring services. There is a trade association, the Factors and Commercial Financing Conference of Canada.

factors of production Productive resources used in a variety of combinations to create additional goods or services; sometimes called inputs. The three traditional factors of production are: **1.** Land, which includes not only land but also the quality of the soil, water, natural resources, and forests. **2.** Capital, which includes the accumulated stock of factories, transportation systems, commercial buildings, computers, and other machinery and equipment. **3.** Labour, which includes not only physical capacity but all the accumulated knowledge and skills of people. Some economists take the view that entrepreneurial or management ability and innovation should be considered additional factors of production. In any enterprise, production results from the combination of factors of production; managerial know-how should lead to the most efficient mix. Rent is the income earned by land, interest the income earned by capital, wages and salaries the income earned by labour, and profit the income earned by entrepreneurial effort and innovation.

fair-employment laws Laws designed to protect workers against discrimination based on race, colour, religion, or national origin. The federal and provincial governments have various laws to provide such protection. The federal law is contained in the Canadian Human Rights Code. It prohibits discrimination by employers, unions, or employment agencies in any place of employment under federal jurisdiction. It bans the use of any form or application for employment, any job advertising, or any written or oral statement that suggests any discrimination or preference based on race, colour, religion, or national origin. The CANADIAN HUMAN RIGHTS COMMISSION provides protection against job discrimination.

fair market value The amount that a buyer would readily pay for something and at which a seller would readily sell it in a free market. It is a price freely arrived at without pressure or obligation on either side.

fallacy of composition A fallacy based on the assumption that something that is good for each person alone is therefore good for the entire community. It may be good for each individual to save more and spend less; but if everyone did this, the economy would slow down, unemployment would increase, and everyone would end up worse off.

family Statistics Canada has three definitions: **1.** For census purposes, a family is a husband and wife with or without children, or a parent with one or more unmarried children, living together in the same dwelling. **2.** In surveys on family income and income distribution, a family is considered to be an economic unit, or a group of individuals sharing a common dwelling and related by blood, marriage, or adoption, a definition that includes all relatives. **3.** In family-spending surveys, a family is defined as a group of people who depend on a common or pooled income for all major expenses in the same dwelling, a definition that includes students sharing an apartment, for example.

family allowance A monthly allowance paid to families with children to help cover the costs of child maintenance. The program was started in 1944, but has undergone a number of changes since then. Originally, all families received the same tax-free benefits, depending on the age of the children up to eighteen. In 1972 the program was changed, with the allowances being sharply increased and indexed to changes in the consumer price index. But the allowances henceforth were treated as taxable income. In 1979, family allowances were frozen, but a new supplementary scheme was introduced to provide additional payments to families with lower incomes if they claimed it by filing an income-tax return. Thus, the revised version provides a minimum universal payment, but uses the tax system to redistribute additional income to families who need it. The legislation allows individual provinces to have their own set of benefits, provided that they meet certain federal criteria, and provided that the cost is the same as if federal benefits were being paid. Alberta and Quebec have opted for their own schemes.

family business A business owned and operated by a family; usually, a small business. In most instances the various members of the family all work in the business. Many of today's largest corporations started off as family businesses.

farm A holding of land on which agricultural products are raised or grown with the purpose of selling this output to others. For census purposes in Canada, a farm is defined as a holding of at least one acre or 0.4 hectares and with sales of agricultural products of fifty dollars or more. There are four main types of farms, according to Statistics Canada. They are: **1.** Livestock farms, where cattle, hogs, dairy products, and poultry for eggs and meats are raised. **2.** Grain farms, which produce wheat, oats, barley, flax, and rapeseed. **3.** Special-crop farms, which produce vegetables, fruits, potatoes, and various root crops. **4.** Other farms, including those that combine livestock and grain production.

farm-assistance programs The range of federal and provincial programs to sustain farm income, to modernize and expand farms, to finance irrigation and drainage, to develop better farming methods and improved seeds and livestock through research and development, to promote the sale of farm products, and to assist farm ownership. Such programs are designed to ensure that the country has an efficient agricultural industry, and to make sure that individual farmers get a fair share of national income. Many farm-assistance programs deal with specific problems, such as crop failure, drought, depressed prices, farm credit, transportation, and rural poverty. See also AGRICULTURAL STABILIZATION BOARD, CANADIAN DAIRY COMMISSION, CANADIAN WHEAT BOARD, CROP INSURANCE, FARM CREDIT CORPORATION, FARM MARKETING BOARDS, FARM PRODUCTS MARKETING AGENCIES ACT, PRAIRIE GRAIN ADVANCE PAYMENTS ACT, PRAIRIE FARM REHABILITATION ADMINISTRATION.

farm cash receipts The cash income of farmers from the sale of farm products, advance payments for grain, and payments from various farm-assistance programs. Farmers must pay all their costs out of these receipts. The figure is published monthly by Statistics Canada. See also FARM NET INCOME.

Farm Credit Corporation (**FCC**) A crown corporation set up in 1959 to replace the Canadian Farm Loan Board. It administers federal farm-credit programs that help groups of farmers form syndicates to purchase jointly farm machinery, equipment, and buildings; it provides mortgage loans to individual farmers as well. It also administers the federal government's Small Farm Development Program, which, since 1972, has helped marginal farmers to retire early or to stop farming, by buying up their land. Where possible, the land is sold to other farmers who can use the land to improve their productivity.

Farm Improvement Loans Act A federal law to help farmers get loans from banks and other financial institutions for new machinery, livestock, installation of farm electrical systems, major repairs, fencing and drainage, repair and construction of farm buildings, and for the acquisition of additional land. The act, administered through the Department of Finance, provides guarantees to financial institutions making such loans.

farm-machinery arrangement An arrangement between Canada and the United States permitting the duty-free movement of farm machinery between the two countries. In 1913, at the urging of its farmers, the United States removed its tariff on most farm machinery produced in Canada. In 1944, Canada granted duty-free access for U.S.-made farm machinery. The purpose of the tariff elimination was to help farmers get farm machinery at lower prices; about 95 per cent of farm machinery traded between the two countries is shipped duty-free.

farm marketing boards Boards established under federal or provincial law to set prices of farm products, to allocate production quotas to farmers, to market farm products and collect levies from farmers to pay marketing-board costs, and to maintain reserve stocks for some commodities. Membership is compulsory for farmers. Individual provinces operate their own marketing boards, but a number of national marketing agencies have been formed for commodities in which there is considerable interprovincial or international trade. Important national marketing boards include the CANADIAN WHEAT BOARD (1935), the CANADIAN DAIRY COMMISSION (1966), the Canadian Egg Marketing Agency (1973), the Canadian Turkey Marketing Agency (1974), and the Canadian Chicken Marketing Agency (1979).

Both Ottawa and the provinces acted in the 1930s to set up producer marketing boards, but initial efforts were turned back by the courts. British Columbia passed a Produce Marketing Act to set up marketing boards for certain fruits and vegetables, but this was ruled unconstitutional by the Supreme Court of Canada in 1931, on the grounds that it affected interprovincial trade and that the levy on producers was an INDIRECT TAX. The federal Natural Products Marketing Act of 1934 tried to establish a system of national marketing boards, but it was ruled unconstitutional on the grounds that it interfered with provincial powers. Finally, the British Columbia Natural Products Marketing Act of 1936 was upheld by the courts, and became the model legislation for all of the provinces. It permitted provincial marketing boards to regulate and control, within provincial boundaries, the pricing, production, transportation, storage, and marketing of farm products, and to collect levies from farmers to pay the costs. In 1956, Parliament passed the Agricultural Products Marketing Act, which allowed it to delegate to provincial marketing boards the power to regulate interprovincial and export trade and to collect levies for such purposes. This allowed the provinces to use a federal law to raise money for a provincial purpose. In 1960, the Supreme Court upheld the federal law, and declared that marketing-board levies on producers were not an indirect tax but a contractual payment.

In 1972, Parliament passed the FARM PRODUCTS MARKETING AGENCIES ACT, which permitted the provinces and Ottawa to work together to form national farm marketing boards. Since then, national marketing boards have been formed for eggs, turkeys, and chickens. Today, about 60 per cent of farm cash income is earned through marketing boards, with the products controlled ranging from poultry, eggs, honey, and hogs, to milk, fruit, grains, tobacco, soybeans, and maple syrup. Farmers maintain that marketing boards lead to more stable prices and protect them against boom-bust cycles. In the long run, they argue, this benefits the consumer, because it ensures adequate production at reasonable prices. Consumer critics contend that marketing boards lead to higher prices by subsidizing inefficient farmers through quotas, thus preventing efficient farmers from producing more at less cost.

farm net income The annual income that farmers have left over for family income, personal taxes, and new investments, after paying their farm expenses. It includes an estimate for the value of farm products consumed on the farm. Farm net income is calculated by adding together the cash receipts farmers get for the sale of their products, supplementary payments from various farm-assistance programs, and income in kind, which includes not only farm products consumed on the farm but an imputed rental value for the farm dwelling; and then deducting farm expenses, such as fuel, electricity, fertilizer, commercial feed, interest on farm loans, machinery, wages to farm labour, and depreciation. In calculating the role of agriculture in the gross national product, Statistics Canada calculates a second version of farm net income, which includes changes in the value of livestock and crop inventories.

Farm Products Marketing Agencies Act A federal law passed in 1972 that permits the establishment of national farm marketing agencies and boards for specific agricultural products when provincial governments see a need. Such a need may occur if it is difficult to market a farm product effectively within the jurisdiction of individual provincial marketing boards because of extensive interprovincial trade. Under the act, national farm marketing agencies have been established for eggs, turkeys, and chickens. The federal agencies work with their provincial counterparts; they have no direct dealings with local farmers. The act also established a National Farm Products Marketing Council, which monitors the performance of national agencies and assists the provinces to establish new marketing agencies when they wish.

fascism An authoritarian political system that retains private industry and private property but subjects them to extensive government control. So long as they co-operate with the state, corporate leaders are able to run their enterprises and earn profits; co-operative business leaders may fare handsomely in a fascist state. Labour, on the other hand, loses its rights to organize and to engage in collective bargaining.

fast write-off A tax incentive to encourage new investment by business. Instead of depreciating, for tax purposes, a new investment over five to ten years, business firms are permitted, but for a limited period only, to depreciate new investments at a much faster rate —in, say, a two-year period. This increases the after-tax income of the firm in the first two years of the project, and reduces the initial cost of the investment. Although such schemes have been included in federal budgets in the 1960s and 1970s, research shows that they may have only limited impact on investment decisions.

feasibility study The examination of a proposed project to see whether it makes technical and financial sense. This type of review is made before any major capital project is undertaken.

featherbedding A rule imposed by a union in a collective agreement to increase artificially the number of jobs in an organization. Such rules may limit the number of bricks a bricklayer may lay in a day, break a job down into many different segments, each requiring a different worker, or require workers to repeat the work already performed automatically by a machine.

fecundity The capacity of a woman to bear children, as opposed to fertility, which is the actual bearing of children. See also FERTILITY RATE.

Federal Business Development Bank (FBDB) A crown corporation that came into being in 1975, replacing the Industrial Development Bank. Its purpose is to help business expansion in Canada by providing loans to businesses that have difficulty in obtaining money on commercial terms. It also provides management training and counselling for small business, and is empowered to make EQUITY investments if it so chooses. It reports to the minister of INDUSTRY, TRADE AND COMMERCE.

Federal Court of Canada A federal court created in 1970 to hear appeals by citizens against the rulings or actions of federal government agencies and departments, including claims against the Crown, and appeals on the actions of federal boards, tribunals, and other commissions. This includes appeals from assessments under the Income Tax Act and the Citizenship Act. The Federal Court also hears claims by the Crown and adjudicates disputes between citizens over intellectual-property violations, such as the infringement of copyright, trademarks, or patents. The Federal Court as well hears complaints on the manner in which federal boards, commissions, or tribunals have reached decisions or are conducting hearings—complaints, for example, that a tribunal has failed to observe a principle of natural justice, has acted beyond its jurisdiction, or has conducted its hearings in a capricious manner.

Federal Environmental Assessment and Review Office A federal review agency established in 1973 to assess the environmental impact of federal projects. When a federal department finds that a project could have significant environmental impact, the minister refers the project to the review office, which appoints a panel of experts to make an assessment. The project cannot proceed until the minister of the ENVIRONMENT has reached a decision on the panel's report. The originator of the project must prepare an ENVIRONMENTAL-IMPACT STATEMENT.

federal-provincial conference An important institution in the Canadian federal system, which brings the federal and provincial governments together to deal with important issues that concern them both. Although there is no reference to federal-provincial conferences in the BRITISH NORTH AMERICA ACT or in law, they have come to play an important negotiating and co-ordinating role in setting economic, energy, tax, government-spending, and many other policies. In addition to meetings of the prime minister and the provincial premiers on the constitution, the economy, or other matters of concern, there are federal-provincial conferences on a regular basis on finance, energy, mining, consumer laws, communications, labour, industrial development, health, social policy, and law. Such conferences have increased in importance as the actions and policies of the federal and provincial governments have come increasingly to affect one another. They are attended by the relevant ministers from the federal and provincial governments; the federal cabinet minister usually chairs such conferences.

There are two types of federal-provincial conference: continuing conferences, which meet regularly to discuss common problems in such areas as labour relations, consumer laws, finance and social policy; and ad hoc conferences, which are called to deal with specific problems. The continuing conferences are supported by working committees of officials from the federal and provincial governments; if the meetings of the officials are included, there are more than five hundred federal-provincial meetings a year. To facilitate such meetings, the federal government, in 1973, established the Canadian Intergovernmental Conference Secretariat, to provide staff support for the organization of federal-provincial conferences. See also CONFERENCE OF FIRST MINISTERS, FEDERALISM.

Federal-Provincial Relations Office An office responsible to the prime minister, created in 1975 out of the federal-provincial-relations division of the PRIVY COUNCIL OFFICE. The role of the office is to assist the prime minister and the minister of state for Federal-Provincial Relations in their responsibilities for federal-provincial affairs, to help individual government departments to deal with federal-provincial issues, and to increase federal-provincial consultation on a wide range of issues. The office organizes CONFERENCES OF FIRST MINISTERS, monitors provincial views of federal programs and provincial policies that affect federal responsibilities, and advises the cabinet on federal-provincial matters.

Federal Reserve System The central bank system of the United States. It was created in 1913. There are twelve regional Federal Reserve banks in the United States and a national board of governors, operating under the chairman of the Federal Reserve Board, based in Washington. The Federal Reserve Board sets reserve requirements for U.S. banks, supervises the banking system, sets interest rates, reviews the activities of district reserve banks, controls the production of currency, and takes part in the Open Market Committee (which also includes the presidents of five federal-reserve banks, including always the president of the Federal Reserve Bank of New York). The Open Market Committee determines monetary policy and exchange-rate policy. The Federal Reserve System operates in the open market through the Federal Reserve Bank of New York. The chairman of the Federal Reserve is appointed by the U.S. president for a fixed term; his appointment must be approved by the U.S. Senate.

federal spending power The power of the federal government to spend or lend money, as set out in the BRITISH NORTH AMERICA ACT. The federal government has wide jurisdiction over all matters of general or national concern. Section 91 of the BNA Act gives the federal government the general power to make laws "for the Peace, Order, and good Government of Canada," and lists the areas in which the federal government, through Parliament, has exclusive authority. This list of thirty-one classes of federal power—ranging from trade and commerce, defence and postal services to shipping, navigation, and weights and measures—illustrates but does not restrict the federal power. The federal government can spend directly in any field; there is no constitutional barrier, for example, to it establishing a CROWN CORPORATION to engage in any kind of business. In such cases it is exercising its power to legislate and spend on public property under section 91 (1A) of the BNA Act.

The federal government can also spend in areas normally falling under provincial jurisdiction by introducing SHARED-COST PROGRAMS, which make federal grants to the provinces conditional on the provinces abiding by federal legislation setting out the terms under which conditional grants can be made. In this way, for example, the federal government introduced shared-cost programs for health insurance and the Trans-Canada Highway system. Similarly, the federal government can use its power to lend money—for housing and urban development, for example, through the CANADA MORTGAGE AND HOUSING CORPORATION. Section 95 gives the federal and provincial governments concurrent power over agriculture and immigration, with federal law paramount in cases of conflict. Similar concurrent powers exist for old-age pensions and various supplemental benefits, but, in this area, federal law cannot override provincial law.

The federal government has significant and powerful spending—and taxing—powers; it has been able to act in such areas as health, education, and housing, and to fund cultural programs, such as the Canada Council, where there is a clear provincial responsibility as well. The greatest restraint on federal power may be its limited power to regulate. See also FEDERAL TAXING POWER, PROVINCIAL SPENDING POWER, PROVINCIAL TAXING POWER.

federal taxing power The federal government, under section 91 (3) of the BRITISH NORTH AMERICA ACT, is given the power to raise money by any mode or system of taxation. Thus, it can levy DIRECT TAXES such as income tax, and INDIRECT TAXES such as customs and excise duties. The federal government can also use its powers of taxation to regulate the economy, under its general power under section 91 to make laws for "the Peace, Order, and good Government of Canada." It is much less clear how far the federal government can go in using its taxing power to regulate activities that otherwise fall under provincial jurisdiction. See also FEDERAL SPENDING POWER, PROVINCIAL SPENDING POWER, PROVINCIAL TAXING POWER.

federalism A form of political union in which the national and provincial governments are each sovereign within their own areas of jurisdiction and in which there is a wide range of interdependence, since the actions of one level of government will frequently affect the other level. Thus, in any working federal system, there has to be a great deal of co-operation between the two levels of government if the citizens of the country, who frequently are not concerned about the fine print of a constitution, are to have the economic, social, and other policies that bring them maximum benefits. In Canada, a great many formal and informal arrangements exist to achieve co-operation. See, for example, FEDERAL-PROVINCIAL CONFERENCE. But no matter how carefully the division of spending, taxing, and other powers is defined, there are bound to be arguments and confrontations from time to time when important issues are at stake. See also DISTRIBUTION OF POWERS.

federation of labour A province-wide association of union locals and community labour councils set up to deal with their provincial and municipal governments on provincial labour laws and other matters of interest or concern. Provincial labour federations are chartered by the CANADIAN LABOUR CONGRESS.

fee The payment made for a professional service or for the right to do something—a payment for legal or medical services, for example, for a hunting or fishing licence, or for entry to a government campsite or a cultural institution such as an art gallery or museum.

feedstock The raw material—crude oil or natural gas—used in an oil refinery or petrochemicals plant.

fertility rate The number of live births per year, per thousand women of child-bearing age, at mid-year. The definition of child-bearing age varies; it usually starts at age 15 and extends to either age 44, 45, or 49, depending on the statistical agency. Statistics Canada uses age 45, while the United Nations uses age 49. The total fertility rate is the number of children, on average, that a woman would bear if her child-bearing experience were the same as that of a cross-section of women of different age groups in a given year. It is sometimes used to estimate the average number of children per completed family. Demographers also calculate age-specific fertility rates for women in different age groups. Throughout the world, the fertility rate is falling below family-fecundity or biological-reproductive capacity. See also ZERO POPULATION GROWTH.

fiat money Paper money that has the value stated on it, not because it is backed by gold or silver, but because the government has declared it to be legal tender and the public accepts it as such. All currency in circulation in Canada is fiat money; it cannot be converted into gold or silver and there are no gold or silver reserves to back its face value. The Bank of Canada Act of 1934 called for the maintenance of a gold reserve of at least 25 per cent of the Bank of Canada's note and deposit liabilities. This requirement was withdrawn in 1940, when Canada's gold reserves became part of the country's foreign-exchange reserves, where they have remained ever since.

fibre optics The use of hair-thin glass cables to carry messages in the form of light pulses. Such cables are expected to replace existing copper-wire systems currently in use for telephone and other forms of wired communication, and are expected to bring dramatic changes in communications systems. Fibre optics can carry a much higher volume of messages than copper wire, have a lower transmission loss, and are much less susceptible to interference; they should also become much cheaper over time. Because of their enormous carrying capacity, fibre optics are expected to provide consumers with access to libraries and data banks, electronic newspapers, two-way message systems, and shopping from the home through direct access to computers and computer networks. Fibre optics may even enable much of the work currently being done in offices to be done at home instead. The use of fibre optics is also expected to reduce significantly the congestion of wires and cables running beneath city streets.

fiduciary A person—for example, a trust-company officer—who holds and manages assets in trust for someone else. Trust companies in Canada are the only financial institutions empowered to play a fiduciary role.

fifo See FIRST IN, FIRST OUT.

final good Goods or services purchased by the final or ultimate consumer. These are the only kinds of goods and services included in the GROSS NATIONAL PRODUCT. See also INTERMEDIATE GOOD, RAW MATERIAL.

final payment In the western grains industry,

the payment the federal cabinet authorizes the CANADIAN WHEAT BOARD to make to farmers at the end of the CROP YEAR. Whether or not there is a final payment, and how large it is, depends on the funds left over with the wheat board after the year's crop is sold and its marketing and other costs are met. See also INITIAL PAYMENT.

final-utility theory of value The theory that value depends on final or MARGINAL UTILITY. Thus, necessities of life, such as air and water, are cheap because additional units are freely available, while diamonds and gold, while of limited practical use, are costly because of the difficulty in obtaining additional units.

Finance, Department of The principal economic-policy-making department of the federal government. Its responsibilities range from management of the economy, the balance of payments, and the tax system, to tariffs and trade policy, federal-provincial financial relations, relations with international agencies such as the International Monetary Fund, debt management, and the structure of the banking system and financial markets. It advises the cabinet on economic and financial policies, sets out the annual FISCAL FRAMEWORK for government spending, taxing, and borrowing, prepares the budget, conducts economic negotiations with foreign countries on tax treaties and other commercial arrangements, looks after Canada's interests in the world monetary and trading systems, monitors the spending programs of other government departments, co-ordinates tax and fiscal policies with the provinces, reviews the capital budgets and financial arrangements of crown corporations, and undertakes medium-term economic planning. The department is divided into five branches: tax policy and federal-provincial relations; economic programs and government finance; international trade and finance; fiscal policy and economic analysis; and long-range economic planning. The minister of Finance reports to Parliament for the ANTI-DUMPING TRIBUNAL, the TARIFF BOARD, the INSPECTOR GENERAL OF BANKS, the DEPARTMENT OF INSURANCE, the CANADA DEPOSIT INSURANCE CORPORATION, and the BANK OF CANADA. The department was created in 1869. It publishes an annual *Economic Review*.

Financial Administration Act Federal legislation, dating back to Confederation but frequently amended since then, that establishes the rules and regulations for the handling of public funds. It sets out what is to be done with monies that are collected, the rules on how these monies are to be spent, and what kind of financial-reporting system is to be used. It provides for the system of PUBLIC ACCOUNTS, the operation of the CONSOLIDATED REVENUE FUND, and the establishment of the Department of FINANCE and the TREASURY BOARD, and of such offices as the OFFICE OF THE COMPTROLLER GENERAL.

financial asset On a balance sheet, either cash or an investment that can be converted into cash—for example, bonds, shares, and certificates of deposit.

financial-flow accounts Part of the system of NATIONAL ACCOUNTS produced quarterly by Statistics Canada. These accounts show the source and disposition of savings in the economy, including savings flowing into or out of Canada. The economy is divided into various sectors: different levels of government, private households, industrial corporations, financial intermediaries, and the rest of the world. The accounts give the lending and borrowing for each sector by type of financial asset (shares, bonds, loans, trade receivables, and mortgages, for example). The movement of funds among the different sectors is also shown, giving an overall view of where savings have originated in the economy and where they have been used. The flow of funds out of one sector becomes its financial asset; the receipt of those funds in another sector becomes its liability. Financial assets and liabilities in the economy are balanced out.

financial future A FUTURES contract in which a buyer and a seller agree, through a futures broker, to purchase or deliver a specified dollar volume of a particular financial security such as a TREASURY BILL at a price and on a date agreed to at the time of the sale of the contract. The existence of a financial futures market allows investors to speculate on changing interest rates. Changes in rates will change the price of the financial securities.

financial intermediary A financial institution that accepts savings as deposits and re-lends the money to borrowers, earning a profit on the difference between the interest rate it pays savers and the interest rate it charges borrowers. Financial intermediaries play a vital role in the economy, channelling the funds of millions of savers, with a wide variety of saving needs, into the hands of borrowers with widely different needs. In effect, such institutions are the middlemen between savers and borrowers. Examples of financial intermediaries include chartered banks, trust companies, credit unions, caisses populaires, life-insurance companies, investment dealers, and stockbrokers. Many intermediaries are highly specialized, and, in sophisticated financial markets, many transactions may be between different financial intermediaries. See also CAPITAL MARKET, MONEY MARKET.

financial-management budget The method of presenting government revenues and expenditures according to function instead of department. Thus, all social-welfare spending is lumped together, whereas the BUDGETARY-ACCOUNTS BUDGET lists spending by department; the problem with the latter system is that identification of, say, social-welfare spending is more difficult, since some comes under the Department of National Health and Welfare, some comes under the Canada Employment and Immigration Commission, and some may come under other departments. Details are published by Statistics Canada in its annual publication, *Federal Government Finance*.

financial statement The annual accounting statement of a business. It includes the BALANCE SHEET, the EARNINGS STATEMENT, and the statement of RETAINED EARNINGS or surplus. See also ANNUAL REPORT.

financial year See FISCAL YEAR.

finder An agent who succeeds in finding a buyer or a seller, who hence enables a transaction to take place. The agent is paid a fee or commission, known as a finder's fee.

fine-tuning Using the levers of economic policy—monetary and fiscal policy, for example—to smooth out the peaks and valleys of the business cycle. Experience in the 1970s has led economists to reconsider hopes they once had of being able to moderate short-term fluctuations in the economy quickly. Not only does it take time for changes in economic policy to make themselves felt, but statistics may be slow in picking up economic changes and alerting policy-makers to the need for fine-tuning; politicians, moreover, are often reluctant to act quickly.

fire insurance Insurance purchased to provide protection against losses caused by a fire. Fire-insurance policies often provide protection against other forms of property damage, such as burst pipes, explosions, and lightning, as well.

firm A business organization, large or small, that produces goods or services for a profit. It can be an owner-operated business, a partnership, a medium-sized firm, or a giant multinational. Aside from the profit motive, all firms have certain common characteristics: they employ various FACTORS OF PRODUCTION, add value, and sell what they produce to someone else.

first in, first out The most widely used method in Canada of determining the value, in a company's books, of INVENTORY. It assumes that the first goods purchased or produced for the company's inventory are the first ones used up or sold from the company's inventory. In periods of rapid inflation, this method of inventory valuation is disliked by many companies because it tends to overvalue inventories and lead to higher taxable income. See also LAST IN, FIRST OUT, and INVENTORY.

first-ministers' conference See CONFERENCE OF FIRST MINISTERS.

first mortgage The mortgage that has first claim on a property; the mortgage that is paid off first in the event of foreclosure.

first world The rich, highly industrialized nations of the world, including Canada, the United States, Japan, the European Economic Community, Australia, and New Zealand. These countries are also called the developed countries, the North (in the NORTH-SOUTH DIALOGUE), and are the members of the ORGANIZATION FOR ECONOMIC CO-OPERATION AND DEVELOPMENT.

fiscal agent An investment dealer appointed by a government or corporation to give it financial advice on the management of its debt and the planning of its future financial needs, and to manage new issues of its bonds, shares, or other securities.

fiscal drag The reduction of purchasing power or demand in the economy that occurs during a period of real growth or inflation because tax revenues in a progressive-income-tax system rise faster than government spending. The effect is to weaken the economy's capacity for future growth unless something is done—taxes cut or government spending increased—to get that purchasing power back into the economy. The marginal tax rate in the income-tax system takes a greater tax bite with each income increase, so government revenues can rise sharply in a period of rapid inflation or growth, while government spending shows less of an increase. Indeed, government spending may even be reduced in a period of rapid growth, because unemployment-insurance, welfare, and other such payments will be reduced, thus adding to the fiscal drag. To some extent, the fiscal drag caused by inflation is offset in Canada, because the income-tax rates are adjusted each year to take inflation into account.

fiscal framework The economic parameters developed each year by the Department of FINANCE as the critical first step in preparing the BUDGET and the spending ESTIMATES. The department projects expected revenues and spending, based on existing tax rates and government programs, economic conditions and legal obligations, and, if there is a projected deficit, it shows the various ways in which the deficit might be financed (through tax increases, borrowing, or some combination of such measures). It shows the cabinet how much elbow room there is for new spending programs, and gives some idea of the leeway for tax cuts or extra spending to stimulate the economy.

fiscal policy The use of the government's taxing and spending powers to achieve a full-employment economy with stable prices and to smooth out sharp swings in the business cycle. The use of fiscal policy to maintain economic growth and employment has been one of the great lessons of KEYNESIAN ECONOMICS. Through its taxing and spending powers, the government can run deficits to boost demand and create jobs; or it can increase taxes and spending to achieve a surplus, to hold back the level of demand, and to check inflation.

There are many different ways in which the use of the tax system can affect the performance of the economy: tax increases reduce consumption, and hence the purchasing power of consumers, and discourage investment by business; tax cuts can add to purchasing power and encourage economic growth; tax incentives to business can accelerate business investment; a tax surcharge on corporate income tax will slow down investment; cuts in tariffs and sales taxes will reduce prices for consumers. Similarly, government spending can have an important effect on economic behaviour: a reduction in government spending on goods and services will reduce the overall level of demand in the economy and slow economic growth, while an increase will boost demand and growth; government spending on public works can give an extra spurt to job creation, while a cutback on public works can quickly reduce employment in the construction industry; a government increase in transfer payments, such as pension supplements to the needy, can quickly boost consumer spending, and hence the overall level of demand in the economy.

Because of the division of spending and taxing powers in the Canadian form of FEDERALISM, the fiscal impact of the provinces is significant, and the federal and provincial governments have to ensure that there is a degree of co-ordination in fiscal policy. Fiscal policy cannot be used in isolation from

MONETARY POLICY, but economists place different emphases on the relative importance of each. See also FULL-EMPLOYMENT BUDGET, BUILT-IN STABILIZER.

fiscal year The financial or accounting year for any government, corporation, or other organization. It is any consecutive twelve months; for most corporations and other organizations, it coincides with the calendar year of 1 January to 31 December. But for the federal government and provincial governments, it runs from 1 April to 31 March.

Fisheries and Oceans, Department of The federal government department responsible for the management and conservation of fishery resources in Canada's coastal waters and inland waters. The department's role has increased significantly since January 1977, when Canada proclaimed jurisdiction over a two-hundred-mile fishing zone along its coasts. The department looks after Canada's participation in INTERNATIONAL FISHERIES CONVENTIONS, the inspection of fishing practices and gear, adherence to fishing quotas, management of programs to build up Canada's fishing fleets, programs to market fishery products, and the negotiation of federal-provincial fishing agreements. The department also carries out fisheries and oceans research.

Fisheries Prices Support Board A federal agency that provides price support for fishery products when prices are declining. It can purchase and stockpile fishery products and pay DEFICIENCY PAYMENTS to the fishing industry. It reports to the minister of FISHERIES AND OCEANS.

Fisheries Research Board A federal research organization that advises the minister of FISHERIES AND OCEANS on needed fisheries and marine research. The board members include scientists from provincial agencies and universities and executives from the fishing industry.

fishing zones The zones along Canada's east and west coasts where Canada has full control over fishing rights and activities. Since 1 January 1977, Canada has claimed jurisdiction for two hundred miles (370 kilometres) from its coastline. This means that fishermen from other countries who wish to fish in these waters have to have Canada's permission, and have to follow Canadian fisheries-conservation and -management regulations. Foreign fishermen are allowed to catch fish declared surplus to Canada's fishing capacity and within total fishing-catch quotas. As Canadian fishing capacity increases, the role of foreign fishermen will be reduced. A number of foreign countries have signed fishing agreements with Canada, so that they can fish in Canada's fishing zones. See also INTERNATIONAL FISHERIES CONVENTIONS.

fixed asset An asset of a more or less permanent nature that is essential to the operation of a business, and thus is used to produce goods and services and is not for sale. Fixed assets include the land, building, machinery, furniture, and trucks owned by a business. They have a reasonably long life and, for accounting and tax purposes, their declining value, due to wear and tear or eventual obsolescence, is written off through DEPRECIATION. See also CURRENT ASSET.

fixed cost Costs that do not change in a business, at least in the short run, regardless of the level of production. Such costs, often described as overhead, include rent, maintenance, interest, property taxes, insurance, and administrative salaries. Even if production fell by 50 per cent, these costs would remain the same. However, if it appeared that production would remain much lower for a long time, then some of these costs could be reduced. Some administrative staff might be fired; or the firm could move to a smaller building and save on rent, maintenance, insurance, and property taxes.

fixed exchange rate A system under which individual countries are required to maintain the exchange rate of their currency within a narrow band on either side of its par value. This was the monetary system agreed on at BRETTON WOODS in 1944, and which the world used, through the INTERNATIONAL MONETARY FUND, from 1945 to the early 1970s. It was replaced by a system of FLOATING EXCHANGE RATES.

Under the fixed-exchange-rate system, countries had to intervene in foreign-exchange markets to maintain the value of their currencies and to raise or lower their official exchange rates when their balances of payment were in FUNDAMENTAL DISEQUILIBRIUM. They had to follow international rules set out in the articles of agreement of the IMF. In the early 1970s, as international conditions became unsettled due to the big U.S. balance-of-payments deficit, continued global inflation, and shifts in the balance of economic power among nations, fixed exchange rates became increasingly difficult to maintain. After the United States abandoned the gold standard, and hence, its fixed exchange rate, in 1971, other major nations soon followed suit. In March 1973, the IMF officially ended the fixed-exchange-rate system, though it could be reintroduced.

Canada had a fixed exchange rate through most of its history to 1950, and from 1962–70. Its dollar floated between 1950 and 1962, and was floated again in 1970 with permission from the IMF. See also EUROPEAN MONETARY SYSTEM.

fixed-interest securities Any security whose yield is fixed. Corporate and government bonds, guaranteed-investment certificates, preferred shares, and certificates of deposit would all fall into this category. Common shares, whose dividend rate may vary from year to year, are not fixed-interest securities.

fixed-price contract A contract someone has agreed to fulfil for a specified price, regardless of any increase in his own costs. See also COST-PLUS CONTRACT, ESCALATION CLAUSE.

fixed shift The policy of keeping the same workers on the same shift in a business or other organization that has several shifts of workers and operates twenty-four hours a day. This means that a worker will always work the same shift. See also SPLIT SHIFT.

flag of convenience A flag flown by a ship, indicating that it has been registered in a country that offers low taxation, has lax laws on minimum wages and benefits, and has only modest safety regulations. While a ship may be owned in Canada, the United States, or Western Europe, it may be registered in Liberia, Panama, Honduras, or other states that offer such flags of convenience, which thus enables the owners to pay low taxes and wages and to minimize their costs for safety and pollution control.

flexwork The practice of letting employees set their own starting and finishing times each day, provided that they work a stipulated number of hours.

floating exchange rate A system in which the exchange rates of currencies are set by the daily forces of supply and demand in international foreign-exchange markets. Unlike the FIXED EXCHANGE RATE, the floating exchange rate does not bind a country to keep its exchange rate within a narrow band on either side of its PAR VALUE. Exchange markets automatically adjust a country's exchange rate for changes in rates of domestic inflation, productivity, or balance-of-payments surpluses or deficits. By using the price mechanism of supply and demand to set exchange rates, individual nations need not intervene in foreign-exchange markets to protect the value of their currency. None the less, countries do intervene to smooth out fluctuations in their exchange rates or to counter speculators. Occasional intervention of this sort is known as a clean float. Intervention by a country deliberately to change the value of its currency, or to prevent market forces from changing the value, is known as a dirty float.

Floating exchange rates became the rule rather than the exception in 1971, after the U.S. government took the U.S. dollar off the gold standard. In March 1973, the INTERNATIONAL MONETARY FUND ended the régime of fixed exchange rates that had been adopted in 1944 as part of the BRETTON WOODS AGREEMENT. Exchange rates thus can float on the market in response to supply and demand, central-bank interventions, or changes in interest rates, which draw in or drive out capital and thus affect the demand for particular currencies.

The floating-exchange-rate system has its drawbacks, as the fixed-exchange-rate system did. Speculators can still cause an exchange crisis, and the existence of floating rates adds an element of uncertainty to international trade and investment. Nor are floating exchange rates a substitute for domestic policies to deal with the problems of inflation, excessive foreign borrowing, and uncompetitive industry. Canada has had more experience with the floating dollar than any other Western nation. The Canadian dollar floated from 1950 to 1962, and has floated again since 1970.

floor trader An employee of a stockbroker or commodity dealer who is qualified to trade on the floor of a stock exchange or commodities exchange on behalf of his firm and its clients.

flurry A surge of buying in a foreign-exchange, stock, or commodity market, usually by speculators anticipating an announcement of some sort that will lead to high prices.

Food and Agriculture Organization (FAO) An important United Nations agency headquartered in Rome. It was founded by a special conference held in Quebec City in October 1945 to help deal with the food problems of countries whose economies had been devastated by the Second World War. But it quickly assumed a much broader role, helping to solve world-wide problems of food supply and distribution. It provides a wide range of technical and other assistance to the LESS-DEVELOPED COUNTRIES to improve their production and distribution of agricultural, fisheries, and forest products. It also is responsible for monitoring the balance between world food supply and demand, for handling emergency food-aid programs, and for the preparation of emergency relief planning. It has been responsible for the 1960 Freedom from Hunger Campaign, the 1969 World Agricultural Development Program for 1985, and the 1974 WORLD FOOD CONFERENCE. Canada has been a member from the start, and, because of its agricultural, fisheries, and forestry expertise, is a member of the FAO Council and many specialized FAO bodies. See also WORLD FOOD COUNCIL.

Food and Drug Act A federal law, administered by the Department of National Health and Welfare, designed to protect consumers against risk to health, or against fraud or deception in the foods, drugs, and cosmetics they buy. The law's scope ranges from protection against harmful and unsanitary food to protection against misleading or deceptive claims for medicines.

Food Prices Review Board A federal board established in April 1973, to report quarterly on the reasons for food-price changes by product-group, and to make policy recommendations when appropriate. It was subsequently empowered to investigate any price increase in any food product by any producer or firm where such an increase appeared unwarranted, to publish a report, and to make recommendations, if any, to correct the situation or to prevent it from recurring in the future. Thus, it monitored food prices, handled public complaints, investigated price increases, and advocated food- and agriculture-industry policy changes. It was replaced by the much broader ANTI-INFLATION BOARD in October 1975.

fool's gold A piece of rock that, superficially, appears to contain gold. In reality, it is pyrite, a shiny, yellow mineral that is known as sulphide of iron.

force majeure A clause in a contract that permits the supplier of a commodity such as oil or natural gas to deliver less than promised, due to an act of God such as a flood, or an act of war, an act of a government, or other causes, such as a strike.

forced sale A sale instigated by creditors who want their money, rather than a sale willingly made by the owner of the property.

forced saving Unwilling savings by consumers who have no choice because goods are not available, government is taking their income to prevent consumption, or corporations are withholding dividends instead of paying them out to shareholders. In a period of inflation arising from strong growth, prices are bid up and some consumers are forced to withdraw from the market. Government tax increases to cool consumer demand or to finance investments also force consumers to reduce their purchases. Totalitarian countries can force consumers to save by compelling them to buy government bonds, or simply by refusing to make consumer goods available.

forecasting The projection or estimation of future economic or technological performance. Forecasts can be short-term, medium-term or long-term. They can be for a country or group of countries; or they can be for a firm, industry, or community. Techniques can range from simple projection forward of past trends, can be calculated from an analysis of LEADING INDICATORS, or can be based on the use of computer ECONOMETRIC models of the economy that use thousands of equations to describe a vast multitude of relationships.

Banks, investment dealers, and independent economic-research organizations all publish annual economic forecasts, and many of them publish quarterly or semi-annual changes in their forecasts based on more up-to-date statistics. The federal government publishes a few figures from its vast array of internal economic forecasts, but withholds most of its information. The ECONOMIC COUNCIL OF CANADA publishes forecasts, as do some of the provincial governments. And the ORGANIZATION FOR ECONOMIC CO-OPERATION AND DEVELOPMENT publishes forecasts twice a year for the Western world and for individual OECD members, including Canada.

Forecasts do not often turn out to be exactly right, but they represent the best available information at the time they are made and can give some reasonably clear indications of economic trends. See also DELPHI TECHNIQUE.

foreclose To bring about the sale of a property because the owner has failed to make payments on his mortgage, his taxes, or on other debts. Foreclosure has to be approved through a court order before a sale can take place.

foreign aid Assistance by DEVELOPED COUNTRIES to help the LESS-DEVELOPED COUNTRIES to carry out programs of economic development and thus raise their standard of living; foreign aid may also be provided as emergency relief in the case of famine, flooding, earthquakes, or other natural disasters. Canada provides different forms of foreign aid, including financial, technical, and food aid. Part of the foreign-aid budget is channelled through international agencies, such as the World Bank, or INTERNATIONAL BANK FOR RECONSTRUCTION AND DEVELOPMENT (IBRD), or the United Nations; part is channelled through regional-development banks and the COLOMBO PLAN; and part of it is handled on a bilateral basis, through the CANADIAN INTERNATIONAL DEVELOPMENT AGENCY.

Foreign Claims Commission A federal commission created in 1970 to help Canadian citizens to settle outstanding claims against foreign governments. The bulk of the commission's work has been to deal with claims of Canadians against the governments of Hungary, Romania, Poland, and Czechoslovakia, for payments that predate the forced establishment of communist governments in those countries.

foreign direct investment Investment by a foreign corporation or individual for the purposes of owning, controlling, and operating a business in another country. MULTINATIONAL CORPORATIONS account for much of the foreign direct investment that takes place, operating through their FOREIGN SUBSIDIARIES. There are many different motives for foreign direct investment, though they are all related to the profits of the parent company. A multinational corporation may establish a foreign subsidiary to secure supplies of raw materials, to take advantage of low-cost labour or low taxes, to establish a strong enough presence in a foreign market to discourage the creation of local competitors, to buy out foreign firms that could become competitors, to increase its market share and profits, to develop new markets, or because this is the cheapest way to serve a foreign market. Foreign direct investment does not include purchases by non-residents of bonds or of shares purchased strictly for dividends and potential capital gains.

Statistics Canada measures foreign direct investment in terms of the proportion of foreign-owned capital to total long-term capital employed in different industries, and in terms of the total capital employed in non-resident-controlled businesses. Three regular

Statistics Canada reports are published: an annual report on foreign direct investment, published under the CORPORATIONS AND LABOUR UNIONS RETURNS ACT; a report on *Canada's International Investment Position,* published roughly every two years; and BALANCE-OF-PAYMENTS statistics, published each quarter, which show the amount of new foreign direct investment in Canada by non-residents and the amount of new foreign direct investment abroad by Canadians. Foreign-controlled corporations in Canada today depend more on the reinvestment of their retained earnings than on fresh flows of direct investment capital for their growth.

Foreign Direct Investment in Canada A federal report, published in 1972, usually known as the Gray Report since the study into ways to increase Canadian ownership and control was headed by National Revenue Minister Herb Gray. The report outlined the implications for Canada of a high level of foreign control of manufacturing and resource industries, and concluded that foreign direct investment was very much a cost-benefit problem. As the report put it: "Foreign direct investment is a complex combination of costs and benefits: easy access to foreign entrepreneurial talent, technology, capital, and markets must be offset against TRUNCATION; the competitive stimulation in certain cases must be counterbalanced by the restrictions on competition in others; the provision of export markets in certain cases must be counterbalanced by export restrictions in other cases; increased economic growth, jobs, tax revenues, etc., must be offset against the long-term effects of foreign direct investment on our industrial structure."

The report considered a number of alternatives to increase the benefits and reduce the costs. It rejected a policy of requiring 51 per cent Canadian ownership in all business enterprises as too costly. It found some value in policies to require Canadian ownership in key sectors of the economy, such as banking, broadcasting, and transportation, but only as a supplement to other national policies. It further recommended creation of a review agency, either in the form of an independent tribunal or as an administrative agency responsible to a cabinet minister.

The agency was to review six aspects of foreign investment: foreign takeovers of Canadian firms; the establishment of new business enterprises in Canada by foreign investors; new licensing and franchise arrangements by Canadians with foreign interests; major new investments by existing foreign-controlled enterprises in Canada; existing foreign-controlled enterprises in Canada, even if they were not planning new investment; and major new investments abroad by Canadian-owned multinational corporations. However the review process was handled, the report said, the criteria for approving, rejecting, or otherwise dealing with foreign direct investments should be set out in legislation. Each proposal received should be reviewed according to its contribution to productivity and industrial efficiency, its compatibility with the government's own industrial strategy, the contribution it made to economic growth and new employment, its geographic location within Canada, its effect on competition within the industry in question, and its other economic benefits. The report also said that the proposed agency should be the central agency dealing with foreign direct investment in Canada, and should gather data on foreign investment, engage in research on the effects of foreign investment and policies to deal with it, and serve as a registry of the activities of Canadian-controlled multinationals. See also FOREIGN INVESTMENT REVIEW AGENCY.

foreign exchange The currencies of other countries used to pay for imported goods and services, foreign travel, and foreign investment. The ownership of foreign exchange gives the residents of one country financial claims on another. The convertibility of major currencies means that hundreds of thousands of individuals, firms, and governments can buy and sell from one another, invest in each other's countries, travel abroad, and engage in a wide range of economic relationships. If a Canadian firm needs U.S. dollars, Japanese yen, or Italian lira to pay for imports, it can obtain them from a FOREIGN-EXCHANGE MARKET through a bank or other financial institution; similarly, if a German or British importer needs Canadian dollars to pay for imports from Canada, these can also be obtained on foreign-exchange markets, as can Canadian dollars for a U.S. investor buying a Canadian company, or a Canadian going to Florida or Hawaii in the winter.

Foreign exchange allows individuals, corporations, or governments to settle foreign debts. In settlements between countries, a central bank can use or accept its own currency, other currencies, or SPECIAL DRAWING RIGHTS issued by the INTERNATIONAL MONETARY FUND. Individual countries maintain foreign-exchange reserves to settle international debts arising from financial claims held by foreigners, and to use on foreign-exchange markets to smooth out fluctuations in the value of their own currencies.

Foreign Exchange Control Board A board created in 1939 under the Foreign Exchange Control Act to restrict capital flows from Canada and to limit the use of Canada's scarce foreign-exchange reserves to essential purposes. The board had the power to license imports and exports of goods, currency, and capital, including stocks and bonds. It regulated all transactions with residents of other countries. In April 1940, all Canadians were required, under the foreign-exchange-acquisition order, to sell their holdings of foreign exchange to the foreign-exchange board; at the same time, the Bank of Canada turned over its gold holdings to the board, so that all of Canada's foreign-exchange reserves were under the control of a single body. In July 1940, the board ceased selling foreign exchange to Canadians for pleasure travel. In the latter days of the Second World War, the board began to lift its controls. But it was not until December 1951 that the government revoked its foreign-exchange regulations. The Foreign Exchange Control Act was repealed in 1952.

foreign-exchange dealer Banks and other institutions that buy and sell foreign currencies on the FOREIGN-EXCHANGE MARKET. Most of the trading in Canada is done by the banks on behalf of customers, on their own account, or on behalf of the Bank of Canada.

foreign-exchange market A market where foreign currencies are traded, and the daily or spot and future prices of currencies are decided. The Canadian market is centred in Toronto and consists of an electronic communications network linking the chartered banks, the Bank of Canada, currency dealers, and other traders. This market, in turn, is linked to other financial centres, such as New York and London, so that, for most currencies, there is a global market. It is on the foreign-exchange market that companies buy and sell the currencies that they need for trade and investment or have earned for trade and investment. It is also the market in which a central bank intervenes to defend its country's exchange rate, by buying or selling its own currency or the currencies of others, and thus affecting supply and demand.

foreign-exchange reserves Currencies and liquid assets held by a country that can be used to settle its international BALANCE OF PAYMENTS or to intervene in foreign-exchange markets to defend its exchange rate. In Canada's case, foreign-exchange reserves consist mainly of U.S. dollars and U.S. treasury bills, gold, and SPECIAL DRAWING RIGHTS. These reserves are held in the EXCHANGE-FUND ACCOUNT; the Department of FINANCE publishes a monthly report on changes in the account.

foreign investment The purchase by non-residents of business enterprises, mineral deposits or rights, timber or fishing licences, buildings, land, shares, bonds, futures contracts, certificates of deposit, short-term money-market instruments, bank deposits, or other assets capable of yielding a return. Foreign investment is classified as short-term or long-term, and as debt investment (investment in financial assets) or equity investment (investment in the ownership of physical assets). Equity investment, in turn, may consist of PORTFOLIO INVESTMENT in shares and bonds for capital gain, interest and dividends, or DIRECT INVESTMENT in shares or productive assets to own or operate a business. See also FOREIGN DIRECT INVESTMENT. The various types of foreign investment are shown each quarter in the BALANCE-OF-PAYMENTS report of Statistics Canada.

Foreign Investment Review Agency (FIRA) A federal agency created to screen foreign takeovers of Canadian firms and the establishment of new foreign-owned businesses, to determine whether they result in "significant benefit" for Canadians. The agency was approved by Parliament in 1973 in the Foreign Investment Review Act, following publication in 1972 of the government report, FOREIGN DIRECT INVESTMENT IN CANADA (the Gray Report). The agency began screening foreign takeovers in April 1974 and new foreign businesses in October 1975.

The agency makes a recommendation to cabinet through the minister of INDUSTRY, TRADE AND COMMERCE, while the cabinet makes the final decision to allow or disallow. The task of the agency is not to block foreign investment, but to make sure that the significant-benefit test is met; this means that the agency can negotiate with a foreign corporation to get it to agree to do certain things to meet the significant-benefit test. Agreements between foreign companies and the agency are not made public; but the agency is supposed to police the agreements, to make sure that they are lived up to. If a foreign corporation refuses to carry out agreements it made earlier, then the agency can force disvestiture through the courts.

The significant-benefit test considers the impact of a takeover or new investment on employment, research and development, exports, Canadian participation in management and ownership, the purchase of Canadian goods and services, and capital investment. The agency must also seek out provincial government views on proposed takeovers and new businesses. The criteria of significant benefit spelled out in the Foreign Investment Review Act are: **1.** The effect of the investment on the level and nature of economic activity in Canada, including the effect on employment, on resource processing, on the utilization of parts, components, and services produced in Canada, and on exports from Canada. **2.** The degree and significance of participation by Canadians in the business enterprise and in the industry sector to which the enterprise belongs. **3.** The effect on productivity, industrial efficiency, technological development, innovation, and product variety in Canada. **4.** The effect on competition within any industry or industries in Canada. **5.** The compatibility of the investment with national industrial and economic policies, taking into consideration industrial and economic-policy objectives enunciated by a province likely to be significantly affected by the proposed investment.

Effective October 1975, existing foreign-owned businesses in Canada also had to obtain FIRA approval if they expanded into an unrelated business. A related business was defined to include vertical integration, both backward towards raw materials or forward towards distribution; manufacturing of a substitute product for an old line; a new business providing new products with essentially the same technology and production processes used in the old business; the marketing of new products resulting from research and development carried out by private companies in Canada; and a new business that is classified in a special list issued by the federal government as being in the same field as the old business. FIRA publishes an annual report of its activities. It reports to Parliament through the minister of Industry, Trade and Commerce.

foreign ownership See FOREIGN DIRECT INVESTMENT.

foreign sector Economic activities conducted with non-residents. Thus, the foreign sector of the economy includes exports and imports, travel, interest and dividend payments to or from non-residents, income and payments for international banking services, international payments for management fees, patent rights, franchises, and transportation services, and long-term and short-term capital flows.

foreign subsidiary A company that is controlled by a foreign corporation. Many foreign corporations have subsidiaries in Canada, while a number of Canadian firms have subsidiaries abroad. Most foreign subsidiaries established in Canada were set up to develop the Canadian market for the foreign parent or to exploit Canadian natural resources. A few carry out specialized manufacturing activities for world-wide markets on behalf of the foreign parent. See also TRUNCATION, FOREIGN-SUBSIDIARY GUIDELINES.

foreign-subsidiary guidelines Federal government guidelines for good corporate behaviour by foreign subsidiaries in Canada. See NEW PRINCIPLES FOR INTERNATIONAL BUSINESS (1975), and GUIDING PRINCIPLES OF GOOD CORPORATE BEHAVIOUR (1966).

forgery A white-collar crime in which a false document, such as a cheque, is made, or in which a legal document is altered. A cheque may have a false signature; or the amount on the cheque may be altered.

forward exchange A foreign currency that is bought or sold at a specified price for delivery at some specified future date. For example, an importer who is to take delivery of products in three months and who wants to protect himself against higher prices caused by a decline in his own country's exchange rate, will buy a three-month futures contract, enabling him to take delivery of the foreign currency he will need then at a price that protects him against a loss on his import transaction. Exporters who are being paid in foreign currencies will do the same thing. See also FUTURES MARKET.

forward exchange rate The exchange rate being quoted for a currency for delivery thirty or ninety days into the future. The rate for immediate transactions is the SPOT PRICE.

forward integration A merger or takeover by a business enterprise of another business enterprise that takes the acquiring firm one step further up the ladder in the production-distribution process. A mining company, for example, may take over a processing or manufacturing firm; an oil-producing company may buy a chain of independent gasoline stations or a home fuel-oil distribution company; a manufacturer of auto parts may acquire a chain of auto-repair shops.

forward market A market on which traders buy and sell futures contracts, such as commodities or foreign currencies, for delivery at prices fixed when the contract is originally made. See also FUTURES MARKET.

forwarding agent A business firm that collects merchandise from factories, warehouse, and other locations and delivers it to a dock, railway station, or airport for shipment to its ultimate destination. Forwarding agents carry out a specialized role in the transportation industry, acting as middlemen between the transportation companies and firms that need products shipped. Forwarding agents make all the arrangements necessary for their customers, including booking space with the railways, ship companies, and airlines.

fossil fuel Hydrocarbon fuels formed over millions of years through the heat and pressure exerted on decaying vegetable matter. Oil, natural gas, and coal are examples.

fourth world The poorest of the LESS-DEVELOPED COUNTRIES, with the lowest per capita incomes, few prospects for economic growth without massive outside assistance, and few if any natural resources. These are also the countries most seriously affected by the oil-price increases of 1973–74. Countries in this group include most of those in central Africa, India, Pakistan, and Bangladesh, and have per capita gross national products of two hundred dollars or less.

Framework Agreement for Commercial and Economic Co-operation between Canada and the European Communities A formal treaty signed by Canada and the members of the EUROPEAN ECONOMIC COMMUNITY on 6 July 1976, following the enunciation by Canada of its new foreign-economic policy, the so-called THIRD OPTION, in 1972. Under the treaty, Canada and members of the EEC agreed to develop closer economic relations and to consult regularly on ways to increase trade and investment ties. A Joint Co-operation Committee was established, consisting of cabinet ministers from Canada and the EEC, to monitor progress under the agreement and to suggest ways of increasing economic co-operation. The first such meeting was held in Brussels in December 1976, and the second in Ottawa, in March 1978.

Subcommittees of officials have been established to pursue progress in particular areas —for example, non-ferrous metals, forest products, aerospace products, nuclear equipment, and construction and information equipment. The agreement is intended to increase joint ventures by Canadian and EEC industries, to increase two-way investment, to encourage licensing agreements, to facilitate joint research and development, and to boost joint activities in third countries.

One area of disagreement between Canada and the EEC has been over the treatment of natural resources. The EEC members want secure supplies of raw materials; Canada wants greater processing of resources before they are exported. Failure to agree on accessibility to resources led to the exclusion of commitments on resources from the treaty. Following the signing of the treaty, Canada has been trying to persuade Canadian business to follow up with direct discussions with European industries and with more vigorous sales efforts in Europe.

franchise A licence or privilege granted by a corporation or government to sell a particular product or to offer a service in a given area; often an advertised trade name is part of the franchise. Governments may grant a franchise to operate a radio or television station on a certain part of the airwaves, or to provide transportation services between particular communities. Many small businesses are operated as franchises—fast-food outlets, for example, or auto-parts and repair shops. In a business-franchise contract, the franchisor (the person who grants the franchise) will sell the use of his trade name, and frequently certain equipment and supplies, to the franchisee (the person obtaining the franchise), in exchange for a one-time payment, royalties based on sales, and an agreement to meet all the standards for product or service quality, such as staffing and decor, imposed by the franchisor.

Fraser Institute An economic and social-research organization, founded in 1974 to identify the benefits to Canadians of a free-market economy, and to identify ways to strengthen competitive forces within the economy. The institute also analyzes the impact of government controls and regulations on the well-being of Canadians. It is funded by its corporate and individual supporters and by the sale of its studies. It is based in Vancouver.

fraud A white-collar crime in which an individual, using false information or documents, cheats another person or organization out of money or other assets, or deceives a person or organization into signing a disadvantageous contract. Fraud is a criminal offence; but the offended party can also sue for damages.

fraudulent bankruptcy A deliberate bankruptcy designed to cheat creditors or suppliers of money. A person may, for example, establish a store, obtain goods on credit, sell them, and not pay his suppliers; the money is diverted out of the business so that it cannot be recovered by creditors, whereupon the retailer declares bankruptcy. It is a criminal offence.

free and clear A statement signifying that there are no outstanding claims or liens on a property. Thus, a vendor is free to sell a property and a purchaser can buy it, without fear that a third party will appear with a claim on the property.

free economy See FREE-MARKET ECONOMY.

free enterprise See PRIVATE ENTERPRISE.

free good Goods that are available in such abundance that they can be obtained without cost—fresh air, sunshine, and a climate favourable to high agricultural productivity are examples; as opposed to an ECONOMIC GOOD, which is scarce and requires cost and effort to obtain. With the development of the concept of EXTERNALITIES, economists are re-examining the idea of free goods. With air pollution in cities, for example, it is questionable whether clean air is a free good; someone has to pay to keep it clean. See also FINAL-UTILITY THEORY OF VALUE.

free list A list of goods that are not subject to import duties.

free-market economy An economy in which prices and production are largely determined by the unrestricted play of market forces through the LAW OF SUPPLY AND DEMAND. But many of the virtues of efficiency and low prices claimed for a free-market economy exist only under conditions of PERFECT

COMPETITION. In the real world of IMPERFECT COMPETITION, market forces have a role to play, but they may need to be backed by government intervention to deal with MONOPOLY or OLIGOPOLY and to ensure an equitable distribution of income. See also MIXED ECONOMY.

free on board (f.o.b.) The delivery of goods without charge to a specified location, where the buyer obtains actual ownership. For example, a truckload of lightbulbs delivered from Toronto to Winnipeg f.o.b. would be delivered without charge to the buyers in Winnipeg.

free port A port at which goods are accepted without the payment of customs duties. Such a port is usually used to attract tourists or to assemble products for reshipment.

free trade International trade that takes place without the imposition of any tariffs or other barriers to the free movement of goods and services, such as quotas, government procurement rules, or import or export licences. Proponents of free trade cite the doctrine of COMPARATIVE ADVANTAGE. They say that free trade would lead to the most advantageous international division of labour and specialization, increase the potential output of all nations, and improve the standard of living of everyone. But opponents fear that, like LAISSEZ-FAIRE conditions in domestic markets, free trade would lead to monopoly power and worsen rather than reduce disparities in income, while reducing the political sovereignty of individual nations. Since the end of the Second World War, however, there has been a gradual reduction in international tariff and other trade barriers, and the establishment of a number of FREE-TRADE AREAS around the world. See also GENERAL AGREEMENT ON TARIFFS AND TRADE, MERCANTILISM, NEO-MERCANTILISM.

free-trade area An agreement between two or more countries to abolish TARIFF and NON-TARIFF BARRIERS on some or all goods and services moving between them. They may agree to apply a common external tariff on imports from other countries, or to let each member set its own tariff policy. Examples include the EUROPEAN ECONOMIC COMMUNITY, the EUROPEAN FREE TRADE ASSOCIATION, and the LATIN AMERICAN FREE TRADE ASSOCIATION. Canada and the United States have free-trade arrangements in certain products—farm machinery, for example. See also CANADA-UNITED STATES AUTOMOTIVE PRODUCTS AGREEMENT.

free-trade zone A duty-free area near a port or airport where goods are imported and re-exported, sometimes with some assembly or other manufacturing activity taking place.

Freedman Report An important report by Mr. Justice Freedman of the Manitoba Court of Appeal, under the Industrial Relations and Disputes Investigations Act, which dealt with the rights of management and labour in the introduction of technological and other changes not covered in a collective agreement. The investigation was initiated in November 1964, after railway trainmen, conductors, firemen, and engineers launched a WILDCAT STRIKE when the Canadian National Railway Company tried to eliminate crew changes at several divisional points.

Mr. Justice Freedman found that the CNR had acted legally in reducing crew changes when technological improvements made this possible. But he said that the issue none the less should have been a matter of negotiation. "The present situation which permits management to make unilateral changes in working conditions during the contract period is a manifest inequity which clamours for correction," he said. Either party should have the right to refer the issue to an arbitrator, picked either by the affected unions and their employer or by the minister of LABOUR, to determine whether the proposed change would cause a material change in the working conditions of the employees. If it didn't, Mr. Justice Freedman said, the change would be permitted to be carried out immediately. If it did, the employer should be required to delay the change until the next collective-bargaining period, unless the union agreed to the changes.

Mr. Justice Freedman dealt only with the CNR case, but said that the procedures and policies he recommended for that case could be applied to similar situations in other instances of technological change. "The old concept of labour as a commodity simply will not suffice; it is at once wrong and dangerous. Hence there is a responsibility upon the entrepreneur who introduces technological change to see that it is not effected at the expense of his work force." Mr. Justice Freedman also said that communities affected by technological change were entitled to a hearing on the reasonableness of the CNR's proposals, and that the federal and provincial governments had a responsibility to compensate them for the economic loss. The CNR, he said, also had a responsibility to compensate affected workers and to pay their expenses in moving to jobs in other communities.

freedom of entry The ability of new firms to enter the market freely. In a world of PERFECT COMPETITION, no one firm has any particular advantage over any other, so that new firms can enter with ease; the consumer benefits, because new firms will eliminate the excess profits that existing firms in the industry may have earned. In the real world of IMPERFECT COMPETITION, existing firms may enjoy an advantage, such as recognized brand names, superior technology, or ECONOMIES OF SCALE, so that freedom of entry does not exist and established firms are able to earn higher profits. Freedom of entry implies an absence of BARRIERS TO ENTRY.

freight rates The rates charged by railways, airlines, and trucking firms to move goods and commodities. Freight rates are not subsidized and, in Canada, except for air-cargo rates, they are unregulated. See CROW'S NEST PASS AGREEMENT.

frequency distribution A statistical technique used to organize a large volume of data into understandable groups. For example, the income of Canada's several million families can be organized by broad classification: under $1,999, $2,000 to $2,999, $3,000 to $3,999, $4,000 to $4,999, and so on. This technique greatly simplifies analysis of statistics.

frictional unemployment Unemployment due to lags between the time people leave old jobs and the time they take new ones. Even when there is FULL EMPLOYMENT, there is always some frictional unemployment. People may not be sure which new job they want, or they may lack information about the jobs available, and therefore have to spend time getting that information. Frictional unemployment can be reduced to some extent by improving labour markets, so that more information is available about job vacancies and skills that are needed, or by providing labour-mobility assistance so that people can move more easily to new jobs in other communities.

fringe benefits Benefits, other than wages or salary, provided by an employer for an employee. They include paid vacations, group life and disability insurance, dental and supplementary hospital and drug insurance, reimbursement for educational courses, a share of pension costs, and share purchase plans. In Canada, fringe benefits account for about one-third of payroll costs, with wages and salaries accounting for the other two-thirds. Fringe benefits can also include the cost of subsidizing staff cafeterias, employee recreation programs, and similar activities.

front-end loading The practice of insurance companies, mutual funds, and sellers of registered retirement savings plans, of claiming the initial premiums or payments for administrative, interest, and other costs. Thus, if a person cancels a policy or takes early redemption, he may find that much of his investment has been claimed by the financial institution to cover its costs and risk.

frontage The measurement of a parcel of land where it fronts on to a street, highway, or body of water.

frontier reserves Reserves of crude oil and natural gas that may have great potential but which, at present, cannot be shipped to market at competitive prices and for which no physical distribution system, such as a pipeline, exists. Canada's frontier areas include the Mackenzie delta, the Beaufort Sea, the Arctic islands, and the offshore areas of eastern Canada.

frozen asset An asset that cannot readily be converted into cash or used for the owner's personal benefit, except at great inconvenience or loss. Assets of enemy nationals may be frozen in wartime; similarly, in legal, business, or nationalization disputes, assets may be frozen until disagreements have been resolved.

full employment The condition existing when everyone who is able and willing to work can find a job. This does not mean that there will be zero unemployment, because there is always some FRICTIONAL UNEMPLOYMENT, due to people in the process of changing jobs or people who turn down available jobs because they are confident that something better is imminent; there is also always some SEASONAL UNEMPLOYMENT. Full employment is a fundamental goal of economic policy; the condition of full employment should mean that the economy is operating at its full capacity. Economists today differ on what constitutes full employment. For a long time, it was held to be 4 per cent unemployment. Some economists and policy-makers have argued in recent years that, with more generous unemployment-insurance benefits and with more families with more than one income, people take longer to choose new jobs, and that full employment should therefore be considered an unemployment rate of 5 or 6 per cent.

full-employment budget A calculation that measures what the country's fiscal position would be if the economy were operating at full employment and existing tax policies and spending programs were in place—hence the terms full-employment surplus or full-employment deficit. The full-employment budget is a useful analytical tool, for it may show, for example, that a government could afford to double its deficit to fight unemployment, since FISCAL POLICY, in full-employment conditions, would yield a surplus or balance. Or it may show that the deficit is so large that, even with full employment, there would still be a deficit. Economic growth yields tax revenues at a rate faster than the growth of the economy, due to the progressive nature of the income-tax system; similarly, a growing economy has a declining need for unemployment assistance and welfare benefits. Hence, using the full-employment budget, policy-makers can see not only how much room they have for economic stimulus, but whether or not they should be planning a tax cut or new spending programs to counter the FISCAL DRAG that could prevent the economy from reaching full-employment output.

functions of money The different uses of money in a modern economy. It is a medium of exchange, a standard of value, a store of value, and a standard of deferred payments when a debt is to be repaid.

fund Money and other financial assets that are held in reserve for a specified purpose. Examples include a trust fund for heirs, an endowment fund for a charity, a stabilization fund for commodities, a contingency fund for emergencies, or a sinking fund for the repayment of debts.

Fund for Rural Economic Development (FRED) A federal regional-development program introduced in 1966 to promote the social and economic growth of low-income, high-unemployment, and predominantly rural areas. A total of five agreements with four provinces were signed, to aid the Manitoba Inter-Lake region, Prince Edward Island, the Gaspé region of Quebec, and the Mactaquac and northeastern regions of New Brunswick. By 1979 the program had expired, with only the P.E.I. agreement still in effect.

fundamental disequilibrium The condition described in the articles of agreement of the INTERNATIONAL MONETARY FUND when the system of FIXED EXCHANGE RATES operated, indicating the need for a country to revalue or devalue its exchange rate and to take other measures to correct its BALANCE-OF-PAYMENTS problems. It meant that the actual exchange rate of a country was so much higher or lower than the official exchange rate, or was under such extreme market pressure to change, that the official exchange rate or par value had to be changed and other economic policies adopted to improve economic performance. The condition of fundamental disequilibrium does not technically exist in a system of FLOATING EXCHANGE RATES; but balance-of-payments problems and the need for changes in domestic economic policies have not disappeared.

funded debt The outstanding debt of a company, in the form of bonds, debentures, and other securities, that must be repaid within the next twelve months.

futures market A market in which speculators buy and sell commodities and foreign exchange for future delivery. While the market is speculative in nature, it performs the important economic function of spreading risk, and provides a year-round market for commodities. In the case of agricultural crops, it means that prices are not set simply on the day they come to market but are based on the willingness of investors to trade on future needs. Commodity dealers are able to protect themselves against wide swings in prices by HEDGING. There are two prices quoted—the spot or actual price and the futures price, for delivery, say, three months ahead. Futures traders are speculating on the difference between the futures price and the spot price three months later. Futures markets trade in a wide range of commodities, from grain and pork bellies to orange juice, cotton, gold, copper, and the Canadian dollar.

futurology The science of long-range forecasting. It is concerned with showing the alternative futures available to man, rather than with simply trying to predict the future. Futurologists are particularly active in the areas of economic, social, technological, ecological, and political change. Although their science is still in its infancy, they have developed a number of computer-assisted techniques to improve their skills and usefulness.

G

Galbraith, John Kenneth A leading POST-KEYNESIAN economist, born in Canada in 1908 but for most of his life a U.S. citizen and professor of economics at Harvard University. He is a strong advocate of a permanent INCOMES POLICY to control inflation. In his book, *American Capitalism: The Concept of Countervailing Power* (Boston, 1952), Galbraith argued that equilibrium is achieved in the economy not by intensive competition but by the checks and balances of big units. Big labour acts as a check on big corporations, big retail chains as a check on big manufacturers; big government, by its purchasing power, acts as a check on other big units. Throughout the economy, the countervailing power of big buyers and big sellers serves as the main form of restraint on OLIGOPOLY.

In *The Affluent Society* (Boston, 1958), Galbraith argued that sufficient abundance existed to allow all members of industrial countries to enjoy a comfortable standard of living; scarcity was not the problem. But the emphasis on private-sector production had led to a distortion in the distribution of society's resources, so that private affluence was accompanied by public squalour. Thus, there was an abundance of television sets and fast-food restaurants, but a shortage of parks and decent schools. Mass-market advertising and widespread consumer credit only served to increase the demand for private consumer goods at a time when the real need was to increase spending on public goods. Hence, gross national product was not a useful measure of economic progress. While it showed steadily rising output, this did not necessarily signify improvements in human welfare, if public goods such as hospitals, libraries, schools, parks, transit, public housing, and other needs were being neglected.

In *The New Industrial State* (Boston, 1967),

Galbraith depicted the mature corporation as the strategic planning unit of society, desiring social stability and stable growth. Entrepreneurs were replaced by corporate bureaucrats, who used scientific techniques, ranging from engineering to social psychology, to shape demand and set long-term goals. These scientific and bureaucratic corporate managers, Galbraith argued, had their like-minded counterparts in government; together, they formed modern society's technostructure or planning apparatus. Galbraith predicted a world-wide convergence towards a uniform technostructure and value system.

In *Economics and the Public Purpose* (Boston, 1973), Galbraith pointed to the unequal development of modern economies; on one side is the planned economy of the large corporation, while on the other is the market economy of farmers, small businesses, and entrepreneurs. The modern state, according to Galbraith, serves the interest of the powerful planning sector, while neglecting the market sector. He proposed major changes in economic policy-making: a reallocation of public spending to meet public needs rather than the needs of major corporations; comprehensive tax reform, to tax alike all increases in the command over resources; the use of public spending on needed projects rather than tax cuts to stimulate the economy during a recession; a sharply reduced role for monetary policy; a guaranteed annual income; permanent wage and price controls to deal with big corporations and big unions; and creation of a public planning authority to meet public needs in the economy.

galloping inflation See HYPERINFLATION.

game theory A technique used in business education to give students experience in devising competitive corporate strategies. Game theory deals with conflicts; players are given a simulated business situation and then handed the task of achieving certain objectives in competition with other players representing other firms. A player has to calculate how another player—a "business competitor"—will react if he cuts prices, changes his product mix, boosts advertising, or makes other decisions that corporate management makes in real life. Computers are used so that the results of decisions can be quickly seen. See also ZERO-SUM GAME.

garnishment A court judgement that allows a creditor to go to an employer and have part of an employee's pay deducted each week until an overdue loan or debt has been paid off. The employer transfers the money to the creditor before the employee gets his paycheque or deposit.

General Agreement on Tariffs and Trade (GATT) An international agreement whose objectives include the gradual reduction of trade barriers, and which sets out international rules on trade practices that all its signatories are pledged to respect. It has a secretariat in Geneva to monitor trade practices and to see that the GATT rules are followed.

GATT was one of several multilateral institutions formed in the aftermath of the Second World War to prevent a return to the protectionism and discriminatory policies of the 1930s. It hoped to promote instead international trade and investment in a world economy governed by non-discriminatory policies and international agreements on codes of conduct. Expanding world trade, it was argued, would benefit all nations by encouraging efficient production based on comparative advantage; such international specialization, it was expected, would raise the standard of living of people throughout the world.

GATT initially was signed by twenty-three countries, including Canada, in 1947, and came into effect in 1948. When it was first set up, it was planned as a temporary agreement until the International Trade Organization came into being; but in 1950, the U.S. Senate rejected the ITO, and GATT became the permanent institution.

GATT emphasized non-discriminatory trade policies—that is, trade policies in which a country would treat all of its trading partners alike. It opposed bilateral or discriminatory trade agreements, since such policies could lead to trade wars, retaliation, further protectionism, and reduced volumes of international trade. It has tried to curb the use of quotas and to prescribe rules where they are used, has established procedures that individual nations should follow in dealing with DUMPING and other improper trade practices, worked out agreements to control contentious trade problems such as low-cost textiles from the less-developed countries, achieved a system of generalized trade preferences for the less-developed countries, reduced the role of NON-TARIFF BARRIERS, and helped create rules for dealing with state trading companies from communist nations.

GATT rules permit the formation of free-trade areas such as the EUROPEAN ECONOMIC COMMUNITY. Its three basic objectives are the multilateral reduction of tariffs by negotiation; the non-discriminatory application of tariffs to all trading partners; and the gradual elimination of non-tariff barriers such as quotas, subsidies, and the use of health and other regulations to block imports. Major reductions of trade barriers were negotiated in the Geneva Round of 1956, the Dillon Round of 1960–62, the Kennedy Round of 1964–67, and the Tokyo round of 1974–79.

General Arrangements To Borrow A plan in which a group of ten nations, including Canada, made available a stand-by credit of seven billion dollars to the INTERNATIONAL MONETARY FUND in 1962. The purpose was to provide additional financing to protect currencies against speculative attacks. The countries—Canada, the United States, Britain, France, Germany, Japan, the Netherlands, Belgium, Italy, and Sweden—had to give prior approval before the IMF could make use of the credit. The fund was renewed for five years in 1979. See also GROUP OF TEN.

general equilibrium The existence in an economy of an equilibrium or balance between supply and demand in all industries and markets. General equilibrium is achieved when the competing demands for scarce goods and services and factors of production have been allocated through the price system in an on-going and interdependent process. For example, in labour markets, differences in wages will encourage mobility among firms and among industries. But the labour market will evolve towards a network of wage differences that reflects a matching of supply and demand for labour; when this is achieved, wage differences will tend to stabilize—thus, equilibrium is achieved. When such equilibrium exists in all markets for factors of production and supply of goods and services, then general equilibrium has been achieved.

General equilibrium analysis is the study of the conditions necessary to achieve general equilibrium and of the impact on general equilibrium of changes in one sector of the economy. It is a useful tool in helping to analyze the interdependence of different sectors of the economy; however, general equilibrium is never achieved in real life, since any economic system is always in a state of change. Technological innovation, new consumer tastes, oil-price increases, and changes in tax laws, for example, all affect general equilibrium.

General Investment Corporation A Quebec government corporation established in 1962 to invest in industrial enterprises, and thus to help develop Quebec's industrial base under local ownership. It was intended that the ownership would be shared equally among the Quebec government, the CAISSES POPULAIRES, and the public. Shares were sold to the public in 1963, but the Quebec government repurchased them in 1972, in exchange for Quebec government bonds, because of the corporation's poor financial performance. The corporation can be both a majority owner of a subsidiary enterprise and a partner in a joint venture. Its most important holdings include: Marine Industries Limited of Sorel, a shipbuilding, turbine, and railway-car manufacturer; Donohue Company Limited of Quebec City, a pulp and paper company; Forana Limited of Plessisville, a manufacturer of sawmill and pulp and paper equipment; and Cegelec Enterprises Incorporated of Laprairie, a manufacturer of electrical equipment. In 1979, the corporation formed a joint venture with Gulf Canada Limited and Union Carbide Canada Limited to establish a new petrochemical company, Petromont Incorporated. The headquarters of General Investment Corporation are in Montreal.

general strike A general work stoppage by union members in an attempt to paralyze the economy, either throughout a nation or in a particular region, in a bid to win their demands. In 1976, Canadian unions organized a "day of protest" against the federal government's wage- and price-controls program; they did not call it a strike, since a strike would have been illegal under their collective agreements. See also WINNIPEG GENERAL STRIKE.

generalized system of preferences A system of preferential or lower tariffs for LESS-DEVELOPED COUNTRIES, adopted by the GENERAL AGREEMENT ON TARIFFS AND TRADE in 1971 to help stimulate the economic growth of developing countries. Canada implemented the system in 1974.

generally accepted accounting principles The guidelines and techniques used by auditors to verify the financial statements and annual reports of a company. The guidelines are prepared by the Canadian Institute of Chartered Accountants. The AUDITOR'S REPORT in a company's financial statement must indicate whether or not the statements are based on generally accepted accounting principles; if there is any discrepancy, it must be indicated by the auditors.

Geological Survey of Canada A branch of the Department of ENERGY, MINES AND RESOURCES that carries out geological research and survey work to determine Canada's oil, natural-gas, uranium, and other mineral-resource reserves. It also carries out research into geological and geophysical techniques. GSC operates the Institute of Sedimentary and Petroleum Geology in Calgary and the Atlantic Geoscience Centre in Dartmouth, N.S. GSC publishes occasional assessments of Canada's oil and natural-gas reserves, including assessments of the country's ULTIMATE POTENTIAL RESERVES. Its most recent assessment was completed in 1979.

geophysics Prospecting for minerals using scientific methods; in particular, geophysicists try to detect the presence and size of mineral ores. Different minerals have different levels of magnetism, radioactivity, or electrical conductivity, for example, which can be detected by instruments above ground.

gift tax A tax levied on a donor when he makes a gift to another person. The federal government imposed a gift tax until the beginning of 1972, when the CAPITAL-GAINS TAX came into effect. The gift tax was turned over to the provinces, but only Quebec imposes such a tax; Ontario abolished it in 1979.

The federal government assumes deemed realization of the capital gain when a person makes a gift to someone else—except when the gift is to the spouse, or consists of a farm or small business given to other members of the family. In the case of farms and small businesses, the recipient has to pay the capital gain that would have been paid by the donor, if the recipient ever sells the farm or business.

Quebec imposes a 20 per cent tax on the donor of any gift of more than $3,000 per person, and imposes an annual maximum on all tax-free gifts by an individual of $15,000. Quebec provides an exemption for family farms and businesses, and requires that gifts made a certain number of years before death also be subject to SUCCESSION DUTY.

glamour stock A COMMON SHARE that is widely traded and that investors believe will enjoy a continuing and significant increase in earnings. Such a share usually sells at a high PRICE-EARNINGS RATIO.

gnomes of Zurich A name for Swiss bankers and financiers who, operating behind the secrecy of Swiss banks and numbered accounts, are alleged to exert significant influence on foreign exchange, gold, and money markets. Their role is exaggerated, but they do still have an important influence and can contribute to sudden speculation around a national currency.

go public A term used to describe a privately owned company's decision to get its shares listed on a stock exchange and to sell its shares to the public. A company going public in Canada has to get the approval of a provincial SECURITIES COMMISSION and file a PROSPECTUS. It must also be accepted for listing by a STOCK EXCHANGE.

go slow See WORK TO RULE.

gold exchange standard The system under which countries expressed their exchange rates in gold but, instead of keeping gold in their foreign-exchange reserves, kept a stable currency that was freely convertible into gold. India was on the gold exchange standard in the early part of the twentieth century; it kept its reserves in the British pound sterling.

gold market In Canada, gold can be purchased from banks and gold futures can be traded on the WINNIPEG COMMODITY EXCHANGE. The international price of gold, which affects trading in gold and gold futures around the world, is set daily in two different centres, London and Zurich, in London as a result of daily trades among five bullion dealers, and in Zurich by three major banks that operate a gold pool.

gold pool An agreement among eight central banks, that lasted from 1961 to 1968, to maintain the price of gold at U.S. $35.19875, by buying and selling gold out of their exchange reserves on the London market. The pool originally consisted of the United States, Britain, France, Germany, Italy, Belgium, the Netherlands, and Switzerland, and operated through the BANK FOR INTERNATIONAL SETTLEMENTS. France withdrew early in 1968 and, with the price of gold soaring, the arrangement was replaced by the even shorter-lived TWO-TIER GOLD PRICE.

gold reserves Gold held by individual countries as part of their foreign-exchange reserves. While gold is no longer used to back up paper money or as an official part of the international monetary system, it is still an important part of many countries' foreign-exchange reserves. The INTERNATIONAL MONETARY FUND is developing a common method of valuing the gold that individual countries still hold in their foreign-exchange reserves. See also GOLD STANDARD.

gold standard The use of a fixed amount of gold as the basic standard of value of a currency. Before the First World War, Britain was the leading country on the gold standard. Many other nations found it just as convenient to hold British pounds as to hold gold in their reserves, not only to settle their international balances of payment, but also to back their domestic currencies. Britain went off the gold standard during the First World War, returned to it briefly in the 1920s, and went off it permanently in 1931. The United States remained on the gold standard until 1971. Canada was on the gold standard at the time of Confederation. At the start of the First World War, Canada went off the gold standard, along with Britain; after the war, Canada returned briefly to the gold standard, between July 1926 and January 1929, but Canada was not officially declared off the gold standard until September 1931.

Under the gold standard, a country's currency is defined in terms of a specific weight and fineness of gold. The appeal of the gold standard was that it imposed a strict discipline on governments, who were anxious to retain their gold reserves and were thus disposed to take harsh measures to keep their inflation rate down and international creditors happy. Investors also liked gold because it was international and had a relatively stable value. But the standard also had great flaws. It tied world economic growth and the expansion of trade and investment to the supply of a metal dug out of the ground in just a few countries.

good Any commodity, product, or service that serves a human want. Economists talk of two types of good, an ECONOMIC GOOD, which is a scarce good and therefore bears a price, and a FREE GOOD, which is so abundant that it cannot command a price.

good faith The assumption in business and in collective bargaining that the parties to a transaction or agreement are sincere in their actions, want to reach an agreement, and will honour it when it is made.

goodwill The value placed on the reputation, know-how and trademarks of a company. Goodwill is the difference between what one company pays for another and the value of the acquired company's TANGIBLE ASSETS. It is an INTANGIBLE ASSET and represents earning power, just as machines and buildings do. A company with a good reputation has usually invested in that reputation, through the quality of its product or service, its willingness to deal with customer problems, the non-business role it plays in the community (for example, through its support of charities), and the advertising and promotion money it has spent to make sure that the public is aware of its name, product, and reputation. Goodwill is the money value of a firm's reputation.

Gordon Commission See ROYAL COMMISSION ON CANADA'S ECONOMIC PROSPECTS.

government bond A BOND issued by a federal, provincial, or municipal government, school board, or other government agency.

government procurement Purchases by government of goods and services, including goods and services for its own use, such as computers, computer terminals, trucks, and consulting advice, and goods and services to provide a public service, such as airports, nuclear-power stations, telecommunications services, and military equipment. Some policy-makers argue that government procurement should be used as a tool of INDUSTRIAL STRATEGY, by giving a preference to domestic firms and thus assuring them of a market if they develop new technologies or products. Others argue that there is a limit to such a policy, because other countries would retaliate and because it can be considered a NON-TARIFF BARRIER. Some provincial governments give their own firms a preference when awarding contracts, to encourage their growth and development.

government revenues All income received by a government. It includes tax and tariff revenues, royalty income from natural resources, proceeds from the sale of crown lands or licences for the use of crown lands for forest or mineral exploitation, profits from crown corporations, fee and licence revenues, direct charges to users of government services, investment income, the sale of government assets, and the proceeds from the sale of government bonds. See also FEDERAL TAXING POWER, PROVINCIAL TAXING POWER.

government spending The total spending by the federal, provincial, and municipal governments and their agencies, such as local school boards and universities. Government spending can take several forms: direct spending on goods and services; capital investment in housing, airports, power stations, and the like; transfer payments to individuals, other levels of government, or corporations; and the foregone revenue or value of all the tax incentives and write-offs that governments give to industry and individuals. Although direct government spending, capital investment, and transfer payments are all measurable, no level of government in Canada has made a serious effort to calculate the cost to the public of so-called TAX EXPENDITURES—that is, the value of incentives and exemptions in the tax system. Without such a calculation, it is impossible to measure the overall level of government spending in the economy. The federal government was considering presenting a tax-expenditure budget at the time of its 1980–81 BUDGET.

governor-in-council Decisions of a federal or provincial government made by the Crown —that is, the governor general or a lieutenant-governor—on the advice of the Privy Council, which, in practice, is the cabinet. Confirmation of a cabinet decision by the governor-in-council gives the decision the force of law; such confirmations are known as orders-in-council. In the early days of Confederation, the governor general exercised considerable discretion: between 1867 and 1878, he refused to give royal assent to twenty-one bills passed by Parliament and would sit in on cabinet meetings. Today, he plays only a ceremonial role.

grace period A short period of time after an interest payment or debt payment falls due in which the debtor can still meet his obligation without penalty. The period is usually three days, and covers such contingencies as a cheque being delayed in the mail.

grain-handling system The system that handles the movement of grain from country elevators to final destinations. It includes country elevators, terminal and transfer elevators, mill elevators, the railways that move grain, grain inspection, weighing and cleaning services, and loading facilities at ports where grain ships pick up their cargoes. It is a large network of different companies, co-operatives, and government agencies and departments, engaged in assembling, storing, processing, and transporting grains. A strike in any one part of the grain-handling system can close the entire system down.

grain trade The international traders who sell Canadian grains. In addition to the CANADIAN WHEAT BOARD, the grain trade includes a number of firms that act as selling agents on behalf of the board.

Grains Group A federal body created in 1970 that advises the cabinet minister responsible for the CANADIAN WHEAT BOARD. The minister serves as chairman of the group, which is made up of advisers from the Department of AGRICULTURE, Department of INDUSTRY, TRADE AND COMMERCE, and the Ministry of TRANSPORT. It reviews problems in grain handling and marketing, transportation, and production.

grandfather clause A clause inserted in new legislation when the new legislation prohibits or restricts certain activities that had been permitted until then; the purpose of the grandfather clause is to exempt all existing persons or firms that had already been engaged in the now-prohibited or -restricted activity before the legislation was introduced. For example, Ontario securities legislation restricting the entry of new, foreign-owned securities firms contained a grandfather clause permitting foreign-owned securities firms already active in the province to continue to operate.

grant A government payment intended as an incentive to an individual, organization, or corporation, to perform a certain task. For example, governments give grants to individuals and firms to carry out research and development, and to firms to make investments in areas with chronically high unemployment.

gratuity A tip, given in return for a service rendered.

Gray Report See FOREIGN DIRECT INVESTMENT IN CANADA.

Great Lakes Water Quality Agreement An agreement signed by Canada and the United States in April 1972 to achieve specified clean-up targets for the Great Lakes and the international section of the St. Lawrence River, with specific programs to be in place by 1975. The agreement followed the report of the INTERNATIONAL JOINT COMMISSION in 1970, which pointed to the urgent need to halt the deterioration of the Great Lakes, resulting from the presence of phosphates, mercury, lead, DDT, and bacteria. Pollution had severely damaged the Great Lakes fishing industry and spoiled recreational beaches; through eutrophication, oxygen was being consumed, thus destroying life in the water.

Canada and the United States agreed on a set of water-quality standards; on measures to deal with municipal and industrial-waste disposal, including pollution from the pulp and paper, petrochemicals, base-metal-mining, and food-processing industries; a 50 per cent reduction in the amount of phosphates dumped into the Great Lakes each year; and on contingency plans to deal with oil spills and other wastes from Great Lakes shipping. The agreement was extended, in November 1978, to the end of 1983. Objectives included tighter controls to deal with oil wastes from Great Lakes shipping, new objectives on the control of wastes from municipalities and industry, tougher curbs on toxic pollutants, the identification of airborne pollutants entering the Great Lakes, the identification and control of pollution from agriculture, forestry, and other land-use activities, further reductions on phosphates entering the Great Lakes, and new limits on radioactivity. The International Joint Commission monitors the agreement's progress. The Canadian costs are shared by the federal and Ontario governments under a federal-provincial agreement.

green paper A document published by the government that contains proposals for change. The proposals do not represent government policies or intentions, but are put forward to generate public discussion and debate. See also WHITE PAPER.

green revolution The introduction of new, high-yielding wheat and rice seeds especially suited to the conditions of the LESS-DEVELOPED COUNTRIES, along with scientific methods of agricultural production that were introduced in the 1960s. The use of new hybrid seeds, along with irrigation, chemical fertilizers, pesticides, and modern farming techniques, gave less-developed countries the potential to raise their food output significantly.

Gresham's law Bad money drives out good; when two moneys of equal legal-tender value but different real value are in circulation, the more valuable of the two will be hoarded rather than spent. Thus, if gold and silver coins are in circulation, with equal legal-tender value but with the gold coins actually worth more than the silver, then the gold coins will be hoarded and the silver ones used for commerce. It could be argued that the law also applied to international exchange markets in the late 1960s: the U.S. dollar and gold had fixed legal-tender values, but the real value of gold was so much higher than its U.S. dollar value that some countries and investors hoarded gold and cashed in their U.S. dollars for gold. The law is named after Sir Thomas Gresham (1519–79), an adviser to Queen Elizabeth I.

grey market A market in which a scarce commodity is sold at above-market prices for immediate delivery. Unlike a BLACK MARKET, which is illegal, a grey market is legal, but prices are much higher than those prevailing in the normal market.

grievance A formal complaint against an employer by an employee or group of employees, or by a union contending that there has been a breach of the COLLECTIVE AGREEMENT. It can also consist of a formal complaint by an employer against a union or an employee, also on the grounds that the collective agreement has been broken, although such grievances by employers are more rare. Once a grievance has been filed, a number of steps must be followed, steps that are usually spelled out in the collective agreement. Normally, the union and the employer will try to settle the grievance in the department where it happened. If this fails, then higher levels of both management and the union will try to reach a settlement. Should they fail, then the grievance goes to ARBITRATION, where a ruling is made that is binding on the employer, the union, and the employees concerned.

gross domestic product (GDP) The value of production of goods and services in the economy resulting from the factors of production, in particular from capital, whether of Canadians or of non-residents. It does not include the returns from Canadian investment abroad, but does include the returns on foreign capital invested in Canada. GROSS NATIONAL PRODUCT, on the other hand, includes the value of goods and services produced by Canadians, whether earned inside or outside Canada, but excludes the returns to non-residents on capital they have invested in Canada. Statistics Canada breaks the gross domestic product down into fifteen major industrial categories, and gives detailed information for each on wages, inventory changes, profits, investment, and taxes. The figures are extremely useful in sectoral analysis of the economy. See also NATIONAL ACCOUNTS, GROSS PROVINCIAL PRODUCT.

gross fixed-capital formation An important element of GROSS NATIONAL EXPENDITURE; the total capital investment in the economy by government and industry, including spending on new housing, before deducting DEPRECIATION for the normal wear and tear or obsolescence of capital stock. Gross fixed-capital formation minus depreciation or capital-cost allowances equals net new-capital formation, or the addition to the nation's capital stock.

gross income The total income of an individual or enterprise before expenses and taxes have been deducted. In some business enterprises, it may be the total income after deducting the cost of goods sold, but before deducting other expenses and taxes.

gross national expenditure (GNE) The total level of demand in the economy for goods and services; it shows how the GROSS NATIONAL PRODUCT, the total output of goods and services, is consumed through consumer spending, investment, and government spending.

The main elements of demand are: **1.** Personal spending on consumer goods and services, including rents and imputed rents for people living in their own homes. **2.** Government spending on goods and services. **3.** Capital investment by government and business, including construction of new homes, factories, power plants, mines, shopping centres, mineral exploration, and industrial machinery and equipment. **4.** The value of physical increases or reductions in inventories. **5.** The net contribution of the foreign sector of the economy—that is, of exports of goods and services minus imports of goods and services. **6.** The residual error of estimate, a small statistical adjustment to round out the calculations.

Gross national expenditure can be adjusted for inflation, by deducting the GROSS-NATIONAL-PRODUCT DEFLATOR, to indicate the physical or real changes in demand in the economy. Gross-national-expenditure figures are important in economic analysis since they permit economists to study the strengths and weaknesses of the various elements of demand in the economy and to recommend policy changes to improve economic performance.

gross national product (GNP) A nation's total output of goods and services, expressed either in current dollar value or, by adjusting for inflation, in real terms or by changes in physical volume. The change in the gross national product each year is the growth rate of the economy. In spite of its imperfections—it includes the costs of fighting crime or of reducing pollution as part of the nation's output, but fails to measure such benefits as increased leisure time—the gross national product is the best overall measure of economic performance.

The principal components of the GNP are: **1.** Wages, salaries, and supplementary labour income such as paid holidays, tips, and commissions. **2.** Military pay and allowances, including payments to military personnel stationed outside Canada. **3.** Corporation profits before taxes, minus dividends paid to non-residents. **4.** Interest and miscellaneous investment income, including the investment income of individuals, pension funds, insurance companies, and other institutions, except for interest from consumer loans, and government income from crown corporations. **5.** Accrued net income of farm operators from farm production, which represents the pre-tax profits of farmers and the physical change in farm inventories. **6.** Net income of non-farm unincorporated businesses, professional incomes of doctors, lawyers, and others, and rental income, including an imputed rent on owner-occupied buildings. **7.** An adjustment for changes in the value of inventories, due to price changes. All of these items together constitute net national income at factor cost—in other words, the earnings of the various FACTORS OF PRODUCTION.

To arrive at the GNP, other costs of production also have to be included. These are: **8.** INDIRECT TAXES less subsidies, which include the manufacturers' sales tax, business property taxes, customs and excise taxes, and other taxes that are levied on businesses but are paid ultimately by consumers, minus various subsidies paid out by governments, such as direct grants to industry or subsidies to consumers to hold down prices. **9.** Capital-cost allowances and miscellaneous valuation adjustments, which consist mainly of DEPRECIATION of the normal wear and tear of business assets. **10.** A residual error of estimate, a small statistical figure to balance out the numbers.

GNP figures are published quarterly, at seasonally adjusted annual rates, and annually for the year as a whole. See also GROSS-NATIONAL-PRODUCT DEFLATOR, GROSS-NATIONAL-PRODUCT GAP, GROSS NATIONAL EXPENDITURE, GROSS PROVINCIAL PRODUCT, GROSS DOMESTIC PRODUCT.

gross-national-product deflator The price index for the entire economy. Unlike the CONSUMER PRICE INDEX, which measures changes in consumer prices, the deflator measures price changes for all the goods and services used in the economy; for example, in addition to consumer prices, it measures changes in wholesale prices, construction costs, machinery prices, and import and export prices. It is the best overall measure of inflation in the economy. The deflator is produced at the same time as quarterly GROSS-NATIONAL-PRODUCT statistics; it is deducted from the current dollar rate of economic growth, to yield the real rate of growth or physical-volume rate of growth. The deflator is broken down into a variety of price indexes, measuring, for instance, construction costs, machinery prices, or import and export prices.

gross-national-product gap The difference between an economy's GROSS NATIONAL PRODUCT at FULL EMPLOYMENT and its actual output when it is operating below full-employment rates. Calculations can be made of the lost output of the economy for each percentage point of unemployment above the full-employment rate. See also POTENTIAL GROSS NATIONAL PRODUCT.

gross profit An accounting term, meaning sales revenue left over after deducting the cost of producing the goods sold, but before deducting sales, administrative, and other indirect business costs. It consists of net sales minus the cost of the goods sold.

gross provincial product (GPP) The value of goods and services produced within the geographic boundaries of each province; the provincial equivalent of the GROSS DOMESTIC PRODUCT. Statistics are produced annually for each province by Statistics Canada, and date back to 1961.

gross-up and credit system See DIVIDEND TAX CREDIT.

group insurance A single life- and disability-insurance policy covering all members of an organization; often used by an employer to provide relatively low-cost life and disability insurance for all of his employees. The cost is low because the administrative costs are low. The contract is between the insurance company and the employer; individuals enter and leave the plan as they enter and leave employment with the firm.

Group of Seven The seven major non-communist powers that have met at formal economic summits since 1975. The group includes the United States, Canada, Britain, West Germany, Japan, France, and Italy. Canada was excluded from the economic summit at Rambouillet, France, in November 1975, but has attended subsequent summits, including those at Dorado Beach, Puerto Rico, in June 1976, in London in May 1977, in Bonn in June 1978, and in Tokyo in June 1979.

Group of Seventy-seven See UNITED NATIONS CONFERENCE ON TRADE AND DEVELOPMENT (UNCTAD).

Group of Ten (G-10) The finance ministers and central-bank governors, or their officials, of the leading industrial countries, who meet on a regular basis to discuss problems of the international monetary system and ways to make the system function more effectively. The group came into being after the GENERAL ARRANGEMENTS TO BORROW fund was created in 1962 by the same ten nations, to help the INTERNATIONAL MONETARY FUND to deal with balance-of-payments problems. The fund of seven billion dollars was extended for another five years in 1979. The Group of Ten remains an influential body; it is the forum in which the western nations attempt, not only to reach a consensus on needed changes in the monetary system, but also to co-ordinate their monetary policies. Its members are Canada, the United States, Britain, Germany, France, Italy, Belgium, Japan, the Netherlands, and Sweden. Chairmanship rotates among members of the group.

Group of Twenty (G-20) The Interim Committee of Finance Ministers of the INTERNATIONAL MONETARY FUND, created in 1974 to advise the fund on improvements to the structure of the world financial system. Members include the finance ministers of the United States, West Germany, Japan, Britain, Canada, and France, plus fifteen others elected from the fund's members. In 1976, the G-20 presented a series of proposals to the fund for reform, including a recommendation that the G-20 become a decision-making council of governors of the IMF.

growth stock Shares of a company that is expected to have exceptionally good prospects for growth in dividends and capital gain.

grubstake Financial assistance, or supplies of equipment, food, and clothing, provided to a prospector, with the promise that he will reciprocate with a share in any discovery he may make.

guarantee 1. The promise by a third party to a lender to pay back a loan if the borrower fails to do so. Sometimes a bank is unwilling to make a loan to an individual without a promise by a third party to pay back the debt if need be. The person providing such an assurance is a guarantor. **2.** A synonym for an expressed WARRANTY that comes with certain consumer products, such as electrical appliances.

guaranteed annual income Automatic payments from government to individuals or families to ensure that everyone in society has a minimum level of income. This could be achieved, for example, through a NEGATIVE INCOME TAX. The difference between existing income-maintenance schemes and a guaranteed annual income is that existing schemes tend to discourage recipients from trying to supplement their income, whereas a guaranteed annual income could be designed to include a strong work incentive by letting recipients keep part of their earnings. It is also argued that a guaranteed-annual-income system would be much cheaper to administer and would eliminate the need for the great variety of assistance programs that now exist, each of them designed to deal with a particular kind of income need. Canada has a form of guaranteed annual income for senior citizens; it is the guaranteed-income supplement, a payment that is made in addition to the old-age pension to senior citizens whose total income is below a certain level. The amount of the payment depends on the gap between the total income of a pensioner and the income ceiling set under the guaranteed-income supplement.

guaranteed-investment certificate A debt security, issued by a trust company, that pays a fixed rate of interest, usually at least one percentage point higher than can be earned on a savings account at the time the security is purchased. These investment certificates are issued in denominations of five hundred dollars or more for terms of one to five years; they are issued in denominations of five thousand dollars or more for terms of 364 days or less.

guideline A government attempt to influence behaviour by setting out a standard of desired behaviour that lacks the force of law. Guidelines may be used, for example, to restrain pay and price increases, to persuade foreign-owned subsidiaries to do more research and development, to reduce industrial pollution to a certain level, or to discourage corporations from borrowing abroad. See also MORAL SUASION.

Guiding Principles of Good Corporate Behaviour Guidelines issued by the federal government on 31 March 1966, to define good corporate citizenship for foreign-controlled subsidiaries operating in Canada. The objectives encouraged were: **1.** Pursuit of sound growth and full realization of the company's productive potential, thereby to share the national objective of full and effective use of the nation's resources. **2.** Realization of maximum competitiveness through the most effective use of the company's own resources, recognizing the desirability of achieving appropriate specialization of productive operations within the internationally affiliated group of companies. **3.** Maximum development of market opportunities in other countries as well as Canada. **4.** Where applicable, the extension of processing of natural-resource products to the degree practicable on an economic basis. **5.** Pursuit of a pricing policy designed to assure a fair and reasonable return to the company and to Canada for all goods and services sold abroad, including sales to the parent company and other foreign affiliates. **6.** In matters of procurement, the search for and development of economic sources of supply in Canada. **7.** The development, as an integral part of the Canadian operation wherever practicable, of the technological research and design capability necessary to enable the company to pursue appropriate product-development programs, so as to take full advantage of market opportunities domestically and abroad. **8.** Retention of a sufficient share of earnings to give appropriate financial support to the growth requirements of the Canadian operation, having in mind a fair return to shareholders on capital invested. **9.** The development of a Canadian outlook within management, through purposeful training programs, promotion of qualified Canadian personnel, and inclusion of a major proportion of Canadian citizens on the company's board of directors. **10.** The development of a financial structure that provides opportunity for equity participation in the Canadian enterprise by the Canadian public. **11.** Periodic publication of information on the financial position and operations of the company. **12.** Appropriate attention to and support for recognized national objectives and established government programs designed to further Canada's economic development, and encouragement and support for Canadian institutions directed towards the intellectual, social, and cultural advancement of the community. Large and medium-sized subsidiary companies were also asked to provide confidential information on their operations from time to time. In 1975, the guidelines were replaced by the NEW PRINCIPLES FOR INTERNATIONAL BUSINESS.

guns and butter A metaphor used to illustrate the point that economics is about choice, and how to allocate resources to achieve the maximum welfare for the community. No country can have all the guns it wants and all the butter it wants; economics helps society to determine the combinations of both that can be produced, with the knowledge that in choosing more of one, society is sacrificing some of the other. In a FULL-EMPLOYMENT economy, extra production of one product means less production of another.

H

harbour commission A semi-autonomous federal body, which includes local as well as federal appointees, that is responsible for the administration of a port. The commissions report to the minister of TRANSPORT. The ports operated by commissions include Toronto, Hamilton, Windsor, the Lakehead, Oshawa, Belleville, and a number of west-coast ports, including New Westminster, Nanaimo, and Port Alberni. See also NATIONAL HARBOURS BOARD.

hard currency A currency that is freely convertible and enjoys a stable exchange rate. Nations of the industrialized world tend to have hard currencies, while the LESS-DEVELOPED COUNTRIES have SOFT CURRENCIES. Frequently, poor countries find that they have to pay for the products of industrial countries in hard currencies, since no one wants their currencies—there may be nothing to buy with soft currencies, or no profitable investments to be made. This means that poor countries have to scramble hard to earn the hard currencies they need for essential imports. The Canadian dollar is a hard currency.

hard sell An intensive sales effort that puts considerable pressure on consumers to buy. Sometimes, a hard-sell effort can backfire, because consumers rebel against the pressure.

hardware The physical elements in a computer system, including the central processing unit, the various memory and filing systems, and the terminals through which information is entered into the computer or received from it. See also SOFTWARE.

haulage The term used to describe the rates charged by trucking companies to carry goods.

hedging A way of reducing, and perhaps even eliminating, the risk of a loss from changes in the price of commodities or foreign exchange. The risk is covered by buying futures on the FUTURES MARKET; a profit on futures will cover a loss on the commodity or foreign exchange, while a loss on the futures can be covered by a profit on the commodity or foreign exchange. For example, a flour company may buy wheat at, say, four dollars a bushel to be milled into flour for delivery in three months' time. To protect itself against a sudden drop in wheat prices, which would also reduce flour prices, the flour company will contract to deliver an equal amount of wheat at four dollars a bushel in three months. If the price of wheat has dropped to three dollars a bushel in three months, the flour company will have lost money on its flour; but it can buy wheat in the market for three dollars a bushel, which it can instantly resell, through its futures contract, at a profit. The profit on the futures contract should cancel out the loss on the flour, so that the flour company will end up with the rate of profit it had expected from its normal processing of the wheat. If the price of wheat instead shoots up to five dollars a bushel, the flour company would make an extra profit on its flour; but that extra profit would be used to cover the loss on the futures contract, since the flour company has to buy wheat at five dollars a bushel and deliver it to someone who will pay only four dollars a bushel.

An importer who has to pay a bill in a foreign currency or an exporter who is expecting to be paid in a foreign currency will go through the same exercise, with a futures contract on a foreign currency, if he feels there is any likelihood that the exchange rate will change before the delivery and billing dates. Hedging protects normal profits, but eliminates the opportunity for windfall profits, since any big gain in the value of the commodity or foreign exchange will be offset by the loss on the futures contract.

hedonistic principle The notion that individuals are motivated in their actions by the pursuit of pleasure, self-interest, or the avoidance of pain or discomfort. This principle is the basis of the theory of UTILITY as an economic concept.

Heeney-Merchant Report A report on *Principles for Partnership* between Canada and the United States, written by Arnold Heeney, twice Canadian ambassador to the United States, and Livingstone Merchant, twice U.S. ambassador to Canada. In January 1964, Prime Minister Lester B. Pearson and U.S. President Lyndon Johnson asked the two men to produce guidelines "to make it easier to avoid divergencies in economic and other policies of the two countries." Heeney and Merchant investigated a number of recent causes of friction, including Canadian trade with Cuba, union disputes in Great Lakes shipping, U.S. magazines in Canada, and oil and gas export and import policies, and asked the officials involved in both countries how these disputes might have been better handled.

In their July 1965 report, *Principles for Partnership,* Heeney and Merchant recommended an ongoing committee of Canadian and U.S. government officials to back up the work of the JOINT MINISTERIAL COMMITTEE ON TRADE AND ECONOMIC AFFAIRS, a wider role for the INTERNATIONAL JOINT COMMISSION, more effective use of the Permanent Joint Board on Defence, and a joint study of U.S.-Canada energy policies. Canadian authorities, the report said, "must have confidence that the practice of quiet diplomacy is not only neighbourly and convenient to the United States but that it is in fact more effective than the alternative of raising a row and being unpleasant in Canada." The report caused controversy in Canada, both for its advocacy of quiet diplomacy in dealing with Canada-U.S. disputes, and because of its recommendation that Canada strive to avoid public disagreement with the United States on international questions, "especially upon critical issues." This was taken to mean that Canada should not express itself publicly on U.S. foreign policy; at the time, the U.S. was engaged in the war in Vietnam.

hidden inflation Inflation that does not show up in the form of price increases, but in a decline in the size or quality of a product or service. For example, the size of a chocolate bar may be reduced instead of its price being raised; this means that the consumer gets less chocolate bar for the same price.

hidden tax A tax that is included in the price of goods or services, but is not separately identified to the consumer; usually an INDIRECT

TAX, ranging from a tariff or excise tax to a manufacturer's sales tax, which raises the price of the product or service. While it is paid in the first instance by the importer, manufacturer, or other business firm, the tax is added into the price of the product or service and shifted on to the consumer.

hidden unemployment People who are unemployed but who don't show up in the unemployment statistics compiled by Statistics Canada in its monthly LABOUR-FORCE SURVEY. The hidden unemployed include discouraged workers who have stopped looking for work because of their age, health, or lack of skills, or because they live in an area of chronic unemployment; and people who would like to work but don't try to find a job because they don't think they have a chance to find one. Indians living on reservations who don't have jobs are also among the hidden unemployed. The term can also be applied to workers with part-time jobs who really want full-time jobs.

historical cost An asset in a balance sheet whose value is expressed as the actual cost at the time it was acquired; in today's dollars, it might cost much more to replace. Historical cost is the acquisition cost. It also means that property and other assets may be worth considerably more than the BALANCE SHEET shows.

hoarding The accumulation of goods or money far in excess of normal, everyday needs, by a business or individual. The main motives for hoarding are the belief that there will be a shortage or the belief that prices will rise significantly. A person who believes that a currency—say, the Swiss franc—is going to rise sharply in value may buy Swiss francs in the form of traveller's cheques and store them in his safety-deposit box.

hog fuel A by-product fuel made from the scraps of pulp mills, plywood mills, and sawmills, scraps such as bark, shavings, sawdust, and rejected lumber scraps.

holding company A company set up to own a controlling block of shares in another company or other companies, and thus to run those companies; hence, it is more than simply an investment company. The investors controlling a holding company do not need to own all the shares, simply enough to control it. The holding company, in turn, can control many other companies. Thus, from a relatively small financial base, an investor or group of investors can end up controlling a large corporate empire. The shares of a holding company are sometimes traded on a STOCK EXCHANGE.

home-improvement loan A loan for up to ten years to property owners to repair and renovate their homes or apartments. CANADA MORTGAGE AND HOUSING CORPORATION gives a limited guarantee for such loans, made by banks and other financial institutions at a lending rate slightly above the long-term government-bond rate.

horizontal expansion The expansion of a firm within the industry in which it is already active; the purpose is to increase its share of the market for a particular product or service. An example would be a truck manufacturer who expands by taking over another truck manufacturer, or by building a major facility to increase his truck-making capacity.

horizontal integration The situation in which a company takes over another in the same business, thus eliminating a competitor and achieving both a broader market and greater economies of scale. See also VERTICAL INTEGRATION.

hot money Funds flowing out of a country for speculative reasons. These can range from anticipated exchange controls or increased taxation to changes in monetary policy. Expectations of a change in the country's exchange rate can also be a reason for money to flee to another financial centre.

household A person or group of persons occupying the same dwelling. Usually a household is a family, but it may consist of a group of unrelated persons, of two or more unrelated families living together, or of one person living alone. Statistics Canada measures households in several ways: by average size; by type—that is, family or non-family; and by age and marital status of the head of the household. See also FAMILY.

household formation An important statistic that shows the net increase in a year of new households. The rate of household formation is used to estimate the demand for new homes and CONSUMER GOODS. The rate can increase faster than overall population growth if there is a large number of young people in their late teens and early twenties who expect to leave home and live on their own.

household survey A survey by a public-opinion firm or by STATISTICS CANADA to get information from the various members of households, as opposed to individual opinions or information. Household surveys are often used in MARKET RESEARCH; they are also widely used by Statistics Canada to calculate statistics on unemployment, family income, eating habits, and spending, for example.

housing starts A monthly statistic compiled by both Statistics Canada and CANADA MORTGAGE AND HOUSING CORPORATION, showing the number of new housing units on which construction has begun. The statistic is often expressed in terms of an annual rate. The statistic is based mainly on the number of building permits issued by Canadian municipalities, with some adjustment made for the length of time it normally takes before excavation work begins. The figure includes single-family homes, duplexes, townhouses, and rental and condominium apartments.

Howe Research Institute (HRI) An economic-research organization that deals mainly in public-policy issues and international economic issues. It was formed in 1973 through the merger of the C.D. Howe Memorial Foundation and the Private Planning Association of Canada. It has continued the work of three committees established by the Private Planning Association: the Canadian Economic Policy Committee, which concentrates on Canadian economic issues; the Canadian-American Committee, which deals with North American trade and other economic issues; and the British–North American Committee, which deals with international economic issues. The institute has its own research staff and also sponsors outside research. Among its publications is its annual *Policy Review and Outlook*, which reviews the economic outlook and suggests priorities for national economic policy. The institute is based in Montreal.

human capital Investments in the health, education, and skills of the workforce. The assumption is that a healthy, well-educated, and skilled workforce will have a high rate of productivity and thus contribute to economic growth. The concept of human capital is used to help justify public spending on health and education.

Hyde Park Agreement An agreement between Canada and the United States, signed 20 April 1941, in which the two countries agreed to share their industrial capacity and resources in the defence of the North American continent. The agreement was of more immediate importance to Canada, which was already heavily involved in the war effort and seriously short of U.S. dollars to buy strategic materials and parts; the United States agreed to accelerate its purchases of defence materials and supplies from Canada, and to broaden its lend-lease arrangements, so that U.S. parts obtained for weapons assembled in Canada for British use could be included under U.S. lend-lease financing of the British war effort. The agreement paved the way for close economic co-operation and joint production planning once the United States entered the Second World War, following the Japanese attack on Pearl Harbor on 7 December 1941.

hydro-electric power Electricity created by the exploitation of Canada's major rivers through the use of power dams and power-generating facilities. The electricity is carried to market by long-distance transmission lines. About 60 per cent of Canada's electrical-generating capacity is derived from hydro-electric facilities.

hyperinflation Sharp and escalating increases in prices, increases so immense that they lead to the collapse of ordinary commercial dealings, the disorganization of production, and social breakdown. The wealth of large groups may be wiped out in a matter of weeks. Money becomes worthless and the monetary system ceases to function. Such economic collapses usually take only a few months to run their course; fortunately, there are few cases in modern history. The best known was in Germany in 1920–23; inflation soared 2,500 per cent in one month. Hyperinflation also created anarchy in China, Hungary, and Greece after the Second World War. Hyperinflation is sometimes called galloping inflation.

hypothecate To pledge real property or securities as collateral for a loan.

I

idle capacity The unused productive capacity of a firm, due to a lack of demand for its products, or a lack of raw materials or parts. Statistics Canada publishes quarterly statistics on excess capacity in the manufacturing industry in its CAPACITY-UTILIZATION series.

idle money Bank deposits that are not being used. These are deposits in excess of what the banks need to have on hand to meet daily transactions and BANK OF CANADA reserve requirements. It is from those excess reserves that new loans can be made; through its MONETARY POLICY, the Bank of Canada manipulates the volume of loanable funds.

illegal strike Any work stoppage by union members in violation of labour laws or a COLLECTIVE AGREEMENT. In Canada, strikes may not take place during the life of a collective agreement except under unusual circumstances and with government approval. An illegal strike is sometimes called a WILDCAT STRIKE.

immigrant remittances Money sent by immigrants to their families in their country of origin. These remittances are an important source of income for families in less-developed countries and an important source of foreign exchange for their governments. Statistics Canada measures the outflow of such remittances in its BALANCE-OF-PAYMENTS figures. The remittances contribute to a balance-of-payments deficit for the country from which they are sent and to a surplus for the countries to which they are sent.

immigration The movement of people into a country, say Canada, from another country for permanent residence. Immigrants usually come to a new country to seek a better economic life, political freedom, or to escape persecution. For the recipient country, immigrants contribute to economic growth and bring needed skills, as they also contribute to the social, political, and cultural life of their new country. Canada's immigration regulations favour immigrants who possess skills, are relatives of people already here, have entrepreneurial plans to start new businesses, or who are political refugees.

imperfect competition The condition that prevails in a market when one producer is able to increase the price that he charges without the loss of a significant volume of sales; this may be due to successful PRODUCT DIFFERENTIATION, barriers to entry for would-be competitors, or the possession of various MONOPOLY powers. This differs from a market in which perfect competition prevails and no single producer has sufficient market power to affect prices. The notion of perfect competition is built on the assumption that products are homogeneous and interchangeable. But in the world of imperfect competition, producers invest heavily in advertising, packaging, design, and other forms of product differentiation, so that products are no longer homogeneous. Such investments can act as barriers to entry for new firms wishing to enter an industry, and thus protect a monopoly or oligopoly from new competition. Imperfect competition may also exist because consumers are unable to obtain all the market information they need about alternative products, or, at least, they are unable to obtain it without going to a great deal of trouble. Most major industries operate in a world of imperfect competition. But perfect competition is assumed in the free-market model of CLASSICAL and NEOCLASSICAL ECONOMICS.

imperial preference See BRITISH PREFERENTIAL TARIFF.

import controls Various measures to restrict the flow of all imports, of imports of specific items, or of imports from specific countries. Controls range from the imposition of IMPORT SURCHARGES and TRADE EMBARGOES to IMPORT QUOTAS imposed on the recommendation of such groups as the TEXTILE AND CLOTHING BOARD, or negotiated in the form of export-restraint agreements with exporting countries. Specific controls can also be imposed under the EXPORT AND IMPORT PERMITS ACT or on agricultural products under other trade legislation.

import duty See TARIFF.

import leakage The proportion of purchasing power in a country that is spent on imports rather than on domestically made goods and services. When the government implements tax cuts or adopts other measures to boost domestic purchasing power and thus to create more jobs, the extent to which the extra income is spent on imports will reduce the full impact of the tax cuts or other measures designed to increase domestic demand.

import licence A licence issued by the federal government to allow an importer to bring into the country a specified quantity of goods that meet specified standards. Normally, an import licence is not required, but it may be if the imported good is subject to an import quota, strict health standards, or some other restriction. See also EXPORT AND IMPORT PERMITS ACT.

import-price index A Statistics Canada monthly index of changes in import prices. See also TERMS OF TRADE.

import quota A limit on the amount of a commodity, product, or class of product that can be imported during a specified period of time. Canada, for example, imposes quotas or negotiates export-restraint agreements for imports of textiles, clothing, shoes, electronic products, and other goods. See also TEXTILE AND CLOTHING BOARD. Import quotas raise prices for consumers; they are designed to encourage domestic production, by guaranteeing domestic firms protection against strong import competition and ensuring domestic producers of a fixed portion of the total market.

import restrictions Any kind of measure that limits imports. Examples would be artificial import valuations, import quotas, government purchasing policies that favour domestic companies, or health, engineering, safety, and other standards designed to limit imports. See also NON-TARIFF BARRIERS.

import surcharge An additional tariff imposed on top of existing tariffs to reduce imports and thus to help correct a major BALANCE-OF-PAYMENTS deficit. Canada imposed import surcharges during its 1962 exchange crisis, as did the United States in its 1971 balance-of-payments crisis.

import valuation The estimated value of a product for import-duty purposes. Import valuation can be a matter of dispute. A foreign subsidiary in Canada importing parts and components from its parent firm may be charged a TRANSFER PRICE that is lower than its market value so as to avoid full payment of customs duties. Import valuation can also be used as a NON-TARIFF BARRIER when a country imposes an artifically high value on imports for import-duty purposes.

imports Goods and services that are consumed in one country—say, Canada—but produced in other countries. See also EXPORTS, TRADE DEFICIT, BALANCE OF PAYMENTS.

improved good A commodity or good that is further processed or used in another product, with value being added, before it is ready for use by a consumer.

impulse buying A spur-of-the-moment purchase, usually motivated by packaging or design, resulting from a consumer seeing the product on display. This kind of consumer purchase helps to explain the large investments some consumer-goods companies make in appealing packaging and design.

imputed income The estimated value of non-money income, such as the food a farmer grows and consumes himself, free board and meals for employees, the personal use of a company car, or other employee non-money benefits. Some forms of imputed income are taxed; they are treated as TAXABLE BENEFITS. Some forms of imputed income are also included in the GROSS NATIONAL PRODUCT.

imputed rent An estimate of the benefits a homeowner receives, after allowing for maintenance, financing, and other costs, from living in his own home, similar to the rent a landlord would receive if he owned and rented out the building.

in kind Payment in goods or services, as opposed to money.

in situ recovery When used in reference to the OIL SANDS, the recovery of the oil without having to engage in open-pit mining of the sands. Heat techniques and steam pressure are used to extract the oil. The technique has not yet been developed for commercial use but will be essential if large-scale development of the tar sands is to take place.

incentive A measure to encourage someone to do something. For example, if the government wants the public to save more, it can make interest on savings income-tax free; if it wants people to conserve energy by buying smaller cars or insulating their homes, it can reduce the sales tax on smaller cars or raise it on larger cars, and let people deduct the cost of insulation from their income tax; if it wants industry to speed up investment plans, it can introduce an INVESTMENT TAX CREDIT; if it wants industry to increase research and development, it can let industry write off 150 per cent of such costs. There are many different ways the tax system can be used, as a carrot or a stick, to provide incentives. Direct grants can also be used as incentives.

incidence of taxation The point at which a tax is actually paid; in other words, the taxpayer who ultimately pays a particular tax. Many taxes can be shifted from the person or corporation on whom they are levied, backward on to suppliers or forward on to consumers. For example, it is argued that corporate income taxes are passed forward to consumers in the prices that corporations charge. Similarly, the manufacturer's sales tax is included in consumer prices, while the sales tax on building materials is included in the price of housing.

income **1.** The money and other benefits flowing to individuals, firms, and other groups in the economy. Income accrues from the sale of goods and services, including labour, from the return to capital, such as INTEREST and dividends, and from the return to land, RENT. See also PERSONAL INCOME. **2.** For a corporation or individual, money income and taxable benefits, such as the use of a company car, from all sources before the payment of taxes. Net income is a synonym for profits. **3.** In tax theory, any increase in the command of an individual over goods and services. Thus income would include spending on goods and services and increases in net worth arising from all sources, including CAPITAL GAINS, BEQUESTS, and LOTTERY winnings. See also PERSONAL INCOME TAX, CORPORATE INCOME TAX.

income averaging A method of reducing the income-tax liability for unexpected lump-sum or windfall payments by spreading out the tax liability over a number of years. Otherwise, the taxpayer would have to pay a much higher share of this income in taxes, leaving less of the money for his own use. Since 1972, athletes, entertainers, film producers, and musicians receiving a large payment, individuals getting lump-sum payments from pension plans or stock-option benefits, or others getting large payments from profits on the sale of a private business or from other sources, have been able to reduce their tax liability by buying an income-averaging annuity. All the money is paid into the annuity, and the individual is taxed only on the money received from the annuity each year. The amount of money must be the same each year; the annuity can be for a fixed number of years or for life.

income distribution The share of total income in society that goes to each fifth of the population. Between 1967 and 1976, the top 20 per cent of the Canadian population averaged 42.7 per cent of total income, while the bottom 20 per cent received 4.0 per cent of income. Statistics Canada publishes an annual review of income distribution in its report, *Income Distribution by Size in Canada*. See also INCOME INEQUALITY, INCOME REDISTRIBUTION.

income effect The change in a person's purchasing power, resulting from a change in the price a person has to pay for a good or service. If, for example, a consumer has to pay a higher price for a particular good, this has the effect of reducing that consumer's total purchasing power or income. This change will affect the range of goods and services the person can buy. The effect will depend on whether there are substitutes, the size of the price increase or decrease, and how essential certain goods or services may be.

income inequality Differences in income among individuals, groups of individuals, or regions. Differences may be due to differences in property wealth, including inherited wealth, in personal ability, in education and training, in opportunity, including social connection, in family support, or in age and health. One of the purposes of the income-tax system, based on ability to pay, is to redistribute income and thus to reduce inequality. See also INCOME REDISTRIBUTION.

income-maintenance programs Programs that provide cash payments to individuals to raise their income to some minimum level —above the POVERTY LINE, for example, or to a minimum subsistence level, or up to a minimum comfort level. Examples include unemployment insurance, social assistance from provincial and municipal governments, the guaranteed-income supplement for senior citizens, and workmen's compensation.

income redistribution Policies to reduce INCOME INEQUALITY. The income-tax system is one of the principal means of redistributing income, since it collects proportionately more taxes from those with higher incomes and enables society to provide social assistance and free or low-cost public services, such as health care, education, and subsidized housing, to those with low incomes. Taxes on wealth or capital, including inherited wealth, also help to redistribute income, and reduce great inequalities in wealth in society. Hence tax policies, the provision of essential public services at little or no cost, and transfer payments to individuals, all help to redistribute income. See also NEGATIVE INCOME TAX.

income statement See EARNINGS STATEMENT.

income tax A tax levied on the income of individuals and corporations. The tax is levied on taxable income—that is, on the income remaining after allowable tax deductions have been made. Under the BRITISH NORTH AMERICA ACT, both the federal and provincial governments can levy an income tax. In the case of PERSONAL INCOME TAX, all the provinces except Quebec have a tax rate that is a per cent of the basic federal tax, and that is collected for them by the federal government; Quebec has its own personal income-tax system and collects the tax directly from Quebec residents. In the case of CORPORATE INCOME TAX, the provinces levy a tax that is a per cent of taxable corporate income as established under the federal income-tax act, and that is collected by the federal government for all of the provinces except Ontario, Quebec, and Alberta, which collect their own corporate income taxes. Income tax was introduced in Canada in 1917, through the Income War Tax Act, to help finance the costs of the First World War, although some provinces had imposed a corporate income tax at the turn of the century. Income-tax revenues today account for close to 60 per cent of budgetary revenues: about 41 per cent from personal income taxes, and about 18 per cent from corporate income tax. Canada's income-tax system underwent a major revision in 1972. One of the most controversial questions in income-tax systems is the definition of income. Ideally, the definition would include actual spending by an individual during the course of a year on goods and services, and increases in his net worth. But most income-tax systems fall far short of maintaining such a definition in practice. See also ROYAL COMMISSION ON TAXATION, TAX EXPENDITURES.

incomes policy Government policies to limit the growth of money incomes, such as wages, salaries, profits, dividends, and rents, and thus to help reduce or restrain the rate of inflation. Examples of incomes policies include wage and price controls, a wage and price freeze, voluntary wage and price guidelines, tax-based incomes policies that tax away excessive wage or profit increases, and government-business-labour consensus agreements on wage and price restraint. Incomes policies are used to deal with COST-PUSH INFLATION rather than DEMAND-PULL INFLATION. They have two effects: they can curb actual income increases, and they can alter expectations of future inflation, hence reducing the need for big wage, price, and rent increases.

Canada imposed an incomes policy in the Second World War; see WARTIME PRICES AND TRADE BOARD. Since the mid-1960s, Canada has reviewed and implemented various forms of incomes policy. In its third annual review in 1966, the Economic Council of Canada concluded that "a formal incomes policy would not be an effective way of meeting the problem in Canada, except possibly under rare emergency conditions and then only on a temporary basis." In its 1966 annual report, the Bank of Canada hinted at the need for an incomes policy. A 1968 federal government white paper, *Policies for Price Stability,* recommended the creation of a prices and incomes commission to "discover the facts, analyze the causes, processes and consequences of inflation, and to inform the public and the government on how price stability might be achieved." In 1969, the PRICES AND INCOMES COMMISSION was established, and in 1970, it implemented a program of price and profit controls. The commission was wound up in 1972. In 1973, the federal government created the FOOD PRICES REVIEW BOARD. In 1975, full wage and price controls were imposed through the ANTI-INFLATION BOARD. It ran until the end of 1978, and was succeeded by the CENTRE FOR THE STUDY OF INFLATION AND PRODUCTIVITY. In March 1979, the centre was replaced by the NATIONAL COMMISSION ON INFLATION; it was abolished in July 1979.

incorporation The legal steps taken by an individual or group of individuals to obtain a charter from the federal or a provincial government to establish and operate a LIMITED-LIABILITY company. If the application is granted, a charter is issued in the form of LETTERS PATENT or articles of incorporation. Some companies are created by a special act of Parliament or a provincial legislature—telephone companies, for example, some railways, and, until now, chartered banks. The rules governing incorporation of companies are set out in federal and provincial CORPORATION LAW.

increasing costs Costs that rise for each unit of output as the volume of production increases. At some point in the production process, the average cost per unit of output begins to rise instead of continuing to decline. This can be due to production putting additional strain on the assembly line, the increased costs of overtime for labour, or the increased difficulty in extracting a natural resource. As pressure in a natural-gas or oilfield declines after much production, for example, more expensive recovery methods become necessary. See also LAW OF DIMINISHING RETURNS.

increasing returns The circumstances in which the application of an additional FACTOR OF PRODUCTION yields progressively greater increases in output. At some point in production, DIMINISHING RETURNS set in. See also ECONOMIES OF SCALE.

increment A small increase either in costs or in income.

indemnity Payment for damages. Some life-insurance policies carry a double-indemnity clause, which doubles the insurance paid in the event of death in certain types of accidents, such as an air crash.

independent union A union that has no affiliation with a national or international labour congress or organization.

index A figure used in statistics to show average values and their percentage change over a period of time, with the change being measured from a base period. For example, if the CONSUMER PRICE INDEX is 189.5 and the base year is 1971, then 1971 equals 100 and consumer prices are 89.5 per cent higher than they were in 1971. Any year, month, or week can be a base period; it is made equal to 100 and the percentage change in whatever is being measured is calculated from that point. The consumer price index is an average value of consumer prices for many different products, with the different products being weighted according to their importance in the household budget. Statistics Canada produces many useful indexes, in addition to the monthly consumer price index—an employment index, for example, an INDEX OF INDUSTRIAL PRODUCTION, and a price index for new housing. Major stock exchanges also produce indexes, showing the average change of prices on a daily basis. See also TORONTO STOCK EXCHANGE INDICES.

index of industrial production A monthly index published by Statistics Canada showing changes in the volume of output by mines, quarries, oil wells, and manufacturing industries, and by electric-power, natural-gas, and water utilities. The index is based on 1971 (1971=100).

index of real domestic product A monthly index of the value-added, in 1971 dollars, of the output of all Canadian industry, including goods-producing and service industries, agriculture, fisheries, and construction. The index, published by Statistics Canada, gives a detailed monthly breakdown of major economic sectors—of the agriculture, forestry, fishing and trapping, mines, and manufacturing industries, of construction, transportation, storage, and communications, of electric-power, gas, and water utilities, of the retail-trade, finance, insurance and real-estate, community, business, and personal-service industries, and of public administration and defence—and further breakdowns within many of these sectors.

indexation The adjustment of pensions, wages, social-assistance benefits and income-tax rates for inflation. The reason for adjusting pensions, wages, and social-assistance benefits is to ensure that there is no decline in the real purchasing power of these payments as a result of inflation. Similarly, Canada's income-tax system has been indexed since 1973; the basic exemptions and the rate schedule are adjusted for inflation so that taxpayers are not pushed into higher tax brackets as their pay goes up, unless they have had a real increase in their income. See also COLA CLAUSE.

Indian Affairs and Northern Development, Department of The federal department responsible for northern economic development, including oil, gas, and other mineral development, and for looking after the economic interests of northern native peoples, including their land claims. It also administers the Indian Act, which sets out its legal obligations to native people, including economic development, jobs, and community planning. The department also administers all federal crown lands north of the sixtieth parallel.

Indian Claims Commission A one-man commission established by the federal government in 1969 to study Indian claims and grievances and, in consultation with representatives of the Indians, to propose settlements. The commissioner reports to the cabinet through the prime minister.

indicative planning A form of government planning in which targets are set for the economy and for individual industries and economic sectors. These targets may be set by the government alone, or by government in consultation with industry and labour. Indicative planning is not usually compulsory, but it may include fairly strong pressure by government, along with incentives, to see that the targets are met. French industrial recovery and modernization after the Second World War was aided by extremely detailed indicative planning.

indirect cost Any expense in a business that cannot be identified with a specific part of the production process. It is allocated by dividing it by the number of units produced and attributing an equal portion to the price of each unit of output. It includes property taxes, rent, property maintenance, and administrative costs; it is a synonym for overhead.

indirect production The production of machinery, equipment, and productive facilities that in turn are used for the production of consumer goods.

indirect tax A tax that is not levied on the final consumer of a good or service, but is usually paid by the final consumer in the price of the good or service; in other words, a tax that can be shifted on to someone else. Indirect taxes include customs duties, excise taxes, and the federal manufacturer's sales tax. Under the British North America Act, indirect taxation is the exclusive preserve of the federal government. One reason for this is that the Fathers of Confederation wanted Canada to be a single market; they feared that, if the provinces were allowed to impose indirect taxes, they would use them as barriers to trade from other provinces. Indirect taxes are not the major source of revenue today, but, until the First World War, they provided almost all of federal revenues. See also DIRECT TAX.

induced consumption The increase in consumer spending that results from new capital investment. An increase in capital investment leads to a rise in wages in the construction, machinery, and related industries, which in turn has a MULTIPLIER effect on other industries, including consumer goods and services. Thus, an investment-led recovery can stimulate consumer spending.

induced investment The increase in capital investment that results from an increase in spending by consumers. As consumer spending rises, industry approaches its productive capacity or sees the opportunity to introduce new products. A consumer-spending-led recovery can stimulate additional capital investment.

industrial-assistance programs Federal and provincial programs to assist industrial growth or aid industries that need to modernize. Such programs include loan guarantees or subsidized financing, managerial counselling and assistance, export financing, trade missions, and direct grants. The shipbuilding and textile industries, for example, have benefitted from industrial-assistance programs.

Industrial Defence Board An advisory body created by the federal government in April 1948 to advise the cabinet on the industrial war potential of Canada, to maintain a plan for war-time industrial production, and to work with the Canadian armed forces and defence and resource industries. It included senior government officials and businessmen, and worked closely with its U.S. counterpart, the National Security Resources Board.

industrial democracy A term that covers a wide range of methods to give employees a say in the management of the firm or organization for which they work. It can include anything from job-safety councils to freedom for employees to organize their working hours or patterns, so long as they maintain a specified production level, and may include the compulsory seating of employee representatives on the boards of directors of a firm. For the most part, Canadian unions have resisted forms of industrial democracy, and have emphasized collective bargaining instead.

industrial-development corporations Public corporations established by the federal and provincial governments to assist industrial development. They provide low-interest loans, direct grants, equity participation, industrial parks, negotiated energy rates, local tax concessions, leasebacks, and other assistance, to attract industry and thus to create jobs. Examples include the Alberta Opportunity Company, the B.C. Development Corporation, the New Brunswick Industrial Development Board, the Newfoundland and Labrador Development Corporation, the Northern Ontario Development Corporation, the Ontario Development Corporation, Prince Edward Island's Industrial Enterprises Incorporated, the Quebec Industrial Development Corporation, the Saskatchewan Economic Development Corporation, and the CAPE BRETON DEVELOPMENT CORPORATION.

industrial dispute A STRIKE, LOCKOUT, slowdown, WORK-TO-RULE, or any other quarrel between a union and employer that results in a reduction or stoppage of work. The Department of LABOUR publishes monthly statistics on strikes and lockouts in Canada.

industrial espionage Underhanded efforts by one company to learn the commercial secrets, such as design changes, investment plans, marketing strategies, or new product plans, of a competitor. These efforts range from the hiring away of key employees and wiretapping, to overflying drilling sights, theft, and bribery. Many of these techniques are illegal.

industrial organization A specialized area of economics that deals with the structure of an industry and the behaviour of individual firms within that industry. It studies factors affecting the ownership of the industry, mergers, pricing policy, oligopoly and monopoly, trade practices, and profits.

industrial psychology The field of psychology concerned with the management of people, on-the-job relations among people or between people and machines, the psychological needs of workers and their career objectives, personnel policies, including hiring, training, and appraisal, and work practices and productivity.

industrial relations See LABOUR RELATIONS.

industrial strategy A set of policies to strengthen the competitive position of a country's manufacturing and supportive service industries. These policies include direct incentives for research and development, government financial assistance to develop costly new technologies, the use of government purchasing power to ensure a market for new, advanced products, measures to increase managerial abilities, changes in the tax system to encourage investors, forced or encouraged mergers to create bigger firms, specific programs to modernize selected industries in which a country wishes to specialize, and INDICATIVE PLANNING. Government can play a direct role, as well, through publicly owned enterprises or joint ventures with private industry. It can set out such a strategy on its own or in consultation with industry and labour. See also CANADA DEVELOPMENT CORPORATION.

industrial union A union that represents all or almost all of the employees in a particular firm or industry, regardless of job or level of skill; it is sometimes called a vertical union. Examples include the unions in the steel and pulp and paper industries and in the public service. See also CRAFT UNION.

industrialization The process of transforming an agricultural and cottage-industry economy into one in which production is organized in factories, utilizing new technology and mechanization to achieve ECONOMIES OF SCALE. Industrialization brings with it major changes in the way society is organized and in the relations among different groups in society. It gives new importance to managers and engineers and creates a large class of wage-earners. Modern society tries to continue the process of industrialization, but, unlike the early industrial societies of the late eighteenth and early nineteenth centuries, attempts to control its growth through laws on pollution, COMPETITION, and UNFAIR LABOUR PRACTICES, and to redistribute the benefits of growth through the tax system and through transfer payments.

industry A producer or distributor of goods or services. The term can refer to a single firm, or collectively to all producers in a nation or all producers of a particular product or service (the oil industry, the trucking industry, the mining industry, the steel industry, the auto industry, or the aviation industry). A separate term, commerce, is used to describe banking, retailing, and other financial and retail or wholesale activities.

Industry, Trade and Commerce, Department of (ITC) The federal government department responsible for trade expansion, industrial policies, and the administration of various trade quotas and other restrictions. Through trade-expansion programs, the department seeks out new markets for Canadian goods and services, tries to ensure continued access to existing markets, administers export-financing assistance through the EXPORT DEVELOPMENT CORPORATION, runs trade-promotion offices in foreign countries, and conducts trade relations with other governments. In its industrial-growth program, it promotes industrial research and development, develops expansion strategies for specific industries, encourages greater emphasis on industrial design, administers a number of industrial-assistance programs, monitors the activities of foreign-owned industry in Canada, and develops policies to increase productivity, raise managerial skills, encourage modernization and new product development, and increase the level of processing of Canada's natural resources.

Through other programs, the department is responsible for the expansion of Canada's tourism industry, conversion to the metric system, and the sales of turn-key projects, arms, and other products through the CANADIAN COMMERCIAL CORPORATION. ITC participates with other departments in developing government policy on trade, regional development, energy, research and development, and agriculture, including grains. The minister is responsible for the FOREIGN INVESTMENT REVIEW AGENCY, the FEDERAL BUSINESS DEVELOPMENT BANK, the CANADA–UNITED STATES AUTOMOTIVE PRODUCTS AGREEMENT, the ENTERPRISE DEVELOPMENT PROGRAM, the METRIC COMMISSION, the MACHINERY AND EQUIPMENT ADVISORY BOARD, the STANDARDS COUNCIL OF CANADA, and the TEXTILE AND CLOTHING BOARD, as well as the Export Development Corporation, the Canadian Commercial Corporation, and a number of smaller agencies and advisory councils.

industry-wide bargaining Collective bargaining in which all the unions and employers in an industry negotiate a uniform contract. It can be nation-wide, province-wide, or cover a metropolitan area. The goal is to avoid a multiplicity of strikes occurring in different parts of the year in the same industry. In Canada, the various railway unions negotiate at the same time with the railway companies. Industry-wide bargaining also occurs in the pulp and paper industry, and in the construction industry in some regions or provinces.

inedible end product A term used by Statistics Canada in export and import statistics to describe manufactured products.

inelastic demand Demand that shows little change as a result of a price change. An increase in price will not reduce demand by much; a reduction in price will not increase demand by much. The demand for life's necessities is inelastic: for example, no matter how much producers lower the price of sugar or bread, it is unlikely that they can increase the demand very much; even with an increase in price, consumers will continue to buy the product unless the price rise is significant, persists, and there is a ready and acceptable substitute (tea instead of coffee, for example). See also ELASTICITY OF DEMAND.

inelastic supply Supply that shows little change as a result of a price change. An increase in the price will not increase the supply by very much; a reduction in price will not reduce the supply by very much.

infant industry A new and underdeveloped industry that is said to be capable of establishing itself and becoming competitive if it is given the chance to develop ECONOMIES OF SCALE and its own technology. Thus, the temporary protection of high tariffs to keep out foreign competition is justified. Initially this would force consumers to pay higher prices, but, in theory, once the industry becomes efficient, the high tariff protection will no longer be necessary and consumers will benefit through lower prices. The view that new industries should be protected by high tariffs until they have established themselves in their own market was popular in the nineteenth century, and retains followers in the LESS-DEVELOPED COUNTRIES today. Sir John A. Macdonald used the argument of infant industries to justify high tariffs as part of his NATIONAL POLICY following Confederation.

infant-mortality rate The number of infant deaths per thousand live births in a given year.

inferior good A good whose consumption falls as the income of consumers rises. As their incomes rise, consumers will switch from bologna and macaroni to ham and steaks, or from black-and-white television sets to colour television sets.

inflation A persistent rise in the price of goods, services, and factors of production over an extended period of time, as measured by a price index such as the CONSUMER PRICE INDEX or the GROSS-NATIONAL-PRODUCT DEFLATOR. Inflation reduces the purchasing power of the dollar or any other unit of money, and tends to redistribute income from those with savings, including pensioners or those on fixed incomes, to those who owe money or have sufficient bargaining power in the economy to raise their prices, wages, or professional fees above the rate of inflation. In the postwar period, inflation of 2 per cent or less had been regarded as acceptable but, since the mid-1960s, the rate has been much higher. There are various types of inflation. See also COST-PUSH INFLATION, DEMAND-PULL INFLATION, STRUCTURAL INFLATION, INCOMES POLICY.

inflation accounting The recalculation of a company's financial statements to show the effects of inflation on the company's assets and earnings. In a period of prolonged and high inflation, real profits are overstated, while the replacement costs of plant, of machinery and equipment, and of inventories are understated; this also means that depreciation deductions are too low to replace assets as they wear out. The result is a misleading presentation of a company's real financial performance. This is particularly true in the case of CAPITAL-INTENSIVE industries such as steel, petrochemicals, and pulp and paper. In inflation accounting, BALANCE-SHEET items such as plant, machinery and equipment, and inventories, which are carried at historical cost, are adjusted either for the general rate of inflation since they were acquired or are revalued in terms of their current replacement cost. This means that on the INCOME STATEMENT, figures for both the cost of goods sold and depreciation must also be increased to reflect the changes made in the balance sheet. The result is either a smaller profit or perhaps even a loss. Thus, rising profits in a period of strong inflation are often called paper profits.

inflationary expectations The belief that inflation is going to continue and will probably get worse; if this belief becomes entrenched it leads firms and unions to build future inflation into their prices and wage demands.

inflationary gap The extent to which planned investment in the economy exceeds the savings available under full-employment conditions. The result is inflation, since the demand for goods and services will exceed the available supply, thus bidding up prices for the available goods and services. The government response usually is to curb consumption through tax and interest-rate increases and other dampening measures.

inflationary spiral A situation in which labour, business, and investors are all seeking to increase their share of the national product, with the result that their collective demands add up to more than 100 per cent of national product. The rivalry among different groups leads to a self-reinforcing upward push on prices. Business seeks to raise or maintain its share of the national product by raising prices to boost profits; labour responds by demanding higher wages, which in turn are passed on in the form of still higher prices. As the inflation spiral takes root, expectations of increased inflation lead various groups in the economy to build these expectations into their price and wage increases, accelerating the inflation process. See also COST-PUSH INFLATION, INCOMES POLICY.

infrastructure The basic capital assets of a country; these assets are important to industrial development and economic growth. Infrastructure includes roads, electric-power systems, water-supply systems, railways, telephone systems, serviced land for industry and housing, and other such facilities. Since the health and education of the workforce are important in economic development, investment in hospitals, schools, universities, and the like are also a part of infrastructure.

inheritance tax See SUCCESSION DUTY, GIFT TAX.

initial established reserves Reserves of oil or natural gas that can be produced with current technology and at current prices prior to the start of production. See also ESTABLISHED RESERVES.

initial payment In the western grains industry, the payment the federal cabinet authorizes the CANADIAN WHEAT BOARD to make at the start of the CROP YEAR to grain farmers. Handling costs at local grain elevators and transportation costs to Thunder Bay or to west-coast ports are deducted, giving the farmer his guaranteed floor price. If the wheat board is unable to recover this price in world grain markets, the deficit is paid by the federal government. See also FINAL PAYMENT.

initial volume in place The total volume of crude oil, tar sands, heavy oil, and raw natural gas calculated to exist in a reservoir before any volume has been produced.

injunction A court order that requires certain things either to be done or not to be done. In labour relations, it is a court order telling an employer or union to do or not to do something. An employer in a strike, for example, may seek an injunction ordering a union to reduce the scale of its picketing. An *ex parte* injunction is one in which the party affected is absent during the application hearing. An interim injunction is one that prohibits something from happening until another action has been completed—the sale of goods whose ownership is in dispute in a trial, for example.

Innis, Harold A. Canada's leading economic historian. Innis (1894-1952) explained the growth and settlement of Canada and the development of its political, cultural, and financial institutions in terms of the exploitation of successive commodities or staples for export markets. This is the so-called STAPLE THEORY of Canadian development. In Innis' view, a new country—New France and, later, Canada—had to grow by serving as a supplier of commodities to the much more highly specialized and developed economies of older nations. This emphasis on commodities, in turn, determined where communities would be located, the role of government in maintaining the economic system (through support for transportation, for example), the types of jobs that would exist, the nature of social relationships, and many other aspects of life.

Innis first outlined his theory of Canadian development in 1930 in his book, *The Fur Trade in Canada: An Introduction to Canadian Economic History*. He showed how the fur trade, based on the demand of Europeans for beaver fur and the need of Indians for manufactured goods, spread settlements and transportation links through the interconnected lakes and rivers of central Canada. From the fur trade, Innis demonstrated, through the economic development of fish, timber, wheat, and minerals, Canada grew as a country because of its geography and not in spite of it, as so many economic and political historians had maintained. In other words, there was an east-west unity to the country, as development spread from the St. Lawrence system westward, along the Canadian Pacific Railway to the wheat economy. This development, especially its importance in ensuring transportation links, helped to account for the active role of government in the Canadian economy.

Other works by Innis expanded on or reinforced the staple theory. See, for example, *Problems of Staple Production in Canada* (1933), *Settlement and the Mining Frontier* (1936), and *The Cod Fisheries* (1940). Later in his career, Innis became fascinated by the role of communications in developing and shaping civilization. He wrote *Political Economy in the Modern State* (1946), *Empire and Communications* (1950), *The Bias of Communication* (1951), and *Changing Concepts of Time* (1952). Innis was a major figure in Canadian intellectual history, and spent most of his career at the University of Toronto.

innovation The use of a new idea, material, or technology by an industry to change either the goods or services produced or the way in which the goods or services are produced or distributed. See also INVENTION, which is the actual discovery of something new; innovation is the application of something new. Innovation can include improved managerial systems, new production techniques, new technology, the industrial results of research and development, or the application of computer systems to a business. Joseph Schumpeter (1883–1950)—*The Theory of Economic Development* (Cambridge, Mass., 1934) and *Capitalism, Socialism, and Democracy* (New York, 1942)—regarded the innovator as the crucial figure in capitalism. He also argued that only big corporations could afford to bear the risks and make the capital investments necessary for innovation. Innovation is vital in a dynamic economy, which raises the standard of living of its people through constant gains in productivity.

input The factors—land, labour, capital, know-how—used in the production process to obtain output—that is, goods and services.

input device Any type of computer terminal that is used to put information into a terminal; such devices convert data in various ways into computer-manageable electrical signals. The earliest input devices used punched cards or punched paper tape to feed information into a computer; today, information can be typed in, or it can be read by devices such as those that read optical characters or coded price-inventory labels in supermarkets.

input-output analysis The branch of economics that analyzes the relationships between changes in output in particular industries and the effect those changes have on the output of other industries. Input-output tables are composed with, say, horizontal columns listing inputs and vertical tables listing outputs.

Input-output analysis is an important tool for economists because it itemizes the production of an industry or the economy and analyzes the raw materials, parts, and components that production will require from other industries. By developing descriptions of such relationships, it is possible to calculate in detail the industrial impact of an increase or a reduction in demand for a product, such as motor vehicles. Input-output analysis for the automobile industry will show, for example, how much steel, plastics, glass, carpeting, or electrical wiring is needed to produce a specific number of cars. Similarly, it is possible to determine how much steel will be needed in a given year by adding up the steel demand of key users, assuming certain levels of output, such as the auto, construction, aircraft, pipeline, electrical, and other industries. In turn, it is possible to calculate how much iron ore, coal, and energy will be needed to produce the estimated level of steel required.

Input-output analysis is also part of the system of NATIONAL ACCOUNTS. The total of all the inputs must equal the total of all the outputs. Input-output analysis was developed by the U.S. economist, Wassily Leontief. It is a highly refined tool of analysis today because computer systems can be used to collect and manipulate data.

insider Any senior company officer, director, or major shareholder who has access to information about his company's affairs or prospects that is not generally available to ordinary shareholders or to members of the public. The possession of inside information may permit an insider, for example, to sell his company's shares before an unexpected loss is announced to the public, or to buy additional shares before the announcement of an exceptional profit or a takeover bid. For this reason, federal and provincial laws restrict the right of insiders to buy and sell shares, either directly, or indirectly through a relative, partner, or associate company, and require insiders to report regularly all changes in their holdings of a company's shares. Insiders are usually defined as all directors of a corporation, all senior officers (including the chairman, vice-chairman, president, vice-presidents, secretary, treasurer, and general manager), the five highest-paid officers of the company, and anyone owning or controlling more than 10 per cent of the voting shares of the company. Insiders may also include directors and senior officers of another company that has more than 10 per cent of the voting shares of the company concerned. Federal law also includes directors and senior officers of subsidiary companies as insiders.

insider report A report, usually monthly, of any changes in total holdings of shares in a company by an INSIDER, to a provincial securities commission. Such filing must be made by anyone within ten days of becoming an insider, showing his direct and indirect ownership of shares in the company. Any subsequent changes in those holdings must be reported as they occur. The purpose of such reports, which are made public, is to inform shareholders and the public of the trading activities of insiders. Failure by an insider to make a timely or accurate report is an offence punishable by provincial law.

insider trading The buying and selling of shares by INSIDERS of a company. If an insider makes use of confidential information to trade in shares directly or through relatives or partners before the information is made public, he can be sued and forced to compensate anyone for direct losses suffered, as well as being forced to return his profit to the company. There are also restrictions on insider trading during takeover bids.

insolvency The inability of a company, individual, or government to repay debts when they become due. Insolvency occurs when liabilities exceed assets, excluding ownership assets. Insolvency does not necessarily mean bankruptcy; a firm, for example, may be able to sell certain assets and arrange new financing, or to bring in a new investor.

inspector general of banks A federal office that monitors the activities of the chartered banks incorporated under the BANK ACT, and other banks incorporated under the Quebec Savings Bank Act, to ensure that they are in a sound financial position and that they are acting within the terms and conditions set out under banking laws. The office was created after the failure of the Home Bank in 1923; a total of nine banks had failed or had had their charters repealed between 1900 and 1923. The office reports to Parliament through the minister of FINANCE.

instalment credit A form of consumer credit in which the consumer makes regular repayments of equal amounts on specified dates, each payment including interest and principal. This form of credit is used to purchase automobiles, electrical appliances, furniture, and other major CONSUMER GOODS, with a downpayment frequently being required as part of the agreement.

Institute for Research on Public Policy (IRPC) A national, non-profit research institute incorporated in 1972, that began operation in 1974. It is funded by the federal government, the provincial governments (except Quebec, Manitoba, and British Columbia), and private industry. The institute sponsors research studies on a wide range of public-policy issues. Its headquarters are in Montreal.

institutional investor A financial organization, such as a PENSION FUND, INSURANCE company, or MUTUAL FUND, that manages a large portfolio of bonds and other securities, and has a steady flow of money to invest. Such organizations have become the main buyers and sellers on stock exchanges and are major buyers and sellers in bond and mortgage markets as well. While such investors can influence prices on a stock exchange, they tend not to exercise any direct influence in the companies whose shares they buy; instead, they act as passive investors.

instrument A document; for example, a PROMISSORY NOTE, or the legal document incorporating a company. A negotiable instrument is a promissory note or other debt instrument that can be signed over to another party.

insurance A contractual arrangement under which an insurer will provide protection against risk in return for payment of a premium. Almost any kind of risk can be protected against by an insurance company. The most common forms of insurance policy are those for the loss of life, disability, theft, accident and sickness, fire, and automobile accidents. The insurance company provides compensation to make up for the loss or damages. Insurance companies use the premium income as investment capital from which future claims are paid; the types of investments they can make are regulated—for example, under the Canadian and British Insurance Companies Act. The Department of INSURANCE regulates the activities of insurance companies; the minister of Finance is responsible for the Department of Insurance. See also LIFE INSURANCE, CASUALTY INSURANCE, NO-FAULT AUTOMOBILE INSURANCE.

insurance agent A person who arranges insurance coverage, acting as a middleman between clients who have a great variety of insurance needs, and different insurance companies offering a range of specialized coverage. He seeks out the best available price for his clients, but is paid commissions by the insurance companies. He also handles claims arising from the insurance contracts he has arranged.

Insurance, Department of The federal government department that administers laws applying to federally incorporated insurance, trust, loan, and investment companies, foreign insurance companies operating in Canada, certain pension funds, small loan companies, licensed moneylenders, co-operative credit societies operating under the Co-operative Credit Associations Act, and provincially incorporated insurance companies registered with the department. The deputy minister is the superintendent of Insurance; the minister of FINANCE acts as the minister of Insurance. One of the most important roles of the department is to ensure that the financial institutions it monitors comply with federal regulations intended to ensure their financial soundness. The department was set up in 1910; for the previous twenty-five years, it had been a branch of the Department of Finance.

intangible assets Assets that are non-physical—that is, they cannot be touched or measured. They include patents, trademarks, franchises, goodwill, and copyrights. They are essential to the operation of a business but hard to value, and are usually included as miscellaneous items on a BALANCE SHEET at only nominal value—say, at one dollar.

integration Increasing the ties that bind the economies of different countries together. For example, the integration of the Canadian and U.S. economies can result from growing trade and the progressive reduction of tariffs, the construction of energy-supply systems that cross the border, the tendency to harmonize economic policies, and increasing linkages between the banking systems and the financial markets of the two countries, along with special bilateral arrangements worked out in tax treaties, trade agreements, exemptions (such as Canada's exemption from the U.S. INTEREST-EQUALIZATION TAX), and dependence on each other for travel and tourism business.

intellectual property The ownership of knowledge and information, consisting of COPYRIGHTS, PATENTS, TRADEMARKS, and industrial designs. Laws governing intellectual property can have an important impact on the rate of innovation in an economy; inventors, designers, authors, filmmakers, and entrepreneurs are likely to be more active if the economic benefits of what they create are protected and adequately rewarded with royalties or other payments. In Canada, laws dealing with intellectual property are the responsibility of the Department of CONSUMER AND CORPORATE AFFAIRS. International protection is co-ordinated through the WORLD INTELLECTUAL PROPERTY ORGANIZATION.

intensive cultivation The use of modern agricultural methods to increase yields from land. These methods include the application of chemical fertilizers and pesticides, mechanized agricultural equipment, new seed varieties, and highly trained farm labour.

Inter-American Development Bank A development bank established in 1959 to provide loans to public and private organizations in Latin America for development projects. The bank, through affiliates, also makes SOFT LOANS. Canada became a member in 1972.

interdependence The mutual dependence that exists among individuals, communities, and regions of a country or among different countries in the world. No nation makes everything its consumers consume; indeed, with increasing specialization, nations are becoming even more dependent on one another. Similarly, citizens in a country or nations in the world have a common stake in the functioning of their economic systems. Industrial countries are dependent on Saudi Arabia for their oil, for example, but the Saudis are dependent on a stable Western economy so they can safely invest their PETRODOLLARS, and on Western industry to supply the industrial goods they need to modernize their economy and meet their health and INFRASTRUCTURE needs. Similarly, Quebec is dependent on a healthy economy in the rest of Canada, while Ontario manufacturers need a growing market in Quebec. Canadian prosperity, in turn, depends on economic growth in the United States, Europe, and Japan, and on the smooth functioning of the world monetary system. Interdependence is a characteristic of modern economic life.

interest The price paid by a borrower for the temporary use of someone else's money or, conversely, the price charged by a lender for the temporary use by someone else of his money. It is expressed as a per cent of the amount borrowed or lent; this is the RATE OF INTEREST. Individuals pay interest on their mortgages, consumer loans, and unpaid balances on their credit cards; they earn interest on their savings bonds, bank accounts, GUARANTEED-INVESTMENT CERTIFICATES, and REGISTERED RETIREMENT SAVINGS PLANS. Businesses pay interest on their corporate bonds, inventory, and working-capital loans, mortgages, sales financing, and other debts, while earning interest on their cash balances and other financial assets. Governments pay interest on their bonds and treasury bills. See also BANK RATE, PRIME RATE.

interest futures A means of speculating on short-term and long-term interest rates. Investors can buy futures contracts on the Chicago Board of Trade and Mercantile Exchange for U.S. treasury bills and U.S. government mortgages. See also FUTURES MARKET.

interest-equalization tax A U.S. tax levied from 1963 to 1974 on the interest and dividends earned by U.S. citizens, financial institutions, and corporations, on foreign bonds, shares, short-term financial paper, and other such investments. Its purpose was to halt the flow of U.S. funds abroad because U.S. interest rates were lower than foreign interest rates. The tax, which was announced on 18 July 1963, underlined Canada's strong dependence on U.S. capital markets when it sparked a crisis in Canadian financial markets. Canada obtained an exemption, announced on 23 July; but there was the implied threat that, if Canadian borrowing increased over traditional levels, the exemption would be lifted. Canada had also to agree not to increase the level of its foreign-exchange reserves through the proceeds of new U.S. borrowings. This ceiling imposed a strong need on the Bank of Canada to monitor Canadian foreign borrowing, and, in some cases, to ask would-be borrowers to use the Canadian market instead.

The interest-equalization tax consisted of a 15 per cent tax on purchases by Americans of shares in foreign corporations, and a tax, ranging from 2.75 per cent on short-term securities to 15 per cent on long-term bonds, on interest paid to Americans on new loans they made to non-residents. New FOREIGN DIRECT INVESTMENT by U.S. corporations was excluded. The new tax led to a plunge in Canadian financial markets and a sharp decline in the Canadian dollar when it was first announced, since it would have almost completely barred Canadian borrowers from using U.S. financial markets. The U.S. government agreed to a conditional exemption for Canada, which turned the market around; the U.S. Congress made a number of other changes in the tax to benefit Canada, before passing it in 1964.

In 1966, Canada announced co-operation with new U.S. controls on foreign investment by U.S. corporations, announced late in 1965, in order to maintain exemption from the interest-equalization tax. Canadian investors were asked not to buy securities issued by U.S. corporations or their non-Canadian subsidiaries that would be subject to the tax if purchased by Americans; this was to prevent Canada from being used as a pass-through by Americans trying to avoid the tax. It was feared, for example, that Canadians might buy such securities and then turn to U.S. capital markets for additional borrowing. A more serious problem with the U.S. guidelines, however, was that U.S. multinationals were asked to reduce the funds they transferred to their foreign subsidiaries, including their

Canadian subsidiaries. Depending on decisions made by U.S. parent companies, funds for Canadian subsidiaries could be cut back much more than the overall global reduction, shifting their requirements to Canadian financial institutions. Such a shift, in turn, could crowd out higher-risk Canadian borrowers on Canadian financial markets.

In 1968 the U.S. guidelines were made mandatory, and U.S. multinationals were also ordered to increase the repatriation of earnings from their foreign subsidiaries, including those in Canada. With such a high level of U.S. ownership of Canadian industry, such policies could have caused serious damage to the Canadian economy. This was reflected in the Canadian-dollar crisis in early 1968; eventually, Canada obtained an exemption from the U.S. guidelines for non-financial corporations, and, at the end of 1968, the U.S. lifted its ceiling on Canada's foreign-exchange reserves, which had been imposed in 1963 in exchange for an exemption for the interest-equalization tax.

One result of the U.S. policies was that Canadian borrowers began to make more use of the EUROCURRENCY MARKET. On 29 January 1974, the United States announced that it was terminating its guidelines on foreign investment and the interest-equalization tax. The next day, Canada discontinued the guidelines it had imposed to prevent Canada being used as a pass-through by U.S. investors.

interest-rate spread In a financial institution, the difference between the interest paid on deposits and the interest charged on loans. The term also refers to the difference in the level of interest rates between two countries—for example, the difference between interest rates in Canada and in the United States.

Inter-Governmental Maritime Consultative Organization A United Nations agency formed in 1959 to combat ocean and coastline pollution and to promote safety at sea. Canada, with its long coastline, has been an active member from the start. One of the agency's major concerns is the intentional or accidental discharge of oil and other pollutants at sea.

Interim Committee of Finance Ministers See GROUP OF TWENTY.

interim report A financial statement published by a public company for its shareholders, showing semi-annual or quarterly financial results, including earnings per share. Such statements, unlike a company's annual report, are not usually audited by the company's outside auditors. Its purpose is to give shareholders a progress report on how the company is doing; it is not intended as a complete financial accounting.

inter-industry competition Competition among companies in different industries where there is a high degree of substitution for their products. For example, the steel, plastics, and aluminum industries may compete with one another as suppliers of materials for auto bodies. Soft-drink, mineral-water, iced-tea, and wine and beer companies compete for summertime beverage sales. Poured-concrete, steel, brick, and glass companies compete in providing building materials for apartment and office towers. Inter-industry competition can also occur in the pursuit of consumer sales —the travel industry, the summer-cottage industry, stockbrokers, financial institutions selling investment certificates and retirement plans, and encyclopedia salesmen, are all competing with one another for discretionary consumer spending.

interlisted share A share in a company that is listed on more than one stock exchange. Many important Canadian companies are listed on the Toronto, Vancouver, and Montreal stock exchanges. Some large Canadian companies are also listed on U.S. stock exchanges, frequently the American Stock Exchange, and some blue-chip American corporations are listed on the TORONTO STOCK EXCHANGE. When a share is listed on more than one exchange, there is sometimes an opportunity to make a profit through ARBITRAGE.

interlocking directorate The situation that exists when a person sits on the board of directors of two or more companies that may compete with one another, or have a business relationship with one another that can give rise to a conflict of interest. The public concern is that interlocking directorates may reduce competition or lead to a conflict of interest. The BANK ACT prohibits a person from serving on the boards of both a CHARTERED BANK and a TRUST COMPANY.

intermediate good A good used in the production of another good; as opposed to a final good, which is ready for consumption by a consumer. All the parts and components that go into the production of a television set, along with the machinery used in the manufacture of the television set, are intermediate goods; the television set is a final good. Intermediate goods are not counted in the calculation of the GROSS NATIONAL PRODUCT; their value is accounted for in the value of final goods.

intermediation The vital role in the economy of financial institutions that serve as middlemen between savers and borrowers. Intermediation is the act of accepting deposits, on which interest is paid, and making loans, on which interest is charged.

internal audit A review or audit of the financial accounts of a company or other organization by its own accounting staff, as opposed to an annual audit conducted by an outside accounting firm to verify the accuracy of the accounts.

internal migration The movement of people from one region of Canada to another, from one province to another, or from rural to urban society. Statistics Canada publishes a variety of figures showing internal migration in Canada.

International Atomic Energy Agency (IAEA) An international organization affiliated with the United Nations, set up in 1957 in Vienna to promote the peaceful use of atomic energy, in particular the use of nuclear power, under controlled and safe conditions. Canada has been a member of its board of governors from the start, due to its important role in the world nuclear industry. Under the terms of the 1968 Treaty for the Non-Proliferation of Nuclear Weapons, the IAEA inspects nuclear-sales agreements to individual nations to make sure that the facilities cannot be used for possible military purposes. It inspects individual nuclear facilities to make sure that the safeguards set out under the treaty are being complied with. The IAEA also conducts research into the peaceful uses of atomic energy and into nuclear safety and the disposal of nuclear wastes.

International Bank for Reconstruction and Development (IBRD) A United Nations –affiliated development bank, known as the World Bank, which provides commercial and low-interest loans and other assistance to the LESS-DEVELOPED COUNTRIES. It was created in 1945 as an agency to assist the postwar reconstruction of war-torn Europe, but shifted its emphasis to the less-developed countries after the U.S. provided Marshall Plan aid to Europe. The IBRD gets its money from the capital subscribed by its member countries, the bonds it sells in the wealthier countries, and from its retained earnings from the interest earned on earlier loans; the repayment of loans also provides a flow of capital that can be relent. Canada, a member from the start, had 4.12 per cent of the votes and had contributed about 6.2 per cent of the IBRD's capitalization up to 1978. The bank makes loans for productive purposes—for infrastructure projects such as highways, for example, for electric-power plants, water and sewage systems, ports and airports, telecommunications systems, agricultural colleges, irrigation systems, or for urban-development, educational, and farm-credit programs, which aid economic development. It has in recent years begun, partly at Canada's urging, to lend money to developing countries for oil and natural-gas exploration. In recent years, special emphasis has been put on projects that aid the poorest people in the less-developed countries, such as programs to boost nutrition and health, low-cost housing, clean water, small industries, and improved productivity on small farms. The bank also provides development-planning assistance and supports family-planning programs. The IBRD created the INTERNATIONAL FINANCE CORPORATION (IFC) in 1956 and the INTERNATIONAL DEVELOPMENT ASSOCIATION (IDA) in 1960, to provide specialized aid for the less-developed countries. Its headquarters are in Washington, D.C.

International Bauxite Association A cartel of bauxite-producing nations set up in 1974 to get higher prices for bauxite-alumina, and to prevent competitive price-cutting by members. The founding members were Australia, Guinea, Guyana, Jamaica, Sierra Leone, Surinam and Yugoslavia. Since then, the Dominican Republic, Ghana, and Haiti have joined, while Greece, India, and Trinidad have been accepted as official observer nations. IBA members account for about 65 per cent of world bauxite production. The principal activity of member nations has been to increase state ownership of bauxite reserves and to raise substantially the tax and royalty revenues from bauxite production. The members have also explored methods of increasing processing and manufacturing in the resource countries. The secretariat is in Kingston, Jamaica.

International Chamber of Commerce A Paris-based association of chambers of commerce from many different countries, including Canada, which seeks to develop common views on international economic issues, such as a policy on the role of multinational corporations. It also promotes the expansion of world trade and the free flow of investment.

International Civil Aviation Organization (ICAO) A United Nations agency, with headquarters in Montreal, concerned with the growth and safety of international civil aviation. Its activities include international agreement on the conditions under which aircraft fly over another nation's territory, safety standards and procedures, arrangements under which all nations can share in the growth of civil aviation, and the compilation of statistics on civil aviation. The agency was formally established in 1947 after twenty-six nations, including Canada, approved a Convention on International Civil Aviation. It has about 130 members today, with a governing council of thirty nations, including Canada.

international commodity agreement See COMMODITY AGREEMENT.

International Confederation of Free Trade Unions (ICFTU) An international association of trade unions formed in 1949 by a number of national trade-union congresses, including the CANADIAN LABOUR CONGRESS. It was formed as an alternative to the World Federation of Trade Unions, a largely communist organization formed in 1945. ICFTU supports efforts to strengthen free unions in countries where they are weak or almost non-existent, and also attempts to achieve some co-operation among unions from different countries in dealing with the spread of MULTINATIONAL CORPORATIONS. In particular, it is concerned about efforts by multinationals to move out of countries with strong unions and labour laws to countries with weak unions and weak labour laws. Canada has played an important role in the organization; in 1972, a CLC president, Donald Macdonald, became the organization's first president from outside Europe. The AFL-CIO of the United States withdrew in 1969 because it objected to the number of contacts by British and German unions with unions in communist nations. It has not returned to the organization. Headquarters of ICFTU are in Brussels.

International Convention for the High Seas Fisheries of the North Pacific Ocean An agreement among Canada, the United States, and Japan, to manage the fisheries of the high seas of the North Pacific to get the maximum sustainable production, and to implement conservation procedures that will ensure the long-term availability of fish. The agreement is also important to Canada because the practices followed in the high seas affect the level of salmon and other fish within Canadian coastal waters. The International North Pacific Fisheries Commission, which administers the convention, is located in New Westminster, B.C. Canada signed the convention in 1952.

International Convention on Dumping Wastes at Sea An international agreement to help protect the oceans by regulating the manner in which ships may dispose of garbage and other wastes at sea. It was negotiated in 1972, following the United Nations Conference on the Environment in Stockholm. Canada has signed the convention and is an active supporter of measures to enforce it.

International Council of Copper Exporting

Countries (CIPEC) A cartel-like organization formed in 1967 by four copper-exporting countries—Chile, Peru, Zaire, and Zambia—to try to achieve continuous growth of real earnings from copper. The four countries account for about 35 per cent of non-communist copper production and about 65 per cent of world primary copper exports. But the cartel is weak, because for most of the years of its existence there has been a surplus of copper in world markets. In addition, all of the countries in the cartel rely heavily on export earnings from copper, and they cannot afford to cut back production; nor do they have the financial resources to build up a buffer stock to maintain prices during periods of excess supply. The main achievement of CIPEC has been to increase the knowledge of the four members of how the mining industry works and of how copper markets function. The prospect of copper mining on the ocean floor raises the prospect of even more competition for CIPEC members.

International Development Association (IDA) An affiliate of the INTERNATIONAL BANK FOR RECONSTRUCTION AND DEVELOPMENT, formed in 1960, which gives loans at little or no interest to the poorest of the LESS-DEVELOPED COUNTRIES, who are unable to raise money on commercial terms except at very high cost; the IDA allows them to repay, in some cases, in their own currencies. The IDA loans are long-term loans and are usually made for INFRASTRUCTURE projects, such as roads, hospitals, and schools. Canada has been one of IDA's financial supporters from the start and has been one of the largest sources of capital. In the period 1960 to 1979, Canada supplied $1.013 billion to IDA, making it the sixth largest supporter and providing 5.5 per cent of IDA funds. Only the United States, Britain, and Germany have supplied more. The IDA is based in Washington.

International Development Research Centre (IDRC) A unique Canadian centre created to help the LESS-DEVELOPED COUNTRIES solve their problems through research and development. The centre was established in 1970 by the Canadian government to help less-developed countries build up their research facilities, scientific skills, and specialized institutions, to solve their problems in such areas as agriculture, the food and nutrition sciences, the population and health sciences, and the information sciences. The centre is now funding research and training programs in many different parts of the less-developed world. It has a board of twenty-one of whom eleven, including the chairman and the vice-chairman, are Canadians; the remaining eight are from other countries. The IDRC's headquarters are in Ottawa.

international economics The area of economics concerned with international trade and investment, including the role of international economic institutions, the problems of the world monetary system, capital flows, the role of multinational corporations, commodity agreements, economic development, and co-ordination of economic policy among the major nations.

International Energy Agency (IEA) An organization of oil-consuming nations belonging to the ORGANIZATION FOR ECONOMIC CO-OPERATION AND DEVELOPMENT, set up in 1974 to deal with problems of oil supplies and prices after the 1973 embargo by Arab oil-exporting nations against the United States and the Netherlands. It started off with sixteen members, including Canada, and now has twenty. It has developed a number of plans to reduce the growth of oil consumption and to share oil in a shortage, and has also co-ordinated a number of energy-research and -development projects to find future alternatives to oil.

Under the IEA's emergency plan to share oil in an emergency, each country is required to have emergency oil reserves equal to ninety days of net imports by 1980, to have rationing and other demand-restraint programs ready to apply in an emergency, to participate in an emergency oil-sharing arrangement, and to have established an emergency oil-sharing agency. The IEA emergency plan comes into effect when the IEA secretariat in Paris finds that the member countries as a whole have suffered a shortage in supplies equal to 7 per cent of average oil consumption. Each country would then agree to reduce consumption by 7 per cent, and draw on emergency stored oil; the remaining oil would be shared among the IEA members. This procedure works on a progressive basis until the shortage reaches 50 per cent of normal average consumption; the IEA would then have to decide on further co-operative measures of restraint.

The IEA also co-ordinates the energy policies of member countries to avert a major oil shortage by the mid-1980s. IEA members have agreed to adopt policies of energy conservation and alternative energy sources, so that, in 1985, their total oil imports will be limited to 26 million barrels a day, compared to 22 million barrels a day in 1977. Each country has set its own import target, at which the 26-million-barrel target can be reached while economic growth is still maintained. Canada's share was originally to restrict net oil imports to 800,000 barrels a day, or one-third of consumption, whichever was lower, by 1985. This has since been reduced to 600,000 barrels a day. The IEA publishes a regular assessment of member countries' energy policies. Its members are: Australia, Austria, Belgium, Britain, Canada, Denmark, Germany, Greece, Ireland, Italy, Japan, Luxembourg, the Netherlands, New Zealand, Norway, Spain, Sweden, Switzerland, Turkey, and the United States. The IEA is based in Paris.

International Finance Corporation (IFC) An affiliate of the INTERNATIONAL BANK FOR RECONSTRUCTION AND DEVELOPMENT, created in 1956 to provide financial assistance to private industry undertaking important projects in the less-developed countries. It can invest directly in up to 25 per cent of the ownership of a project, provide direct loans or loan guarantees to private lenders, and provide loan capital to foreign-development banks for private-industry projects. The IFC can get capital from the paid-up capital of its member nations, including Canada, from the sale of shares or notes it holds in existing projects, or in the form of loans from the IBRD. It is based in Washington.

international fisheries conventions An agreement among Canada and other nations on the maximum level of catch, the type of gear that can be used, and on conservation- and scientific-research programs in the fishing area and for the species covered by individual conventions. Each convention is implemented by a commission set up under the agreement. Canada's first fisheries convention, signed in 1923, was the Canada-U.S. convention for the preservation of the halibut fishery of the North Pacific Ocean and Bering Sea. There are now about ten such conventions, the most recent being the 1979 Canada-U.S. East Coast Fishery Resources Agreement, covering fishing on George's Bank off eastern Canada. Fishing conventions exist for seals, tuna, whales, Great Lakes fisheries, and salmon. See also NORTHWEST ATLANTIC FISHERIES ORGANIZATION and the INTERNATIONAL CONVENTION FOR THE HIGH SEAS FISHERIES OF THE NORTH PACIFIC OCEAN.

International Fuel Cycle Evaluation A program to study the nuclear-fuel cycle, from a non-proliferation point of view, to reach an international consensus on alternate fuel cycles, safeguard methods, adequacy of fuel supplies, and environmental safety. The concern of the nations and agencies participating in the program is to control the paths where material from nuclear-power systems could be diverted into weapons-use in the reprocessing and enrichment processes. The study was proposed by the United States at an October 1977 conference of four international organizations and forty countries, including Canada. The four organizations were the EUROPEAN ECONOMIC COMMUNITY, the INTERNATIONAL ATOMIC ENERGY AGENCY, the ORGANIZATION FOR ECONOMIC CO-OPERATION AND DEVELOPMENT's Nuclear Energy Agency, and the INTERNATIONAL ENERGY AGENCY. The participants in the project were to report in 1980.

International Fund for Agricultural Development A specialized United Nations agency· created in 1976 to help the LESS-DEVELOPED COUNTRIES to raise their food production by providing low-interest loans. The fund was proposed by the U.N.'s 1974 WORLD FOOD CONFERENCE, and more than one billion dollars was provided by DEVELOPED and less-developed countries, including thirty-three million dollars from Canada during the fund's first three years. Decisions of the fund are shared equally among developed countries, less-developed countries, and members of the ORGANIZATION OF PETROLEUM EXPORTING COUNTRIES, which has supplied close to one-third of the funds from the OPEC Special Fund. The fund, which is based in Rome, began operating in December 1977, and made its first loan in April 1978. See also WORLD FOOD COUNCIL.

international indebtedness The amount of money that countries owe to foreign lenders, in particular to foreign governments, international agencies, foreign banks, and foreign corporations. The international indebtedness of certain LESS-DEVELOPED COUNTRIES and of some East European nations has become a matter of concern to bankers and Western governments. Canada's international indebtedness is reported periodically by Statistics Canada in its publication, *Canada's International Investment Position*. Canada is a net debtor, which means that the amount of money it owes to foreign lenders is greater than the amount owed to Canadians by foreign borrowers. Canada's international debts include bonds, bank deposits, shares, various short-term financial investments, the retained earnings in foreign-controlled firms here, and FOREIGN DIRECT INVESTMENT in Canadian industry. A country is expected to be a net debtor as its economy is being developed and a net creditor once its economy has been developed. But Canada has remained a net debtor, with the increase in its international obligations creating future claims by non-residents for interest and dividends from Canada.

International Joint Commission (IJC) A Canada–United States agency set up in 1911, following the Boundary Waters Treaty of 1909, to settle disputes between the two countries over the use of the thousands of different waterways that cross their common border. A set of principles on the use of these waterways for transportation, hydro-electric power, and irrigation is set out in the Boundary Waters Act, and these principles are, in effect, terms of reference for the IJC. Canada and the U.S. each have three members, and the IJC's approval is required for any use of, construction on, or diversion of a body of water that crosses the border where it would affect the natural level or flow in the other country, or which would raise the level of water on the other side of the border.

The IJC has a long record of dealing with Canada-U.S. problems in the past, including problems with power developments such as the Columbia power project, and in transportaion and agricultural disputes. In recent years it has taken an increasingly active role in reviewing water-pollution problems on the Great Lakes and along other parts of the Canada-U.S. border. It is responsible for monitoring progress under the GREAT LAKES WATER QUALITY AGREEMENT. It has also dealt with some problems of air pollution. In Canada it reports to the secretary of state for EXTERNAL AFFAIRS, and in the United States to the Secretary of State.

International Labour Organization (ILO) An international organization representing governments, unions, and employers, formed under the Treaty of Versailles in 1919 to set international labour standards, such as limitations on child labour, minimum wages, the right to organize unions freely, vacations with pay, maximum hours of work, non-discrimination, job safety, and the provision of social assistance. Canada has been a member from the start; Prime Minister R.B. Bennett, introducing his "New Deal" in 1935, justified his legislating in areas of provincial jurisdiction on the grounds that he was implementing ILO standards. In 1946, the ILO became a U.N. agency headquartered in Geneva; it was based in Montreal during the Second World War.

In recent years, the ILO has paid increasing attention to job needs, particularly in the LESS-DEVELOPED COUNTRIES, and to improving social security. It also disseminates a great deal of labour information and provides technical help to less-developed countries in setting up collective bargaining, job safety, and other labour-law provisions. Canada has ratified twenty-four of the ILO's more than 135 conventions. Each country's delegation consists of four members, one an employer, one from a union, and two from government. In 1977, the former president of the CANADIAN

LABOUR CONGRESS, Joe Morris, became chairman of the ILO's governing body.

international migration The movement of people from a country or group of countries to another country or countries.

International Monetary Fund (IMF) A specialized United Nations agency, created to maintain and enforce a world monetary system, that facilitates the expansion of international trade and investment and thus helps to raise world living standards. The IMF was formed at the U.N.'s Monetary and Financial Conference at BRETTON WOODS, New Hampshire, in July 1944, as one of the postwar agencies to assist the orderly growth of an international economy. It was designed to avoid a return to the destructive policies of exchange controls, competitive devaluations, and bilateral arrangements that had sprung up during the depression of the 1930s. The IMF created a system of convertible currencies with fixed exchange rates and various provisions to help countries within the system to solve their balance-of-payments problems, with rules to ensure compliance. Without a system of FIXED EXCHANGE RATES, strict conditions under which they could be changed, and the ability to convert different currencies into other currencies, postwar planners believed that it would not be feasible for international trade, borrowing, investment, and travel to take place, especially on the enlarged scale envisaged in the postwar world.

Under the original IMF system, each country was to have a fixed exchange rate, with fluctuations permitted only within a very narrow range; each country was also to try to make its currency fully convertible into the currencies of other IMF members. If an individual nation's currency moved up or down beyond the permitted narrow range of fluctuation, due to that country's own economic mismanagement or to structural difficulties, the country concerned was supposed to correct its internal economic policies—by bringing down inflation, for example, or by stimulating growth. Changes in the exchange rate were permitted only in conditions of "fundamental disequilibrium"—that is, when a country could no longer afford to defend its existing exchange rate without imposing unacceptably high costs, such as extreme unemployment, on its people. The IMF also had financial reserves of foreign currencies and gold to help individual countries to get over balance-of-payments difficulties, which it backed up with the GENERAL ARRANGEMENTS TO BORROW, an agreement of standby credit from leading industrial nations, plus swap arrangements with the BANK FOR INTERNATIONAL SETTLEMENTS.

Although Canada had an exemption, permitted under IMF rules for "exceptional circumstances," which allowed its dollar to float between 1950 and 1962 and again starting in 1970, the fixed-exchange-rate system worked fairly well until the late 1960s, when growing international concern over the huge surplus of U.S. dollars and the inability of the U.S. government to solve its balance-of-payments problems led to the breakdown of the fixed-exchange-rate system. In 1969, the IMF created a new form of international money, SPECIAL DRAWING RIGHTS, which was intended eventually to replace gold and the U.S. dollar as the principal reserve asset of the system used to settle balances of payment among nations. But the pressures on a U.S. dollar pegged to a heavily undervalued gold standard, and a fixed-exchange-rate system with the U.S. dollar as its linchpin, led to further pressure for change, and to the 1971 decision by the U.S. to unpeg the U.S. dollar from gold and let it float in international currency markets.

At the end of 1972, the fixed-exchange-rate system had been replaced by a FLOATING-rate system. IMF members began negotiation of a new monetary system, to preserve the international framework of rules and measures to help individual nations to deal with balance-of-payments problems, but also to permit a more flexible method of determining exchange rates. In January 1976, agreement was reached at a conference in Jamaica. Changes were subsequently made in the IMF's articles of agreement, formalizing the replacement of the system of fixed exchange rates by a system of floating exchange rates, subject to IMF surveillance so that individual nations would not artificially manipulate the value of their currencies for competitive reasons. At the same time, the IMF further reduced the role of gold in the world monetary system. The IMF retained its power to police the system, since nations needing IMF assistance to solve their balance-of-payments and international-debt problems had to agree to economic policies worked out in consultation with the IMF.

IMF assistance is important for two reasons: the fund is able to provide significant credit assistance, and its participation in helping a country to solve its balance-of-payments problems makes it easier for the country to raise capital from other sources, including banks. Since the sharp rise in world oil prices in 1973, the IMF has strengthened its ability to help nations solve their balance-of-payments problems. In 1974 and 1975, it created an Oil Facility to help poor nations finance balance-of-payments deficits caused by the sharp increase in oil prices. In 1979, the supplementary financing facility, which provides additional financing help to IMF members, came into effect.

Canada has been an IMF member since 1945, its participation being authorized under the BRETTON WOODS AGREEMENT Act. Initially, there were only forty-five IMF members; today there are about 130. Each member has a quota of exchange reserves it must deposit with the IMF, depending on its importance in the world economy. The U.S. quota is 21.5 per cent of the total, Germany's 5.5 per cent, Canada's 3.5 per cent, and India's 1.2 per cent. The IMF has a formal committee of twenty executive directors, who represent their own countries and, in some cases, a group of countries, in the day-to-day operations of the IMF. Canada is an executive director and represents the Bahamas, Barbados, Grenada, Jamaica, and Ireland. Approval of changes in the IMF rules requires approval from 60 per cent of its members and 85 per cent of the votes as represented by quotas. See also GROUP OF TWENTY.

international oil price The price charged for crude oil in world markets. Since 1973, this has been the price set by the ORGANIZATION OF PETROLEUM EXPORTING COUNTRIES at periodic price-setting meetings. But the going price can fluctuate below the OPEC price in times of surplus world supply, and has risen above the OPEC price on SPOT MARKETS in times of unanticipated world shortages, such as the halt in oil production in Iran in late 1978 and early 1979. The pricing policy in Canada is to move the Canadian oil price gradually to world-price levels, with the output from TAR-SANDS and heavy-oil plants getting the international oil price immediately.

International Telecommunications Union (ITU) An international agency, founded in 1865 but now a U.N. agency, which establishes and monitors international conventions and standards on telecommunications services, including the allocation and use of radio frequencies, standardization of equipment, the improvement of international telecommunications services, and the delineation of policy issues on new technologies, such as broadcasting satellites. Canada is a member of the thirty-six-nation ITU council, which is headquartered in Geneva and now has about 140 nations as members.

International Tin Agreements A series of international commodity agreements between tin-exporting and tin-importing nations, designed to provide stable and reasonable prices, ensure adequate supplies, and promote export earnings through new uses for tin. There have been five agreements so far, 1956–61, 1961–66, 1966–71, 1971–76, and 1976–81. Membership is open to all exporting and importing countries, and Canada is a signatory. The agreements are administered by the International Tin Council, which is made up of both exporting and importing nations. The council has three methods to control prices and supply: it maintains a buffer stock, selling into the market when prices rise too far and buying when they fall too low; it can impose export controls on producing countries; and it can change the price range for tin, which triggers buying and selling activities from the buffer stock. While the agreements have helped to achieve stable prices, they have been less successful in increasing the level of processing and manufacturing in the tin-exporting countries. The main tin exporters are Malaysia, Bolivia, Thailand, and Indonesia.

international transit Free and uninterrupted passage through another country's territory, waters, or airspace, by ships, planes, trains, trucks, or pipelines. For the most part, the passage through territorial waters or airspace is covered by international agreement or law; for example, the INTERNATIONAL CIVIL AVIATION ORGANIZATION has helped to develop the transit rules for civil aviation. Canada has treaty agreements with the United States that provide for the free and uninterrupted passage of oil and natural-gas pipelines through each other's territory; each pipeline project requires a separate treaty. In 1977, Canada and the United States signed two pipeline treaties, one concerning transit pipelines and the other concerning the pipeline to carry Alaska natural gas through western Canada to the United States. The purpose of such treaties is to make sure that at some date after the pipeline is built, the other country doesn't impose new conditions or taxes, or interfere with the project.

international union In Canada, a union with members in both Canada and the United States, whose headquarters is almost certain to be in the United States. About half of all Canadian union members belong to international unions; a much higher percentage of industrial and construction workers belong to international unions, since the principal Canadian unions tend to be those representing public-sector employees. The autonomy of Canadian locals in international unions has been an issue, and, in 1970, the CANADIAN LABOUR CONGRESS adopted a restlution to strengthen autonomy. The resolution urged the election of Canadian union officers by Canadian members, urged that elected Canadian representatives be the ones authorized to speak for the union in Canada, and that elected Canadian officers and Canadian union members determine policy stands in dealing with Canadian issues and the Canadian government. The bigger international unions have tended to encourage Canadian autonomy, but some international unions are more rigid. In 1974, the CLC passed another resolution calling for stiffer enforcement of its 1970 policy. See also CANADIAN STANDARDS OF SELF-GOVERNMENT.

International Wheat Council (IWC) An international organization of major wheat-exporting and -importing countries, established in 1949 to promote international wheat trade, to stabilize world prices for wheat when this is in the interest of exporters and importers, to resolve world wheat problems, to keep close records of crop forecasts and importer needs, and to negotiate international agreements on minimum and maximum prices, when this is possible. The council maintains a secretariat in London, which collects up-to-date information on world wheat supply and demand, and publishes an annual review of the world wheat situation. The council administers successive international wheat agreements and food-aid conventions. The wheat agreements provide the framework under which the wheat council functions. The food-aid conventions provide for the allocation, by wheat-exporting and wealthy industrial nations, of a portion of their crops or cash equivalents to buy wheat as a gift to the LESS-DEVELOPED COUNTRIES. The last international wheat agreement and the last food-aid convention were signed in 1971. These agreements have been renewed several times since, and run until mid-1981.

interpolation The calculation of a figure from within a known range of figures, as opposed to EXTRAPOLATION. For example, Canada carries out a full census once every ten years; taking the census figures for 1951, 1961, and 1971, it would be possible to make fairly detailed interpolations for, say, the year 1968.

interprovincial conferences Meetings of representatives of provincial governments without the participation of the federal government. See also PREMIERS' CONFERENCE, WESTERN PREMIERS' CONFERENCE, COUNCIL OF MARITIME PREMIERS, FEDERAL-PROVINCIAL CONFERENCE, CONFERENCE OF FIRST MINISTERS.

interprovincial trade Trade that crosses provincial boundaries and thus falls under federal regulation. It includes the movement of farm products and energy. Section 91 of the British North America Act gives the federal government general powers over trade and commerce in Canada.

interprovincial trade barriers Provincial laws or policies restricting the movement of goods or services from one province to another. These can include government purchasing policies, health or other regulations, FARM MARKETING-BOARD policies, trucking regulations, or other such policies. To limit the use of such barriers, the Fathers of Confederation decided not to allow the provinces to impose INDIRECT TAXES. Section 121 of the British North America Act states: "All articles of the growth, produce, or manufacture of any one of the provinces shall, from and after the Union, be admitted free into each of the other provinces." Thus, Canada was created as a single economic market.

intervention currency A strong, stable currency used by different nations to settle their balances of payments, and employed by nations in foreign-exchange markets when controlling fluctuations in their own currency's exchange rate. For most of the postwar period, it was the U.S. dollar alone, but today it may include the German mark and the Japanese yen. Canada, for example, uses these intervention currencies to influence the value of the Canadian dollar in foreign-exchange markets. But the Canadian dollar is not used as an intervention currency by other countries, one reason being that there are not enough in circulation outside Canada; Canada lacks the strength and size of economy to justify the use of its dollar as an intervention currency.

intestate The circumstance in which someone dies without leaving a will.

intrinsic value The underlying usefulness of a commodity or product; for example, the ability of an item of food to satisfy a person's hunger. In a modern economy, it is the supply and demand of the food product, rather than its intrinsic value, that determines its price.

invention The creation of a new technology or process, as opposed to its application. See also INNOVATION, PATENT.

inventory The various raw materials, parts, and finished goods plus work-in-progress of a firm, and their total value. Inventory in raw materials and parts is held in order to meet the future production needs of a firm, while an inventory of finished products is held to meet new orders. A manufacturer, for example, needs to have sufficient materials so that his production lines can operate efficiently and will not have to slow down due to insufficient raw materials or parts. If a manufacturer fears a strike in one of his suppliers or in a transportation industry, he will build up his inventory to tide him over the expected strike; otherwise, he may have to shut down while his competitors keep working and gain some of his customers. Similarly, a retailer wants to make sure that he has enough winter coats on hand to supply his customers. If he under-orders, he loses sales; by the time he can get delivery on a new order, the season may be over. Excessive inventories, however, are costly; a manufacturer may find himself stuck with a supply of outdated products, or a retailer may find himself with too many coats at the end of the winter season that may be out of style the following winter.

Changes in the physical volume of inventories are important in determining the economic outlook and the need for changes in economic policies. If inventories are low, then business may feel the need to rebuild them to more satisfactory levels; if they are high and not moving, then it is unlikely that there will be much growth in business output. Changes in the physical volume of inventories are thus an important element of demand in the economy, and help to determine the rate of economic growth. The size of inventories also reflects business confidence or lack of confidence about the economic outlook. The two principal forms of inventory in the gross national product are the inventories of non-farm businesses—in other words, business and government enterprises—and farm inventories, which include farm-stored grain and livestock and farm products in commercial channels.

inventory control Since inventories represent tied-up capital and can also spoil or become obsolete, businesses try to maintain inventories as low as possible but sufficient to meet business needs. This is an important element of management, and has become more scientific with the use of computerized control systems and financial-management techniques.

inventory profit The profits of a firm resulting from the fact that it had large inventories in stock during a period of rapid inflation, and increased the price of its products accordingly.

inventory turnover The number of times a firm's average inventory is replaced during the course of a year. The turnover rate is determined by dividing the cost of goods sold during the year by the average inventory.

inventory valuation The method used in a company's BALANCE SHEET, under current assets, to determine the value of inventories. The most widely used method is FIRST IN, FIRST OUT (fifo), which assumes that the items acquired earliest for the inventory are the first used or sold. Two other methods of valuation are LAST IN, FIRST OUT (lifo), which assumes that the most recently acquired inventory items are the first to be used or sold; and the average-cost method, in which an average value is determined for all items in the inventory. The method of inventory valuation used helps to determine the profitability of a firm. A large profit made on inventories due to inflation may be illusory, since the inventory will have to be replaced at much higher prices, and part of the profit just earned will have to finance inventory-replacement costs.

inventory-valuation adjustment A figure used by Statistics Canada in its GROSS-NATIONAL-PRODUCT calculation, to show the change in the value of inventories due to price changes. This enables Statistics Canada to separate out the physical change in inventories, a figure that is important in analyzing economic performance and in calculating future business performance and economic growth, from changes due simply to inflation.

invested capital The total of SHAREHOLDERS' EQUITY in a corporation, plus outstanding long-term debt, minus the portion of long-term debt to be paid off in the following twelve-month period. In other words, invested capital consists of the total assets of a business minus its current liabilities. It represents the capital at work in a corporation. One useful way of measuring the profitability of a corporation is to calculate profits as a per cent of invested capital; this is known as return on invested capital, and shows how well management is using the resources of the corporation, including its credit.

investment 1. As used in economics, spending on CAPITAL GOODS such as factories, mines, and machinery, so as to increase the productive capacity of the economy. New investment is an important source of economic growth and PRODUCTIVITY improvement; it is undertaken to increase profits. It depends on the expected level of demand in the economy and the existing level of productive capacity, on the need to replace obsolete equipment so as to remain competitive, the anticipated growth in population and income, new inventions, changes in public tastes, new export markets, and other such factors. Economic policy-makers have to find ways of encouraging investment so that enough of it takes place but in an orderly way, so that it will not contribute to inflation. Gross investment in the economy is the total amount of investment spending; net investment is the actual addition to the nation's productive capacity, and is obtained by deducting depreciation or capital-consumption allowances from gross investment. **2.** In its broader meaning, investment is any purchase of an asset to increase future income. It represents savings, as opposed to consumption, and includes purchases of shares, bonds, property, works of art, and a wide range of short-term financial securities, such as certificates of deposit, guaranteed-investment certificates, treasury bills, and finance-company paper.

investment banking See INVESTMENT DEALER, UNDERWRITER.

investment club A group of individuals who put their savings together into one investment fund, usually adding an agreed-on amount to it on a monthly basis, and invest the money in shares and other securities as a single investor. In this way they are able to invest in a variety of securities and to spread their risk. Some clubs make their own investment decisions, while others retain an investment analyst to make recommendations on investments or to manage the funds directly.

investment company A company that invests its capital in the shares, bonds, and other securities of other companies. There are two types: **1.** CLOSED-END INVESTMENT COMPANIES have fixed capitalization; their shares may be listed on stock exchanges, where they can be bought or sold. **2.** OPEN-END INVESTMENT COMPANIES, or MUTUAL FUNDS, which have unlimited capitalization, with shares being issued as they are sold and shares redeemed when shareholders wish to liquidate their holdings. Mutual funds are not listed on stock exchanges.

investment counsellor A professional who advises clients how to invest their funds. Investment counsellors must be registered, under provincial securities laws, with a SECURITIES COMMISSION.

investment dealer A financial firm that has two principal functions: **1.** To help corporations and industries who need investment capital to raise it on the best possible terms, and to help pension funds, insurance companies, trust funds, corporations, and individuals with investment capital to get the best return on their funds. **2.** To help provide a secondary market for outstanding BONDS, COMMERCIAL PAPER, finance paper, TREASURY BILLS, and UNLISTED SHARES. Investment dealers play an important role in advising governments and corporations on the size, type, and timing of new offerings, including such questions as whether to issue bonds, PREFERRED SHARES, or COMMON SHARES, whether there should be a PRIVATE PLACEMENT or PUBLIC ISSUE, along with advice on whether a company should go public, how to prepare a PROSPECTUS, how to handle mergers, and the like. Investment dealers also buy and sell new and outstanding debt and other invested securities on their own account, maintaining an inventory so that there is always a ready market. They UNDERWRITE new issues, and buy and sell outstanding issues. Some of them also operate the MONEY MARKET, dealing in short-term funds and thus playing an important role in the BANK OF CANADA's implementation of MONETARY POLICY through OPEN-MARKET OPERATIONS. Most investment dealers are part of a securities firm that is a STOCKBROKER as well, acting as an agent for clients in buying and selling SHARES on recognized STOCK EXCHANGES.

Investment Dealers Association (IDA) An association of INVESTMENT DEALERS and STOCKBROKERS, both individuals and firms, established to encourage saving and investment by providing safe financial markets for investors through self-regulation of the securities industry, the adoption of high standards of behaviour by members, and the provision of training courses for those working in the industry. The present non-profit body was created in 1916 as the Bond Dealers Association of Canada; it adopted its present name in 1934. Members of the IDA must meet a set of standards before they are accepted and must continue to meet those standards if they wish to remain as members; the most important standards have to do with the safety of client funds, and the maintenance of a minimum amount of net free capital to meet emergencies. The IDA is to a large extent responsible for the rules governing the operation of the MONEY MARKET and the OVER-THE-COUNTER MARKET in Canada. It works closely with provincial SECURITIES COMMISSIONS and operates a number of programs to protect the investing public. It administers, with the Toronto, Montreal, and Vancouver stock exchanges, a national contingency fund of $1.5 million, to provide assistance to clients in the event of a collapse of a member's firm. It is based in Toronto. See also CANADIAN SECURITIES INSTITUTE.

investment guarantee A government program to encourage corporations to invest in LESS-DEVELOPED COUNTRIES; the government promises to reimburse the corporation for all or most of its investment costs in a less-developed country if an investment is expropriated with little or no compensation. Such guarantees are provided to Canadian firms through the EXPORT DEVELOPMENT CORPORATION.

investment incentives Government measures

to encourage business firms to invest in new facilities, to undertake a particular type of investment, such as new spending on research and development or on pollution-control equipment, or to invest in areas of chronic unemployment and slow economic growth. There are many types of subsidy or incentive. They range from direct grants, such as those offered by the Department of REGIONAL ECONOMIC EXPANSION, and low-interest loans, to various tax measures, such as an INVESTMENT TAX CREDIT or ACCELERATED DEPRECIATION (sometimes called accelerated capital-cost allowances), a tax cut, or special write-off provisions and DEPLETION ALLOWANCES. An investment incentive can also consist of low-cost power supplies or natural resources, or direct government spending on INFRASTRUCTURE that would normally be part of a corporation's costs.

investment income The investment received by an individual, corporation, or pension or endowment fund, trust, or other organization, from its holdings in securities and property. It includes rent from property, dividends from shares in corporations, and interest from bonds, guaranteed-investment certificates, bank accounts, certificates of deposit, treasury bills, and other financial securities.

investment portfolio The list of investments held by an individual, pension fund, or other investor. The portfolio should reflect the investment strategy of the owner; the emphasis may be on income or on capital gain, or on some particular combination, depending on the needs of the investor.

investment tax credit A subsidy from the government to corporations to encourage them to expand their operations generally or to undertake a specific kind of investment, such as more investment in research and development facilities, in pollution equipment, or investments in areas of chronic unemployment. It takes the form of a credit, equal to a percentage of investment spending, that can be deducted by a corporation from the income tax it owes to the government. An investment tax credit thus reduces the tax liability of a corporation making an investment. For example, the investment tax credit running from 1975 to 1980 allowed corporations to deduct from the taxes they owed the federal government 5 per cent of the cost of new buildings, machinery, and equipment used in manufacturing, processing, petroleum and mineral exploration and development, and logging, fishing, and farming.

invisible hand A concept developed by ADAM SMITH; the theory that, although each individual pursues his own selfish interests, the welfare of society is achieved through the competing interplay of these market forces. The competing forces of supply and demand, acted out through hundreds of thousands of individual transactions, achieve an EQUILIBRIUM that represents the best interests of society. Smith put it this way in *An Inquiry into the Nature and Causes of the Wealth of Nations* in 1776: ". . . every individual, therefore, endeavours . . . to employ his capital . . . that its produce may be of the greatest value . . . He generally, indeed, neither intends to promote the public interest, nor knows how much he is promoting it . . . he intends only his own security; . . . only his own gain, and he is in this, as in many other cases, led by an invisible hand to promote an end which was no part of his intention . . . By pursuing his own interest he frequently promotes that of the society more effectually than when he really intends to promote it."

This concept is at the core of LAISSEZ-FAIRE economics, and is used by advocates of the FREE-MARKET ECONOMY to argue against government interference. But the invisible hand assumes PERFECT COMPETITION. If there is IMPERFECT COMPETITION, then there is no invisible hand to ensure that the economy functions in the best interests of society. Government intervention is needed to deal with MONOPOLY or OLIGOPOLY, with EXTERNAL DISECONOMIES such as pollution, and to make sure that public wants ignored by monopolists or oligopolists are met.

invisibles The non-merchandise part of a country's current account in its BALANCE OF PAYMENTS. It includes the wide range of payments and receipts for all kinds of services, including interest and dividends, travel, patent and royalty payments, management and other fees between subsidiaries and head offices, insurance and banking services, transportation including shipping, various gifts, and the funds immigrants bring to a country or remit to their homelands. The balance in trade or VISIBLES plus the balance in invisibles equals the current-account surplus or deficit. Canada usually has a visibles surplus and an invisibles deficit, and tends to run an overall current-account deficit that is offset by inflows of foreign capital.

invoice An itemized statement, usually a bill, sent by a seller of goods or services to the purchaser. It lists the goods or services purchased, the quantity, and the amount owed.

iron law of wages The theory that wages can never be sustained above the level necessary for minimal subsistence. If wages rise above that level, the number of workers will increase, and families will be able to afford to have more children. This, in turn, will increase the supply of workers, and force wage rates below the subsistence level. As workers stop working because wages do not even provide subsistence, production will fall. Employers will then offer higher wages to attract workers, with wages once more temporarily rising above the subsistence level. But soon they will slip below subsistence levels again, as the cycle repeats itself.

This gloomy nineteenth-century view was an outgrowth of the MALTHUSIAN view of the world, and its conviction that man's limited ability to increase the food supply was a great constraint on all human activity. Experience tells a different story. The reserve army of the unemployed, which was supposed to be available to replace workers wanting more money, does not exist. It ignores, as well, the fact that employers have a need for an enormous variety of skills that are not interchangeable, and in competitive labour markets have to bid for these skills. It also ignores the role of unions in negotiating wages and protecting jobs and the role of government in setting minimum wages. By the middle of the nineteenth century, a new wage theory, the WAGE-FUND THEORY, had been developed to explain how wages were set. It has been replaced, in this century, by the MARGINAL-PRODUCTIVITY THEORY OF WAGES.

irrigation Methods of bringing water to agricultural land to increase output or to make farming possible; techniques include the use of pipes or ditches. See PRAIRIE FARM REHABILITATION ADMINISTRATION.

issue See NEW ISSUE.

issued capital The proportion of AUTHORIZED CAPITAL that has been sold to the public in the form of PREFERRED and COMMON SHARES. Issued capital is usually less than authorized capital; a company anxious to raise new investment capital will, if stock-market conditions are good, issue new shares if the company hasn't reached its authorized limit, instead of borrowing money, which increases its future interest costs.

J

J-curve The curve followed by a country's BALANCE OF PAYMENTS after its currency has been devalued. Initially, the balance of payments will worsen, because of the flow of goods already in inventory and transit, and contracts signed before the devaluation occurred. But as importers and exporters adjust to the price impact of the devaluation, the country's balance of payments will turn around and begin to improve. There is nothing automatic about this; there may be other factors that mitigate against the J-curve to some extent, in addition to the time it takes for firms to adjust. For example, in spite of price reductions for exports, industry's capacity to produce more may be too low to take advantage of new market opportunities, or there may not be an increase in demand for these products in other countries, even with lower export prices. But the J-curve expresses what should happen and usually does happen following a devaluation.

jawbone economics Efforts by a government to restrain price and wage increases by talking up the need for restraint to fight inflation. This talk may be accompanied by suggested price and wage guidelines and by singling out individual firms and unions for public attention if they disregard the guidelines or need for restraint. Sometimes a government may threaten action, in public or behind closed doors, against a firm or union that ignores the need for restraint. See also MORAL SUASION. Jawbone economics may be successful for a short period, but often they are the first stage of an INCOMES POLICY that eventually includes some kind of legal controls or punishment for misbehaving firms and unions.

job description An outline of the various duties of a person doing a particular job, along with a description of his authority and the authority to whom he reports. A job description is used to determine the qualifications needed for a job and as a benchmark to assess how well a person is doing it.

job enrichment Attempts to increase personal satisfaction and motivation on the job. Techniques include giving workers more say in how they organize their activities, adoption of the so-called open office and generally more open work environment, opportunities for workers to discuss how their jobs should be performed, and efforts to increase challenges and worker responsibilities. The purpose is to reduce absenteeism and dissatisfaction, and to increase productivity.

job evaluation An organized assessment of the skills needed to perform a particular job, used as the basis for differential rates of pay in an industry or firm.

job-safety laws Federal and provincial laws to protect the health and safety of workers. They cover such items as heating, lighting, ventilation, tunnelling, the protection of dangerous machinery, electrical installations, boiler pressure, and sanitation. There may be special laws dealing with more dangerous industries, such as construction and excavation, mining, and forestry.

job security Various provisions in a collective agreement that give workers protection in the event of automation or of new production methods or products.

jobber A middleman or local wholesaler who buys from manufacturers, importers, and national wholesalers, and sells to local retailers.

joint account A bank account in which two or more persons have signing authority and thus can write cheques and make deposits. The account may require at least two signatures on a cheque or only one, depending on the arrangement made. But each party to the account is liable for any overdraft. Joint accounts are widely used by husbands and wives to manage their household budgets.

joint agreement In labour relations, a collective agreement among three or more parties. It may consist of an industry-wide contract between many different employers and a single union or several unions. Or it may consist of an agreement between one employer and several different unions representing different groups of workers in the firm.

joint costs The costs incurred in producing two or more products simultaneously. For example, in petroleum refining, gasoline, fuel oil, kerosene, and naphtha are all produced at the same time. In flour milling, different types of flour and wheat germ are produced simultaneously. In meatpacking, various meat products, hides, and shortening are produced simultaneously. The problem for accountants is to allocate these joint costs in the early, simultaneous stage of production. At a more advanced level of production, costing becomes easier because the products reach a stage at which they require separate types of processing.

joint demand The demand for two or more products that normally must be used together—in the auto industry, for example, the demand for steel, glass, rubber, carpeting, paint, plastics, electrical wiring, and other products used in the manufacture of a car. A change in the demand for cars will also result in a change in demand for tires and other products used in autos, such as car radios. An understanding of joint demand is important in understanding the economic impact of, say, a major price increase or decrease for one commodity on the demand for other products.

Joint Ministerial Committee on Trade and Economic Affairs A means of cabinet consultation between Canada and the United States that began in 1953 and continued until 1970. The committee met almost every year, under the chairmanship of the Canadian secretary of state for EXTERNAL AFFAIRS and the U.S. secretary of state, and included cabinet ministers from both countries concerned with finance, trade, agriculture, energy, industrial development, balances of payment, mining, and other such matters of joint concern. The governor of the BANK OF CANADA and the chairman of the U.S. FEDERAL RESERVE Board also attended these meetings, which alternated between Ottawa and Washington.

joint tenancy A form of ownership of land and the buildings on it, in which two or more persons have a common interest and equal rights and in which there is a right of survivorship. This means that, upon the death of one of the owners, the surviving owners automatically own the portion held by the deceased partner. See also TENANTS IN COMMON.

joint venture A specific project carried out by two or more firms. The Syncrude TAR-SANDS plant in Alberta was a joint venture of oil companies and of the federal, Ontario, and Alberta governments. One of the purposes of the CANADA DEVELOPMENT CORPORATION is to participate in joint ventures to develop industry in Canada. It is sometimes an alternative to complete foreign control of a firm; a joint venture may be possible between Canadian investors and a foreign firm that has expertise in a particular new technology, for example. Joint ventures are often undertaken if one firm is too small to carry out a project by itself or if the various partners have complementary skills or technologies.

journeyman A skilled worker—for example, a carpenter or electrician—who has completed his apprenticeship program.

junior company A company that, from an investment point of view, does not have an established earnings or dividend record.

jurisdictional dispute A conflict between two or more unions over who shall represent workers in a particular firm or industry, or over which union members should work on a particular job. It may also be a conflict between two different levels of government over taxing, spending, or regulatory powers, or between different countries over who controls the resources in a disputed body of water.

K

key sector A branch of the economy that is considered essential to the cultural or economic life of the country. The Canadian government has identified certain sectors of the economy that must be under complete or near-complete control of Canadian-owned companies. These include railways, banking, broadcasting, and publishing. This approach doesn't always guarantee that the Canadian-controlled firms will meet Canadian objectives. Hence, for example, the government has also had to impose Canadian-content requirements on the broadcasting industry so that broadcasters will devote sufficient time to Canadian programs.

Keynes, John Maynard The British economist (1883–1946) who provided the theoretical basis for government intervention in the economy, through FISCAL POLICY, to achieve FULL EMPLOYMENT. He developed his main economic theory on the importance of total aggregate demand in the economy during the depression of the 1930s, in *The General Theory of Employment, Interest and Money,* published in 1936. (See also KEYNESIAN ECONOMICS.) Keynes rejected the view of the NEOCLASSICAL ECONOMISTS, who believed that full employment was the normal state of the economy and that the economic system would self-correct and return to full employment if there was any lapse. Keynes argued that LAISSEZ-FAIRE economics could not ensure stable economic growth and full employment, and maintained that government intervention in many forms, including budget deficits, was needed.

After a brief career in the civil service in India, Keynes spent most of his life working for the British Treasury or teaching economics at Cambridge University. He was a British delegate to the Versailles Peace Conference in 1919, but opposed allied demands for huge reparations from Germany. He wrote a book that year, *The Economic Consequences of the Peace* (1920), in which he argued that the reparations demanded from Germany were not only immoral, but placed an impossible burden on the country.

For the next twenty years, Keynes taught economics and took an active part in public-policy debates of the time. In 1936, he published his *General Theory*, after the economists of his day had failed to find a cure for the Great Depression. During the Second World War, he worked as an adviser in the British Treasury. He was one of the architects of the postwar multilateral institutions, having played an active role at BRETTON WOODS. However, the resulting INTERNATIONAL MONETARY FUND, built around a central role for gold and the U.S. dollar, fell far short of his own ideas of how to reform the world monetary system.

Keynes called for a world clearing bank and an international currency to be called the bancor. The clearing bank would finance balance-of-payments deficits. If a country's balance of payments fell into a chronic and unsustainable deficit, then surplus countries and the deficit country would all have to take corrective steps. Keynes argued that this would give all countries a stake in achieving equilibrium in the international economy, instead of placing most of the burden on deficit countries.

Keynesian economics The school of economics developed by JOHN MAYNARD KEYNES and his followers, and based largely on Keynes' major work published in 1936, *The General Theory of Employment, Interest and Money*. Keynesian economists rejected the NEOCLASSICAL view that the economy, left to its own devices, tended to operate at full-employment levels. They argued that it was possible for the economy to achieve an equilibrium level at less than full employment, and hence for high unemployment to continue for lengthy periods of time. Neoclassical economists had assumed that all national income would be spent on either consumption or investment goods, and that monetary policy could be used, by adjusting interest rates, to determine the levels of consumption, savings, and investment. Keynes and his followers showed that not all income would necessarily be spent, but that, if it was not, the level of demand in the economy would be insufficient to maintain full employment.

Keynesian economists also rejected the view that the level of interest rates could determine how much people would spend, save, and invest. They argued that the level of saving and spending depended not on interest rates but on how much income a person had; as a person's income rose, the proportion of income spent tended to decline and the proportion saved tended to rise (see also MARGINAL PROPENSITY TO CONSUME). The decision to invest would depend not simply on the cost of borrowed goods but also on the expected rate of return on the investment, something affected very much by an investor's confidence in the future. But as investment increased, the rate of return would decline (see also

MARGINAL EFFICIENCY OF CAPITAL). This meant, according to Keynesian economists, that a rich, industrial economy would have to find new opportunities for investment, to achieve and maintain full employment. Hence, the role of government in running a deficit, to make sure that the level of spending on consumption or investment goods in the economy matched the full-employment level of savings. The MULTIPLIER would then ensure that this additional government spending would generate higher levels of income and employment, and hence, new opportunities for private investment.

Keynes and his followers thus put considerably less emphasis on MONETARY POLICY, and introduced a much bigger role for fiscal policy in achieving full employment. They also paved the way for a more significant role for government in economic management, and therefore reduced reliance on free-market forces. They believed that a free-market, capitalist economy, left to its own devices, would fail to achieve long-term full employment, and that any kind of private-enterprise system could only be maintained through government intervention in a MIXED ECONOMY. See also POST-KEYNESIAN ECONOMICS.

kickback An illegal or improper payment —by a supplier to a retailer, for example, by a contractor to a government or private builder, or by a worker to a union official—to get a job.

kiting A method, sometimes with fraudulent intent, of juggling one's bank accounts to make it look as though there is more money on hand than there really is, or to cover a temporary cash shortage. For example, someone kiting cheques is counting on delays in the banking system to enable him to cover a cash shortage. If a cheque is coming due for payment on a certain day at his bank, he can cover it by depositing a cheque from an account in another bank, even though there isn't enough money in the second account to cover this new cheque. But he may be gambling that, in the meantime, he will receive a cheque due him that he can deposit in the second bank account before the second cheque he issued is presented at the second bank for payment. While kiting was a widespread practice in the days before computerized banking, it is harder to get away with today, with much speedier CLEARING of cheques.

knowledge industry A broad term describing an industry that produces information goods and services, and whose employees are scientists, technicians, and managers. Examples include the telecommunications industry, research and development organizations, the mass media, accounting, education, and banking.

Kondratyev cycle The theory that business cycles run for long periods of fifty to sixty years, named after a Russian economist, Nikolai Kondratyev, who made important studies of long-term cycles during the 1920s. He argued that these long cycles are due to fundamental changes in investment, production techniques, technology, and new markets, and were part of the rhythm of long waves inherent in the capitalist system; several decades of prosperity are followed by several decades of slump. According to Kondratyev, the start of a new wave or cycle brings with it great changes in society and the expansion into new markets, which in turn can provoke revolution and war. Examples of his cycles include the Industrial Revolution of the late eighteenth and early nineteenth centuries, the new steelmaking technology and use of steam at sea in the last half of the nineteenth century, the introduction of electricity, the internal-combustion engine, and chemicals in the first half of the twentieth century, and possibly the computer, telecommunications, and micro-electronic technologies of the late twentieth century.

L

labour One of the FACTORS OF PRODUCTION, labour is the human effort employed in the production of goods and services. It consists not only of the number of workers and the hours they have worked, but also of their physical and mental effort, skills, and initiative. This effort is rewarded by salaries, wages, professional fees, commissions, bonuses, and other payments.

labour agreement A contract between a union and an employer setting out pay and various conditions of work for a specified period —one, two, or three years. It is usually called a COLLECTIVE AGREEMENT.

labour council An association of union locals in a metropolitan area or district that work together to represent union interests and concerns in local matters. The locals usually belong to CANADIAN LABOUR CONGRESS–affiliated unions.

Labour, Department of The federal government department, established in 1900, that is responsible for labour laws and policies affecting unions, management, and workers under federal jurisdiction. This sector accounts for about 10 per cent of the labour force and includes such industries as banking, railways, airlines, shipping, and the employees of the federal government and its agencies and crown corporations. The department influences provincial labour laws indirectly, since reforms at the federal level encourage others at the provincial level to push for similar reforms. The department is responsible for the CANADA LABOUR CODE, the CANADA LABOUR RELATIONS BOARD and the CANADA LABOUR RELATIONS COUNCIL, which deal with the basic administration of federal labour law. The department also publishes nation-wide statistics on wage settlements and time lost due to strikes and lockouts, investigates labour-management questions to reduce the incidence of strikes and lockouts, administers programs to help workers laid off due to trade agreements and lowered tariffs, including the ADJUSTMENT-ASSISTANCE-Benefits Program, publishes detailed data on wage rates for communities across Canada, and attempts to work with union leaders to represent their concerns and interests in the formulation of government policy. The department is also Canada's liaison with the INTERNATIONAL LABOUR ORGANIZATION.

labour force As defined in the LABOUR-FORCE SURVEY of Statistics Canada, all Canadians fifteen years and over who are employed or unemployed. It does not include members of the Canadian armed forces, inmates in penitentiaries, or residents of Indian reservations, the Yukon, and the Northwest Territories. Included among the employed are people who, during the survey week, did any kind of work, full- or part-time, including people who weren't paid but who contributed to a family-owned business, and people who had jobs but weren't working due to illness, a strike or lockout, bad weather, or vacation. Included among the unemployed are those who are actively looking for work, were laid-off, or who were unemployed but had a new job to start in four weeks or less. The size of the labour force is calculated from a monthly survey of fifty-five thousand households across Canada.

labour-force survey A monthly survey by Statistics Canada to determine the actual and SEASONALLY ADJUSTED UNEMPLOYMENT RATES, as well as growth in employment and in the size of the labour force, breaking all these down by sex, age and province; some information is also available for major cities. The survey gives a detailed picture of employment changes in major industries, information on numbers of workers not working due to labour disputes, and other labour-force data. It is based on a survey of fifty-five thousand households across Canada, taken during a reference week each month. It started in 1946 as a quarterly survey, but became a monthly survey in 1952. See also UNEMPLOYMENT RATE, EMPLOYMENT INDEX, LABOUR FORCE.

labour hoarding The policy followed in some companies of retaining skilled employees during a recession, even though not all workers will be fully employed and unit costs will thus rise. The reason for this policy is that management has an investment in the employees, in the form of their on-the-job training and experience. If a firm has to hire new employees at the time of the next economic recovery, it will have to invest in training new workers. Retaining employees during a recession also means that the firm avoids the problems and costs of attracting new workers during the next recovery. Labour hoarding occurs mainly during short-lived recessions. If a recession is prolonged, an employer will lay off workers, starting with the least experienced and least skilled.

labour income An important measure of demand in the economy. As measured by Statistics Canada, it includes wages and salaries paid to employees, along with payments by employers for the future benefits of employees, such as pension-plan contributions and unemployment-insurance and workmen's-compensation premiums. Wages and salaries include bonuses, commissions, taxable allowances and benefits, and directors' fees. Labour income does not include the salaries of the armed forces.

labour-intensive A term used to describe an industry or company that uses a high degree of labour per unit of output and a relatively low proportion of capital. Wages will thus form a large part of the industry's or firm's total costs. Examples include the clothing, footwear, and retailing industries. Some industries have shifted from labour-intensive to CAPITAL-INTENSIVE; these include the automobile, steel, and food-processing industries.

labour legislation Federal and provincial laws that spell out the rights of labour and management, how labour relations are to be conducted, and the procedures for union certification and decertification, collective bargaining, mediation, and strikes and lockouts. Such laws also deal with minimum wages, job safety, accident prevention, job discrimination, maternity protection, layoffs and termination of employment, vacations with pay, public holidays, hours of work, technological change, and overtime. Labour laws guarantee workers the right to organize; they establish labour-relations boards to certify unions as bargaining agents, and compel employers to bargain in good faith with a certified union. These laws also prohibit employers from interfering in union efforts to organize and guard against other unfair labour practices. They set out strict rules on collective bargaining, and the steps, including CONCILIATION and MEDIATION, that must be followed before a strike or lockout can legally take place. Strikes and lockouts are prohibited during the life of the contract. See also CANADA LABOUR CODE.

labour market The market in which wages and the quantity of labour employed are determined. It includes many submarkets for particular skills and industries; but these many submarkets affect one another, since relative pay relationships are important and since there may also be a high or low degree of labour mobility between one skill or industry and another. Economists often talk of the efficiency of labour markets—the speed with which news on job vacancies reaches workers seeking jobs, the mobility of workers from one job to another, the skills-training available. The FRICTIONAL UNEMPLOYMENT rate can be reduced somewhat if labour markets are efficient in matching job vacancies with workers, encourage mobility to better jobs, and make skills-training available.

labour mobility The ability of workers to change jobs or move into new careers. Government can aid labour mobility by providing up-to-date information about available jobs, grants for workers to move to new communities where jobs exist, or skills training so that workers can move up the occupational ladder to better-paying jobs. A high degree of labour mobility shows that labour markets are working well, and that the social system is open and does not put barriers in the way of people who have the talents or skills to move into better jobs. The main barriers to labour mobility are lack of knowledge of job vacancies, money to move out of an area of chronic unemployment into one where jobs are available, access to education and skills-training, or union and professional restrictions, which make it hard for newcomers to enter the skill or profession.

labour relations A specialized field that deals with the relations between employers and employees, including COLLECTIVE BARGAINING. Most employers have a labour-relations staff, while some universities designate the field as a special area of study. Increasingly, the field of labour relations is subject to regulation under federal and provincial labour laws. The term INDUSTRIAL RELATIONS is sometimes used in manufacturing companies.

labour-relations board A federal or provincial board that administers labour laws and deals with some forms of labour-management grievances. Such boards, among other things, monitor the certification of unions as bargaining agents. See also CANADA LABOUR RELATIONS BOARD.

labour-saving machinery Machinery that can produce the same volume of output with a much smaller number of workers than would be required to produce it by hand, or with less sophisticated machinery.

labour slowdown A form of labour protest that falls short of a complete work stoppage, but is designed to put pressure on an employer to resolve an outstanding dispute with the union or to settle a contract. The advantage to the union members is that the employer must continue to pay them, even though they are producing less than they normally would. See also WORK TO RULE.

labour theory of value The theory that labour is the source of all value. The idea was first expressed by the CLASSICAL ECONOMISTS, but it is usually associated with KARL MARX, who adopted the idea from the classical school. According to the theory, only labour—the amount of labour needed to produce something—gives a good or service value. No account is taken of the part played by CAPITAL or LAND in the production process; no provision is made for rent or profits. The theory also disregards such sources of value as SCARCITY or UTILITY. Thus, if a product requires five hours of labour to make, it is worth five times as much as a product that takes one hour to make. Marx used the theory to argue that workers were exploited by capitalists. He complained that a product that took, say, five hours of labour to make, might require ten hours of labour to buy, the difference between the wages paid the workers and the value of the goods produced, the profit, being the extent to which capitalists exploited labour.

labour union See union.

lagging indicator A statistical series that follows on the heels of changes in economic conditions to provide evidence of changes in the economy—statistics on labour costs per unit of output, for example, indicating changes in cost pressures on profit margins. See also LEADING INDICATOR, COINCIDENT INDICATOR.

laissez-faire An economic doctrine that asserts that the best way to achieve strong economic growth and a high standard of living is to limit strictly government intervention in the economy to maintaining the value of the currency and protecting private property. The belief in unrestricted private enterprise emerged in the eighteenth century as a reaction against government interference and MERCANTILISM. Laissez-faire economists, among them ADAM SMITH, argued that self-interest should be allowed a free rein, since this would result in the optimal allocation of resources and provide the surest protection of political liberties in the process. Laissez-faire began to lose its appeal in the late nineteenth century, because it led to the growth of MONOPOLY and OLIGOPOLY, resulted in an unacceptably wide inequality of income, and required government interference to deal with harsh social conditions, such as the use of child labour and the arbitrary treatment of workers. See also MIXED ECONOMY.

land One of the FACTORS OF PRODUCTION, which includes all of the limited natural resources found on land, such as minerals, oil and gas, forests, and the fertility of the soil; it also includes the resources of the sea, such as fish and offshore minerals. RENT is the return on land; it may consist of a royalty paid on mineral resources, a direct payment or rent for the use of the land, or a tax or fee.

land assembly The acquisition of adjoining parcels of land from different owners, often through middlemen or brokers, for a major commercial or housing project. Land assembly is usually carried out by private developers, but the federal and provincial governments sometimes work together to assemble land for a public-housing project, airport, or other such facility.

land reform The break-up of large landholdings in less-developed countries and the distribution of this land to individual farmers in smaller holdings, so that they can retain the income they earn through their own effort. Such reform is carried out not only for reasons of equity; it is also argued that land reform should lead to higher agricultural output, since individual farmers will have a greater incentive to work hard and increase their output.

land registry A provincial office where the titles to all individual parcels of land and buildings are registered. Titles are searched at such offices whenever a property is bought or sold, to ensure that there are no outstanding claims against the property.

land-transfer tax A tax levied on the sale of land or real estate. It is a percentage of the sale price.

land-use planning The designation of land for specific purposes or the banning of certain types of activity on particular parcels of land. For example, municipalities designate which land can be used for low- or high-density housing, industry, office buildings, and stores, through ZONING by-laws. Provincial governments may restrict the conversion of prime agricultural land into other uses such as housing projects, shopping centres, and industrial parks. Federal and provincial parks are a form of land-use planning; land is set aside for recreational use. In some cases, provision is made for mixed use—for example, in a municipality, land may be used for apartments or offices; federal or provincial land may be used for forestry and as recreational parkland.

landlord The owner of a property who leases out the use of his property to others in return for payment or rent.

landlord and tenant laws Provincial laws that set out the rights of landlords or property owners, and tenants, the people who rent the property. Such laws set out the conditions under which a tenant may be evicted, the responsibilities of the landlord and tenant for the care of the property, lease rights, and other such matters. Such laws may also cover rent controls or procedures for tenants to appeal large rent increases.

language of work The language used by an employee on the job. In most parts of Canada it is English; in Quebec, it is French, with some government-approved exceptions for head-office activities. In federal government activities, the general principle is that public employees should be able to work in the language in which they feel most at home, although this does not always apply. This reflects the spirit of the Official Languages Act, passed by Parliament in 1969, which said that English and French "possess and enjoy equality of status and equal rights and privileges as to their use in all the institutions of the Parliament and Government of Canada."

last in, first out (lifo) A method of determining the value, in a company's books, of its INVENTORY. It assumes that the first items removed or sold from inventory were the last ones to be placed in the inventory. It thus values the items in the inventory according to what it would cost to replace them. This approach is favoured during periods of high inflation, since it results in a more accurate assessment of the replacement value of the inventory. It results in higher expenses being reported in a company's books and hence, lower reported profits. See also FIRST IN, FIRST OUT.

Latin American Free Trade Association (LAFTA) A free-trade agreement signed in 1960 by Argentina, Brazil, Chile, Mexico,

Paraguay, Peru, and Uruguay. Since then Ecuador, Colombia, and Venezuela have joined. Progress has been made in reducing tariffs among the LAFTA members, but not on achieving a common external tariff. In 1968, LAFTA agreed in principle with the members of the CENTRAL AMERICAN COMMON MARKET to establish a single common market for Latin America by 1985. But progress towards this target has been slow.

laundering A term to describe the way in which criminal and other hot money is made respectable. For example, funds from organized crime in Canada may be sent to Switzerland or a TAX HAVEN, given anonymity, and reappear in Canada in the form of a real-estate holding company or an investment company, or be used directly to purchase a respectable business.

law of diminishing marginal utility An economic law stating that, as a consumer buys more of a good, the satisfaction derived from each extra unit is less and less, even though his total satisfaction may increase with additional consumption. For example, a steak-lover may want to eat a good many steaks in a week, but at some point each additional steak yields less and less satisfaction, although each one continues to add some satisfaction. The first steak in the week will yield a great deal of satisfaction, but the fourth, while still yielding some satisfaction, will yield less, and the fifth less still. The ability of the consumer to appreciate more steaks declines, although it does not disappear. This law can be used to justify a tax system based on the ability to pay. Since each dollar of income yields some but less and less satisfaction, taxing away from those with high incomes to help those with low incomes adds to the total utility or satisfaction in the community.

law of diminishing returns An economic law stating that, although an increase in one of the factors of production while the other factors remain fixed will cause total output to increase, at some point each extra unit of that factor of production will yield successively smaller increases in output. This is because the extra units of that factor of production have less and less of the other factors of production, which are fixed, to work with. For example, in a factory with a fixed amount of machinery and space, the addition of extra workers will at some point add less and less output, because there will be less and less space and machinery for each worker to use.

law of downward-sloping demand An economic law stating that, if the price of a good is raised while all other prices are unchanged, less of the good will be demanded. Similarly, if the supply of a good is increased, the extra supply can only be sold if the price is reduced.

law of supply and demand The basic law governing what is produced, in what quantity, and at what price in a free-market economy. If the demand for a product is greater than the supply, the price will rise; in this way, a scarce resource will be allocated to those willing to pay a higher price. At the same time, rising prices will encourage new producers to enter the market, so that supply will increase and prices will decline. Similarly, if supply rises, prices will fall, unless demand increases at the same time. If supply rises and the demand remains constant, prices will fall. Through the market mechanism, the equilibrium price is the price at which goods are willingly produced and willingly purchased. The law of supply and demand thus operates to allocate scarce resources in society, assuming that conditions of PERFECT COMPETITION exist, by determining stable prices based on the intersection of supply and demand forces.

law of the sea See UNITED NATIONS CONFERENCE ON THE LAW OF THE SEA.

Law Reform Commission of Canada A federal commission created in 1970 to study the country's laws and legal procedures, including laws affecting business, administrative law, and the legal powers of regulatory agencies, and to recommend improvements and reforms. The commission reports to Parliament through the minister of Justice.

layoff The temporary or permanent loss of a job. An employer may temporarily lay off workers if there is a strike at a supplier or because inventories of the finished product are too high; or he may permanently lay off workers if the economy is soft and the prospects for recovery are distant. In the latter case, the workers laid off may have first chance at jobs when the company begins rehiring; but that may not be for eighteen months or longer, so it is more likely that the workers will seek out jobs elsewhere.

lead time The amount of time it takes for an economic action to be completed. The term is used in several senses—to describe the amount of time, for example, that elapses before a change in economic policy, a tax cut, for instance, starts to have any effect, in this case to increase consumer spending. It can refer to the amount of time it takes to build a major project, such as a nuclear-power plant or natural-gas pipeline; in such a case it might be ten years before engineering design, regulatory hearings, financing, and construction are all completed. Or it may refer to the time that elapses between the ordering of goods or parts and the date they are actually delivered. Knowledge of lead times is important in economic and business planning.

leading indicator A statistical series that provides advance warning of changes in economic activity. Leading indicators represent decisions already made that will affect the future performance of the economy, or reflect expectations by investors and others about future economic prospects. Examples include statistics on the deflated value of building permits, indicating future construction activity; primary steel production, indicating orders by auto, construction, and other industries; the deflated value of pre-tax profits, indicating the resources available for business expansion; the deflated value of the money supply, indicating credit conditions; the Toronto Stock Exchange composite index, indicating investors' expectations of future profits and dividends; the average hours worked in manufacturing, indicating the intensity with which labour is being used and the likelihood of new hiring; and the ratio of selling prices to unit labour costs, indicating profit margins. Two Canadian banks publish their own leading-indicator indexes: the Royal Bank of Canada, with its quarterly Trendicator, and the Canadian Imperial Bank of Commerce, with its Commerce Leading Indicator. See also LAGGING INDICATOR, COINCIDENT INDICATOR.

leads and lags The speed-up or delay in the payment of trade and other international debts that may occur when there is uncertainty about a country's future exchange rate. If the Canadian dollar is expected to rise in value, then Canadian importers will delay paying (a lag) until the change takes place, since the expected rise means that they will need fewer Canadian dollars to pay the bill. But if the Canadian dollar is expected to decline in value, a Canadian importer will speed up (a lead) payment to his foreign supplier because, if he delays payment, he will need extra Canadian dollars to pay his bill. International corporations and active importers and exporters are always watching for possible exchange-rate changes, and try to time their payments and billings to earn an extra profit or to avoid an unnecessary cost if they can. Such actions can have an unsettling effect on a country's balance of payments, and may add to the need for exchange-rate adjustment.

leakage The extent to which outside influences decrease the impact of economic-policy changes on national income. For example, a tax cut to increase consumer spending and thus stimulate new business investment may not have the impact anticipated, because too much of the increased purchasing power goes to imports instead of to domestic-made goods and services; thus, demand for domestic-made goods and services is not raised sufficiently to generate the level of new business investment that had been expected. Leakage may also occur if consumers decide to pay off old debts instead of increasing their spending, or if an accelerating rate of inflation offsets the higher purchasing power from a tax cut.

lease 1. A contractual agreement between the owner of a property and someone who pays for its exclusive use for a specified period of time; the owner is the lessor and the user is the lessee. A lease may be for a house, apartment, commercial building, piece of land, automobile, aircraft, oil tanker, or other major capital good. A lease sets out the terms and conditions under which the contract is made, including the rights and responsibilities of both the lessor and lessee. **2.** A contract between an oil, natural-gas, or mining company and the federal or a provincial government; it gives the company the right to extract resources in return for a royalty payment. See also PERMIT.

leaseback A method of business financing in which a firm sells a plant, office building, or various capital assets to a financial institution or other private investor, on condition that the firm can lease the plant, building, or other asset back for a specified number of years at a negotiated rent. There are many advantages to such an arrangement. For the firm, it means that the business is assured of the facilities it needs; in the meantime, it can also obtain the proceeds from the sale to use as working capital to expand, while writing off the leaseback costs as a business expense. For the investor, the arrangement represents a reasonably safe investment with an assured rate of return.

leasehold land Land on which a person or firm may build a property but which is owned by someone else; the person or firm building the property has a long-term lease for the land.

leasing A method of business financing in which a firm determines its need for major capital goods—say, oil tankers, aircraft, or heavy machinery—and approaches a financial institution or private investors and arranges to lease the capital goods from them, instead of buying them itself. There may be a tax advantage to the financial institution or private investors, and the firm thus does not have to tie up its working capital or utilize its line of credit at the bank. Another form of leasing is that in which a business firm acquires capital goods—say, cars and trucks—and leases them to a variety of users for short periods of time.

least-developed countries See FOURTH WORLD.

ledger The book in which the accounts of a firm or other organization are initially recorded. Separate ledgers may be maintained for different activities of the firm or other organization.

legacy See BEQUEST.

legal tender Money that, under a country's laws, must be accepted in the settlement of any obligation or debt. In Canada, the Canadian dollar is the legal medium of exchange.

leisure A form of non-monetary income that is not measured in national-income and other statistics that are designed to illustrate improvements in the standard of living. Leisure is earned when workers get a shorter work week with no cut in pay and is purchased when workers refuse overtime. It is reflected in many practices—in shorter work weeks, longer vacations with pay, more public holidays, and less discretionary overtime. It is made possible by improved productivity, which raises total output in the economy at a faster rate than the growth in population.

lend-lease A U.S. program of assistance to its allies, introduced in 1941, which did not require repayment as such but which expected the equipment to be returned after the war. The United States also expected the recipients to agree to an open, multilateral trade and investment environment after the war. The program was important to Canada because, under the HYDE PARK AGREEMENT, British lend-lease assistance could be used for material and components from the United States that Canada needed for inclusion in military equipment it was supplying to Britain. This relieved the drain on Canada's low supply of U.S. dollars to pay for such material and components.

lender of last resort An important function of the Bank of Canada and other central banks; their responsibility to lend funds to the chartered banks when the chartered banks have temporary shortages of funds. This happens only rarely, and the funds are usually not needed for more than a few days, but the presence of the central bank as a lender of last resort adds an important element of strength to the banking system, and is one reason why a repeat of the Great Depression of the 1930s would be unlikely. The term is sometimes applied to government development corporations if they take on the function of assisting private firms that cannot obtain financing from any private source, such as a chartered bank or venture-capital firm.

less-developed country (LDC) A term that is applied to more than one hundred countries at varying stages of economic development, all of which have a relatively low real per capita income, a low rate of domestic savings, a large part of the population engaged in agriculture, a low level of industrialization, inadequate infrastructure, large segments of the population living near the subsistence level, a dependence on foreign capital and development assistance, and considerable disguised unemployment. LDCs range from countries with strong economic prospects whose main needs are capital, education, infrastructure, and markets, such as Mexico, Yugoslavia, and South Korea, to those with serious but surmountable difficulties, such as India, Egypt, Jamaica, and Nigeria, and those with scarce resources, a strong poverty cycle, burdensome population problems, and extremely low per capita incomes, such as Bangladesh, Ethiopia, and Afghanistan. The LDCs include most of Central and South America, all of Asia except Japan, most of Africa except for South Africa, southeast Europe, and the Caribbean Islands, and account for more than 70 per cent of the world's population. See also THIRD WORLD, FOURTH WORLD, NEW INTERNATIONAL ECONOMIC ORDER, UNITED NATIONS CONFERENCE ON TRADE AND DEVELOPMENT, CANADIAN INTERNATIONAL DEVELOPMENT AGENCY, NORTH-SOUTH DIALOGUE, DEVELOPMENT ASSISTANCE, FOREIGN AID, INTERNATIONAL BANK FOR RECONSTRUCTION AND DEVELOPMENT.

letter of credit An instruction from a bank to a CORRESPONDENT BANK in another country or a foreign or domestic branch of its own to pay the bearer a specified sum, provided that the attached conditions are met. The issuing bank guarantees repayment to the correspondent bank. Letters of credit are important in trade, especially foreign trade, since they give exporters an assurance of payment. A Canadian exporter shipping goods to, say, Mexico, will get a letter of credit through his Mexican customer, in which the customer's Mexican bank instructs its Canadian correspondent bank to pay the Canadian exporter a certain sum, the Mexican bank guaranteeing the Canadian bank repayment. If the Mexican customer defaults, this becomes a problem for his Mexican bank.

letters patent A synonym for articles of incorporation; the charter granted to a company when it is incorporated under federal or provincial law. The document sets out the company's proposed name, the purposes of the company, its AUTHORIZED CAPITAL, and the number of directors.

leverage The ability to borrow money and reinvest it to earn a higher return than the interest payments that have to be made. A firm may borrow large sums of money in the form, say, of corporate bonds, preferred shares, and medium-term bank financing, thus relying heavily on DEBT CAPITAL, as opposed to another firm that may obtain more of its financing through the issue of COMMON SHARES, thus relying heavily on EQUITY CAPITAL. If the firm relying heavily on debt capital earns a higher rate of return on this capital than it must pay in interest and preferred dividends, then the extra earnings are attributed to the common shares, thus boosting their value and, in all likelihood, their dividends. In a company relying heavily on equity capital, the profits would have to be spread among a larger number of common shares, so that earnings per share would be lower even if total profits were identical.

A company may succeed in significantly improving the position of its common shareholders by borrowing large sums of money and using them profitably. But, if the market turns and the firm earns a lower return on its borrowed capital, even if it still earns a profit, the decline can cause a significant drop in earnings per common share, and hence cause a sharp fall in the value of common shares. If the firm finds that it is no longer able to earn a profit on its borrowed capital, it may have to halt dividends to common shareholders and sell off assets. Leverage can be a risky method of raising common-share earnings, as many real-estate and other firms have found in the 1960s and

1970s—especially those that relied heavily on borrowed funds at high interest rates for expansion capital.

liabilities All the debts of a corporation, partnership, or individual; one part of the BALANCE SHEET. Liabilities include short-term or current liabilities such as accounts payable, short-term debts, income and other taxes due, and the amount of long-term debt that must be paid within twelve months; and long-term liabilities, which include long-term debts and deferred income taxes. Liabilities are the contributions by creditors to a business, and increase as a result of increases in assets through borrowing or as a result of incurring new, unpaid expenses. On a balance sheet, liabilities are subtracted from assets—what remains is the SHAREHOLDERS' EQUITY, or ownership in the business. Thus assets always equal liabilities plus shareholders' equity.

liability insurance A form of insurance that protects the holder by paying legal claims, usually up to a specified maximum, arising from injury, death, or other damage to a third party, resulting from negligence in the care of property or manufacturing of a product, or from mistakes made by an employee.

licence A certificate permitting a person, firm, or organization to do something legally. Licences are widely used by governments—to permit someone to operate a radio or television station or a cable-television system, for example, to permit someone to export uranium, to import certain agricultural products, to work in a certain occupation or profession, to hunt or fish, or to sell hot dogs from a stand on the main street of a city or town. Owners of PATENTS and COPYRIGHTS grant others a licence to use their works in return for a fee or royalty.

licensed moneylender A lender in Canada who is licensed under the federal Small Loans Act. The act, passed in 1939, limits the interest rates that may be charged on cash loans of up to fifteen hundred dollars. It does not apply to instalment financing of department stores, motor-vehicle dealers, and finance companies that finance the purchase of consumer durables; nor does it apply to credit-card financing or to the consumer loans of chartered banks.

lien The right of a creditor to attach a claim to someone else's property or to take possession of that property until a debt is paid. It means that the actual owner of the property cannot sell it to a third party until he has first paid off his creditor. But the creditor cannot sell the property without the permission of the courts after all other efforts have failed to secure payment of the debt. There are various types of liens. A bank or mortgage company, for example, may attach a claim to a property if the owner is behind in his payments. A builder-repairman may attach a mechanic's lien to a property if he has performed repair, renovation, or other such work and has not been paid. A landlord may seize the possessions of a tenant who is behind in his rent, while a hotel owner may seize the baggage of a hotel guest who has not paid his bill. And a government may attach a claim to property if taxes are unpaid.

life insurance A contract between an individual and an insurance company in which the insurance company promises to pay a sum to the family or other beneficiaries of the individual if he should die while the contract is in force; in return, the insured person agrees to pay a regular and specified premium. Sometimes the insurance is paid by a third party, who is usually the beneficiary; for example, a partnership may place an insurance policy on the life of each partner, with the surviving partners the beneficiaries. Employers may also provide life insurance for their employees, with their families as beneficiaries, as a fringe benefit. In endowment life-insurance policies, the insured person collects a cash sum if he reaches a certain age.

The most common forms of life insurance are: **1.** Term insurance, in which insurance is provided for short periods of time, ranging from a trip, in the case of air travel, to, say, five years, in the case of normal term insurance. Premiums increase with age and the insured has no claim for cash once the term is up. This form of insurance is popular with people who want considerable protection when their families are young and they have few other assets, but who expect to accumulate other assets, such as their own home, shares, and a valuable pension plan as they grow older. **2.** Whole life insurance, in which the person whose life is insured continues to pay premiums as long as he lives or until he reaches a certain age—say, sixty-five.

life table A calculation of life expectancy that shows how many people would survive out of, say, one hundred thousand persons born in a particular year, based on past death rates prevailing over a certain period of time. Successive calculations are made for all those in the same group who reach two years of age, three years, and so on, all the way through the lifespan. Thus, a life expectancy is calculated, for example, for all those born in 1941 who reach the age of forty. The life table is an important demographic tool used to calculate the future size of the population and has important specific-use applications—in the life-insurance industry, for example, in pension and labour-force planning, and in the calculation of future school and university populations. Life tables may understate the lifespans of a generation because they do not always take into account medical progress.

lifo See LAST IN, FIRST OUT.

limit-pricing The practice of a MONOPOLIST in holding down his prices so as to discourage the entry of a competitor into a particular industry or product line.

limited company A private or public company with LIMITED LIABILITY. It is designated as such by the use of the word Limited or Ltd. in its name.

limited liability The limitation of a shareholder's liability for losses incurred in his business to the money he has invested in the business; creditors cannot attach a claim to the shareholder's other possessions, such as his house and family savings. If a limited-liability company has a big debt, its creditors can demand that its assets be sold; if these do not meet the creditors' claims, the creditors are out of luck—they cannot sue the shareholders.

The legal distinction between a company and its shareholders was developed in the nineteenth century. Without limited liability, it would not be possible to organize large corporations and persuade individuals to invest in them. It is an important legal concept that makes modern corporations, large pools of savings, and dynamic economic growth possible and encourages individuals to risk their money without fear of losing all they own in the event of the failure of a company they invest in. In particular, its absence would prevent pension funds and insurance companies from investing in shares; it would expose even the small investor to the loss of all he owned, even if he bought just a few shares in a company that failed.

limits to growth A view of the world's future that sees the combination of population growth and rising standards of living creating an unsustainable pressure on the world's supply of natural resources, its ability to produce food, and the functioning of the ecological system. Unless the world reverts to ZERO POPULATION GROWTH, undertakes large-scale recycling of resources, practises conservation, and aims for zero economic growth, it faces famine, the collapse of the environmental support systems, drastic declines in standards of living, and exhaustion of energy and mineral resources within the next hundred years. This gloomy view of man's future, which resurrects some of the fears of THOMAS ROBERT MALTHUS, is based on two studies, Jay Forrester's *World Dynamics* (Cambridge, Mass., 1971), and *The Limits to Growth* (New York, 1972), a CLUB OF ROME study by Dennis Meadows and others. While many economists accept the need for population control, the careful use of resources, and measures to safeguard the environment, they reject the computer model of man's future devised by Forrester, Meadows, and others. They point out that the pricing system can ration the use of resources and encourage the development of substitutes, and note that man's history is one of adapting technology to raise productivity and overcome natural barriers to growth. There is no reason, they argue, to believe that man will be any less inventive in the future. See also RIO PROJECT.

line of credit The agreement by a bank or other lender to make credit up to a certain upper limit available to a borrower, which the borrower can draw on as his needs arise. The financial institution may require notice that a drawing on the credit is to be made. All businesses establish a line of credit with their bankers, with the amount of such lines being renegotiated from time to time. Lines of credit are negotiated in advance of the need for credit. Banks usually retain the right to revise a company's line of credit if its financial circumstances should change.

linear programming A mathematical technique used to solve certain business and economic problems, usually those in which the best course of action has to be chosen from among several alternatives. The technique may be used, for example, to help firms to choose their most profitable product mix, the best location of a plant site, or the most economic cattle-feed mix that meets a specified nutritional standard.

linkage 1. The effect that the growth of one industry has on the growth of others. The growth of the petrochemicals industry can stimulate the growth of the oil and natural-gas industries as suppliers, and the growth of the plastics, fertilizer, and synthetic-fabrics industries as users of its output. Similarly, the basic steel industry influences the growth of supplier industries such as iron ore and coking coal, and user industries such as those making finished steel products. **2.** In trade and other international negotiations, the linking of agreement on one issue with settlement of a disagreement on another issue. For example, in the late 1960s, when the United States had oil-import quotas, Canada told the U.S. that it could only get more Canadian natural gas, which the U.S. wanted, if it also agreed to buy more Canadian oil, which the U.S. was refusing to do.

liquid asset Cash, plus any assets that can be quickly converted to cash. These include CANADA SAVINGS BONDS, certificates of deposit, bank term deposits, and guaranteed-investment certificates. Other assets that are also liquid but that, depending on the market, may lead to a loss if they are sold to other investors, include government and corporate bonds and shares.

liquidation 1. The selling off of assets to improve a company's cash position. **2.** The termination of a business, a process also known as winding up a business. An intermediary—a liquidator—is usually appointed to sell the company and get the best price he can for the assets, to pay off the creditors, and to distribute the remaining cash to the eligible shareholders or owners.

liquidator The person who takes over the affairs of a company when it is being wound up to make sure that the creditors are paid off before the owners or shareholders get their proceeds.

liquidity 1. The capacity of a firm to meet its obligations or to handle unanticipated costs. There are two ways of measuring this. The first is the current-ratio test, which is the ratio of current assets to current liabilities. The second is the quick ratio or acid-test ratio, which is the ratio of current assets minus inventories to current liabilities. The second method is preferred, because inventories may not always be readily saleable. **2.** The availability of money to meet the obligations of a particular industry or the private sector generally, or of individual nations to obtain strong currencies, SPECIAL DRAWING RIGHTS, or gold, to settle their international balances of payments and thus to finance their trade and investment. **3.** The ability to convert an asset into cash without a substantial loss. A person is said to be highly liquid if he has considerable cash, or assets that can be quickly converted to cash at little cost.

liquidity preference The desire by savers to hold their money in cash or bank accounts rather than to invest it in shares, bonds, mortgages, and other such investments, which are less easy to convert back to cash. A high liquidity preference represents an unwillingness to save. People have a variety of motives for preferring to hold their money in highly liquid forms. These include the normal-transactions desire to have enough money on hand to meet everyday needs, the precautionary desire to have money readily available to meet an emergency, and the speculative desire to hang on to cash in the belief that stock-market conditions will improve or interest rates go up. Thus, the demand for money on hand is influenced by many factors, including the level of income a person has, his expectations about investment opportunities, the current level of interest rates, and cultural attitudes.

list price The published price of a product before any markdown has been made for high-volume purchases, dealer discounts, or other trade rebates.

listed share A share that meets the listing requirements of a STOCK EXCHANGE and is traded on the exchange. Each stock exchange has its own listing requirements. The required level of earnings, net working capital, and minimum net tangible assets for a company to be listed depend on the size and importance of the exchange. The TORONTO STOCK EXCHANGE has the most demanding requirements and the ALBERTA STOCK EXCHANGE the least demanding. Lower requirements are imposed for JUNIOR oil, natural-gas, and mining companies.

Companies must meet a number of requirements to maintain their listed status on a stock exchange; if they fail to meet these requirements or break stock-exchange rules, they may be suspended from trading or lose their listed status altogether. Listing requirements range from engraving company share certificates so that they cannot be forged and filing quarterly financial statements, to filing an annual report in response to a standard stock-exchange questionnaire on general corporate information, and reporting any changes in dividends and in other financial arrangements, including sale of new shares and any proposed material change in the company's business or affairs. This last requirement is important and covers such matters as the speedy reporting of takeover bids, of acquisition or sale of a major block of shares or such assets as a mining or oil property, of any change in ownership that may affect control, of any change in the directors or principal officers of the firm, and of any change in the nature of the business.

listed stock See LISTED SHARES.

livestock Agricultural production of cattle, sheep, hogs, and chickens for consumption.

loading The charges in an insurance contract, mutual-fund contract, registered retirement savings plan, and other such investments to cover administration and selling costs, including a salesman's commission. In front-end loading, all of these costs are collected from the first payments made by the purchaser; thus, he may find at the end of a year of payments that his asset value is still zero or close to zero because the insurance company, mutual-fund, or other financial institution has collected its costs for the total life of the contract first.

loan A sum of money borrowed by a government, firm, small businessman, individual, or other organization from a lender, at an agreed rate of interest and usually for a specified period of time. There are many different types of loans—for example, SECURED LOANS and UNSECURED LOANS, VENTURE-CAPITAL loans, BRIDGE FINANCING, and MARGIN loans. Loans are made by many institutions, including banks, trust companies, sales-finance companies, acceptance companies, stockbrokers, and mortgage-loan companies.

loan insurance Insurance that is available for consumers on consumer and mortgage loans. Consumers pay a premium and, in the event of their death, the lender is paid off so that there is no claim against the estate.

loan shark An unlicensed moneylender who lends money at unconscionable rates of interest and who may resort to violence and other illegal means to force repayment. There is little legal protection in Canada against loan sharks unless the loan shark resorts to violence and the borrower is willing to testify in court. The federal government is considering definition of a criminal rate of interest to help prosecute loan sharks.

loanable funds The potential supply of money available to be lent to governments, business, other organizations, and individuals. It consists of current savings, including retained earnings in business firms, dishoarding or a reduction in business cash balances, or a transfer of funds from bank chequing accounts to non-chequing accounts, investment certificates, and the like, and increases by the central bank in the money supply. These are the funds available for use by government, business, other organizations, and consumers.

lobby An organized attempt by any special-interest group to persuade government to do something or not to do something. Lobbying is not illegal in Canada and there are many types of lobbying and lobbyists. Most industry groups maintain staffs to influence government decision-making and politicians; so do unions, cultural organizations, and groups concerned with social-welfare policies. Lobbying practices range from the formal presentation of briefs to government, personal meetings with politicians and civil servants, to mail-in campaigns to politicians, and entertainment and other social activities.

local The smallest unit in a union. A union usually consists of a national or international body made up of dozens or hundreds of locals, depending on its size; sometimes, for administrative convenience, locals are organized into regional bodies. Each local elects its own officers, handles its own negotiations with employers, and administers local union matters.

local taxes Taxes levied and collected by municipalities for municipal purposes, including, in most provinces, local school boards. Municipalities may only impose DIRECT TAXES, since they are creations of the provinces, which, in turn, under the British North America Act, are limited to direct taxation to raise revenue. The main types of local taxation are PROPERTY TAXES on land and buildings; business taxes that are levied on the operators of local businesses; and water taxes, which are designed to recover all or part of the cost of providing residents with clean, drinkable water.

location theory The branch of economics that attempts to determine the factors that influence where a firm will locate a plant or other activity. The factors range from straight economic considerations, such as access to resources or closeness to markets, to less-quantifiable considerations, such as political stability and the desire of professional employees to live in or near a city that has a wide range of cultural and social activities.

The factors affecting the location of a firm differ for individual industries. It is simple enough to see that a food-processing plant will be located near the source of supply, or that a smelter will be located near a mineral ore-body because the costs of transporting a heavy ore with considerable waste would be high; but if the transportation cost is low, for oil moved by pipeline, for example, then the oil may be refined close to market, since it is easier to refine the oil into many different oil products close to market than to arrange the transportation of each product separately over a long distance. But, although aluminum or nickel may be processed in a remote area, finished aluminum and nickel products tend to be produced close to where they are consumed, or where labour costs are low and productivity is high. Closeness to markets, costs of transportation, availability of skilled labour, local labour and environmental laws, the chance of a complementary industry, tax and government incentives, the availability of cheap energy in energy-intensive industries, and the need for supporting service industries and local infrastructure, are all factors affecting the location of industry. See also REGIONAL DEVELOPMENT, Department of REGIONAL ECONOMIC EXPANSION.

lockout A labour dispute in which the employer closes his establishment so that his employees cannot work and are not paid. Like a STRIKE, a lockout can only follow certain other legal steps after a COLLECTIVE AGREEMENT has expired. While lockouts are much less frequent than strikes, they are sometimes resorted to by employers, either to force a settlement or to weaken the power of the union. In some industries, such as meatpacking, where a number of contracts in major firms expire at about the same time, some meatpackers may bring on a lockout if another firm has been struck. The purpose is to reduce the pressure on the struck packer to agree to a high settlement, which he might have to do if the other firms stayed open and picked up part of his business.

lode A mineral deposit that is found in a body of soil or rock.

logical fallacy of composition The mistaken conclusion that, because something is good for each individual, it is therefore good for the community as a whole. For example, it may be a good idea for individuals to save more and borrow less: but if everyone did this, the economy would suffer from a fall in consumer demand; workers would be laid off, and people would end up having less to save or having to dip into their savings to get by.

London inter-bank offer rate (LIBOR) The reference point for many international syndicated loans, especially those made in EUROCURRENCY markets. The rate is not set by the central bank but is determined by the leading banks in much the same way that they set rates for CERTIFICATE-OF-DEPOSIT rates in individual countries. International loans are often made at a specified number of BASIS POINTS above LIBOR, depending on the risk.

London Metal Exchange (LME) The world's principal spot and futures market for metals such as copper, lead, zinc, nickel, tin, and silver. Although much of the output of the world's metal mines is sold through negotiated contracts between producers and consumers, the LME plays an important role in the pricing of metals. The exchange dates back to 1881.

long-range planning Planning for a decade ahead or longer. Long-range planning by governments or business attempts to take account of major changes taking place in technology, the supply and demand for natural resources and fuels, changing social and political attitudes, demographic changes, and the evolution of new international relationships. It is strategic planning.

long-selling The selling of shares that the seller already owns, as opposed to SELLING SHORT.

long term A period of time that is long enough so that all the factors of production in a firm or the economy can be varied, to achieve a more efficient level of output. This means long enough to retool industrial plants, to install new methods of production, to train workers in new skills, to adapt new technologies, and to build new production facilities. In the long run, such fundamental changes can be made; but in the short run, a firm or economy has to work with its existing facilities and methods and can only increase output by making better use of its existing factors of production, or by adding inputs, such as more labour.

long-term asset Sometimes called a fixed asset. Long-term assets may consist of buildings, plant and equipment, land, and other assets of a relatively permanent nature or assets that at least have a long life. Long-term assets are listed on the BALANCE SHEET below CURRENT ASSETS.

long-term debt A bond, debenture, or other form of debt maturing after ten years.

long-term forecast An economic forecast that looks five years or longer ahead.

long-term liability A debt that does not have to be repaid within the next twelve months. As a long-term debt, or a portion of it, approaches the repayment date, it will cease to be a long-term liability and will become a short-term liability instead. Long-term liabilities are listed on the BALANCE SHEET after short-term or current liabilities.

loophole An unexpected interpretation of a law or contract, usually a tax law, resulting from it being badly or vaguely worded, that allows someone to do something that was not intended—to evade taxes, for example, or to get out of an onerous requirement in a contract.

Lorenz curve A curve that can be used to show the degree of inequality of distribution of wealth, income, or some other variable in a country.

loss In a corporation's financial year, the failure to earn sufficient revenues to cover costs. In an investment, the sale of an asset for less than the sum paid for it.

loss leader A product sold by a retailer at a loss to attract customers into his store. The expectation is that, once the consumer is in the store, he or she will decide to buy a better-quality product or to buy other products in addition to the loss-leader item.

lottery A game of chance designed to raise money. Participants buy tickets that have a series of numbers printed on them; a sequence of numbers is selected, and the winners, the people holding tickets containing those numbers, get the prizes. Lotteries are operated in Canada by the federal and provincial governments and by charitable organizations. An amendment to the Criminal Code in 1969 legalized lotteries in Canada by making it no longer an offence to organize and operate a lottery. In 1970, Loto-Quebec was set up as the first government-operated lottery. In 1973, Parliament created the Olympic Lottery to help finance the 1976 Olympic Games in Montreal; the lottery, in nine draws between April 1974 and August 1976, raised $230 million for the Olympics and $25 million for the provinces, while awarding $190 million in prizes. In 1975–76, Ontario and the western provinces launched their lottery schemes. Also in 1976, the federal government created Loto-Canada, a crown corporation, to operate a national lottery to reduce the debt of the 1976 Olympics; funds have also been used to help finance the 1978 Commonwealth Games in Edmonton, the 1979 Canada Games, and amateur sport and fitness programs across Canada. In 1979, the federal government announced its intention to get out of the lottery business and leave it to the provinces; Loto-Canada would be wound up.

Luddite A term used today to describe those opposed to technological change. It was originally applied to British workers who, in the early nineteenth century, destroyed labour-saving machinery, which they said was contributing to unemployment. The term is said to come from a Ned Lud who, late in the eighteenth century, was reputed to have destroyed machinery in anger over the loss of jobs it caused.

lump-of-labour fallacy The belief that there is only so much useful work to be done in society; as a consequence, the supporters of this belief resist the introduction of technological change, seek shorter working hours, and justify various work rules that lead to featherbedding. It is a static view of economics and ignores the possibilities for new consumer wants and new industries, as well as the role of government in stimulating economic growth and creating more jobs.

lump-sum payment An unusual or one-time payment: for example, the payout from a registered retirement savings plan, the receipt by an author of a large payment for the film rights to a book, the payment to a beneficiary of an insurance policy, or the receipt by an individual of all his past payments into a pension plan when he changes jobs. Income-tax authorities allow taxpayers to lessen the tax load on such payments, which otherwise would be treated as ordinary income in the year received and thus be subject to the top marginal tax rate. Registered retirement savings plans and lump-sum income to authors can be converted into annuities, for example, and taxed as the annuity pays out an annual sum to the recipient. See also INCOME AVERAGING.

luxury tax A tax on articles not considered essential to everyday life. Canada, for example, imposes at the federal level an excise tax on alcohol, cigarettes, perfume, jewellery, and other luxury items.

M

M-1, M-2, M-3 See MONEY SUPPLY.

Machinery and Equipment Advisory Board A federal board created in 1968 to consider applications for duty remission on imported machinery and equipment. The board, consisting of a chairman and the deputy ministers of Industry, Trade and Commerce, Finance, and National Revenue, may grant the remission of duty on imported machinery and equipment if it is not available from a Canadian source and if it is in the public interest to do so. Under Canada's import policy on machinery and equipment, tariffs are remitted on imports to reduce the cost of business expansion, unless there is a Canadian producer of the machinery. The board is also in a position to identify types of machinery for which demand is high enough to justify production in Canada.

MacPherson Commission on Transportation See ROYAL COMMISSION ON TRANSPORTATION.

macroeconomics The study of the economy as a whole, as opposed to MICROECONOMICS, which concerns itself with the study of sectors of the economy. Macroeconomics concerns itself with the big picture, the overall level of consumption, investment, and government spending in the economy. It looks at the aggregate of demand, the workings of monetary and fiscal policy, the banking system, prices, savings, trade, and the balance of payments. It is concerned with the gross national product, total employment, economic growth, and inflation. Macroeconomists deal with policies to achieve full employment and stable prices.

maintenance of membership A clause in a collective agreement that requires all union members to remain in good standing in their union for the life of the contract if they wish to keep their jobs. A union member who breaks union rules and thus is no longer a member in good standing would have to be fired by his employer.

make-work project A method of increasing jobs without necessarily accomplishing anything of great usefulness. For example, a union may insist on certain job practices to inflate the number of employees, and hence membership, artificially. See also FEATHERBEDDING. In times of unemployment, the government may pay unemployed workers to carry out miscellaneous jobs, such as cleaning out culverts alongside highways, washing windows in senior citizens' homes, or other such tasks, simply to get purchasing power into the economy and to help speed up economic recovery.

Malthus, Thomas Robert A British clergyman and professor of political economy (1766-1834), best remembered for the pessimistic warning about population growth contained in *An Essay on the Principle of Population*. The essay was first published anonymously in 1798 and was revised six times, with the final edition published in 1826.

Population, Malthus said, could not exceed food supply. But there was a tendency for population to grow at a geometric rate (1, 2, 4, 8, 16, 32), while food production could only be increased at an arithmetic rate (1, 2, 3, 4, 5, 6, 7). Thus, an expanding population would put enormous and increasing pressures on the prevailing standard of living. Efforts to increase the productivity of the land, Malthus argued, would be thwarted by the LAW OF DIMINISHING RETURNS. At the same time, the costs of producing extra food would rise, so that real wage rates would decline and the growth of population would reduce mankind to the margin of subsistence. Malthus refrained from advocating population controls, but campaigned for late marriages and sexual abstinence.

It was the gloomy view of Malthus, that man was doomed to a subsistence existence and periodic bouts of famine to hold population in check, that led Thomas Carlyle to call economics the "dismal science." What Malthus failed to foresee were the great gains in agricultural productivity achieved in the nineteenth and twentieth centuries. Nor did he anticipate the decline in FERTILITY RATES. None the less, the Malthusian view of population pressures on food supplies may have some relevance to some LESS-DEVELOPED COUNTRIES. See also NEO-MALTHUSIANISM.

man-hour The amount of work done by one employee in an hour. It is a unit used to measure productivity and to calculate labour and other costs.

man-year See PERSON-YEAR.

managed float A floating-exchange-rate system in which the central bank intervenes in foreign-exchange markets to moderate sharp fluctuations in the nation's exchange rate or to push the exchange rate, over time, either up or down. While some intervention is accepted by the major nations to moderate unusual fluctuations, interventions to push a currency up or down deliberately are regarded as improper. The former is considered a clean float, the latter a dirty float.

management **1.** The people in a firm or other organization who have authority and make decisions, as opposed to labour, which carries out the decisions so that the tasks set by management are fulfilled. **2.** The running of a firm or other organization, including the setting of objectives, the planning of new products and services, the co-ordination of all the different activities of the organization, the setting of policies for employees, customer relations, sales, and other practices, and the utilization of the various factors of production to achieve the most efficient level of output or provision of services. In a typical organization, there is senior management, which sets policies and objectives, middle management, which takes charge of various functions such as sales or accounting, and on-the-floor or supervisory management, at the level of foreman or office manager.

management by exception A form of management control in which higher-level management intervenes only when actual performance deviates significantly from planned performance. It means that management has only to concern itself with details of an operation when something is going wrong.

management by objectives A form of management control in which employees are motivated, and their performance assessed, through personal job goals that are defined by the employee and his supervisor or senior executive together. Firms can also set corporate objectives that are agreed to by the board of directors and become the performance targets for senior executives.

management consultant A person or firm that specializes in helping business and other organizations to improve their managerial efficiency or to solve particular management problems, such as poor inventory control or sour employee relations. A management consultant may be called in to help reorganize a company, to introduce a computer system, to help find new top executives, to train senior employees in management skills, or to reorganize lines of command.

management fee A fee charged by an INVESTMENT COMPANY to a mutual fund or pension plan for advice on investments or management of the investment portfolio.

management-information system The use of accounting and other systems, usually with the assistance of computers to store and manipulate information, to keep management fully informed of the operations of the firm or other organization. Management can be supplied with detailed information, ranging from up-to-date data on sales, inventories, orders, and cash flow, to such detailed information as the number of employees scheduled to retire in the next two years, the location of all trucks in the firm at any particular time, or unusual increases in spending. More sophisticated systems allow a firm to calculate the impact of various corporate decisions, such as price changes or the shut-down of declining product lines, on overall profitability.

management science The application of modern mathematical and computer techniques to management. For example, the use of OPERATIONS RESEARCH, GAME THEORY, or

LINEAR PROGRAMMING to make investment or pricing decisions.

management services The charge made by a parent company to its foreign subsidiaries, to cover head-office costs in administering the subsidiary or to recover costs for the use of head-office know-how by the subsidiary. Up to a point, such charges are legitimate, but they can be abused to get profits out of a Canadian subsidiary without paying corporate income tax or withholding tax. When subsidiaries are overcharged, there is abuse, and Canada is deprived of taxes it should get. The Department of NATIONAL REVENUE has strict rules on charges that can be deducted as management services.

manifest An itemized inventory of the cargo of a ship, plane, freight car, long-distance truck, or the contents of a warehouse.

manpower planning Planning that assesses the future supply and demand for labour, including types of skills needed, regional growth in supply and demand, and the role of immigrant labour. Such planning should also include policies to ensure that the necessary skills-training is being carried out in advance, so that inflation-producing bottlenecks do not occur in labour markets, as well as job-creation programs to help maintain employment during periods of economic decline.

manpower policy Any policy that deals with labour supply. Manpower policies include programs to facilitate the mobility of labour to jobs, placement services for the unemployed, job training and retraining, policies to help workers adapt to technological change, and improved methods of letting workers know where job vacancies exist.

manufacturers' new orders, shipments, and inventories An important monthly indicator published by Statistics Canada that helps to identify economic trends. It shows, by province and for twenty industries, the dollar value of shipments, new orders, and inventories held by manufacturers. A coming recession could be signalled by a decline in the growth of new orders and a build-up in inventories. Conversely, an upsurge in new orders and a decline in manufacturers' inventories could be a sign of economic recovery.

manufacturing industry An industry that takes raw materials, semi-finished products, or finished parts and components, and uses them to produce final goods or goods used in the production of final goods.

margin The amount an investor pays towards the total cost of shares when the shares are bought on credit; in such accounts with stockbrokers, called margin accounts, the balance is a loan from the broker. Such loans must be backed by collateral. Stock exchanges strictly regulate the margin—the difference between the market value of the shares and the loan the broker will make against it—and the total amount of credit extended to investors. Investors are required to put up at least 80 per cent of the cost of shares selling from $1.50 to $1.74; this is reduced to 50 per cent for shares selling for $2 or more. Margin buying is not permitted on shares selling for less than $1.50. If the price of a share purchased on margin falls, then the investor has to supply additional funds to the broker since the broker has to reduce the credit available; alternatively, the investor can sell his shares and take a loss.

One reason for the Great Crash in 1929 was that investors were able to buy shares on margin with very little downpayment. This encouraged speculation. But when margin loans were called, investors panicked and dumped their shares in a futile attempt to cut their losses. One of the lessons of that crash was the need for strict margin rules and significant up-front money from investors.

marginal borrower A borrower who, in effect, will decide not to borrow if the rate of interest is raised any further; either the higher rate will exceed the return he can expect from the use of the borrowed money, or he will be unable to afford the loan if the rate is raised. As interest rates rise, businessmen will be deterred from expanding their facilities, and would-be home buyers may postpone a decision to buy a house. Conversely, as interest rates fall, business will find a greater incentive to invest and families to buy houses.

marginal buyer A consumer who decides not to make a purchase if the price of the product or service rises any higher. Thus, a corporation has to assess the impact of price increases on the volume of sales it can expect to make as a result.

marginal cost An important concept in determining the price of goods, the quantity produced, and hence the allocation of resources in society. At a given level of output, the marginal cost is the extra cost incurred by a firm in producing an additional unit of output. Marginal cost tends to decline at first, due to ECONOMIES OF SCALE, to level out, and then to rise again, due to the LAW OF DIMINISHING RETURNS. The optimal level of production will be the optimal profit level, which is reached when the marginal cost is equal to the selling price. All production in excess of that level will be made at a loss; all production up to that level is made at a profit. If a firm wants to expand production and profits, it has to reduce its marginal cost through improved managerial know-how, a more highly skilled labour force, or technological change.

marginal land Land whose productivity is such that its output will only just recover the cost of production. Whether land is marginal or not depends on prevailing prices for the commodities produced. If prices rise, the amount of land considered marginal declines, whereas if prices fall, the amount of land considered marginal goes up.

marginal mine A mine whose quality of ore or accessibility of ore is such that its output just recovers the cost of production. Whether or not a mine is marginal depends on existing prices. If the price of, say, copper or nickel rises, then mines that were marginal and hence not worth operating become profitable and hence worth operating. Similarly, if mineral prices decline, then the mine will have to be closed down if a loss is to be avoided. The rise or fall in mineral prices also determines, in an economic sense, the level of available mineral reserves.

marginal producer A producer who is just able to recover his production costs at the existing price for his product—for example, a farmer who just recovers his production cost at the prevailing price of, say, corn or milk. See also MARGINAL MINE.

marginal product The increase in output that results from the addition of one unit of input—an extra worker, an extra machine, an extra acre of land, for example—while the other factors of production are held constant. The marginal product of labour is the extra output achieved by a worker in a factory when all the other factors, such as machinery, are held constant. The marginal product of land is the extra output of a farm, achieved when the number of acres farmed is increased but the number of workers and amount of farm machinery remains unchanged. The concept of marginal product helps to determine the distribution of income in a society; the different factors of production are arranged to achieve maximum profit. Since wages are the marginal product of labour, interest or profits the marginal product of capital, and rent the marginal product of land, the way in which society arranges the use of these factors will determine the way in which national income is distributed.

marginal-productivity theory of wages The theory that wages are determined by the value of the extra product that an additional worker can produce. If, in a factory employing one hundred men, the number is reduced to ninety-nine, the reduction in the value of output is equal to the marginal product of that man, and is the basis for determining the wages of all the workers. The number of workers increases to the point where marginal productivity reduces the wage level to the point where it is no longer attractive to work. If the wage level is negotiated, the number of workers will be increased until the wage level is equal to the marginal product. Once the marginal product becomes less than the wage rate, it no longer pays an employer to hire additional workers. According to this theory, wages can only be increased if the marginal productivity of the workers is increased or, up to a point, if the number of workers is reduced. It establishes the relationship between wage increases and productivity increases. An increase in marginal productivity not only results from workers working harder or getting additional skills; it can also result from technological change, larger markets, and hence, economies of scale or improved managerial know-how.

marginal propensity to consume The amount of extra consumption that will result from an increase in income. When a person gets an increase—say, a pay raise or a tax cut—he is likely to spend some of the money and save some. The behaviour will differ from individual to individual, depending on existing disposable income and consumer tastes. The ratio is determined by dividing the increase in spending by the increase in income. Suppose someone gets a raise of $400 and spends $300 of it; the marginal propensity to consume equals 300 divided by 400, or .75. It is an important consideration in determining whether an across-the-board tax cut will stimulate new consumer spending, or whether it is better to concentrate the tax cut among lower-income earners with a higher marginal propensity to consume.

marginal propensity to save The amount of extra saving that will result from an increase in income. When a person gets an increase in income—say, a pay raise or tax cut—he is likely to save some of the money and spend some of it. The behaviour will differ from individual to individual, depending on existing disposable income and consumer tastes. The ratio is determined by dividing the increase in saving by the increase in income. Suppose someone gets a raise of $400 and saves $100 of it; the marginal propensity to save equals 100 divided by 400, or .25. If the government wants to encourage consumer spending through a tax cut and the marginal propensity to save is high among those with high incomes and low among those with lower incomes, the government will likely give the greatest tax-cut benefit to those with lower incomes, since it knows that the money is more likely to be spent and spent quickly.

marginal revenue The extra revenue that a seller gets from the sale of an extra unit of output. To realize its maximum profit, a firm will keep producing until its marginal revenue is equal to its MARGINAL COST. After that, it will lose money on additional products sold. A producer tries to reach the point where the extra revenue from the last unit sold equals the extra cost of making it.

marginal tax rate In the income-tax system, the rate of tax levied on each additional unit of taxable income. In a progressive income-tax system, the marginal tax rate rises with each unit, say each thousand dollars, of taxable income. Thus, the marginal tax rate on taxable income in excess of, say, $30,000, and up to $30,999, may be 42 per cent, on taxable income from $31,000 to $31,999 may be 43 per cent, and so forth, up to the top marginal rate—for example, 62 per cent on all taxable income in excess of $60,000.

marginal utility The extra satisfaction that a consumer derives from an extra unit of a particular good or service. As consumption increases, the utility or satisfaction yielded by each extra unit declines, although the total utility continues to increase. The price a consumer is said to be willing to pay is the price he is willing to pay for the last unit consumed. Thus, to increase sales, the price of the good will have to be lowered. In economic theory, the intersection of marginal utility with MARGINAL COST determines the kind and volume of goods society should produce and at what price. See also LAW OF DIMINISHING MARGINAL UTILITY, PARADOX OF VALUE.

Maritime Energy Corporation (MEC) A federal-provincial corporation established by the governments of Nova Scotia, New Brunswick, Prince Edward Island, and Canada to ensure adequate electrical supplies in the Maritime provinces. A feasibility study was completed in 1977 and the corporation was incorporated in 1979, with the provincial power utilities holding 52 per cent of the shares and the federal Department of ENERGY, MINES AND RESOURCES holding 48 per cent. Its purposes are: to plan a bulk-transmission system supplying the three provinces; to finance and build electrical generating stations; to oversee the operation of the entire Maritime provinces' system of power generation and transmission; to carry out energy research and development and energy-conservation measures; to take over any future major work on the Fundy tidal-power project; and to take over the Point Lepreau nuclear-power station in New Brunswick.

Maritime provinces The provinces of New Brunswick, Nova Scotia, and Prince Edward Island. See also ATLANTIC PROVINCES.

Maritime Union Study A study sponsored by the three Maritime provinces of New Brunswick, Nova Scotia, and Prince Edward Island, and carried out under the supervision of John Deutsch, principal of Queen's University, to investigate the opportunities for economic and other forms of regional co-ordination and co-operation. Begun in March 1968, the study was completed and published in October 1970. It recommended creation of the COUNCIL OF MARITIME PREMIERS, a Maritime Provinces Commission to carry out regional economic planning, and a joint legislative assembly. The assembly would meet once a year and carry out regional economic planning and regional negotiation with the federal government, establish common administrative services and uniform legislation, and co-ordinate existing provincial policies. The assembly would also prepare a constitution for a single Maritimes government and implement the various steps necessary to achieve political union. The assembly would review its activities at the end of five years and, if the prospects for union were not encouraging, review the entire program. Political union was rejected by the Maritime premiers, but the Council of Maritime Premiers was established.

mark-up The difference between what it costs to make or buy a product and the price charged when it is sold to someone else. Many corporations and stores price their products by marking up the product by a fixed percentage, so that whenever costs rise, these are passed along to the consumer. The mark-up, normally a percentage of the cost, covers the seller's costs of production, selling costs, and profit.

market **1.** The place where buyers and sellers meet to exchange goods for money or for other goods, at a price that is arrived at through an implied auction in which buyers and sellers negotiate price. A market need not be in one place; it can be world-wide. But in economics, the concept of a single market is often used to explain the workings of PERFECT COMPETITION, the way the law of SUPPLY AND DEMAND determines prices, and the allocation of resources. For examples of real-life markets, see STOCK EXCHANGE, COMMODITY MARKETS, AUCTION. **2.** The demand, actual or potential, for a product or service.

market economy An economy in which the setting of prices and allocating of resources are determined largely by the forces of supply and demand. The greater part of economic activity results from the actions of private corporations and individuals, while the role of government is held to a minimum. The market economy has been largely replaced by the MIXED ECONOMY, which combines the use of the market system in some sectors and government intervention in others, with government setting the overall rules and regulations under which businesses and individuals operate.

market forces The forces of supply and demand, which, in a market economy, determine prices, output, and method of production. Market forces play a significant role in some industries, such as cattle, copper, and fast-food restaurants, but only a limited role in industries with administered or regulated prices.

market penetration See MARKET SATURATION, MARKET SHARE.

market research Research, including consumer surveys, to determine consumer attitudes to existing products and those of competitors, or to a possible new product. Such research examines consumer buying habits, use of leisure time, consumer needs or wants, criticisms of existing products, perceptions of competitors' products, and other such information. Market research is used by management to determine MARKETING strategies, including product changes, new packaging, changes in product design, or revisions in advertising and promotion. It is also used to help decide whether a new product should be launched, and may include test marketing in a small number of communities, to see what the consumer reaction is likely to be.

market saturation The extent to which a potential market for a particular product has been filled. If, for example, 95 per cent of households have a colour television set, then there is much less growth available in the market, without a technological or design breakthrough, than if only 25 per cent of households had a colour television set. As market saturation increases, a business is forced to rely more heavily on replacement sales or on product changes that enlarge the market—in this case, the development of a smaller and cheaper colour television that could be sold as a second set.

market share The percentage of a company's sales for a particular product as a percentage of total industry sales for that product. A basic aim of a corporation's strategy is either to retain its market share or to expand its market share. It is used as an indicator of COMPETITION or CONCENTRATION in an industry; where no firm has more than, say, 5 per cent of the market, there is considerable competition, but where one or two firms control, say, 80 per cent of the market, there is little competition.

market structure The basic characteristics of a market, indicating the degree of competition among sellers and their ability to administer prices, or the degree of concentration among buyers and their ability to control prices. Among the factors affecting the power of sellers are the size of market share held by the largest firms, the BARRIERS TO ENTRY for new firms, and the degree of product differentiation. But not all the market power is on the side of the sellers. If there is a small number of large buyers—say, department-store chains —and a large number of sellers—say, clothing manufacturers—and significant barriers to entry for new department-store chains, then the buyers will have a big say in determining prices.

market value The going price. See also FAIR MARKET VALUE.

market-value assessment A method of assessing land and buildings for property-tax purposes. The tax or MILL RATE is levied on the periodically redetermined fair market value of the property. The advantage is that all assessment is based on the same standard, as opposed to methods of assessment based on historic value or special use, where the same-sized properties just a few blocks apart may end up paying much different property taxes because of different assessment formulae. The system is used in New Brunswick, Nova Scotia, and British Columbia.

marketable A security that can easily be traded because a ready group of buyers exists and because there are no legal or other impediments to the sale.

marketing The planning and implementation of a strategy for the sale, distribution, and servicing of a product or service. Marketing starts with MARKET RESEARCH, in which consumer needs and attitudes and competitors' products are assessed, and continues through into ADVERTISING, promotion, distribution, and, where applicable, customer servicing and repair, packaging, and sales and distribution. In the case of consumer durables, marketing often includes servicing, repair, and WARRANTY policies. Marketing is an important responsibility of corporate management, especially in consumer-goods industries. Marketing plans form an important part of corporate strategy for new products and business expansion.

marketing board A board of producers operating under legal authority that is empowered to control production, pricing, and the distribution of a commodity. See also FARM MARKETING BOARD.

Marshall, Alfred A leading British economist (1842–1924) and architect of the NEO-CLASSICAL school. Marshall also helped to develop MICROECONOMICS as an important form of economic analysis. He argued that the entire economic system was too complicated to be studied as one huge activity, and urged that it be examined "a bit at a time"; from these separate studies, a picture of the total economic system would emerge.

Marshall developed a new approach to price determination, as well as the concept of equilibrium price. He argued that demand was related to the additional satisfaction or utility that each unit of a good purchased would yield, and recognized that there would be declining utility with each additional unit purchased—diminishing marginal utility. Hence, at some point, a consumer will decide that he would sooner hold on to his money rather than purchase additional units. But, if the price is reduced, then demand should increase again—the so-called elasticity of demand. From this model, Marshall was able to construct a demand curve. Similarly, a supply curve could be constructed, showing the quantity of units that suppliers would be willing to produce at different price levels. The intersection point of the two curves—what Marshall called the bite of the scissors—represented the equilibrium price, at which consumers would willingly buy and suppliers willingly produce. If the price was higher, there would be overproduction; if it was under, there would be shortages.

Marshall believed that competition was effective in allocating resources in society, and, while he saw the danger that firms in areas of new technology would become large entities with great market power to achieve economies of scale, he was skeptical about the dangers of OLIGOPOLY or MONOPOLY. He believed that a number of restraints existed on bigness, not the least of them being the natural lifespan that he believed a corporation traced, from birth and expansion to decline and death. Marshall was also confident that full employment was the natural state of the economy; market forces, left to adjust for market fluctuations, would always return the economy to full employment.

Marshall introduced a number of other ideas into economics, in addition to his concepts of equilibrium, prices, and the relationship between demand and value or satisfaction. For example, he introduced the idea of short-run and long-run considerations, so that the time element became important in considering changes in supply and demand and the effect on prices. Marshall also rejected the idea held by CLASSICAL and MARXIST economists that labour was the only source of value in production and that all income in excess of payments to labour represented profits. He included in the income of labour, salaries paid to management and wages imputed to management in owner-operated business. He also argued that much of what was called profit was really interest that was due to owners of capital in return for abstaining from consumption. Profits in excess of management income, and interest paid to the owners of capital and reinvested in the business, were a temporary phenomenon or the sign of a monopoly, he said.

Marshall spent most of his academic life at Cambridge University; his major contributions to the study of economics are contained in his most important book, published in 1890, *Principles of Economics*.

Marshall Plan See EUROPEAN RECOVERY PROGRAM.

Marx, Karl A German-born economist, sociologist, historian, and revolutionary. Marx is one of the most important thinkers in modern political and economic history. He was born in Germany in 1818 and spent much of his early life in radical activities in Germany and France. In 1849, he moved to Britain with the help of his friend Friedrich Engels, and settled in London, where he lived until his death in 1883.

Marx's grim views on industrial society and the crisis of capitalism were elaborated in a period when many workers were confined to slums and paid subsistence wages, while capitalists lived lives of ostentatious luxury, exploited workers, including children, and used the limited powers of the state to protect their own privilege. Economic instability was chronic; workers had no protection, and were doomed to miserable and often short lives. For Marx, this type of society could not survive. But he rejected the possibility of reform, and said that, by the scientific laws of history, capitalist society would collapse, to be replaced by a new and better society. He and Engels published the *Communist Manifesto* in 1848. In 1859, Marx published the first part of his *Contribution to the Critique of Political Economy,* and in 1867 the first volume of his monumental work, *Das Kapital*. It and the two subsequent volumes published posthumously, in 1885 and 1894, provided the foundation for MARXIST ECONOMICS and COMMUNISM.

Marxist economics The school of economics originating with Karl Marx (1818–83) and developed by his followers. Marxism asserts the inevitability of an historical evolution of society from capitalism to socialism and then to communism, but most of its analysis is concerned with the collapse of capitalism rather than the workings of post-capitalist societies. The basis for Marxist thought was set out in Marx's monumental work in three volumes, *Das Kapital*. In it, Marx claimed to have discovered the laws governing the unfolding of history and their inevitability, asserting that no degree of reforming zeal could prevent the collapse of capitalism, although it could delay it. Marx also made the important sociological connection between the nature of the economic system and the social behaviour, attitudes, and roles of people in it. The economic system, he said, determined the way that people thought and the types of social relationships they had with one another.

Marx argued that capitalism was inherently unstable and doomed because it was based on conflicts and tensions that were fixed in the capitalist system, and that could only be eliminated by destruction of the system. These conflicts were rooted in the fact that the means of production were privately owned, thus making workers dependent on capitalists for their jobs and creating two distinct classes in society, capitalists and workers. Marx argued that all value came from labour and that capital in the form of machinery merely represented stored-up labour. But, by their control over the means of production, capitalists were able to exploit workers. According to Marx, workers might need to work only six hours a day to acquire the necessities of life; capitalists were able to force them to work twelve hours a day, the product or surplus from the other six hours of work going to the capitalist. This surplus value of labour led to the accumulation of additional capital (machinery) by the capitalists, reducing the need for labour per unit of output and making workers even more dependent on the capitalists. At the same time, growing mechanization reduced the need for skills and allowed employers to use the lower-priced labour of women and children.

But, Marx argued, capitalists were simultaneously caught in their own competitive struggle with one another, with their declining rate of profit (resulting from intense competition) forcing them to mechanize faster and faster, with big firms increasing in size and small and medium firms being driven out of business. Thus, the drive of capitalists to accumulate would lead to the demise of competition and the growth of monopoly power, which in turn would widen even further the inequalities of income in society. Moreover, the drive for mechanization would increase the "reserve army of the unemployed," so that capitalists could depress wages by threatening to replace workers who were dissatisfied with others who were unemployed.

As capitalism moved towards its inevitable crisis, the misery of the growing number of unemployed and the chronic instability of the system would worsen. Finally, a cataclysmic depression would result in revolution, with the workers overturning the huge combine of capitalist power in a violent upheaval. Thus, according to Marx, "the expropriators [of surplus labour value] are expropriated," paving the way for socialism, from there to communism, which emancipates mankind, eliminates the class struggle and division resulting from the private ownership of the means of production, ends exploitation, and produces a new society based on the withering away of the state and on the ethic, from each according to his abilities, to each according to his needs.

Subsequent Marxist thinkers have attributed the failure of the capitalist system to collapse to the growth of great colonial empires, which delayed the fall in the rate of profit and slowed down the growth of mass unemployment at home. Capitalist prosperity, according to Marxists, has thus come to depend on exploiting third-world countries for their natural resources and their markets. At the same time, Marxists believe that imperialism has only delayed capitalism's collapse, while internationalizing the class struggle and inevitable revolution, and sowing the seeds of conflict among the great imperial powers as they struggle for markets.

Other economists question not only Marx's

assumptions about the inevitable laws of historical change based on economic determinism, but also his analysis of capitalism and the inevitability of a falling rate of profit, declining real wages for workers, mass unemployment, and a falling wage share of the GROSS NATIONAL PRODUCT. KEYNESIAN ECONOMICS, which uses fiscal policy to maintain domestic demand, along with new techniques and rising productivity, which support new industries and new investment opportunities, has led to the MIXED ECONOMY, with rising real per capita incomes, that Marx did not foresee.

mass market The market for a widely used consumer product that is sold to many different income and age groups. Typical mass-market products include soaps, cosmetics and detergents, food products, cigarettes, alcohol, automobiles, and cameras. They are promoted heavily through advertising during prime-time television viewing, through mass-circulation newspapers, and other media reaching large audiences. Mass-market products tend to have high advertising and promotion budgets.

mass production The production of large quantities of identical goods using standardized parts and modern machinery, while limiting the role of labour to the performance of the simplest tasks in an assembly line, where work has been broken down into the greatest possible division of labour. By using modern machinery and computerized production controls, along with standardized parts, and by limiting workers to routine, repetitive tasks, management is able to achieve great savings in production costs and to benefit from ECONOMIES OF SCALE.

master of business administration (MBA) A graduate degree earned for passing a university program designed to train managers or executives. Business-management skills taught include finance, marketing, personnel management, corporate planning, business ethics, computer science, accounting, business-government relations, corporate law, mergers and takeovers, management of research and development, and the role of business in modern society.

Materials Co-ordination Committee A Canada-U.S. committee established in the spring of 1941, more than six months before the United States entered the Second World War, to co-ordinate efforts to meet the raw-material needs of industry for military purposes. The committee was a step towards integrating the raw-materials industries of both countries and allocating raw materials to industry on either side of the border, according to military priorities. Expansion in production of a particular raw material was to be made in the country in which the increase could be achieved most rapidly. The close working relationship between the governments and natural-resource industries during the Second World War continued after the war was over, although the committee did not. In the period prior to and during the Korean War, Canada became an increasingly important supplier of raw materials to the United States, with much of the expansion in raw-materials-production capacity financed through direct investment by U.S. corporations.

mature economy A stage of economic development in which the rate of population growth begins to decline, leading to a decline in the proportion of gross national product going to new capital investment and an increase going to consumer goods. There is no evidence that modern industrial economies necessarily reach a mature stage where they stop growing.

maturity The date when a bond, preferred share, or other security or debt becomes due and the principal must be repaid.

mean average The mathematical or simple average that is obtained by adding together a series of numbers and dividing the resulting figure by the number of numbers that have been added together. For example, if the rate of economic growth in the Canadian economy was 3.6 per cent in 1974, 1.2 in 1975, 5.4 in 1976, 2.4 in 1977, and 3.4 in 1978, the mean average, or simply the average, from 1974 to 1978, was 3.2 per cent a year.

means test A test to determine whether a person qualifies for a welfare grant or other social benefit. It usually consists of an effort to determine the income and wealth of the applicant, along with other information, such as number of dependents, personal health, employability, and other such considerations. Means tests were for a long time considered demeaning but, with the rising cost of universal social-welfare programs, which are said to give too much money to those who don't need help and too little to those who do, there is a move back to wider use of the means test. Now, the emphasis is on using a person's income-tax form to determine need. See also NEGATIVE INCOME TAX.

mechanic's lien See LIEN.

mechanization The use of machinery to replace human labour in agriculture and industry. While the term is still used to describe the changes taking place in less-developed countries, in the major industrial countries the word AUTOMATION is more frequently used; it includes the use by industry of computerized control systems with self-adjusting feedback.

median An average calculated by taking the middle number in a range of values. For example, in determining median income, the numbers are arranged by size and the middle number picked as the median number, assuming that there is an odd set of numbers. If there is an even set of numbers, then the two central numbers (the second and third if there are four numbers, or the 13th and 14th if there are 26) are added together and divided by two. Suppose there are 400 families and that 110 have an annual income of $10,000; 100 get $12,500; 100 get $13,750; 50 get $15,000; and 40 get $15,500. The median income is $13,750. Suppose, instead, that there are 360 families and that 110 get an annual income of $10,000; 100 get an annual income of $12,500; 100 get an income of $13,750; and 50 get an annual income of $15,000. Since there is no middle number, the second and third numbers ($12,500 and $13,750) are added together and divided by 2, yielding a median income of $13,125.

mediation A final effort to prevent a strike or lockout in a labour dispute, using a third party to help find a compromise solution. Mediation may follow the collapse of CONCILIATION, with the mediator meeting separately with each side in an effort to avert a strike or lockout or to end one that has already started. See also ARBITRATION, COMPULSORY ARBITRATION.

medium-term bond A bond or other security maturing in three to ten years.

medium-term forecast An economic forecast that looks three to five years ahead. This is usually long enough to determine when recovery from a recession should begin, or when a current period of economic expansion will start to weaken and turn downward towards a recession.

Mercantile Bank affair A dispute between the Canadian government and the First National City Bank of New York (Citibank) over the sale of the Mercantile Bank of Canada. In 1963, Citibank told the Bank of Canada and Finance Minister Walter Gordon that it proposed to buy the Mercantile Bank of Canada, the only foreign-controlled bank in Canada, from its Dutch owners. Mr. Gordon told the U.S. bank that he opposed the sale, that the charter of the Mercantile Bank would be up for renewal in 1964, and that it would not necessarily be renewed. He said that the government viewed the banking industry as a vital part of the economy and that, if Mercantile fell under aggressive U.S. control, it would become a significant participant in the Canadian banking system and would lead to a flood of applications from other foreign banks to establish themselves in Canada. Mr. Gordon advised Citibank against completing the transaction, indicating that, if it did, it would do so at its peril. He pointed out that the Bank Act was about to be reviewed. Citibank went ahead with the takeover anyway.

In 1965, amendments to the Bank Act were proposed by the government that would have frozen the growth of any bank if more than 25 per cent of its voting shares were owned by non-residents; Mercantile was 100 per cent owned by Citibank. Following intensive negotiations, Citibank was given five years in the eventual 1967 amendments to the Bank Act to reduce its ownership to 25 per cent or to cut back its liabilities (deposits) to twenty times its authorized capital. If it did not, it would be subject to a fine of one thousand dollars a day. In 1971, Mercantile and the government agreed to plans for the sale of new shares to Canadians that would lead to 75 per cent Canadian ownership by 1980.

mercantilism The economic doctrine of the seventeenth and early eighteenth centuries that stressed the importance of gold, obtained by running a trade surplus, as a measure of a nation's prestige and power. By obtaining gold from other nations in settlement of its trade surplus, according to the mercantilists, a country increased its own capacity to expand its domestic economy and finance military activities. Hence, mercantilist economic policies stressed the importance of obtaining a surplus of exports over imports, and justified government intervention in the form of tariffs, subsidies for domestic industries, monopolistic privileges for trading companies, and quotas.

However, at the same time that a trade surplus strengthened some countries, trade deficits weakened others, since they had to give up gold reserves. The mercantilists were challenged on this score by the CLASSICAL economists, led by ADAM SMITH, who rejected international trade as a ZERO-SUM GAME in which one country's growth had to lead to another country's decline. The classical economists contended that consumers suffered as a result of mercantilist protectionism and subsidies for industry; they argued that everyone would be better off in a world without restrictions, and advocated FREE TRADE. NEO-MERCANTILISTS today argue that a liberal world-trading and -investment order benefits mainly the stronger nations and corporations; the neo-mercantilists support state intervention to obtain greater benefits for their own countries. Free traders see neo-mercantilism simply as old-fashioned protectionism, dressed up in a new vocabulary of INDUSTRIAL STRATEGY.

merchant bank A specialized financial institution that deals in corporate finance and, more particularly, in corporate takeovers, mergers, and corporate reorganization. A merchant bank has industry and finance experts who can analyze the resources and prospects of individual firms, advise them on how to grow, and find acquisitions for them as part of their growth strategy. There are few such organizations in Canada, although there is a recognition by financial authorities that this is a gap in the Canadian financial system that needs to be filled. Merchant banks can play a vital role in assisting the growth of local firms.

merchant marine Ocean-going freighters, tankers, and other commercial ships. Canada has, for all intents and purposes, no merchant marine of its own. Its exports and imports are carried almost entirely in the merchant marines of other nations.

merger The combining together of the assets of two or more companies into a larger, single firm. Most mergers result from one company taking over another company and absorbing the acquired corporate assets into its own corporate structure; in such mergers, the acquired company loses its separate corporate identity. A horizontal merger is one in which competitive companies in the same industry are merged. A vertical merger is one in which companies at different stages of production or distribution in the same industry are merged. A conglomerate merger is one in which companies in totally unrelated businesses are merged. While mergers can sometimes make an industry more efficient, or may be necessary to enable any of the firms in the industry to survive, they can also lead to OLIGOPOLY, and hence are subject to review under the COMBINES INVESTIGATION ACT.

merit pay The additional pay in excess of the base rate that an employee gets for superior performance on the job.

merit rating An evaluation of an employee's work to determine whether he or she should be promoted to a higher job, or be given MERIT PAY for performing an existing job in a superior manner.

Metric Commission of Canada A commission created in 1971, with a full-time chairman and twenty part-time commissioners, to develop a plan to convert some one hundred different sectors of the economy to the metric system and to monitor their progress. It reports to the minister of INDUSTRY, TRADE AND COMMERCE.

metric conversion The program of the federal government to convert to the metric system. Although the metric system had been legal in Canada since 1871, it was not widely used. After the British decision in 1965 to convert to the metric system, the Canadian government considered similar action in Canada; in 1970, a white paper on metric conversion that urged adoption of the metric system was published. The following year, the METRIC COMMISSION OF CANADA was appointed to achieve conversion by 1980. The national program of guideline dates was approved by the government, which affirmed 1980 as the target for the completion of conversion to the metric system. The principal reasons given for conversion were that the metric system is the system used by most of Canada's trading partners and that the system itself is a simpler one, since everything is a multiple or division of ten. The main reasons many Canadians opposed the conversion were the large costs of converting, the inconvenience caused the public in having to learn a new system, and the fact that the United States, Canada's largest trading partner, was delaying conversion to the metric system.

metropolitan area For census purposes in Canada, the main labour market of a large, built-up area with a population of one hundred thousand or more. There are twenty-three such areas, accounting for about 60 per cent of the country's population. They are: Calgary, Chicoutimi-Jonquière, Edmonton, Halifax, Hamilton, Kitchener, London, Montreal, Oshawa, Ottawa-Hull, Quebec, Regina, St. John, N.B., St. Catharines-Niagara, St. John's, Nfld., Saskatoon, Sudbury, Thunder Bay, Toronto, Vancouver, Victoria, Windsor, and Winnipeg. Metropolitan areas define not only labour markets, but trading markets for stores, newspapers, and various other producers of goods and services.

microeconomics That part of economics concerned with individual economic sectors or groups of decision-makers, such as consumers, savers, sellers, and producers, as opposed to MACROECONOMICS, which studies the economy as a whole. Microeconomics puts the economy under a microscope, and tries to deal with such questions as how prices are set in particular industries, how labour markets work, the factors contributing to increased demand for a particular commodity, the theory of the firm, the distribution of income, and the consequences of IMPERFECT COMPETITION.

microfiche A device for storing information; it consists of a small piece of film, which has printed on it a large number of pages that are far too small to be read directly. But with a magnifying reading device, individual pages smaller than postage stamps can easily be read. Corporate and government files can be transferred to microfiche, thus eliminating the need to maintain large volumes of older files in their original and bulky form.

middle distillates Refined products made from crude oil, including diesel fuel, light fuel oil, kerosene, and stove oil.

middleman A person or firm serving as an intermediary between producers and consumers, sellers and buyers. A middleman may be a WHOLESALER, a BROKER, or a JOBBER.

mill A production facility where an ore is treated so that metals are recovered from it, or where wheat or other grains are processed to produce flour.

Mill, John Stuart A British economist (1806–73) in the CLASSICAL school of economics. He is best known, though, for his break from classical orthodoxy, and in particular for his view that the state could play an important role in improving the well-being of the people. He noted, for example, the failure of economic progress under free-market forces to improve the standard of living of the needy.

Mill spent most of his life as an employee of the East India Company, his work there giving him considerable spare time to develop his ideas in political economics. His most important work, *Principles of Political Economy*, was published in 1848. Mill helped to develop the theory of COMPARATIVE ADVANTAGE, but he turned his attention largely to the optimistic view that education and improved economic security for the people would lead to reduced population growth and higher aspirations.

Mill maintained that there was nothing inevitable about the unfair distribution of income in society, and said that it could and should be altered. The state, he said, could play a much more significant role than was usually assumed in classical economics. It could be a civilizing influence by spreading education and decent facilities, such as parks and museums. It could also levy taxes to pay for socially useful projects. He also regarded the economic system of his day as one step along the road to socialism, but a form of socialism in which the state would not play a dominant role.

Mill was also a sharp-tongued social critic. While he was aware of the rapid economic growth of the United States, he noted that this was mainly to the benefit of white males: "All that these advantages seem to have done for them is that the life of the whole of one sex is devoted to dollar hunting, and of the other to breeding dollar hunters." Mill, who campaigned for an extension of the vote to working people and women, was defeated in his bid for re-election to Parliament after serving one term.

mill rate The property-tax rate, expressed usually as a per cent rate per one thousand dollars of the assessed value of a property.

mineral reserves Mineral-ore reserves that are known, physically, to exist, or are considered likely to exist and that may or may not be economically exploited. Such reserves fall into four categories: proven ore reserves; probable ore reserves; possible ore reserves; and indicated ore reserves.

mini-budget A term used to describe an economic statement by the minister of FINANCE in the House of Commons, in which tax, tariff, spending or other economic-policy changes are announced. But it does not include the full range of BUDGET information and budget papers, and is not treated in the House of Commons rules as a budget. Mini-budgets are usually brought in by a government to deal with changed economic circumstances since the full budget was introduced earlier in the year, or because the official budget has not had the impact that was expected. A mini-budget is also called a baby budget.

minimax principle A cautious approach to decision-making in which the best decision among several choices is the one that would produce the least harmful results if something went wrong.

minimum wage The lowest wage, expressed as so much an hour, that an employer may legally pay an employee. The purpose of the minimum wage is to protect employees against exploitation and to ensure that they are able to earn at least a subsistence level of income. There are separate federal and provincial minimum wages, each applying to workers under their own jurisdiction. Minimum-wage laws also differentiate for some industries or according to age, and, in some sectors, may exempt workers altogether. Ontario minimum-wage laws, for example, provide a lower minimum wage for those working in the tourist industry. The federal minimum wage differentiates between workers seventeen and over and those under seventeen. People working as maids are excluded from minimum-wage protection almost everywhere in Canada, and farm labour is also excluded in some provinces. Quebec, under its Collective Agreement Decrees Act, may order that the wages agreed on in a collective agreement for a particularly large firm in an industry, also be paid by the other firms in the same industry.

The full effect of minimum wages is still a matter of dispute among economists. Some argue that minimum wages are essential to prevent exploitation. Others contend that high minimum wages result in fewer jobs, since employers cannot afford to hire as many people; as a result, the people who are supposed to be helped by minimum wages actually suffer through higher unemployment. A national minimum wage was introduced in Canada in 1965; it was $1.25 an hour. The first minimum wage, for women, was introduced in Manitoba in 1918, while the first minimum wage for men was introduced in British Columbia in

1925. Minimum-wage rates are usually changed every twelve to eighteen months.

Mining Association of Canada An association of producing mining companies, exploration companies, and mineral refineries and smelters, that presents the views of the mining industry to the federal government on matters of mining, exploration, development, and exports. It deals with policies ranging from taxation to environmental protection. The association also has a research and environmental co-ordinator, who keeps track of improvements in mining techniques and environmental safeguards. It has about one hundred mining-company members who account for about 95 per cent of mining production in Canada, excluding coal. It was founded in 1935 as the Canadian Metal Mining Association, but changed its name in 1965. It is based in Ottawa.

minority interest Shareholders in a company who do not own enough shares to control the enterprise alone or in concert with a small number of other shareholders; all the shareholders other than those who have a controlling or majority interest.

mint The government-controlled enterprise that produces metal coins for everyday use and gold and silver for commemorative purposes. See also ROYAL CANADIAN MINT.

misleading advertising Advertising that misrepresents the price or quality of an article, or makes a claim about the performance, efficacy, or length of life of a product without adequate testing. Misleading advertising is an offence under the COMBINES INVESTIGATION ACT.

misrepresentation A false statement intended to deceive a person into buying a good or service or entering into a contract. The harmed party may sue for damages and have the contract rescinded. Consumer-protection laws provide some remedy for the public. See, for example, MISLEADING ADVERTISING, which is a criminal offence.

mixed economy An economic system in which both government and the private sector have important roles to play; Canada is an example. Private corporations operate alongside public corporations, while the government, through laws, regulatory agencies, moral suasion, and its sheer economic power, modifies the workings of market forces to protect the public and to achieve public goals that are not necessarily the goals of private corporations. The mixed economy is a compromise between capitalism and socialism that has evolved during the twentieth century, to retain the dynamics and innovation of the profit motive of private initiative, while also seeking to limit the powers of private corporations and individuals where they act against the perceived public interest. The mixed economy uses the resources of the economy to achieve social goals, including greater opportunity for those on the lowest rungs of the economic ladder and a guaranteed income for all of its citizens.

mobility of labour See LABOUR MOBILITY.

mode The number in a series of numbers that occurs most frequently. Where 300 cars are for sale and the price for 65 of them is $3,000, the price for 80 of them is $3,820, the price for 40 of them is $3,975, the price for 75 of them is $4,085, and the price for 40 of them is $5,880, the mode is $3,820, since there are more cars marked at this price than at any other.

model See ECONOMIC MODEL.

modified union shop A workplace where a union has been recognized as the BARGAINING AGENT, but in which existing non-union employees are not required to join the union. However, new employees and those who joined the union during or after CERTIFICATION proceedings must remain union members.

monetarism The school of economic thought that argues that economic performance depends mainly on the rate of growth of the MONEY SUPPLY. In other words, the control of inflation, stimulus of economic growth, and creation of jobs depend on MONETARY POLICY alone, according to this school. It is identified with the University of Chicago and Nobel

Prize winner Milton Friedman. Friedman and his followers argue that the best economic performance is achieved by having the central bank set a long-term growth rate in money supply, and then letting the free market allocate resources within society. Monetarists reject short-term manipulation of money-supply growth, or fine-tuning, contending that it is ineffective and may do more harm than good. They also reject the use of FISCAL POLICY as an important instrument of economic policy, and argue that it has little or no impact on the level of economic growth, the rate of inflation, or the creation of jobs; fiscal policy decides how the gross national product is divided between the public and private sectors, but not the size of gross national product.

monetary aggregates A synonym for MONEY SUPPLY, however defined.

monetary base The portion of the MONEY SUPPLY that represents the balance-sheet liabilities of the BANK OF CANADA to the private sector and that can be defined to include currency in circulation plus deposits by the chartered banks at the Bank of Canada. MONETARISTS argue that control over the monetary base should allow the central bank to control money supply readily. The Bank of Canada does not use this approach to control the rate of monetary expansion; instead, it adjusts short-term interest rates to influence the level of transaction balances held by the private sector. See also MONETARY POLICY.

monetary policy The money-supply and credit policies of the BANK OF CANADA, which determine the availability and cost of credit in the economy and, hence, the rate of economic growth and the rate of inflation. The Bank of Canada controls the rate of growth of the money supply through the control of interest rates. The policy objective of the central bank is to achieve rates of monetary growth consistent with a satisfactory rate of real economic growth and price stability. In November 1975, the governor of the Bank of Canada announced an explicit target range for the growth of the MONETARY AGGREGATE M-1 (defined as currency in circulation plus the public's holdings of chartered-bank demand deposits). The initial target rate of growth was not less than 10 per cent but well below 15 per cent, measured from the average level of money holdings over the three months centred on May 1975. Since then, the target range has been systematically lowered and, in September 1978, stood at 6 per cent to 10 per cent, measured from the average June 1978 level.

Controlling the growth of the money supply tends to stabilize total spending on goods and services in the economy. For example, if the rate of spending exceeds the rate of monetary expansion, interest rates tend to rise, which in turn induces firms and individuals to moderate their spending; in this way, it is argued, inflationary pressures arising from excess demand are curbed. Monetary policy is also influenced by other developments, such as changes in the BALANCE OF PAYMENTS and the EXCHANGE RATE. This can lead to conflicting pressures. For example, even if the economy is weak, if interest rates are not increased an outflow of Canadian capital to other countries may occur, thus reducing the exchange rate of the Canadian dollar and adding to inflation.

The Bank of Canada has two basic ways to influence interest rates:

1. Through its cash-management policies and OPEN-MARKET OPERATIONS, it can, on a day-to-day basis, influence the level of government deposits in the chartered banks, and thus control the level of excess reserves of the chartered banks available for lending and to meet the current cash or other needs of their customers. The Bank of Canada always knows a day ahead whether there will be a significant change in its cash balances in the chartered banks, resulting from a large flow of government cheques for income-tax rebates, family-allowance and other such social-security payments, or government-payroll payments. It can decide to let existing government cash balances in the chartered banks cover the cheques, thus running down the level of reserves held by each of the chartered banks close to or even below their legal requirements. This forces the chartered banks to seek new funds; they will usually do this by raising short-term interest rates. Thus, if the Bank of Canada wants to raise short-term rates, it can reduce government cash balances with the chartered banks. Conversely, if it wants to re-

duce short-term rates, it can increase cash balances in the banks, thus increasing the excess reserves of the chartered banks and, hence, the supply of loanable funds.
2. The Bank of Canada can also alter interest rates through its sale and purchase of government securities. It holds a large portfolio of TREASURY BILLS and government bonds. By selling from its portfolio, it can increase the supply of government securities in the market. This has the paradoxical result of reducing the market value of government treasury bills and bonds, and thus increasing their effective yield or interest rate. Similarly, if the Bank of Canada wants to reduce short-term rates, it can buy government treasury bills and bonds, thus raising the demand for such securities and, hence, their market value. This, in turn, reduces their effective yield or interest rate.

Interest rates are also influenced by the changes the Bank of Canada makes in the BANK RATE. This is a signal that the bank wants interest rates to be raised or lowered. See also BANK OF CANADA, MONEY SUPPLY. The Bank of Canada publishes weekly statistics that show changes in money supply, the level of government cash balances, Bank of Canada balance-sheet items, and a variety of interest rates. These statistics indicate the direction of monetary policy.

money A medium of exchange for goods and services; it consists of anything that is generally accepted in the settlement of debts or purchase of goods or services. Money has a variety of functions. The first is as a medium of exchange that allows an economic system based on the division of labour to function; the alternative would be a BARTER system. Second, money is a unit of account, or a yardstick in which prices, debts, and wages are expressed. Third, it is a means of storing value or holding one's wealth for future consumption. Without money, it is hard to see how an economy could function at anything more than the most primitive level.

money illusion The failure of a person to appreciate that, although he has more money than he had before—due, for example, to a raise—he is no better off than before because inflation means that the purchasing power of a dollar is less than it was before. Thus, a person whose annual income has risen from $8,500 a year to $11,000 a year over a five-year period might think that he had made a real gain in his earning power. But if inflation has risen 35 per cent over those same five years, he is actually worse off; he would need an annual income of $11,475 to have the same purchasing power he had five years earlier, when he was earning $8,500 a year.

money market The sector of the CAPITAL MARKET in which short-term capital is raised and invested and in which short-term securities, such as treasury bills, commercial paper, guaranteed-investment certificates, acceptance-company notes, and other securities maturing in three years or less are traded. The money market as a national, organized market came into being in 1953, to assist the BANK OF CANADA to carry out its responsibility for MONETARY POLICY and to increase the opportunities for investment of short-term funds in the economy. The principal participants in the money market are the federal, provincial, and municipal governments, the chartered banks, the Bank of Canada, and major corporations and nonprofit organizations. The market is operated through a telephone network organized by thirteen investment dealers known as MONEY-MARKET DEALERS. Since these dealers also hold large inventories of short-term securities, which are essential for the smooth operation of the market, they qualify for day-to-day loans from the banks and, if needed, short-term credit from the Bank of Canada.

money-market dealers Investment dealers who trade in and hold inventories of government short-term bonds and treasury bills, who thus, as jobbers, form the heart of the MONEY MARKET. Because these thirteen dealers hold inventories, they are able to meet the various needs of the Bank of Canada, the chartered banks, and other institutions participating in the money market. To help finance their activities they can get day-to-day loans from the chartered banks or short-term loans from the Bank of Canada. The money-market dealers operate the money market through a telephone network connecting their various offices.

money order A cheque issued by a telegraph or post office, bank, or other institution, which can be cashed on demand. It is purchased for a fee plus the face value and made out to a person, company, or organization designated by the purchaser. The recipient can instantly convert it to cash.

money supply The total amount of money in an economy at any point in time that is available to make payments to others. Money supply includes not only cash, but bank deposits, deposits in financial institutions, certain types of short-term notes, and, in its broadest definition, even credit cards. The data used to calculate money supply is published weekly by the Bank of Canada. There are several definitions of the money supply, progressing from a fairly narrow definition to a fairly broad one. The main definitions used in Canada are:

M-1 This consists of currency in circulation outside of the chartered banks, along with all Canadian-dollar demand and pure chequing deposits, which can be withdrawn by depositors at any time without prior notice. This definition is the one used by the Bank of Canada when it talks of targets for growth in the money supply. It is not the same as the U.S. definition of M-1. In Canada, M-1b is equivalent to the U.S. M-1. It consists of the Canadian M-1 plus chequable savings deposits, which usually can be withdrawn at any time, even though formally they can require advance notice of withdrawal.

M-2 This consists of M-1b along with non-chequing personal term and savings deposits and some corporate chequable and non-chequable notice deposits. Canadian M-2 corresponds to U.S. M-2.

M-3 This consists of M-2 along with all non-personal term deposits, including certificates of deposit held by business corporations.

The Bank of Canada tries to maintain a growth rate of money supply that is sufficient to meet the growth needs of the economy, but not so high that it contributes to inflation. The central bank's ability to manipulate the growth rate of the money supply also gives it an important tool with which to influence the growth of the economy and the rate of inflation. See also MONETARY POLICY.

money wage The wages paid in money to an employee. The money value does not necessarily indicate its real value or purchasing power, since prices may have increased and may thus have made the money worth less in actual purchasing power. So long as money wages keep pace with inflation, there is no decline in real wages. But if money wages rise more slowly than prices, then real wages have declined. Thus, stating an increase in a money wage by itself, without reference to price changes, does not indicate much about the real value of the wage increase. A person might get a money-wage increase and still suffer a real-wage loss.

monopoly The situation in a market in which there is only one producer but many buyers, thus enabling the single producer to exercise considerable power over the price, quantity, and quality of the product. It usually means that the consumer has to pay higher prices than he should because the monopolist is in a position to seek higher profits. Fewer of the products are available, since one way to maintain artificially high prices is to create artificial scarcity by withholding products from the market. The extent of a monopolist's power depends on the ability of consumers to substitute other products.

Governments can regulate monopolists by reducing tariffs, so that imports provide competition; or governments can regulate prices or the rate of return through a regulatory agency, threaten to break up a monopolist, impose an excess-profits tax to take away the monopoly profit, introduce more liberal patent or other laws, which give would-be competitors access to the technology of the monopolist, or threaten to nationalize the monopolist. Sometimes a monopoly is unavoidable—for example, in the provision of telephone or cable-television services; in such cases, government can regulate the rate of return for the utility. See also COMBINES INVESTIGATION ACT, UTILITY RATE OF RETURN, OLIGOPOLY.

monopsony A market in which there is only a single buyer for a product, service or commodity; this enables the buyer to exercise considerable power over the price that the producer is able to charge. It is the opposite of MONOPOLY.

Monopsony occurs only rarely—for example, in a one-company town, where there is only one employer who is able to check demands for higher wages. A monopsony-type situation can arise in other industries—for example, wherever the retail market is dominated by two or three major department-store or supermarket chains who buy from a multitude of suppliers of, say, shoes, blouses, or furniture. A similar situation would arise for competing shopping-centre developers, who would need a supermarket but would have only two or three chains with whom to negotiate.

Montreal Stock Exchange (MSE) A stock exchange created in Montreal in 1874, following eleven years of operation as an informal exchange. In 1926, the Montreal Cash Exchange was founded so that shares not listed on the MSE could be traded; in 1953 this became the Canadian Stock Exchange, which reached an agreement with the MSE to share trading facilities. In 1974, the Canadian Stock Exchange merged with the MSE. The MSE has three categories of shares, each with its own listing requirements: senior industrials, junior industrials, and mines and oils.

Montreal Stock Exchange indices Since 1974 the MSE has published hourly indices on price changes in a composite group of stocks, industrials, and various industrial sectors. The MSE has published indices of share prices since 1926.

moonlighting The holding of two or more paying jobs at the same time by a single individual. A person who works during the day, for example, may get a second job during the evening or on weekends.

Moore Report A report on the implications of foreign ownership of brokerage and investment houses and on alternative methods of financing the securities industry, published in June 1970. It recommended a freeze on the foreign ownership of Canadian securities firms. "Canada has recognized that the national interest requires the retention of Canadian control over banks, loan companies, life insurance companies, and finance companies. The same conclusion should apply to securities firms," it said. The report also opposed allowing securities firms to go public. Instead, it proposed that up to 40 per cent of a securities firm's invested capital could be owned by approved outside investors, including up to 25 per cent of the voting shares; no single approved outside investor would be allowed to own more than 10 per cent of a firm's total equity.

The study was sponsored by the INVESTMENT DEALERS ASSOCIATION and the Toronto, Montreal, and Vancouver stock exchanges in May 1969, following the takeover of Royal Securities Corporation, a Canadian-owned MONEY-MARKET DEALER, by the U.S.-owned brokerage firm of Merrill, Lynch, Pierce, Fenner and Smith Incorporated. Trevor Moore, senior vice-president of Imperial Oil Limited, chaired the study. In July 1971, the Ontario government announced that the ONTARIO SECURITIES COMMISSION would require that all new entrants into the securities industry be limited to 25 per cent non-resident ownership; however, the commission could grant exemptions, while a GRANDFATHER CLAUSE exempted all existing firms with greater than 25 per cent foreign ownership. Similar rules were adopted by the TORONTO STOCK EXCHANGE.

moose pasture A term for worthless land.

moral suasion Efforts by the government or the BANK OF CANADA to persuade companies, including financial institutions, either to do something or not to do something. Such requests lack the weight of laws to back them up and are based on the moral authority of government or the implied threat of legislation. The federal government, for example, may want the provinces, municipalities, and corporations to limit their foreign borrowing; to accomplish this, the minister of FINANCE may appeal to these groups not to borrow abroad unless absolutely necessary, arguing that such restraint is necessary for the economic welfare of the country. Similarly, the Bank of Canada may appeal to the banks to increase their loans to small business or to regions with chronic unemployment, arguing that the banks and other institutions have a moral obligation to the country to do this. Moral suasion is also used when governments try to persuade business and unions to restrain price and wage increases in order to prevent inflation and protect other workers from a loss of jobs, or pensioners from hardship caused by the erosion in the value of their pensions.

moratorium A period of time during which debtors are freed from an obligation to pay their debts. A moratorium may be declared on the debts of a poor country that is undergoing a balance-of-payments crisis, the moratorium being one of the remedies to help the country bring its balance-of-payments problems under control. Similarly, a moratorium may be declared on certain types of debts—for example, mortgages on farms and personal residences—during a domestic economic crisis.

morbidity The extent of sickness and disease in a population. It is one way of measuring the health of a population.

mortality table See LIFE TABLE.

mortgage A loan to buy land, a building, or other major piece of property. In return for the loan, the borrower or mortgagee transfers ownership but not possession to the lender or mortgagor as security for the loan. The transfer of ownership expires when the mortgage is repaid. If the borrower defaults, the mortgagor has the right to sell the property to recover the amount of the loan that is still outstanding; but he has to get court permission first. There are various types of mortgages, depending on the priority of claim they have on the property. The holder of the first mortgage has first claim, the second mortgage second claim, and so on. Hence, the interest rate for the second mortgage is higher than the interest on the first, since the holder of the second mortgage incurs somewhat greater risk.

mortgage broker A person or firm whose business it is to bring mortgagors and mortgagees together for a commission or fee. A mortgage broker arranges mortgages for people seeking such loans, places funds in mortgages for investors, and borrows on his own account to finance mortgages; he may also buy and sell mortgages.

mortgage debenture A fixed-interest loan, obtained by a company or other organization, in which the loan is secured by real property of the company or organization.

mortgage insurance Insurance obtained to pay off the outstanding balance of a mortgage should the mortgagee die. Since the outstanding balance of a mortgage declines over time, homeowners often obtain a form of TERM INSURANCE to cover the mortgage.

mortgage-loan company A federally or provincially incorporated company that borrows money, usually for terms of one to five years, and re-lends it in the form of mortgage loans. Most such companies either own trust companies as subsidiaries or are affiliated with the chartered banks. Hence, the borrowed funds can be obtained by the guaranteed-investment certificates and other term deposits of the trust companies and banks.

most-favoured nation (MFN) A clause in trade agreements, in particular in the GENERAL AGREEMENT ON TARIFFS AND TRADE, which ensures that, when one country grants a trade concession to another, the same concession is available to its other trading partners as well. GATT signatories adhere to the most-favoured-nation principle. It is the opposite of trade discrimination. Canada is a signatory to GATT and has MFN arrangements with most of its trading partners.

motivational research Psychological research into the behaviour of consumers' attitudes and preferences. Motivational research is an important marketing tool, used in the preparation of advertising, promotional, and packaging plans. It may, for example, be used to determine why consumers prefer brand A instant coffee over brand B, or how consumers would react to a change in a product.

moving average An average calculated from a changing series of figures, so that, as the latest figure is added, the earliest is dropped. This type of average is useful in measuring changing economic conditions, such as unemployment and inflation. Over the course of the year, the moving average will, successively, represent the average of the figures for January, February, and March; for February, March, and April; for March, April, and May; and so on.

Multi-Fibre Arrangement An international agreement first negotiated in 1973 and now extended through to 1981, which sets out the rules under which the developed and LESS-DEVELOPED COUNTRIES negotiate bilateral quotas on different groups of textile products shipped from less-developed countries to industrial countries. Its purpose is to control the growth of textile exports from third-world countries to the industrial countries. Canada is a signatory.

multilateralism The negotiation of trade, investment, and other international agreements that apply to virtually all countries, as opposed to BILATERAL AGREEMENTS, which define trade and other relationships between just two countries, to the exclusion of others. Since the end of the Second World War, the major nations have attempted to develop and strengthen multilateral arrangements and to curb discriminatory or bilateral agreements among small numbers of countries. Examples of such arrangements include the INTERNATIONAL MONETARY FUND and the GENERAL AGREEMENT ON TARIFFS AND TRADE. The underlying philosophy is that multilateralism will lead to a greater expansion of world trade and economic growth. Bilateralism, it is argued, encourages restrictive trade blocs, protectionism, and beggar-thy-neighbour policies, which restrict the growth of trade and investment.

Canada was a strong advocate of the multilateral approach after the Second World War, in large part because it was felt that this would give the country some chance to curb the unilateral exercise of economic power by the United States. In the absence of strong multilateral institutions and arrangements, it was also feared that Canada would be forced into closer bilateral arrangements with the United States, in which Canada would be by far the weaker partner and would hence lose much of its independence in economic and foreign policy.

multinational corporation A corporation that has subsidiaries in more than one other country, and that operates from an international or global perspective. Multinational corporations are able to use their financial resources, technology, managerial know-how, established systems of distribution, product identity, and economies of scale to set up subsidiaries in countries around the world, and to allocate production according to local labour costs and skills, tax policies and incentives, distribution costs, and other such factors. They have become an important means of TECHNOLOGY TRANSFER and job creation. But they also have a number of significant drawbacks: **1.** The real transfer of technology does not occur, since research and development for the most part remain in the country of the parent company; thus, host countries may get less technological knowledge than they would if they tried other arrangements, such as joint ventures and technology licensing. **2.** The existence of a large number of multinationals in a host country can mean that local people do not develop top-level management skills, since these may be left to the parent-company head office. **3.** The entry of multinational corporations into a nation can prevent the creation of local companies in the same industry, since multinationals can quickly and more cheaply establish local subsidiaries. In particular, multinationals may pre-empt the development of high-technology industries, while leaving the less profitable, declining industries to local business. **4.** The existence of a large number of foreign subsidiaries weakens the ability of the government to control its economy, since many decisions on investment, research, product lines, exports, wage policies, and corporate practices are made in foreign parent-company head offices. **5.** The existence of many subsidiaries of multinationals leads to a fragmented industrial structure that is weak in research and development and that lacks the capacity to meet the challenge of changing technology and growing third-world imports on its own. **6.** Foreign subsidiaries may have an unwelcome effect on local cultures, shaping consumer tastes and values away from local traditions and values. **7.** Multinationals may deprive local treasuries of taxes to which they are entitled, by overpaying their head offices for management services and research and by manipulating transfer prices between the local subsidiary and the multinational's companies elsewhere in the world. **8.** Since multinationals tend to seek a higher rate of return on capital invested abroad, consumers in countries where the multinational has established affiliate operations may pay higher prices. **9.** Multinationals can frustrate local aspirations, by refusing to sell shares in a subsidiary to local investors and by refusing to place local citizens in positions of top management. **10.** Multinationals may increase foreign domination, by bringing with them their own bankers, their own advertising and insurance agencies, and the like, and by using the same suppliers and engineers they use in their home countries. Multinationals are also called transnational corporations.

multiple-listing service (MLS) The listing of a property for sale or rent with all members of local real-estate boards; whichever firm arranges the sale or lease, collects the commission. See also EXCLUSIVE LISTING.

multiplier The number by which the change in investment or some other element of aggregate demand in the economy is multiplied, to calculate the resulting total change in GROSS NATIONAL PRODUCT. The decision of a firm to build a new factory, for example, sets off a long chain of spending and employment. If a firm decides to build a one-million-dollar factory, it will pay out one million dollars to the contractor, building-materials suppliers, and others. These people, in turn, will spend at least some of the money; if their MARGINAL PROPENSITY TO CONSUME is 80 per cent, then they will spend $800,000. The people and firms who get the $800,000 may have a marginal propensity to consume of 75 per cent, so they will spend $600,000. Thus, without tracing the initial investment very far, it is possible to see how a one-million-dollar investment decision has already resulted in the spending of $1.4 million more than the cost of the original project. The same kinds of calculations can be made to measure the multiplier effect of a tax cut that increases purchasing power, or a government decision to accelerate public-works spending to create jobs. And the multiplier effect amplifies reductions in investment or aggregate demand as well as increases; a one-billion-dollar decline in investment will have a much larger multiplier effect on total gross national product and employment.

The multiplier has become an important tool of economic management and analysis since JOHN MAYNARD KEYNES used it in the 1930s. It allows the government to calculate the resulting investment from a tax cut, the total growth in national income resulting from the increased investment, and the additional tax revenue that, in turn, will be generated through the multiplier effect as it increases the gross national product.

municipal debenture A debt security that is issued by a municipality and is much the same as a bond, except that it is not secured by any municipal assets but is based on the general credit-worthiness of the municipality. There are two types of municipal debenture: serial debentures, in which a percentage of the principal is repaid each year; and term debentures, which mature on a specified date.

Municipal Development and Loan Fund A special fund established by the federal government in 1963 to help create jobs by making low-cost loans available to municipalities, to carry out needed public works. The fund was launched with four hundred million dollars to finance loans covering two-thirds of the cost of eligible projects that were approved by the provinces; 25 per cent of the loan would be forgiven if the projects were completed by 31 March 1966, the planned terminal date of the program. Eligible projects included hospital and school construction, transit projects, and water and sewer projects. See also WINTER-WORKS PROGRAM.

Munitions and Supply, Department of A federal government department established in 1940 to handle all purchasing for the armed forces, to control the allocation of commodities and products essential to the war effort, such as coal, rubber, oil, timber, steel, machine tools, motor vehicles, ships, chemicals, and electric power, and to help set up new industries for war production. Many wartime plants were built and machines purchased with government money, but these facilities were for the most part operated by private industry under government supervision. In some instances, CROWN CORPORATIONS were created—to manufacture, for example, synthetic rubber, precision instruments, small arms, and ships.

mutual fund An investment company that invests in the shares, bonds, or other securities of other companies. It is an open-ended investment company, because it does not have a fixed or authorized number of shares that are traded on a stock exchange, as a CLOSED-END INVESTMENT COMPANY does. There is no limit on the number of shares it may issue. Shares are issued in as great a number as can be sold. Shareholders who wish to liquidate their holdings do not sell them to other investors on a stock exchange, but sell them back to the mutual fund, which redeems them at prevailing market value minus a commission or handling charge. Some funds impose other charges as well on investors. The money obtained from the sale of shares provides the basic capital for the fund's investments. To get the net asset-value per share, total liabilities are deducted from total assets, and the net assets are divided by the number of shares outstanding. Mutual funds are established for different types of investors, some emphasizing yield and some capital gain; some have diversified portfolios, while others may specialize in bonds, growth stocks, real estate, or oil and gas companies. Mutual funds have to be registered with provincial securities commissions. Their purpose is to allow small investors to participate in equity markets through a diversified portfolio, with investment decisions being made by professional investment managers.

N

narrow market See THIN MARKET.

national accounts See SYSTEM OF NATIONAL ACCOUNTS.

national-accounts budget A method of presenting the federal government's budget so that its full economic impact can be assessed; as opposed to the BUDGETARY-ACCOUNTS BUDGET. The national-accounts budget measures only the government income and spending that has an immediate effect on the flow of income in the economy. It thus includes, in addition to government spending on goods and services and transfer payments, all the expenditures and income of the unemployment-insurance program, the expenditures and income of the government's pension funds for its own employees, and the net profit or loss of government business enterprises. This method of budget presentation also shows revenues as they are earned or become due, and expenditures when the liabilities are incurred, rather than when the money is actually received or paid out, as is the case in the budgetary-accounts budget. That means, for example, that corporation tax revenues are credited to the government's revenue accounts when the taxable income is earned, instead of when it is paid to the government, several months later. The national-accounts budget can be extended to include provincial and municipal data as well, making it possible to assess the total economic impact of activities of all three levels of government. It is also the budget that can be compared with those of other countries, since the national-accounts system is the only one that is at all compatible with the budget systems of other countries.

The national-accounts-budget forecast has been included in the annual BUDGET SPEECH since 1964. Details are published quarterly by Statistics Canada in its GROSS-NATIONAL-PRODUCT and government-finance statistics. Past details of the national-accounts budget are also contained in the PUBLIC ACCOUNTS. See also CASH-NEEDS BUDGET, FINANCIAL-MANAGEMENT BUDGET.

National Commission on Inflation (NCI) A post-controls agency established in March 1979 to monitor prices, profits, costs, and compensation, and to make reports to the federal cabinet on any increases that appeared prejudicial to efforts to reduce inflation or to maintain or improve the competitiveness of Canadian industry. It was given broad powers to obtain company and other records. It was not given rollback powers, but could make reports to the government on out-of-line increases and recommend steps that could be taken against firms, professional associations, or unions that made inflationary gains. The commission replaced the CENTRE FOR THE STUDY OF INFLATION AND PRODUCTIVITY; its mandate was to expire 30 June 1980 but it was abolished in July 1979.

national debt The outstanding debt of the federal government and its agencies. It consists of outstanding government bonds, including CANADA SAVINGS BONDS, TREASURY BILLS, the debts of crown corporations, and Canadian drawings from foreign central banks and from the INTERNATIONAL MONETARY FUND. See also PUBLIC DEBT, which consists of the debts of all levels of government.

National Design Council A federal advisory body created in 1961 to encourage Canadian industry to pay more attention to the distinctive design of its products and to encourage the development of a strong industrial-design industry in Canada. The council believes that distinctive Canadian designs will lead to a more competitive Canadian manufacturing industry, and hence boost output and employment. It reports to the minister of INDUSTRY, TRADE AND COMMERCE.

National Energy Board (NEB) One of Canada's most important regulatory agencies, created in 1959 to ensure that Canada's energy needs were properly met. It conducts regular hearings on the supply and demand for oil and natural gas, to see whether Canada has sufficient supplies for its own needs and to determine whether there is an exportable surplus. It administers Canada's oil-export program; it holds hearings for natural-gas export licences and determines who gets the licences, and under what conditions, if there is a gas surplus. It was also responsible for the administration of the NATIONAL OIL POLICY from 1961 to 1974; under the PETROLEUM ADMINISTRATION ACT of 1975, it administers the export tax on Canadian oil and the export price of Canadian gas. It holds hearings on the construction of oil and gas pipelines that cross provincial or international boundaries, to determine the availability of supplies to justify a new or expanded pipeline, the environmental safety of the pipeline, and the need for the pipeline. It may raise other public-interest questions about the pipeline and can set down conditions for Canadian content and financing. It also holds hearings on pipeline tariff changes and other oil and gas questions, such as the location of liquefied-natural-gas plants. The board must also approve the import or export of electricity and the construction of transmission lines to carry imports or exports. On all such questions, it makes a recommendation, which the cabinet is free to overrule. As a separate responsibility, it is required to advise the government, through the minister of ENERGY, MINES AND RESOURCES, on energy policy generally, including energy relations with the United States, and to make recommendations whenever it feels it should.

National Farm Products Marketing Council An advisory body created in 1972, under the FARM PRODUCTS MARKETING AGENCIES ACT, to advise the federal minister of AGRICULTURE on the most effective ways of using FARM MARKETING BOARDS in interprovincial and export trade. It consults with farmers, consumer groups, provincial and national marketing boards, and the federal and provincial governments, on the operation of marketing boards and the identification of possible new marketing boards.

National Farmers Union A national organization of farmers established in 1969 through a merger of provincial organizations, some of which dated back to the late nineteenth century. Unlike the CANADIAN FEDERATION OF AGRICULTURE, the National Farmers Union restricts its membership to farmers and does not permit other agricultural interests to become members. It acts as a spokesman for farmers. Its headquarters are in Saskatoon.

National Harbours Board (NHB) A federal board created in 1935 to administer most of Canada's major ports, including St. John's, Nfld., Halifax, St. John, N.B., Quebec, Montreal, Sept-Isles, Que., Churchill, Vancouver, and Prince Rupert. See also HARBOUR COMMISSION.

National Health and Welfare, Department of A federal government department created in 1944 to administer Canada's social-welfare and health programs. It has been responsible for the introduction of family allowances, hospital insurance, medicare, the CANADA PENSION PLAN, the CANADA ASSISTANCE PLAN, and limited forms of a guaranteed annual income for Canadians. Its welfare division runs the Canada Pension Plan, old-age pensions and the guaranteed-income supplement for pensioners, the Canada Assistance Plan, and family allowances, and is responsible for research into income-maintenance and income-redistribution policies and pension reform. Its health division is responsible for drug and food safety, including the Food and Drug Act, the maintenance of minimum standards of hospital and medical care across Canada, the health care of native peoples, and federal environmental-health concerns. The minister is responsible for the Medical Research Council, which allocates federal medical-research funds to Canadian universities and hospitals. An advisory body, the National Council of Welfare, advises the minister on social-security needs.

National Housing Act (NHA) The principal housing legislation of the federal government, the purposes of which are to maintain an adequate flow of mortgage funds into housing at reasonable rates by insuring mortgages or new housing, to help finance rental housing for low-income and elderly Canadians and for students, to assist average wage-earners to buy houses through various mortgage subsidies and other such schemes, and to provide government assistance, in the form of loans and grants, to assemble and service land for housing and to assist public housing, non-profit housing, and neighbourhood improvements. The act is administered by CANADA MORTGAGE AND HOUSING CORPORATION. The original housing legislation was contained in the Dominion Housing Act of 1935. The first National Housing Act was passed in 1938. It has been completely revised and amended many times since then.

national income and expenditure accounts An important part of the SYSTEM OF NATIONAL ACCOUNTS, consisting of a combined statement of GROSS NATIONAL PRODUCT and GROSS NATIONAL EXPENDITURE, produced by Statistics Canada. The combined statement shows all the different sources of national income, such as wages and salaries, corporate profits, farm and small-business income, dividend and other investment income, and other factors that make up gross national product, along with all the various forms of spending in the economy, by consumers, government, and investors, including business investment in new facilities, exports, and imports, which together make up gross national expenditure.

national oil policy Canada's oil policy, which designates which parts of the country should be served by domestic oil and which parts by imported oil. The original policy, announced on 1 February 1961, set production targets of 625,000 barrels a day by mid-1961, rising to 800,000 barrels a day by 1963. The policy rejected proposals for extending the oil-pipeline system from western Canada beyond the Ontario border to Montreal. Instead, it drew a line down the Ottawa River valley, banning the sale of foreign oil west of the Ottawa valley in Ontario, and reserving oil markets east of the line in Quebec and the Atlantic provinces for foreign oil. Since the price of foreign oil was low, it was felt that eastern Canada should not have to buy more costly oil from Alberta and Saskatchewan; it was left to Ontario and the United States to help develop western Canada's oil industry by providing a market. Instead of a pipeline to Montreal, increased sales of western Canadian oil would have to be made through increased exports to the United States.

This oil policy continued until 1973. On 6 December 1973, a new national oil policy was announced, which included a plan to extend Canada's oil pipeline into Montreal and, eventually, to Halifax. So far, the line has been extended only to Montreal, and plans to extend it as far as Halifax have been dropped. Under the new policy, Canada was to have a single-price oil policy, with the Canadian oil price below the international price; a tax on oil exported to the United States and general federal tax revenues were to be used to subsidize the cost of imported oil in eastern Canada. Plans were also announced to establish a Canadian company in the oil and gas industry to operate in all phases of the industry, from exploration to refining and marketing. See also PETRO-CANADA.

National Policy The nation-building policies of the Canadian government following Confederation in 1867. The government's purpose was to create an east-west transcontinental economy that could counter the north-south pull of the much stronger U.S. economy, and could develop the economic basis for a separate Canadian nation. The National Policy implied an active role for government in creating the conditions under which a separate Canadian nation and economy could develop. The three principal elements of the National Policy were: **1.** The construction of the Canadian Pacific Railway, under Canadian control, across the prairies to the Pacific coast. **2.** Mass settlement of the prairies, made possible by generous land grants and an open-door policy on immigration, to ensure Canadian sovereignty and to provide an economic reason for the railway to exist. **3.** The Protective Tariff of 1879, introduced after the depression of 1876–79, to foster the growth of the Canadian manufacturing industry and, by discouraging imports from the United States, to encourage east-west trade in Canada. See also DOMINION LANDS POLICY.

National Research Council (NRC) A federal body created in 1916 to carry out scientific research and engineering and to finance and encourage scientific activities in Canadian universities and industry. In addition to pure research in its own science laboratories, the council carries out research into problems of national concern and develops scientific standards—for building codes and durability of basic materials, for example. It provides scholarships to promising young scientists. The council also plays a major role in disseminating scientific information; one of its activities is the Canadian Institute for Scientific and Technical Information. It operates a subsidiary, CANADIAN PATENTS AND DEVELOPMENT LIMITED, which makes council inventions available to would-be users. The council is run by a president, three vice-presidents, and a board of seventeen, picked from universities, industry, and unions.

National Revenue, Department of The federal government department that collects taxes, customs revenues, Canada Pension Plan and unemployment-insurance premiums, and other federal levies. The department also interprets the application of tax laws for the government of Canada, directs inquiries into tax evasion, and carries out certain import-valuation duties for the government, including preliminary investigations into cases of alleged DUMPING. The department is divided into two principal branches: Customs and Excise, and Taxation. The department has twenty-eight district taxation offices from coast to coast and computerized tax-processing centres in Ottawa and Winnipeg. It also maintains customs offices at all ports of entry, including highway border points, airports, and ports.

national union A union that operates only in Canada; as opposed to an INTERNATIONAL UNION, which recruits members on both sides of the border. The major national unions in Canada are the Canadian Union of Public Employees, the Public Service Alliance, and the Canadian Paperworkers' Union. Most national unions are affiliated with the CANADIAN LABOUR CONGRESS, but some are affiliated with the CONFEDERATION OF NATIONAL TRADE UNIONS or the CONFEDERATION OF CANADIAN UNIONS.

nationalization The takeover of a privately owned corporation by the government so that it can be operated as a publicly owned corporation. Compensation is normally, although not always, paid. In most countries it is paid at FAIR MARKET VALUE, but in some countries it may be set artificially low. Examples in Canada include the takeover of private power companies in Quebec and British Columbia during the 1960s and the takeover of potash mines by Saskatchewan in the 1970s. Nationalization does not include all sales of private companies to a government; it consists of those cases in which the government identifies a company that it wants and acquires it, even though the owner may not want to sell it.

native claims Claims by native groups for recognition of rights and interests in lands across Canada, including the North. Their claims are based on their traditional use and occupancy, or are made for re-negotiation of their rights under treaties already negotiated with the Crown. Aboriginal claims are based on the traditional use and occupancy of lands by native groups, such as the Inuit in the North, as opposed to claims based on treaties signed by native groups and the Crown before or after Confederation where there is disagreement over the meaning of the terms, as it is argued that treaties were signed under duress. Native peoples have a number of issues they want settled, including some form of self-government on the lands claimed, along with recognition of limited sovereignty, the recognition of traditional hunting and fishing rights, the ownership of land, a share of mineral rights, and cash payments. In 1974, the Department of INDIAN AFFAIRS AND NORTHERN DEVELOPMENT formed the Office of Native Claims to represent the government of Canada in negotiations with native groups. In 1975, a settlement with the Cree and Inuit people of the James Bay area was signed. Other claims are under negotiation with the Indians, Inuit, and Métis of the Yukon and Northwest Territories and Indians in other parts of Canada. The native peoples represent less than 2 per cent of Canada's population—about 300,000 Indians and 18,000 Inuit. See also DENE NATION.

natural-gas reserves See ESTABLISHED RESERVES, INITIAL ESTABLISHED RESERVES, REMAINING ESTABLISHED RESERVES, ULTIMATE POTENTIAL RESERVES.

natural increase The difference between the CRUDE BIRTH RATE and the CRUDE DEATH RATE.

natural monopoly Industries in which the basic investment costs are so high that it does not pay for more than one firm to supply the product or service—a telephone company, for example, an electricity utility, or a natural-gas pipeline. It is much cheaper for the existing firm to increase its output or to lower its prices slightly than for a second firm to make the capital investment necessary to compete. Natural monopolies tend to be regulated, to protect the public against excessively high prices.

natural resources The living and non-living elements of man's environment that can be used to sustain life and to produce goods and services. These include mineral deposits, fish and wildlife, fertile soil, water for electric power, agriculture, and transportation. Natural resources are usually classified as renewable resources (examples would be timber, fish, and water), which means that they reproduce themselves in reasonably short order or can be used over and over again; or as non-renewable resources (an example would be mineral deposits), which means that, once used, they cannot readily be replaced. A natural resource is of no value if there is no known use for it; if a use is discovered, it has utility or value. Similarly, the size of reserves of various natural resources depends on the costs of exploitation and their use; if the cost of iron ore is, say, $100 a ton, and it would cost $150 a ton to mine a particular ore-body, then the ore-body is of no use. Man can sometimes offset a decline in one natural resource by developing a natural or synthetic substitute; during the Second World War, for example, synthetic rubber was developed as a replacement for natural rubber.

near bank A financial institution that possesses almost all of the characteristics of a chartered bank, including the taking of deposits and making of loans, except that it cannot borrow from the BANK OF CANADA as a lender of last resort and is not subject to the regulations of the BANK ACT. Near banks include federally and provincially incorporated trust companies, caisses populaires, and credit unions.

near money An asset that can be used to settle a debt but is not legal tender. Examples include CANADA SAVINGS BONDS and TREASURY BILLS. Near money is not included in definitions of MONEY SUPPLY.

negative income tax A system of social assistance that uses the tax system to determine the benefits a person receives. It can be used to replace income-maintenance and other social-welfare programs and to provide benefits to special groups, such as the working poor. The tax return is used as a form of means test. Just as the progressive tax system imposes an increasing marginal rate of taxation on increasing levels of taxable income, so a negative income tax would include a negative marginal tax rate below a defined poverty line, so that people with income below that line would be paid money to raise their income to the poverty-line level. The amount would depend on the gap between their income and the defined poverty line. A person with no income would get 100 per cent of the poverty-line amount.

Two of the advantages of the negative income tax are that it provides a single system of assistance and therefore is much easier and cheaper to administer; and that it includes, unlike many direct forms of social assistance, an incentive for a person with a low income to work, since the income he earns just above the poverty line would be taxed at a low marginal rate. This would leave him with most of his earned income, so he would be better off than if he did not work. A key question in such a system would be the level chosen for the poverty line. If it were quite low, it would provide little assistance to the working poor and other groups. If it were fairly high, then it would be a major exercise in income redistribution.

negligence A form of TORT or civil action to recover damages from someone who has failed to carry out his legal responsibility to take reasonable care to prevent death, injury, or financial loss of another person. For example, a building owner who fails to put salt or sand on ice outside his building during winter is liable to a negligence action if a passerby slips and injures himself.

negotiability The ability to transfer ownership of a cheque, promissory note, bond, or other financial paper by endorsing it over or delivering it directly to another person. The new owner acquires full legal title to the money that the financial paper represents.

neoclassical economics The school of economics that flourished in the late nineteenth and early twentieth centuries, and held sway until it was challenged by KEYNESIAN ECONOMICS in the 1930s. The neoclassical school, in its economic model, assumed that the economy would normally operate at full employment, and that any deviation would be temporary because the economic system was self-adjusting. It assumed that full employment was the normal condition because it assumed that all national income would be spent; hence, ongoing unemployment was impossible. It also assumed that, if economic activity declined and unemployment increased, wage rates would fall, thus raising the demand for workers and reducing unemployment. It assumed as well conditions of PERFECT COMPETITION and that government, by adjusting interest rates through its monetary policy, could always ensure an adequate flow of savings and investment.

Neoclassical economists introduced mathematics into the study of economics and began the study of what is today known as MICROECONOMICS. While they emphasized, as the classical economists had done, the role of market forces in allocating resources and setting prices, the neoclassical economists acknowledged that market imperfections could exist, and studied small groups, such as firms and households, to understand the decision-making process and to find ways to correct market imperfections. Neoclassical economists also studied the relationships among different sectors of the economy, and how resources were allocated in the free-market economy. The leading economists in the neoclassical school included ALFRED MARSHALL of Britain, Leon Walras of Switzerland, John Bates Clark of the United States, Eugen von Bohm-Bawerk of Austria, and Knut Wicksell of Sweden.

neo-Malthusianism The view that, while THOMAS ROBERT MALTHUS (1766–1834) was correct in his belief that population growth would outpace increases in food production, he was wrong in his belief that moral restraint and later marriages were the only acceptable means to counter rising population. Neo-Malthusians advocate policies of birth control to check population growth.

neo-mercantilism A term used by free-market economists who see a revival of MERCANTILIST policies in modern plans to develop industry by adopting various non-tariff barriers, including subsidies, to strengthen domestic firms or even to limit FOREIGN DIRECT INVESTMENT. The term was coined by Canadian economist Harry Johnson, who argued that modern industrial policies to strengthen industries based on new technologies through various forms of government support were simply old-fashioned protectionism in new clothes.

net asset value The value of total assets of a corporation remaining after total liabilities have been deducted.

net economic welfare A measure developed by two U.S. economists, James Tobin and William Nordhaus, to give a better estimate of standard of living than the usual measure of per capita gross national product. They add to the gross national product an estimate for the value of leisure, represented by the decline in the work week, and for the value of work performed by housewives in the home. At the same time, certain parts of the gross national product, such as the costs of fighting pollution or crime, are deducted from the gross national product. The gross national product by itself fails to measure such non-monetary gains as more leisure time; it also treats the costs of dealing with such social problems as prisons, for example, as contributions to economic growth.

net income The profit of a company after all of its expenses, including taxes, depreciation, and interest on long-term debt, have been deducted. It is the money available to pay dividends to shareholders and to reinvest in the expansion of the firm.

net investment The net change in capital formation in a country or firm. Net investment indicates whether the productive resources of the economy or firm have increased or declined after the cost of replacing obsolete or worn-out equipment has been taken into account. It is calculated in GROSS-NATIONAL-EXPENDITURE statistics by subtracting capital-cost allowances or depreciation from gross fixed-capital formation or capital investment.

net loss The loss of a company after all of its expenses, including taxes, depreciation, and interest on long-term debt, have been deducted from its revenues.

net national income The total flow of income earned in the economy by labour, capital, and land. Net national income consists of wages, salaries, and other labour income, military pay and allowances, corporation profits before taxes but minus dividends paid to non-residents, interest and other investment income, accrued net income of farmers from farm operations, and the net income of non-farm unincorporated businesses, including rent and changes in the value of inventories. If INDIRECT TAXES and depreciation (capital-cost allowances) are added to net national income, the result is GROSS NATIONAL PRODUCT. Net national-income statistics, produced quarterly by Statistics Canada, are sometimes used to analyze changes in the distribution of income among labour, business, and other groups in the economy.

net present value The total costs and revenues expected for an investment project over the life of the project, adjusted or discounted so that future cash inflows and outflows are expressed in their PRESENT VALUE. For example, future revenue from a project, to be expressed in terms of its present value, is discounted to reflect current interest rates and risk; a dollar earned five years from now, for example, would be worth less than a dollar today and therefore, in this form of investment analysis, might have a net present value of, perhaps, seventy-five cents. Net present value is an important analytical tool for corporations and others in making investment choices; faced with several possible projects, investors will choose the one with the highest net present value or reject all the projects if the rate of return is less than prevailing interest rates. In such a situation, they would be better off to invest their money in government bonds or other financial securities. See also DISCOUNTED CASH FLOW.

net price The price paid after all discounts have been deducted.

net profit See NET INCOME.

net reproduction rate A measure of population change; the number of daughters, expressed per thousand women, that the current generation of women in their child-bearing years will have during those years, based on current age-specific fertility and mortality rates. It is thus a projection of the number of women there will be in the next generation, or the female reproduction rate. A net reproduction rate greater than 1:1 means that the population should increase; of less than 1:1, that it should decline; and at unity or 1:1, should remain stationary.

net worth The value of the remaining assets after a firm's or a person's liabilities have been deducted from total assets. In a company, the net worth of the firm is calculated on the balance sheet by deducting total liabilities from total assets, to yield what is known as SHAREHOLDERS' EQUITY, or net worth. This is what the shareholders would get if the company was wound up. A similar calculation can be made for an individual by adding together such assets as his home, pension-plan contributions, savings, assets such as furniture, car, and cottage, and any other assets, and then deducting liabilities, such as the unpaid balance on a mortgage and outstanding loans and consumer debt.

New Brunswick Royal Commission on Finance and Municipal Taxation A royal commission appointed in 1962, headed by E.G. Byrne, which reported its recommendations in 1964. It proposed sweeping changes to municipal finance in the province, including having the province take over all the costs of education, public health, hospital services, social assistance, and justice, and the adoption of a uniform tax code throughout the province. The province-wide code would include a provincial property tax for education, greater reliance by the province on the retail-sales tax to finance local responsibilities, a new automobile tax, and the complete renegotiation of tax concessions to industry. Money for local purposes would be raised in a property-tax system based on MARKET-VALUE ASSESSMENT. The commission also proposed a substantial consolidation of local governments and school boards, reducing their number by more than half. The provincial government followed up on many of the recommendations. It was the first province to reorganize completely its system of municipal finance and taxation in the postwar period.

New Deal See BENNETT NEW DEAL.

new economics A term used to describe economic policies introduced in the United States in the early 1960s. These policies included efforts to fine-tune economic performance and the use of a major tax cut to stimulate the economy when there was already a budget deficit.

new international economic order (NIEO) Proposals by the LESS-DEVELOPED COUNTRIES for a substantial change in their economic relations with the industrialized world, including Canada. The less-developed countries maintain that significant changes are necessary if they are to achieve a rate of economic growth sufficient to solve their problems of poverty and to improve the standard of living of their people. They complain that the world is divided into exporters of commodities (the less-developed countries) and the exporters of manufactured goods (the developed countries); that the terms of trade work against them; that they are too dependent on the industrial world for the finance needed for development, a fact that they say is burdening them with an excessive load of debt and a need to earn increasing amounts of foreign exchange simply to pay interest; and that they are forced to depend on the growth rate of the industrial world for their own economic growth. In their view, the political colonialism of the past has been replaced by economic colonialism, with the industrial countries holding down the price of raw materials while charging increasingly higher prices for manufactured goods. They further complain that the trade policies of the industrial countries restrict their ability to export, because industrial countries have low tariffs on raw materials but higher tariffs and quotas on manufactured imports from the less-developed countries. They want much better access for their manufactured products, sharply increased flows of foreign aid, full control over their natural resources, including prices that at least keep pace with the rising costs of manufactured imports, renegotiation or elimination of much of their outstanding debt, and a greater role in determining the policies of the INTERNATIONAL MONETARY FUND, the GENERAL AGREEMENT ON TARIFFS AND TRADE, and other international bodies.

The formation of the UNITED NATIONS CONFERENCE ON TRADE AND DEVELOPMENT (UNCTAD) was an early effort by the less-developed countries to try to get a better economic deal. It was followed, in 1974, by the adoption of two resolutions by the U.N. General Assembly setting out new principles for economic co-operation on trade, aid, debt management, and other concerns. See also CONFERENCE ON INTERNATIONAL ECONOMIC CO-OPERATION, CHARTER OF ECONOMIC RIGHTS AND DUTIES OF STATES.

new issue The raising of new long-term capital by the sale to investors of common shares, preferred shares, or bonds. The sale may be made directly to the public or through a PRIVATE PLACEMENT to institutional investors. If it is to be sold to the public, the issue must first be approved by a provincial SECURITIES COMMISSION. See also PRIMARY DISTRIBUTION.

new orders See MANUFACTURERS' NEW ORDERS, SHIPMENTS, AND INVENTORIES.

New Principles for International Business Federal government guidelines for good corporate behaviour by foreign-controlled subsidiaries in Canada, tabled in the House of Commons on 18 July 1975. They replaced the 1966 guidelines, the GUIDING PRINCIPLES OF GOOD CORPORATE BEHAVIOUR. The new guidelines, like the ones they replaced, represented government policy and had been approved by cabinet. According to the new guidelines, foreign-controlled firms doing business in Canada should: **1.** Pursue a high degree of autonomy in decision-making and risk-taking functions, including innovative activity in the marketing of resulting new products. **2.** Develop as an integral part of the Canadian operation an autonomous capability for technological innovation, including research and development, engineering, and industrial design and preproduction activities. **3.** Retain in Canada a sufficient share of earnings to give strong financial support to the growth and entrepreneurial potential of the Canadian operation. **4.** Strive for a full international mandate for innovation in market development, when it would enable the Canadian company to improve its efficiency by specializing collective operations. **5.** Aggressively pursue and develop market opportunities throughout international markets. **6.** Extend the processing in Canada of natural-resource products to the maximum extent feasible on an economic basis. **7.** Search out and develop economic sources of supply in Canada for domestically produced goods and for professional and other services. **8.** Foster a Canadian outlook among management, as well as larger career opportunities within Canada. **9.** Create a financial structure that provides opportunity for substantial equity participation in the Canadian enterprise by the Canadian public. **10.** Pursue a pricing policy designed to ensure a fair and reasonable return to the company and to Canada for all goods and services sold abroad, including sales to parent companies and other affiliates. **11.** Regularly publish information on the operations and financial position of the firm. **12.** Give appropriate support to recognized national objectives and established government programs, while resisting any direct or indirect pressures from foreign governments or associated companies to act in a contrary manner. **13.** Participate in Canadian social and cultural life, and support those institutions that are concerned with the intellectual, social, and cultural advancement of the Canadian community. **14.** Endeavour to ensure that access to foreign resources, including technology and know-how, is not associated with terms and conditions that restrain the firm from observing these principles.

New York Stock Exchange (NYSE) The world's leading stock exchange, based on Wall Street in New York.

newly industrialized countries (NICs) A term describing LESS-DEVELOPED COUNTRIES in the process of rapid industrialization but whose per capita income is still too low to include them among the DEVELOPED COUNTRIES. A large portion of the exports of the newly industrialized countries consists of industrial products such as electrical machinery, consumer goods, and steel and wood products. Examples include Brazil, Greece, Hong Kong, Mexico, Portugal, Singapore, Spain, Taiwan, and Yugoslavia.

no-fault automobile insurance A system of automobile insurance in which there is, in the courts, no determination of blame for an automobile accident before payments for bodily harm and perhaps automobile damages are made by insurance companies. In most provinces, the courts, under the TORT system, have to determine who is responsible for an accident before damages can be paid. Under a no-fault system, the court hearing is not needed, so there are significant savings in legal and other costs. Each person in the accident is recompensed according to the bodily damages suffered, but according to some set of schedules—for example, $250 for a broken wrist. Everyone is treated in the same way regardless of income, wealth, or occupation, and the courts are used to seek damages only in cases of death or serious injury. The elimination of fault has to be voted by a provincial legislature before a no-fault scheme can be introduced. Saskatchewan brought in the world's first no-fault system of automobile insurance in 1946. Quebec introduced a similar plan in 1978.

no par value Common shares that have no face value. When they are first sold to the public, a price is set by the underwriters, in line with what investors are believed to be willing to pay. The value of such shares depends on total SHAREHOLDERS' EQUITY divided by the number of common shares outstanding.

nominal price **1.** The estimated price of a commodity or product for which there is no recent price. **2.** The face value of a bond or preferred share, which may differ from the market price.

nominal yield The interest or dividends received on a bond or preferred share, expressed as a percentage of its face or par value. The nominal yield may differ from its actual yield, which is a percentage of the market value.

nominee holding The purchase and holding of shares, land, or other assets in the name of a stockbroker, bank, or trust company, rather than in the name of the actual owner. Sometimes nominee holdings are established to conceal the identity of the true owner. For example, developers trying to assemble a large parcel of land from a variety of different owners may use this approach, employing several real-estate brokers, to avoid speculation and a sharp increase in price.

non-durable goods Consumer goods that have only a short life, such as food products, clothing, drugs, toiletries, and the like.

non-negotiable A bond, debenture, or other security whose ownership cannot be changed simply by an endorsement on the back of the certificate or by delivery to the would-be buyer.

non-price competition The type of competition that occurs in an OLIGOPOLISTIC industry. Competition is not based on price-cutting but on advertising, contests, packaging, giveaways, design, and various other techniques of product differentiation. Sometimes such competition can lead to improved products or services, but it may mean that consumers end up paying more than they would if there were price competition.

non-profit corporation A corporation formed to carry out a charitable, educational, religious, social, or environmental activity for the benefit of its members or of the public at large, and that is not expected to operate at a profit. Such corporations may depend for income on public donations; with approval from the Department of NATIONAL REVENUE, such donations are tax-deductible. Non-profit corporations are usually tax-exempt if they show a surplus and may get certain other tax exemptions—from sales and property taxes, for example.

non-recurring expense An unusual expense in a business, such as a large payment in a lawsuit, clean-up costs in an unexpected environmental accident, or loss of a plant or mine due to an earthquake, revolution, or other such event.

non-renewable resource A natural resource that cannot be replaced within a reasonable period of time. The most common non-renewable resources are oil, natural gas, coal, uranium, and metal minerals; all of them were formed more than one hundred million years ago. See also RENEWABLE RESOURCES.

non-tariff barrier (NTB) A government policy designed to discourage or block imports. As tariff rates have declined in importance, non-tariff barriers have become a more important protectionist device, although the Tokyo Round of the GENERAL AGREEMENT ON TARIFFS AND TRADE, completed in 1979, reduced non-tariff barriers to some extent. Examples of non-tariff barriers include quotas on imports; government regulations written to accommodate domestic producers but to exclude imports (for example, restrictive food and drug laws, or engineering, environmental, and safety standards); government purchasing policies that favour domestic producers; agricultural subsidies and marketing arrangements; the tying of foreign aid, so that recipients have to use the money in the donor country; and subsidies to encourage import substitution, or to underwrite exports. See also NEO-MERCANTILISM.

non-voting shares Common shares in a corporation that do not include the right to vote, but share, with voting common shares, the right to dividends. Non-voting shares are not widely used. Their main purpose is to enable a company to raise additional equity capital, while allowing the existing owners of the firm to retain their control. For investors, such shares have less appeal, since they offer little say in a firm's affairs and are of no consequence in a takeover bid for a company.

North Atlantic Treaty Organization (NATO) A mutual-defence treaty among Canada, the United States, and the nations of Western Europe, signed in 1949. Article two in the treaty is known as the Canadian article. It encouraged economic co-operation among NATO members, and was seen by the Canadian government as a way to reduce Canada's economic dependence on the United States and to reduce the capacity of the United States for unilateral economic-policy measures. In a broader forum, such as NATO, Canada hoped to exert a greater influence on U.S. policies than it could in BILATERAL discussions. The article was another expression of Canada's MULTILATERAL approach to economic problems after the Second World War.

North-South dialogue The ongoing discussions between the rich, industrialized nations of the northern hemisphere, including Canada, and the poor, less-developed countries of the southern hemisphere, over a NEW INTERNATIONAL ECONOMIC ORDER. These discussions were formally organized at the Conference on International Economic Co-operation in 1975–77, but also take place in the UNITED NATIONS CONFERENCE ON TRADE AND DEVELOPMENT, the INTERNATIONAL MONETARY FUND, the INTERNATIONAL BANK FOR RECONSTRUCTION AND DEVELOPMENT (World Bank), and the GENERAL AGREEMENT ON TARIFFS AND TRADE. The Communist nations do not participate in the dialogue; they contend that the plight of the poor countries is the result of colonialism by the capitalist countries.

North-South Institute A non-profit organization formed in Canada in 1976 to conduct research into international development and aid issues from a Canadian perspective. It has studied Canadian efforts in dealing with world food problems and with the debt problems of the less-developed countries; it has conducted evaluations of Canadian aid in the form of skim milk and commodity trade, and of Canada's performance in the North-South debate. It also publishes an annual overview of aid and development issues, and does contract research work for agencies such as the CANADIAN INTERNATIONAL DEVELOPMENT AGENCY and the INTERNATIONAL BANK FOR RECONSTRUCTION AND DEVELOPMENT (IBRD), or World Bank. It is funded by private foundations, private industry, and government. It is based in Ottawa.

northern-tier refineries Oil refineries located in U.S. states along the Canadian border that were originally built to use Canadian oil and therefore have priority in the export of Canadian oil.

Northern Pipeline Agency A federal agency established in 1978 to implement the Northern Pipeline Act, passed by Parliament in April 1978. Its establishment followed the September 1977 Canada-U.S. agreement on the construction of a natural-gas pipeline from Alaska and the Canadian far North to U.S. and Canadian markets. The Northern Pipeline Act implemented the terms of the Canadian-U.S. agreement, provided a CERTIFICATE OF PUBLIC CONVENIENCE AND NECESSITY to the pipeline company for the Canadian portions of the project, and contained provisions to ensure energy, industrial, and economic benefits for Canada and to reduce social and environmental damage from the project. The legislation also created the pipeline agency to co-ordinate and supervise pipeline activities, according to the law, and to act as the single regulatory agency responsible for the project. The regulatory and administrative powers exercised by other government agencies and departments have been delegated to it.

Northwest Atlantic Fisheries Organization (NAFO) A successor to the International Convention for the North Atlantic Fisheries, which Canada had signed in 1949. NAFO has its headquarters in Halifax-Dartmouth and held its first meeting in March 1979. Its purpose is to supervise the level of fishing in the Northwest Atlantic, to allocate shares of quotas beyond Canada's two-hundred-mile zone, and to adopt and implement fisheries-conservation and -research programs. Members include Canada, the United States, the Soviet Union, East Germany, Portugal, the European Economic Community, Cuba, and Bulgaria.

not-sufficient-funds (nsf) cheque A cheque that a bank refuses to honour and returns to the payee because there are not sufficient funds in the account to pay the cheque. Banks impose a penalty on the person writing the cheque, in the form of a handling fee. Because such situations can arise from a miscalculation by a customer, most banks recognize that they have an obligation to try to reach the customer before they return the cheque to the payee, so that the customer can make other arrangements to pay it.

notary A provincially appointed official who can administer oaths, certify copies of documents, take depositions, and carry out other such public responsibilities.

note Evidence of a debt and a promise to pay issued by a borrower, such as a corporation or government agency. Depending on the terms and conditions, notes may be negotiable—that is, they can be sold at a discount to third parties, and they may be payable to the bearer or to the person named in the note.

notes to financial statements A series of footnotes in a company annual report that need to be read along with the figures presented in the company's EARNINGS STATEMENT and BALANCE SHEET in order for its financial affairs to be fully understood. These notes include many important details, such as information on company accounting practices, the treatment of income from affiliated companies, the valuation of fixed assets and goodwill, an explanation of long-term debt, details on the remuneration of officers and directors, intercorporate transactions, information on the company's tax position, details of any lawsuits that might affect the company's profits, the treatment of foreign exchange in earnings, stock options and pension benefits for senior officers, valuation of inventories, and details of the company's capital structure. These notes can sometimes be more important to understanding a company's true financial position or future prospects than the actual financial figures in the annual report.

nuclear energy Electricity produced during a controlled nuclear chain-reaction in a nuclear-power reactor.

nuclear safeguards Measures to prevent the spread of nuclear weapons to non-weapons states through controls on the export of nuclear-power technology and fuels. The safeguards were devised by the INTERNATIONAL ATOMIC ENERGY AGENCY, a U.N. body based in Vienna. Countries using nuclear-power systems are required to file regular, detailed reports to the IAEA, and to allow international inspection of their facilities to ensure that there is no diversion of nuclear materials from civilian to military use. The development of the safeguards followed the signing of the Treaty on the Non-Proliferation of Nuclear Weapons in 1968.

Nuclear Suppliers' Group The fifteen principal suppliers of nuclear-power technology, including Canada, who have met annually in London since 1975 to develop stronger safeguards against the misuse of nuclear power and fuel. In 1977, the group agreed on an international code of conduct on nuclear exports. The original seven members were Britain, Canada, France, Japan, the Soviet Union, the United States, and West Germany. Since 1975, Belgium, Czechoslovakia, East Germany, Italy, the Netherlands, Poland, Sweden, and Switzerland have joined.

nugget A piece of precious metal, such as gold, usually found in rivers and streams, that has been worn down by water.

nuisance tax A tax that raises little revenue but causes considerable work for those who must pay it. For example, a one per cent tariff might produce almost no revenue, but importers would still have to go through a certain amount of paperwork to pay it.

numbered bank account A bank account whose owner is identified by number rather than name, thus giving the account a secret identity. Such accounts are common in Switzerland, where only a senior officer of a bank usually knows the identity of the account holders. Because of this facility, Swiss banks have become a favoured haven for hot money, in particular for the funds of criminal elements, corrupt officials, and politicians accumulating funds outside their own country in case they have to leave in a hurry some day. Such Swiss accounts may also be used by Canadians to hide income and wealth and thus illegally evade taxes they should be paying in Canada.

numéraire The standard against which the prices of other currencies or goods are expressed. For example, gold, the U.S. dollar, or SPECIAL DRAWING RIGHTS can be used as a numéraire for expressing the value of other currencies.

obsolescence The reduction in the useful life of an asset, such as productive machinery or a major consumer product, caused by new technology or a switch in consumer tastes rather than by normal wear and tear. In industry, obsolescence often occurs because a new invention enables a competitor to reduce production costs significantly, even though existing productive facilities are still in good working order. Some consumer-goods industries resort to planned obsolescence, either by making frequent product changes or by building a product so that it does not last for as long as it could.

occupational health and safety laws Federal and provincial laws designed to reduce the risk of accidents and disease in industry.

odd lot The sale or purchase of shares in a small or uneven number. Such transactions often require a higher commission because they may be harder to buy or sell than so-called ROUND LOTS of 100. The sale of 85 shares or 115 shares is an odd lot; the sale of any multiple of 100 shares is a round lot.

offer 1. The price a would-be purchaser is willing to pay for a property. In the real-estate industry, an offer to purchase a house, for example, is usually accompanied by a deposit to show that the offer is serious. If the offer is accepted but the would-be purchaser changes his mind, he loses his deposit. **2.** In stock and bond markets, the lowest price at which a person is willing to sell. See also BID.

Office of Native Claims See NATIVE CLAIMS.

Office of the Comptroller General of Canada An office reporting to the president of the TREASURY BOARD, established in 1978 and responsible for improving financial-management practices within the federal government. The comptroller general's role is similar to that of a CONTROLLER in a corporation, setting out the financial-reporting and -control systems, developing financial managers, monitoring the way that financial controls are applied, and revising the system when need be. The office was established in response to complaints from the AUDITOR GENERAL and others over a lack of adequate financial controls within the government to prevent waste in public spending.

official development assistance (ODA) Government financial aid given or lent to less-developed countries on concessionary terms for non-military purposes. Its purpose is to promote the economic development and welfare of the recipient countries; it must either be a grant or a concessionary loan containing a grant element of at least 25 per cent. Thus, ODA consists of multilateral and bilateral financial assistance in the form of grants or soft loans. In 1970, the U.N. DEVELOPMENT DECADE adopted a target of 0.7 per cent of the GNP from each developed country, including Canada, in the form of ODA; the PEARSON COMMISSION made a similar recommendation. In 1970, Canada's aid programs amounted to 0.42 per cent of GNP; in 1978, this figure had reached 0.52 per cent, but in 1980, due to government cutbacks, was expected to fall to 0.40 per cent. See also CANADIAN INTERNATIONAL DEVELOPMENT AGENCY.

offset agreement An agreement in a government contract, in which the supplier of a major item, such as military or civilian aircraft, agrees to carry out industrial work in Canada equivalent to a specific amount of Canadian content, although the actual aircraft or other major equipment to be supplied is to be imported from another country. It usually does not make economic sense to manufacture the actual aircraft or other equipment in Canada, since this would raise the costs significantly. But if the government wants a certain level of CANADIAN CONTENT out of a multi-million-dollar contract, it can insist on production of certain parts or components of the aircraft in Canada for world-wide distribution, or on the supplier setting up an unrelated industrial activity in Canada that meets the desired level of Canadian content. Offset agreements are sought on big contracts because it is felt that Canada should use this government purchasing power to help strengthen its own industrial development, rather than simply pay out the entire sum on imports that benefit the industrial development of other countries.

offshore drilling The drilling for oil or natural gas from drilling platforms erected in Canada's coastal waters.

offshore mineral rights The ownership of mineral-resources rights on the ocean floor along Canada's coastline. This is a matter of dispute between the federal and provincial governments. At stake is the question of who controls exploration and development, and which level of government gets the royalty income from oil, natural-gas, and mineral exploitation. The Supreme Court of Canada, in 1967, ruled that the offshore resources along the Pacific coast belonged to the federal government. But the provinces have been attempting to negotiate full or shared jurisdiction. In 1979 the federal government announced that it would turn over jurisdiction to the provinces, but this may require an amendment to the BRITISH NORTH AMERICA ACT.

oil reserves See ESTABLISHED RESERVES, INITIAL ESTABLISHED RESERVES, REMAINING ESTABLISHED RESERVES, ULTIMATE POTENTIAL RESERVES.

oil sands Deposits of sand and other rock aggregates, that contain a heavy, viscous oil mixture known as crude bitumen. The oil cannot be recovered through oil wells, but has to be mined and processed to separate the oil from the sand and into a form in which it can be used by refineries as an oil interchangeable with conventional crude oil. Western Canada has enormous potential reserves at Athabasca, Buffalo Head Hills, Cold Lake, Peace River, and Wabasca. But large-scale exploitation depends on the development of an effective and economic IN SITU recovery system.

old-age pension See PENSION.

oligopoly An industry in which there are only a few large sellers but many buyers, and which is characterized by limited or intermittent price competition. The main forms of competition consist of advertising, packaging, product differentiation, and servicing. In an oligopolistic industry, each firm is able to calculate the effect of its pricing and production decisions on the other firms. It is possible for tacit collusion to exist in such a situation, possibly through the price leadership exercised by the largest firm. In some oligopolistic industries, the firms may manufacture an identical product, such as steel or petrochemicals, or similar products in which there is considerable product differentiation based on styling or packaging, such as in the refrigerator, automobile, and cigarette industries. Oligopolistic firms tend to be large and require significant capital investment to achieve economies of scale. They are therefore difficult to break up. These high start-up costs or the existence of BARRIERS TO ENTRY usually account for the existence of oligopolies. See also IMPERFECT COMPETITION, CONCENTRATION RATIOS.

oligopsony An industry in which there are only a few large buyers and many sellers, and which therefore allows the buyers to depress the prices that can be earned by the sellers. Examples include big department-store or supermarket chains, which may buy a product, such as women's blouses or bread, from a great many different sellers.

Ontario Economic Council (OEC) An advisory body created by the Ontario government in 1968, consisting of businessmen, union leaders, university economists, and other representatives of the community. The council makes its own recommendations to the government, in published reports. It also assigns research projects to economists, out of a research budget allocated to it by the provincial government, to investigate questions that the council believes to be of great importance. Much of its activity to date has been in the area of public finance and the examination of the province's future economic prospects. The council is based in Toronto.

Ontario Energy Board An Ontario regulatory agency whose principal activities are to regulate natural-gas prices and to review Ontario Hydro electricity rates. The board was established in 1960 as a successor agency to the Ontario Fuel Board. The board regulates natural-gas utility rates, approves the construction and expropriation of land for natural-gas pipelines wholly within the province, designates gas-storage areas, reviews Ontario Hydro plans for electricity-rate increases if the minister of energy so wishes, and reviews other energy-policy questions on reference from the minister of energy (a recent example is a review of the cost and pricing policies of Ontario Hydro). The board holds public hearings, and is based in Toronto.

Ontario Energy Corporation A government-owned energy company created by Ontario in 1974 to invest in oil, natural gas, and other energy projects. It held Ontario's 5 per cent interest in Syncrude Canada Limited, a major tar-sands project, which it sold in 1978. Other major investments include participation in the Polar Gas natural-gas-pipeline project for the Arctic, and funding of by-product heat projects—the use of by-product heat for power plants to heat commercial greenhouses and fish farms, for example. The purpose of the corporation is to invest in energy projects anywhere in Canada or elsewhere, to increase the supply of energy in Ontario, to stimulate the exploration for and development of sources of energy, to stimulate the expansion of the capability to produce energy, and to encourage and invest in energy-conservation projects.

Ontario Municipal Board (OMB) An Ontario government agency made up of officials appointed to supervise the activities of Ontario municipalities. It must approve many municipal actions, such as zoning changes, official plans, subdivision plans, restricted-area bylaws, municipal capital spending, changes in boundaries, and changes in municipal charters. Its decisions can be appealed to the Ontario cabinet.

Ontario Securities Commission (OSC) The principal provincial securities commission in Canada, which regulates the securities industry in the province with the purpose of protecting the investing public. Its responsibilities include the registration and approval of all securities, such as common shares, preferred shares, and bonds, to the public; the registration of salesmen, investment counsellors, and others in the securities industry; the maintenance of up-to-date records of INSIDER TRADING and other corporate disclosures; the regulation of the TORONTO STOCK EXCHANGE; the supervision of MUTUAL FUNDS; and the regulation of COMMODITY-FUTURES trading. The OSC, which is based in Toronto, was first established in 1928, but has acted as a full-time regulatory agency only since broader securities legislation was passed in 1945.

Ontario White Paper on Tax Reform A 1969 Ontario government white paper that proposed sweeping changes in the provincial tax system. Its major proposals included a new provincial income-tax system; the use of tax credits to replace various income-maintenance or welfare schemes, leading to a guaranteed annual income; introduction of a capital-gains tax; the assumption by the province of a greater share of municipal costs, including local school costs currently paid out of property-tax revenues; and reform of the property-tax system, by introducing MARKET-VALUE ASSESSMENT.

open-cut mine A mine that is open at the surface, as opposed to a mine that is worked deep underground and can only be worked by sinking a shaft and operating through a network of underground tunnels.

open economy An economy in which there is a high inflow and outflow of trade and investment relative to the size of the gross national product. A smaller country like Canada is more likely to be an open economy, since it lacks the internal market to produce or consume many of the types of goods and services that are needed. A big country like the Soviet Union is less likely to be an open economy, since it is not as dependent on foreign markets or foreign sources of supply.

open-end investment company See MUTUAL FUND.

open-market operations Action by the Bank of Canada to influence interest rates and thus to help implement MONETARY POLICY by buying and selling government securities, such as government bonds and treasury bills. The purpose of these sales and purchases is to alter the level of cash reserves in the banking system, thereby altering the ability of the chartered banks to make loans, to purchase securities, and thus to finance the expansion of the economy. By selling government securities, the Bank of Canada reduces the cash reserves of the banking system, and hence its lending ability, while raising interest rates, thus encouraging Canadians to save rather than spend. Interest rates are raised because the increased supply of government securities reduces their face value, which raises their effective yield. By purchasing government securities from the banking system, the Bank of Canada increases the cash reserves, thereby increasing the lending ability of the chartered banks. It also lowers interest rates and increases money supply by encouraging spending instead of saving. Rates are lowered because the central bank has reduced the supply of outstanding securities, thus raising their face value and lowering their effective yield or interest rate, and by the effect of the announcement that the bank is entering the market.

open mortgage A MORTGAGE that can be partially or fully paid off at any time without penalty.

open shop A place of employment in which a union is recognized as the bargaining agent for employees, but where new employees are not forced to join the union.

operating company A company that is actively engaged in the production of goods or services, as opposed to an investment or holding company, which may be incorporated for tax or other purposes to hold and make investments.

operating profit The profit from the normal operations of the business, as opposed to an extraordinary gain from an investment or sale of a company-owned asset.

operations research A mathematical technique used to decide the best of a series of alternative courses of action. It originated in the Second World War as an important tool in military planning, but is now widely used by business and government, with the aid of computers, to help reach difficult solutions where there are a great many factors and considerable information to take into account. The firm or government agency using operations research has to define the criteria to be met —profitability, for example, or greatest possible public access. Typical operations-research applications include the best location of manufacturing and distribution centres of a company; inventory management; calculation of the minimum number of boxcars, trucks, or planes a transportation company needs to meet its schedules; planning the number of runways and unloading gates an airport needs; or estimation of the best construction schedule to meet the future needs of an electrical utility.

opportunity cost A term that describes the benefits sacrificed by taking one course of action instead of another. It is an economic rather than an accounting concept, since it measures the costs of not doing something else, whereas accounting measures the costs of what is actually being done. The opportunity cost of taking action A—say, building a shopping centre—is the sacrifice of the profits that would have been made by taking action B—building an office tower instead. Similarly, the income from renting out a paid-for building should at least equal the opportunity cost of selling the building and using the proceeds to make another investment.

Opportunity cost is an important concept in making investment choices and allocating resources. It does not make sense to use a FACTOR OF PRODUCTION—land, labour, capital, technology—for a particular purpose, if it yields less than the opportunity cost of using the factor in some other way. Similarly, it doesn't make sense for a worker to take a job in one industry, when he or she could make more money for the same skills and responsibilities in another industry; opportunity cost is therefore an important consideration in setting wages in different industries. Opportunity cost identifies choices that have to be made, since every factor of production can be said to have an alternative use.

optical character recognition A computer-readable form of type that is read by a scanner and converted into electrical signals, which can be stored in a computer or which can activate a computer. An example is the coding that appears at the bottom of personal and business cheques.

opting out The right of a province not to participate in a federal-provincial shared-cost program; in return, the federal government reduces its income-tax points in the opting-out province so that the province can gain additional income by raising its tax rates. The additional income raised by the province is supposed to match the funds the province would have received from the federal government under the shared-cost program. In 1965, the Established Programs (Interim Arrangements) Act gave all provinces the right to opt out of certain shared-cost programs, and gave them six months to decide; only Quebec exercised the option. The legislation covered hospital insurance, vocational training, and various social-welfare programs, such as payments to the blind and disabled, and payments under the CANADA ASSISTANCE PLAN. The only programs covered under the act now are the allowances for blind and disabled persons and the Canada Assistance Plan.

option A contract in which the owner of a piece of land, building, block of shares, film script, or some other property, agrees to sell the property to another party for a specified price during a specified period of time if the other party decides that he wants to buy it. In return, the buyer of this right or option pays a sum of money, whether the option is exercised or not. The purchaser of an option loses money if he doesn't exercise the option, but this is a small price to pay if it turns out that purchasing the property would have been a poor investment. It is a convenient way of obtaining the right to buy something, and hence to consider an investment without having to put up a lot of money all at once. A property developer, for example, may buy options on adjoining pieces of land with the intention of undertaking a major project. But if the market turns sour or municipal authorities indicate that they will not approve the project, he will not exercise the option.

Options also represent a cheaper way of speculating in the stock and commodities markets. Two types of options can be purchased: a CALL option, which gives the purchaser the right to buy shares or a commodity at a fixed price within a specified period of time; and a PUT option, which allows the purchaser of the option the right to sell someone a fixed number of shares at a fixed price within a specified period of time. The options market has taken on greater importance in Canadian stock markets in recent years.

order-in-council See GOVERNOR-IN-COUNCIL.

ore Various types of rock formations containing minerals that can be extracted economically.

Organization for Economic Co-operation and Development (OECD) An organization of industrial nations, with a permanent staff of officials, established in 1961 to improve trade and investment flows among its members, to help analyze and deal with balance-of-payments and other economic problems, and to co-ordinate foreign-aid policies through a separate DEVELOPMENT ASSISTANCE COMMITTEE (DAC). Its original members were Canada, West Germany, Britain, Ireland, France, Austria, Sweden, Iceland, Denmark, Italy, the United States, Norway, the Netherlands, Turkey, Greece, Belgium, Portugal, Spain, Switzerland, and Luxembourg. Since then Japan, Finland, Australia, and New Zealand have become members, while Yugoslavia has an associate status.

The OECD plays a number of important roles in the world economy. **1.** It attempts to harmonize economic policies among member nations, to check inflation or to achieve better economic growth. **2.** It studies common economic-policy problems, such as inflation, manpower training, taxation, and investment incentives, and recommends possible solutions. **3.** It prepares its own semi-annual forecasts of economic performance, for the OECD as a whole and for individual OECD members, along with policy recommendations. **4.** It carries out comparative studies among OECD members, to see how they deal with specific problems, such as worker retraining, regional development, environmental controls, industrial development, or early retirement, or how they compare, for example, in spending on research and development, unemployment insurance, or social assistance. **5.** It co-ordinates policies among OECD members—in defining a code for behaviour by MULTINATIONAL CORPORATIONS, for example, by establishing ground rules on export subsidies, by dealing with nuclear-energy policies or with restrictive business practices, or by formulating responses for the industrialized world to the demands of the LESS-DEVELOPED COUNTRIES for a NEW INTERNATIONAL ECONOMIC ORDER.

The finance ministers of OECD countries meet regularly as members of its Economic Policy Committee; an important subcommittee is Working Party Three (WP3), which deals with balance-of-payments problems. Meetings of OECD committees in other policy areas, such as science, the environment, social policy, manpower training, and industrial development, also bring OECD-nation cabinet ministers together. Individual nations in the OECD are represented by officials of ambassadorial rank. Agencies related to the OECD include the INTERNATIONAL ENERGY AGENCY and the Nuclear Energy Agency. OECD headquarters are in Paris.

Organization for European Economic Cooperation An organization of West European countries formed in 1948 to work with the United States and Canada, which were associate members, to plan the postwar reconstruction of their economies and to administer the EUROPEAN RECOVERY PROGRAM, better known as the Marshall Plan. After U.S. aid was discontinued, the organization continued to promote trade and investment among the member countries. It was replaced in 1960 by the ORGANIZATION FOR ECONOMIC CO-OPERATION AND DEVELOPMENT.

Organization of Arab Petroleum Exporting Countries (OAPEC) An association of the oil-exporting nations in the Arab world, formed in 1968 to co-ordinate economic policies, undertake joint projects, share expertise, and provide training and employment for each other's citizens. Joint projects include the Arab Maritime Petroleum Transportation Company, the Arab Shipbuilding and Repair Company, the Arab Petroleum Investment and Repair Company, the Arab Petroleum Investment Company, and the Arab Petroleum Service Company. Members include Iran, Iraq, Saudi Arabia, Kuwait, the Persian Gulf emirates, Algeria, and Libya.

Organization of Petroleum Exporting Countries (OPEC) A cartel of oil-exporting nations created in 1960 to raise the producing nations' revenues from oil, following the 1959 and 1960 reductions in posted oil prices by big international oil companies. At that time, oil production and pricing was, for the most part, controlled by the major international oil companies. The original members met in Baghdad in September 1960 to form OPEC: they were Iran, Iraq, Kuwait, Saudi Arabia, and Venezuela.

During the 1960s, although OPEC had little impact on prices, it was expanding its membership to thirteen nations accounting for 85 per cent of world oil exports. In 1968, OPEC issued a statement asserting that the governments of oil states had the right to participate in the ownership of the oil companies operating in their countries, and to set the posted price of oil to ensure that prices kept up with inflation; OPEC members contended that the oil companies should transfer a part of their "excessively high earnings" to the oil-producing states. In its first test of strength in 1970, OPEC raised the posted price of oil and raised its tax rate from 50 per cent of the posted price to 55 per cent. But the true significance of OPEC's strength became clear in 1973–74, when the posted price of oil was raised almost fourfold. Since then, OPEC has also taken other steps to strengthen its hand and to increase the benefits of oil and natural-gas reserves for the producer nations. The foreign oil-producing companies have been for the most part nationalized, and OPEC members have sought to increase their economic benefit by moving into refining, petrochemicals production, and the ownership of tanker fleets. OPEC members argue that their oil and gas reserves will not last forever, and that they are therefore entitled to try to use their oil and gas wealth to strengthen and diversify their economies for the benefit of future generations.

OPEC's members today include Algeria, Ecuador, Indonesia, Iran, Iraq, Kuwait, Libya, Nigeria, the Persian Gulf emirates, Saudi Arabia, and Venezuela. OPEC maintains its headquarters in Vienna, where it has a highly trained staff of oil experts. Its members meet regularly to discuss world oil-production trends, to allocate production cutbacks in the event of a temporary glut so as to avoid price-cutting, which could undermine the cartel, to negotiate price increases, and to discuss strategies to increase the benefits OPEC members get from oil production, strategies such as demanding a bigger share of world refining and petrochemical production. In 1976, the OPEC Special Fund was created, with eight hundred million dollars in capital, to assist less-developed countries hurt by oil-price increases. See also INTERNATIONAL ENERGY AGENCY.

Ottawa Agreements A series of trade agreements made among Britain and the members of the British Commonwealth at the Imperial Economic Conference held in Ottawa in 1932. The agreements, consisting of twelve bilateral treaties, raised tariffs against the rest of the world and established lower, preferential-tariff rates among members of the Commonwealth. Prime Minister R.B. Bennett of Canada was one of the driving forces behind the conference, practising his 1930 election promise to put "Canada first, then the Empire." But he was successful in persuading the British to agree to the scheme in large part because the United States had already made significant increases in its tariffs.

outside director A director of a company who is not an officer of the company and has no important holding in the company. He is usually appointed because he is a community figure, a well-known businessman whose ideas can be used in the company, or a prominent academic.

outstanding shares The preferred or common shares of a corporation that are held by investors. The number of outstanding shares can be increased if a NEW ISSUE is sold to the public. The number can be reduced if a corporation redeems some of its preferred shares or buys back some of its shares from the public, but the total number of shares is limited by a firm's AUTHORIZED CAPITAL, as set out in its charter.

over-the-counter market (OTC) The market for corporate and government bonds and unlisted shares, usually conducted over the telephone or by telex, with prices reached through negotiation. Taken together, the dollar value of trading for bonds and shares in the over-the-counter market is greater than the dollar value of trading for LISTED SHARES on recognized STOCK EXCHANGES. But the greatest proportion of this trading is represented by the BOND MARKET. The over-the-counter market for unlisted shares is quite small, but none the less provides an opportunity to develop a market for shares in small and relatively young companies. The INVESTMENT DEALERS ASSOCIATION provides daily quotation lists for bonds and unlisted shares, and plays a major role in monitoring the operation and standards of behaviour on the over-the-counter market for bonds and unlisted shares.

overburden A mining-industry term that describes the sand, soil, and other surface material covering a mineral deposit.

overdraft The movement of a person's bank account into a debit position because the cheques written on the account exceed the amount in the account. Canadian banks discourage overdrafts in personal accounts.

overhead See FIXED COSTS.

overheating Economic policies that generate a level of demand in excess of the productive capacity of the economy, and lead to DEMAND-PULL INFLATION.

overpopulation The situation of a country or region when its per capita gross national product is smaller than the GNP that could be achieved with a smaller population, or when its population is so large that it can neither feed itself nor earn sufficient foreign exchange through other means to import its food needs.

overproduction The production of more goods or commodities than can be sold at a break-even or profitable price.

oversaving A level of saving in the economy that is too high to be profitably reinvested to meet prevailing levels of consumer demand. It can be a sign of an excessively uneven distribution of income, in which lower-income families have too little to spend and higher-income families far too much. Oversaving is another way of saying that consumer spending is too low, relative to the size of the economy.

oversubscription The situation that occurs when the total demand for a NEW ISSUE of shares or bonds exceeds the size of the issue. When this happens, all the would-be purchasers are allocated a correspondingly smaller number than they wanted to purchase.

overtime The number of hours worked in excess of the number set out in a collective agreement or in federal or provincial labour laws. Employees must be paid a higher rate of pay, usually one and a half times the normal hourly rate, for the overtime hours they work. Some contracts call for the payment of two or even three times the normal hourly rate if employees work on holidays, Sundays, or seven consecutive days. If an employer requires a great deal of overtime work by his employees, the union will push for an increase in the number of employees. But employers may prefer to build up a high overtime bill, rather than to increase their workforce, since a larger workforce means additional payments for fringe benefits, and problems if business slackens and employees have to be laid off.

ownership The legal right to possess a piece of property. Ownership is demonstrated in different ways—by the possession of a share certificate indicating ownership of a portion of a company, for example, or by a deed indicating ownership of land and buildings, by a bond indicating ownership of a claim on a company's assets, or by a receipted bill of sale, indicating that a possession has been paid for in full.

P

pace-setter In labour relations, a union with significant bargaining power, representing a large number of workers, whose wage settlement in a new collective agreement will therefore set a pattern for other unions and employers.

paid-up capital The money that shareholders have paid for shares in a corporation and that is available for use by the corporation for the growth of the business. Paid-up capital and RETAINED EARNINGS represent the bulk of SHAREHOLDERS' EQUITY in a corporation.

pan A method of searching for gold and other precious metals in a stream. Rock from the streambed is washed in a pan to see if it contains gold or other precious metals.

Panarctic Oils Limited A company formed by a group of Canadian mining and oil and gas companies and the federal government in 1967 to explore for oil and gas in the Arctic region. The consortium was formed on the initiative of Canadians in the oil and gas industry who lacked the capital to sustain the kind of exploration effort needed in the far North. Almost all the other exploration in the northern regions was in the hands of the large, foreign-controlled oil companies. PETRO-CANADA holds the federal interest in Panarctic, which amounts to about 45 per cent of the voting shares. Panarctic is not a crown corporation; it is a private corporation in which the federal government, through a crown corporation, is the largest single shareholder.

panic A wave of fear in financial and foreign-exchange markets of impending economic collapse. Such fears usually worsen the situation because investors become anxious to sell at any price, thus causing an even sharper drop in the price of shares, currencies, real estate, and other investments.

paper gold See SPECIAL DRAWING RIGHTS.

paper loss A loss stemming from the decline in value of an asset, such as a share or work of art, that has not been realized because the asset has not yet been sold. An investor, faced with a paper loss, has to decide whether to cut his loss or hope that, if he holds on to the asset, it will again go up in value. See also PAPER PROFIT.

paper money Most narrowly defined, the paper currency issued by the central bank of a country. It is usually money because the government says it is and guarantees its use as legal tender. In the past, paper money was backed by gold and other precious metals, but this is not the case today. Paper money can be more broadly defined to include other forms of paper that can be used as money, such as cheques, and certain debt securities, such as CANADA SAVINGS BONDS.

paper profit An increase in the value of an asset, such as a share or work of art, that cannot be spent because it has not been realized. The profit can only be spent when the asset is sold. See also PAPER LOSS.

par value The face value of a bond, preferred share, or other security, that appears on the certificate of ownership. The interest or dividend paid on the security is a fixed percentage of the face value. But the MARKET VALUE may be quite different, depending on prevailing interest rates and other factors. For example, the market value of a corporate bond with a face value of ten thousand dollars, and paying 11.5 per cent interest, will be much more than ten thousand dollars if the prevailing level of interest rates declines to, say, 9 per cent. Most common shares are issued at NO PAR VALUE, since dividends are not paid as a percentage of the issue price but are tied to profitability of the firm and the number of common shares outstanding.

paradox of thrift While saving is usually considered a virtue, JOHN MAYNARD KEYNES argued that, if everyone tries to save more and consume less when the economy is operating below its full-employment potential, then the economy will decline and consumers will end up with less income—and, therefore, less to save. Cutbacks in consumption represent cutbacks in the level of demand or purchasing power in the economy; when the economy is weak, society needs more spending—higher demand, not less. In such circumstances, saving is a vice rather than a virtue.

paradox of value The explanation as to why water, a necessity of life, is cheap, while diamonds, which are of extremely limited usefulness in society, are worth so much. It is a question that concerned ADAM SMITH in his *Wealth of Nations* (1776). Neoclassical economists, such as ALFRED MARSHALL, argued that the MARGINAL UTILITY of a product is the explanation. Water is plentiful and the utility or satisfaction of an extra ounce of water is low, while the cost of getting an extra ounce is also low. Diamonds, though, are scarce, so the marginal utility or satisfaction from getting one more diamond is high, while the cost of getting an extra diamond is also high. Under MARGINAL-COST pricing, the price of getting that last extra unit of water or diamond determines the price of all water and all diamonds. In other words, the total utility of water versus that of diamonds is not the key consideration.

parent company The company that owns a majority of the shares and hence controls subsidiaries and affiliated companies. A multinational corporation, for example, usually consists of a parent company in one country and wholly owned or controlled subsidiaries in other countries. The policies of the subsidiary companies will be set by the parent company; it will also allocate to its subsidiaries a share of the cost of parent-company activities, such as research and development, corporate planning, and major managerial services.

Pareto optimum The state of equilibrium that exists when no one in society can be made better off without making someone else in society worse off. This concept, which helped to contribute to the idea of GENERAL EQUILIBRIUM, is named after an Italian sociologist, Vilfredo Pareto (1848–1923). Pareto was dealing with economic efficiency rather than equity or fairness. To make one person better off, you have to take something from someone else, and hence make him worse off.

Pareto's law The belief that nothing can be done to correct income inequality. Vilfredo Pareto (1848–1923), the Italian sociologist, believed that there was an inevitable tendency for income to be distributed in the same way in all countries, in spite of special tax, social, or other policies to correct great disparities in income distribution.

parity 1. Equality. For example, Canadian workers in a particular industry may try to negotiate wage parity with workers in the same industry in the United States. Or workers in one city may seek wage parity with workers in the same industry or occupation in another

Canadian city—teachers in Windsor and Ottawa, for example, or policemen in Calgary and Edmonton, carpenters in Ontario and Quebec. **2.** A system of pricing. In energy, for example, there is a tendency to price different forms of energy in terms of a common energy equivalent—say, British Thermal Units. In agriculture, certain farm products may be priced to yield farms an income equal to some level of income in the non-farm economy. **3.** An official exchange rate or par value used in a system of fixed exchange rates as the central rate in pegging a currency. Currencies had to stay within 1 per cent either side of parity under the fixed-exchange-rate system of the INTERNATIONAL MONETARY FUND.

Parkinson's law In fact, a series of laws drawn up by C. Northcote Parkinson, a British political scientist, which, while satirical in tone, expresses some basic problems of modern management and bureaucratic organization. His best-known law is "Work expands so as to fill the time available for its completion." A second of his well-known laws is that expenditure in an organization rises to meet the income that is available. See his book, *Parkinson's Law* (Boston, 1957).

partial-equilibrium analysis A system of economic analysis—say, of a particular industry or sector of the economy—in which one variable is changed, with the other variables left unchanged. This form of analysis can be used to determine the effect of tax, price, and other changes on a particular industry, for example. GENERAL-EQUILIBRIUM analysis is used to determine all the effects of a change in one variable throughout the economy, including the resulting changes in other variables.

participation rate The percentage of the population fifteen years of age and older that is in the labour force; in other words, the percentage of Canadians fifteen years and older who have jobs or who are looking for jobs. The participation rates for the entire population and for different age and sex groups are published monthly by Statistics Canada in its LABOUR-FORCE SURVEY. Changes in the participation rate also affect the unemployment rate. For example, if the participation rate of women in the labour force rises faster than the growth in jobs for women, then the unemployment rate will also increase.

partnership An agreement between two or more individuals to contribute capital or other resources to a business and to share in the profits, losses, and debts of the business. While this kind of arrangement is satisfactory for relatively small businesses, it becomes less so as the business, and its debts, grow, since the partners have unlimited liability for the debts of the business. It then makes more sense to establish a LIMITED-LIABILITY COMPANY.

patent The legal right to ownership of an invention issued, in Canada, under the Patent Act. By granting this right to inventors, society hopes to encourage invention and innovation, and thus to benefit from increased economic efficiency and growth. The benefit to the inventor is that, for a limited period, he can charge a royalty for the use and application of his invention, or sell such rights to another person. For a corporate inventor, it means that the firm can produce a distinctive product, which other firms are forbidden from duplicating; without such protection, there would be less incentive for corporations to spend money on research and development. In Canada, patent protection is provided to the originator of the invention, although this can lead to conflicting claims. Disputes are adjudicated by the Patent Appeal Board and the FEDERAL COURT OF CANADA. In many other countries, patent rights are granted to the first to file. Exclusive protection under the Patent Act is provided for seventeen years from the date the patent is granted.

Patent Office A division of the Bureau of Intellectual Property within the Department of CONSUMER AND CORPORATE AFFAIRS, that administers the Patent Act and publishes a weekly abstract of patents granted.

pawnbroker A provincially licensed moneylender who makes loans on valuable goods left with him as security. The pawnbroker issues a ticket to the borrower and cannot sell the goods left with him until a certain period of time has elapsed.

pay-back period A calculation that is made to determine how long it will take a new investment in new machinery or a new project to pay back the original investment cost. This is not the same thing as determining the full return that can be made from the investment over its productive life. But, since investors normally are anxious to recover their original costs as quickly as possible, it is one of several important calculations made in judging any investment proposal.

pay-out ratio The proportion of a company's after-tax profits paid out to shareholders in the form of DIVIDENDS.

payment in kind A barter-type arrangement in which one person pays for goods and services in other goods and services. While it is illegal to pay wages this way, private tradesmen and others doing extra work outside their normal jobs sometimes arrange for payment in kind to avoid income taxes.

payola Money or gifts paid to people for their help in promoting company products surreptitiously. A record company may make such payments to a radio-station disc jockey, for example, if the disc jockey promotes a certain record or recording store, or a food company may make such payments to a supermarket manager if he gives extra shelf space or shows other preference for a particular product.

Pearson Commission The Commission on International Development, appointed in 1968 by Robert McNamara, president of the INTERNATIONAL BANK FOR RECONSTRUCTION AND DEVELOPMENT (World Bank, or IBRD). It was headed by Lester Pearson, former prime minister of Canada, and included seven other experts from around the world. The commission was asked to study the effectiveness of international programs of development assistance and to recommend improved programs. In 1969, it published its report, *Partners in Development*. It recommended a development strategy for the 1970s, including adoption by the developed countries of an aid commitment equal to 0.7 per cent of gross national product, with at least 10 to 20 per cent of such aid being channelled through multilateral institutions. It said that aid should not be considered a substitute for foreign direct investment and expanded international trade as means of development.

peg In a system of fixed exchange rates, the intervention rate or exchange rate at which the Bank of Canada would intervene in foreign-exchange markets to keep the Canadian dollar from rising or falling. Normally, there are two pegs, an official selling price and an official buying price. The gap between the two can be a wide band or a narrow band, depending on the degree of currency fluctuation permitted in the system.

penalty clause A contract clause that makes one of the parties to a contract pay a certain sum of money to the other if the contract obligations are not fulfilled.

penny stock A stock that sells for less than one dollar and that is speculative. Penny stocks are often available for small mining, oil, and gas companies.

pension Payments to persons who are no longer of working age, who have retired from the workforce before reaching the mandatory retirement age, or who are unable to work because of some type of disability. There are five basic sources of pension income for Canadians: **1.** The federal old-age pension, which, since 1951, has been payable to everyone who meets the age and residency requirements. **2.** The federal guaranteed-income supplement, which, since 1967, is payable to pensioners who have little or no income other than the old-age pension. **3.** The CANADA PENSION PLAN (or QUEBEC PENSION PLAN), which, since 1967, has paid pensions to members of the workforce based on their wages or salaries up to an annual maximum amount, and which requires workers and their employers to pay premiums during their working lives; there are also some benefits for spouses and their families. **4.** Private pension plans, based on contributions from employers and employees. **5.** Annuity income from REGISTERED RETIREMENT SAVINGS PLANS.

In addition, there are special pension benefits, such as pensions for veterans and their widows, and disability pensions paid through provincial workmen's compensation boards. The provincial governments also provide tax credits and supplementary pension income for senior citizens with low retirement incomes. Some pensions also provide free drug and medical and hospital care, and subsidized housing.

pension fund The contributions of employers and employees into a managed fund, which is invested in bonds, mortgages, shares, and other assets, to earn income that will pay for future pension benefits. Pension funds are usually managed by trust companies or other specialized investment experts who, with their vast pool of dollars, represent one of the most important sources of investment capital in the economy; they are leading INSTITUTIONAL INVESTORS. They are subject to federal and provincial regulation to protect beneficiaries and to ensure that the funds are invested mainly in Canada.

pentanes plus A hydrocarbon liquid very similar to oil and used as oil; it is obtained as a by-product in the processing of natural gas.

per capita In statistics, the division of any output or consumption figure by the population for that year, to obtain output or consumption per individual. Since population is not static, changes in consumption or output by themselves do not give a true picture, on average, of how much growth in output or consumption is due to population change and how much is due to each person producing and consuming more. Per capita gross national product is used as a crude measure of the relative standard of living of different countries; such an average, of course, may conceal great disparities of income within a country. In some consumer products, such as sugar or milk, production may rise each year although per capita consumption remains static; the growth is due to population increases. Other products may show increased production, due both to population growth and to increasing per capita consumption; wine is a recent example.

per capita tax In a union, the ongoing payment by individual locals to their national or international headquarters or to a provincial or regional labour council or federation.

per diem A daily charge by a professional, such as an accountant or a lawyer, or by a consultant for his services. The term means daily or by the day.

perfect competition A market in which the laws of supply and demand work to bring about the most efficient allocation of resources and the lowest possible prices. Such an economy is supposed to work according to a number of ideal rules: **1.** There are large numbers of both buyers and sellers, with no one a large enough buyer or seller to influence prices or supplies. **2.** Products are homogeneous or identical, so that the buyer will always buy at the lowest price, thus forcing all suppliers to have the same low price. **3.** Buyers and suppliers have perfect knowledge of prices and products throughout the economy. **4.** Perfect freedom of entry and exit exists, so that new suppliers face no barriers if they want to enter the market, while old suppliers are free to leave. **5.** It is assumed that there are no transportation or other such costs. **6.** There are no profits other than the minimum return to the factors of production, to ensure that they remain in the market.

Perfect competition is a concept used by economists in constructing theoretical models of economic systems. It does not exist in the real world, although FREE-MARKET economists see it as the ideal towards which public policy should aim. See also CLASSICAL ECONOMICS, NEOCLASSICAL ECONOMICS, IMPERFECT COMPETITION, MONOPOLY, OLIGOPOLY, INVISIBLE HAND.

performance bond A bond posted by a major contractor or supplier of capital equipment to make sure that a project is completed.

permit A certificate that is issued giving the holder permission to do something—a permit to export natural gas or uranium, for example, a permit to cut timber, a permit to fish, or a permit to import live animals. Under a permit granted an oil or natural-gas company by the federal or a provincial government to search for oil and gas, the company must complete a certain dollar-value of work within a specified period of time. In return, it usually has the right to choose up to half the land and to obtain a LEASE without having to bid in an auction. The other half of the land is leased to the highest bidder, or to the same company for payment of an additional fee.

perpetual bond A bond that has no maturity date on which the borrower is required to repay the principal. In 1936, the government of Canada sold fifty-five million dollars' worth of a 3 per cent perpetual bond. In September 1966, it issued new certificates, with another thirty years of annual interest coupons. In 1975, it announced that the bonds would mature on 15 September 1996, when the last of the existing interest coupons had been cashed in.

person-year The period of time worked by a person in one year if he or she was employed full time for an entire year, or the equivalent—for example, 3 persons each working for 4 months, or 2 persons each working for 6 months. Federal government departments have their staffing budgets set out in terms of person-years needed to carry out the departmental responsibilities, leaving the individual departments to decide the details of staffing. The term used to be man-year.

personal income The income received by individuals from all possible sources. It includes not only wages, salaries, and pensions, but also rents, dividends, interest, welfare payments, profits of personal businesses, and realized capital gains.

personal income tax A tax levied as a per cent of personal income. It is both a federal and a provincial tax and the tax rate is graduated, rising with the level of a taxpayer's personal taxable income, according to the ability-to-pay principle.

Under the Income Tax Act, income means income from almost all sources, except certain social-assistance payments, gifts, capital gains from the sale of personal residences, half the capital gains from investments, one thousand dollars of interest income, and certain other exemptions. Thus, the tax base includes salary and wages, unemployment insurance, interest and dividends, capital gains, alimony payments, pensions, fees, commissions, and scholarships. In calculating taxable income, deductions permitted under the Income Tax Act, such as pension-plan contributions, charitable donations, basic exemptions, and union dues, are subtracted from total or gross income. The resulting figure is taxable income, or the federal tax base for taxpayers in all provinces except Quebec. The federal tax rate is then applied, starting at about 6 per cent of taxable income at the bottom of the tax table, rising to a top rate of 43 per cent. In addition, there is a provincial tax rate, ranging in 1978 from 38.5 per cent of the federal tax base for Alberta taxpayers, to 58 per cent for Newfoundland taxpayers. The combined federal-provincial top rate thus ranges from 60 to 70 per cent, depending on the province in which the taxpayer lives.

The federal government's tax-collecting activities are covered under the Fiscal Arrangements Act of 1977. Quebec has its own personal income-tax system. Personal income today accounts for just over 40 per cent of budgetary revenues, compared to 8 per cent in 1939–40. In 1972, the income-tax system was overhauled, with the tax base being significantly broadened to include one-half of CAPITAL GAINS, unemployment-insurance benefits, and scholarships. While the personal income tax is a major source of government revenue, it is also an important tool for INCOME REDISTRIBUTION, since it is based on ability to pay, and also for DEMAND MANAGEMENT, since tax increases and tax reductions can significantly affect the level of demand or purchasing power in the economy. The federal personal income tax was introduced in 1917. See also CORPORATE INCOME TAX, ROYAL COMMISSION ON TAXATION, TAX EXPENDITURES.

personal property Property aside from REAL ESTATE, owned by an individual. It can include furniture, automobiles, jewellery, clothing, shares and bonds, and works of art.

personnel management The field of management that deals with the hiring, training, promotion, and motivation of employees. Its responsibilities also include the management of fringe benefits, the development of hiring and firing policies, and special needs, such as employee counselling to deal with problems such as alcoholism.

Peter principle The principle attributed to Laurence J. Peter and Raymond Hull in their book, *The Peter Principle* (New York, 1969), that employees tend to rise to their level of incompetence. Thus, for example, the top salesman is almost certain to be made the sales manager, even though his real skills are in sales rather than in management, while a poor salesman who could be a good sales manager probably will never get a chance at the management job.

Petro-Canada A federal crown corporation created in 1975 to help the government to formulate its national energy policies, to increase Canadian energy supplies, to undertake energy research and development and exploration programs that are in the national interest, to give the government a view of oil-industry operating practices and finances, and to increase the Canadian presence in the petroleum industry, which was heavily foreign controlled. Since it began operating in 1976, Petro-Canada has acquired control of two foreign-owned oil companies in Canada, Atlantic Richfield Canada Limited and Pacific Petroleums Limited, as well as a major share of Western Transmission Company. It holds the government's 45 per cent interest in PANARCTIC OILS LIMITED and in Syncrude Canada Limited, a major oil-sands plant. It has joined in exploration efforts with private oil companies in the Canadian North and Atlantic offshore region. Petro-Canada has also made arrangements to participate in heavy oils development, and is investigating ways to transport liquefied natural gas out of the Arctic to eastern Canada. It has supported the planning for a natural-gas pipeline to Quebec City. It has also launched a research and development program to devise new energy sources. And it has become an important oil-importing agency for Canadians, negotiating oil-supply arrangements with Mexico and Venezuela. Its head office is in Calgary.

In September 1979, the federal government appointed a task force to recommend ways in which major assets of Petro-Canada could be returned to the private sector, while the federal government retained the capacity to arrange state-to-state oil sales, to support high-risk exploration in the frontier regions, and to promote energy research and development. In October 1979 the task force proposed that all of the profitable assets of Petro-Canada be vested in one company, with the federal government taking over its debt, and that the shares be distributed without charge to Canadians. No Canadian would be allowed to own more than 1 per cent of the shares and no institutional investor more than 3 per cent. A separate company, to be a non-operating company, would be set up as a government-owned entity to make state-to-state deals, to finance frontier development, and to promote research. These changes would have to be approved by Parliament.

petrodollars The surplus foreign-currency funds of members of the ORGANIZATION OF PETROLEUM EXPORTING COUNTRIES. While some OPEC members, such as Nigeria, Indonesia, and Venezuela, have been able to use the great bulk of their oil-export earnings since the rapid escalation of oil prices starting in 1973, other oil-producing nations, such as Saudi Arabia, Kuwait, and the Persian Gulf emirates, have tiny populations and cannot spend a good part of the money they earn from oil. These surplus funds, to a large extent U.S. dollars, have been recycled into EURO-CURRENCY markets, U.S. government treasury bills, or into real estate and other corporate investments. This recycling helps to offset the huge trade deficits of many industrial nations, caused by sharp increases in the price of oil.

Some economists worry about the huge accumulation of these petrodollars, and fear they may become a threat to the international banking system. To a large extent, petrodollars have been placed as short-term funds in Eurocurrency markets, with Western banks in turn re-lending a large volume of these funds in long-term credits to LESS-DEVELOPED COUNTRIES, which may find that they are unable to repay the interest and principal. Thus, the Western banks rather than the oil countries are bearing the risk of such loans, and a default could have severe repercussions throughout the banking system. Others fear that the oil-rich countries may use their petrodollars to buy large blocks of prime agricultural and resort land in Western nations, or to buy control of major corporations.

Petroleum Administration Act An act passed by Parliament in June 1975, permitting the federal government to regulate the price of oil and natural gas and to allocate supplies. It allowed the federal government to have a single price for oil and natural gas within Canada and to set a higher price for export markets.

The act is divided into five parts. Part I allowed the NATIONAL ENERGY BOARD to levy an oil-export tax on exporters. Part II allowed the federal government to negotiate a domestic oil price with the producer provinces and, if the negotiations failed, to set the domestic oil price itself. Part III allowed the federal government to negotiate natural-gas prices with the producer provinces, and, should the negotiations fail, to set natural-gas prices itself. Part IV allowed the federal government to operate a cost-compensation program, to stabilize the cost of foreign oil used in eastern Canada and thus to help maintain the single Canadian price below the international price. Part V gave the minister of ENERGY, MINES AND RESOURCES the power to obtain information from oil and natural-gas producers, to seize documents, and to inspect their premises. It also required the Energy minister to make an annual report on the administration of the act.

Parts of the legislation, namely parts I and III, were made retroactive to 1 January 1974. The domestic price for oil and natural gas, according to the act, should balance the interests of consumers and producers, should protect consumers against price instability, and should encourage the discovery and development of oil and natural gas, to achieve self-sufficiency in Canada. In 1978, the act was amended to allow tar-sands oil and heavy oil to be sold in Canada at the international price, with the price being subsidized by a levy imposed on Canadian refineries.

petty cash Money kept available in a business or other organization to pay small expenses.

philanthropy The donation by wealthy people of large amounts of their wealth for charitable, educational, social, and cultural causes.

Phillips curve A graphic representation showing the trade-off between full employment and low inflation. The relationship, the work of British economist A. W. Phillips, showed that, as unemployment declined, the rate of inflation, represented by the rate of increase in money wages, rose. Similarly, as the rate of unemployment rose, the rate of inflation, represented by the rate of increase in money wages, declined. Since 1958, when Phillips first published his work on the unemployment-inflation trade-off, economic policy-makers have had less and less success in achieving their goal of a better curve with less inflation and lower unemployment. Instead, both inflation and unemployment have become more firmly entrenched at higher levels, and some economists question the relevance of the Phillips curve as a tool of economic analysis in the modern, mixed economy.

In its sixteenth annual review in 1979, the ECONOMIC COUNCIL OF CANADA argued that policy-makers could no longer treat unemployment and inflation in a framework that assumes a direct trade-off between the two within a steadily growing economy. Inflation, for example, is not caused only by excess demand; other factors include changes in world oil and other commodity prices, exchange-rate fluctuations, excessive wage demands, declining productivity growth, and changes in relative prices. Similarly, insufficient demand is not the only cause of unemployment; other factors include a mismatch of jobs and skills, poor labour-market information and changes in work attitudes, and financial benefits for those who choose not to work.

physical quality-of-life index (PQLI) An indicator of national economic progress, used as a supplement to per capita gross national product to compare the standard of living of different countries. It takes three physical factors—life expectancy, low infant mortality, and the rate of literacy—and averages them together. The measure was devised in 1977 by the Overseas Development Council, a U.S.

non-profit agency interested in the problems of the less-developed countries. It shows that a nation may have a low per capita gross national product and a high physical quality-of-life index—Sri Lanka, for example. Conversely, a country such as Mexico can have a higher per capita gross national product and a lower physical quality-of-life index. A developed country is one that has a PQLI of 90 or more, as well as a per capita income of more than $2,000. Canada had a PQLI of 95 and a per capita income of $7,510 in 1977. Sweden, Norway, and Iceland are the highest, at 97, while the United States also has a PQLI of 95.

Physiocrats An eighteenth-century school of French economists led by François Quesnay (1694–1774), which emphasized land as the sole source of wealth or surplus value and, hence, the only factor of production that should be taxed. The physiocrats believed in LAISSEZ-FAIRE economics and in FREE TRADE. Quesnay devised the tableau économique, which showed the interdependence of the many different participants in economic life; in some respects, the tableau was an early predecessor to modern INPUT-OUTPUT tables. The physiocrats were among the first thinkers to attempt to turn economics into a specialized field of study and a science.

picket line A line of striking union members at the entrances to their place of work; the purpose is to inform the public that a strike is taking place. Picketing workers hope to persuade customers not to do business with the firm, suppliers not to deal with the firm, would-be workers not to enter the place of business, and other unions in the same firm or other firms to support the strike by not crossing the picket line. Picketing is a legal activity so long as it is peaceful and does not interfere with the rights of third parties to use the streets and sidewalks, or the right of the firm to try to continue operating the business.

piecework A method of paying wages that depends in part on the number of items produced by each individual worker. While no employer can pay less than the minimum wage, an employer can tie wages above the minimum wage or other base rate to actual production.

pig iron The cast iron that is produced from a blast furnace, but has yet to be converted into basic steel products, such as steel rods and beams.

Pigou effect A theoretical concept named after the British economist Arthur C. Pigou (1877–1959), who wanted to show that an economy could automatically return to full employment, something that JOHN MAYNARD KEYNES denied. Pigou argued that unemployment could be cured by letting wage rates fall, which would in turn lead to a drop in prices. This decline in prices would increase the real value of money, thus encouraging people with savings to spend and invest. This increased economic activity, resulting from the increased purchasing power of liquid money, would return the economy to full-employment conditions. Pigou was attempting to show that an economy with flexible wages and prices could return to full employment without government intervention. But he did not advocate this, preferring instead to increase the money supply and achieve the same results at much less cost to people. Pigou is also well known for his work in WELFARE ECONOMICS, in particular for showing that governments could make comparisons of the effects of different social policies on different income groups in society, and thus determine the utility of those policies.

pilot plant A test plant to see whether a new production process works, and to improve the production process before a major investment is made in a full-scale production plant. The construction of pilot plants allowed, for example, the oil and engineering companies planning extraction plants for the Alberta tar sands to improve their production processes before huge investments in fully operating plants were made.

pitchblende A valuable uranium ore that contains a fairly high percentage of uranium oxide and is highly radioactive.

placing The issuing of new shares or bonds through an investment dealer or bank. In a public issue or placement, the new shares or bonds will be made available to the public. In a PRIVATE PLACEMENT they will be made available only to a few large INSTITUTIONAL INVESTORS. In either case, the planned issue must be approved by a provincial SECURITIES COMMISSION.

planned economy An economic system in which all the basic decisions on production, investment, manpower, and distribution are made by the government, rather than through the price mechanism or market forces. Thus, the allocation of resources is the function of the state rather than of the mixture of market forces, supply and demand, consumer tastes, profitability, corporation strategies, and government policies and regulations, that affects and helps to determine decisions in a MIXED ECONOMY such as Canada's. While it is possible for a planned economy to provide for a fairer distribution of income among its citizens, a mixed economy should yield a higher average standard of living, since it allows more scope for innovation and risk. Communist countries and some less-developed countries operate planned economies, where central government agencies set economic goals, allocate resources, and set prices. But most countries live with some form of mixed economy. Economic planning is something quite different, since it does not necessarily mean economic decision-making by government alone, using arbitrary powers to allocate resources and decide what should be produced. Economic planning usually means an effort by government, along with other groups in the economy, such as business and labour, to foresee economic problems, to agree on priorities, and to develop policies to ensure full employment and low inflation.

planned obsolescence Design or other changes in a product, to persuade consumers to buy a new product—a car or a dress, for example—before the old one has worn out.

planning 1. The activity of government in defining and reaching economic goals. There are many forms of planning, ranging from the rigid and centralized PLANNED ECONOMY of totalitarian states such as the Soviet Union and China, to the co-ordinating role played by the governments of social democracies, such as Sweden, where the government, with business and labour, sets investment goals and pay policy, to the looser, consensus-style planning tried, so far with little success, in the mixed economies of Canada and the United States. Other types of planning include the INDICATIVE PLANNING of France, where the government sets various industrial goals and industry is free to co-operate, receiving various forms of government assistance if it does, or the INDUSTRIAL-STRATEGY planning tried in Canada through the Board of Economic Development, starting in 1978, in which various industries and their unions produced joint reports containing recommendations on how to improve their efficiency and output. **2.** A normal function of major corporations, which devise five-year plans setting out product, investment, and market plans, and relate these to future financial needs, competition, and profitability. **3.** The determination, by municipalities, of how land is to be used—commercial versus residential construction, for example, the DENSITY of land use, or the location of major roads and expressways.

planning-programming-budgeting system (PPBS) A system of planning, organizing, and monitoring government spending. It was designed to help government make choices—a new highway instead of a new airport, for example—in situations where profitability is not the determining factor. Introduced in the U.S. government in 1965, it was subsequently adopted by the Canadian government. Spending was to be set out in terms of programs and objectives, and was supposed to allow policy-makers to compare alternative programs in terms of costs and benefits. Government officials preparing spending plans were supposed to devise criteria for weighing the benefits generated by their programs; in preparing a spending submission, officials had to set goals, define objectives, and develop planned programs to achieve those objectives. Although it was hoped that PPBS would allow government officials to make better choices among competing programs because the system provided a clearer picture of the benefits of different programs, less reliance has been put on PPBS by itself in recent years because it resulted in a loss of control over operating costs and staffing. See also ZERO-BASE BUDGETING SYSTEM.

plant Major capital assets, including mines, smelters, refineries, factories, commercial buildings, power stations, and government buildings.

plant-gate price The price for natural gas charged by a natural-gas-producing company to a pipeline company. It is the price for gas that has been gathered and processed from surrounding producing wells, so that it is ready for transmission. See also CITY-GATE PRICE.

plutocracy A government or society that is dominated by a relatively small group of wealthy people, and whose policies are designed primarily to protect the interests of the wealthy.

point A way of measuring a change in the price of a share, bond, or currency. A point is a one-dollar change in the price of a share, a 1 per cent change in the par value of a bond, and one one-hundredth of a cent change in the value of the dollar. Hence, a share that goes up one dollar has risen a point; a thousand-dollar bond that goes up ten dollars has risen a point; and a Canadian dollar that goes from 86.125 to 86.126 U.S. cents has risen a point.

policy **1.** An insurance contract in which an insurance company agrees to provide protection against a particular risk, in return for payment of a premium. **2.** In a government or corporation, a statement of rules to be followed in dealing with a particular situation or a set of desired objectives, along with an outline of the methods to be used in reaching those objectives. The policy statement provides the goals and operating instructions for public servants, or corporate employees and middle managers.

policy mix The set of policies used by a government to achieve the economic performance it desires. For example, to control inflation, a government may use a combination of monetary, fiscal, and supply policies. Rarely is one policy alone sufficient to achieve an economic objective.

political economy The study of political and economic institutions and models together, to achieve a better understanding of how the real world functions. For example, it is difficult to analyze the role of the corporation in the economy without also understanding the political system in which it functions, and its political influence; the same is true of the role of unions. It is necessary to link the study of political science and economics together to understand, for example, how income and wealth are distributed, how economic priorities are set, what political barriers exist to effective economic management, and what types of competition policies exist.

pollution control Laws and regulations to reduce the contaminents that can pollute the air, water, or land. Contaminents such as gases in the air, toxic chemical wastes in the soil or water, or phosphates, mercury, and other metals in water, can endanger human health and the natural ecological balance if they are allowed to build up in large concentrations. Both the federal and provincial governments have laws and regulations to reduce or even eliminate the pollution resulting from industrial, human, and government activity.

population The total number of inhabitants in a particular area, or a sub-group of the population—for example, the labour-force population, the school-age population, the urban population.

population forecast An attempt by demographers to calculate the future population of a community, province, country, or the world, using standard demographic tools such as fertility, mortality, and migration trends. Such forecasts are vital to governments and corporations in planning investment and other policies. World population figures, such as those developed by the United Nations Fund for Population Activities in 1973–75, help policy-makers and -planners to assess future world food, employment, housing, and other needs. National forecasts, such as those prepared by the demographers of Statistics Canada, help to determine future housing, education, hospital, and job needs, and, when these projections are broken into different age groups, can determine the outlook for particular industries, such as baby foods or industries serving senior citizens, as well as the outlook for consumer durables resulting from the rate of new household formation. Community projections are useful in determining future water and sewage needs, land use, numbers of classrooms and homes for senior citizens.

population pyramid A graphic representation of the age distribution of the population. It will not necessarily be in the exact shape of a pyramid; there may be more ten-to-fourteen-year-olds than there are younger age groups. But there will be far fewer older people at the top of the pyramid, thus illustrating the fact that younger people outnumber older people.

port of entry A port, airport, or border-crossing point, where customs and immigration officers are stationed to determine whether individuals or imported goods may enter the country.

portable pension The right to future pension benefits, represented by the accumulated pension contributions of an employee and an employer, which can be carried by an employee from one job to another. At present, the only pensions that are truly portable in Canada are the CANADA PENSION PLAN and the QUEBEC PENSION PLAN. Within some industries and within the public sector, there is some portability. But in most private-industry jobs, an employee who moves from one company to another loses his right to future pension benefits and his employer's matching pension contributions, unless the plan is VESTED. Thus, the fear of losing pension benefits becomes, as workers grow older, a barrier to changing jobs. One solution would be to make the Canada Pension Plan a much more significant pension plan for all Canadians.

portfolio A list of all the shares, bonds, and other investments of an individual or INSTITUTIONAL INVESTOR. The make-up of an investment portfolio will depend on the investment objectives of the investor. Some investors put more of an emphasis on income, while others emphasize capital gain.

portfolio investment The purchase of shares and bonds for the income they yield or the capital gains they may bring; such investment is not made for the purpose of acquiring control of a company. For example, foreign portfolio investment in Canada consists of the purchase of government and corporation bonds and the purchase of shares on Canadian stock exchanges. See also DIRECT INVESTMENT, FOREIGN DIRECT INVESTMENT.

possession utility The satisfaction of a consumer in the possession of particular goods or services, and the satisfaction of the seller in the possession of what he received in exchange for particular goods or services.

post-dated cheque A cheque that is dated for future rather than immediate payment.

post-industrial society A society characterized by the production of knowledge rather than goods. The term was first used by Daniel Bell, an American sociologist, in the mid-1960s. He saw Western societies shifting more and more into economic and social structures based on the development of new knowledge and the use of this knowledge to achieve technological innovation. The traditional goods-producing industries would shift to the less-developed countries, while the industrialized world, increasingly dominated by the scientific, technical, and professional classes, moved into a knowledge or information economy. The ECONOMIC COUNCIL OF CANADA, in its 1975 study, *Looking Outward,* studied the implications of the post-industrial society for Canadians.

post-Keynesian economics The school of economic thought that, while accepting the great contributions of JOHN MAYNARD KEYNES, contends that Keynesian solutions are no longer enough to achieve satisfactory economic performance and to improve general economic welfare. Whereas Keynes believed that the fundamental need in economic management was to maintain an aggregate level of demand in the economy in order to provide full employment and stable prices, he also had reasonable faith that the market system could take over, once the level of demand was sufficient. Post-Keynesian economists believe that the structure of the economy has changed so much in the past thirty years that, not only does the market system no longer work; it cannot be made to work. The growth of large corporations and unions, the increasing role of government in meeting consumer needs such as health, education, and housing, and in regulating business activity, the use of non-market institutions such as FARM MARKETING BOARDS in agriculture, and the appearance of resource cartels, have all diminished the role of market forces. As a result, new policies are needed—INCOMES POLICY, for example, to control inflation. The purpose of post-Keynesian economics is to improve the functioning of the modern MIXED ECONOMY.

Potash Corporation of Saskatchewan A crown corporation created in 1976 to acquire a major interest in the province's potash industry by purchasing or expropriating existing, privately owned potash mines. In August 1976, the crown corporation acquired its first potash mine for $128.5 million; it has taken over several other potash companies since then.

Potash Development Act Legislation passed by the Saskatchewan legislature on 28 January 1976, authorizing the provincial government to acquire the assets of producing potash mines. The POTASH CORPORATION OF SASKATCHEWAN was incorporated to act on behalf of the provincial government and to operate mines taken over by the province. The legislation drew official protests from the U.S. government, and was also criticized by the federal government. The United States feared that Saskatchewan would use its ownership to seek monopoly prices for its potash.

potential gross national product The output of goods and services in the economy that would occur under conditions of full employment without generating COST-PUSH INFLATION. It is thus the highest level of real GROSS-NATIONAL-PRODUCT growth that can be sustained without causing accelerating inflation, using the existing FACTORS OF PRODUCTION. It is defined by the ECONOMIC COUNCIL OF CANADA as "the output that can be produced with the available capital stock and available labour, given the productivity of both." The gap between potential output and the actual output of goods and services under conditions of high unemployment is known as the production gap. The gap equals the loss to society each year from the failure to achieve full employment. One of the goals of economic policy is to reduce or eliminate this gap.

According to Statistics Canada, the economy operated very close to its potential in the 1960s, aside from a recession in 1960–61 and another in 1970. Since early 1974 the economy has for the most part operated well below its potential. In recent years, according to the Economic Council, the growth of the productive potential of the Canadian economy has declined because of a significant drop in the growth of labour productivity due to inadequate business investment. According to the council, potential output grew at 4.2 per cent a year in 1973–78, while actual output grew 4.0 per cent a year; potential employment grew 3.1 per cent, while actual employment grew 2.9 per cent.

poverty The absence of sufficient income to obtain either a subsistence standard of living or the basic necessities of life, as defined by the society in which a person lives. Absolute poverty refers to a standard of living so low that a person is not even able to obtain adequate nutrition or shelter. Relative poverty refers to a standard of living in which a person may be able to obtain sufficient nutrition and adequate shelter, but has no income left over for what have become necessities of life—a television set, for example, or cigarettes, magazines, and other such items. While absolute poverty may be the inevitable consequence of a poor society, relative poverty may be due to the uneven distribution of income and wealth in an affluent society. According to Statistics Canada, families that spend 62 per cent or more of their income on the basic necessities of food, shelter, and clothing live in poverty; they have little income left over for discretionary purposes. A person who lives in relative poverty in one country may be considered wealthy in another; for example, a person living in officially defined poverty in Canada might be considered wealthy in India.

poverty line The level of income below which a family in Canada is considered to be living in poverty. Statistics Canada publishes periodic calculations of the poverty line, based on nation-wide surveys of family spending habits and living costs. Any family that spends 62 per cent or more of its income on the necessities of food, shelter, and clothing is considered to be poor. According to Statistics Canada, the percentage of families of two or more people living below the poverty line declined from 18.4 per cent in 1967 to 11.3 per cent in 1974; in 1977 it rose to 11.9 per cent. In the case of single individuals, the percentage living below the poverty line moved from 38.9 per cent in 1967 to 37.4 per cent in 1974 and 37.9 per cent in 1977. The Canadian Council on Social Development, a non-profit organization, calculates its poverty line as 50 per cent of average family income. According to this definition, 18.2 per cent of Canadians lived below the poverty line in 1973.

power of attorney A written authorization by one person designating another person to act on his behalf; the delegated power may be tightly defined for specific purposes and with strictly limited authority, or it may be of a more general nature, enabling, for example, the designated person to have wide decision-making powers.

prairie economic conference An annual conference of the three prairie premiers held from 1965 to 1972. The meetings dealt with regional problems, including economic and transportation problems. In 1973, the conference was enlarged to include British Columbia and renamed the WESTERN PREMIERS' CONFERENCE.

Prairie Farm Rehabilitation Administration (PFRA) An important federal program established in 1935 to help prairie farmers to restore their farmlands after the severe drought and soil drifting that hit Alberta, Saskatchewan, and Manitoba in the 1930s. Under the program, more than one hundred community pastures have been established on some 2.5 million acres of marginal land. PFRA assistance has also been used to finance major irrigation and water-supply projects, to help farmers find on-farm sources of water supply, and to provide millions of trees to be planted as shelterbelts, to prevent soil being carried away by the wind in periods of dryness.

Prairie Grain Advance Payments Act A federal law passed in 1957 that provides interest-free advance payments to prairie grain producers for farm-stored wheat, oats, and barley, along with financial assistance for grain drying and harvesting.

prairie provinces Manitoba, Saskatchewan, and Alberta.

preclusive buying The purchase of raw materials, parts, or other goods and services, so that a competitor is not able to buy and use them.

predatory practice An activity designed by a firm or firms in an industry to eliminate a competitor; the activities may be costly in the short run but, if successful, may allow the remaining firms to raise their prices and earn higher profits. Examples include a sharp reduction in prices so that the competitor is unable to compete, or the takeover of a supplier who provides parts or components for the competitor. Such activities, when they reduce or are intended to reduce competition, are illegal under the COMBINES INVESTIGATION ACT.

predatory pricing An attempt to eliminate or discourage competition by setting prices unreasonably low or by setting them much lower in one part of the country, where competition is feared, than in others. Such attempts to restrict competition are illegal under the COMBINES INVESTIGATION ACT.

preferential tariff A tariff that is lower for the imports from some countries than it is for the same imports from other countries. Under the GENERAL AGREEMENT ON TARIFFS AND TRADE, commodities from less-developed countries are imported into most Western industrial countries at a lower tariff rate than would be imposed on the same imports from other countries. The BRITISH PREFERENTIAL TARIFF, which established lower tariffs on trade among Commonwealth countries, is another example. See also OTTAWA AGREEMENTS. The European

Economic Community has entered into preferential arrangements with some associate-member states, mainly less-developed countries.

preferred creditor A creditor who has first claim on the assets of a bankrupt firm or deceased individual; his claim must be paid in full, before any of the UNSECURED CREDITORS can receive even partial payment of their claims. Sometimes preferred or secured creditors will take all of the assets, leaving nothing for the unsecured creditors.

preferred share A share in a company that entitles the shareholder to a fixed rate of return on his investment. Like the owner of COMMON SHARES, an owner of preferred shares of a corporation is an owner of the company, and, in the event it is wound up, he is entitled to a share of the assets, after creditors, including bondholders, have been paid. He must be paid his annual dividend before common shareholders get a dividend. If a company cannot pay its preferred shareholders their dividends in a particular year, then common shareholders must be deprived of their dividends as well; in fact, common shareholders cannot receive a dividend until past-due dividends owed to preferred shareholders are paid in full. Preferred shareholders do not usually have a vote at company annual or other meetings, but they may be entitled to vote if their dividend payments are in arrears. Sometimes preferred shares are convertible into common shares. They may also be participating preferred shares; that is, their holders may share in the rising profits of a company along with common shareholders and may get an extra dividend. Some but not all preferred shares are callable; that is, they can be bought back by the issuing company if it so wishes. Preferred shares are traded, just as common shares are, on the stock market.

premiers' conference The annual gathering of provincial premiers that has been held every year since 1960; the idea was suggested by the Quebec government, and the first of these conferences was held in Quebec City. The agenda of these conferences covers many areas of economic concern, such as inflation, unemployment, capital investment, energy policy, pensions, securities legislation, provincial purchasing policies, provincial incentives to industry, and tax policy. The premiers also deal with language policy, the constitution, and social and cultural policy. See also WESTERN PREMIERS' CONFERENCE, COUNCIL OF MARITIME PREMIERS.

premium **1.** The annual, semi-annual, or monthly payment to keep an insurance policy in force. **2.** The amount by which the market price of a bond or preferred share exceeds its issue price or face value.

premium pay The rate of pay that is paid for overtime, work under unusual conditions, or work on scheduled days off or public holidays. It is higher than the pay scale for straight time; for example, overtime pay is usually one and a half times the pay for straight time.

present value The value, in today's dollars, of a future inflow or outflow of funds in a proposed investment project. It is a tool used by corporations in assessing investment alternatives in which the future inflow and outflow of funds is discounted to reflect the TIME VALUE OF MONEY. See also NET PRESENT VALUE, DISCOUNTED CASH FLOW.

president The top operating officer of a corporation, and usually the chief executive officer as well, which would also make him the chief policy-maker in the corporation. In some corporations, though, the chairman rather than the president is the chief executive officer.

price The cost of a good or service, expressed in terms of the amount of money that must be exchanged to obtain it. Price rations goods or services to those who want them the most, since an increase in demand will normally lead to an increase in price; a decline in supply will have the same effect. Price is sometimes described as what you must give up to get what you want. The way prices are set and the role they play in allocating resources are two of the most important questions in economics.

price controls Measures by government to fix the price of all goods or services or particular goods or services. General price controls are imposed as part of an anti-inflation policy; for examples, see WARTIME PRICES AND TRADE BOARD, PRICES AND INCOMES COMMISSION, ANTI-INFLATION BOARD. When controls are applied to a particular good or service, the purpose is to prevent the price from rising excessively. For example, the government regulates telephone and cable-television rates to prevent monopoly services from exploiting the public; the prices of oil and natural gas are controlled so that price increases can be phased and windfall profits prevented. Sometimes prices are controlled—which usually means increased—to make sure that producers earn enough—farm prices set by FARM MARKETING BOARDS, for example.

price-cutting An attempt by a firm to increase its share of the market by cutting its prices; price-cutting may also be necessary for a firm anxious to retain its market share, if competitors are cutting their prices. Price-cutting can be illegal if it is designed to prevent a would-be competitor from entering the business; see also PREDATORY PRICING.

price differentiation The practice of charging different prices to different customers for goods of like quality and quantity, when the price differences cannot be justified by cost differences. The practice is illegal under the COMBINES INVESTIGATION ACT if it injures an otherwise efficient competitor and the supplier is unable to show that the differences in price are based on differences in cost of supply.

price-earnings ratio The ratio obtained by dividing the current market price of a share by its annual earnings per share, a figure obtained from the EARNINGS STATEMENT in the annual or quarterly report of a publicly traded corporation. A share selling at $20 on a stock exchange and having earnings of $2 per share has a price-earnings ratio of 10; this indicates that an investor is willing to pay $10 for the ownership of $1 of that company's earnings. If the price-earnings ratio were 12, then investors would be willing to pay $12 for ownership of $1 of the company's earnings. Price-earnings ratios differ for different industries; but a high price-earnings ratio usually indicates that investors are optimistic about a company's future profit growth, and thus willing to pay a high price for ownership of $1 of its earnings today and the right to higher earnings in the future. High future profits would indicate an ability to pay higher dividends in the future.

price effect The impact on the demand for a product as the result of a change in price. If the income of consumers is fixed and the price goes up, then consumers will be able to buy less of the product, or, if they maintain their level of demand for that product, less of something else. Higher prices can also lead to substitution of a cheaper alternative.

price elasticity The effect on the demand for a product of a change in its price. If a change in price results in a change in demand, then the product is price-elastic. If a change in price has little or no effect on demand, then the product is price-inelastic. One reason given for raising Canadian oil prices is that demand is price-elastic, and that higher prices may thus lead to reduced demand and hence energy conservation.

price-fixing A conspiracy by competing firms to charge the same price, usually an excessively high price, and thus to avoid the lower prices and lower profits that might result from price competition. Price-fixing is a criminal offence in Canada under the COMBINES INVESTIGATION ACT.

price index An INDEX that shows changes in the overall inflation rate or the rate of price change for a particular sector of the economy, with the base year equal to 100. The CONSUMER PRICE INDEX measures the rate of change in a typical basket of consumer goods and services, including housing, food, and health care. It can be broken down into food and non-food items, goods and services, and other components. The GROSS-NATIONAL-PRODUCT DEFLATOR measures the overall rate of inflation in the economy, including consumer prices, construction prices, import and export prices, and investment prices. Statistics Canada publishes a large number of price indexes, in addition to these—indexes for industrial selling prices, for example, housing prices for selected cities, and building-material prices.

price leadership The role of a major firm in an industry, usually the largest firm, in determining the timing and size of price increases for all of the largest firms in an OLIGOPOLISTIC industry. Formal agreement to set prices this way is illegal, but the same results can be obtained if one firm is tacitly recognized as the price leader and the other firms act accordingly. This type of price behaviour avoids price competition, which oligopolistic firms fear because it could reduce their prices and profits without gaining them an extra share of the market. While consumers would be better off, all of the firms would probably be worse off.

price level The general level of prices in the economy, expressed as an INDEX, or a percentage change from a previous year.

price-maker A large firm that has a major share of a market; its price decisions thus have an affect on its competitors' prices.

price mechanism See PRICE SYSTEM.

price rigidity The relative insensitivity of the price of a commodity to changes in supply or demand; most frequently, it refers to the failure of prices to drop in the face of increased supply or reduced demand.

price stability A level of price increase that is so small that it protects the long-term purchasing power of the dollar. The historic price-stability target for Canada has been a 2 per cent inflation rate. Along with FULL EMPLOYMENT, price stability is one of the basic goals of economic policy.

price support Government subsidies or other assistance to maintain the market price of a commodity at a minimum price level.

price system A system in which the allocation of resources, hence the production of goods and services, is determined by the prices that consumers are willing to pay and sellers or producers are willing to accept. When the price system functions freely, the LAW OF SUPPLY AND DEMAND is the operating mechanism that sorts out the countless independent desires of consumers and sellers. For example, if the economy needs more computer programmers, the price or wage will go up to attract more people to train for such jobs.

The effective functioning of the price system as an efficient allocator of resources, however, depends on the existence of competitive markets. If competition is not perfect or near-perfect and oligopoly or monopoly power exists, then the price system will fail to achieve the most efficient allocation of resources. Moreover, there are some goods, so-called PUBLIC GOODS, whose production cannot be based on the law of supply and demand; for example, hospitals have to be built according to need, and not according to a pricing system where access is based on income. Nor does the price system fully take into account so-called EXTERNALITIES, such as pollution. The consumer of a good may pay only part of the cost of cleaning up the pollution caused by the manufacturer of the product; the rest of the cost may be paid for by the public out of public funds.

price-taker A company whose output is so small that the price it pays for parts, raw materials, and labour, or the price it charges for its goods or services, has no effect on the overall level of prices in its particular industry or in the economy. If it charges a higher price than its bigger competitors, they are unlikely to react by raising their prices as well.

price war A series of price reductions by competitors, usually of a temporary nature, so that each can retain its market share. Price wars usually occur when there is a surplus of a product that cannot easily be stored. For example, a temporary surplus of gasoline may lead to a price war among competing gas-station chains; when the surplus is gone, prices will return to their normal level.

Prices and Incomes Commission (PIC) An anti-inflation agency established by the federal government in January 1969, following the publication of the white paper, *Policies for*

Price Stability, in December 1968. The white paper said that existing economic institutions did not give the government the scope it needed "to resolve the very real conflict which exists at the present time between the objectives of maintaining high-level employment and restoring the price stability that is necessary for sustained economic growth." In its original terms of reference in 1969, the three-man commission was "to inquire into and report upon the causes, processes and consequences of inflation and to inform those making current price and income decisions, the general public and the government on how price stability may best be achieved." A Commons-Senate committee on price stability, incomes, and employment was to be appointed (it never was), to hold hearings on the commission's reports.

The role of the Prices and Incomes Commission was subsequently enlarged to include the negotiation of a voluntary-restraint agreement by business and labour. Business leaders met at a national conference on price stability in February 1970, and agreed to limit price increases to amounts clearly less than the increased costs that businesses were experiencing. The commission had full powers under the Inquiries Act to investigate company costs and income, and to recommend action to the government to punish firms disregarding the guideline. The formal restraint agreement expired at the end of 1970. The commission also tried to persuade labour leaders to agree to a 6 per cent wage guideline, but failed to get labour to co-operate.

The commission was wound up after its final report and accompanying research were published in August 1972. In its final report, the commission argued that the exercise of economic power by unions and corporations did not emerge as a major cause of Canada's inflation. It put the blame instead on shortcomings in government economic management, holding government responsible, in particular, for allowing the economy to overheat in the late 1960s. It also argued that, while the existence of monopoly power is an explanation of high prices, it is not an explanation of rising prices. One of the main costs of inflation, the commission said, is that of trying to bring it down once it is decided that the inflation rate is too high. The principal way to cure and prevent inflation, the commission said, is to improve the management of the economy, principally through better use of monetary, fiscal, and supply policies. It said that temporary price and income controls can be helpful in changing public expectations during periods of high inflation, thus reducing the need for harsh monetary and fiscal restraint; but it argued that controls would only work when there was wide public support and the government was determined to enforce them, as well as to stick to its restrained monetary and fiscal policies. The report rejected the use of voluntary restraint or punitive taxes to secure compliance with voluntary price and income guidelines.

pricing out of the market The circumstances that exist when a country's or firm's prices are so high that its goods cannot be sold in their normal markets. This can happen when the cost of raw materials increases, when wage settlements are too high, when an exchange rate is overvalued, or when domestic inflation robs a country or firm of its competitiveness against foreign producers.

primary distribution The sale of an issue of common or preferred shares, bonds, or other securities for the first time. These are securities that have not previously been distributed or issued, and therefore represent new capital. Such an issue must be preceded by a prospectus approved by a provincial SECURITIES COMMISSION.

primary industry An industry that produces the raw materials employed in an economy. Its products range from agricultural and fishing-industry products to products such as oil and gas, minerals, and pulp and paper, which have been subject to only a limited degree of processing. Their conversion into products ready for consumers or for goods used to produce consumer goods is the role of SECONDARY INDUSTRY or TERTIARY INDUSTRY.

primary recovery The crude oil that can be recovered from an oil reservoir by natural pressure that moves the oil into the oil wells.

primary reserve ratio The cash reserves that

a chartered bank must, under the BANK ACT, set aside from new deposits before it can make additional loans and buy new securities. The primary reserves consist of cash balances that the chartered banks must maintain in the form of notes of, or deposits with, the BANK OF CANADA and on which no interest is earned. The requirements under the 1967 revisions to the Bank Act set the primary reserve ratio at 12 per cent of each bank's demand deposits—that is, 12 per cent of current and personal chequing accounts—and 4 per cent of notice deposits. The chartered banks are required to meet their minimum cash-reserve ratio on a half-monthly basis. The proposed 1979 revisions to the Bank Act would alter the requirements, so that the primary or cash-reserve ratios maintained by each chartered bank would consist of 10 per cent of Canadian-dollar demand deposits, 2 per cent of Canadian-dollar notice deposits for the first $500 million, 3 per cent of all Canadian-dollar notice deposits above that amount, and 3 per cent of foreign-currency deposits used to finance domestic transactions. The primary reserve ratio is fixed by law. See also SECONDARY RESERVE RATIO.

prime contractor The chief contractor on a major project, who is responsible for its completion. The prime contractor will often use the services of many different subcontractors to carry out and complete the project.

Prime Minister's Office (PMO) The office of experts that advises the prime minister on government policies. It has an important role to play in setting government economic policy, since the priorities and objectives of the government are set and co-ordinated within the cabinet and the PMO. The prime minister's staff usually includes advisers on economic and energy policy. See also PRIVY COUNCIL OFFICE.

prime rate The interest rate the chartered banks charge on business loans to their strongest corporate customers. It is usually changed in step with changes in the BANK RATE.

principal 1. The amount of money owed by an individual, corporation, or government, on which interest is paid. A borrower must pay interest while he has the use of the principal and must repay the principal before the loan is considered to be repaid. **2.** The person, firm, or government whose interests are represented by an agent in negotiations with a third party. **3.** The owner of a business.

principles of taxation The basis for a sound and acceptable tax policy. ADAM SMITH, in his *Wealth of Nations* (1776), said that taxes should be: levied according to a person's ability to pay, as indicated by his income; certain as to the amount and method of payment, and should not depend on arbitrary rulings by officials; levied and collected at a time most convenient to taxpayers; and cost as little as possible to collect. Since then, other considerations have come into play, such as the desirability of using the tax system to redistribute income from the wealthy to the needy, or to encourage or restrain economic growth.

private brand A product manufactured by one company and sold under the name of another. For example, most foodstore chains arrange with food-processing companies that sell products under their own brand name to manufacture a similar product that is sold under the supermarket's name.

private company A company whose charter of incorporation limits the number of shareholders to fifty, whose shares cannot be bought or sold by members of the public, and whose shares cannot be sold by one shareholder to anyone else without the approval of the board of directors and, in some cases, the prior offer of shares to existing shareholders. A private company, if it is federally incorporated, must file a public annual financial return with the Department of CONSUMER AND CORPORATE AFFAIRS if it is above a certain size in assets or sales.

private enterprise An economic system in which individuals have the right to own private property and to engage in economic activities of their choice to earn a profit. In such a system, private property has limited legal rights; governments, for example, must regulate some business activities and prices, how capital is to be raised, the liabilities of borrowers, the conditions under which trade takes place, and the circumstances under which an investor is barred from acquiring other business enterprises. An economic system that emphasizes the role of private enterprise is also likely to emphasize the role of market forces and competition. In a MIXED ECONOMY such as Canada's, there are roles for both private enterprise and government in achieving economic goals and adding to economic output.

private good A good or service consumed by an individual or family and purchased from after-tax income, as opposed to a PUBLIC GOOD paid for out of taxes or user fees. Much of the political debate in the Western world is over the ratio of private to public goods: in general, society seems to want more of both; thus, the argument is over how to provide a desired level of public services, while leaving individuals with a desired level of personal disposable income.

private placement The sale of a new issue of corporate bonds, preferred shares, or other debt securities to INSTITUTIONAL INVESTORS, such as pension funds and insurance companies, instead of offering the issue for sale to the public. Usually no PROSPECTUS is required, although securities commissions must be informed of the placement.

private property The legal right of a person or corporation to use an economic good. It may consist of a building, land, patent, copyright, trademark, work of art, security such as a share or bond, machinery, or other possessions, including personal possessions. Ownership of personal property may be represented by a deed or title, certificate, receipted bill of sale, or simple possession. Private-property rights are both protected and limited by law.

private sector That part of the economy under private ownership and control. It includes all privately owned corporations, small businesses, farms, professional firms, and individual entrepreneurial activity, and non-commercial organizations such as unions, non-profit corporations, and churches. In effect, it represents that part of economic activity accounted for by consumer spending and business investment in machinery, buildings, and inventories. It is one of two major sectors in the MIXED ECONOMY, the other being the PUBLIC SECTOR.

Privy Council Office (PCO) The department in the federal government that serves the prime minister. Its senior official is the clerk of the Privy Council, who is also secretary to the cabinet. The main roles of the PCO are to coordinate and support the cabinet and its committees, to prepare material for the prime minister, to liaise with government departments and agencies on cabinet matters, to carry out special studies, and to organize the work of interdepartmental committees of government officials. The PCO has operating secretariats serving different cabinet committees, and thus has its own staff of experts, including those who deal with the economy, energy, native affairs, social policy, defence, external affairs, and government operations and organization. It also has a planning group, which deals with the longer-term needs of public policy, and a security, intelligence, and emergency-planning secretariat. A separate FEDERAL-PROVINCIAL RELATIONS OFFICE advises on federal-provincial relations. See also PRIME MINISTER'S OFFICE.

pro forma statement A draft financial statement for a new business, showing estimated revenues and expenses, and how various costs and income will be defined so as to give a true financial picture of the new enterprise's financial condition. It can also be a future projection of an existing firm's financial statements, to estimate, for example, future CASH FLOW or WORKING CAPITAL.

pro rata The distribution or division of an asset or benefit based on some proportional relationship: for example, the offer of a RIGHTS ISSUE to buy additional shares according to the number of shares already owned by each shareholder in a firm.

probable reserves In the mining industry, an

identified ore-body but one that hasn't been fully blocked out, and hence cannot be classified as a proven or positive ore.

probate The procedure under which a court approves a particular WILL as the true and last testament of someone who has died, that as such represents his final wishes on how the estate is to be distributed among various beneficiaries. The court also confirms the executor named in the will.

proceeds **1.** The amount of money remaining from a new issue of shares or bonds after the sales costs, including commissions, have been deducted. **2.** The net yield from the sale of a home, farm, business, or other asset, after the cost of selling the asset, such as a real-estate broker's commission and legal fees, have been paid and any claims against the asset, such as mortgage debt, have been paid off. **3.** The yield from the tax system after the costs of collecting the tax have been deducted.

process control An on-line computer system that is used to monitor and control automatically the workings of a continuous operation, such as a refinery, nuclear-power plant, petrochemicals facility, or highly automated production line. Human intervention is only required when the system signals a problem that it cannot handle on its own.

procurement The purchase of needed goods and services. The term is frequently used to describe government purchasing of goods and services. Government procurement policies can be used as a non-tariff barrier to keep out imports and protect local industries, or as a tool in industrial strategy, to encourage the development of a domestic industry, for example, in areas of new technology.

producer goods Goods used in the production of other goods—for example, machinery, machine tools, process-control computers, motors, trucks, or freight cars.

product Something that can be sold.

product differentiation Efforts to make similar or nearly identical products seem different, and thus to allow firms to compete through these differences rather than through price competition. Sometimes product differentiation results from real differences in quality, but frequently the differences result from styling, packaging, brand-name identification, model changes, advertising, or service and warranty claims. Many mass-consumer products, from gasoline, toothpaste, and detergents to beer, shampoos, and automobiles, rely heavily on product-differentiation techniques to retain or increase their share of the market. Such competition is a sign of IMPERFECT COMPETITION; in PERFECT-COMPETITION models, products are assumed to be homogeneous or perfectly interchangeable, so that the consumer makes his choice on the basis of price alone, and is thus able to force down prices. In a world of imperfect competition, the consumer probably pays more than he would in a world of perfect competition.

production The use of raw materials to create producer and consumer goods through various refining, processing, and manufacturing activities.

production function The amount of output of a specific good or service that can be produced by different combinations of the factors of production, such as labour, machinery and equipment, or land and raw materials, at an existing level of technology. The calculation of different production functions allows a firm to determine the most profitable mix of factors. For example, it is possible to use different combinations of labour and capital in a firm that produces twenty-five thousand men's suits; the firm will try to find the combination of factors that produces the cheapest suit, bearing in mind that it also has to meet the demands of customers, such as delivery deadlines. If the cost of labour rises and the tax system provides incentives for capital investment, then the firm will recalculate its production function, and most likely substitute capital equipment for labour to the extent that it can. Whenever technological change occurs, the production function has to be recalculated.

production gap See POTENTIAL GROSS NATIONAL PRODUCT.

productivity The output of goods and services in the economy or in an industry from the effective use of various inputs, such as skilled workers, capital equipment, managerial know-how, technological innovation, and entrepreneurial activity, used to produce those goods and services. Real improvements in standard of living depend on the ability to raise productivity—that is, to increase the physical volume of output for a fixed level of inputs. Wage increases in excess of productivity increases can be inflationary because they are not backed by increases in output. The most common measures of productivity are changes in the volume of output per person employed or volume of output per man-hour. But, while productivity is measured in terms of labour output, the role of labour in achieving productivity gains may be quite small. Much of the responsibility rests with management, to ensure that technological change is taking place, new markets are developed, the workplace is organized to achieve the most efficient level of output, labour-management relations are well managed, programs exist to improve the skills of workers, and the level of managerial know-how is constantly improving. In recent years, technological change has been found to be one of the most important sources of productivity improvement.

productivity of capital stock The ratio of physical output in the economy, an industry, or firm, to the real value of capital stock, represented by buildings, equipment, and technology. The level of productivity will depend on how the capital stock is organized and used, advances in technology, the level of care, maintenance, and replacement, and the skills of the workers using it.

profit What is left over for the owners of a business after all expenses have been deducted from the revenues of a firm. Gross profit is the profit before corporate income taxes, or before extraordinary items such as the write-off of a bad investment have been deducted, and before minority interests in a firm have been taken into account. Net profit is the final profit of the firm after all deductions have been made; it is the amount of money that is available for distribution to shareholders as DIVIDENDS, or for reinvestment in the firm for business expansion in the form of RETAINED EARNINGS. Profitability for a firm or industry can be measured in several ways: through year-to-year changes in EARNINGS PER SHARE; through net profit as a per cent of sales; through net profit as a per cent of SHAREHOLDERS' EQUITY; or through net profit as a RATE OF RETURN ON INVESTED CAPITAL. Net profits for individual firms are available from corporate annual and quarterly reports, and for industry as a whole or individual industries from various quarterly and annual reports of Statistics Canada. The annual and quarterly figures on GROSS NATIONAL PRODUCT show pre-tax corporate profits and the share of national income represented by pre-tax profits.

Economists have a number of different ways of treating profits—as returns on various FACTORS OF PRODUCTION, for example, or as a reward for innovation and entrepreneurial skills, as a premium or return for risk, as an ECONOMIC RENT or QUASI-RENT, as a monopoly return resulting from a contrived scarcity, or, in the case of KARL MARX, as the surplus value of labour's contribution to production.

profit and loss statement See EARNINGS STATEMENT.

profit centre Any division of a firm that is clearly identifiable for accounting purposes, that can be held responsible for its activities, and whose goal is to earn the highest possible profit.

profit margin The profitability of a firm or industry, calculated by taking the after-tax profit as a percentage of sales, shareholders' equity, or invested capital. Profit margins can be calculated for the private sector as a whole or for a single industry, and the results for a particular firm measured against industry averages to determine the efficiency of the individual firm.

profit maximization The attempt to calculate and to reach the most profitable level of output by keeping costs at the lowest possible level per unit of output. Under these conditions, output can be increased until the MARGINAL REVENUE from the last unit produced and sold is equal to the MARGINAL COST of producing that unit. So long as marginal revenue is greater than marginal cost, it will always pay to produce more; once marginal cost passes marginal revenue, then extra production will reduce profits. In economic models, it is assumed that firms seek to maximize profits and thus to achieve the most efficient allocation of resources in the economy; but in real life this may not always be the strategy of the individual firm, especially in the short run. For example, in an OLIGOPOLISTIC industry, the existing firms may be satisfied to live with existing market shares, instead of seeking to maximize profits through competition for a bigger market share at the expense of their rivals.

profit motive The instinctive desire that is said to exist among entrepreneurs in a free-market economy for the highest possible profit, and is viewed by free-market economists as the engine of economic growth and the source of economic and social progress. Free-market economists contend that every firm seeks to maximize its profits. See also INVISIBLE HAND.

profit-sharing A plan under which employees in a firm receive a share in their employer's profits in addition to their regular wages. The profit-sharing can be in the form of money or shares in the firm, and is usually based on a percentage of after-tax profits set aside for employees. Profit-sharing can be paid out on an annual basis, or can be accumulated as a form of retirement fund or pension, in which case it is treated differently for tax purposes. The proponents of profit-sharing schemes argue that such schemes can lead to better employee morale and improved productivity in the firm. Union critics say that they prefer to bargain for better wages and working conditions, instead of relying on management to decide whether there should be a profit-sharing bonus in a particular year, or what the bonus will be.

profit-taking The sale of shares to realize the profit from an increase in the value of the shares. Until the shares are sold and the profits received, all the shareholder has as a result of the increase in the value of his shares is a PAPER PROFIT.

program A sequential series of commands, in a machine-readable language, that instructs a computer to carry out a particular function. Programs can be designed for the general operation of a computer system, or to deal with a specific situation. Problem-solving programs are usually written in special programming languages, such as PL/1, ALGOL, COBOL, and FORTRAN. Programming or software firms are often used to write programs for a computer system so that it can deliver the specialized applications sought by a particular firm, government agency, or other organization. Software production is one of today's growth industries.

program-evaluation and -review technique (PERT) A scientific method of setting completion dates for projects and of ensuring that the completion time is kept as short as possible. In most applications, a computer system is used to keep track of progress; a project is broken down into all of its separate steps, and calculations are made as to which steps can be done independently, which steps must be completed before others can be started or completed, and how much time must be allowed for the delivery of materials or components, skilled workers, and raw materials. From this information it is possible to chart out the sequence of steps and to determine dates for orders, completion dates for individual stages of the project, the time to start hiring workers, and so forth. The computer can keep track of progress, and give management a periodic review to show whether or not a project is likely to meet its targeted completion date, or whether special steps, such as overtime, are needed to reach the completion date on schedule. The technique was developed in 1958 by the U.S. Navy for the Polaris submarine project, and was used later in Canada to schedule the construction of Expo 67 in Montreal. See also CRITICAL-PATH METHOD.

progressive tax A tax in which the tax rate increases in line with increases in the tax base; this means that the larger the tax base—for example, the larger a person's taxable income—the greater the percentage collected as tax. Progressive taxes are based on the ABILITY-TO-PAY PRINCIPLE, with the MARGINAL

TAX RATE rising as the tax base rises.

The best-known progressive tax is the INCOME TAX. A person with a taxable income of, say, $3,000, would pay a low tax rate. But as his taxable income rises, so does his rate of tax, so that the taxable income between, say, $25,000 and $27,000, is taxed at a much higher rate than the first $3,000, with the rate rising to a top marginal rate on all taxable income over, say, $60,000.

Tax experts point out that the other side of the coin in a progressive-tax system is that tax deductions end up being worth much more to people with high taxable incomes than to those with low taxable incomes. For example, the person who has a taxable income of $27,000 in the above example, and who invests $2,000 in a registered retirement savings plan, will get a much bigger tax refund than the person with only $3,000 of taxable income; this means that the $2,000 of savings for the first taxpayer's old age have cost him much less than it would have cost the second taxpayer to get the same retirement benefit. Thus, in determining the progressive nature of an income-tax system, many factors have to be taken into account, such as the marginal-tax-rate schedule itself, the forms of income that are tax exempt or tax deductible, and various incentives that are built into the tax system. See also TAX EXPENDITURES.

proletariat In MARXIST ECONOMICS, the working or wage-earning class. KARL MARX argued that the wages of the working class were held at a subsistence level to allow capitalists to exploit the workers and to accumulate capital. He predicted that the proletariat would someday rebel at this condition, overthrow the capitalists, and establish a socialist society that would represent the next stage in the inevitable evolution of man towards a communist society.

promissory note A signed promise by a borrower to repay a lender a stated sum of money plus a stated amount of interest, by or on a stated date. In some cases, such notes may be negotiable.

promoter A term, sometimes pejorative, used to describe a person trying to raise capital for a business enterprise, or to get approval for a change in local by-laws so that he can put up a new building. The term is sometimes used to describe those who tout shares in penny mining stocks, or who try to attract private capital into backing a new venture.

promotion 1. An organized effort to raise new capital or to make a stock-market profit by pushing the sale of a company's shares. **2.** A marketing effort to launch a new product or to strengthen the sales of an existing product through such devices as contests, sponsorship of sports or other events, a special discount sale, or intensive advertising. **3.** An advance in the career of an employee to a higher level of responsibility and pay.

propensity to consume The proportion of his income that a person will spend instead of save, at any given level of income. Most people tend to spend a smaller proportion of their incomes as their incomes rise. At the lowest levels of income, people are likely to spend their entire incomes, and perhaps even more than their total incomes.

propensity to save The proportion of his income that a person will save instead of spend, at any given level of income. Most people tend to save more as their incomes rise. At the lowest income levels, there is likely to be no saving and perhaps even DISSAVING.

property The legal right to possess and use economic goods and to derive both present and future benefits from such use. There are different types of property: real property, consisting of land and buildings, for example; personal property, consisting of such assets as furniture and a car; or intellectual property, consisting of such things as copyright, patents, and trademarks.

property tax A direct tax levied on the assessed value of land and buildings; the tax is usually expressed as a mill rate or per cent of each thousand dollars of assessed value. Property tax is within the taxing powers of the provinces under the British North America Act. All the provinces have delegated the power to levy a property tax to their municipalities, although two provinces, New Brunswick and Prince Edward Island, also levy a property tax directly on real property. Methods of assessment differ from province to province. In some provinces, assessment is based on MARKET VALUE; in others, it is based on a multitude of assessment rules that have been developed over the years, which, as a result, may lead to similarly valued properties being assessed at quite different amounts. The main criticism levied against property tax is that it is not based on ability to pay.

proportional tax A flat-rate tax, which collects the same percentage from the taxable asset regardless of its value. Examples would be sales taxes, the mill rates of property taxes, or tariffs.

proprietorship A business owned and operated by one person—for example, most small shops and many other small businesses.

prorationing A method of apportioning oil or other mineral production among all of the producers in relation to their reserves when the supply of a resource is greater than the demand for it.

prospect A property on which minerals have been discovered, but whose exact mineral value has not yet been determined by geological calculation and exploration.

prospector An individual acting on his own or retained by a mining company or group of investors to search for mineral prospects.

prospectus A document that describes a new issue of COMMON or PREFERRED SHARES or BONDS being issued for sale to the public; the prospectus must meet the disclosure and other requirements of the provincial SECURITIES COMMISSION under whose jurisdiction the new issue is to be made, and must be approved by the securities commission before any of the new shares or bonds can be offered for sale to the public. A "full, true, and plain disclosure of all material facts" in respect of the offering of such securities must be made. These facts include the price to the public of the shares or bonds, the commission being earned by the UNDERWRITER, the use to which the funds being raised are to be put, a financial history of the company, including its dividend record over the past five years, a commentary on the company's financial statements signed by an outside auditor or accountant, names, addresses, and occupations of the company officers plus their total remuneration, details of principal shareholders in the company, a statement of the company's capitalization, information on current legal suits, and other details, along with a certificate signed by the company's chief executive officer, chief financial officer, and two directors, stating that the information is full, true, and plain disclosure, along with a similar statement signed by the UNDERWRITERS.

protectionism Policies to restrict trade, such as high tariffs, quotas, import licences, and a wide variety of NON-TARIFF BARRIERS, such as government purchasing policies, health standards, and artificial import valuations. The purpose of all of these measures is to keep out imports and to protect local industries and jobs. Protectionist policies are more difficult to implement with the adoption of increasingly liberal trade rules under the GENERAL AGREEMENT ON TARIFFS AND TRADE—but not impossible. A popular device these days is to negotiate so-called voluntary quotas with exporters, using political and economic threats to get agreement; under voluntary quotas, exporting nations agree to limit their exports.

Protestant ethic A term applied by the German sociologist, Max Weber, to his thesis that Protestantism, from the seventeenth century on, gave a particular impetus to the capitalist drive for material success by making a virtue of hard work and the accumulation of wealth. Yet there are many examples of societies that have had no connection with Protestantism where communities have worked hard and striven for riches—Japan, for example, or Israel, France, Singapore, and South Korea.

provincial savings institution Savings banks operated by the Alberta and Ontario governments. The Province of Ontario Savings Office opened its doors for business in 1922; it pays interest on deposits, but does not make consumer loans. The Province of Alberta Treasury Branch began operation in 1938; it provides regular chequing and savings services and makes consumer, business, and agricultural loans and mortgages.

provincial spending power The principal spending powers of the provinces, set out in section 92 of the BRITISH NORTH AMERICA ACT. These powers include spending for the management and sale of public lands, including the timber on those lands, for provincial jails, hospitals, municipalities, local works and undertakings, and for the administration of justice within the province, on matters affecting civil property and civil rights in the province and on all matters of a merely local or private nature within the province. Section 92 also spells out the provincial responsibility for education. Section 95 gives the federal and provincial governments concurrent powers over agriculture and immigration; but federal law prevails if federal and provincial laws conflict. A 1951 amendment to the British North America Act, section 94 (A), gives the federal and provincial governments concurrent powers over old-age pensions, but federal pension laws cannot affect provincial pension laws. The provinces are able to spend in a wide range of areas, including social welfare, education, industrial development, environmental protection, highways, trade promotion, agriculture, resource development, telecommunications, hydro-electric power, consumer protection, health care, labour relations, law enforcement, municipal services, and tourism. See also PROVINCIAL TAXING POWER, FEDERAL SPENDING POWER, FEDERAL TAXING POWER, SHARED-COST PROGRAM, EQUALIZATION PAYMENTS, TRANSFER PAYMENT.

provincial taxing power The principal taxing powers of the provinces, set out mainly in section 92 of the BRITISH NORTH AMERICA ACT. Section 92 (2) allows the provinces to levy DIRECT TAXES, such as income taxes, property taxes, mineral, oil, natural-gas, and timber royalties, retail-sales taxes, corporation taxes, and death and succession duties. The tax must be levied within the province to raise revenue for a provincial purpose. Section 92 (9) permits provinces to raise money by regulating shops, saloons, taverns, and auctioneers, and by other licensing activities for provincial, local, or municipal purposes. Section 124 is of minor importance, but does permit New Brunswick to raise money by levying lumber-export duties, a condition imposed by the province on entering Confederation. The provinces may also raise money through charges levied for services under various regulatory powers. Provincial taxing powers may be delegated to municipalities; for example, the provinces have given the municipalities the power to levy PROPERTY TAXES.

Although the provinces have wide powers to levy direct taxes, the courts have been careful to restrict the most blatant misuse of such powers. For example, the courts in the late nineteenth century ruled that harsh British Columbia taxes on Chinese people were *ultra vires,* because they were not levied to raise revenue but to drive the Chinese out of the province. The Fathers of Confederation decided not to let the provinces impose INDIRECT TAXES because they wanted to make sure that Canada remained a common market; they feared that the provinces might use indirect taxes to raise trade barriers against one another. Section 121 of the British North America Act underlines their intention, by stating that the products of each province are to be admitted duty free to the other provinces.

proxy A document signed by a shareholder of a corporation designating another person to vote his shares at the annual or other meeting of a corporation. The management of a corporation solicits the proxies of shareholders who don't plan to attend corporation meetings, or who support management and do not wish to vote their shares. Proxy documents are mailed out before annual and other meetings. However, a shareholder can assign his vote to any other person he chooses, including critics of management; he assigns this right to vote his shares simply by writing that person's name on the proxy document and signing it. A shareholder can also limit the voting rights of management or anyone else named in his proxy statement. Securities legislation in Canada requires that all management motions planned for annual and other meetings be included in proxy statements, and that the statements must be mailed well in advance of the meeting. Under provincial securities laws, rival shareholder groups must also be given access to the shareholder mailing lists, so that they can also solicit proxies from shareholders.

proxy battle A competition between management and a rival group of shareholders, or between various groups of shareholders, to get control of the proxies of other shareholders so that they can win votes at annual or other corporation meetings. Such battles may take place when there is a contest for control of a company, or when a group of shareholders wants to elect a member to the board of directors to represent their interests.

prudent-man rule The requirement that a trustee, such as a trust-company officer, invest only in securities that a prudent man would buy if he were investing for other people for whom he felt morally bound to provide. Some provinces and the federal government designate the type of securities that a trustee or fiduciary may buy. See also REASONABLE MAN.

Prudential Finance Corporation affair The 1966 collapse and bankruptcy of a financial company, incorporated in Ontario, which subsequently helped lead to a major overhaul of Ontario securities laws. See also ATLANTIC ACCEPTANCE AFFAIR. The company, on bankruptcy, had assets of $23.5 million and liabilities of $27 million. The company president was arrested and charged with theft, forgery, and uttering, and the Ontario Securities Commission was ordered by the Ontario attorney general to investigate the company's affairs. As events proceeded, a number of other companies were placed in receivership, including North American General Insurance Company, the first federally incorporated insurance company to declare bankruptcy since the early 1920s. Reports tabled in the Ontario legislature in 1968 showed that Prudential had been under investigation by the Ontario Securities Commission since 1963, but that no action had been taken.

psychic income The pleasure or satisfaction that is derived from a job and is a factor in a person's decision to seek or hold a job, even though it may pay less than another job that the same person could get. A person might work for a charitable organization where pay is lower because of the satisfaction received from doing a job that clearly helps the less fortunate. A person who enjoys the outdoors or dislikes the regimentation of an assembly line may work as a mailman or garbageman instead of in a factory, even if the pay is lower.

psychological theory of the business cycle The theory that changes in the business cycle result from business and general public attitudes about the economic outlook. If confidence is high, then consumers will buy and business will invest. If people are pessimistic about the future, even for non-economic reasons, then consumers may hold on to their money and buy less, while business will delay new investment plans. While economists generally do not attach much significance to public attitudes in explaining the business cycle, it is recognized that public attitudes or confidence can affect the overall level of economic activity.

public accounts The books of account published by the Canadian government once a year, which show in detail how public funds have been spent in the past fiscal year. The accounts list spending, department by department, for the fiscal year ending the previous 31 March, and provide other information, including itemization of government assets and liabilities, to give as true a picture as possible of the financial position of the Canadian government and its agencies. Similar reports are published by each of the provincial governments.

Public Accounts Committee A standing committee of the House of Commons established in the first session of the first Parliament, in 1867, to give members of Parliament the opportunity to review the PUBLIC ACCOUNTS or spending records of the government and to examine the reports of the AUDITOR GENERAL. The public accounts and report of the auditor general are automatically referred to the committee: it is the financial watchdog of Parliament. Since 1957, an opposition member has chaired the committee; it also has a research officer.

public company A company whose shares are traded by members of the public through a recognized STOCK EXCHANGE or OVER-THE-COUNTER MARKET. This means that they are subject to regulation by a provincial SECURITIES COMMISSION and by the stock exchanges on which they are listed.

public corporation See CROWN CORPORATION.

public debt The outstanding debt of all levels of government and their agencies. In Canada, it includes the debts of the federal, provincial, and municipal governments, school boards, crown corporations, and other government agencies. It consists of bonds, treasury bills, and preferred shares held by residents or non-residents; the portion of public debt held by non-residents is the potentially worrisome part of the public debt, since the interest and principal must usually be repaid in foreign currencies, which have to be earned and which represent debit entries in the country's balance of payments.

public finance The field of economics that studies the economic and social impact of government tax and spending activities. Among the areas it is concerned with are: the economic and social impact of various forms of taxation and the total level of taxation, including the impact on individuals, different income groups, regions, industries, and the economy as a whole; government spending, including its control, budgeting, and economic and social impact; debt management; and fiscal relations among different levels of government.

public good A good obtained by government spending and consumed collectively by members of the community. Examples include roads, parks, education, museums, and hospitals. See also PRIVATE GOOD, FREE GOOD. Economist JOHN KENNETH GALBRAITH has argued that society overproduces private goods and underproduces public goods. The benefits of private goods are often more immediately evident than the benefits of public goods; moreover, there are aggressive producers of private goods who are able to stimulate consumer demand through advertising. In contrast, it is harder for the public to voice clearly its demand for public goods.

public housing Housing that is owned and operated by government agencies. Although provincial governments were once the main operators of public housing, municipal governments, with the assistance of federal and provincial funds, are increasingly establishing their own local housing corporations to provide subsidized housing for needy families and individuals, senior citizens, and the handicapped.

public issue Shares or bonds offered for sale to the public for the first time. Such public offers must first be approved by a provincial SECURITIES COMMISSION. See also PRIMARY DISTRIBUTION.

public lending right The right of authors to receive a royalty from a public library for the repeated use of their books. The amount received could be based on the number of times the book is circulated; or it could be based on the number of copies of books held in public libraries. Authors are seeking recognition of this right in Canada and the United States, arguing that, while they receive a royalty for every copy of their book that is sold, they are at present not compensated for the repeated use of their book by library users. Some authors argue that libraries reduce the potential sale of their books, and hence reduce their potential royalty income. Legal recognition of the public lending right exists in Denmark and Sweden and is about to be introduced in Britain.

public-opinion survey A scientific polling of the adult population as a whole, or of specific groups according to age, occupation, sex, income, or region, to obtain opinions on public issues.

public ownership The ownership and operation by a government of a corporation that produces a good or service. Generally speaking, such corporations are established or acquired to advance or protect the public interest, or to undertake an important activity that private enterprise is unwilling or unable to undertake. Examples of publicly owned corporations in Canada include Air Canada, the provincial power utilities, local bus or transit utilities, Canadian National Railways, Pacific Western Airlines, the Potash Corporation of Saskatchewan, the Alberta Energy Company (which is 50 per cent government owned), and the Canadian Broadcasting Corporation.

public relations Activities designed to cast a firm, industry, individual, or government in a favourable light with the public. Public-relations departments of firms advise clients or employers on how to cast themselves or their activities in a way likely to win favour with the public, how to get publicity, how to provide information to the press and public, and how to deal with elected politicians and government agencies.

public revenue Total government revenues. Public revenue includes income from taxes, tariffs, fees, and licences, interest on loans, profits of crown corporations, royalties, revenues from the sale of mineral, timber, or other rights, and all other forms of government income.

public sector The part of the economy under direct government ownership and control. It includes all federal, provincial, and municipal governments, hospitals, schools and universities, federal and provincial crown corporations and agencies, municipal transit, housing, and other services. It is one of two major sectors in a MIXED ECONOMY, the other being the PRIVATE SECTOR.

Public Service Commission (PSC) The hiring agency of the federal government. Its role is to hire employees for the federal government, except for crown corporations, and to promote them on the basis of merit rather than political patronage. The original Civil Service Commission was created in 1908. In 1918, the principle of merit was protected in law with the passage of the Civil Service Act, which gave the commission responsibility for the hiring and classification of government employees and for recommending pay scales. The Civil Service Act of 1961 reaffirmed the merit principle, and also gave employee associations the right to be consulted on pay and on working conditions. The Public Service Employment Act in 1967 again gave the commission responsibility for government hiring based on the merit principle; but with the introduction of collective bargaining in the public service, responsibility for negotiating pay scales and working conditions passed to the TREASURY BOARD. The secretary of state reports to Parliament for the commission.

Public Service Staff Relations Act Federal legislation that, since 1967, has given federal employees the right to collective bargaining and the right to strike. The act sets out the conditions under which collective bargaining takes place; these rights are not as broad as those available to industries covered by the CANADA LABOUR CODE. Bargaining is limited to pay scales, hours of work, vacations, and matters related to these. Under the act, bargaining units must indicate whether they want the right to strike if negotiations reach a stalemate, or whether they want arbitration.

Public Service Staff Relations Board A labour-relations board created in 1967 by the Public Service Staff Relations Act to determine public-service bargaining units, to certify bargaining agents, to handle complaints of unfair labour practices, and to supervise collective bargaining in the public service. It includes a pay-research bureau, which collects information on pay and employment conditions in Canada that can be used by both sides in collective bargaining as objective information.

public utility A corporation, often government-owned but sometimes privately owned, that provides an essential good or service to the public, usually under monopoly conditions. Examples include the provincial power companies, telephone companies, cable television, local transit services, and, in some instances, pipelines. Prices charged by public utilities are usually regulated. Provincial hydro companies, for example, may have to get approval for rate increases from provincial energy boards. Some utilities—for example, Bell Canada—are subject to a regulated UTILITY RATE OF RETURN, while others, such as cable operators, have to get government approval for rate increases.

public welfare **1.** Income maintenance and other programs of public support to the needy. **2.** A more general term that refers to the welfare of society as a whole, as opposed to the interests of a special group.

public works Government construction projects to meet the economic, social, or cultural needs of the nation, province, or community. Examples include airports, harbours, highways, bridges, theatre centres, hospitals, schools, universities, public housing, subways, government office buildings, and research laboratories. While such works are undertaken according to need and the financial resources of government, they can be accelerated during periods of recession, as a counter-cyclical measure; they provide jobs, boost demand for building materials, and, through the MULTIPLIER effect, generate economic activity throughout the economy. Similarly, during periods of full employment, it may make sense for government to delay public works and thus reduce the level of demand in the economy.

Public Works, Department of One of the first government departments to be established at the time of Confederation, it is the principal construction and real-estate manager for the federal government and its agencies. It supervises government construction projects, manages government buildings and other property, arranges the leasing of commercial buildings for the government, and plans future government property needs, including the need for office space.

pump priming The use of government spending on public projects to stimulate the economy and to create jobs.

purchasing power **1.** Money in the hands of consumers, or credit available to them to purchase goods and services. In times of recession, a government may cut taxes to increase the purchasing power of consumers, and thus raise the level of demand in the economy. In turn, this should lead to increased investment by business, as rising consumer demand pushes industrial production closer to full capacity. Conversely, purchasing power may be curbed during periods of full employment and rising inflation by increasing taxes. **2.** The physical volume of goods and services that a Canadian dollar can buy. As inflation increases, the purchasing power of the dollar—or any other monetary unit—declines.

purchasing-power parity The theory that the exchange rates between two currencies are in equilibrium when their purchasing power is the same in each of the two countries. Under this theory, exchange rates change to reflect relative changes in purchasing power caused by inflation in one country or the other; if the exchange rates did not adjust, then it would pay to make all of one's purchases in the country with the least inflation. Thus, if the Canadian dollar is at par with the U.S. dollar, and Canada has 10 per cent inflation and the U.S. has none, then the new Canadian exchange rate should be one Canadian dollar equals ninety U.S. cents. The problem with this theory is that goods and services are not traded between two countries in the same proportion as the representative bundle of goods and services that would be used to calculate typical purchasing power in each country. Trade is more specialized; nor does this method of setting exchange rates take into account other factors that affect exchange rates, such as investment flows, and travel based on climatic differences.

pure interest The actual rate of interest paid for the use of someone else's capital, after deducting the administrative and paperwork costs of the loan and the premium charged to cover the risk of default or loss. It is a theoretical concept used in economic analysis.

put A contract that gives the holder the right to sell a specified number of shares, during a specified period of time, to someone who has agreed that he will buy the shares; in return, the holder of the put pays a fee to the would-be buyer of the shares for the privilege, whether or not he ever exercises his option to sell. Puts may be written for anywhere between thirty days and six months and, like the direct sale and purchase of shares, are arranged through stockbrokers. A person purchasing a put option does so because he expects a sizeable drop in the value of the shares during the life of the put. See also CALL, OPTION, STRADDLE.

pyramid selling A method of selling in which agents or salesmen pay a fee to participate, and earn money by finding and charging others to participate as salesmen. Salesmen, in addition to paying a hefty fee to participate, are usually also required to purchase a minimum quota of goods even before they have made any sales. Pyramid selling is, generally speaking, a dubious and often fraudulent form of enterprise that employs high-pressure tactics and misleading claims to persuade people to pay money for the privilege of becoming salesmen. Federal and provincial laws restrict such enterprises. For example, Ontario's Pyramidic Sales Repeal Act licenses companies engaged in pyramidal selling, and stipulates that no more than 10 per cent of any investment by an individual in a sales plan can be used as a finder's fee or other such benefit for the other participants.

Q

qualifying share A single share or small number of shares owned by a person serving as a director of a corporation. Ownership of at least one share is necessary if a person is to serve as a company director.

quality control The inspection and testing of products off the assembly line to make sure that product standards are being met. Almost all firms have quality-control inspectors who systematically examine the firm's production, to ensure that the expected level of workmanship is being maintained by the firm's employees.

quality of life A concept of standard of living that includes material and non-material well-being. Attempts have been made to measure quality of life—through the development of SOCIAL INDICATORS, for example—but it remains a highly subjective and thus extremely difficult concept to measure. What is known is that, with rising incomes, people are more likely to take non-economic factors into account—by taking leisure time instead of working overtime, for example, or by blocking commercial development to preserve a landscape or create a park.

quantity theory of money and prices A theory that explains the level of prices and pace of economic activity in terms of the relationship between the level of output and the money supply. Although the theory dates back to the CLASSICAL ECONOMISTS, it is associated today with Milton Friedman of the University of Chicago and the MONETARIST SCHOOL, which argues that the way to control inflation and manage economic activity is to control the supply of money.

The theory can be expressed in mathematical terms as the equation of exchange: total supply in the economy, expressed as the total supply of money multiplied by the velocity of money, equals total demand in the economy, expressed as total physical output or real gross national product multiplied by the price level. Where M is the money supply and V the velocity of money, P the price level and Q the real gross national product, $MV=PQ$. The velocity of money, which depends on the way the banking system works and on the spending and saving habits of the population, is assumed to be constant in the short run. The level of output in the economy under full-employment conditions is also assumed to be fixed in the short run. Thus, the variables in the short run are the supply of money and the price level. According to the theory, increases in money supply will lead to inflation as the economy approaches full employment. Similarly, a decline in the money supply can lead to deflation.

quarterly report **1.** A financial statement issued by a public corporation every three months to keep shareholders up to date on its performance. Such reports are usually not audited by the firm's outside auditors, and contain mainly EARNINGS-STATEMENT rather than BALANCE-SHEET information. **2.** Quarterly statistics under the SYSTEM OF NATIONAL ACCOUNTS—for example, on the gross national product, balance of payments, and financial flows—published by Statistics Canada.

quasi-rent Although rent is normally associated with land and the resources contained on the land, the British economist Alfred Marshall argued that firms also earn a quasi-rent or extra profit on their other factors of production when demand exceeds supply and there is a delay in expanding productive capacity in an industry. Since it takes time to construct new buildings, heavy engineering works, and other productive facilities, there is a period of time during which existing producers can raise prices without affecting demand. This extra profit they earn is a rent they can exact from their customers. It is called a quasi-rent because it should be temporary, ending when productive capacity in the industry has been expanded to meet consumer demand under normal pricing and profit conditions.

Quebec Deposit Insurance Board A provincial agency responsible for licensing financial institutions (other than banks) that accept deposits, and for insuring customer deposits. It is also a lender of last resort to provincial trust and mortgage-loan companies and caisses populaires. The board may borrow funds in turn from the CANADA DEPOSIT INSURANCE CORPORATION.

Quebec Pension Plan (**QPP**) The Quebec equivalent of the CANADA PENSION PLAN, established in 1965. It is fully portable with the Canada Pension Plan and offers similar benefits. Its investment policy differs, however. While the Canada Pension Plan funds are lent to the provinces at the rate of interest paid on outstanding government bonds, the Quebec Pension Plan funds are deposited with the Quebec Deposit and Investment Fund, and are used to help develop the industrial base of the province. Its main investments are government bonds, but the investment fund also purchases the bonds, shares, and mortgages of Quebec businesses.

queuing theory A mathematical technique that is used to help management decide the level of service to provide in a facility where customers or users expect to be treated on a first-come-first-served basis—the number of loading gates at an airport, for example, the number of check-out counters at a supermarket, the number of turnstiles in a subway station. While a system that did not provide for some queuing during periods of peak use would probably be unjustifiably expensive, queuing theory helps management to find ways to keep queues to a minimum, and to move people, planes, or ships in a seaway or canal most effectively.

quick asset An asset that is readily convertible into cash at roughly its face value or book value, such as a certificate of deposit or bond, accounts receivable, or cash itself. Such assets are listed as CURRENT ASSETS and are usually considered to include all current assets other than inventories.

quick ratio See ACID-TEST RATIO.

quiet enjoyment The continuous use and possession of one's property without interruption due to trespass, pollution, noise, or construction that eliminates sunlight or has some other harmful effect.

quota A limitation: for example, on the volume of imports, exports, immigration, production, or consumption. Quotas may be expressed as a percentage of a base period or as an actual number. Import quotas are often adopted as a protectionist device to protect local industry from foreign competition; sometimes they are imposed directly by the importing country and sometimes they are negotiated with exporting countries, which impose "voluntary" export quotas. Quotas may also be imposed on the export of a commodity in short supply or on domestic consumption during a shortage. In international trade, the use of quotas is gradually being restricted and controlled through changes in GENERAL AGREEMENT ON TARIFFS AND TRADE rules. Quotas are also imposed by FARM MARKETING BOARDS on the output of farmers.

quotation 1. The closing price for a share listed on a stock exchange, a commodity on a commodity market, or a bond on a bond market. **2.** During the course of the trading day, the highest bid to buy and the lowest offer to sell. Quotations are published daily in the financial pages of newspapers.

R

RIO (Reshaping the International Order) Project A study sponsored, in 1974, by the CLUB OF ROME and the Dutch government, to describe "what new international order should be recommended to the world's statesmen and social groups so as to meet, to the extent practically and realistically possible, the urgent needs of today's population and the probable needs of future generations." The study was headed by Jan Tinbergen, a Dutch economist and winner of the Nobel Prize for economics, who assembled twenty-one international experts to devise a new international economic order.

The report, published in 1976, proposed an international treaty, similar to the Treaty of Rome that had established the European Economic Community, and modelled on the CHARTER OF ECONOMIC RIGHTS AND DUTIES OF STATES. This framework treaty would lay the legally binding foundation for a new set of international economic relations, and would provide a legal basis for the negotiation of the agreements needed to implement a new international economic order. The report said that the LESS-DEVELOPED COUNTRIES must have full sovereignty over their natural resources. It also developed the concept of "the common heritage of mankind," which it took to include not only the oceans and space, but also minerals, science and technology, the means of production, and other sources of wealth. It proposed specific medium-range (1976–85) and long-range (1985–2000) policies in ten areas: the international monetary system; income redistribution and financing of development; food production; industrialization, trade, and the international division of labour; energy, ores, and minerals; scientific research and technological development; multinational corporations; the human environment; arms reduction; and ocean management.

raiding An effort by a union to persuade members of another union to switch ranks and have it certified as their new bargaining agent. Federal and provincial labour laws restrict the rights of one union to raid another to a relatively short period of time, called an open season, each year or in the life of a collective agreement, while individual labour federations, such as the CANADIAN LABOUR CONGRESS, impose penalties on affiliated unions that engage in such practices unless there is clear evidence that a union is not serving its members adequately. Raiding, when it does occur, is usually launched by a union that is affiliated with a competing labour federation. A raiding union, to be certified as the new bargaining agent for a group of members, has to be able to show that it speaks for a majority of the workers and thus have the existing bargaining agent decertified.

rally A stock-market term indicating a firm recovery and rise in the price of a share, or of shares generally, following a decline in the price of a share or shares generally.

Rand formula A clause in a collective agreement under which the employer agrees to collect union dues or an amount equivalent to union dues from all employees in the bargaining unit, whether or not they are union members, during the life of the collective agreement. The formula is attributed to a 1946 decision by Mr. Justice Ivan C. Rand of the Supreme Court of Canada, in a conflict between the Ford Motor Company and its union, the United Auto Workers. Mr. Justice Rand said that the company had to make a compulsory check-off for all employees, but that all members of the bargaining unit did not have to be members of the union. Such an arrangement is sometimes called an agency shop, as opposed to a UNION SHOP. Most collective agreements now have a Rand-type formula, and two provinces, Manitoba and Quebec, have made the Rand formula compulsory in all collective agreements.

rate of interest See INTEREST.

rate of return on invested capital A measure of the profitability of a company that shows how well the management has used the resources at its disposal. It is calculated by dividing net earnings by the company's INVESTED CAPITAL. This ratio allows the financial performance of different firms in the same or different industries to be compared.

rationalization In industrial policy, the reorganization of firms in an industry—through mergers, for example—to achieve ECONOMIES OF SCALE in production, and sufficient size and cash-flow to support research and development and similar essential corporate activities. Rationalization usually occurs in industries where there are too many competing firms, each too small to achieve the benefits of mass-production techniques and other economies of scale or to support product innovation and plant modernization. In Canada, it is argued, too many industries have too many producers; an industrial strategy is needed, it is also argued, to rationalize many of these industries through mergers, so that they can compete against imports and produce distinctive products that are competitively priced for world markets. One explanation for the proliferation of firms in Canada is that many MULTINATIONAL CORPORATIONS have established BRANCHPLANTS here just to serve the Canadian market by assembling many of the products developed and designed within their parent-company operations.

rationing The allocation of consumer goods or industrial materials in time of shortage, to make sure that all essential needs are first met and that allocation does not depend on who can pay the highest price. Rationing may be introduced for a single commodity—say, oil—by having a government agency allocate the oil among refineries and by rating customers, giving high priority to hospitals and homes, railways, trucking companies, and farmers, and lower priority to commercial enterprises and private automobiles. During the Second World War, the WARTIME PRICES AND TRADE BOARD had wide power to allocate scarce raw materials to industry for military and other essential purposes, and to ban the manufacture of certain non-essential consumer goods. The board imposed coupon rationing for meat, tea, coffee, butter, and sugar, for example. Coupons were issued to all Canadians for equal amounts of such necessities, with the coupons being required at the time of purchase. Retailers, in turn, had to turn in coupons to get new supplies. The Department of MUNITIONS AND SUPPLY rationed the sale of automobiles, trucks, tires, gasoline, steel, non-ferrous metals, rubber, chemicals, oil, coal, wood fuel, and other raw, semi-processed, and processed materials.

raw land Land that has no services, such as water, sewers, or streets, and therefore cannot immediately be used for new housing, commercial buildings, or other such purposes.

raw material A natural or semi-processed material that is used by a manufacturer in the production of a good. For example, lumber is a raw material for a furniture company, iron ore for a steel company, or steel for a manufacturer of rail cars.

real domestic product A measure of the contribution, in real or constant-dollar terms or in physical output, of major industries to the

GROSS DOMESTIC PRODUCT. The figures, produced monthly by Statistics Canada, show the changes in production by more than one hundred different goods- or service-producing industries and by key industrial categories, such as agriculture, forestry, fishing and trapping, mining, manufacturing, construction, transportation, storage and communication, electric power, gas and water utilities, retail trade, finance, insurance, real estate, public administration, and defence. The changes in output are measured as an index, with 1971 equal to 100.

real estate Property, such as land and buildings, that is not movable. See also CHATTEL.

real-estate board An association of real-estate brokers in a community, that supervises the activities of brokers, organizes and oversees co-operative services, such as the MULTIPLE-LISTING SERVICE, and that, until amendments to the Combines Investigation Act came into effect in 1976, fixed commission rates charged by member-brokers on the sale of land and buildings.

real-estate broker A person who buys and sells land and buildings on behalf of buyers and sellers, and who also arranges the leasing of land and buildings.

real-estate investment trust (**REIT**) An investment vehicle established by a bank or other financial institution, that raises money by selling shares or debt securities to the public and invests the proceeds in mortgages, real estate, and sale and leaseback arrangements; it may also make construction loans. REITs do not pay corporate income tax on their profits or capital gains; but the owners are taxed at their personal rates, which may be lower than the corporate rate, on the income paid to them, or on one-half of the distributed capital gains.

real growth The growth of the economy, or a sector of the economy, after the money-value of the increase is deflated by the amount of inflation during the same period. It gives a true picture of the growth in output, as opposed to illusory growth represented simply by inflation. In a given year, the real growth of the economy may be 3.5 per cent, although the growth in current dollars may be 11 per cent; the difference is inflation. When talking about economic growth, economists mean real growth and not current money-value growth.

real wages The actual purchasing power of wages, as opposed to money wages. If wages are increased 5 per cent but inflation also increases 5 per cent, then real wages have not changed at all. If wages increased 5 per cent but inflation increased 7 per cent, then real wages, or purchasing power, have actually declined; similarly, a 5 per cent wage increase when inflation is 3 per cent means that real wages have increased.

reasonable man A man who never does anything without first considering the effect of his act or failure to act on other persons; he is always aware of the need to consider the welfare of others. In negligence cases, the defendant's behaviour is usually compared with the behaviour one would expect from a reasonable man. See also PRUDENT-MAN RULE.

rebate The return of part of the payment already made for a good or service. Rebates may be offered for high-volume purchases, prompt payment, or other such reasons. Under Canadian law, the same rebate must be offered to all customers in the same circumstances. See also DISCOUNT, which is deducted before the account is paid.

receipt A written document that shows that delivered goods have been received, a service rendered, or payment made.

receiver A person either appointed by a court or by a creditor to take temporary charge of a business and operate it, until the business is either liquidated or wound up and the creditors paid off, or until the owners can arrange new financing to pay off creditors. The receiver's job includes making sure that the records of the business are maintained, and making an inventory of the firm's assets.

receiver general of Canada The chief financial officer of the federal government, who receives all revenues of the government and deposits them in the CONSOLIDATED REVENUE FUND. Each government payment, no matter how small, must be authorized by a specific law of Parliament (such as, say, the family-allowance legislation), or by annual APPROPRIATION ACTS, which authorize cabinet ministers or their deputies to make requisitions for payment to the receiver general. He is usually the minister of SUPPLY AND SERVICES.

receivership The status of a firm whose affairs have been put in the hands of a receiver because it is unable to pay its bills and other obligations.

recession The down-side of the business cycle. A recession is technically a period of weak economic activity, characterized by two consecutive quarters showing a decline in real gross national product. The term is more generally used today to describe reduced economic activity and increased unemployment, even though there may still be slight economic growth.

reciprocal trade agreement An agreement between two nations, giving each other special and equal tariff and other trade concessions; or an agreement among a larger number of nations, giving one another tariff and trade agreements of approximately equal value. The most important reciprocal trade agreement in existence today is the GENERAL AGREEMENT ON TARIFFS AND TRADE (GATT). Canada has reciprocal trade agreements with Australia and New Zealand, and the CANADA–UNITED STATES AUTOMOTIVE PRODUCTS AGREEMENT may also be considered a form of reciprocal trade agreement. Canada and the United States had a reciprocal trade agreement from 1854 to 1866; a new reciprocity agreement was proposed in 1911, but, while it was passed by the U.S. Congress, it was turned down by Canada after a general election that saw the government of Sir Wilfrid Laurier, who had proposed the agreement, defeated by Sir Robert Borden. During the 1920s and the 1930s, Canada negotiated reciprocal trade agreements with many of its trading partners, including Britain, and, following passage by the U.S. Congress in 1934 of the Reciprocal Trade Agreements Act, with the United States. Since the end of the Second World War, most nations have abandoned the negotiation of bilateral reciprocal trade agreements, and have participated in GATT and in regional common-market arrangements instead. See also OTTAWA AGREEMENTS.

reciprocity The exchange of tariff reductions and other trade concessions by one nation, in exchange for similar concessions from another.

reconstruction A wide series of measures adopted in 1944–45, to convert the Canadian economy to peacetime activities and to ensure high levels of employment and stable prices following the Second World War. The federal government feared that, without major planning and intervention, the economy might return to the Depression levels of unemployment that had existed before the Second World War; it also feared that postwar shortages of necessities might lead to severe inflation.

In 1944, the federal government embarked on a number of steps to ease the transition from a wartime economy to a peacetime economy. These included: creation of federal and federal-provincial planning committees; passage of the Agricultural Prices Support Act and the Fisheries Prices Support Act, to control agricultural and fisheries prices; passage of a new NATIONAL HOUSING ACT to stimulate postwar housing construction; establishment of the Export Credits Insurance Corporation (now the EXPORT DEVELOPMENT CORPORATION) to finance export trade; establishment of the Industrial Development Bank (now the FEDERAL BUSINESS DEVELOPMENT BANK) to finance business expansion; establishment of the Department of NATIONAL HEALTH AND WELFARE to improve social welfare for Canadians by implementing a program of FAMILY ALLOWANCES, and through other programs; establishment of the Department of Veterans Affairs, to take charge of the re-establishment in civilian life of Canadians who had served in the armed forces, or otherwise to care for them; and the creation of the Department of RECONSTRUCTION, to take charge of postwar programs to convert the economy back to peacetime activities, to stimulate economic growth, and to control prices. The following year, the federal government spelled out a broad program of measures to achieve full employment and stable prices in its WHITE PAPER ON EMPLOYMENT AND INCOME. Its proposals formed the basis for future government fiscal and other policies to promote growth and check inflation.

Reconstruction, Department of A federal government department created in June 1944 to take charge of converting Canada's economy from its wartime footing to peacetime activities, while averting a return to the high unemployment of prewar Canada and ensuring that postwar shortages did not lead to rapid inflation. The responsibilities of the department were: to determine the employment needs of Canadians being demobilized from the armed forces or laid off from war-related industries as the Second World War drew to an end, and to outline the opportunities to provide new jobs for them; to co-ordinate the activities of other government departments and agencies, so that the transition to a peacetime economy occurred as smoothly as possible; and to devise plans for industrial development and conversion, public works, housing and urban planning, industrial research and development, and the development of Canada's natural resources.

The department was organized into several divisions. The industrial-reconversion division helped industry to convert plants developed for war purposes to peacetime uses, and to find the most efficient postwar use of prewar plants, while trying to ensure a normal flow of employment and income. The surplus-war-assets division advised the government on policies to follow in disposing of a huge inventory of war assets, with the War Assets Corporation actually disposing of the assets. The industrial-research division developed a technical- and scientific-information service for industry, promoted research and development activities, including specific projects to help solve particular industrial and development problems, and co-ordinated the government's long-term scientific programs. The NATIONAL RESEARCH COUNCIL was also made responsible to the minister of Reconstruction. The depreciation-allowances division advised the minister of National Revenue on the level of incentive depreciation rates that should be granted for specific new capital spending by industry on plant and equipment. The co-ordinator of controls, a division of the department, advised the government on when specific wartime controls could be lifted without causing inflation due to shortages. The public-works division worked with provincial and municipal governments to help plan and carry out needed public-works projects that would create jobs and help improve the country's infrastructure. The natural-resources-development division, working with the provinces, planned hydro-electric, forestry, and mining projects, and government-assistance programs needed to see that such projects were carried out. The civil-aviation division promoted the use of civil aviation to improve the economic well-being of the country. The liaison division worked with other federal departments, such as Trade and Commerce (now INDUSTRY, TRADE AND COMMERCE) and LABOUR, and with provincial planning councils established for reconstruction purposes. The department, renamed Reconstruction and Supply in 1946, was wound up in 1949.

recovery The up-side of the business cycle, reflecting an increase in economic activity as the economy moves out of its recession or trough. It is characterized by increased demand and employment, setting the stage for increased investment and further increases in economic growth and employment.

recycling 1. The investment of surplus funds, from countries with strong balance-of-payments surpluses, in countries with serious balance-of-payments deficits or in commercial money markets. For example, the surplus funds or PETRODOLLARS of such oil-rich nations as Saudi Arabia, Kuwait, and the Persian Gulf emirates have been recycled through the EUROCURRENCY market into bonds and other securities issued by deficit nations, many of them LESS-DEVELOPED COUNTRIES, into corporate bonds and shares, or into U.S.-government TREASURY BILLS. Similarly, the surplus oil and gas royalty income of Alberta, through its Heritage Savings Trust Fund, is reinvested in bonds and other securities issued by other governments in Canada. **2.** The re-use of materials after they are no longer needed for their original purpose. For example, old newspapers and other wastepaper products can be converted or recycled into new paper products, while scrap steel can be re-melted into new steel products, and aluminum soft-drink cans can be converted or recycled into aluminum that can be used again for other purposes.

redeemable bond A bond, also known as a callable bond, that can be paid off before maturity by the issuer; the reasons for doing so would either be to take advantage of lower interest rates, or to eliminate interest costs. Most government and corporate bonds are redeemable.

redeemable preferred share A preferred share that may be recalled and paid off by the issuing corporation. Most preferred shares are redeemable.

redemption The paying off of outstanding bonds or other debt securities. This occurs either on the redemption date specified on the bond or other security, or at some earlier date if the bond or other security is redeemable. See also REDEEMABLE BOND, REDEEMABLE PREFERRED SHARE.

redistribution of income Measures adopted by the federal or provincial governments to reduce great inequalities in income among Canadians. These policies include direct government spending to assure free education, accessible health care for all regardless of income, adequate housing, a minimum income (through welfare payments, unemployment insurance, or other programs) to purchase the necessities of life, and a progressive INCOME-TAX system based on ability to pay.

redundancy A term used in government and some business enterprises to indicate the elimination of a job because the function is no longer required. It can result from changing technology, from cancellation of a program or product, or from a shift in demand.

refinancing The issuing of new bonds or other securities by a government or corporation, with the proceeds being used to retire an existing bond or other security. Sometimes the refinancing may be accomplished by exchanging a new security for an outstanding security. See, for example, the CONVERSION LOAN OF 1958. The reasons for refinancing may include a reduction in interest costs, if prevailing rates are lower than those of the outstanding securities, or the extension of the maturity of the outstanding debt. Thus refinancing may occur to roll over an existing debt that is maturing or to replace one form of debt, say a long-term bond, with another—for example, an issue of PREFERRED SHARES.

reflation The adoption of expansionary economic policies to stimulate business activity and to achieve full employment. Such policies usually lead to an increase in the rate of inflation as well.

reforestation The replanting of harvested forests by the pulp and paper and lumber companies, or by provincial agencies, to ensure future supplies. Reforestation is usually a condition of a timber licence, although provincial governments may subsidize replanting costs.

regional development Policies to improve economic conditions in parts of a country that suffer from chronically high unemployment and a general economic performance well below that of the country as a whole. Canada has had such policies in varying degrees almost since Confederation, although they have become much more significant since the start of the 1960s. Typical regional-development policies include: direct government grants to develop INFRASTRUCTURE, such as roads, power plants, water-supply systems, transportation, and industrial parks in slow-growth regions; government grants; LEASEBACKS; more generous tax rates to corporations investing in slow-growth regions; agreements to provide industry with cheap power; and government participation, as a minority equity partner or provider of low-cost loans, through provincial development corporations. See also Department of REGIONAL ECONOMIC EXPANSION.

Regional Economic Expansion, Department

of (DREE) A federal government department created in 1969 to stimulate economic growth and social adjustment in slow-growth parts of Canada that are characterized by chronically high levels of unemployment and per capita income significantly below the national average. To meet its responsibilities to reduce regional economic disparities, DREE provides direct funding for INFRASTRUCTURE projects such as roads and industrial parks, pays capital-investment grants to firms locating in designated areas under the Regional Development Incentives Act, and works with the provinces to devise long-term general-development agreements to establish growth strategies, backed by funding, for slow-growth areas. DREE also administers other regional-development programs, including the PRAIRIE FARM REHABILITATION ADMINISTRATION (PFRA). It is responsible for the CAPE BRETON DEVELOPMENT CORPORATION and the ATLANTIC DEVELOPMENT COUNCIL.

registered home-ownership savings plan (RHOSP) A tax-incentive plan to encourage Canadians to save downpayments to buy their own homes. To qualify for the tax advantage, which permits a taxpayer to save and deduct one thousand dollars a year—to a lifetime maximum of ten thousand dollars—from his taxable income, an individual must be at least eighteen, not previously have benefited from a RHOSP, and not own nor have a spouse who owns a home. If the proceeds of a RHOSP are invested in a home, they are not taxable; if not, they are. RHOSPs are trusts managed by Canadian trust companies, although the trust companies may authorize other financial institutions, such as banks, credit unions, and caisses populaires, to act as selling agents. A RHOSP is an example of a TAX SHELTER.

registered industrial accountant (RIA) An accountant trained specifically for internal-management accounting rather than for public practice. An RIA is trained to design and operate accounting systems in business and government and to provide management with the information it needs to operate the business or government department. An RIA is an accountant who has met the professional standards of the Society of Management Accountants.

registered retirement savings plan (RRSP) A tax-deferral scheme that encourages Canadians to save for their retirement. Most financial institutions, such as banks, trust companies, life-insurance companies, and even mutual funds, offer managed RRSPs. Individuals may invest up to $5,000 a year or 20 per cent of their earned income, whichever is less, if they do not also belong to a registered pension plan, or $3,500 or 20 per cent of their earned income, whichever is less, if they do belong to a registered pension plan. The amount invested each year is deductible from taxable income, with the tax deferred until the purchaser starts to receive benefits on retirement; this will probably be at a lower tax rate, since his income will usually be lower on retirement. Holders of RRSPs must deregister their plans by the age of seventy-one, and use the proceeds to purchase one of several different types of annuities or retirement-income funds. If the money is not invested in this way, it is taxed as a LUMP-SUM PAYMENT the year it is received. Provisions also exist to permit individuals, under certain conditions, to operate their own RRSPs. Financial institutions must invest 90 per cent of the investment funds from RRSPs in Canadian shares, bonds, mortgages, and other Canadian investments.

registered security A bond, share, or other security that is registered in the name of its owner on the books of a company or government agency, and that can only be transferred to a new owner when the existing owner endorses the bond, share certificate, or other security.

registered trademark A TRADEMARK registered or recorded in the TRADE MARKS OFFICE of the BUREAU OF INTELLECTUAL PROPERTY in the Department of CONSUMER AND CORPORATE AFFAIRS.

registrar A trust company or other agent designated by a corporation, that oversees the sale and purchase of the corporation's shares. The registrar receives cancelled share certificates from sellers of shares, and, through the corporation's TRANSFER AGENT, records the new share certificates in the name of the new owner, makes sure that all shares are accounted for, and makes sure that the number of shares registered tallies with the number that are supposed to be OUTSTANDING.

registration The filing of a PROSPECTUS for a new issue of shares or bonds with a provincial SECURITIES COMMISSION in the province or provinces in which they are to be sold to the public.

registry A public record of ownership of land, buildings, shipping, shares, bonds, or other major assets, or of certain types of claims against assets, such as mortgages or chattel mortgages. Registries are maintained by municipalities or provinces for land and buildings, by corporations for shareholders and owners of bonds, and by national governments for shipping and aircraft.

regressive tax A tax whose burden falls more heavily on those with low incomes than on those with high incomes. A retail-sales tax is an example of a regressive tax, since it takes a larger percentage of the total income of a low-income person than of a higher-income person.

regulation The control of the behaviour of corporations or individuals by government rules set out under the authority of federal and provincial laws.

regulatory agency A government agency that regulates the behaviour of corporations or of individuals. Examples include the NATIONAL ENERGY BOARD, the CANADIAN TRANSPORT COMMISSION, the ALBERTA ENERGY RESOURCES CONSERVATION BOARD, and the ONTARIO SECURITIES COMMISSION.

reinsurance The assumption of part of the risk insured by one insurance company, by a second insurance company, to reduce the risk.

remainder To sell off at a substantially reduced price the surplus stocks of a firm—the remaining copies of a book, for example, or a seasonal line of clothing.

remaining established reserves Oil or natural-gas reserves yet to be recovered, but recoverable under current technology and economic conditions, and proved by drilling, production, or other means; or contiguous recoverable reserves, which are judged to exist because of geological, geophysical, or other information. See also ESTABLISHED RESERVES, INITIAL ESTABLISHED RESERVES, and ULTIMATE POTENTIAL RESERVES.

renewable resources Natural resources whose supply can be replaced as they are used. Examples include forests, fisheries, and fur-bearing animals. See also NON-RENEWABLE RESOURCE.

rent **1.** The amount paid for the use of land and buildings that belong to someone else—the monthly amount paid by a tenant to his landlord, for example. See also RENT CONTROL. **2.** The surplus return to land, broadly defined as land, buildings, minerals, oil and natural gas, water, forests, fisheries, and wildlife, above that required to meet the demands of investors and workers to exploit the land. This surplus can be taxed away without depriving corporations and workers of their normal returns, and is known as ECONOMIC RENT. **3.** The rent paid by a person to himself. If a person lives in his own home, the difference between his mortgage interest and other costs, and what he could earn if he rented the house to someone else, is his IMPUTED RENT.

rent control The limitation of rent increases under provincial law. In Canada, rent controls were implemented during the Second World War and, through the provinces, as part of the ANTI-INFLATION BOARD program introduced in 1975. Rent controls can range from a freeze on rents or a fixed-percentage rent increase, to an increase related to the cost increases of landlords. Some provinces retained rent controls after the AIB program ended in 1978.

rentier Someone who receives his or her income from shares, bonds, annuities, real-estate rents, trusts, and other such assets. The income consists of dividends, interest, and rent.

reparations The payment of money and goods

demanded by victorious nations from defeated nations following a war. In 1919, under the Treaty of Versailles, the victorious allies imposed heavy reparations on Germany, although JOHN MAYNARD KEYNES warned that the payments would cripple the German economy. After the Second World War the allies, with the exception of the Soviet Union, refrained from demanding reparations; however, Germany was required to pay damages to Jewish families who survived the Holocaust.

repatriation The transfer of ownership of local corporations from non-residents to residents, or the transfer of capital from abroad for investment at home. When Canadians talk of repatriating their economy, they are talking of reducing foreign ownership of Canadian corporations by buying back ownership from the non-resident owners.

replacement-cost standard A method of VALUATION that determines the value of an asset in terms of what it would cost to replace it at today's prices, as opposed to the original cost of the asset. See also INFLATION ACCOUNTING.

repossession The taking back of an item of personal property, such as an automobile, appliance, or article of furniture, by a bank, sales-finance company, acceptance company, or retailer, when the purchaser fails to keep up payments under the terms of a consumer-credit contract.

repudiation The refusal by a creditor to pay off a debt, or by a party to a contract to live up to the terms of the contract.

resale-price maintenance An attempt by a supplier of goods for resale to set the final price at which the goods may be sold to consumers, and to cut off any retailer who refuses to abide by the dictated price. This practice is illegal in Canada; it is an offence under the COMBINES INVESTIGATION ACT. No supplier of goods is permitted to set the final selling price of a product or to cut off a retailer for selling at a low price; all he may do is publish a suggested retail price. An exception is made if it can be shown that a retailer is regularly using a particular product as a LOSS LEADER, or in BAIT-AND-SWITCH advertising.

research and development Scientific, engineering, and design activities that result in new or improved products or production processes. Such spending is considered a significant indicator of a country's capacity for innovation, and hence for economic growth. Some economists regard it as a factor of production much like land, labour, or capital, and some analysts believe that it is the single most important source of PRODUCTIVITY growth. Canada has one of the lowest rates of research and development spending, as a percentage of GROSS NATIONAL PRODUCT or GROSS DOMESTIC PRODUCT, of any of the Western industrial nations. One reason is said to be the high level of foreign ownership of Canadian manufacturing, which means that Canada imports much of its new technology from the parent companies of foreign subsidiaries instead of developing it itself.

Research and development starts with basic research, usually in a university or government laboratory, where the emphasis is on scientific knowledge, and proceeds to applied research, carried out in a university, government laboratory, or in a corporation, where the focus shifts to commercial possibilities in the form of new products or new techniques. The development phase, usually carried out by a corporation, consists of perfecting the new product or process, engineering and design work, and the creation of a prototype product or process. Research and development is costly and, in many industries, such as petrochemicals and tar-sands technology, it can usually only be carried out by large firms, which can afford to invest in research and development that does not pan out and which can also afford to finance a new product or process from its earliest stages until it reaches the market.

reservation price The price below which producers or suppliers will hold their goods or services off the market. The price is influenced by such factors as expectations of future price changes, storage costs, and the need for cash.

reserve appreciation An increase in oil and gas reserves in a particular pool or reservoir, resulting from additional drilling or the application of improved recovery techniques.

reserve army of the unemployed The lines of unemployed people at factory gates who, according to KARL MARX, were pointed out to the workers by bosses intent on depressing wages. According to Marx, the workers were told that they had to settle for low wages, or the unemployed would come in and work for less. In fact, employers often have to bid up wages to attract skilled workers.

reserve bid The minimum price permitted for an item at an auction. It is set by the owner of the goods being sold.

reserve currency A national currency that is widely accepted and used in financing international trade, in maintaining exchange rates in foreign-exchange markets, and in settling individual countries' balances of payments. As such, a reserve currency is held in the foreign-exchange reserves of individual nations, along with gold and SPECIAL DRAWING RIGHTS; indeed, it usually constitutes the major component of a nation's foreign-exchange reserves. A reserve currency is also the major component of working balances held by banks and corporations heavily engaged in international trade and investment. Through the late nineteenth century and into the 1920s, the British pound was the principal reserve currency. Starting in the 1930s, the U.S. dollar took on increasing importance as the world's reserve currency, a role that became even more significant after the Second World War. But, by the mid-1970s, the West German mark and the Swiss franc also were used as reserve currencies, although there were far too few in international circulation to permit them to be widely used.

reserve requirement The percentage of deposits by customers that a CHARTERED BANK must keep on deposit with the BANK OF CANADA. See also PRIMARY RESERVE RATIO, SECONDARY RESERVE RATIO.

residual-rights clause A clause in a collective agreement leaving all matters not covered in the contract to the prerogative of management.

Resources for Tomorrow Conference A move in the early 1960s by the federal government to co-ordinate federal and provincial policies on water and land use and on the management of other resources, such as forests. A conference held in Montreal in October 1961 brought together seven hundred representatives of federal and provincial governments, industry, the universities, and private groups, to discuss eighty papers on agriculture, water resources, regional development, forests, fisheries, wildlife, and outdoor recreation. The federal government proposed a national-resources council to encourage conservation, and to promote regional and intergovernmental co-operation, the creation of a national advisory land- and water-use board, and the holding of further resources conferences every three to four years. These proposals were not adopted, but the conference led to the creation of the Canadian Council of Resource Ministers; the council was active in co-ordinating federal and provincial activities in the early 1960s, but later played a much less significant role.

restitution The return of property to its legal owner, or the compensation for the damage to or loss of such property.

restraint of trade Any form of collusion among producers, or any practice by a single producer that reduces competition. Examples include PRICE-FIXING, PRICE DISCRIMINATION, a refusal to sell to certain buyers, and RESALE-PRICE MAINTENANCE. See also COMBINES INVESTIGATION ACT.

Restrictive Trade Practices Commission An investigatory commission established under the COMBINES INVESTIGATION ACT. It has two areas of responsibility: **1.** It investigates and holds hearings on complaints from the director of Investigation and Research of the BUREAU OF COMPETITION POLICY in the Department of CONSUMER AND CORPORATE AFFAIRS, complaints dealing with trade practices such as EXCLUSIVE DEALING and tied selling, which are banned under part IV (1) of the act. The commission, after hearing the evidence, may issue an order banning the action or practice. **2.** The commission appraises evidence submitted to it, under part V of the act (dealing with restrictive trade practices, such as combinations in restraint of trade), by the director of Investigation and Research and the parties against whom allegations have been made. The commission then advises the minister of Consumer and Corporate Affairs on whether charges should be laid. The commission was established in 1952, and has four members, including a chairman.

retail price The price charged to consumers. See also WHOLESALE PRICE. The CONSUMER PRICE INDEX measures changes in retail prices.

retail sales Sales to the ultimate consumers of goods and services. The volume of retail sales, measured monthly by Statistics Canada, is an important indicator of economic activity, since retail sales account for more than half the total level of demand in the economy. A rising level of retail sales, for example, is likely to indicate rising industrial production, and investment as well (assuming that the increased volume of sales is not made up mainly by a rising demand for imports). The monthly figures are contained in the Statistics Canada publication, *Retail Trade*.

retail trade The distribution of goods and services to the ultimate consumer. The retail trade includes department and chain stores, supermarkets, independently owned and operated stores, mail-order houses, door-to-door salesmen, co-operatives, and even the person selling jewellery, candles, and leather belts and purses from a street-corner stand.

retained earnings The portion of annual after-tax profits left over, after dividends have been paid to shareholders, for reinvestment in the business. Retained earnings are the single most important source of funds for business expansion. A corporation's BALANCE SHEET shows, under SHAREHOLDERS' EQUITY, the value of retained earnings for the year, and the accumulated retained earnings for previous years. The role of retained earnings in business expansion helps to explain the steady growth of foreign-controlled enterprises in Canada, even though flows of new FOREIGN DIRECT INVESTMENT into Canada fluctuate from year to year.

retained-earnings statement In a corporation's annual report, a statement showing the accumulated RETAINED EARNINGS of the corporation, along with the dividends paid out and retained earnings for the current year.

return on equity After-tax profits expressed as a percentage of SHAREHOLDERS' EQUITY. See also RATE OF RETURN ON INVESTED CAPITAL, which includes both shareholders' equity and long-term debt.

return on investment The after-tax profits earned on an investment, expressed as a percentage of the original cost of investment or purchase price. See also RATE OF RETURN ON INVESTED CAPITAL.

returns to scale The increase in production that results from additional units of various factors of production, such as labour and machinery. The typical business enterprise is assumed to get a proportionately greater increase in output from the application of additional labour or machinery in the early life of the enterprise, thus achieving increasing returns. After it reaches a certain size, the additional units of the factors of production are said to yield roughly proportionate increases in output, or constant returns. And if the firm grows ever larger in size, it is assumed to yield proportionately smaller gains in output from the application of additional units of the factors of production, resulting in decreasing returns. There is some disagreement as to whether the ECONOMIES OF SCALE achieved by a large and efficient firm yield to DISECONOMIES OF SCALE if a firm becomes ever larger. It is argued that, beyond a certain size, the increasing bureaucratization and delegation of responsibility in a firm makes it harder for management to respond to market changes and to reach decisions. At the same time, some of the world's largest corporations are also among the most successful.

revaluation An increase in the value of a country's exchange rate; as opposed to

DEVALUATION. If, by intervention on foreign-exchange markets, Canada's dollar is raised from 85 U.S. cents to 88 U.S. cents, it is said to have been revalued. If a country is running a high and persistent BALANCE-OF-PAYMENTS surplus, it may revalue its currency to reduce the cost of imported goods, and raise the cost to others of its exports, thus bringing its international transactions into closer balance.

revenue The total income a business firm or government receives from all sources.

reverse takeover The acquisition of a larger corporation by a smaller one. It can also mean the acquisition of control of a parent company by an affiliate or subsidiary.

revolving-credit account A type of consumer-credit account used by department stores, in which individual customers are allowed to run purchases up to a predetermined credit limit, and on which customers must make a minimum monthly payment, depending on the amount outstanding. Holders of bank credit cards can also operate their accounts this way. Interest is charged on the outstanding monthly balance.

Ricardo, David A British CLASSICAL economist (1772–1823), who had little formal education but was able to retire at the age of forty-two after becoming a millionaire by trading in government securities. His most important work was *On the Principles of Political Economy, and Taxation,* published in 1817, in which he attempted to construct an economic model to explain the distribution of income in society. He was anxious to determine the laws that governed the distribution of economic output among workers, capitalists, and landowners; his analysis led him to the concept of ECONOMIC RENT. But, while his model-building led to a new tool for economic analysis, his own model failed to provide an explanation for the distribution of income.

Ricardo also helped to develop the concept of COMPARATIVE ADVANTAGE, which is the basis for present-day theories of international trade and specialization; he arrived as well at a theory of value. Value, he argued, was based on the scarcity of a good and the quantity of labour required to obtain it: while scarcity accounted for the value of a limited number of commodities, in most cases value depended on labour. But in today's world of shrinking natural-resource supplies and pressures on global food supplies, Ricardo's views on scarcity are attracting fresh attention.

rigged bid A form of collusion among a group of firms bidding on a public contract. The firms decide ahead of time which one should get the contract, and fix the price of their bids so that the chosen firm makes the lowest bid and thus gets the contract. Usually, in such an arrangement, the bids will be arranged so that each of the firms gets its share of the business, but at higher levels of profit than if the firms were actively competing with one another. The practice is illegal and is punishable by jail terms and fines.

rigged market A market in which prices are manipulated, so that those doing the manipulating can make a windfall profit. For example, commodity speculators who CORNER THE MARKET in a specific commodity can distort prices; similarly, a small group of investors may be able to rig prices of a company's shares on a STOCK EXCHANGE or OVER-THE-COUNTER MARKET.

right-of-way The legal right of one party to cross through another party's land. This is usually indicated on the title to the land.

right-to-work law A law that makes illegal the negotiation, in a collective agreement, of a UNION SHOP or other arrangement to maintain union membership in a BARGAINING UNIT.

rights issue A method of raising new equity capital. A company planning to issue new shares will issue to all existing shareholders on a certain date the right to purchase new shares at a specified price in proportion to their existing holdings. A shareholder who does not want to exercise his rights can sell the rights on a stock exchange if the shares of the issuing company are already listed. The shares purchased under a rights offering are acquired directly from the issuing company, and no commission has to be paid to a stockbroker.

risk The danger of a loss or low yield from an investment, which is accepted by an investor in weighing all the possible outcomes from his investment. Generally speaking, the greater the risk in an investment, the greater the profit that is demanded if the investment is successful. Thus, a mining company will seek a high profit from a successful discovery, to offset the risk of losses from the possibility of unsuccessful exploration efforts. Similarly, an investor in a new apartment building in a growing city will be facing less of a risk in his investment, and therefore may be satisfied with a lower rate of return.

risk capital Capital invested in new or small business enterprises, and hence subject to greater risk than an investment in an established business enterprise. See also VENTURE CAPITAL.

rollback The power of government to ban a price increase and force a supplier to charge an earlier and lower price. Governments sometimes exercise this power by MORAL SUASION, or threats. For example, if a corporation with a significant market share raises its prices and refuses to withdraw the price increases in spite of government requests to do so, the government may threaten to lower tariffs on the product, thus putting price pressure on the offending company, or will refuse to let the corporation's products be used in government-financed projects. Rollback powers may be granted as part of an INCOMES POLICY. See also ANTI-INFLATION BOARD.

rolling stock The diesel engines, freight cars, tanker cars, passenger coaches, and other equipment for railways that are used to carry people or goods.

round lot The normal unit of trading on a stock exchange. On Canadian stock exchanges, it is usually 100 shares or a multiple of 100—for example, 600, 1,100, 12,500. Blocks of less than 100 are known as ODD LOTS, and usually command a higher commission because they have to be organized into round lots for trading purposes.

Rowell-Sirois Report See ROYAL COMMISSION ON DOMINION-PROVINCIAL RELATIONS.

Royal Canadian Mint The federal crown corporation responsible for the production of coins used as money in Canada. It was first established as the Ottawa Mint, a branch of Britain's Royal Mint, operating as a branch of the Department of FINANCE. In 1969 it became a crown corporation, enabling it not only to maintain its principal role as producer of Canadian coinage, but also to get more actively into the business of issuing commemorative and other coins for commercial purposes, and to seek, on a competitive basis, coinage business from other countries and from private firms. The chief executive of the Mint is known as the master of the Mint.

royal commission A study or investigation appointed by a federal or provincial government, and headed by an individual or panel of individuals known either for their experience or for their capacity for independent and objective judgement, into a particular problem or incident. Royal commissions usually have full power to obtain documents, to summon witnesses, and to hear evidence under oath. They can hire research staffs and counsel, commission studies, and publish their own analysis and research. Royal commissions have played a significant role in exploring federal and provincial issues. Examples include the commissions on Dominion-Provincial Relations, Canada's Economic Prospects, Banking and Finance, and Taxation. Royal commissions are also known as commissions of inquiry.

Royal Commission of Inquiry on Constitutional Problems A royal commission appointed by the Quebec government in February 1953, to examine fiscal relations between the federal and provincial governments and to demonstrate that the power of direct taxation, including personal income taxes, rested exclusively with the provinces—in spite of section 91 (3) of the BRITISH NORTH AMERICA ACT, giving Parliament the power to raise money "by any mode or system of taxation." The commission was headed by Quebec Chief Justice Thomas Tremblay, who produced a five-volume report in 1954 that not only proposed a radical restructuring of Canada, but also advanced a remarkable analysis of the nature and roots of French-

Canadian society and the importance of Quebec as the French-Canadian homeland.

The Tremblay Commission took the Quebec conservative-nationalist view that the federal government was the creation of the provinces, who made a compact among themselves; the purpose of the federal government was to establish the framework within which the French and English communities could live their separate lives, side by side, in a single state. The federal government was, in this view, largely an administrative agency that looked after military, technical, and co-ordinating services required by the provinces. It was the responsibility of the provinces to deal with everything that affected people's lives—social and cultural policy, education, municipalities, and family life; indeed, even the notion of a loyalty to Canada was contrary to the spirit of Confederation. Loyalty was to be to the provinces, which, according to this view, represented the real interests of the people. Confederation was simply an administrative arrangement, not the establishment of a new nation. But the growth of the federal government, through its dominance of income taxes and social security, was undermining the basis of Confederation—in particular, the right of the provinces to be the principal force in the lives of their people.

The Tremblay Commission called for much greater autonomy for the provinces and a return to what it called the spirit of Confederation. It urged that the federal and provincial governments agree on a maximum level or percentage of gross national product that should be allocated to the state, and that this sector then be divided between the federal and provincial governments, according to their responsibilities. The provinces should have all taxes on income, including personal income tax, and estate, gift, and succession taxes. The federal government should have all taxes having to do with the economy, namely corporate income taxes, sales taxes, and tariffs and excise duties and taxes; sales taxes would have to be established on a progressive scale, so as not to hit low-income Canadians too harshly.

The commission also proposed that all social programs be under the jurisdiction of the provinces. It proposed that the provinces should be given the right to sell bonds to the Bank of Canada, and that a permanent committee of federal-provincial conferences be established, along with a council of the provinces; the latter would facilitate co-operation among the provinces, and thus eliminate the need for federal programs or intervention. The commission saw little need for EQUALIZATION PAYMENTS to the poorer provinces if the proposals were adopted, with only the Maritime provinces requiring modest help. The other provinces, it said, could establish an equalization fund on their own, without federal participation.

Royal Commission on Banking and Finance
A royal commission headed by Chief Justice Dana Porter of the Supreme Court of Ontario. It was appointed in October 1961, to examine "all aspects of money, banking, credit and finance," including all existing financial institutions and the BANK OF CANADA, and the laws regulating their activities.

The commission's report was published in April 1964. It recommended a number of important changes in the banking system, including: abolition of the 6 per cent interest-rate ceiling on bank loans, so that the banks could play a bigger role in providing consumer credit; disclosure of bank-loan costs; the entry of banks into conventional mortgage financing; legislation to prohibit banks from agreeing to set common interest, chequing, and other customer charges; a ban on banks owning more than 10 per cent of the shares of any non-financial business; and a limit on interlocking directorships by bank officers.

Other proposals included: government approval for any purchase of Canadian bank shares by foreign interests; the bringing of trust companies, finance companies, credit unions, and other near banks under the authority of the Bank of Canada; the removal of restrictions on personal and business loans by trust and loan companies; regulation of the investment funds of pension plans, including increasing to 25 per cent from 15 per cent the amount they could invest from their funds in Canadian common shares; amendments to the BANK ACT, so that the government, through an order-in-council, could overrule the central bank on monetary policy; creation of a national securities commission to ensure high standards of regulation across Canada; much tougher stock-exchange rules to protect investors, including higher listing standards, INSIDER-TRADING penalties, full disclosure by corporations and mutual funds, and improved supervision of securities salesmen; new legislation to control takeover bids; government regulations to control mergers between banks and trust companies, or bank takeovers of other financial institutions; and an interest-rate ceiling on all personal loans made by financial institutions, running to 24 per cent a year on the first $300, and 12 per cent on amounts above $300 and up to $5,000. Many of its recommendations were incorporated into the Bank Act when it was amended in 1967.

Royal Commission on Bilingualism and Biculturalism A commission appointed in 1963, with André Laurendeau, editor of *Le Devoir*, and Davidson Dunton, president of Carleton University, as co-chairmen, and with eight other members. It was asked to review the status of bilingualism in Canada, to find ways to improve bilingualism and strengthen the bicultural nature of the Canadian federal state.

Altogether, the commission produced six volumes of recommendations. Among them was volume 3, published in 1969, entitled *The Work World*. It called for the use of French as the principal language of work at all levels in Quebec, as an equal language of work in New Brunswick, and as a significant language of work in those parts of Ontario with significant French-speaking populations. In the federal public service, it found that the use of English dominated; it said that the solution was not to emphasize individual bilingualism, but to establish French-language work units.

The commission summarized its findings on the work world this way: "In every area affecting the work world that we have examined, Francophones are at a disadvantage vis-à-vis their Anglophone colleagues. Their incomes are conspicuously lower in Canada as a whole, in the individual provinces, in specific cities, and in specific industries and occupations. There are comparable disparities in educational attainment. In Canada's work position—including industrial and commercial concerns, the federal public service, and the military—Francophones are much less likely than Anglophones to hold top-level positions. Moreover, the Francophones who do hold high positions are very often required to use English as their language of work. Finally, the Francophone share of ownership in industry is disproportionately small, even when the high incidence of Canadian ownership of the country's industry is taken into account."

Royal Commission on Canada's Economic Prospects A royal commission appointed in 1955 to investigate Canada's economic prospects over the next twenty-five years. Specifically, the commission was asked to review Canada's long-term economic prospects and the problems of economic development that were likely to occur. These included developments in the supply of raw materials and energy, population growth, prospects for changes in domestic and foreign markets for Canadian producers, trends in productivity and standard of living, and the requirements for industrial and social capital. The commission, headed by Walter Gordon of Toronto, produced its final report in 1958; it also published a large number of separate studies on different sectors of the Canadian economy.

The commission took an optimistic view of Canada's future, but called for policies to reduce foreign ownership and control of the economy, and to encourage Canadians to invest in their own country. It said that anti-combines laws should be modified to permit mergers among Canadian companies, so that they could achieve more efficient production and compete against foreign firms. To prevent foreign control of Canadian banks and insurance companies, which the commission said must remain under Canadian ownership and control because of their central role in the economy, foreign shareholders of such financial institutions should lose their voting rights. The commission called for a program of continued immigration into Canada, even during recessions, because a growing population would encourage new industries to be established in Canada, and thus help to diversify the economy. A growing population, the commission said, offered great hope for "more control over our economic welfare than we have at present."

In calling for policies to increase Canadian ownership in the economy and to direct the activities of foreign-controlled firms, the commission said that Canada should look to foreigners for DEBT CAPITAL for mortgages and bonds, but rely on Canadians for EQUITY CAPITAL, which represents ownership in the form of shares. In Canada, it said, "there is concern that as the position of American capital in the dynamic resource and manufacturing sectors becomes even more dominant, our economy will inevitably become more and more integrated with that of the United States. Behind this is the fear that continuing integration might lead to economic domination by the United States and eventually the loss of our political independence."

The commission saw little prospect of major new free-trade moves, and said that Canada should stick with the existing levels of tariffs. It also predicted that a growing proportion of Canada's trade would be with the United States. It was doubtful about the prospects for significantly increasing the processing of mineral resources in Canada before they were exported. Concerning energy, it said that Canada should extend an oil pipeline to Montreal if the United States was not willing to buy more Canadian oil; and it urged the establishment of a national energy agency to supervise the development, export, import, and consumption of all forms of energy.

The commission called for policies to make Canadian transportation systems pay their way, and policies to help residents of the Atlantic provinces to move to other parts of Canada if local jobs were not available; it encouraged greater urban planning, as more Canadians moved into cities, and warned against overproduction in agriculture. It said that the provinces should help to finance municipal transit systems, and municipalities should boost their own revenues by imposing sewer and motor-vehicle taxes, or be assured of a proportion of provincial motor-vehicle revenues. The commission also endorsed KEYNESIAN economic policies of tax cuts and increased government spending to fight recession.

Royal Commission on Dominion-Provincial Relations A royal commission appointed in August 1937, to re-examine "the economic and financial basis of Confederation and of the distribution of legislative powers in the light of the economic and social developments of the last seventy years." The commission was specifically asked to inquire into the constitutional allocation of taxing and spending powers, to review public expenditure and public debts to see whether the existing allocations were equitable, and to review federal grants and subsidies to the provinces. The commission was appointed after the Depression of the 1930s had created a financial crisis in several provinces, and revealed confusing differences of opinion over the division of powers and tax responsibilities, which in turn had hampered the introduction of effective policies to deal with the country's grave economic condition. The five-man commission was originally headed by Newton Rowell, chief justice of the Supreme Court of Ontario; he resigned due to ill health in November 1938, and was succeeded by Joseph Sirois, professor of constitutional and administrative law at Laval University.

The commission's three-volume report, which included an economic history of Canada from 1867 to 1939, was published in May 1940. The commission found that changes in the economy and society since Confederation had produced major imbalances that needed correcting. It proposed changes in the federal system so that the provinces would always be assured of sufficient financial resources, regardless of the state of the economy, to carry out social, health, and education policies, while leaving the federal government with the principal taxing powers and the responsibility to see that the provinces had the funds they needed to carry out their obligations. The commission assigned responsibility for unemployment relief, aid to primary industries such as agriculture, and the payment of contributory and non-contributory pensions to the federal government.

In its financial proposals, the commission recommended that the federal government alone levy personal income taxes, corporation taxes, and succession duties. In return, the federal government was to refrain from competing with the provinces in the tax fields left to them; with respect to the natural-resource wealth of the provinces, the federal government would pay over to the province concerned 10 per cent of the corporate income derived from the exploitation of natural resources.

To ensure that each province was able to provide a Canadian standard of services, the commission called for an annual national-adjustment grant from the federal government, to enable each province to provide a Canadian standard of services at normal Canadian taxation rates. A finance commission was to be set up to calculate and review such grants every five years. If voters in a province wanted a higher standard of services than those provided through meeting Canadian standards, then a provincial government could raise additional tax revenues to improve the services.

In other areas, the commission recommended: concurrent federal and provincial powers to set up farm marketing boards, and thus end constitutional confusions in this area; establishment of a transportation-planning commission, which would enable the federal government and the provinces to solve the country's transportation policies; the holding of federal-provincial conferences at least once a year, along with the creation of a small secretariat to serve the federal-provincial conferences and to facilitate federal-provincial co-operation; and establishment of a social-science research council, to co-ordinate and fund social-science research in Canada.

The recommendations of the commission were considered at a federal-provincial conference in June 1941. But the opposition of a number of provinces, along with pre-occupation with the war effort, led to the report being shelved.

Royal Commission on Price Spreads and Mass Buying The most sweeping public investigation ever undertaken in Canada into the market power of department and chain stores; the relationship between manufacturers, such as cigarette companies, canners, bakeries, and meatpackers, and the farmers and fishermen who supplied them; working conditions in chain and department stores and in manufacturing industries, including sweatshop conditions in the textiles industry; and unfair practices affecting consumers, such as misleading advertising and inaccurate weights and measures. The principal purpose of the inquiry was to determine the causes of "the large spread" between prices paid to farmers and fishermen by industry, and the prices charged consumers by department and chain stores. The study originated as a Special Committee of the House of Commons on 2 February 1934. Trade and Commerce Minister H.H. Stevens was the chairman. The committee became a royal commission later that year. On 1 November 1934, W.W. Kennedy, MP, became chairman, after Stevens resigned following a dispute with Prime Minister R.B. Bennett.

The commission's report was tabled in the House of Commons on 12 April 1935. It made a number of significant recommendations, among them: **1.** The creation of a Dominion trade and industry commission to enforce the Combines Investigation Act, to regulate industrial monopolies, to promote competition, to provide leadership on laws dealing with merchandising, to administer new consumer-protection laws, and to provide national protection for investors in securities markets. **2.** Much greater protection for workers, including strictly enforced minimum wages, reduction of hours of work, with a uniform forty-four-hour work week throughout the country, encouragement of trade unions and a greater role for collective agreements among employers and workers, and establishment of a special group in the Department of Labour to study industrial relations, to draft model labour laws, and to plan federal-provincial conferences on labour matters. **3.** Greater protection for farmers and fishermen in their dealings with food companies, including marketing boards for fruit and vegetable growers, licensing of all food processors, public livestock yards to reduce the powers of the meat packers, and encouragement of co-operatives for fishermen. **4.** Increased competition, through amendments to the Combines Investigation Act, and improved protection for investors through amendments to the Companies Act, including much greater financial disclosure and more stringent responsibilities for company directors and stock promoters.

Royal Commission on Publications A royal commission appointed in September 1960 to study the problems and prospects of Canadian magazines in the face of strong foreign competition, including Canadian editions of foreign magazines, and to study ways to strengthen the development of a Canadian identity through genuinely Canadian magazines. The commission, in its report published in June 1961, called for the removal of tax deductions for advertising by Canadian advertisers in foreign magazines aimed at the Canadian market, and a ban on foreign magazines entering Canada, including so-called Canadian editions of foreign magazines, when they contained advertising directed mainly at the Canadian market.

Royal Commission on Taxation Appointed in 1962 under the chairmanship of Kenneth Carter, to study every aspect of the federal tax system and to recommend reforms, including tax legislation to encourage Canadian ownership of Canadian industry without discouraging the continued inflow of foreign capital.

In February 1967, the six-volume report, containing hundreds of proposals for changes in the tax system, was published. The commission, recognizing the tax system as one of the fundamental tools of economic and social policy, found the existing tax system to be extremely unfair, since too many people in similar circumstances and with similar purchasing power paid quite different amounts of tax. The commission argued that this also contributed to an inefficient allocation of resources, and hence a lower standard of living for Canadians. The commission said that the system should be made much fairer, and that it should also be much better utilized to promote economic growth, to contain inflation, to increase Canadian ownership of the economy, and to achieve other important economic goals.

The fundamental concern of the commission was equity or fairness, with taxation based on the ability-to-pay principle. In any conflict between the goals of fairness and economic growth, fairness must prevail. Carter said: "Preserving and developing the system by scrupulously fair taxes must override all other objectives." To this end, the commission proposed a new, comprehensive tax base, which would include all net gains in purchasing power, or command over goods and services in cash or kind, for tax purposes. Reflecting its "a buck is a buck" philosophy, the commission recommended that capital gains, windfall gains, family allowances, unemployment insurance, and many other forms of income that were then tax exempt be made taxable. "If a man obtains increased command over goods and services for his personal satisfaction we do not believe it matters, from the point of view of taxation, whether he earned it through working, gained it through operating a business, received it because he held property, made it selling property or was given it by a relative."

The commission proposed that all capital gains, including those on personal residences, be taxable, with a lifetime exemption of twenty-five thousand dollars on homes and farms. It called for the abolition of federal estate and gift taxes, and recommended that gifts and inheritances be taxed as income—with an exemption for gifts and bequests between spouses and a modest exemption on gifts and inheritances for other individuals. The commission also argued that families should be allowed to file a joint return. Tax deductions for children would be replaced by TAX CREDITS, which would be worth more to lower-income families. The top marginal tax rate would be reduced to 50 per cent from 80 per cent, but wealthy people would pay more in taxes because of a much more comprehensive tax base.

The commission also proposed major changes in the taxation of corporations, including abolition of the low 21 per cent rate for small businesses, and a system of accelerated depreciation allowances for new and small businesses instead. In addition, Canadian shareholders of Canadian corporations would be credited with a 100 per cent credit for the corporation taxes paid on their behalf by the corporation, thus giving Canadians an incentive to invest in Canadian shares and reducing the cost of new capital for Canadian companies. The commission recommended that co-operatives and credit unions be taxed, that the existing three-year tax holiday for new mines be abolished, that the depletion allowances for the mining, oil, and natural-gas industries be sharply reduced, and that life-insurance companies be taxed as any other business. It proposed a halt to expense-account living, with ceilings on the amount an individual could claim on travelling and entertainment expenses, and the treatment as taxable income of any expenditure by an individual above the ceiling.

The commission proposed that employees be allowed to deduct employment expenses, such as tools and uniforms, and that there be greater tax incentives for individuals to save for their retirement. It called for the abolition of the federal 11 per cent manufacturer's sales tax, along with a halt by the federal government to turning over additional shares of the income-tax field to the provinces. If the provinces wanted more tax room, then the federal government should make room by reducing its sales tax. The commission also said that the federal government should assume full control of the corporation income tax. It called for a new tax court to replace the Tax Appeal Board, and a new board of revenue commissioners to take over federal tax collection and administration from the Department of NATIONAL REVENUE.

The proposed changes were calculated to yield more tax revenue from wealthy Canadians and foreign-owned corporations, but less from the ordinary taxpayer. The resulting redistribution of income, the commission said, was necessary, "if we are to achieve greater equality of opportunity for all Canadians and make it possible for those with little economic power to attain a decent standard of living."

Royal Commission on Transportation A commission appointed in 1959 to investigate transportation problems in Canada, in particular in the railway industry. The original chairman was Mr. Justice Charles McTague but he was replaced by Mr. Justice Murdoch A. MacPherson.

The report, in three volumes, was published in 1961–62. It called for a significant increase in the freedom of railways to end uneconomic passenger services and to eliminate, over a fifteen-year period, uneconomic branch lines. While it did not call for the abolition of the CROW'S NEST grain rates, it said that the railways should receive extra subsidies to carry out the grain-handling responsibilities imposed on them by Parliament. The commission pointed to the great changes occurring in transportation in Canada—the great growth in air travel and increasing use of highways and pipelines, for example—and said that new public policies would be needed to ensure a competitive environment that worked to the public benefit. It emphasized that the railways could only compete effectively with other carriers if uneconomic responsibilities were eliminated. The commission led eventually to a new National Transportation Act, and the establishment of the CANADIAN TRANSPORT COMMISSION.

royalty A payment for the use or exploitation of someone else's property. Examples include royalties paid to government by oil, natural-gas, or mining companies for the right to extract natural resources, and royalties paid to the owners of PATENTS or COPYRIGHTS to use their INTELLECTUAL PROPERTY. Royalties are usually fixed as a percentage of production, sales revenue, or sales. Under section 109 of the BRITISH NORTH AMERICA ACT, the provinces are empowered to impose royalties on the exploitation of land, forests, minerals, oil, and natural gas.

rule of law The underlying principle governing Canadian society, namely, that the law as passed by elected representatives is supreme, and that everyone, including the different levels of government and all their officials and agents, including the police, must obey the country's laws. The rule of law is intended to protect citizens from the arbitrary exercise of power by government and from the abuse of power by government.

runaway inflation Unusually high and rapidly increasing inflation.

S

safety-deposit box An area maintained in the vault of a bank or trust-company branch, in which a number of individual drawers are rented out to customers for the safekeeping of securities, jewels, records, and other valuable items. Each drawer needs two keys to be opened, one belonging to the customer and the other to the financial institution.

St. Lawrence Seaway Authority The Canadian agency that came into being on 1 July 1954, to construct, maintain, and operate the Canadian sections of the St. Lawrence Seaway, a deep waterway between Montreal and Lake Erie. The authority also co-operated with its U.S. counterpart, the St. Lawrence Seaway Development Corporation, in jointly building, maintaining, and operating international segments of the seaway. The St. Lawrence Seaway opened for commercial use on 1 April 1959.

salary Compensation paid to an employee each week, fortnight, or month, as opposed to a WAGE, which is paid according to the number of hours worked. Industrial employees tend to be paid wages, while administrative or white-collar workers are usually paid salaries.

sale and leaseback A technique of business financing, in which a business sells an asset, such as a plant or item of heavy machinery or equipment, to an investor or financial institution, and then promptly leases it back under a long-term agreement. The business thus gets immediate cash but retains the use of the asset.

sales-finance company A company that finances instalment-credit purchases of durable goods by consumers, farmers, and small business. Goods purchased in this way include cars, trucks, tractors, farm implements, and household appliances. Many retailers sell sales contracts they have signed with consumers to a sales-finance or acceptance company; car dealers, for example, often handle car sales this way, reselling the sales contract to a finance company, which frequently is owned and operated by the automotive manufacturer.

sales tax A tax that is applied when goods or services are sold. It can be applied at many different stages of production and sale. Canada has a manufacturer's sales tax that is applied at the federal level, while all the provinces except Alberta have a retail-sales tax. The federal manufacturer's sales tax is an indirect tax, since manufacturers pass it along to consumers in their prices. Provincial retail-sales taxes are direct taxes, because they are paid by the consumer and cannot be passed along to anyone else. Sales taxes are considered regressive by many economists, because they take a larger fraction of income from people with lower incomes and a lower fraction from those with higher incomes, when both groups are purchasing the same goods and services. The federal manufacturer's sales tax was introduced in 1924. The first province to bring in a retail-sales tax was Alberta in 1936, but the province dropped the tax the same year, due to protests by Albertans. The city of Montreal collected its own sales tax from 1935 until 1940, when Quebec introduced a province-wide sales tax. Most provinces adopted retail-sales taxes in the 1950s and 1960s. See also VALUE-ADDED TAX.

salvage value The amount of money an asset would fetch if it were scrapped.

sample **1.** A small portion of ore or rock that is taken to assess the possible mineral content. **2.** A representative segment of a statistical group—the entire population, the labour force, farms, or consumer prices, for example—from which conclusions can be drawn about the entire group.

sanctions The severing of trade, investment, and other economic relations with another state, to force it to halt a military act, to withdraw from occupied territory, to alter a domestic policy, such as racial discrimination, or to take some other desired step. In 1966, the United Nations adopted trade sanctions on selected products from Rhodesia because it would not grant majority rule to its black citizens; these sanctions were later widened to a complete embargo on trade and other economic dealings with Rhodesia, until it changed its racial policies.

savings Income that is not spent when it is earned, but is set aside for future consumption. Individuals save either by putting part of their current income into pension plans and insurance policies, by paying off mortgage principal, by investing their money in shares, bonds, mutual funds, commodity futures, and savings certificates, or by holding their money in bank, trust-company, and credit-union savings accounts. Corporations save by retaining part of their profits each year and by reinvesting the money in their own operations, or by using it to acquire other companies. Savings provide the funds for capital formation, and hence, productive facilities, for the future. There are many different reasons why individuals save; they include acquiring a home or recreation cottage, providing for emergency family needs, and building up a reserve to meet personal needs in old age. The decision to save may be encouraged by higher interest rates or tax incentives, and may be discouraged by high inflation. Savings are also affected by a person's level of income, with the PROPENSITY TO SAVE rising with income. See also MARGINAL PROPENSITY TO SAVE. The level of personal savings in the gross national product can be calculated by subtracting from personal disposable income, total personal spending on consumer goods and services, interest on consumer debt, and payments to non-residents; the remaining figure is the level of personal savings in the economy.

savings bond A bond sold to the public in low denominations and through payroll-deduction and other savings plans. See also CANADA SAVINGS BOND.

Say's law The assertion that there can never be a shortage of purchasing power, because supply creates its own demand. This was a fundamental tenet of economics from the time it was expressed by the French businessman, Jean Baptiste Say (1767–1832), until it was effectively demolished by JOHN MAYNARD KEYNES in 1936. Say argued that every time something was produced and sold, the equivalent amount of demand was generated in the economy, in wages, rents, profits, and other forms of income. If some people saved their income, others would borrow it for consumption purchases; if they did not, prices would fall until supply and demand were again in balance. As Say saw it, the economic system was self-correcting and would tend to operate at about full employment, though this would mean that, during periods of adjustment, wages would have to fall. Keynes argued that it was possible to have overproduction or a shortage of purchasing power. Left to its own devices, the economic system would restore EQUILIBRIUM, but at a lower level of output and higher level of unemployment. Keynes argued that the government should borrow excess savings and spend them in the economy to restore a full-employment equilibrium.

scab See STRIKEBREAKER.

scarcity The condition that exists when we can't satisfy all our wants; it is a normal condition of economic life. For scarcity to exist, goods and services must be wanted and there must be some difficulty in obtaining all that we want of them. The study of economics is built around the notion of scarcity. The existence of scarcity creates the need for some kind of system—whether free-market forces and the price system, or government planning—to allocate scarce resources. Even though some consumer goods, such as toasters or transistor radios, may appear plentiful, they are still scarce in the sense that there are not enough of them to distribute freely, and those who want toasters or transistor radios have to forego some other good or service to satisfy their wants. The idea of scarcity is based on the fact that there are limited amounts of human and material resources, and that no combination of these can produce everything that everyone would want.

scenario A forecast of a likely outcome based on a particular set of assumptions. In determining the likely demand for oil and natural gas, for example, the NATIONAL ENERGY BOARD calculates a series of scenarios of supply and demand, based on different assumptions about Canada's future rate of economic and population growth, and future energy prices.

Science and Technology, Ministry of State for (MOSST) A policy ministry created in 1971 to advise the government on science policy, including measures to increase basic research, to attain greater application of the research already underway, to increase research and development in private industry, and to negotiate technology-sharing and research and development projects with other countries.

Science Council of Canada A scientific advisory body to the federal government, created in 1966 and given greater independence as a crown corporation in 1969. The council has twenty-five members, selected from industry, the universities, and government, who have a special interest in science and technology; the council also has a full-time staff of experts. Its job is to identify areas of scientific opportunity for Canada, to assess Canada's scientific capabilities and weaknesses, and to recommend policies to improve the contribution of science and technology to the Canadian economy and to the well-being of Canadians. The council has carried out major studies on the need for an INDUSTRIAL STRATEGY, the impact of multinational corporations on Canada's research and development efforts, the status of university research, science opportunities in agriculture, forestry, and the North, occupational health, health care, and energy, and has recommended major science programs in such areas as transportation, telecommunications, water-resource management, and energy. The council has also completed a major study on the CONSERVER SOCIETY. It reports to Parliament through the minister of state for SCIENCE AND TECHNOLOGY.

science policy Policy to encourage basic and applied research and development. Tools include direct funding to government laboratories and universities, the contracting-out of government research projects to universities and private industry, scholarships, government sponsorship of major industry projects, and tax incentives and grants to private industry to carry out research and development projects.

seasonal adjustment A statistical adjustment to take account of unusual seasonal factors, so that statistical series more accurately reflect underlying trends. The main seasonal factors are climatic (affecting the fishing, farming, forest, construction, and energy industries) and institutional (such as the build-up of retail sales at Christmas and Easter). For example, Statistics Canada makes an allowance each summer for the temporary presence of large numbers of students in the labour force, in order to calculate the seasonally adjusted unemployment rate for the summer months. Similarly, a statistical series on prices could be affected by the sharp increase in vegetable prices each winter.

seasonal industry An industry that operates for only part of the year. Examples include fruit and vegetable processing, tourism, shipping on the Great Lakes, fishing, and farming.

seasonal unemployment Unemployment caused by climatic and other conditions each year. Such unemployment is predictable in certain industries, such as tourism, forestry, fishing, and Great Lakes shipping, and less predictable than it used to be in others, such as construction. There is also seasonal employment—in the retail industry at Christmas, for example.

seasonally adjusted unemployment rate See UNEMPLOYMENT RATE.

second mortgage An additional mortgage put on a property that already has an existing or first mortgage against it. The holder of the second mortgage cannot be paid, in the event of default, until the holder of the first mortgage has been paid. That is why a second mortgage usually commands a higher rate of interest than a first mortgage.

second world The communist countries of Eastern Europe and the Soviet Union. The second-world nations play virtually no role in the NORTH-SOUTH DIALOGUE and the debate over a NEW INTERNATIONAL ECONOMIC ORDER; in spite of their relatively high standard of living, they provide little non-military foreign aid to the LESS-DEVELOPED COUNTRIES.

secondary distribution The sale to the public of a large block of company shares that had previously been distributed, and hence is not a new issue. The shares may come from a significant investor who wants to liquidate his holdings, from an institution such as a pension fund, or from the trustees of an estate. The shares are purchased by an investment dealer or group of dealers, and resold to the public.

secondary industry A synonym for manufacturing industry.

secondary recovery In the oil and gas industry, the use of proven and feasible techniques to obtain production from oil and natural-gas reservoirs additional to that resulting from the normal pressures in the reservoirs. Common techniques include water flooding and gas or steam injection. See also PRIMARY RECOVERY, TERTIARY RECOVERY.

secondary reserve ratio The second reserve that must be maintained by each of the chartered banks under the BANK ACT; the other reserve requirement is the PRIMARY RESERVE RATIO. The BANK OF CANADA can manipulate the country's money supply by altering the secondary reserve requirements, and thus increase or reduce the ability of the banking system to make loans or to purchase securities. The secondary reserve consists of TREASURY BILLS held by the banks, and the day-to-day loans that the banks make to MONEY-MARKET DEALERS. The Bank of Canada can require each chartered bank to maintain a secondary reserve in these securities, equal to up to 12 per cent of its Canadian-dollar deposits; since the mid-1970s, however, it has not used this power to manipulate the money supply and thus implement its monetary policy. The secondary reserve ratio in recent years has been about 5 per cent of Canadian-dollar deposits.

sector A division of the economy that can be studied by itself. Examples include the private and public sectors, the agricultural and non-agricultural sectors, the primary-industry sector, the goods-producing sector, the service sector, and specific industries such as steel, textiles, machinery, motor vehicles, computers, and petrochemicals.

secular stagnation The belief that, as economies mature, they lose their dynamic capacity for technological innovation, which in turn leads to less investment, reduced aggregate demand, slower growth, and higher unemployment. This view was advanced by U.S. economist Alvin Hansen in 1938 to explain the slowdown in the U.S. and British economies. The U.S., he argued, was experiencing a slowdown in population growth, had settled its remaining frontier lands, had accumulated enormous productive capacity, and, by its emphasis on labour-saving and high technology, had reached the point where corporate profits could no longer find new investment opportunities. This meant that new policies, such as increased public spending, were needed to increase demand and to create jobs.

secular trends A persistent trend that reflects the effect of long-term forces at work in the economy. It is a term used in statistics to describe a trend in a particular series. Examples include the rising participation rate for women in the labour force, the growth of service-sector jobs in the economy, and the growth of real per capita income.

secured loan A loan that is backed by collateral, such as bonds, insurance policies, shares, or real estate, which the borrower must relinquish to the lender if he is unable to repay the loan. A secured loan, because it is backed by collateral, which reduces the risk, commands a lower rate of interest than an UNSECURED LOAN.

securities commission A provincial body responsible for the administration of a province's SECURITIES LEGISLATION, including the maintenance and disclosure of corporate information, the issuing of a PROSPECTUS, the proper observance of rules on TAKEOVER bids, the registration of securities-industry firms and employees, and the supervision of STOCK EXCHANGES and OVER-THE-COUNTER MARKETS. Each provincial body, usually a commission but sometimes a branch of a government department, meets with its provincial counterparts twice a year to improve the uniformity of laws and regulations and to work out national policies—to reduce the paperwork and costs for firms filing a prospectus in more than one province, for example. The most important securities commissions in Canada are in Ontario, Quebec, British Columbia, and Alberta.

securities legislation Provincial laws to regulate the underwriting, distribution, and sale of securities, and to protect the buyers and sellers of securities such as shares, bonds, commodity futures, tax-shelter packages for motion pictures, oil and gas drilling, real estate, mutual funds, and scholarship plans. Such laws, for example, require any corporation planning to sell a new security to the public to file a PROSPECTUS containing complete and true information. Until the prospectus is approved by a provincial SECURITIES COMMISSION, the new security issue cannot be sold to the public. Securities laws also require the registration of all INVESTMENT DEALERS, stockbrokers, INVESTMENT COUNSELLORS, and others who buy and sell securities or investment advice and management. The laws also require the registration of the securities salesmen, analysts, portfolio managers, and other employees of these firms. Securities laws cover the operation of STOCK EXCHANGES and OVER-THE-COUNTER MARKETS, and deal specifically with the manner in which securities can be traded, INSIDER information, PROXIES and proxy solicitation, the full and timely disclosure of financial information, advertising, conflict of interest, and TAKEOVER bids.

While securities regulation is a provincial activity in Canada, as opposed to a federal activity, as in the United States, the provincial securities laws have achieved a degree of uniformity since the Ontario Securities Act was passed in 1966. Agreements among the provinces on securities trading also give the securities industry a national focus.

security **1.** A BOND, SHARE, TREASURY BILL, or other financial asset that yields income and can readily be converted into cash by sale on the bond market, a stock exchange, or other financial market. **2.** Property pledged as collateral for a loan.

security of supply A consideration in making long-term import arrangements for essential raw materials. The supply must be readily available from a politically stable country that is unlikely to halt supplies suddenly, and it must be obtained through a militarily secure route. For example, the United States would probably prefer to obtain its oil and gas imports from Canada—because Canada is politically stable, likely to live up to its contracts, and can be defended by U.S. armed forces against military attack by an enemy—as opposed to obtaining its oil from Saudi Arabia, whose supply route to the United States is several thousand miles long, and therefore hard to defend.

seigniorage The profit made by the ROYAL CANADIAN MINT, and hence the federal government, from converting metals into coins that have a higher face value than their metallic content.

seismic exploration The use of geophysical techniques, such as the speed and reflection of sound waves against different types of rock formations on land or on the ocean bottom, to indicate the possible presence of oil, natural gas, or other minerals.

self-employed People in the labour force who work for themselves. Examples include doctors, some lawyers and accountants, operators of small stores, consultants, and farmers.

self-reliance The ability of a country to meet a significant proportion of its essential needs out of its resources and skills; it falls short of SELF-SUFFICIENCY, but means that the country is not overly dependent on imports to meet an essential need for a particular commodity or technology, or a group of commodities or technologies. For example, in 1977, Canada set a self-reliance target for oil that would limit oil imports to one-third of its refinery needs, or 800,000 barrels a day, whichever is less, by

1985. At the Tokyo economic summit in June 1979, that target was reduced to 600,000 barrels a day of imports. Provided that an emergency stockpile exists, along with plans that would allow rationing or allocation of supplies, a country that aims for self-reliance instead of self-sufficiency in a key commodity should be able to withstand a temporary loss of imports without undue hardship.

self-sufficiency The ability of a nation to meet its needs for a single commodity or product, or for a range of essential commodities and products, from its own resources and skills. Most nations would like to be self-sufficient in basic foodstuffs, energy, key technologies, and the most important RAW MATERIALS. But this is usually impossible; the alternative is to develop secure sources of supply, or to build up emergency stockpiles of key foodstuffs and raw materials. In fact, in a world in which the principle of COMPARATIVE ADVANTAGE has been encouraged by the growth of international trade, self-sufficiency has declined and interdependence has increased. Canada has one of the world's best chances to be self-sufficient in food, energy, forest products, and raw materials, but is at its present stage of development still highly dependent on other nations for technology. See also SELF-RELIANCE.

seller's market A market in which supply is low and demand high, so that sellers are able to demand and get higher prices. See also BUYER'S MARKET.

selling costs The costs that are incurred in selling a good or service. These costs include market research, advertising, promotion, salesmen's salaries and commissions, and distribution.

selling group Investment dealers and others who are brought in by a BANKING GROUP or SYNDICATE handling a new issue of shares or bonds, to help sell the issue. The members of the selling group buy the securities from the banking group at a discount and resell them to their customers. While the banking group is responsible for the sale of the issue, the members of the selling group have no financial liability if the entire issue is not sold.

selling short The sale, by a speculative investor, of shares or commodity futures that he does not own, in the belief that the price will decline, he will be able to buy them back at a lower price and thus replace the shares, pay the stockbroker's commission, and still make a profit. When the short-sale is made, the stockbroker borrows the shares sold from someone else (usually someone who has a MARGIN account with the same broker), while the short-seller must also deposit cash with the broker to cover the sale. This cash is used to buy the same number of shares, if and when the price declines, the share certificates being returned to the account from which they were borrowed and the stockbroker collecting his commission. What is left over goes to the short-seller; if the shares go up in price, rather than decline, then he has to pay a deficit and thus suffer a loss. Canadian stock exchanges have strict rules governing short-selling. See also LONG-SELLING.

semi-finished goods Partially manufactured or processed goods that are not yet ready for consumption and cannot be sold in their present condition.

semi-skilled worker A worker who has some job experience in a particular skill, but who has not gone through an apprenticeship or other extended training program. The skills possessed are of less value than those of a SKILLED WORKER. See also UNSKILLED WORKER.

senior debt The debt that has to be paid off before any other claims can be considered.

seniority The length of service of an employee in a firm, determining his status when it comes to layoffs, call-backs after layoffs, promotions, length of vacation, or early retirement. Most collective agreements give preferential treatment to workers with the greatest seniority. Length of service may not be the only consideration; service as a union officer may also add to an individual's seniority, for example. Thus, when a firm lays off workers, it lays off those with the least seniority first; when it recalls laid-off workers, it recalls those with the greatest seniority first.

separation rate The percentage of workers in the labour force—or in a firm or industry—who quit, are laid off, or who retire in any defined period of time. It is an important labour-market indicator, since a rising separation rate usually indicates slackening economic activity, and vice versa.

serial bond A bond issue that is redeemed by a predetermined amount each year, so that, by the final year, only a small amount of the original loan remains to be paid off. Much municipal financing is done through such issues. In a serial bond issue, the shorter maturities may be sold to banks and trust companies, and the longer maturities to individuals and to institutional investors, such as pension funds and insurance companies.

service An intangible consumer or producer good that is usually consumed at the time it is produced and purchased. Examples include banking, teaching, engineering, computer software, musical entertainment, and hairdressing. Sometimes a service industry will produce an economic good that is not altogether intangible—architectural or engineering blueprints, for example, accounting statements, or computer print-outs.

service industry An industry that produces a SERVICE rather than a tangible good, for which someone will pay money. A growing proportion of Canadians are employed in service industries rather than in goods-producing industries.

settlement date The date by which the purchaser for shares, bonds, or other securities must pay for the purchase, or by which the seller of shares, bonds, or other securities must deliver the certificates representing the securities he has sold. For most transactions, it is the fifth business day after the transaction itself.

severance pay A payment made to an employee who is fired, or whose job disappears due to automation or a shutdown of a branch or plant of a firm. The amount may be as little as two weeks' pay in the case of dismissal, or as much as a year's pay if the employee has a long record of service with the firm.

share Ownership of part of the capital stock of a corporation, as represented by the possession of share certificates registered in the name of the shareholder. When a company is incorporated, it is authorized to issue a maximum number of PREFERRED and COMMON SHARES. The number of shares issued is the number that have actually been sold to investors, while the number outstanding is the number issued minus any that have been bought back—or redeemed, in the case of preferred shares—by the corporation. If the corporation has issued the maximum number of shares authorized, it can increase its authorized capital by SUPPLEMENTARY LETTERS PATENT. Shares are bought and sold on STOCK EXCHANGES or on the OVER-THE-COUNTER MARKET through STOCKBROKERS. The ownership of 5 per cent of the common shares of a corporation entitles the owner to 5 per cent of the issued dividends, 5 per cent of the votes at the annual or other meetings, and 5 per cent of the net assets if the corporation is wound up.

share register See REGISTRAR.

share-split See STOCK SPLIT.

shared-cost program A program whose costs are shared by more than one level of government. For example, the federal government introduced hospital insurance, medicare, and the Canada Assistance Plan as cost-sharing programs, paying half the costs to those provinces that agreed to participate. Similarly, provincial governments have shared-cost programs with their municipalities—to encourage the construction of transit systems, for example, to build roads, or to provide day-care and other social services. Sometimes, shared-cost programs may bring together all three levels of government—in some federal housing and urban-redevelopment programs, for example.

For the senior level of government, such programs are a way of stimulating activity by a lower level of government, where the senior level of government sees a need but cannot act on its own for constitutional or other reasons. Thus, the federal government, by introducing hospital insurance and medicare programs, was able to push all the provinces into providing universal health care for Canadians; left on their own, the provinces might have taken much longer, but they could not afford to ignore the incentive of federal funding for half the cost. Such funding is also known as a conditional grant, since another level of government offers to pay a grant if certain conditions are met.

The provinces have resented the introduction of shared-cost programs, contending that the federal government has used this device to enter fields that are really under provincial jurisdiction, and to alter a province's own choice of spending priorities. The federal government has responded that it has a duty to see that all Canadians, regardless of where they live, have access to a uniform set of basic services, such as health, welfare, housing, and post-secondary education. Today there are many different types of shared-cost programs, including some in which the federal government and only a few of the provinces participate. Examples include tourism development, manpower training, assistance to the blind and disabled, regional development, and sewer and water-supply projects. See also OPTING OUT, UNCONDITIONAL GRANT.

shareholder The owner of voting or non-voting shares in a corporation; shareholders are entitled to receive dividends and annual and quarterly reports of the corporation's affairs. Most shares traded are voting shares, which entitle the owner to attend annual meetings to elect directors, approve the auditor's report, and question management on the corporation's policies and plans. Owners of voting shares are also entitled to attend special meetings to approve mergers or changes in the corporation's charter. If shareholders cannot attend a corporation meeting, they are entitled to transfer their votes to others by signing PROXY statements.

shareholder of record A shareholder whose name and ownership of shares are recorded in the company register as of a certain date, and who is thus entitled to receive a dividend that has been declared, or to participate in a RIGHTS ISSUE.

shareholders' equity The interest of the shareholders in a corporation if all of its liabilities were to be paid off. It is calculated from a corporation's BALANCE SHEET by deducting total liabilities from total assets; what is left over is shareholders' equity. It consists of several items: **1.** Capital stock, which is the money raised by the corporation from the sale of its shares. **2.** Retained earnings, which are the after-tax profits over the life of the corporation that have not been paid out as dividends to shareholders but have been reinvested in the business instead. **3.** Contributed surplus, the funds raised from the sale of shares in excess of the par value or market value of the shares when they were offered for sale. **4.** The excess of appraised value of fixed assets over their original cost, an item that appears when a major fixed asset is reappraised and found to be worth much more than its original cost.

One way of measuring the profitability of a corporation is to determine its after-tax profits as a percentage of shareholders' equity; its performance can be compared with that of other firms in the same industry or in other industries. If a corporation suffers a loss, the loss is deducted from the retained earnings of the firm, thus reducing the shareholders' equity.

shift The scheduled working hours for a group of employees in a firm or government agency. See also SPLIT SHIFT.

shift differential Extra pay for those who work on shifts other than the normal daytime shift. Employees who work, say, from 4 P.M. to midnight, or midnight to 8 A.M., may get an extra 10 per cent above the base rate of pay for daytime workers, to compensate for having to work less attractive hours.

shipping conference A group of ocean-going shipping companies that sets shipping rates, routes, and schedules for shipping between designated ports. Most countries agree to such price-fixing arrangements, to ensure regular service at their ports. Such arrangements have an exemption from the COMBINES INVESTIGATION ACT through the Shipping Conferences Exemption Act; rate, route, and schedule information must be filed with the CANADIAN TRANSPORT COMMISSION. Canadian companies negotiate with shipping companies through the Canadian Shippers Council, an association of thirteen trade and commodity groups. Among those most directly concerned are the CANADIAN EXPORT ASSOCIATION, the CANADIAN IMPORTERS ASSOCIATION, and the CANADIAN MANUFACTURERS' ASSOCIATION. Different shipping-conference agreements are negotiated for different shipping routes. See also UNITED NATIONS CODE OF CONDUCT ON CONFERENCE SHIPPING.

shop steward A union member, usually chosen by fellow workers in the same work area, who handles grievances and other union matters for that group of workers. Although this is the lowest elected job in a union, it is also a very important post, because the shop steward handles so many day-to-day issues with management.

short term A period of time—generally speaking, less than two years—during which a firm is unable to alter all of its FACTORS OF PRODUCTION. For example, while it may be able to recruit and train new workers in a relatively short period of time—say, four to six months—it may take up to two years to purchase and install new production machinery, or to build a new factory. Thus, in the short term, the main way a firm can increase its production is to make more effective use of its existing factors of production. See also LONG TERM, in which all the factors of production, including factory buildings and heavy machinery, can be varied.

short-term bond A bond that will mature within three years.

short-term debt Debt that must be repaid within twelve months.

short-term forecast An economic forecast that attempts to outline economic performance for the next twelve to eighteen months.

short-term rate of interest The rate of interest charged on commercial loans of six months or less.

silent partner A partner who invests in a business enterprise or other investment project, but who does not participate in its management.

simple interest Interest calculated as a percentage of the outstanding principal; it does not include a percentage of any previous interest paid on the same outstanding principal. See also COMPOUND INTEREST.

sinking fund Money set aside by a corporation each year from its earnings to pay off a long-term debt or preferred share issue, or to replace productive assets. Cash in a sinking fund is usually invested in various securities until the money is needed.

sinking-fund debentures Bonds that contain a sinking-fund clause that requires the corporation to set aside a specified amount of money each year for the eventual redemption of the bonds. The money must be deposited with a trustee, who either redeems a number of bonds each year, or holds and invests the money until the maturity date.

sit-down strike A strike in which union members refuse to continue working, and may also refuse to leave their place of work.

skewness An unequal distribution of resources in a country—Saudi Arabia's huge surplus of oil and severe shortages of water and agricultural land, for example.

skilled worker A trained and experienced worker who has completed an apprenticeship or other skill-building education, and who has worked for several years in his skill.

slowdown A planned reduction by union members of their production or work effort, to put pressure on an employer during COLLECTIVE BARGAINING without going on strike, or to force an employer to settle a GRIEVANCE. See also WORK TO RULE.

small business A firm with twenty or fewer employees: this is the definition used in Statistics Canada's monthly employment survey. According to the Ministry of State for Small Business, a small business is any manufacturing firm with fewer than one hundred employees, or, in any other sector, a firm with fewer than fifty employees. Using either definition, small business accounts for between 80 and 90 per cent of all businesses in Canada, but for a much smaller percentage of business activity.

Small Business, Ministry of State for A federal government cabinet post, created in 1976 to assist the minister of INDUSTRY, TRADE AND COMMERCE to aid small business. The responsibility includes designing and running specific programs to assist small business, assessing the impact of government policies and regulations on small business, representing the interests of small business to other government departments, and disseminating information to small business.

Smith, Adam The father of political economy and of the CLASSICAL SCHOOL of economics. Smith (1723–90) believed that sustained economic growth offered the best hope for improving the well-being of the people. In his monumental work published in 1776, *An Inquiry into the Nature and Causes of the Wealth of Nations,* he argued that the greatest rate of economic growth was most likely to be achieved through the free play of market forces, under which each individual pursued his own best interest. It was from this premise that he formulated his notion of the invisible hand: ". . . every individual, therefore, endeavours . . . to employ his capital . . . that its produce may be of the greatest value. . . He generally, indeed, neither intends to promote the public interest, nor knows how much he is promoting it . . . he intends only his own security; . . . only his own gain, and he is in this, as in many other cases, led by an invisible hand to promote an end which was no part of his intention. . . By pursuing his own interest he frequently promotes that of the society more effectually than when he really intends to promote it."

Smith spelled out the advantages of the DIVISION OF LABOUR in raising productivity and output. He used the example of the pin factory, contending that each worker could only produce a few complete pins each day; but if each worker carried out only one stage in pin production, the output of the same group of workers would be much higher. He also contributed to the concept of COMPARATIVE ADVANTAGE, or specialization by nations in the things they do best, with each nation trading with the others to meet its needs. By unleashing man's competitive instincts, Smith said, the vital goal of dynamic economic growth would be achieved automatically.

While Smith feared the tendency of businessmen to seek out ways to circumvent competition and join in collusion against the consumer, he believed that government intervention would be worse because it would slow economic growth. The role of government, he contended, was to protect property rights, to provide essential public works, such as roads and docks, and to maintain an effective national defence. Competition, he maintained, could best be ensured by maintaining a climate of strong economic growth; this would reduce the motive for collusion among businessmen.

Smith also formulated the LABOUR THEORY OF VALUE, the theory that the amount of labour required to produce a good or service was the value of that good or service. This concept was taken up by KARL MARX, but rejected by ALFRED MARSHALL. Smith is also important because he was the first to attempt to devise a method of measuring changes in the value of national output.

Smithsonian Agreement An agreement, reached in Washington on 18 December 1971 by the GROUP OF TEN, that officially devalued the U.S. dollar by 11 per cent, set out new exchange rates for the other G-10 currencies, including that of Canada, and allowed currencies to float by 2.25 per cent on either side of their official rate, instead of 1 per cent, as set out under the INTERNATIONAL MONETARY FUND's rules for fixed exchange rates. The devaluation was less than the United States had sought: for example, it wanted the Canadian dollar pegged above par with the U.S. dollar; instead, the Canadian dollar was set at 97.5 U.S. cents. In less than a year, new exchange rates were adopted, which led to a further devaluation of the U.S. dollar; eventually, a system of floating exchange rates was adopted. Under the Smithsonian Agreement, the United

States also dropped its 10 per cent import surcharge and its proposed job-development tax credit, with Canada, the European Economic Community, and Japan agreeing to undertake urgent negotiations on outstanding trade issues.

smuggling Importing goods into a country without declaring them to customs officials of the Department of NATIONAL REVENUE, and thus avoiding the payment of import duties on them.

social capital The total resources of a society, including its agricultural land, its natural resources, its buildings, the machinery and equipment used to produce goods and services, its public facilities and infrastructure, ranging from roads, hospitals, schools, and airports to museums, art galleries, and theatres, and the skills and talents of its people.

social contract The consensus that exists among members of a society, reflecting their mutual dependence, on the nature of their society, its institutions and principles, its goals, and the rights and responsibilities of its citizens, which makes possible the democratic governing and functioning of the society. In modern economic policy, a social contract or compact implies a bargain among various groups in society, such as business, labour, agriculture, and government, to restrain wage and price increases to reduce inflation, in return for various social and economic policies that are in the public interest. The term came into wide use in the eighteenth century after the French political philosopher, Jean-Jacques Rousseau (1712–78), published his important work, *Le Contrat social,* in 1762.

social costs The cost of private actions, such as the production of goods or services, that are paid for by the public. Examples include the pollution of the environment and the health-care costs of injured or ill workers. See also EXTERNALITIES.

social credit An economic and political theory originating with a Scottish engineer, Major C.H. Douglas (1879–1972), after the First World War. Douglas argued that the underlying economic problem of society was a lack of purchasing power, which meant that workers could not buy all of the goods and services produced in the economy. He blamed this in large part on the banks, which, he said, forced producers to raise their prices to repay the interest on loans they needed to run and expand their businesses. As a solution, he proposed social-credit governments, which would aim to increase total purchasing power; their methods would include easy credit and low interest rates, which would result in lower prices, and social credit, consisting of discounts to retailers and national dividends to all citizens.

A social-credit government headed by William Aberhart was elected in Alberta in 1935, but it lacked the constitutional power to implement social-credit policies; several of its programs were disallowed by the federal government, with the disallowance upheld by the SUPREME COURT OF CANADA and the Judicial Committee of the Privy Council.

social indicators Social statistics used to show the social well-being of Canadians, much like the economic statistics used to indicate economic trends. Examples include statistics on levels of education, birth and death rates, illness and life expectancy, standards of housing, the per capita possession of such consumer goods as automobiles, telephones, colour television sets, and motor boats, suicides, divorce, alcoholism, crime, poverty, the state of the environment, and nutrition. In recent years, social scientists have begun to use these statistics to analyze social trends and to establish social relationships, projects much like the analysis, forecasting, and model-building activities of economists. Social scientists have, for example, attempted to show the relationships that exist between rates of illness and levels of education, and between rates of alcoholism and rates of urbanization. The ECONOMIC COUNCIL OF CANADA established a social-indicators group in 1972. Statistics Canada has prepared a periodic collection of social indicators since 1973, entitled *Perspectives Canada*.

social-insurance number (SIN) A national

registry of all Canadians who have ever worked, filled in an income-tax return, or paid Canada Pension Plan premiums. The allocation of numbers began in 1964 as a preliminary step to the introduction of the Canada Pension Plan, but the SIN is more widely used today as a means of identification—on income-tax returns, for example, and to receive various government benefits.

social mobility The ability of individuals to advance on the basis of ability or merit, rather than through social, political, and economic connections. This means that education, natural talent, and willingness to work should enable anyone to reach the top positions in the economy. While social mobility has improved in Canada, family background, social connections, and the wealth of one's parents may still give one person an advantage over another, regardless of their comparative talents. See, for example, *The Vertical Mosaic,* by John Porter (Toronto, 1965).

social overhead The public facilities needed by private industry to enable it to function. These include sewer and water systems, roads and airports, schools, and manpower-training facilities. Whether or not these costs are fully recovered from business depends on the way the tax system is designed and administered. See also INFRASTRUCTURE.

social security Various federal, provincial, and municipal programs to ensure that the aged, handicapped, disabled, unemployed, and the working poor have at least a minimum income to enable them to enjoy the basic necessities of life, such as food, shelter, and clothing. Programs include the CANADA ASSISTANCE PLAN and related provincial and municipal welfare services, old-age pensions and a guaranteed-income supplement, the CANADA PENSION PLAN, UNEMPLOYMENT INSURANCE, FAMILY ALLOWANCES, and veterans' assistance. Some of these programs are universal—that is, they are payable to everyone (old-age pensions and basic family allowances). Some are based on contributions (the Canada Pension Plan and unemployment insurance), and some are based on need (the guaranteed-income supplement for pensioners, additional family-allowance payments to families with medium to low incomes, and provincial and municipal welfare programs for the unemployed and for single or deserted mothers).

social services The various services that are available to the needy, the elderly, the handicapped or disabled, and the unemployed. These include support services, such as the distribution of hot meals and homemaker services so that the elderly can live on their own; crisis intervention, to prevent suicides or to help abused wives or children; group homes, which provide care for troubled teenagers or the mentally retarded; family-planning assistance, rehabilitation services for the disabled or handicapped, and family counselling.

social welfare What is best for society as a whole. This is not something that can be measured or quantified easily, but it may be expressed in terms of desirable goals, such as full employment, a tax system based on ability to pay, the redistribution of income to reduce great disparities in wealth and income, a minimum income for all citizens, a clean environment, a labour market that provides opportunities for individuals to advance on the basis of merit, a high level of public services, and reasonable opportunities to start one's own enterprise and retain a fair share of the wealth that is created. Sometimes goals can be in conflict—the desire to improve fairness or equity in the tax system, and the desire to improve productivity and increase economic growth, for example. It is the role of political parties to set out the various social-welfare choices, and the responsibility of voters to understand these choices and to make known their preferences. To a large extent, social-welfare goals or choices are a result of an evolving consensus in society.

socialism A political and economic system in which the state owns all or a large proportion of the means of production, in which planning largely displaces market forces in the allocation of resources, and the reduction of great disparities between individuals in wealth and income is a major objective of social and economic policy. It is a system that has developed a wide range of forms in practice, from the moderate and democratic socialism of Sweden, West Germany, and the New Democratic Party of Canada, to the sharply reduced role assigned to private initiative and private property in many of the less-developed countries, to the complete ownership of the means of production and the absolute system of state planning in communist countries. The idea dates back to France in the 1830s. KARL MARX saw socialism as a stage in the evolution of society, following the collapse of CAPITALISM and preceding the arrival of COMMUNISM.

Société générale de financement du Québec, La See GENERAL INVESTMENT CORPORATION.

soft currency A currency for which there is little demand in foreign-exchange markets, either because it is not freely convertible, or because the economy of the country issuing the currency is weak and unstable, and the currency does not represent a secure store of value. The currencies of many less-developed countries are soft currencies; this means that these countries have to obtain HARD CURRENCIES to finance their foreign trade and to repay their international debts.

soft loan A form of foreign aid or OFFICIAL DEVELOPMENT ASSISTANCE. A soft loan is a loan made to a less-developed country at a low rate of interest or no interest at all, and with a long repayment term of, say, thirty to fifty years. Often such loans may bear no interest in the first years, may require no repayment of principal for, say, the first ten years, and may be repaid in the SOFT CURRENCY of the borrowing country.

software Programs to operate computer systems or to enable a computer system to be used for specialized applications. Software design and production is one of the new knowledge industries in the so-called information society.

soil erosion The loss of agricultural topsoil due to wind or water. In 1935, the federal government created the PRAIRIE FARM REHABILITATION ADMINISTRATION, to help western farmers to avoid a repetition of the 1930s dustbowls. Measures included planting rows of trees to act as windbreaks, and the construction of irrigation and water-supply systems to help prevent farmlands from drying up.

solar energy The heat of the sun, in the form of radiation, which can be captured and stored by various techniques for future or immediate use.

Soldier Land Settlement A program adopted at the end of the First World War to help veterans to obtain farmland in western Canada.

solvency The ability of a firm or government agency to meet its obligations; this usually means that CURRENT ASSETS are greater than CURRENT LIABILITIES on a firm's balance sheet.

source-and-disposition-of-funds statement See STATEMENT OF CHANGES IN FINANCIAL POSITION.

sovereignty-association A new relationship between Quebec and the rest of Canada, advocated by the Parti Québécois as an alternative to existing constitutional arrangements under the federal system. The idea was first outlined in the late 1960s, but it was not until February 1979 that the Parti Québécois spelled it out in any detail, in a document entitled *Among Equals*. The PQ stated that Quebec had the right to self-determination, and, on achieving sovereignty, would negotiate a new economic and monetary relationship with the rest of Canada, negotiating "on the basis of equality between our two nations."

By sovereignty, the Parti Québécois meant the exclusive right to make all laws, collect all taxes, spend all government moneys, administer justice, and make any foreign agreements it wanted to. Its concept of association included: free trade between Canada and Quebec, with no barriers except those needed to protect agricultural production, support regional-economic development, and maintain preferential buying schemes; specific agreements between Canada and Quebec on railways, shipping, and air transportation, and on offshore mineral rights; an agreement between Canada, Quebec, and the United States on the operation of the St. Lawrence Seaway; a common external tariff imposed by Canada and Quebec on all imports from other countries; a common dollar, controlled by a joint monetary policy; the free circulation of money across the Canada-Quebec border without restriction, except insofar as foreign-investment rules and regulations of financial institutions might be affected; the sharing between Canada and Quebec of the outstanding federal debt and federal assets; the free movement of people back and forth across what would be an unguarded and unpoliced border; reciprocal recognition of minority-language rights; and separate responsibility for citizenship and immigration.

A government white paper, *Quebec-Canada: A New Deal,* was tabled in the Quebec National Assembly in November 1979. According to the white paper, an international treaty would be signed between Quebec and Canada defining the relationship between the two nations and establishing the rules and institutions that would ensure the proper functioning of Quebec-Canada. Four institutions would be established: **1.** A community council, to be made up of an equal number of cabinet ministers from Quebec and Canada and chaired alternately by a Canadian and a Québécois; the council would have decision-making powers on matters entrusted to it by the treaty of association. **2.** A commission of experts, acting as the secretariat for the community council. **3.** A court of justice, made up of an equal number of judges from Quebec and Canada, with exclusive jurisdiction over the interpretation and implementation of the treaty of association. **4.** A monetary authority, which would be responsible for money-supply and exchange-rate policies for the common currency of Quebec and Canada. The number of seats on this board would be allocated to Quebec and Canada in proportion to the relative size of their economies, but major questions could be referred to the community council.

Special Drawing Rights (SDRs) A reserve asset created by the INTERNATIONAL MONETARY FUND to replace the use of gold and U.S. dollars in the international monetary system. Sometimes called paper gold, SDRs were adopted by the IMF annual meeting in 1969 as the new international reserve asset for the settlement of balance-of-payments deficits between countries. They were first allocated to IMF members in 1970, according to the size of each nation's quota in the IMF. Originally, the value of the SDR was based on the U.S. dollar and gold, but starting in 1974, it was redefined in terms of a weighted basket of sixteen major currencies valued at their exchange rate for the U.S. dollar. In 1978, the currencies of Saudi Arabia and Iran were added to the basket, while those of South Africa and Denmark were dropped. The Canadian dollar has always been one of the currencies in the SDR basket.

Although the IMF expected to make regular new allotments of SDRs after their first issue in 1970–72, the significant growth in the supply of U.S. dollars, German marks, Swiss francs, and Japanese yen in the international foreign-exchange reserves of individual countries has delayed the issue of additional SDRs. But the new reserve asset has become an important international standard of value. The less-developed countries have sought a special allocation of SDRs to help them meet their foreign-exchange requirements and expand their imports, but so far the industrial nations have opposed such an allocation.

special governor general's warrants Special authorizations by the governor general to permit the federal government to spend money when no APPROPRIATION ACT is before Parliament, or no act has been passed and Parliament itself is not sitting. Since no money can be spent by the government without specific authorization from Parliament, some emergency procedure has to exist to enable the government to meet its everyday bills, such as payroll, fuel, rents, and other costs, during times when Parliament is not sitting. Such warrants had to be obtained from April to October of 1979, for example: Parliament had been dissolved before the government's spending plans had been approved; an election was held, and a new Parliament did not meet until October.

Such warrants have to be sought one month at a time; notice must be published within fifteen days in the *Canada Gazette,* and a full report must be made to the House of Commons within fifteen days after it resumes sitting. These warrants are then included in the ESTIMATES, for approval by Parliament in a subsequent appropriation act. To get such a warrant, a cabinet minister must certify that the money is urgently needed for the public good; the president of the TREASURY BOARD must confirm that there is no other place to which this spending may be charged within the government's accounts, and the cabinet must make an official request to the governor general.

special meeting A meeting of company shareholders, other than the ANNUAL MEETING, called to discuss company actions, such as a takeover, merger, or change in the company's charter, and to seek approval from shareholders. A special meeting can also be organized by dissatisfied shareholders, if enough of them agree, to review the company's policies or proposed actions with which they disagree, and perhaps to replace the BOARD OF DIRECTORS and senior officers.

specialization The division of various functions or production steps in the manufacture of a particular product among different workers in the same firm, or of different goods and services among different firms, regions, or nations. This results in greater output at lower cost, increasing the productivity and output of the economic system, and providing a higher STANDARD OF LIVING. Most economies and firms are highly specialized today, and many seek an even further degree of specialization. Specialization is often an incentive to mechanization and automation, although it can also lead to alienation in the workplace if employees find their jobs monotonous; they may no longer be aware of the product they are helping to manufacture, because their work has become so narrow.

Specialization also increases the interdependence of individuals, firms, and nations, since all of them end up producing only a small proportion of the things they consume. For example, an electronics firm may buy all of its components from suppliers, while an automobile manufacturer is dependent on many independent parts-makers in producing a car or a truck. Nations also end up depending on other nations for certain products or commodities, while this is even more the case with individuals. See also COMPARATIVE ADVANTAGE.

specialization agreement An agreement between competing firms in the same industry, under which each firm agrees not to manufacture certain product lines. This gives the firms that continue to produce those lines the opportunity to establish longer and more efficient production runs.

specie Metal coins that can be converted into paper money—for example, Canadian pennies, nickels, dimes, quarters, half-dollars, and dollars.

specific tariff A tariff applied according to the weight or number of units, rather than to the value of the goods. See also AD VALOREM TAX.

specific tax A tax levied according to the weight or number of units, rather than as a percentage of the value. See also AD VALOREM TAX.

speculation Investment in shares, bonds, commodities, foreign exchange, land, and buildings, not for the purpose of earning income but to sell them again, in as short a period as possible, at a profit. Speculators usually assume greater than normal risks because they hope to make large capital gains in a short period of time. A speculator may buy a share because he expects a takeover bid to be made, a wheat future because he expects pessimistic crop forecasts, a piece of land because he expects that someone will soon need it for a construction project, or a high-interest bond because he expects interest rates to drop.

Speech from the Throne The statement drafted by the prime minister and his staff, and approved by the cabinet, that is read by the governor general to the members of Parliament and senators assembled together in the Senate at the opening of a new session of Parliament. The speech traditionally gives a report on the state of the nation, indicates the concerns and direction of the government, and outlines the main items of legislation to be considered by Parliament in the ensuing months. The reading of the Throne Speech is followed, in the House of Commons, by an eight-day debate of a motion by the government thanking the governor general for his speech. The opposition parties can move amendments criticizing the speech. These are treated as non-confidence amendments; if one were passed, the government would be defeated and a new election would probably be necessary.

spending power In the context of Canada's constitution and federal-provincial fiscal arrangements, the power of either level of government to spend money for a particular purpose. See also FEDERAL SPENDING POWER, PROVINCIAL SPENDING POWER, TAXING POWER. The spending and taxing powers of a particular level of government largely determine what it can or cannot do, although the power to regulate is also important.

spin-off A new industry or technology resulting from some other activity. Spin-offs are most common in areas of high technology. For example, defence and space spending have resulted in new industries and products, ranging from food products and insulation for clothing to improved computer and communications systems. Similarly, the growth of a major industry such as computers, motor vehicles, or petrochemicals, will frequently result in the establishment of new firms that develop new applications or become suppliers of parts or of specialized services; often such industries are created by former employees of the major firms in the industry.

split shift The division of a person's workday into two or more segments to meet peak demand for his or her services. Municipal bus and transit drivers, or waiters and waitresses, may, for example, have their working day split into two segments.

spot contract A contract for immediate rather than future delivery of a commodity. Payment must be made at the time of the contract. See also FUTURES MARKET.

spot market A market in which foreign exchange or commodities are sold for immediate delivery. See also FUTURES MARKET.

spot price The price on the SPOT MARKET for the immediate delivery of commodities or foreign exchange. It is today's price, as opposed to the futures price, the price charged for delivery at a time specified in the future.

spread **1.** The difference between prevailing Canadian and U.S. interest rates. **2.** The difference between the BID and ASK prices on a stock exchange or bond or commodities market; the greater the trading activity for a particular share, bond, or commodity, the narrower the spread. **3.** The difference between the selling price of a good or service and the cost of producing it.

stabilization policy Measures to offset fluctuations in the economy, above and beyond BUILT-IN STABILIZERS. These measures may include changes in FISCAL and MONETARY POLICY, and the introduction of an INCOMES POLICY to achieve full employment and stable prices. For example, in periods of rising prices, stabilization measures usually include higher interest rates, higher taxes, reduced government spending, and, perhaps, wage and price controls. Conversely, during an economic slump, stabilization policies could include lower interest rates, tax cuts, and increased government spending.

stable population A population in which there is no net emigration or immigration, that has reached a constant rate of growth, with the proportion of those in different age groups remaining constant as well. See also STATIONARY POPULATION.

stable prices The maintenance of price levels in the economy at an almost constant level over a sustained period of time. While some prices may rise sharply, others are expected to decline, thus maintaining a very low average rate of inflation. For a long time, economists accepted a 2 per cent inflation rate as attainable with long-term productivity growth and full employment. Today, they would like to reduce it to 4 per cent over a sustained period of time. Like full employment, stable prices are an objective of economic policy.

stagflation The combination of high unemployment and a high rate of inflation at the same time. It used to be that an economy would experience either one or the other. High unemployment was expected to lead to low inflation, while low unemployment was expected to lead to higher inflation. In recent years, though, the mixed economy has achieved slow growth, high unemployment, and high inflation, all at the same time, thus raising new questions for economists about how to achieve basic goals such as full employment and stable prices in a modern industrial economy.

stagnation A chronically poor rate of economic performance, resulting in a declining, zero, or much lower-than-potential rate of economic growth, and a static or declining per capita gross national product. Stagnation results from inadequate aggregate demand and a low rate of technological innovation, and hence an absence of new investment and productivity-boosting opportunities; in less-developed countries, it may arise from a high rate of population growth that outstrips the capacity of the economy to raise per capita income and meet the demand even for necessities, such as food and shelter.

stale-dated cheque A cheque that has been held for longer than six months before being presented to a bank for clearing. Canadian banks will not cash cheques that are older than six months. The holder has to go back to the issuer and have a new cheque written.

stamp tax A method of raising government revenue by requiring the purchase of a stamp, to be affixed to cheques, wills, and legal documents, such as those for the sale of a home or other property. Such taxes were once an important source of government revenue; Canada, for example, imposed a stamp tax on bank cheques, letters and postcards, patent medicines, perfumes, and wines during the First World War. But such taxes are rare today.

standard of living A term that combines economic well-being and certain expectations of quality of life. Although there is no consensus on what constitutes a reasonable standard of living, it is based on wants, rather than on needs, that contribute to the welfare or well-being of individuals. Improvement in a people's standard of living depends on economic factors, such as improvements in productivity or per capita real economic growth, a system of income redistribution through the tax system or direct spending by government, and the availability of public services, such as health, education, transit, and parks, along with non-economic factors, such as protection against unsafe or unpleasant working conditions, opportunities for advancement in work, a clean environment, a low crime rate, freedom of expression, and the RULE OF LAW. Economists often use per capita gross national product as a rough way to compare the standard of living of different countries, since the output of goods and services is an important consideration. But other measures have also been devised, such as SOCIAL INDICATORS, and the PHYSICAL QUALITY-OF-LIFE INDEX.

Standards Council of Canada A federal agency, created by Parliament in 1970, to achieve national product standards to protect consumers, increase economic efficiency, improve health and safety, and expand international trade opportunities. The council's standards include dimensions, quality, safety, and performance. The council has assigned standards-writing and -testing to other organizations, to produce a comprehensive set of national standards. These organizations include the CANADIAN STANDARDS ASSOCIATION, the Underwriters' Laboratories of Canada, the Canadian Government Specifications Board, the Canadian Gas Association, and the Bureau de normalisation du Québec. The council also worked with the METRIC COMMISSION OF CANADA to introduce the metric system. It maintains an international standardization branch in Mississauga, Ontario.

standby control An economic power, passed by Parliament or a provincial legislature, that permits the government or a government agency to take certain actions, should the need arise. For example, the federal government has the power to impose export or import controls on particular goods or commodities, to alter the secondary reserves that must be maintained by the chartered banks, or to allocate oil supplies during an emergency. The federal and provincial cabinets often have the power to overrule the decisions of regulatory agencies.

staple theory An important theory of Canadian economic growth, according to which Canadian economic development has been based on the exploitation of a succession of staples or commodities, such as fur, fish, lumber, wheat, metal minerals, and oil and gas, for international markets. This exploitation, in turn, has determined the growth of Canadian transportation systems, the location of Canadian communities, and the establishment of commercial and investment networks, including the banking system and the financial centres of Montreal, Toronto, Winnipeg, Calgary, and Vancouver. The staple theory of Canadian economic history was developed by W. A. Mackintosh, HAROLD INNIS, and Donald Creighton. The staple theory no longer has the consensus of support it once had among Canadian economic historians, but it is none the less the most persistent theme in Canada's economic history and has not been succeeded by any other theory of Canadian development.

statement of changes in financial position An important part of a company's annual report, showing the net changes in WORKING CAPITAL that have occurred between the previous year's BALANCE SHEET and the current year's balance sheet. The statement shows the various sources of company funds, such as funds from company operations, including DEPRECIATION and DEFERRED INCOME TAXES, issues of securities, and the sale of assets, along with the various applications or uses of funds, including dividend payments, the repayment of long-term debt or redemption of preferred shares, long-term investments in other corporations, and investment in new plant, machinery, and equipment. It is sometimes called the source-and-application-of-funds statement.

stationary population A population with a growth rate of zero; the number of births and deaths in the population is the same.

stationary state The idea of a no-growth economy, developed by a number of classical economists, such as THOMAS MALTHUS, DAVID RICARDO, and JOHN STUART MILL, who believed that investment opportunities were restricted by society's limited capacity for innovation, and that capitalists would therefore be faced with declining profits, under the LAW OF DIMINISHING RETURNS, to the point where they would cease to save and invest. New capital formation would thus fall to zero, while wages would fall to a subsistence level and economic growth would cease. ADAM SMITH foresaw the possibility of a stationary state, but thought it too distant a prospect to worry about, while NEOCLASSICAL economists such as ALFRED MARSHALL rejected the notion.

statistical error An adjustment made to reconcile the incompleteness of numerical data, or their failure to balance completely, based on the recognition that information collected by statisticians can never be perfect. For example, statistics on GROSS NATIONAL PRODUCT normally contain a small "errors and omissions" entry to reflect the incompleteness of the thousands of statistics collected on the economy.

statistician A person who is educated in the science of statistics and who works in this field.

statistics A specialized branch of science or mathematics that deals with the assembly and classification of numerical information to establish various hypotheses of economic behaviour or future economic performance, based on expectations or probabilities drawn from historical experience. Statistics are collected from individuals, groups, industries, corporations, nations, and other sources, and organized into understandable and usable forms. Sometimes representative groups, individuals, or firms are surveyed, and conclusions for the entire group, population, industry, or nation are inferred from them. Sometimes all individuals, groups, or firms are surveyed, as in a CENSUS. There is a large body of statistical theory that devises new methods of organizing and presenting information. The field of applied statistics, which is concerned with the application of existing statistical methods, can be broken down into many different categories, such as demographics, economic forecasting, and SOCIAL INDICATORS. See also SYSTEM OF NATIONAL ACCOUNTS.

Statistics Canada The central statistical agency of the Canadian government. It plays a vital role in collecting, analyzing, and publishing a wide range of statistics on almost every aspect of economic and social life in the country. Without this public agency, policymakers, universities, and business firms would lack, for example, the essential information they need to review economic and social policies, to make investment plans, to measure social and economic progress, and to pinpoint problems in the economic and social structure. One of the most important agencies of the federal government, it was established in 1918 as the Dominion Bureau of Statistics. The chief statistician reports to the president of the TREASURY BOARD. See also CENSUS, SYSTEM OF NATIONAL ACCOUNTS.

status symbol Any possession that suggests that the owner is affluent or has a special standing in the community. It can range from the ownership of an extremely expensive car, the consumption of rare wines, membership in an exclusive club, wearing expensive or designer clothes, and living in a big house, to acquaintance with someone in high places, or the parenting of a successful child. See also CONSPICUOUS CONSUMPTION.

statutory holiday A holiday that all employees are entitled to, according to federal or provincial law. Employees who have to work on a statutory holiday are legally entitled to extra pay or other time off. Examples include Canada Day on 1 July, Labour Day on the first Monday in September, and Christmas Day on 25 December. Altogether there are nine federal statutory holidays: New Year's Day, Good Friday, Victoria Day, Dominion Day, Labour Day, Thanksgiving, Remembrance Day, Christmas Day, and Boxing Day.

sterling A synonym for the British pound.

sterling area Those countries that hold a significant portion of their foreign-exchange reserves in British pounds, deposited in the British banking system. Although this was a natural enough arrangement for many members of the British Commonwealth and certain Middle East nations in the days when the pound was a strong RESERVE CURRENCY, these sterling balances have, since the late 1950s, become a liability for Britain. Various measures have had to be adopted to protect Britain against a sudden withdrawal of these reserves, or their conversion to other currencies, since such an act would cause a sharp drop in the exchange rate of the British pound. The existence of these balances has had some effect on the independence of British foreign and trade policy, since foreign holders of these reserves can threaten to reduce them for political reasons or out of disapproval of British economic and trade policies. In recent years, the importance of these sterling balances has declined.

stock See SHARE.

stock dividend The payment by a company of a dividend in the form of additional shares, instead of cash, to its shareholders; the number of shares received is in proportion to each shareholder's existing share of ownership in the company. The benefit of stock dividends to a company is that it does not have to allocate as large a portion of after-tax earnings to the shareholder but can use more of its earnings to finance expansion. The benefit to shareholders is that they are not taxed on the receipt of the extra shares, but instead pay capital-gains tax when the extra shares are sold, which, for many shareholders, means that they pay less tax than they would on cash DIVIDENDS.

Wholly owned subsidiaries can also use this device to repatriate profits to their foreign-parent companies, and avoid paying Canada's 15 per cent WITHHOLDING TAX. A wholly owned subsidiary may pay out dividends to its parent in the form of preferred shares; the parent can then have the subsidiary redeem the preferred shares by paying the parent the value of the preferred shares. If the money had been repatriated as a cash dividend, it would have been liable to the 15 per cent withholding tax.

stock exchange An organized market on which COMMON and PREFERRED SHARES and WARRANTS that meet exchange listing requirements can be bought and sold on behalf of investors or themselves by stockbrokers who own seats on the exchange and meet membership requirements. While the issuing, sale, and purchase of shares is governed by provincial securities commissions, each stock exchange also has its own board of governors to regulate its activities. Each board sets capital and other requirements for member firms, trading rules, and listing requirements for shares traded on the exchange. A stock exchange plays an important role in the economy: it provides a way for companies to raise new equity capital, and it provides a way for investors to use their savings to buy and sell shares and help finance business expansion. The four stock exchanges in Canada are the MONTREAL STOCK EXCHANGE (1874), the TORONTO STOCK EXCHANGE (1878), the VANCOUVER STOCK EXCHANGE (1907), and the ALBERTA STOCK EXCHANGE (1913).

stock-exchange index An index showing the trend of a representative and significant group of shares traded on a stock exchange. The TORONTO STOCK EXCHANGE publishes a composite index of three hundred representative shares, with 1975 equal to 1,000 points. The MONTREAL STOCK EXCHANGE publishes an industrial index and a composite index. Statistics Canada also publishes a number of indexes of prices of Canadian shares, including an industrial index, a utilities and services index, and a finance index. Other stock-exchange indexes include the Dow Jones Index, the Standard and Poor indexes, and the New York Stock Exchange indexes.

stock-exchange listing See LISTED STOCK.

stock-exchange member A firm or individual who owns a seat on a STOCK EXCHANGE and is thus entitled to buy and sell shares listed on the exchange on its own account or on behalf of others. A stock-exchange member must abide by all the rules of the exchange, including its capital requirements and trading rules.

stock-exchange seat See STOCK-EXCHANGE MEMBER.

stock option 1. In a corporation, the right to purchase, under a stock-option plan, a specified number of a company's TREASURY SHARES at a specified price over a specified period of time. Such a right is often given senior officers of a corporation and is sometimes extended to all employees. **2.** A contract giving the purchaser the right but not the obligation to buy or sell a specific quantity of a company's shares at a specific price for a stipulated period of time. The right to purchase the shares is a CALL; to sell the shares, a PUT.

stock split The division of each outstanding share of a company into two or more common shares of the company. This does not increase the capitalization of a company, but it does reduce the market price of each share, and thus improves the marketability of the shares. Companies usually split their shares when the price of each share has become so high that few investors can afford to purchase a BOARD LOT. Such a rise reduces the marketability of the company's shares, and hence not only checks their potential price increase, but also the ability to issue new common shares successfully.

Splitting the shares also makes it possible for a company to achieve a wider distribution of ownership of its shares. For example, if the market price of a company's shares reaches $160 and there are 200,000 common shares outstanding, a 4 for 1 split would reduce the value of each share to $40 and increase the number of outstanding shares to 800,000. Someone who owned 200 of the $160 shares would get new share certificates indicating that he owned 800 of the new $40 shares. The value of the investment is unchanged, unless the price of the shares rises on a stock exchange, indicating increased demand resulting from the split.

stock yield The yield of a common or preferred share; it is the percentage return of an investor on his shares at the current market price, and is calculated by dividing the annual dividend per share by the current market price.

stockbroker A member of a STOCK EXCHANGE who buys and sells shares for investors on a stock exchange. For this service, the stockbroker is paid a commission based on a schedule set by the stock exchange. Stockbrokers also trade in mutual funds, UNLISTED SHARES, and other securities, and provide credit or MARGIN financing for customers.

stockpile A reserve supply of strategic or essential commodities vital to the national defence or economic life of a nation. Commodities stockpiled may include wheat, oil, copper, and scarce metals used in alloys.

stop-loss order An order by an owner of shares to his stockbroker to sell a specific number of shares of a company once it declines to a certain price. Once the price is reached, the shares are automatically offered for sale on a stock exchange. The purpose of such an order is to limit the possible loss on the value of the shares.

stop payment An order to a bank by someone who has issued a cheque not to honour the cheque when it is presented for payment.

straddle An option or contract giving the purchaser the right to buy or sell a particular number of shares of a company at a specified price for a specified period of time. It is both a PUT and a CALL, although the exercise of either option may eliminate the opportunity of exercising the other option. A purchaser of a straddle for 1,000 shares of company A at $50 would exercise the right to sell the 1,000 shares if they fell to, say, $40, and to buy the shares and resell them if the price rose to, say, $60.

straight-line method of depreciation See DEPRECIATION.

strategic materials Commodities such as oil, copper, chromium, and steel, industrial goods such as certain types of heavy machinery, and advanced technologies such as powerful computers, that are vital to a nation's military capacity or the functioning of a wartime economy.

street certificate A share certificate that is made out in the name of a stockbroker or investment dealer, instead of in the name of the actual owner. This makes the certificate easier to sell in a hurry.

strike A decision by employees in a BARGAINING UNIT to stop working, following the breakdown of COLLECTIVE BARGAINING and the failure of CONCILIATION and MEDIATION to produce an agreement with the employer on a new COLLECTIVE AGREEMENT. A strike is a form of pressure on an employer, who risks losing business and his share of the market; it may also be a way of angering the public and hurting the economy or health of the community, if the employer is a government agency. Generally speaking, strikes are only legal after a collective agreement has expired and certain formal steps, including a STRIKE VOTE, have been taken. Sometimes a union will resort to hit-and-run or rotating strikes, so that only a small number of workers are on strike on any particular day. This means that the other workers will be paid, while the employer has to anticipate where the next strike will occur; sometimes this will provoke the employer into a LOCKOUT of his employees. A WILDCAT strike is a strike by workers that does not have the support of union leaders, and is illegal because it occurs while a collective agreement is in force or before all the legal steps up to a strike have been followed. Federal and provincial labour laws govern strike procedures in Canada.

strike vote A vote by union members in a bargaining unit, giving the bargaining committee the authority to declare a strike. Under federal and provincial labour laws, a strike vote has to take place a specified number of days before a strike can legally take place.

strikebreaker A person who takes a job with an employer whose regular workers are out on strike, or an employee who does not join his fellow workers in going out on strike. Federal and most provincial labour laws allow a struck employer to hire other workers for the duration of a strike and to try to keep on operating. A strikebreaker is also known as a scab.

strip mine A mine in which the topsoil and other overburden has been cleared away, so that the ore can be removed by surface extraction.

structural inflation Inflation resulting from institutional arrangements in the economy, rather than from changes in the business cycle. Union rules that restrict the number of new entrants to a trade can, for example, lead to artificial shortages, and thus to higher pay rates for those in the trade. Similarly, government regulations that prevent competition can cause unnecessary increases in air-transportation costs. The ability of unions to get big wage increases from employers during a period of high unemployment may also be a form of structural inflation if the employers are able simply to pass along those wage increases in the form of higher prices and thus maintain their profit margins.

structural policies Policies to ensure adequate supplies of the FACTORS OF PRODUCTION or to enable unproductive regions or industries to become efficient. For the former, see also SUPPLY MANAGEMENT. Examples of the latter include farm-consolidation programs, to make farms larger and hence more efficient, manpower programs, to retrain workers in ailing industries to obtain employment in new industries, and REGIONAL-DEVELOPMENT policies, to improve the INFRASTRUCTURE of slow-growth regions and to persuade industries, through grants and other incentives, to locate there.

structural unemployment Unemployment, usually long-term in nature, caused by inadequate skills, the general decline of an industry or of a region of the country, automation, or an unwillingness by those unemployed to move to other regions where jobs exist. For example, the unemployment of former textile workers in small Quebec towns reflects an inability to adjust to changing economic conditions. There may be no economic reason for new industries to move to these towns, and an understandable unwillingness of workers in their forties and fifties to leave the part of the country they know and, assuming they had the skills, move to, say, Alberta, as workers in a tar-sands project.

student loan A government-subsidized loan to a full-time student to help pay his tuition, living, and other costs while a student. Under the Canada Student Loan Act, the federal government pays the interest on the loans of full-time students while they are students and for six months afterward, if a provincial government certifies that the student is eligible for such assistance. All the provinces participate except Quebec, which has its own program.

subcontractor A firm or individual hired to carry out one segment of a project. For example, in the construction of an office building, an electrical firm will be hired as a subcontractor to install wiring and lighting, and to see to other electrical needs. The firm responsible for the overall construction is the prime contractor.

sublet The assignment by a tenant of his rights under an existing lease to another person or firm. For example, someone who moves out of an apartment before the lease has expired may rent out the apartment to another person for the remainder of his lease period. The original tenant is responsible for making sure that the landlord is paid.

subordinated debenture A DEBENTURE that is ranked below other securities or obligations of the company, and hence has a lesser claim to repayment in the event of bankruptcy.

subordinated debt The debt of a company that can only be paid off after the SENIOR and fully secured debt has been repaid.

subsidiary A company that is legally controlled by another company. Many subsidiaries are wholly owned by a parent firm; but a subsidiary can be controlled by ownership of a simple majority or a large block of voting shares. Many foreign corporations in Canada are wholly owned subsidiaries, but some have a minority of shares owned by Canadians. Sometimes a company within Canada will establish a wholly owned subsidiary to carry out a different business activity; this also leaves the way open in the future to raise equity capital in the subsidiary by selling off a minority block of shares.

subsidy A direct or indirect payment or other assistance to someone to produce goods or services. The most common examples are direct payments by government to avoid raising prices to reflect the true costs—payments to the Post Office to cover its deficit and thus eliminate the need to raise postal rates, for example, or payments to the railways to maintain passenger rail services without significantly raising fares. But a subsidy can also be paid to a producer so that he can sell his output at a lower price—subsidies to Canadian shipbuilders, for example, to cover a part of their costs of production, and thus enable them to compete with foreign shipyards.

Subsidies can also be paid by forcing consumers to pay higher prices; in this sense, tariffs are a subsidy for domestic manufacturers, and prices obtained by farm marketing boards may be subsidies for farmers. Another form of subsidy is a government loan at a low interest rate, or a government-guaranteed loan that allows the borrower to obtain funds at a lower rate of interest than he would otherwise pay.

subsistence wage The lowest wage that can be paid to a worker so that he can obtain the basic necessities of life and still be able and willing to work. For some economists, such as THOMAS ROBERT MALTHUS (1766–1834), this is the long-term wage, since anything higher will attract too many workers and anything lower will attract too few. See also IRON LAW OF WAGES.

substitutes Rival or competing goods that can be interchanged for one another, since they have the same uses or yield similar satisfaction. Thus, if the price of product A rises, the demand for product B, if it is a substitute, should rise if its price is now lower. Tea and coffee are substitutes as hot beverages; trains, planes, and buses are substitutes in travel; steel, concrete, bricks, and lumber are substitutes in construction, and chicken and beef are substitutes as sources of protein. See also COMPLEMENTARY GOODS.

substitution effect The change in demand for a product if its price is changed while the price of other goods remains unchanged; the extent to which demand changes depends, among other things, on whether or not substitutes exist and are readily available. If the price of raspberries goes up while other prices stay the same, it will benefit consumers to substitute a cheaper product—say, strawberries—to hold down living costs. Similarly, if the price of raspberries falls below the price of strawberries, it will pay to switch to raspberries. Thus, the demand for both strawberries and raspberries will change, depending upon their relative prices. See also INCOME EFFECT. When substitutes exist, the price of one product or service is influenced by the price of the other; for example, increases in railway freight rates may lead shippers to make greater use of trucks, if trucking charges are unchanged.

subvention A synonym for a government grant or subsidy.

succession duty A tax on the wealth received by beneficiaries of an estate. Its purposes are to reduce great inequalities of wealth in society by taxing those who inherit significant wealth, and to raise revenue to help cover the costs of government. The federal government withdrew from the field at the end of 1971, so that the provinces could raise money from this tax. However, virtually all of the provinces have withdrawn from the field as well.

suggested retail selling price A price often printed on consumer goods by manufacturers to show the public what they can expect to pay, unless a particular retailer decides to sell the product for less. See also RESALE-PRICE MAINTENANCE.

supplementary estimates Requests to Parliament for approval of additional government spending, beyond the amounts requested in the main ESTIMATES at the start of the FISCAL YEAR. Additional spending needs can result from unanticipated higher costs, a government decision to increase spending under a particular program, or the introduction of new spending programs during the fiscal year. For example, higher than expected unemployment will lead to a need for additional unemployment-insurance spending; a decision to accelerate housing construction will mean that more money will have to be allocated to housing programs; and the introduction of, say, a new research and development program will entail new spending. One set of supplementary estimates is presented in the second half of the fiscal year, while another set is presented at the end of the fiscal year.

supplementary letters patent Changes in the charter issued to a company that has been incorporated under federal or provincial law. An application has to be made to the same government department that issued the original charter. A company may want, for example, to increase its AUTHORIZED CAPITAL if it has grown much faster than expected. This can only be done through supplementary letters patent.

supply The quantity of a good available for sale at a particular price. Supply thus depends on price. Supply can be increased until the marginal cost of the product—that is, the cost of producing one more unit—is equal to the existing price. At that point, a price increase will be needed if the supply is to be increased.

supply and demand See LAW OF SUPPLY AND DEMAND.

Supply and Services, Department of A federal government department created in 1969 to act as the central purchasing agent of the federal government, to provide centralized services to government departments and agencies (for example, computer and printing services), to provide management-consulting assistance to government departments and agencies, to handle payroll, employee-benefit, and pension services for all government employees, to receive all revenue for the government in the CONSOLIDATED REVENUE FUND, and to issue all cheques (and thus make all payments) on behalf of the government of Canada. In its role as purchasing agent for the federal government, the department is able to impose quality standards, to use its purchasing power to encourage the development of Canadian-designed products, and thus to help the growth of Canadian companies. The minister is the RECEIVER GENERAL OF CANADA, the custodian of enemy property during times of war, and is responsible to Parliament for the ROYAL CANADIAN MINT, the CANADIAN COMMERCIAL CORPORATION, and the Crown Assets Disposal Corporation.

supply management Medium and long-term government policies to ensure adequate supplies of the various FACTORS OF PRODUCTION at reasonably stable prices. Thus, supply management includes policies to ensure adequate supplies of everything from skilled labour and serviced land for housing, to energy supplies, VENTURE CAPITAL, and farm products. Supply management touches on many different policy fields, including competition policy, farm marketing boards, land development, banking, manpower training, and energy policy. It is anti-inflationary, in that it is designed to prevent bottlenecks or shortages, which in turn can cause higher prices and slower economic growth.

supply schedule (curve) A curve that shows the relationship between market price and the volume of goods that producers are willing to supply at any given price. As prices rise, so will the supply, and vice versa. See also DEMAND SCHEDULE (CURVE).

suppressed inflation Inflation that cannot make itself felt in the form of higher prices (because of government wage and price controls or some other factor, such as a temporary oversupply of goods and services), but which will appear once controls are lifted or the temporary surplus disappears.

Supreme Court of Canada The highest court in the country, which deals with criminal, civil, and constitutional cases. Its decisions are final; there is no appeal. The court dates back to 1875; but it could be overruled by the Judicial Committee of the Privy Council in Britain until Parliament made the Supreme Court the court of last resort in all cases in 1949. The court has nine judges, the chief one being the chief justice of Canada. Although most of the court's work consists of handling appeals from the decisions of the top courts of appeal in each province, it also deals with direct references from the federal government, and with constitutional disputes (for example, jurisdiction over offshore mineral rights along the Pacific Coast in 1967, the legality of the federal government's 1975 wage and price controls in 1976, and the federal responsibility for cable television in 1978).

surplus **1.** What is left over—for example, the excess of government revenue after its expenditures have been made, the remaining value of goods or services after deducting all costs, the remaining crops after the year's food needs have been met. **2.** The RETAINED EARNINGS of a corporation. **3.** The contributed surplus of a corporation, which arises when a corporation is able to sell new shares above their par or stated value.

surtax An additional tax levied on either the tax base or on taxable income after the normal tax has been levied; it is usually an additional percentage of the normal tax payable. A surtax is sometimes imposed by a government when it wants to adopt a policy of fiscal restraint to curb excess demand in the economy; it can be applied to consumers or corporations, or both.

survey A method of determining public opinion, attitudes, or expectations, by interviewing a representative sample of the population, based on age, sex, education, occupation, and place of residence, and drawing conclusions for the population as a whole from the results. Surveys can play an important role in setting economic policy, by revealing consumer expectations, and hence buying plans, or by indicating the confidence of business leaders and their investment intentions. Surveys are widely used by corporations in MARKET RESEARCH.

suspended trading On a stock exchange, a halt to trading in the shares of a particular company. Suspension may occur until significant news, such as a takeover bid or a major mineral find, is announced and widely disseminated, or details of a takeover bid are clarified, or because a company breaks the rules of the listing stock exchange. So long as trading is suspended, no member of the stock exchange is allowed to handle an order for the shares in another market. Trading is normally resumed when important corporate news has been disseminated and clarified, or when a listed company has dealt with its infraction of the stock exchange's rules to the satisfaction of the exchange.

sustained-yield basis A form of forest management in which trees are supposed to be replanted at the same rate as they are cut down.

swap arrangement An arrangement among various nations, through their central banks, to help each other deal with speculative attacks on one of their currencies, or to deal with a balance-of-payments problem. Under a swap, a central bank will make available to another country's central bank a specified amount of its currency in return for a credit for the second country's currency, with the exchange to be reversed later but at the same exchange rate as the initial transaction. Such arrangements have been used a number of times since 1961, with the assistance of the BANK FOR INTERNATIONAL SETTLEMENTS, to help solve balance-of-payments and foreign-exchange problems. Canada was a recipient of such assistance during its 1962 foreign-exchange crisis.

sweat shop A company that pays workers the lowest possible wage, provides them with the barest of benefits as required under law, and works them the longest possible hours, under high pressure and often under unhealthy conditions. Although labour laws provide workers with some protection against unscrupulous employers, through minimum-wage, hours-of-work, vacation-with-pay, and job-safety laws, workers are not always aware of their legal rights. Illegal or legal immigrants may also be afraid to speak up.

sweetener A device to make a purchase, lease, investment, or other action more attractive to the would-be buyer, tenant, or investor. For example, a men's clothing shop may offer a free shirt with each new sports jacket purchased within a certain period; a landlord may offer a month's free rent or redecoration to attract a tenant; or a company trying to raise new EQUITY CAPITAL may make its PREFERRED SHARES convertible into COMMON SHARES.

sweetheart contract A collective agreement

negotiated by an employer with a dishonest union leader that benefits mainly the employer. It can also be a contract or sales agreement, negotiated between a company and a supplier or customer, that is to the detriment of the majority of shareholders, but that benefits a particular shareholder or director who has an interest in the supplier or customer with whom the contract or agreement is negotiated.

swing-shift In a corporation or government agency operating twenty-four hours a day, the shift that begins in late afternoon and continues until about midnight.

sympathy strike An illegal strike by union members who have a collective agreement in effect with their own employer and who are not directly involved in the dispute.

syndicalism An economic system in which each industry is organized into an autonomous syndicate under the control of the workers. These various units or syndicates for all of the country's different industries meet as a federation to plan national policies and priorities, thus eliminating the need for a strong central government. The idea generated some interest in the late nineteenth and early twentieth centuries, mainly in France, where it was promoted by Georges Sorel and Hubert Lagardelle. Italy's Benito Mussolini showed some interest in syndicalism in the 1930s, and interest has been shown in Canada more recently by some of the more radical spokesmen for Quebec unions.

syndicate 1. A group of INVESTMENT DEALERS who jointly UNDERWRITE and distribute a new issue of shares or bonds, or who arrange the sale of a large block of an outstanding issue of shares or bonds so as not to disturb the market unduly. Banks may also participate in a syndicate—in a new issue of provincial bonds, for example. **2.** A group of investors who participate together in launching a new business enterprise that has a large start-up cost or a large capital investment.

synergy A situation in which two or more groups achieve greater total effectiveness by working together than by working separately.

synthetic crude oil Crude oil produced from TAR-SANDS or heavy-oil deposits, which is treated in upgrading facilities to reduce its sulphur content and to decrease its viscosity, so that it can be processed by a refinery into gasoline, heating oil, and other products, much like ordinary crude oil.

system of national accounts A comprehensive series of statistics, developed by Statistics Canada since the end of the Second World War; these statistics, taken together, give a complete, overall view of changes taking place in the economy and provide a comprehensive basis for economic analysis. The system consists of a number of different statistical reports: **1.** The national income and expenditure accounts, which show who gets economic output and how it is spent. **2.** The balance of international payments, which shows trade, investment, travel, and other transactions with non-residents. **3.** Input-output tables, which show the contributions of different industries to economic growth. **4.** Indexes of real domestic product, which show the growth in output of different industries and their contribution to GROSS DOMESTIC PRODUCT. **5.** Financial-flow accounts, which show the movement of funds between savers and borrowers.

The system of national accounts is one of the most important concepts in modern statistics; without it, economic policy-makers would be hard pressed to build economic models and to improve their skills in economic management. The system of national accounts also provides a basis for making comparisons with economic developments in other countries. The Canadian system is similar to the systems used by the ORGANIZATION FOR ECONOMIC CO-OPERATION AND DEVELOPMENT and by the United Nations.

systems analysis A management technique, using computer models, to study the range of alternatives and their outcomes for a system, whether the system is a corporation, a local or national economy, an industry, or something much smaller, such as a local river system.

T

tailings The waste materials produced in the initial processing of a mineral ore. The solid wastes are separated out from the water used in the processing, in a body of water known as a tailings pond.

take-home pay The amount of money received by an employee to spend, after his employer has made all the required deductions from his pay for income taxes, pension contributions, unemployment insurance, union dues, and for various fringe benefits, such as accident, sickness, and disability insurance.

takeover The acquisition of control of one company by another, usually by purchasing enough shares to exercise control. It is often more attractive for a company to grow by taking over other companies than by investing in new productive assets, especially if stock markets are weak, shares undervalued, and the costs of new capital investment high. A company can also increase its share of the market by taking over competitors.

Foreign corporations have found the takeover of Canadian corporations to be a convenient way of establishing themselves in the Canadian market. Takeovers in Canada are not illegal, but may be subject to review under the COMBINES INVESTIGATION ACT to see whether they "unduly" prevent or lessen competition. The takeover of Canadian companies by foreign investors requires approval from the FOREIGN INVESTMENT REVIEW AGENCY, which must determine whether such takeovers bring "significant benefit" to Canadians. The takeover of publicly traded companies must follow rules set down by provincial securities commissions and local stock exchanges. The Department of CONSUMER AND CORPORATE AFFAIRS publishes data on takeovers in Canada.

tangible assets The physical assets of a firm or other entity. They include buildings, machinery, and equipment. See also INTANGIBLE ASSETS.

tar sands See OIL SANDS.

tariff A tax on imported goods, levied either as a percentage of their value or according to the number of units shipped. An AD VALOREM tariff or duty is one that is levied as a per cent of the value of the goods being imported or exported. Tariffs are INDIRECT TAXES. In the past they were a major source of revenue for governments; today, their main purpose is to protect domestic industries by giving them a competitive advantage over imports, although NON-TARIFF BARRIERS may be more effective in restraining imports. Critics of tariffs contend that they raise prices for consumers, and discourage the most efficient allocation of resources by frustrating the international location of industries according to COMPARATIVE ADVANTAGE. Defenders claim that tariffs are necessary to countries whose industries are not strongly developed, which must protect themselves against the onslaught of goods and services from countries whose industries are much more advanced. See also GENERAL AGREEMENT ON TARIFFS AND TRADE, GENERALIZED SYSTEM OF PREFERENCES, INFANT INDUSTRY.

Tariff Board A federal board, created in 1931, that has two principal functions: **1.** It carries out inquiries ordered by the minister of FINANCE into the effect of imports on particular industries in Canada, including the impact of tariff levels and other trade regulations. These reports are economic studies and are published. **2.** It hears appeals from importers and others on decisions of the Department of NATIONAL REVENUE on the value for duty, tariff classification, and other such matters affecting the level of duty charged on an import.

tariff war An escalating competition between two or more countries, which impose increasingly harsh barriers against the entry of each other's goods as the war heats up. For example, during the depression of the 1930s, the nations of Europe, the United States, and the

British Empire and Commonwealth tried to solve their own unemployment problems by raising tariff barriers against one another's imports. In this way, they hoped to export their unemployment problems to others. Since the adoption of the GENERAL AGREEMENT ON TARIFFS AND TRADE in 1948, the potential for such tariff wars has been sharply reduced, although not entirely eliminated.

task force A group of experts appointed to investigate a particular problem, to come up with an analysis, and to make proposals to solve it.

Task Force on Foreign Ownership and the Structure of Canadian Industry A task force of eight university economists, headed by Professor Melville H. Watkins of the University of Toronto, and appointed by the federal government in March 1967. Its assignment was to study "the significance—both political and economic—of foreign investment in the development of our country, as well as ways to encourage greater Canadian ownership of our industrial resources while retaining a climate favourable to the inflow of foreign investment, as required for Canada's optimum development."

The task-force report was presented to the government in February 1968. It proposed a wide range of policies, among them: **1.** A new government agency to co-ordinate policies on foreign ownership. It would monitor the activities of foreign-owned corporations in Canada, scrutinize licensing agreements on technology between foreign parents and their Canadian subsidiaries, and seek better ways of importing foreign technology, examine international market-sharing arrangements, work with other countries and international agencies to achieve common policies to control multinational corporations, and examine the tax procedures of the Canadian government and multinational firms, to make sure that Canada got its proper share of corporate taxes. **2.** Publication of increased information on the activities of foreign-controlled firms in Canada. The report proposed amendments to the Canada Corporations Act, to require that all federally incorporated PRIVATE COMPANIES disclose their annual financial results, and to make mandatory replies from foreign-controlled firms to government questionnaires on compliance with the GUIDING PRINCIPLES OF GOOD CORPORATE BEHAVIOUR. **3.** A revised competition policy, with amendments to the COMBINES INVESTIGATION ACT to encourage greater competition in the economy, and to facilitate the RATIONALIZATION of Canadian industry to make it more efficient through mergers. **4.** Establishment of the CANADA DEVELOPMENT CORPORATION, to play a major role in encouraging mergers to create stronger Canadian companies, to promote joint ventures with Canadian capital, and to provide a Canadian presence in industries that were for the most part foreign controlled. Other measures to develop an industrial strategy advocated by the report included encouragement of more research and development in Canada, improved business and management education, and better use of CLOSED-END INVESTMENT funds to facilitate Canadian ownership. **5.** Special steps to block the EXTRATERRITORIAL application of foreign laws to the activities of foreign-controlled firms in Canada. The task force proposed a new government export agency to make sure that sales orders from communist countries were filled by American-controlled subsidiaries here, in spite of prohibitions against parent firms under the U.S. Trading with the Enemy Act. The export agency would be able to purchase products from the American subsidiary in Canada and export them itself. It would be illegal for the subsidiary to refuse to sell to the government export agency. The task force also wanted laws to prevent the removal of commercial records from Canada as a result of foreign court orders, legislation to bar Canadian compliance with foreign antitrust rulings, and questionnaires to foreign subsidiaries here to determine the impact of parent-country antitrust laws on their Canadian operations. **6.** Multilateral tariff reductions, to help Canadian companies get a bigger share of foreign markets and to promote competition in Canada.

Overall, the task force found that, while foreign investment had produced both costs and benefits to the Canadian economy, a new National Policy was needed to ensure Canadian economic independence, and to strengthen the country's capacity for autonomous growth.

tax A mandatory payment made by individuals and corporations to government. Taxes are levied on income or wealth or are imposed on goods and services, to finance the cost of government services, to redistribute income, and to influence the behaviour of consumers and investors. Until the early part of the twentieth century, the purpose of a tax was to enable the government to pay its own bills. Since then, PROGRESSIVE TAXATION has been used to redistribute wealth from the well-off to the needy. With the adoption of KEYNESIAN ECONOMICS, governments began to manipulate tax rates, to encourage or to slow down economic growth. A tax can also be used to encourage desired behaviour; for example, the imposition of higher taxes on cars that consume a large amount of gasoline may help the sale of smaller cars that make more efficient use of gasoline. See DIRECT TAX, INDIRECT TAX, INCOME TAX, EXCISE TAX, PROPERTY TAX, SALES TAX.

tax avoidance The reduction of a person's tax liability to the lowest possible level through legal means. This is done by utilizing all possible deductions, taking advantage of alternative methods of reporting and assessing income, and using all possible TAX LOOPHOLES. See also TAX EVASION.

tax base The amount on which tax rates are levied. In the case of personal income tax, the tax base is a person's income after all permitted exemptions and deductions have been made. In the case of property tax, it is the assessed value of the property. The tax base is income, wealth, or the price of a good or service.

tax burden The total tax an individual or corporation must pay.

tax-collection agreement An agreement under which the federal government collects personal and corporate income taxes on behalf of the provincial governments. The Fiscal Arrangements Act authorizes the federal government to enter into such agreements; it collects personal income taxes on behalf of all the provinces except Quebec, and corporate income taxes on behalf of all the provinces except Quebec and Ontario and, starting in 1980, Alberta. The agreements set out the manner in which the provinces will be paid and the conditions they must meet.

tax credit A credit that is deducted from the income tax that an individual or corporation would otherwise pay. It differs from a TAX DEDUCTION, which is subtracted from a person's or a corporation's total income, lowering the taxable income against which income tax is levied. The value of the tax deduction for an individual depends on his level of income. The higher the income, the higher his top marginal rate of tax, and, hence, the greater the value of his tax deduction. In the case of a tax credit, however, the value is the same to all recipients, since it is deducted from the actual tax they would otherwise pay. The tax credit is considered a preferable way of extending benefits to individuals since it gives all recipients the same amount of money, while a tax deduction gives a greater benefit to people with high incomes. Moreover, a tax credit can be paid to people whose income is too low to require them to pay taxes, under a system of NEGATIVE INCOME TAX, whereas a tax deduction can only benefit people who have taxable income. See also INVESTMENT TAX CREDIT.

tax deduction A deduction permitted under the Income Tax Act from a person's or a corporation's income in calculating tax liability. All the deductions permitted an individual, for example, are subtracted from his gross income. The resulting figure is taxable income, and it is on this amount that federal and provincial income taxes are levied. The greater the number and amount of a person's tax deductions, the lower his taxable income and the less tax he will have to pay. Because Canada's income-tax system is based on the ability-to-pay principle, the income-tax rate is much higher on the top $2,000 of income for someone with a taxable income of $45,000 than it is on someone with a taxable income of $15,000. Similarly, a tax deduction of $2,000 will be worth much more to someone with a taxable income of $45,000 than it will be to someone with a taxable income of $15,000.

A TAX CREDIT differs from a tax deduction; whereas the deduction is made from before-tax income and hence is worth more to a person with a higher income, a tax credit is deducted from the amount of tax a person owes and is therefore worth the same to each taxpayer, regardless of income. Canada's tax system provides many deductions for individuals, ranging from pension contributions and a tax-free portion of interest and dividend income to personal education costs and charitable donations. Self-employed people can deduct a wide range of business expenses, and corporations can deduct their operating, interest, and depreciation costs.

tax deferral A provision in income-tax laws that permits the tax on personal or corporate income to be postponed if the income is spent in certain specified ways. For example, an individual may invest a certain part of his income in a pension plan or REGISTERED RETIREMENT SAVINGS PLAN and defer the income tax on the money invested, either until it is collected some time in the future in the form of a pension or until the money is withdrawn from the pension or savings plan. Similarly, ACCELERATED-DEPRECIATION provisions allow a corporation to postpone payment of taxes on corporate income if the corporation makes certain types of investments.

tax evasion The reduction of a person's tax liability to the lowest possible level through illegal means—by failing to report income or by understating income, for example, by falsifying expenses and deductions so that they are overstated, or by claiming false status. It is a deliberate attempt to defraud tax authorities.

tax exclusion The designation of certain types of income as non-taxable under the Income Tax Act. Examples include gifts and bequests, lottery winnings, WORKMEN'S COMPENSATION payments, free travel passes, discounts and similar employee benefits, capital gains on personal residences, and dividends from active foreign subsidiaries in tax-treaty countries.

tax expenditure Revenue that the government gives up through a special provision in its tax laws to provide an incentive for someone to do something or to provide some kind of relief for an individual or corporation. The federal Income Tax Act contains many provisions, in the form of exemptions, deductions, deferrals of taxes, credits, and exclusions, that reduce the amount of tax revenues that would otherwise be collected. Tax expenditures are an alternative to direct spending by government. But unlike direct spending, the concessions and incentives that government grants to industry and individuals in the form of tax expenditures are rarely subject to close evaluation by Parliament to determine their effectiveness or fairness. See also TAX CREDIT, TAX DEDUCTION, TAX DEFERRAL, TAX EXCLUSION, TAX INCENTIVE, TAX PREFERENCE, TAX SHELTER.

tax haven A country with extremely low tax rates that is used by corporations and wealthy individuals as an address from which to avoid taxes in their own country, where tax rates are much higher. For example, a corporation exporting from Canada to Japan might be able, on paper, to export its products to a subsidiary in a tax haven at a low price and to re-export them from the tax haven to Japan at a high price. Thus, it would earn little profit on the transaction in Canada, where it would be subject to normal corporation taxes, and a high profit in the tax-haven country, where it would pay little if any tax. The corporation would retain the use of those profits earned in the tax haven for its own purposes, while the Canadian public would be deprived of important tax revenues. In recent years, such transactions have been made much more difficult, due to a tightening up of Canadian tax laws. Examples of tax havens are Bermuda, the Bahamas, the Cayman Islands, and Liechtenstein. See also TRANSFER PRICE.

tax incentive A tax measure designed to encourage a particular type of activity. The investment tax credit, for example, is used to encourage business to invest. Fast write-offs may be used to encourage spending on research and development or on anti-pollution devices. An exemption on the first thousand dollars of interest income and capital gains is designed to encourage people to save and invest. Lower tax rates in slow-growth regions can be used to attract investment that would not otherwise go there. Through the use of such incentives, the tax system has considerable potential to influence the behaviour of individuals and corporations.

tax incidence The person by whom the tax burden is eventually paid. When a tax is imposed on one person or firm, it is often possible to shift the burden or cost on to someone else. For example, firms can pass along an increase in the manufacturer's sales tax to consumers, shift it on to their employees by giving smaller wage increases, shift it back to suppliers by paying less for parts or commodities, or shift it on to all of these groups. Workers who find that their income tax has increased may try to shift part of that burden on to consumers by demanding bigger wage increases, which their employer, in turn, passes along by raising his prices. Economists argue over who really pays corporate income taxes, the firm on which it is levied, or the consumer, through the prices he pays for a firm's goods or services.

tax lien A lien or claim that is held by a government against a person's or a firm's assets to cover unpaid taxes. A lien by a municipal government on a person's real estate for nonpayment of property taxes restricts the ability of the owner to sell that property. At some point, the municipality can step in and auction the property to recover the unpaid taxes.

tax loophole A provision in tax law, usually but not always unintended, that permits a person's or a firm's income to go untaxed or to be taxed at a lower rate. Such a loophole may give special and more favourable treatment to a particular group. For example, professionals, such as lawyers and doctors, who are able to incorporate themselves, could end up paying tax at a much lower rate than ordinary wage and salary earners. See also TAX SHELTER.

tax loss **1.** A business loss that can be deducted from profits in future years, thus reducing future taxes, or a loss in one branch or subsidiary of a company that can be deducted from the profits of other branches or subsidiaries of the company in calculating the firm's total tax liability. **2.** The sale of shares at a loss, to realize a capital loss that can be deducted from capital gains on the sale of other shares, thus reducing the amount of tax that must be paid on the capital gains. An investor, for example, may decide to sell certain shares that are trading below the price he paid for them and are unlikely to show any recovery on the market for some time to come. He is able to deduct the capital loss from the capital gains on other shares, for tax purposes, and to use the money for other investments.

tax point One per cent of an individual's federal basic tax on his personal income-tax form. If the federal government plans to transfer 2 tax points to the provinces to compensate them for taking over the full cost of what had been a shared-cost program, it turns over to each province 2 per cent of the federal basic tax collected from the taxpayers of that province.

tax preference A provision under income-tax laws that permits a lower rate of tax for certain types of income; examples of tax preference would include a low rate of taxation for small-business income, the taxation of only one-half of capital gains, and a low rate of taxation for resource income.

Tax Review Board A federal board that acts as a tribunal to resolve disputes between taxpayers and the Department of NATIONAL REVENUE. It deals with tax and Canada Pension Plan disputes. The board consists of a chairman, vice-chairman, and up to five other members. It reports to Parliament through the minister of Justice.

tax sale The seizure and sale of property belonging to an individual or company, to collect unpaid taxes. The sale is by public auction; after the unpaid taxes and interest have been deducted, the remaining proceeds, if any, are turned over to the owner or to other creditors.

tax-sharing The occupancy of the same tax field by two levels of government. For example, both the federal and provincial governments occupy the personal and corporate income-tax fields. But only the provinces collect retail-sales taxes, while only the federal government levies a manufacturer's sales tax.

tax shelter A provision under the Income Tax Act that is designed to encourage individuals to make certain types of high-risk investments that the government wishes to see take place. Examples of tax shelters include investments by Canadians in films, in offshore drilling in the far North, and in certain types of rental residential properties. Tax shelters allow the investor to reduce his income-tax liability significantly or to defer his tax liability.

tax shifting The passing of the tax burden along to someone else by the person or firm on whom it is originally levied. For example, it is argued that CORPORATE INCOME TAX on a firm's profits is usually paid by the firm's customers, because a provision for the tax is included in the price that customers pay for the firm's goods or services. The manufacturer's sales tax, levied by the federal government, is added to the price of the goods sold by the firm, so that its customers really pay that tax as well. Similarly, the VALUE-ADDED TAX used throughout the EUROPEAN ECONOMIC COMMUNITY is shifted by manufacturers and retailers on to consumers. But consumers cannot shift the retail-sales tax they pay on to anyone else.

tax treaty A bilateral treaty between Canada and another country, to make sure that the citizens of both get fair and equal treatment on the income they earn in each other's countries, and to avoid double taxation of the same income. The arrangements may include: provisions to make sure that a citizen of country A, working in country B, gets credit in country A for the income taxes he pays in country B, and vice versa, so that he is not taxed twice on the same income; credits in country A for taxes paid in country B, on profits earned by a corporation headquartered in country A from subsidiary activities in country B, and vice versa; and recognition that either country has exclusive tax jurisdiction on certain types of income. Canada has about twenty-five tax treaties with other countries.

taxable benefit A benefit provided by an employer that must be treated by the recipient as income for tax purposes. It can include the personal use of a company car, paid membership in a club, or any such fringe benefit. In Ontario, it includes the payment by an employer of the employee's share of health-care premiums.

taxable income Income that is subject to tax after all possible deductions and exemptions have been made.

taxation A compulsory levy imposed by law by a public body for public purposes, such as the raising of revenue to pay for the costs of public services, the redistribution of income, and the regulation of economic activity.

taxing power The constitutional right of a federal or provincial government to levy a tax. Under the BRITISH NORTH AMERICA ACT, the FEDERAL TAXING POWER includes all forms of taxation, direct and indirect. The PROVINCIAL TAXING POWER is limited to direct taxes, because the Fathers of Confederation feared that the provinces might use indirect taxes as barriers to interprovincial trade.

technical assistance A form of OFFICIAL DEVELOPMENT ASSISTANCE, consisting of technical knowledge and education. It includes sending experts to a less-developed country to help establish a particular facility, such as a power station, and to train the people there to run it. It may also consist of general technical training offered to a less-developed country in, say, agriculture, health care, education, or management; or it may involve helping to establish training centres for young people, or bringing students from foreign countries to Canada or other advanced nations for technical training. Technical assistance was one of the earliest forms of foreign aid, and is still one of the most important forms.

technical rally A temporary surge in the price of shares generally or of a particular share on a stock exchange; it occurs when the number of would-be buyers exceeds the number of sellers.

technocracy A movement originating in California in 1919 with William Henry Smith, an engineer who coined the term; it gained attention briefly during the depression of the

1930s. Technocrats argued that, with the advance of science, technology, engineering, and economic planning, scientists and engineers should replace politicians and businessmen in running society. According to the technocrats, investors and bankers, not consumers, were the main beneficiaries of technological change, because they absorbed the savings from modern machinery in the form of higher profits, instead of passing along the benefits in the form of lower prices and, hence, increased purchasing power. While technocracy was mainly a U.S. movement, chapters were established in many communities in Canada. Since the 1930s, the movement has lost much of its following and appeal.

technological change Advances in technology and knowledge that increase society's output of goods and services. Such advances lead to higher productivity and lower average production costs, and are hence a critical factor in raising a society's standard of living. Technological change can consist of improved products, better manufacturing processes, advances in managerial know-how, new materials, or improved communications and distribution systems. Such change is probably the single most important factor behind the economic progress of the twentieth century. In agriculture, for example, technological change in the form of chemical fertilizer, improved seeds, advances in farm management, and the introduction of highly mechanized equipment has led to substantially increased production with a significantly smaller farm-labour force; moreover, in real terms, farm prices have declined. Much of the capital investment that takes place today results from technological change. Without such change, modern economies would lose a critical source of growth, and individuals would see little improvement in their real standard of living.

technological forecasting Various systems used to identify potential technological developments and to assess their impact. Such forecasting is vital to governments and large corporations, and, in recent years, has emerged as a highly skilled discipline. Techniques include simple extrapolations from existing state-of-the-art knowledge of particular technologies, the so-called DELPHI TECHNIQUE, which brings various experts together in an attempt to develop a consensus, or highly creative thinking in which a number of possible futures, or scenarios, are drafted. Technological forecasting is an important activity in think-tanks and research centres that assemble expert opinions on future trends and developments. See also FUTUROLOGY.

technological sovereignty The ability of a nation to develop the technological capability it needs to ensure its future economic growth, and hence its political self-determination. The term was first used by the SCIENCE COUNCIL OF CANADA in its eleventh annual report (1976–77). In it, the council argued that, unless Canada developed an international capability in some of the world's new technologies, it would not be able to participate in the new industrial revolution and would have little to sell to the rest of the world to pay for its imports. This would inevitably reduce Canada's political independence, and lower the standard of living of Canadians relative to that of their industrial trading partners. The council's report set out a strategy to achieve technological sovereignty: **1.** Increase the demand for Canadian technology within Canada—by having its federal and provincial governments use their purchasing power as customers for Canadian technology, for example. **2.** Expand the capacity of Canadian industry to develop new technology. **3.** Strengthen the capacity of Canadian firms to absorb new technology. **4.** Improve opportunities for Canadian firms to import technology under conditions more favourable to Canada.

technological unemployment Unemployment that results from the introduction of labour-saving machinery or other forms of technological change. Such unemployment is bound to occur in a healthy economy, and can be countered by manpower-retraining programs, to give workers new skills, and expansionary economic policies, to create new jobs. Since technological change results in improved productivity and real economic growth, new employment opportunities should arise. Technological change has eliminated hundreds of thousands of jobs—for example, farm labour, telephone-switchboard operators, payroll clerks, typesetters in newspapers—but a dynamic economy with proper economic policies is able to generate new industries, products, and jobs. At the same time, unions are properly concerned with the fate of their members affected by technological change, and collective agreements and labour laws today usually contain clauses to ease the impact on workers, especially older workers. See FREEDMAN REPORT.

technology The adaptation of scientific discoveries by industry, resulting in new products, production processes, and distribution systems. New technology is probably the single most important factor in economic growth, and is credited with much of the improvement in man's standard of living since the Industrial Revolution of the late eighteenth and early nineteenth centuries.

technology transfer The transfer of knowledge from the nation in which it is developed to other nations where it is used. The study of technology transfer has to do with the means by which access to technology is spread, and the terms and costs of its use by others. Technology can be sold—through the sale of PATENTS, blueprints, and industrial processes, for example—or it can be spread, through the direct investment of MULTINATIONAL CORPORATIONS, the transfer of ideas through scientific papers, the movement of people, and technical aid. It can also be stolen. Canada has relied heavily on the transfer of technology through the entry of multinational corporations into Canada. Many LESS-DEVELOPED COUNTRIES are demanding better terms for the transfer of Western technology; a United Nations conference was held in 1979 to try to develop a code to regulate technology transfers and improve the access of less-developed countries to modern technology on more favourable terms.

technostructure A term coined by JOHN KENNETH GALBRAITH to describe the professional managers or bureaucrats who run large corporations and government. They are the graduates of business and engineering schools, trained in the scientific method and in the behavioural sciences, who inhabit the top ranks of business and industry around the world, and who, by virtue of their positions, jointly plan the policies and priorities of modern societies. Because of their similarities, Galbraith predicted that this scientific and managerial élite would foster a convergence of values and lifestyles in the various industrial countries.

telecommunications The modern communications network consisting of the telephone and cable-television systems, communications satellites, microwave and land lines, computer communications, and the broadcasting system. Sometimes called the electronic highway, it is the basis of the knowledge or information society of the future, in which computer terminals, the television set, and the telephone will provide major new communications links between individuals and industries. Telecommunications will enable individuals to draw on libraries and data banks and to work at home, will provide for instantaneous banking and inventory management, and will lead to many new industries and services. With the introduction of the microprocessor, which substantially reduces the cost of computer systems, of fibre optics, which enable much more information to be carried over a telephone line into the home or office, of communications satellites, which can provide low-cost and high-volume transmission of data, and of computer systems that have immediate access to one another, upcoming developments in communications are expected to make a significant contribution to economic growth; they have, at the same time, great potential for energy conservation. See also CANADIAN RADIO-TELEVISION AND TELECOMMUNICATIONS COMMISSION, COMMUNICATIONS, TELESAT CANADA.

Teleglobe Canada A crown corporation that is responsible for all communications links between Canada and other countries. It provides access to telephone systems in countries around the world, including links by communications satellites and undersea cables. It speaks for Canada in Intelsat, the international communications-satellite network. Teleglobe was originally established by Parliament in 1950 as the Canadian Overseas Telecommunications Corporation.

Telesat Canada A government-industry corporation created by Parliament in 1969 to establish a commercial communications-satellite service in Canada. It launched Anik I, its first satellite, in November 1972, and began to provide commercial service through a system of earth stations in January 1973. Its shareholders include the federal government and the major telephone companies. It is a member of the TRANSCANADA TELEPHONE SYSTEM.

teller An employee of a bank, trust company, caisse populaire, or provincial savings office, who receives deposits and pays out withdrawals.

tenants in common Two or more persons, each with an undivided interest in a parcel of land or a building. That interest may be sold to another party, or left to someone else in a will. This means that, on the death of one of the owners, the survivors do not have an automatic right to the deceased's interest. See also JOINT TENANCY.

tender 1. A bid made to fill a government contract, setting out price, terms, and conditions that a would-be supplier promises to meet. Most government contracts are awarded after a call for tenders, in which competing firms submit sealed bids by a specified deadline. The bids are all opened at the same time and the contract, unless there are compelling reasons to decide otherwise, will go to the lowest tender bid. It is an offence under the COMBINES INVESTIGATION ACT for companies to collude in submitting their bids; see also RIGGED BID. The tender system is also used by corporations planning major investment projects. **2.** The weekly bid by chartered banks and MONEY-MARKET DEALERS to buy federal treasury bills.

term-deposit receipt A debt security issued by a bank or trust company for a fixed sum of money, running for a fixed length of time and paying a fixed rate of interest. The rate of interest is higher than that paid on non-chequing or premium savings accounts, and depends on the term; the longer the term, the higher the interest rate. Term deposits run anywhere from thirty days to six years. The longer the term, the smaller the denomination: minimum term deposits of less than one year are $5,000; one year or longer, $1,000.

term insurance A life-insurance policy that runs for a limited and specified period of time. If a person outlives the term, he receives no portion of the premiums he has paid. The appeal of term insurance is that it covers a limited period when the insurance is most needed, and is usually cheaper than ordinary life insurance. For example, a father with a young family may want to carry a large amount of insurance while his children are young, so that his wife would be able to raise the children in reasonable comfort if he died. But he may calculate that, as he advances in his career, building up savings and investments, he may have less need for a large life-insurance policy. Other forms of term insurance include travel insurance, and insurance on a mortgage or consumer loan.

term loan A loan that has to be repaid after a fixed period of time, usually more than two years; as opposed to a DEMAND LOAN, which must be repaid whenever the lender decides that he wants his money back. A term loan usually requires annual or more frequent repayments of principal.

terminal 1. A transportation or distribution centre. Examples include airports, railway and bus stations, collection points for food shippers, storage facilities, and buyers. **2.** A machine to get information in and out of computers.

terms of trade An indication of how a nation is faring in international trade. It is the ratio of the price index for merchandise exports to the price index for merchandise imports. A country's terms of trade improve if its export prices rise more than its import prices, since this means that it can buy more imports even if its volume of exports remains the same. Similarly, a country's terms of trade deteriorate if its import prices rise faster than its export prices, since this means that it has to export more to pay for an unchanged volume of imports. Thus, a country with high productivity and unique, desired products should rate better in world trade than a country that exports commodities in surplus supply.

In recent years, the terms of trade of the oil-exporting nations have improved with the industrial world, while the terms of trade of the industrial world with the oil-exporting nations have declined. The oil countries can buy much more for each barrel of oil they export than they could five years ago; the oil-importing countries have to export much more of what they produce to obtain the same barrel of oil. The same concept can be applied within a country—between regions, for example, or between groups such as farmers and consumers. Monthly price-index figures for exports and imports are published by STATISTICS CANADA.

territorial waters The coastal waters of a state over which it claims complete sovereignty, including the right to determine who shall enter those waters and under what conditions. States used to claim three miles for their shorelines, the range of cannon. Today most states, including Canada, claim twelve miles. In addition, most states, including Canada, claim a two-hundred-mile fishing or EXCLUSIVE ECONOMIC ZONE.

tertiary industry An industry that uses knowledge or information as its raw material, or a service industry. Examples would include computer programming, banking, health care, law, or engineering.

tertiary recovery Additional crude oil that can be recovered from oil reservoirs by newer and more costly recovery techniques, by flooding to increase pressure, for example, or by *in situ* combustion and steam flooding, to create heat and move the oil. As oil prices rise, it pays to develop new techniques to recover remaining reserves that cheaper and more traditional techniques have left in the ground. With the rise in prices and the development of new recovery techniques, some of these previously unrecoverable pools can be added to reserve calculations.

Textile and Clothing Board A federal board set up in 1969 to investigate complaints from industry and other groups that clothing or textile imports are causing or threatening to cause serious injury to Canadian manufacturers. The board can recommend to the minister of INDUSTRY, TRADE AND COMMERCE that quotas be imposed, or that other steps be taken to protect the industry; or it can decide that the complaints are unjustified.

thermal power Electricity generated by power stations that burn oil, natural gas, and coal. Nuclear power is also considered to be a form of thermal power.

thin market A market in which either the supply or demand for a commodity or security is so small that even a modest change in supply or demand can cause a large increase or decline in price. For example, if most of the shares of a company are held by a few individuals or institutions, then any unusual sale or purchase of the shares will lead to a big change in price. A thin market is a market with either few buyers or few sellers, or both.

Third Option A foreign-economic-policy decision made by the federal government in October 1972, to reduce Canada's economic dependence on the United States. It came in the aftermath of 1971 U.S. policies that hurt the Canadian economy, and of resulting Canadian worries that its economy was becoming too closely tied to the U.S. economy. The government policy paper noted the strong north-south pull of the U.S. and Canadian economies, and worried that growing interdependence would "impose an unmanageable strain on the concept of a separate Canadian identity, if not on the elements of Canadian independence." It set out three options for Canada: **1.** Maintain more or less the existing relationship with the United States, which would mean few policy changes. **2.** Move deliberately towards closer integration with the U.S. **3.** Pursue a comprehensive, long-term strategy to develop and strengthen the Canadian economy and other aspects of Canadian national life, and thus reduce Canada's vulnerability to sudden changes in U.S. policies, or to the danger of eventual absorption by the U.S.

The government chose the third option, which meant supplementing Canada's economic relationship with the U.S. by developing greater economic and commercial ties with the EUROPEAN ECONOMIC COMMUNITY and with Japan. This option, the government's policy paper said, would "lessen the vulnerability of the Canadian economy to external factors, including, in particular, the impact of the United States and, in the process, strengthen our capacity to advance basic Canadian goals and develop a more confident sense of national identity." It said that to create a stronger, and hence less vulnerable, economic base would require "the specialization and rationalization of production and the emergence of strong Canadian-controlled firms," and that this in turn might "have to entail a somewhat greater measure of government involvement than has been the case in the past."

One of the results of the Third Option was the negotiation of the FRAMEWORK AGREEMENT FOR COMMERCIAL AND ECONOMIC CO-OPERATION BETWEEN CANADA AND THE EUROPEAN COMMUNITIES. The Third Option policy was spelled out in a special edition of the Department of External Affairs publication, *International Perspectives*.

third-party insurance See LIABILITY INSURANCE.

third world Those nations that see themselves as members of neither the developed Western or capitalist world, nor the developed Eastern or communist world of the Soviet Union and its satellites. The third world consists of the LESS-DEVELOPED COUNTRIES, with per capita incomes below $1500 but growing economies. Many of its members include countries that have gained their independence since the end of the Second World War. It includes many of the nations of Asia, Africa, Latin America, and the Middle East. Third-world nations are the driving force behind the quest for a NEW INTERNATIONAL ECONOMIC ORDER. But, because the income gap between developing nations is growing, with some, such as Mexico, Malaysia, Argentina, and South Korea, showing rapid economic growth, and others, such as Bangladesh, Pakistan, India, and many central-African states, showing extremely low per capita incomes, some economists now divide the less-developed world into the third-world nations, which are making steady gains in per capita income and have good prospects for growth, and the FOURTH-WORLD nations, which have abysmally low per capita incomes, few resources, and poor prospects for growth. One separating line between the third and fourth worlds is per capita income of $200. The third- and fourth-world nations are the South in the North-South dialogue.

threshold reserves The necessary level of proven or established reserves of oil, natural gas, or other mineral resources, before investments will be made to extract and exploit them. Without this level of reserves, financiers will be unwilling to lend funds, since they could not reasonably be assured of getting their money back. The threshold level depends, among other things, on distance to market. For example, even small oil and gas reservoirs can be exploited if they are close to existing pipeline and gathering systems. But the threshold level for oil or gas in the far North or off the coast of Labrador will be much higher, since it will have to justify the high costs of installing gathering and distribution systems, such as a major new pipeline or natural-gas liquefaction plants.

tied aid Foreign aid to less-developed countries that attaches conditions to the way in which the soft loan or grant is to be spent. The most common condition is that all or a fixed portion of the aid must be spent in the donor country. The fact that aid is tied and, as such, creates jobs in the donor country, as well as eliminating any adverse balance-of-payments effect, is often used by governments of donor countries to justify aid expenditures to their own taxpayers. But it means that recipient countries must use the aid in ways that do not necessarily conform to their own needs, or that may force them to acquire goods and services that are more expensive than or inferior to those available elsewhere. Most bilateral-aid programs contain some tied-aid requirement, though in recent years, donor nations have been reducing such conditions. An increasing portion of foreign aid is now handled by multilateral institutions such as the

INTERNATIONAL BANK FOR RECONSTRUCTION AND DEVELOPMENT (World Bank) and its affiliated agencies, or through regional-development banks and the United Nations.

tight money The condition that exists when a restrictive MONETARY POLICY is being pursued. Interest rates are high and credit is hard to obtain.

time and motion study The systematic study of the amount of time necessary for an employee under normal conditions to perform a particular task. Such a study helps to establish standards for performance, to calculate production schedules, to determine labour costs, and to analyze how to speed up ways a job is done. These studies are a normal part of a firm's or a government agency's efforts to improve PRODUCTIVITY.

time lag In economic policy, the length of time it takes a change in economic policy to take effect. There is always a delay between the time government changes a policy and the time the economy responds, which policy-makers have to take into account. For example, the government may want to spur economic growth through a tax cut for individuals, hoping that this will eventually increase consumer spending and cause business, in turn, to invest in productive facilities or to increase housing construction. But first the money from the tax cut has to get into consumer pockets, and consumers have then to decide whether to spend or save their extra income. Even when consumers decide to spend, this may not have an immediate impact on production. Business inventories may be high, and these will have to be run down first. Only then will there be an impact on production, and, assuming business believes that the higher level of demand can be sustained, and provided it is operating its factories near or at capacity, only then will important job-creating investment decisions be made. Experience with time lags shows how hard it is for a government to achieve quick changes in economic behaviour, as well as the limitations of economic FINE-TUNING.

time preference An individual's preference for consumption now instead of consumption in the future. This preference will differ for individuals depending on their tastes, levels of income, age, expectations of future income, and other such factors. It supposes that each individual can, in effect, set his own interest rate, which is his time preference. The amount of money required to pay an individual for delaying consumption of one hundred dollars' worth of goods and services for, say, a year, expressed as a percentage of that hundred dollars, is the individual's time preference, or the personal interest rate he has set as the price for delayed consumption. If that interest rate is higher than existing interest rates in the economy, then he is more likely to postpone consumption. The concept is an important element in interest-rate theories and in the analysis of saving and investment. It recognizes that individuals who postpone consumption must be paid for doing so with increased future consumption. But how much extra depends on the individual.

time series A series of particular economic statistics taken at enough different points in time, with seasonal fluctuations removed, to show whether or not there is a particular economic trend. For example, monthly statistics of non-food items in the CONSUMER PRICE INDEX for, say, twelve to sixteen months, may show a definite upward or downward pattern. Similarly, the same statistics over a period of years would show the kind of inflation rate that is "normal," though not necessarily acceptable.

time-sharing The use of the same computer system simultaneously by a number of different users, each through his or her own computer terminal. One of the most common examples is an airline reservation and ticketing system, in which hundreds of different people are using the same computer and computer data base at the same time.

time value of money A concept used in investment analysis, according to which a specific amount of money in the hand at present is worth more than the same amount of money in the future, because money available now can be invested and earn a return. Thus

$100 invested today at 10 per cent would be worth $110 a year from now, and hence would be worth more than $100 received a year from now.

timely disclosure The requirement, by securities commissions and stock exchanges, that corporations act swiftly to disclose to the public any news that may have a favourable or unfavourable effect on the price of their shares. Such news would include takeover bids, mineral discoveries, an unexpected loss, or changes in ownership.

tip An amount of money, usually a small percentage of the cost of the service rendered, given voluntarily to a person performing a service. For example, diners in a restaurant may leave a tip of 10 to 15 per cent of the cost of their meal. Tips constitute an important part of the income of some workers, such as restaurant employees, cab drivers, and hotel doormen. Tax authorities make some allowance for tips when reviewing the income-tax returns of such workers.

title Evidence, in the form of a document, that proves a person's ownership of land and buildings. A title shows the history of changes in the ownership of a particular property and indicates whether there are any tax or other claims against the property. When a property is purchased, a title-search is undertaken, to make sure that the person selling the property is the actual owner and to determine what claims, if any, there are against the property. Generally speaking, titles are registered in provincial registry offices, though in some large cities, the municipality may maintain the office. Different provinces or parts of provinces have different methods of registration. Western Canada and northern Ontario have a land-title system, in which the state guarantees the title, and the person conducting the search has only to look at the most recent record. Southern Ontario and the Maritimes use a land-registry system, in which the state does not guarantee the system and the lawyer making the search has to check back, say, forty years, and personally guarantee the title.

toll The charge made to use an expressway, bridge, canal, tunnel, or ferry. The term is sometimes used to describe long-distance telephone rates. Tolls were once widely used to finance public projects, an example of the user-pay principle. They are also a source of revenue once construction costs have been recovered.

Toronto Stock Exchange (TSE) Canada's principal stock exchange, both in terms of volume of shares traded and value of shares traded. It originated in 1852 with a group of businessmen in Toronto who traded shares for thirty minutes each day. It was incorporated in 1878, and has grown since then to the point where, today, it has more than 125 seats or members. For a time, there were two stock exchanges in Toronto: in 1899, the Toronto Stock and Mining Exchange was established as a second exchange, to provide a market for speculative mining shares. It was replaced by the Standard Stock and Mining Exchange in 1908. But in 1934, the Standard merged with the TSE. The TSE is governed by a board of governors, chosen from member firms, who operate the exchange and have the responsibility to see that TSE rules are followed, so that the investing public is protected.

Toronto Stock Exchange indices A composite index of the share prices of three hundred major corporations traded on the TSE, along with separate indices for fourteen major industrial groups in the composite index. The base year is 1975 equals 1,000. The fourteen major industrial groups are: metals and minerals, gold, oil and gas, paper and forest products, real estate and construction, consumer products, industrial products, transportation, pipelines, utilities, communications, merchandising, financial services, and management companies.

tort A civil offence against another person for which damages can be sought; it does not include the breaking of a contract, which is a separate matter. Examples include all forms of negligence or damages caused by a person's failure to take reasonable care in driving, maintaining a building, manufacturing a product, and so on; nuisance, a form of negligence that prevents a person from having continuous enjoyment of his land, due to fumes, smoke, or erosion caused by a neighbour; and libel and slander, which may damage a person's reputation and, hence, his ability to earn a livelihood. Thus, a tort is a civil wrong for which damages can be sought to compensate for the damages or injuries a person has suffered. The term covers a wide field of legal actions, ranging from suits against manufacturers for faulty products, and neighbours whose activities cause pollution, to suits against municipal authorities who fail to keep sidewalks repaired, and newspapers that publish false information about a person's character.

total utility The sum of all of the utilities of different persons in society added together. Taking this approach, some economists argue that it is possible to use the tax system to increase maximum total utility. Since each extra dollar of income is said to bring less satisfaction to a person, a dollar taxed away from a wealthy person and redistributed to a poor person will add to the total utility or satisfaction of society.

trade The exchange of goods and services for money. Foreign trade consists of exchanges of goods and services for money between Canadians and non-residents.

trade association An association of companies in the same industry for a variety of specific purposes, to advance the interests of the industry. The purposes can include representations to government on proposed legislation or existing policies, the collection of industry-wide statistics and other information for the publication of trade directories, the organization of seminars, conventions, and educational activities, general public-relations work on behalf of the industry, and the organization of overseas trade missions. The COMBINES INVESTIGATION ACT makes it a criminal offence for members of an association to discuss prices or to engage in any kind of activity in restraint of trade or "unduly" affecting competition. Examples of trade associations include the CANADIAN MANUFACTURERS' ASSOCIATION, the Canadian Grocery Product Manufacturers' Association, the CANADIAN PETROLEUM ASSOCIATION, the CANADIAN BANKERS' ASSOCIATION, and the CANADIAN PULP AND PAPER ASSOCIATION.

trade barrier Any government policy that restricts the free movement of goods and services between countries. The best-known barriers are tariffs and quotas. But there are many NON-TARIFF BARRIERS to trade as well, such as health and safety regulations written in such a way as to exclude imports or to restrict imports, excessive delays in the processing of import paperwork, government purchasing preferences in favour of domestic producers, and subsidies to domestic producers. Trade barriers can also exist within a country between different regions. For example, the Fathers of Confederation intended Canada to be a single market, but individual provinces may favour local companies in awarding contracts, or may employ other devices, such as farm marketing boards, to keep out the products of other provinces.

trade bloc A group of two or more countries that agree to increase trade among themselves through reciprocal trade preferences, which they do not grant to countries outside their bloc. A trade bloc can take the form of a COMMON MARKET or a CUSTOMS UNION. Some experts fear that the world may divide into regional trade blocs if there is a world-wide return to PROTECTIONISM. If that happened, Canada would likely be linked in a trade bloc with the United States, Mexico, and other nations of South America.

trade credit The credit that a manufacturer or other supplier extends to his customers.

trade cycle See BUSINESS CYCLE.

trade deficit The situation that exists when the dollar or money value of a country's merchandise imports is greater than the value of merchandise exports. Sometimes the trade deficit is calculated on the value of both goods and services traded. Canada may have a TRADE SURPLUS with some countries but a trade deficit in its total trade with all countries, or vice versa. Monthly figures on Canada's trade are published by Statistics Canada. See also BALANCE OF PAYMENTS, CURRENT ACCOUNT.

trade embargo The cut-off of trade to a country, in a bid to change its policies. In the 1930s, the League of Nations tried to halt Italy's invasion of Ethiopia by cutting off its access to oil. The United States, under its Trading with the Enemy Act, has blocked trade with Cuba to try to force Cuba to pay compensation for U.S. subsidiaries it nationalized, and to curb its support for political insurgency in Latin America and Africa. Members of the United Nations, including Canada, banned trade with Rhodesia to force its white-minority government to recognize the political rights of its black majority. The Arab nations of the Middle East have banned trade with companies that have close contacts with Israel or that have Jewish owners, in an attempt to punish those who deal with or support Israel. Members of the NORTH ATLANTIC TREATY ORGANIZATION withhold strategic materials and military technology from the Soviet Union and its satellites, and other nations of the communist world. See also BOYCOTT.

trade fair A fair or exhibition held to bring together buyers and sellers in a particular industry. They are important commercial events, allowing producers to display their latest wares and buyers to see a wide range of products all under the same roof.

Trade Marks Office A part of the BUREAU OF INTELLECTUAL PROPERTY in the Department of CONSUMER AND CORPORATE AFFAIRS, that administers the Trade Marks Act, maintains a record of all registered TRADEMARKS, and publishes weekly the *Trade Marks Journal*.

trade mission A group of businessmen and government officials who visit another country or countries, usually to sell goods, but sometimes to buy. Trade missions are organized by both the federal and provincial governments, to blitz foreign markets and to increase exports. They may consist of representatives of a group of companies in the same industry, or of a variety of companies, all interested in the same country or countries. Buying missions are frequently undertaken by communist countries.

trade surplus The situation that exists when the dollar or money value of a country's merchandise exports is greater than the value of its merchandise imports. Sometimes the trade surplus is calculated on the value of both goods and services traded. Canada may have a TRADE DEFICIT with some countries but a trade surplus in its total trade with all countries, or vice versa. Monthly figures on Canada's trade are published by Statistics Canada. See also BALANCE OF PAYMENTS, CURRENT ACCOUNT.

trade union See UNION.

trademark A particular word, logo, symbol, or other device, used by a corporation to identify its product or service to consumers. It is used in advertising, promotions, marked on company products or packaging, and used in corporate identification—on letterheads and buildings, for example. Because of its unique character, it is of value to its owner and is protected under law. No one else can use a trademark registered with the TRADE MARKS OFFICE; if they do, they can be sued for infringement. Widespread acceptance by consumers of a trademark can sometimes make it extremely difficult for others to enter an industry. In this sense, a trademark can increase the market power of a corporation.

trading stamp A promotional device, once widely used by supermarkets and other chain stores, but which in recent years has largely fallen out of favour. In such a scheme, stamps would be given by retailers to their customers, usually one stamp for each ten cents of purchase. The customers would build up their collection of stamps until they had enough to exchange for some item of merchandise offered by the retailer. From a marketing point of view, the appeal of trading stamps was that they kept customers coming back to the same store to accumulate stamps.

TransCanada Telephone System (TCTS) An association of all of Canada's major telephone companies and TELESAT CANADA. It was created in 1931 to facilitate long-distance telephone service, by negotiating agreements on levels of service and allocation of costs among members. Since then, it has evolved into an organization to develop a national telephone and TELECOMMUNICATIONS system, including communications satellites. TCTS owns no capital equipment of its own, but co-ordinates the use of the capital equipment of its member firms. Its headquarters are in Ottawa.

transfer A change in ownership of land, buildings, mineral rights, previously issued bonds and stocks, or other such assets. A transfer deed is a document that shows that the transfer has taken place. For example, in the sale of shares, the seller must sign a stock-transfer certificate indicating that he has given up ownership of those shares. In an economic sense, transfers are not investments, since they are only a change in the ownership of existing capital and not the creation of additional real capital. A transfer may be subject to a tax—to a land-transfer tax when real estate is sold, for example.

transfer agent The trust company appointed by a publicly traded corporation, to maintain up-to-date lists of the names and addresses of shareholders and the number of shares each shareholder owns, to issue and cancel share certificates, and to distribute dividend cheques and income-tax statements on dividend income.

transfer payment A payment by a government to an individual, a business, a farmer, or another level of government. Such payments range from family allowances, old-age pensions, and welfare, to business and farm subsidies, federal payments to provinces to help finance social welfare, or subsidized housing and similar payments by provincial governments to municipalities. These payments do not add anything to the gross national product, since they do not represent payments for goods or services produced by the recipient. They represent a form of income redistribution, and are financed from the income produced by others.

transfer price The price charged within a MULTINATIONAL CORPORATION or large industrial enterprise for goods or services shipped from one affiliate or subsidiary, or the parent company, to another affiliate or subsidiary. Such prices are a major concern to tax authorities because they can be non-market or artificial prices, quite different from those that would be charged if the corporate affiliates were separate and unrelated firms. The ability to manipulate prices in this way gives a corporation considerable scope in allocating profits on such transactions to the country with the lowest tax rate. For example, a multinational corporation with a Canadian subsidiary using parts from another subsidiary, say, in Malaysia, could ship the parts from Malaysia to another subsidiary of the company in a TAX HAVEN—say, Bermuda—where taxes are extremely low, and reship the parts to Canada from Bermuda. The parts could be shipped from Malaysia at a barely break-even price, thus depriving tax authorities there of tax revenues from corporate profits, with the Bermuda subsidiary reselling them to Canada at a very high price, thus capturing the profit in Bermuda where it will be virtually untaxed. In this way, the parent company has minimized its taxes by its transfer-pricing policy. In recent years, such practices have become much harder to carry out, because Canadian, U.S., and other taxing authorities have adopted tougher rules on transfer pricing; they have also limited the ability to evade taxes by siphoning international profits into tax havens. Corporate affiliates are supposed to deal with one another on an ARM'S LENGTH basis. None the less, there are still opportunities through transfer pricing to inflate profits in countries with low tax rates and to minimize them in countries with high tax rates.

transnational corporation See MULTINATIONAL CORPORATION.

Transport, Ministry of The federal government department responsible for all aspects of national transportation policy as set out by Parliament—for example, in the National Transportation Act. The ministry has a central policy-planning group that advises the minister of Transport, and five operating groups that carry out transport policy. These are: **1.** The Canadian Marine Transportation Administration, whose responsibilities include the Canadian Coast Guard, the National Harbours Board, and the St. Lawrence Seaway. **2.** The

Canadian Air Transportation Administration, which is responsible for airports, airline services, and aviation safety. **3.** The Canadian Surface Transportation Administration, which is responsible for railways, interprovincial truck and bus transportation, motor-vehicle safety standards, and the federal interest in rail and rapid-transit research. **4.** The Arctic Transportation Agency, which is responsible for transport in the far North. **5.** The Transportation Development Agency, which looks after transportation research and development.

The ministry has some responsibility for three independent crown corporations: Air Canada, the Canadian National Railways Company, and Northern Transportation Company Limited. The minister of Transport reports to Parliament for the CANADIAN TRANSPORT COMMISSION, the NATIONAL HARBOURS BOARD, and the ST. LAWRENCE SEAWAY AUTHORITY.

traveller's cheque A cheque easily usable as money, issued by a company established for that purpose or by a bank. A person buying traveller's cheques signs them once when he acquires them and again when he cashes them; this establishes a means of identification when the cheque is cashed. The appeal of such cheques is that they are safer to carry than money; if stolen or lost, they can be readily replaced at no loss to the traveller. And, since they can be denominated in the currency of the country visited, the traveller avoids problems of foreign-exchange conversion during his trip. The issuing companies or banks make a profit by earning interest on the money paid for the cheques, between the time they are issued and the time they are cashed.

treasury bill A short-term government security, issued for a term of 91 or 182 days and held mainly by large INSTITUTIONAL INVESTORS. Treasury bills represent an important source of funds for the federal government, with more than ten billion dollars' worth outstanding; some provinces, such as Ontario, also issue them. Federal treasury bills are issued in denominations of $1,000, $5,000, $10,000, $25,000, $100,000, and $1 million. They do not pay interest; they are sold below their face or par value, but mature at their par value. The difference between the issue price and the par value is, in effect, the interest rate paid.

Treasury bills are sold by auction each week by the BANK OF CANADA to the highest bidder. Only the chartered banks and thirteen MONEY-MARKET DEALERS, along with some other INVESTMENT DEALERS who make occasional bids, are allowed to bid. They, in turn, resell the treasury bills to large institutional investors and corporations looking for a place to put short-term cash. The amount offered by the Bank of Canada in a particular week may equal the amount maturing, or may be greater or less. This depends on the bank's DEBT-MANAGEMENT policy, and the federal government's cash requirements.

Treasury bills account for almost 15 per cent of the national debt. Before the First World War, Canadian treasury bills payable in sterling were sold in British and European financial markets. With the outbreak of the war, the federal government turned to the Canadian banking system to raise funds through the sale of treasury bills. But the treasury-bill market did not become important until after the Bank of Canada began operating in 1935.

Treasury Board Both a committee of the federal cabinet and a department of the government. It is the manager of the government's spending, hiring, collective-bargaining, and administrative activities. It is responsible for all personnel policies in the public service, financial-management policies and procedures, spending controls, the analysis of long-term spending trends, the allocation of government resources among competing departments and agencies, and implementation of bilingualism programs within the government. Each year, the cabinet sets out the priorities of the government, based on an overall level of spending for the entire federal government. Individual departments must then submit their proposed spending plans in line with these priorities. The Cabinet Committee of the Treasury Board—consisting of the minister responsible for the Treasury Board (known as the president of the Treasury Board) and four other cabinet ministers—then scrutinizes the submissions of individual departments, cutting or adding to programs, depending on the government's priorities.

The Treasury Board has existed as a committee of cabinet since Confederation. In 1869, it was made a statutory committee, the only one there is, with the minister of Finance as chairman and his department carrying out the staff work. It was not until almost a century later, in 1966, that the Treasury Board was made into a separate government department, following the recommendation of the Royal Commission on Government Organization. The Finance Department's role is to manage the economy, while that of the Treasury Board is to manage the government and make sure that its priorities and policies are being implemented. Provincial governments follow similar procedures in implementing their policies, allocating resources, managing staff, and setting procedures to monitor spending.

treasury shares Company shares that are authorized but have not been issued to the public, or shares that were previously issued but have been reacquired by the company. When a company is incorporated, its charter sets out its capitalization, which describes the number of shares it may issue. A publicly traded company rarely issues the total number of shares authorized; the treasury shares are those that have yet to be issued. They can be sold to the public, offered to owners of another company, instead of cash, in a takeover bid, or sold to employees of a firm in an employee stock-purchase plan. Treasury shares are not considered to be an asset of the company.

Treaty of Rome The treaty signed by six nations of Western Europe (France, West Germany, Italy, Belgium, the Netherlands, and Luxembourg) in 1957, creating the EUROPEAN ECONOMIC COMMUNITY. The common market came into effect on 1 January 1958.

The treaty set out the objectives of the EEC and the procedures under which the community would evolve into a full-fledged economic and political unit. The goals of the treaty were to achieve the completely free movement of goods, services, labour, and capital among the community's members, and to establish a common external tariff in dealings with the rest of the world, along with a common policy on mergers and other business practices, a common agricultural policy, a common transportation policy, and a regional-development policy to aid the depressed areas of the community. The treaty also dealt with the political evolution of the EEC, creating a Council of Ministers that deals with policy, an EEC Commission, which is the central bureaucracy of the community, a European parliament and a court of justice. The common external tariff was achieved by July 1968; the free movement of labour by 1969; and the election of a European parliament in 1979. The treaty also envisaged the gradual evolution of a common monetary system; a step in that direction was made in 1979, with the implementation of the EUROPEAN MONETARY SYSTEM.

Tremblay Report See ROYAL COMMISSION OF INQUIRY ON CONSTITUTIONAL PROBLEMS.

trial balance An accounting exercise to determine the accuracy of a company's or an organization's books of account or ledger. All the debit and credit balances are added; total credits should equal total debits. It is a routine part of every audit.

trilateralism The relationship, based on shared economic and security interests and political values, among the United States, Canada, the European Economic Community, and Japan; the term came into use in the 1970s. The members of this trilateral group meet at an economic summit on a regular basis, and are all members of the ORGANIZATION FOR ECONOMIC CO-OPERATION AND DEVELOPMENT. There is also a privately funded Trilateral Commission, headquartered in New York, which researches and debates common issues. It consists of about two hundred private citizens, some of whom are from Canada.

tripartism A new approach to managing the Canadian economy, proposed by the federal government after the introduction of mandatory price and income controls in 1975. The government's proposal envisaged formal consultation with business, labour, and other groups to reach a consensus on economic goals and priorities, and implied acceptance by these groups of a share of responsibility in helping to implement the consensus. Under tripartism, business, labour, and other groups would share responsibility with the government for the performance of the economy. In May 1976, the Canadian Labour Congress adopted a new manifesto, in which it endorsed a form of tripartism that would give unions a much larger voice in setting national policy, including business investment decisions and monetary and fiscal policy. In October 1976, the government published a working paper, *The Way Ahead: A Framework for Discussion*, which drew back from the idea of formal consultation, and put more emphasis on strengthening market forces in the economy and on improving labour-management relations. When Canada emerged from anti-inflation controls at the end of 1978, the idea of tripartite management of the economy had been dropped by the government, in favour of a much less structured form of consultation with business, labour, and other groups.

trough The low point in the BUSINESS CYCLE. It is the turning point between a period of economic decline and the beginning of economic recovery.

truncation The state of an economy in which industry is largely under foreign control, and hence fails to carry out a number of its usual functions. This results in inadequate growth, employment, and trade. Many of the essential functions of individual firms, such as research and development, industrial design, marketing, investment planning, and corporate finance and strategy, are performed by their foreign parents rather than by the subsidiaries in a country such as Canada. Such a situation means that native skills will not be developed fully, and that fewer of the spin-off industries that result from these skills and activities will be created.

The term was used in the 1972 federal government report, FOREIGN DIRECT INVESTMENT IN CANADA. The report said: "Truncated subsidiary operations usually lack the capacity and opportunity over time to develop the full range of activities normally associated with a mature business enterprise." The term describes a BRANCHPLANT ECONOMY, in which subsidiaries are unable to initiate new products or develop new markets, while the country as a whole becomes overly dependent on foreign technology, know-how, and decisions. Too many of the conditions necessary for businesses to pursue their own commercial objectives are absent; they are located in the foreign parent companies.

trust Money or other property that is held by one person, often a TRUST COMPANY, for the benefit of another person or persons. These assets are administered according to the terms of the trust agreement. Each province has a trustee act, which regulates the kinds of investments that can be made by the TRUSTEES of a trust fund. The investments must be of high quality and must yield a reasonable income. Approved investments include federal, provincial, and municipal bonds and debentures, bonds, debentures, and preferred and common shares of blue-chip Canadian companies, debt securities issued by loan or acceptance companies, and the bonds and debentures of stable foreign countries and international institutions. See also PRUDENT-MAN RULE.

trust company A financial institution that operates under either federal or provincial legislation. It can engage in almost all of the same activities as a CHARTERED BANK and, like a bank, operates through a network of branches. There are two important differences: a trust company, unlike a bank, does not have access to the BANK OF CANADA as a lender of last resort; and a trust company can engage in trust or fiduciary activities, whereas a bank cannot.

As a financial intermediary, a trust company can accept deposits from the public, make mortgage, consumer, and business loans, and sell savings certificates known as guaranteed-investment certificates. Customer deposits are protected through the CANADA DEPOSIT INSURANCE CORPORATION or its Quebec equivalent. A trust company must also set aside counterpart funds, similar to bank reserves, to protect depositors and holders of its guaranteed-investment certificates. The volume of a trust company's business and consumer loans is more tightly regulated than that of a bank. General consumer and corporate loans and speculative investments, under federal law, are limited to 15 per cent of shareholder's equity or 7 per cent of company assets under a basket clause. Exemptions may be granted.

In its fiduciary role, a trust company administers estates, pension plans, trusts, and agency contracts. The degree of decision-making power is set out in an agreement between a trust company and a customer. But legislation also controls the types of investments that can be made, generally restricting investments to first mortgages, government bonds, blue-chip stocks, corporate bonds, and similarly secure assets.

A trust company also acts as a financial agent for corporations and municipalities, as a transfer agent and registrar for new stock and bond issues, and as a trustee for a new bond issue. Trust companies may also act as real-estate brokers. While a trust company may be established under either federal or provincial legislation, there is a great deal of uniformity between federal and provincial law.

trustee **1.** A person or company, often a trust company, managing money or property for the benefit of others. The role and investment policies of trustees are regulated by the trustees acts of the different provinces. **2.** In bankruptcy, an administrator appointed by a court to manage the affairs of an insolvent company and to distribute the remaining assets to eligible creditors. **3.** In union administration, the person appointed by the union to take over and manage the affairs of a local that has fallen into corrupt hands, or an official appointed by a federal or provincial government, to manage an entire union that has been found to be operated illegally. **4.** For bondholders, a company, usually a trust company, appointed by the company issuing the bonds to keep a watch on assets pledged as security for the bond, or to ensure that other conditions, such as regular payments to a SINKING FUND, are made on time.

turn-key project A completed project, which a contractor is able to turn over to the purchaser ready for use—in other words, one in which the purchaser has simply to turn the key in the door. Turn-key projects have become an important part of international trade. A consortium of companies operating through a contractor will export an airport, factory, subway system, refinery, or power station to another country, both providing the capital equipment and supervising construction and installation.

turnover The number of times a particular item is replaced in a business or in the entire economy in a specified period of time—the number of times in a year that labour in a plant, or inventory in a store, has to be replaced, for example. If a company has 1,000 employees, and 150 of them leave and have to be replaced during a year, the company has a turnover rate of 15 per cent. Such a calculation can be extended to the economy at large. In Canada's case, there is a large flow of workers in and out of jobs, and Canada is said to have a high labour-turnover rate.

two-tier gold price A 1968 agreement that helped to sever the historic link between gold and the world monetary system. The agreement, made in Stockholm among the central banks of the United States, Britain, West Germany, Switzerland, Italy, the Netherlands, and Belgium, and the INTERNATIONAL MONETARY FUND and the BANK FOR INTERNATIONAL SETTLEMENTS, effectively froze the gold in the official reserves of individual nations. The need for action arose because the world price of gold had risen well above the official U.S. price of thirty-five dollars an ounce, leading some foreign holders of U.S. dollars to cash their U.S. dollars in for gold, and either to hoard it or to sell it at a profit on world gold markets. Action was taken to prevent a huge loss by the U.S. of its gold reserves, a development that could have precipitated an international monetary crisis.

Under the agreement, two gold markets were established. One, the official gold market, would continue to price gold at thirty-five dollars an ounce in transactions between central banks and international monetary institutions; the other, the free market, would operate at supply and demand prices, with gold seeking its own level. Central banks agreed neither to sell nor to buy gold on the free market, nor to acquire gold from one another to replace gold already sold on the market. Canada gave its support to the agreement.

At the same time, the nations participating in the agreement reaffirmed that, in the future, world reserves would be increased through the use of SPECIAL DRAWING RIGHTS, or paper gold. The need for such an agreement came to an end in 1971, when the United States announced that it would no longer allow foreign central banks or international institutions to convert their holdings of U.S. dollars into gold. Early in 1976, the members of the GROUP OF TEN, including Canada, announced that they would not engage in gold purchases, following the Jamaica Agreement; they agreed that the International Monetary Fund would sell part of its gold holdings at world prices, and would use the proceeds to help the LESS-DEVELOPED COUNTRIES to cope with their balance-of-payments problems.

tying contract A contract in which a company forces another company or an individual, who wishes to buy some of its products or services or lease its property, to buy other of its goods and services as well or to deal exclusively in its goods and services. This kind of arrangement is common in franchise-type contracts where, for example, someone operating a gasoline station may also be required to deal only in the tires, batteries, and other products supplied by the oil company that has leased the gasoline station. Similarly, a television or movie-production company may compel a television network or theatre chain to buy other of its programs or films, if it wants to buy particular programs or films.

U

ultimate potential reserves An estimate of the total crude-oil or natural-gas reserves that will have been developed in an area by the time that all exploration and development activity has been completed, having regard for the geological prospects of the area, as well as anticipated technology and economic conditions, including future prices. Ultimate potential reserves include the oil or natural gas produced to date, the REMAINING ESTABLISHED RESERVES recoverable under current technology and anticipated economic conditions, and future additions, from extensions and revisions to existing pools and from the discovery of new pools.

ultra vires A law, regulation, or action by a government, that is unconstitutional under the British North America Act. Both federal and provincial claims to authority have been supported or rejected by the Supreme Court of Canada. Early efforts by British Columbia in the 1930s to establish farm marketing boards were declared *ultra vires*; so were laws passed by Parliament in 1935 to establish a system of unemployment insurance, minimum wages, hours of work, and producer marketing boards. See also FEDERAL SPENDING POWER, FEDERAL TAXING POWER, PROVINCIAL SPENDING POWER, PROVINCIAL TAXING POWER.

unaudited report A financial report whose accuracy has not been confirmed by outside auditors. It is normally an interim report, such as a quarterly report to shareholders.

unconditional grant A grant by the federal government to a province, or by a provincial government to a municipality, with no strings attached to the way the money is spent. See, for example, EQUALIZATION PAYMENTS.

underconsumption theory The theory, enunciated by CLASSICAL and NEOCLASSICAL ECONOMISTS, that overproduction and, hence, underconsumption were impossible. Under conditions of PERFECT COMPETITION—homogeneous products, large numbers of buyers and sellers, full knowledge of market conditions, and easy mobility of producers in and out of the market—the system would automatically adjust and return to full-employment conditions. See also SAY'S LAW. The theory was demolished by John Maynard KEYNES. See also KEYNESIAN ECONOMICS, BUSINESS CYCLE.

underdeveloped country See LESS-DEVELOPED COUNTRY.

undersubscribed A new issue of bonds or

shares whose total sales fall short of the planned size of the issue; as opposed to oversubscribed, where total demand is in excess of the planned issue.

underwriter **1.** An INVESTMENT DEALER who helps corporations and governments to raise capital, by buying new shares, bonds, or other securities from the issuing firm or government at a discount, and reselling them to INSTITUTIONAL INVESTORS and others, either by a public OFFERING or a PRIVATE PLACEMENT. Most underwritings are handled by a syndicate of underwriters known as a BANKING GROUP. They may, in turn, enlist the sales help of other securities firms by forming a SELLING GROUP. If some of the securities are not sold, they usually have to be absorbed by the underwriter. **2.** In the insurance industry, a company that accepts an insurance risk and enters into an insurance contract.

underwriting The purchase of new shares, bonds, or other securities by an INVESTMENT DEALER or group of dealers, from a firm or government, for resale to INSTITUTIONAL or other investors. Agreements setting out the terms and conditions are known as underwriting agreements.

underwriting syndicate See BANKING GROUP.

unearned increment A gain in the value of real estate or some other asset that is not due to something done by the owner. For example, the value of a piece of land can increase sharply because a subway route, major highway, or airport is built near it. Or growth in population can lead to an increase in the demand for housing and, hence, the value of existing housing, even though no money has been spent to improve the property. See also RENT, WINDFALL GAIN.

uneconomic An investment or other activity that would incur a loss, just break even, or fail to earn enough to recover the cost of the investment, or to match the OPPORTUNITY COST of other investments or activities.

unemployed person As defined by Statistics Canada in its monthly LABOUR-FORCE SURVEY, a person who was available for work and had looked unsuccessfully during the previous four weeks; or a person who had not actively looked, but who was laid off for twenty-six weeks or less and expected to return to his job; or a person who had a new job to start in four weeks or less, but who was not working during the week of the survey. Full-time students seeking permanent jobs are not counted as unemployed as long as they remain students; but if they are seeking summer or other part-time jobs and cannot find work, they are considered unemployed.

unemployment The failure to find a paying job at the minimum wage or higher. Unemployment can be caused by a lack of demand, and hence growth, in the economy; this kind of unemployment can be cured by fiscal and monetary policies to increase demand. Unemployment can also be structural in nature —when those without jobs lack the skills that are in demand, lack knowledge about the jobs that exist, or live in areas suffering from chronic unemployment and are unable to move to areas where there are jobs. This type of unemployment can only be cured through manpower-training programs, improved labour-market operations, and special measures to aid slow-growth areas. A third type of unemployment is technological unemployment, caused by the introduction of technological change. It can be dealt with by manpower retraining and by policies that encourage economic growth. Finally, there is frictional unemployment, the unemployment that always exists because there are always some people in the midst of changing jobs, just entering the labour force, or who are affected by seasonal factors, such as the closing of the St. Lawrence Seaway during the winter. See also LABOUR-FORCE SURVEY.

unemployment insurance A government-sponsored program of insurance to provide workers with an assured source of income should they lose their jobs. Employers and employees pay premiums to cover the cost of the program, with the federal government paying the extra costs when the national unemployment rate rises above 4 per cent. Unemployment insurance was introduced in Canada in 1935, but the original legislation was declared *ultra vires*. A new law was passed by Parliament in 1940 that covered mainly blue-collar workers. The legislation was significantly amended in 1971, extending compulsory coverage to all members of the labour force, adding maternity benefits, and increasing the duration and amount of benefits, while reducing the amount of work needed to qualify. In 1978, the scope of benefits was reduced, in the belief that they had become a disincentive to work. See CANADA EMPLOYMENT AND IMMIGRATION COMMISSION (formerly the Unemployment Insurance Commission). Unemployment insurance is an important BUILT-IN STABILIZER in the economy; it cushions the impact of a recession because it automatically ensures that unemployed persons still retain some purchasing power.

Unemployment Insurance Commission (UIC) A federal agency created in 1941 to administer Canada's UNEMPLOYMENT-INSURANCE program. It became part of the CANADA EMPLOYMENT AND IMMIGRATION COMMISSION in 1976, when the UIC and the Department of Manpower and Immigration were merged.

unemployment rate The percentage of persons in the labour force who are unemployed. There are two measures in the LABOUR-FORCE SURVEY: the actual unemployment rate, which is the percentage of people unemployed; and the seasonally adjusted unemployment rate, which shows the percentage of people unemployed after making allowances, based on past experience, for such seasonal fluctuations as the entry of large numbers of students into the labour force for part-time jobs during the summer months, or the loss of jobs in the forest, fishing, and construction industries during the winter months. The seasonally adjusted rate is used to show underlying trends in unemployment and employment.

unfair business practice Any business practice designed to mislead the consumer or to take advantage of consumer ignorance or ill-health. Examples include false claims about the quality, standards, and performance of products or services, excessive prices or phony discounts, and high-pressure sales tactics. Federal and provincial consumer-protection laws now make many unfair business practices illegal.

unfair competition Any practice by a business corporation to restrict or reduce competition. Examples include cutthroat competition to drive someone else out of business, false or misleading advertising, price discrimination, and tying arrangements. Such practices are, for the most part, illegal. The principal legislation is the COMBINES INVESTIGATION ACT.

unfair labour practice Any practice of management or unions designed to prevent free certification of workers in the union of their choice, or to interfere in free collective bargaining. Federal and provincial labour laws set out conditions to prevent such practices. Employers, for example, are not allowed to interfere or participate in a union, or to take any action against employees who attempt to organize a union or who are active in union affairs. Employers are also forbidden to require an employee to sign an undertaking, as a condition of employment, that he will not join a union. Unions are not allowed to strike during the life of a collective agreement, except under narrow and tightly defined conditions; nor are they permitted to intimidate people into joining a union or switching their support to another union.

unfavourable balance of trade See TRADE DEFICIT.

unincorporated business A business enterprise, usually an owner-operated business or a partnership—for example, small stores, restaurants and dry cleaners, and small landlords.

union A recognized organization of workers joined together to improve members' wages, working conditions, retirement pensions, paid vacations, fringe benefits, and other interests. Unions were formed to offset the lopsided power of employers to set wage rates and working conditions. Unions existed before Confederation, a number of them affiliates of U.S. unions. The Toronto Trades Assembly, formed in 1871, was the first local labour council; the first national congress of labour unions, the Canadian Labour Union, was formed in 1873. Unions first gained legal recognition in an act of Parliament passed in 1872.

Today, about a third of civilian workers in Canada belong to unions; but the statistics understate the influence of unions. Unions have an impact on everyone's wages and working conditions, and also help to shape government laws on vacations with pay, minimum wages, hours of work, occupational health and safety, and rights to severance pay and advance notice of layoffs due to technological change. Unions also play a role in campaigning for social policies, such as better pensions and health care.

Most unions in Canada are either national or international. They are made up of hundreds of locals, which represent workers in individual firms or government organizations. The locals' main responsibility is to represent members in collective bargaining, with the locals doing the actual bargaining, and the union head office providing bargaining assistance and, if need be, strike pay. Unions in federally controlled industries, such as banks, railways, the federal public service, and the airlines, are subject to the CANADA LABOUR CODE; those under provincial jurisdiction, and they are the majority, are subject to provincial labour laws. Details of union membership are published annually by the federal Department of LABOUR, in the publication *Labour Organization in Canada*. See also LABOUR COUNCIL, COLLECTIVE BARGAINING, CERTIFICATION, BARGAINING UNIT, CANADIAN LABOUR CONGRESS, CONFEDERATION OF NATIONAL TRADE UNIONS.

union label Some kind of mark, design, or tag on a product, to let the consumer know that it was made by union members. It may also consist of the initials of a union on a letter if the letter has been typed by a union member, or a decal on a bus or cab, if the driver belongs to a union.

union security Any provision in labour law or a collective agreement that protects a union against loss of members or loss of dues. An example would be compulsory check-off of dues by the employer to provide a union with necessary funds, thus also saving the union from spending a good deal of time collecting money from members. Another example is the UNION SHOP, which ensures that everyone or almost everyone joining a company or other employer also joins the union. In most provinces, unions still have to negotiate compulsory check-off with employers. Quebec is one province where employers are compelled by law to collect dues on behalf of a union. See also RAND FORMULA.

union shop A place of work where all employees in a bargaining unit, other than management, must be members of the union, and where all new employees, other than management, must join the union after a specified period of time. New employees don't have to be union members when they are hired, but must join the union after they are hired; the union shop is distinguished from a CLOSED SHOP, where new employees must be union members before they can be hired. Most places of work in Canada represented by unions are union shops.

unit cost The total cost of a single product or service. It is calculated by dividing total costs—FIXED and VARIABLE—by the number of units produced. The term *average cost* is also used.

unit labour costs A measure of productivity, calculated by dividing the total wage bill, including fringe benefits, by the total number of units of a good or service produced. It can be expressed as an index and used in comparison with other countries, to see whether Canada is remaining competitive in its costs or is pricing itself out of international markets. It is unfair, though, to assume, when labour costs rise, that all or perhaps even any of the increase is due to higher wages and fringe benefits. For instance, if production falls off and the workforce remains the same, then unit labour costs will automatically increase, even if wages are frozen. Or workers may be trying hard to increase output, but they may be working with out-of-date equipment, or their firm may be badly managed and unable to increase sales.

Unit labour costs are an important economic

indicator that shows the combined effects of changes in compensation and PRODUCTIVITY on the costs of production and, hence, on the rate of inflation. Unit labour costs for a particular industry, listed in Statistics Canada's CENSUS OF MANUFACTURES, can be calculated by dividing the total VALUE-ADDED of the industry by the total payroll costs. Changes in unit labour costs can also help to indicate productivity changes in an industry; for example, if unit labour costs increase less than increases in compensation, then the difference is accounted for by productivity improvements.

unit profits Profits per unit of output; they are calculated in two different ways. The first is to divide corporate-profit figures, published by Statistics Canada in its publication of gross-national-product data, by the figure for commercial non-farm production contained in another Statistics Canada report, the *Index of Real Domestic Product*. The second way is to divide the manufacturing-profit figures published by Statistics Canada in *Industrial Corporations, Financial Statistics*, by real output in manufacturing published in the *Index of Real Domestic Product*. The result can be expressed as an index, and compared with the index of unit labour costs.

United Nations Code of Conduct on Conference Shipping An international agreement devised within the UNITED NATIONS CONFERENCE ON TRADE AND DEVELOPMENT (UNCTAD) in 1979, to give the less-developed countries the opportunity to obtain a share of the shipping of imports and exports in and out of their ports, and thus to break the monopoly enjoyed by shipping companies operating through shipping conferences. Under the 40-40-20 formula devised by UNCTAD, each of two trading partners would be entitled to 40 per cent of the shipping, with the other 20 per cent up for grabs. Canada has not signed the code because it has no MERCHANT MARINE of its own.

United Nations Commission on Transnational Corporations An intergovernmental body established in 1974 by the United Nations to help the world body to deal with MULTINATIONAL (transnational) corporations. It acts as a U.N. forum to examine issues relating to multinationals; promotes the exchange of views of governments, business, unions, and other groups; helps individual countries to set policies dealing with multinationals; conducts inquiries into the activities of multinationals, and publishes studies and reports; assists the U.N. to develop a code of conduct for multinationals; and recommends priorities and programs for the U.N.'s Centre on Transnational Corporations. The centre, which began operation in 1975, is a research and policy advisory body with its own staff, which reports to the U.N. Economic and Social Council. The commission is an advisory body to the council, and is composed of forty-eight member-nations serving for three-year terms. Canada was a member in 1975–78.

United Nations Conference on the Law of the Sea (UNCLOS) A series of U.N. conferences, dating back to 1958, which have attempted to establish an international body of law on the rights of states in coastal waters, the limits of coastal waters, the conservation of fisheries, and the ownership of seabed oil, natural gas, and minerals. UNCLOS I, held in Geneva in 1958, and UNCLOS II, held in Rome in 1960, reached agreements on sea law to deal with fishing and conservation practices, the territorial sea, the continental shelf, the high seas, and settlement of disputes.

In 1970, the United Nations declared the seabed to be the "common heritage of mankind," and initiated new discussions to develop further the law of the sea. UNCLOS III negotiations began in Caracas, Venezuela, in 1974 and continued through 1979. In that period, agreement was reached on the creation of a two-hundred-mile EXCLUSIVE ECONOMIC ZONE, a twelve-mile territorial limit, the right of passage through international straits, rights for landlocked states, and, in principle, the creation of an International Seabed Authority, to exploit the seabed beyond each country's exclusive economic zone. Still to be negotiated are the details of how the Enterprise, the operating arm of the International Seabed Authority, would carry out mining exploration and development in the seabed, and how it would obtain technology from mining companies. All profits would go to the LESS-DEVELOPED COUNTRIES. On 1 June 1977,

Canada declared a two-hundred-mile fishing zone.

United Nations Conference on Trade and Development (UNCTAD) A United Nations organization established in December 1964 to promote the economic interests of the LESS-DEVELOPED COUNTRIES. In 1964, the first of five major conferences was held to discuss trade, foreign aid, and other concerns. Since then, other conferences have been held in Santiago (1968), Manila (1972), Nairobi (1976), and Manila (1979). UNCTAD maintains a secretariat in Geneva, the site of its first conference. In addition to the less-developed countries, it includes twenty-four developed countries (Canada is one of them) and twelve communist countries.

At UNCTAD, the less-developed nations meet in caucus as the GROUP OF SEVENTY-SEVEN (their number at UNCTAD in 1964; it is now more than one hundred). Among the group's aims are better trade terms with the industrial world, including preferential-tariff treatment; higher commodity prices and commodity agreements; the renegotiation of international debt; improved terms of technology transfer; greater flows of foreign aid; a larger share of new issues of SPECIAL DRAWING RIGHTS, to help members solve balance-of-payments problems; changes in health and other standards, so they can sell more products to industrial customers; control of the activities of multinational corporations; access to world shipping on better terms; and a clear commitment by the Western world to a real transfer of resources and manufacturing jobs to the less-developed countries. Much of the debate over the NEW INTERNATIONAL ECONOMIC ORDER has taken place within UNCTAD. Its executive body, the Trade and Development Board, meets annually in Geneva.

United Nations Development Program (UNDP) A United Nations program providing technical and pre-investment assistance to low-income nations. Created in 1965, by the merging of the U.N. Special Fund and the Expanded Program of Technical Assistance, it is funded by annual voluntary subscriptions from U.N. members, including Canada. It is one of the world's principal multilateral foreign-aid programs.

United Nations Environment Program (UNEP) An agency of the United Nations that helps to co-ordinate a number of programs to protect the earth's environment, to gain more information on the environment, or to alert national governments to environmental problems. It was created following the U.N. Conference on Human Environment, which took place in Stockholm in 1972. The program's headquarters are in Nairobi, Kenya. Canada is a member of its governing council and is a contributor to the U.N. Environment Fund.

United Nations Relief and Rehabilitation Administration (UNRRA) The first multilateral-aid program of the United Nations, financed by Canada, the United States, and Britain to provide emergency relief, such as food and medical supplies, in Western Europe as the Allied armies advanced towards Germany. Although Canada was the third largest contributor to UNRRA after it was created in November 1943, Canada was kept off the central committee by its other members (Britain, the United States, the Soviet Union, and China) until 1945. UNRRA was wound up in 1947.

universal payment A social-security payment that is made to all citizens regardless of need. For example, all Canadians sixty-five and over are paid a federal old-age pension, while all families with children get a family allowance, whether they need this government assistance or not. To some extent, these payments are taxed back from Canadians with higher incomes, but not 100 per cent. Critics argue that social assistance should go only to those who really need it, and that it should be possible to do much more to reduce poverty without raising total social-assistance costs. Advocates of universal payments contend that they are valuable because they eliminate demeaning means tests, in which social workers and government officials question individuals about their income and assets before deciding whether a person should get such assistance. See also GUARANTEED ANNUAL INCOME.

Universal Postal Union (UPU) A United Nations agency that helps to facilitate the international movement of mail through various reciprocal arrangements. Its congress meets once every five years, the most recent meeting taking place in 1979. The agency, which is located in Bern, Switzerland, was founded in 1874. It became an agency of the League of Nations in 1920, and of the United Nations in 1947. Canada has been a member since 1878.

unlisted share A share that is not listed on a stock exchange but is traded in an OVER-THE-COUNTER MARKET.

unofficial strike See ILLEGAL STRIKE.

unsecured creditor A creditor who has lent money to a firm, individual, or other entity without obtaining collateral for protection against possible default. In a BANKRUPTCY, the unsecured creditor is the last to be paid and, in most cases, receives no repayment, since assets are inadequate to cover all liabilities.

unsecured loan A loan that is not backed by collateral. As a result, the lender charges a higher rate of interest, reflecting the greater risk, than he would on a SECURED LOAN.

unskilled worker A worker, such as a labourer, filing clerk, or messenger, who is able to perform simple tasks but who has no special training or skills earned through an apprenticeship or other program.

Uranium Canada Limited A crown corporation established in 1971 to manage government-owned stockpiles of uranium built up between 1963 and 1971, and any future stockpiling that might occur after that. While Uranium Canada has sold off some of its stockpile, it is holding the remainder as a buffer stock. It lends uranium to Canadian companies and utilities, with the proviso that the uranium be replaced. The crown corporation also has the power to increase its stockpile, if this is felt to be in the public interest.

Uranium Resource Appraisal Group A government-industry group established by the federal government in 1974, to provide better information on Canada's uranium resources and to conduct an annual audit of reserves. Resources are categorized as measured or proven resources, which are 100 per cent certain; indicated, and 80 per cent certain; inferred, or 70 per cent certain; and prognosticated.

urban population As defined in the 1971 census, all Canadians living in incorporated cities, towns, and villages with a population of 1,000 or more, or in incorporated communities of 1,000 or more, having a population density of at least 1,000 per square mile (386 per square kilometre). People living on the fringes of cities, towns, and villages are also considered urban, provided they meet the same population and density criteria. See also METROPOLITAN AREA. The percentage of urban population has grown significantly as Canada has industrialized.

urban renewal The redevelopment of downtown areas to reinvigorate city centres. Although Canadian cities have not experienced anything like the decline of downtown areas in U.S. cities, there none the less has been a need to revive and rebuild commercial space and housing. CANADA MORTGAGE AND HOUSING CORPORATION provides urban-redevelopment assistance. Urban-renewal projects may include land assembly for shopping-office complexes, new cultural centres, convention centres, transportation terminals, and high-density housing. Properly planned, urban redevelopment can provide an incentive for other property owners to undertake new projects, or to rehabilitate existing buildings and increase local assessment—and thus, property-tax revenues for municipalities—as well.

urban sprawl The unplanned spread of low-density housing, shopping centres, industry, and service facilities. It represents a poor use of land around cities, and builds up high future servicing costs. For example, it is expensive to offer adequate public transportation to people living in widely scattered subdivisions, since distances are long and passenger volumes low. Similarly, sewer, water, and other services have to be carried long distances to serve relatively small numbers of people. Planners also object to urban sprawl because such areas offer few cultural, recreational, and other facilities that enhance the quality of life.

urbanization The processes under which people increasingly locate in cities and towns. Urbanization means different types of jobs, land use, consumer demands, industry, political and social values, transportation needs, and lifestyles. See also URBAN POPULATION, METROPOLITAN AREA.

user-pay principle of taxation The imposition of a tax, toll, or other levy on the user of a particular government service. For example, Canadians who travel by air pay a tax when they buy their tickets to help cover the cost of operating airports. Tolls are often imposed on bridges, ferries, and tunnels, and sometimes on expressways. Fees are charged to enter campsites and parks, while subsidies may be eliminated or reduced on rail travel, all with the purpose of charging the user all or a larger part of the cost of providing the service.

usury A rate of interest in excess of that set by law, or in excess of a common standard of what is acceptable in a community. Medieval and Islamic thinkers argued that any rate of interest constituted usury. There are some, but not many, legal limits on interest rates in Canada: the federal Small Loans Act, for example, has established some limits, and some provinces also have restrictions. But the lack of a legal definition of usury makes it difficult to prosecute LOAN SHARKS.

utilitarianism A political-economic philosophy that asserts that the basic role of government is to achieve the greatest happiness for the greatest number. It seeks to maximize the total utility of the community, which it sees as the sum of individual utilities. Its best-known advocate was Jeremy Bentham (1748–1832), who saw self-interest as the prime human motivator and the pursuit of happiness as the prime human concern.

utility The capacity of goods and services to satisfy human wants or needs. The utility or value of particular goods or services depends on the extent to which they can fill consumer wants; this utility is reflected in the price a consumer is willing to pay for a particular good or service. The consumer is assumed to rank his preference for goods and services in terms of the utility derived from them. See also MARGINAL UTILITY, LAW OF DIMINISHING MARGINAL UTILITY.

utility rate of return The maximum profit rate that may be earned by a monopoly company operating as a utility. The rate is usually set as a per cent of invested capital; the prices charged by a utility (a telephone company, for example) for its different services are set by a regulating agency (in the case of Bell Canada, the CANADIAN RADIO-TELEVISION AND TELECOMMUNICATIONS COMMISSION), in the context of a potential profit that would result from any changes in those prices. A utility's profit has to be set high enough so that it can attract investment capital; it has to be regulated so that it does not use its monopoly position to earn excessive profit. The regulated rate of return is usually slightly above the prevailing rate of interest earned on government and corporate bonds.

utility theory of value The theory that calculates the value of goods and services according to their ability to satisfy human wants in some order of preference. Assuming a certain level of income, the theory then attempts to provide a basis for calculating consumer demand in a particular period.

utopia A vision of a perfect or ideal society. Many different thinkers have described their particular utopias; models of utopian vision would include Plato's *Republic*, Francis Bacon's *New Atlantis*, Sir Thomas More's *Utopia*, Edward Bellamy's *Looking Backward*, and Karl Marx's dictatorship of the proletariat.

uttering The use of a forged document, in the knowledge that it is forged, with the purpose of obtaining some benefit—cashing a cheque with a forged signature or altered amount, for example, or using a forged bond certificate as collateral to obtain a loan.

V

vacancy rate A statistic showing the availability of apartments and other rental accommodation, published periodically by CANADA MORTGAGE AND HOUSING CORPORATION. It is based on a survey by CMHC of rental accommodation; separate vacancy rates are published for twenty-two different metropolitan regions in Canada. If the rate is low, say less than 1 per cent, then the market is probably tight and there is likely to be upward pressure on rents. A vacancy rate of 3 per cent is said to be needed by tenants to give them bargaining power with landlords over rent increases and other terms of a lease. At that level, tenants should be reasonably confident of finding alternative accommodation, if they are unable to negotiate a satisfactory lease with their existing landlord.

vacation-with-pay legislation Federal or provincial laws that entitle workers to annual vacations; the length of the vacation is normally related to the period of time spent working for a particular employer during the year. In most parts of Canada, paid vacations required by law are equivalent to 4 per cent of an employee's earnings. Vacation-with-pay legislation was first introduced in Canada in 1944, when Ontario passed such a law. Federal vacation-with-pay legislation was passed by Parliament in 1958. Through collective bargaining, many Canadians today have annual vacations that exceed the legal minimum. Most large employers grant an extra week or weeks of vacation after a specified number of years of continuous employment.

valuation 1. The assessment of property to establish a value for tax purposes—to determine the value of paintings or antiques on death for CAPITAL-GAINS TAX and SUCCESSION DUTY, for example, or the assessment of real estate for municipal-tax purposes. **2.** The appraisal of property for insurance purposes by qualified experts. For example, an engineer may check the facilities in a plant, along with fire and safety procedures, to help determine an insurance premium, or a specialist may determine the insurance or replacement value of jewels, rugs, and antiques.

valuation day The base date for the calculation of CAPITAL GAINS for tax purposes. It is 22 December 1971 for Canadian common and preferred shares listed on Canadian stock exchanges, foreign shares listed on Canadian stock exchanges, publicly traded but unlisted Canadian shares, rights, and warrants, and some convertible bonds. It is 31 December 1971 for all other assets subject to the tax, such as bonds, antiques, real estate, art collections, and shares in private companies. Capital gains on all assets except personal residences and on assets worth less than one thousand dollars are subject to tax. On death, the capital gain is deemed to have been realized, even though the asset may not be sold.

value 1. The quantity of one product or service that will be given or accepted in exchange for another—hence, a measure of the economic significance of a particular good or service. This value in exchange depends on the scarcity of the good or service and the extent to which it is desired. **2.** The utility or satisfaction resulting from the consumption of a particular good or service.

value-added The difference between an industry's total revenue and the costs of the materials, parts, and purchased services it has used. This isolates the actual value of work carried out in a particular industry, measuring the value that the industry has added to the raw materials, parts, and services it has used in producing goods and services. The value-added is the money that an industry pays on wages and salaries, taxes, dividends, interest, or that it reinvests. It is a vital figure in assessing the importance of different industries in the economy. GROSS DOMESTIC PRODUCT is the nation's total value-added in a given period; it includes DEPRECIATION. Statistics Canada also publishes a breakdown of value-added figures for all major manufacturing industries.

value-added tax (VAT) An INDIRECT TAX, similar to a sales tax, but levied only on the contribution that each firm in the production-distribution process adds to a product. Everybody in the production-distribution process, from the manufacturer of original components, through the final retailer of the product, to the ultimate consumer, is required to pay a value-added tax on all that he purchases, and to charge a value-added tax on all that he sells, deducting the tax he pays out from the tax he collects. Thus, the value-added tax is passed along through each stage of production and distribution. It is a REGRESSIVE TAX, in that the person with a low income pays a larger proportion of his income than a wealthy person pays to consume the same product. And the entire burden of the tax is shifted to the ultimate consumer, who pays the tax as part of the price of the product he purchases. It is the system of indirect taxation used throughout the EUROPEAN ECONOMIC COMMUNITY.

value of the Canadian dollar The exchange rate of the Canadian dollar, expressed in terms of a key international currency. Initially, this was the British pound; after 1910, the key currency became the U.S. dollar. The value of the Canadian dollar indicates its purchasing power in foreign markets for goods and services, including travel. Conversely, it also indicates the purchasing power of foreigners when buying Canadian goods and services.

Since the end of the First World War, the Canadian dollar has fluctuated widely in value. In 1920 it fell to 82 U.S. cents, but by 1922 it had recovered to 98.73 U.S. cents. When Canada returned to the GOLD STANDARD, from 1 July 1926 to January 1929, the Canadian dollar was close to par with the U.S. dollar. But the Depression pushed the Canadian dollar down. After Britain went off the gold standard, in September 1931, the Canadian dollar went down to 80.5 U.S. cents, in December 1931. The Canadian dollar recovered during the Depression, trading at one point as high as 103.6 U.S. cents.

With the outbreak of the Second World War, Canada established the FOREIGN EXCHANGE CONTROL BOARD, which fixed the value of the Canadian dollar at a buying rate of 110 U.S. cents and a selling rate of 111 U.S. cents. In July 1946, although controls were retained, the buying and selling rates of the Canadian dollar were reduced to 100 U.S. cents and 100.5 U.S. cents. In September 1949, when the British devalued the pound by 30.5 per cent, Canada revalued the dollar to a buying rate of 110 U.S. cents and a selling rate of 110.5 U.S. cents.

In October 1950, the fixed exchange rate was abandoned and the Canadian dollar was allowed to float in foreign-exchange markets. The Foreign Exchange Control Act was repealed by Parliament in 1952. For the next decade, the Canadian dollar was at or near parity with the U.S. dollar; but in May 1962, it was pegged at 92.5 U.S. cents, staying at this rate until May 1970, when it was unpegged again. Since then it has floated, as high as 104 U.S. cents and as low as 82.5 U.S. cents.

Vancouver Curb Exchange A second stock exchange in Vancouver, created in 1974 with the approval of the B.C. Securities Commission. It is an exchange where the shares of JUNIOR COMPANIES are traded; it replaced the Vancouver OVER-THE-COUNTER MARKET. It shares trading and clearing facilities with the VANCOUVER STOCK EXCHANGE.

Vancouver Stock Exchange (VSE) A stock exchange created in 1907 that has been in business ever since. It maintains three boards, for resource and development companies, for industrial companies, and for listings of JUNIOR COMPANIES for the VANCOUVER CURB EXCHANGE.

variable cost A cost that goes up or down, depending on whether production goes up or down. Examples include the costs of raw materials, parts, and labour directly involved in the production process. Such costs are also known as operating costs, as opposed to FIXED COSTS or overhead.

variable interest rate An interest rate that varies directly with changes in the PRIME RATE charged by the banks. If the prime rate rises, so does the rate on loans paying a variable rate of interest, and vice versa. Many small-business, corporate, and personal demand loans have a variable rate of interest that changes as the PRIME RATE changes.

variance The difference between actual spending by a business firm or a department of the firm and the amount previously budgeted for the same period.

vein In mining, an ore that has moved up from some deeper underground source to fill a crack or fault in a rock formation.

velocity of circulation The number of times a unit of money—currency and bank deposits—changes hands within a given period of time. A high velocity of circulation means that people are holding on to their money for a short period of time because the economy is expanding. The speed or velocity with which money changes hands is also based on the sophistication of financial markets; a highly specialized financial system is able to attract savings and to invest them quickly into new activities or assets. Changing technology, such as electronic banking and computer communications, along with changing tastes, lifestyles, and expectations, also influence the velocity of circulation. The rate of turnover, generally, rises during periods of growth and declines during a recession.

venture capital Capital available for new or small-business enterprises, which is invested at greater-than-normal business risk since the business enterprises may not succeed. Venture capital usually includes EQUITY CAPITAL, and may be provided by financial firms specializing in such investments or by private investors who seek out high-risk opportunities because of the rewards these can bring if they are successful.

vertical integration The control by a single firm of successive stages of the production and distribution process. Such control gives it greater command over costs, can bring about certain ECONOMIES OF SCALE, ensures a market for its raw materials, and should increase profits. Examples of vertical integration would include an oil company that engages in exploration and development, operates pipelines, refines its oil into gasoline, fuel oil, and other products, then sells its product through gasoline stations and home-heating-oil distributorships to the public; a steel company that owns iron-ore mines, basic steel-producing facilities, and manufacturing operations that produce finished steel products; an aluminum company that mines bauxite, processes aluminum ingots, and manufactures aluminum products; a chain store that also owns food-processing companies and farms.

vesting Attributing a specified amount of money in a pension plan to a particular individual participating in the plan. This sum of money forms the basis for his future pension. For example, an employee who participates in a company pension plan has vested his contributions, those of his employer, plus accrued interest. If the employee changes jobs or otherwise leaves his job before he reaches retirement age, though, the only amount that belongs to him is his own accumulated contribution, plus the accrued interest on his contributions. However, under federal and most provincially regulated pension plans, an employee can reach a point where his interest in the plan, and his right to future benefits based on his own and his employer's contributions to date, are vested; that is, he cannot get his money out of the plan even if he changes jobs, nor can his employer discontinue his obligation to provide a future pension. For example, in Ontario, if an employee has ten years of continuous employment and has reached the age of forty-five, his contributions and those of his employer are vested in the pension plan to pay him a pension when he retires. Advocates of pension reform argue that the loss of future pension benefits when people change jobs reduces labour mobility, and gives employers an unfair hold over employees who would like to move to another job but cannot afford to give up future pension benefits. See also PORTABLE PENSION.

Via Rail Canada A crown corporation established in January 1977 to operate all passenger rail services in Canada. It is a subsidiary of CANADIAN NATIONAL RAILWAYS, but operates at ARM'S LENGTH from it. It is financed directly by the federal government through the Ministry of TRANSPORT. Its head office is in Montreal.

visibles Merchandise exports and imports; as

opposed to INVISIBLES, such as interest, dividend, and travel payments. Both visible and invisible items of trade are considered in the CURRENT ACCOUNT of a country's BALANCE OF PAYMENTS. The visible balance of trade is simply another name for the balance of trade in tangible goods.

visual-display unit An electronic device that looks like a television set with a typewriter keyboard. It is used to display information—in text or diagram form—stored in a computer. The typewriter keyboard can be used to enter additional information or to give fresh instructions to the computer, and a light-pen can be used to alter the diagrams displayed on the screen. One of the most common uses of the visual-display unit is in airline-reservation systems.

vital statistics Basic statistics of a population; they include birth, death, marriage, divorce, and death rates, and other statistics on disease and health. Statistics Canada has actual vital statistics dating back to 1921 and estimates for earlier periods. Vital statistics are used by demographers in making population forecasts.

volume discount A discount in price given to someone who purchases in larger-than-normal quantities. Such discounts are common in the retailing industry; large chains are able to negotiate lower prices than small, independently owned and operated stores. Volume discounts are legal so long as the same discount is available to everyone who wishes to buy the same volume of goods.

voluntary arbitration A method of resolving differences between an employer and a union in negotiations for a new contract; both parties voluntarily agree to send the outstanding issues to arbitration, and to accept the results. See also COMPULSORY ARBITRATION.

voting shares Shares in a corporation that entitle their owner to a vote at ANNUAL and SPECIAL MEETINGS. Each common share usually carries one vote; the owner of such shares can delegate his votes to others by exercising his PROXY. PREFERRED SHARES generally do not carry a vote but, if the company fails to pay a dividend on time, the owners of preferred shares may get voting rights. The owners of voting shares control the company; they elect the board of directors, which in turn is responsible for selecting the senior officers of the company and for supervising the policies, investments, and operations of the company. If the shareholders are dissatisfied with the way the company is being run, they can vote out the directors and install new directors. If a sufficient number agree, the shareholders of a company can also call a special meeting of shareholders, to examine the company's affairs and policies and to seek remedies.

wage The amount of money earned by an individual during a work-week, calculated by multiplying the number of hours worked by a fixed hourly rate of pay.

wage and price guidelines Proposals by government that business and labour help to fight inflation by holding wage and price increases below a specified ceiling or in line with some specified standard, such as price increases not exceeding cost increases, or wage increases no greater than productivity increases plus some allowance for inflation. Experience in Canada and other countries shows that, while such guidelines may work for a short period of time, they can lead to mandatory controls. While there may be initial support for guidelines, there is usually a call for penalties or rollback powers if the guidelines are broken by major corporations or unions. Without some means of enforcement, public support for the guidelines can quickly disappear.

Wage and price guidelines are one form of INCOMES POLICY. See also PRICE CONTROLS, PRICES AND INCOMES COMMISSION, ANTI-INFLATION BOARD, WARTIME PRICES AND TRADE BOARD.

wage drift The tendency for total wages to exceed basic wage rates set out in a collective agreement. This excess pay consists of overtime, special bonuses for productivity, and other incentives. The difference between the basic wage rate and what an employee gets is the wage drift. Since it is the total purchasing power in the economy that affects inflation rates, the existence of wage drift can undermine a policy of wage restraint.

wage-fund theory The theory that the funds available to pay wages to workers are fixed by the level of savings in society, and that wage increases can therefore only occur if there is a reduction in the number of workers or an increase in the level of savings. According to this theory, developed by JOHN STUART MILL and other CLASSICAL ECONOMISTS, the amount of money available for wages does not come from the sale of goods and services but from a pool of capital in the economy that depends on the rate of savings. In many respects, the wage-fund theory was a restatement of the subsistence theory of wages. See also the MARGINAL-PRODUCTIVITY THEORY OF WAGES.

wage leadership The influence that powerful unions can have on the general level of wage settlements in the economy, by seeking and gaining a larger-than-average increase, or by refraining from seeking such an increase and settling for something more modest.

wage-price spiral A form of inflation that occurs when employers grant significant wage increases and pass along the increased costs to consumers in the form of higher prices; they expect the government to keep the overall level of demand in the economy sufficiently high that the more expensive products can be sold. Higher prices, in turn, lead to fresh demands for higher wages, which again are passed along to consumers in the form of higher prices, the process repeating itself again and again, with wages and prices increasing by bigger steps each rung of the way up the inflation ladder. See COST-PUSH INFLATION. Some economists, such as JOHN KENNETH GALBRAITH, argue that the wage-price spiral is a characteristic of economies dominated by large unions and corporations; their power is such that, even during a recession, they can continue to increase wages and prices. Galbraith uses this argument to justify permanent controls on the wages and prices of large unions and big business. MONETARISTS argue that a wage-price spiral would not be possible if the government refused, by holding down the growth in MONEY SUPPLY to the long-term real growth rate of the economy, to finance the inflation.

wage rate The basic rate of pay for an employee for a specified period of work, such as an hour or a week. In addition to the basic wage rate, an employee may get extra pay based on output, or a commission based on sales. Overtime wage rates are higher than basic wage rates, usually one and a half times the basic wage rate. Statistics Canada publishes a monthly report, *Employment, Earnings and Hours,* which sets out industry wage rates for a variety of industries and communities across Canada. The Department of LABOUR also publishes information on wage rates across Canada.

wage restraints The restriction of wage increases within a specified limit, as part of a policy to help control COST-PUSH INFLATION. The restraint can be voluntary, with unions agreeing to some kind of wage ceiling; it may also consist of guidelines, with government policies to help enforce compliance, or of mandatory controls or a wage freeze.

wage settlements Quarterly statistics published by the federal Department of LABOUR showing the average annual rate of pay increase, for base wage rates, in the life of collective agreements covering five hundred or more workers in all industries except construction. The statistics do not include COLA CLAUSES or the value of fringe benefits, but they do provide the single most important indicator of basic wage trends.

walkout An illegal work stoppage, in which workers walk off the job in protest over some grievance, even though they are not legally allowed to do so when a collective agreement is in force.

Wall Street The financial heart of the United States, and the world's single most important financial market, located at the lower end of Manhattan Island in New York City. In a small, concentrated area are located the New York and American stock exchanges, commodity exchanges, and the major stockbrokers, investment bankers, insurance companies, and trust companies. The name is also a synonym for U.S. capitalism. The Canadian equivalent is BAY STREET in downtown Toronto. In an earlier era, it was St. James Street in downtown Montreal.

want The need or desire for a good or service that is not free. A consumer may have the purchasing power to acquire it, but only by not acquiring something else.

War Exchange Conservation Act Federal legislation passed in December 1940, allowing the Canadian government to clamp tight controls on imports and thus to conserve foreign exchange, mainly U.S. dollars, for essential war needs. The legislation prohibited imports from hard-currency or non-sterling countries of non-essential items such as cigarettes and cigars, wines and spirits, fiction magazines and comics, perfume, china, glass, silverware, electrical appliances, sporting goods, cameras, toys, jewellery, private automobiles, and clothing. The legislation also restricted, through a system of licensing, imports such as tobacco, commercial vehicles, lumber products, and petroleum products. At the same time, imports from Britain were encouraged by means of a sweeping tariff cut, while exports to the United States and other hard-currency countries were encouraged by tax incentives.

warrant An option or right to buy common shares of a corporation at a specified price, up to some specified future date when that right expires. Warrants are issued in two ways. A stock-purchase warrant may be attached to a corporate bond or to preferred shares as a sweetener, to induce investors to accept a lower rate of interest on a bond or to pay a higher price for a preferred share. Such warrants may be traded on a STOCK EXCHANGE or on the OVER-THE-COUNTER MARKET. A second type of warrant is the one that automatically goes with the common shares of some companies, and gives existing shareholders the right to buy a new issue of common shares in proportion to their existing holdings. This is a subscription warrant or right, and can also be traded, if the holder does not want to exercise his warrant. The exercise price of a warrant is the price that the holder must pay for the shares he may buy to obtain a share.

warranty A form of protection for consumers against unsatisfactory merchandise. The federal Sale of Goods Act gives consumers an implied warranty on whatever they buy; it says that a product must be fit for its purpose and be of merchantable quality, and that the person who sold it must be the legal owner. If these conditions are not met, the consumer is legally entitled to a refund or replacement. Some manufacturers also offer an expressed warranty, which comes with the product and gives certain guarantees on replacement, repairs, and durability. Such warranties sometimes include a statement that consumers, by possession of the printed warranty, waive their rights to the implied warranty under the Sale of Goods Act. But a number of provinces have passed laws stating that consumers cannot waive their rights of implied warranty; so, whether a product comes with an expressed warranty or not, consumers still have recourse because of the implied warranty under federal law.

Wartime Prices and Trade Board The principal agency created by the federal government in September 1939, with the outbreak of the Second World War, to control prices and rents, and to ensure adequate supplies and the equitable distribution of food, clothing, housing, and other necessities, through rationing, direct orders on production, or a ban on the production of certain goods. The board consisted of five senior civil servants, who supervised a broad array of subsidiary boards and commissions. A system of selective and usually temporary price controls existed until 1941, when a price ceiling or maximum price was set for all goods for the remainder of the war. Prices could not be increased above the level that prevailed in a base period from 15 September to 11 October 1941. Wage controls were introduced at the same time (see also WARTIME WAGES CONTROL ORDER). Price increases were only granted when real financial need on an overall corporate basis could be shown.

The main problems the board had to deal with were to ensure that product quality was maintained and that black-market activities were thwarted. In 1942, the board banned the establishment of new businesses and new lines of business, except by permit. Prices for "new products" that appeared after 1941 were determined by board officials. Rent controls prevailed through most of the war for residential and commercial space, and special rules had to be introduced to protect tenants against eviction, from having to pay more than one month's rent in advance, from having to rent or buy furniture at artificial prices, or having to make special payments as a condition of getting a lease. The board introduced a system of RATIONING to ensure the fair distribution of meat, tea, coffee, butter, sugar, and gasoline, administering the system through six hundred local ration boards and the national Ration Administration. The board also used its power to order the production of certain essential products, such as some items of clothing, when industrial output was too low. The board was dissolved in 1951, its activities having been gradually phased out after the end of the Second World War.

Wartime Wages Control Order A system of wage controls introduced during the Second World War to help prevent high inflation. The government followed a voluntary program until October 1941, when a wage ceiling was imposed at the same time as across-the-board price controls (see also WARTIME PRICES AND TRADE BOARD). Wage rates were frozen at the wage level as of 15 November 1941, but cost-of-living adjustments were permitted. The program was administered by the National War Labour Board and regional war labour boards, advised by committees of employers and union leaders. The various boards could adjust wage rates to remove any "gross inequality or gross injustice." In December 1943, cost-of-living bonuses were abolished and employers were forbidden to raise any individual's wage rate, except in cases of promotion or demotion, without approval from the Department of Labour, which took over administration from the War Labour Boards. The wage-control program was phased out after the Second World War.

wash sale An attempt to manipulate the stock market through fictitious sales in which no change of ownership occurs. By increasing market activity in a particular share, stock-market manipulators can attract new buyers, and hence raise the value of the shares they own. In transactions known as wash sales, manipulators create the impression of hectic activity by buying and selling shares to themselves. Such activities are illegal in Canada.

wasting asset An asset with a declining life, that becomes less valuable over time until it is finally exhausted. Oil and natural-gas wells, mines, and timber stands are examples of wasting assets. In a BALANCE SHEET, wasting assets are usually listed under FIXED ASSETS. See also DEPLETION ALLOWANCE.

watered stock The issue of new shares of a company below their asset value. This dilutes the value of existing shares, and is thus unfair to existing shareholders. Although this practice was once not uncommon, it is now illegal in Canada.

Watkins Report See TASK FORCE ON FOREIGN OWNERSHIP AND THE STRUCTURE OF CANADIAN INDUSTRY.

ways and means motion A motion introduced at the end of the minister of Finance's BUDGET SPEECH, moving that the budget measures be implemented. It is the motion, or set of motions, that is debated during the budget debate and voted on at the end of the debate. The Finance minister then introduces legislation, usually amendments to existing tax laws, to implement his specific tax and other changes.

This legislation is then debated by the MPs and senators and passed by Parliament. Parliament also debates supply motions, which are motions dealing with the spending of money.

wealth The total possessions of an individual that have a market value. This means that they can be sold. Under this definition, wealth includes not only tangible possessions, such as real estate, antiques, and shares and bonds, but also intangible assets, such as special skills or knowledge that can be used to generate income. Wealth is different from income. Wealth represents a stock of assets that can be used to generate income; the greater the wealth a person has at his disposal, the greater the income he can generate. A person who does not inherit wealth, or acquire wealth in the form of skills and knowledge, has less chance of generating income and accumulating assets surplus to his maintenance needs. National wealth includes the wealth of all individuals and the public assets, such as resources, crown lands, and public buildings.

wealth distribution The way in which the ownership of wealth is distributed among the various members of society. The usual approach is to show how much wealth is owned by each 20 per cent of society. While statistics for Canada are sketchy, in Western societies generally there tends to be much greater inequality in the distribution of wealth than in the distribution of income. Inequalities in the distribution of wealth give some Canadians much greater command over resources than other Canadians have. Inequalities of wealth also help to explain great disparities in income. In the absence of offsetting tax policies, inequalities in the distribution of wealth may increase over time, due to inheritance and capital gains. Hence, taxes such as CAPITAL-GAINS TAXES, ESTATE TAXES, GIFT TAXES, and SUCCESSION DUTIES are devices to reduce huge concentrations of wealth and power. Canada, however, has reduced the impact of such taxes in recent years.

wealth tax A tax that is levied upon what a person owns, rather than what he receives as income. Estate and gift taxes and succession duties are forms of wealth tax. In recent years, there has been a growing interest in a wealth tax or capital levy, the argument being that, if the tax system is truly to be based on the ABILITY-TO-PAY PRINCIPLE, then a person's wealth should also be taken into account.

wear and tear An accounting term used to describe the decline in value of an asset, such as a machine or truck, that results from its normal use. See DEPRECIATION.

weighted average A method of averaging used in statistics, to take into account the relative importance of the different numbers being averaged. Each of the numbers to be averaged is multiplied by another number called a weight, which represents its relative importance. The results are then added, to yield the weighted average. The technique is used, for example, in calculating the CONSUMER PRICE INDEX, where, for example, an increase in the cost of food is given a much larger weight than an increase in the cost of personal recreation, since food is a much bigger portion of the typical consumer's shopping basket. Similarly, in the INDEX OF INDUSTRIAL PRODUCTION, the increase in production of the steel industry is given a larger weight or importance than a production increase in the footwear industry, since the steel industry is much more important in terms of output.

welfare Public support for the needy, disadvantaged, and handicapped. It includes INCOME-MAINTENANCE PROGRAMS, subsidized housing, free medical and dental care, veterans' allowances, nursing-home care, and assistance for native peoples.

welfare economics The branch of economics that deals with economic performance in terms of ethical standards or social values. It may be concerned, for example, with finding ways to reduce disparities in wealth and income, to improve job opportunities, to offset the harmful side effects of market forces, such as the spread of MONOPOLIES, or generally to seek out ways to improve the well-being of the ordinary citizen. In welfare economics, the just society is one in which human welfare is maximized. Welfare economics is also concerned with the social costs of economic activity—of occupational disease and pollution, for example. It rejects the automatic workings of the economic system, and attempts, through policies based on desired goals, to influence or alter the behaviour of the system.

welfare state A society that uses the power of the state to ensure a minimum standard of living for all of its citizens by redistributing income. Most democratic societies operate some kind of welfare state. The government, through pensions, income-maintenance programs, subsidized housing, universal medical care, free education, unemployment insurance, progressive taxation, aid for marginal farmers, and other such measures, tries to make sure that every citizen is able to enjoy a share in the wealth and output of society.

wellhead price The price of oil at the producer end of the distribution system. It is the price established from a delivery point in the crude-oil-production system. The price paid for oil elsewhere in the country or in foreign markets is the wellhead price plus pipeline distribution costs to the destination point.

Western Economic Opportunities Conference (WEOC) A conference of the federal government and the four western provinces of British Columbia, Alberta, Saskatchewan, and Manitoba, planned to stimulate and broaden the economic and industrial base of western Canada, held in July 1973 in Calgary. The federal government published background papers on industrial and trade development, capital financing and financial institutions, mineral-resource development, agriculture, transportation, and regional-development opportunities. For their part, the western premiers published four position papers, on economic and industrial-development opportunities, transportation, agriculture, and regional financial institutions. The western provinces sought decentralized offices for the Department of REGIONAL ECONOMIC EXPANSION, increased federal purchasing in western Canada, selective tariff changes, more funding for industrial development in western Canada, increased agricultural development, the right for provincial governments to own shares in chartered banks, federal funding for certain railway fixed costs, so that freight rates could be reduced, improved port facilities at Prince Rupert, B.C., and Churchill, Manitoba, and increased efforts to promote the development of petrochemicals, steel, and transportation-equipment industries in western Canada, thus diversifying its industrial base.

The federal government agreed to a greater decentralization of its regional-development offices, more government purchasing from suppliers in western Canada, the release to the provincial governments of previously secret information on freight rates, amendments to the BANK ACT to permit the provinces to be shareholders in chartered banks, additional funding for northern transportation, and financing to improve port facilities at Prince Rupert.

Western Grain Stabilization Plan A form of federal assistance to provide prairie grain producers with protection against drops in income, due to poor conditions in international markets, sharp rises in production costs, and other developments beyond the control of farmers or governments. Under the plan, participating farmers and the federal government contribute to the Western Grain Stabilization Fund. The farmers' levy is 2 per cent of sales, to a maximum of twenty-five thousand dollars a year. Support is paid to prevent the net cash flow—the difference between production costs and sales revenues—from falling below the average of the five previous years.

western premiers' conference An annual conference of the premiers of Manitoba, Saskatchewan, Alberta, and British Columbia, to discuss common economic, social, and other problems. The four premiers seek out a common ground for representation to the federal government in such matters as freight rates, tariffs, and grain handling. They also examine ways in which they can co-ordinate their policies with one another. The four western premiers have been holding such an annual conference since 1973; prior to that, the three prairie premiers met annually through the PRAIRIE ECONOMIC CONFERENCE.

western provinces Manitoba, Saskatchewan, Alberta, and British Columbia.

wheat pool A system of country and terminal grain elevators co-operatively owned by farmers. The major pools are the Saskatchewan Wheat Pool, which has branched out to operate fertilizer, seed, and various other business activities, the Alberta Wheat Pool, Manitoba Pool Elevators, and the United Grain Growers.

white-collar crime Crime committed by fraud or deceit, as distinguished from violent crime. Such crime is called white-collar crime because much of it takes place in the business world. It can range from embezzlement within a corporation and stock manipulation, to fraudulent bankruptcy, the use of forged documents improperly to obtain credit or possession of property, TAX EVASION, and so-called computer crimes.

white-collar workers A general term used to describe those who work in offices, or in other areas where little or no physical exertion is needed and ordinary clothing can be worn; as opposed to BLUE-COLLAR WORKERS.

white paper A statement of government intentions or policies. It may also include draft legislation. White papers are often used by a government to declare its policies and to get public reaction before the government presents final legislation to Parliament or to a provincial legislature. Publication of draft legislation in a white paper enables a government to spot possible flaws or unintended results and thus present better legislation to Parliament. See also GREEN PAPER, ROYAL COMMISSION, TASK FORCE.

White Paper on Employment and Income A federal blueprint for postwar conversion of the Canadian economy to a peacetime footing under conditions of full employment and stable prices; the white paper was presented to Parliament by the minister of RECONSTRUCTION in April 1945. It was a statement of the objectives and plans of the Department of Reconstruction, and proposed to combine the demobilization of the armed forces and the winding up of war industry with the task of rebuilding the Canadian economy, without reverting to the depressed economic conditions of the 1930s. The white paper calculated that 900,000 more jobs would be needed than existed in 1939, with a growth of 60,000 a year after that. It put primary emphasis on policies to boost private industry, to stimulate housing construction, to modernize agriculture, and to increase consumer spending. The government said that it would seek a reciprocal reduction in world trade barriers, plus international agreements to promote stability in international food and raw-materials markets, which would help boost exports.

To increase private investment and convert wartime industries to peacetime uses, taxes were to be cut and interest rates held at a low level. Special lending programs for business and agriculture were also expected to help. Housing construction was expected to surge, since housing construction had been far too low for the previous fifteen years. Consumer spending was to be encouraged through income-maintenance programs, such as unemployment insurance and family allowances, and through subsidies to farmers and fishermen to support farm and fishery prices. The government indicated that it was ready to introduce contributory old-age pensions and national health insurance, as soon as agreement could be reached with the provinces.

The white paper also emphasized that public-investment spending could become a permanent method of creating jobs in postwar Canada, and proposed two immediate steps: **1.** The advance planning of a shelf of necessary or desirable projects that could be carried out when jobs were needed. **2.** A federal-provincial spending policy, to develop Canada's hydro-electric, forestry, and mining industries. The white paper also called for a significant increase in research and development, to raise the technical level of Canadian industry.

Other measures proposed to increase Canada's postwar economic performance included increased spending on labour mobility and retraining. The government, through the white paper, also promised a relaxation of wartime controls on prices, supplies, foreign exchange, and other restrictions, as soon as they could be lifted without triggering inflation. Most important, the white paper made it clear that the lesson of the 1930s depression had been learned; it adopted KEYNESIAN ECONOMICS, and promised that, when unemployment threatened, the government would run budgetary deficits and increase the national debt so that employment and income goals could be achieved. Conversely, the white paper said, in times of full employment and high levels of income, budget plans would call for a surplus.

White Paper on Foreign Policy A federal white paper published in June 1970, after a two-year review of Canadian foreign-policy interests. Six major themes were emphasized: sovereignty and independence; peace and security; social justice; quality of life; a harmonious natural environment; and economic growth. The three top priorities, the white paper said, were policies related to economic growth, social justice, and quality of life, with much more emphasis than in the past on a foreign policy that would improve Canadian economic performance. This meant stronger efforts to increase Canadian trade, and to keep up to date "on such key matters as discoveries in science and technology, management of energies and resources, significant trends in world trade and finance, policies of major trading countries and blocs, activities of multinational corporations."

Greater emphasis on social justice meant that Canada would increase its foreign aid, while the priority placed on quality of life meant that Canada would play a larger role in international environmental-protection activities, increase its cultural exchanges, and pay more attention to such matters as curbing the international flow of drugs and finding more effective measures to combat terrorism.

There was no direct discussion of Canada-U.S. relations in the white paper, but the discussion of sovereignty and independence was assumed to include the need to strengthen a Canadian identity, distinct from that of the United States. The white paper consisted of six booklets on policies concerning Europe, Latin America, the Pacific, the United Nations, international development, and a general booklet entitled *Foreign Policy for Canadians*. See also THIRD OPTION.

wholesale price The price paid by a middleman or wholesaler, who buys goods in large quantities from domestic or foreign manufacturers and resells them in smaller quantities to retailers.

wholesaler A middleman who buys products from manufacturers and resells them to retailers, thus playing an indispensable role in the production-distribution system. A wholesaler may also resell to industrial, commercial, institutional, and professional users, or to farmers for farm use. The existence of an active wholesaler network means that manufacturers do not have to maintain their own distribution systems.

wholly owned subsidiary See SUBSIDIARY.

wildcat strike An illegal strike that takes place without the approval of union leaders —and perhaps, over their objections—and without observance of the various steps leading up to a legal strike. A wildcat strike may reflect the anger of union members at the bargaining stance of management; but sometimes it can be a signal from union members to their own leadership that they do not like the way that union affairs are being handled.

will A legal document made by an individual, setting out the ways in which his assets shall be disposed of after his death and naming someone, an executor, who is to make sure that the terms of the will are carried out and administer the estate. When a person dies without making a will—dies, in other words, intestate—a court must appoint someone to administer the estate and to dispose of the assets according to procedures set out in provincial laws.

windfall gain A sudden and unexpected increase in profits or in the value of land, natural resources, and other assets. The gain is not due to anything the owner of the business or asset has done; it is caused by the actions of other people. For example, oil companies in Canada were faced with the prospect of a windfall gain on their Canadian oil-resources reserves when the ORGANIZATION OF PETROLEUM EXPORTING COUNTRIES quadrupled the world price of oil in 1973–74. They did not receive the full windfall gain, however, because the provincial governments sharply increased their royalty charges, while the federal government delayed the introduction of world prices in Canada. A person who owns a piece of land along a subway route, especially if it is nearby a subway station, may enjoy a windfall profit on the sale of his land. Economists and policy-makers question whether the owner should be entitled to the full benefit of a windfall gain. See also ECONOMIC RENT, QUASI-RENT.

Windfall Mines and Oils affair A July 1964 scandal on the Toronto Stock Exchange that resulted in significant changes in Ontario securities legislation, and similar changes subsequently in other provinces. The principal shareholders of Windfall Mines and Oils Limited, Mrs. Viola MacMillan and her husband, George MacMillan, made misleading statements about allegedly rich copper finds where none existed. Rumours sent the price of Windfall spiralling, while Mrs. MacMillan sold all of her family's shares and sold short shares she did not own. The stock moved from 56 cents to $6.50; when Windfall issued a subsequent statement saying that there was no ore, it fell to 35 cents.

The TSE and the Ontario Securities Commission were both sharply criticized in a judicial inquiry, which reported in October 1965. Previously, a director of the Ontario Securities Commission had been forced to resign. The royal commission report said that the MacMillans had deliberately misled the public, while making a personal profit of $1,455,928. The report placed full blame on the TSE for permitting trading to continue when it should have been stopped, and called for a ban on the PRIMARY DISTRIBUTION of shares on the TSE, a strengthening of the Ontario Securities Commission, and the creation of a national body to regulate stock exchanges in Canada. The TSE fined a member-firm one thousand dollars for accommodating trading in the sale of Windfall shares, and reprimanded two others. Subsequently, the TSE took a number of other steps to reassure the public, introducing tighter policies for stockbroker firms, higher educational requirements for floor traders, a suspension and delisting policy for inactive oil and mining companies with less than twenty-five thousand dollars in net liquid assets, and tougher rules to deal with deceptive practices by stockbrokers and to bar WASH SALES.

In 1966, a new Ontario Securities Act was passed, requiring monthly publication of INSIDER REPORTS, fuller disclosure in company annual reports, including year-to-year comparative statistics and a statement of SOURCE AND DISPOSITION OF FUNDS, new rules on takeover bids, changes in prospectus requirements to give investors more information, and improved shareholder PROXY forms, giving shareholders more information on how management intended to use the proxies.

Mr. and Mrs. MacMillan and John Campbell, a securities-commission official, were charged. Mrs. MacMillan was convicted of wash trading and sentenced to nine months in jail in 1968, but was released on probation after nine weeks. She and her husband, along with Mr. Campbell, were acquitted on fraud charges.

winding up The legal process of dissolving an incorporated or limited company.

Winnipeg Commodity Exchange (WCE) The only commodities exchange and futures market in Canada. The main items traded are various grains, gold, interest-rate futures, and lumber. In October 1979, the exchange announced plans to establish a separate division, the Canadian Financial Market, to offer futures trading in TREASURY BILLS, government BONDS, gold, and gold options.

The exchange was founded in 1883 and, for a period before World War Two, it was the world's most important grain exchange; since then, the centre of the grain trade has shifted to Chicago. In 1972, it changed its name from Winnipeg Grain and Produce Exchange to Winnipeg Commodity Exchange, reflecting its ambitions as a commodities exchange and futures market, although futures had been traded at the exchange since 1904. Its policies are set out and administered by a board of governors elected from its more than three hundred member-brokers and more than one hundred associate companies, such as grain shippers and merchants, from around the world.

Winnipeg General Strike A general strike called in Winnipeg in 1919 by the One Big Union, a federation of unions in western Canada. The OBU was a radical labour federation that drew many of its ideas from the British labour movement; it believed in the inevitability of class struggle and in the need for workers to advance their demands through direct action. The general strike was sparked when the building and metals trades went on a city-wide strike, after their employers had refused to grant wage increases or to recognize their union. The Winnipeg Trades and Labour Council sought the advice of the OBU, which called a general strike among all unions in Winnipeg until union demands for recognition, wage increases, and the reinstatement of all striking workers were met. Confrontation quickly developed, as city officials feared that the OBU would attempt to seize control. The leaders of the union were arrested on charges of inciting a revolution; but the strike was subsequently called off, after the employers agreed to collective bargaining and the government threatened to take even tougher steps to deal with the union.

The strike began on 1 May 1919, with sympathy strikes running until 26 June 1919. The most serious disturbance came on 21 June, when one rioter was killed and thirty other persons, including sixteen policemen, were injured, after the Riot Act was read by the mayor of Winnipeg. Troops armed with machine guns were also brought into the city after crowds got out of control.

winter-works program A federal program, launched in the winter of 1958–59, to create winter jobs, by paying half the payroll costs of a municipality, its contractors, or subcontractors, on approved municipal projects. The program was ended in fiscal 1963–64. See also MUNICIPAL DEVELOPMENT AND LOAN FUND.

withholding tax A tax levied by the federal government on interest and dividend payments, pensions, royalties, and other payments to non-residents; the tax is imposed on the recipient of the interest and dividend payments. The tax rate is 25 per cent but, in most instances, is reduced to 15 per cent; this means, for example, that non-residents receive 85 per cent of the dividends and interest that they earn on their Canadian investments. The withholding tax can be altered to help achieve economic-policy goals. For example, in June 1975, the federal government suspended the withholding tax on interest payments on new corporate bonds sold to non-residents, to make it easier for Canadian corporations to borrow abroad.

work in progress A term used in accounting to describe products that are at some uncompleted stage of production during the accounting period. The items are usually included with INVENTORIES in a company's BALANCE SHEET.

work permit A permit issued by the CANADA EMPLOYMENT AND IMMIGRATION COMMISSION, allowing a non-resident to take a temporary job in Canada. Anyone who is neither a Canadian citizen or a landed immigrant has to get a work permit. The permit states the name of the employer, describes the job, indicates the location of the job, and gives an expiry date; generally speaking, the maximum length of a work permit is one year, but it can be renewed. Canada has had a formal system of work permits since 1 January 1973. There are some exemptions, such as foreign diplomats and news correspondents and members of the clergy.

work-sharing A reduction in the work-week of all employees in a firm, to prevent the loss of jobs when there is insufficient business to keep everyone fully employed. A firm may, for example, put all of its employees on a three-day week, so as to spread the work around and avoid layoffs.

work to rule A tactic by a union to slow work down that stops short of bringing work to a complete halt. Workers do this by following, to the smallest detail, every work rule laid down by management. There may, for example, be more shutdowns of machinery to check parts, and much more time than usual spent checking out the safety of equipment before it is turned on. By using such tactics, union members are able to frustrate management, to reduce production or service sharply, and yet continue to earn their full pay.

work-week, average The average number of hours worked in a week by non-government employees. Statistics Canada collects information every month from all employers of twenty or more people, on the number of persons employed, full- or part-time, and the number of hours worked by each person. In addition to government employees, members of religious organizations, farm workers, fishermen, hospital workers, teachers, professors, and health and welfare workers are excluded. Hours worked include paid holidays, vacations, and overtime. Short-term change can indicate whether economic activity is picking up or slowing down; in a recovery, for example, there will be more overtime, and part-time workers will put in longer hours. In the long run, the figures show a decline in the average work-week. In 1952, the average manufacturing work-week was 43.15 hours; in 1977, it was 40.0 hours.

working capital The funds available for carrying on the activities of a business after an allowance is made for bills that have to be paid within the year. Working capital is calculated by deducting the current liabilities from the current assets of a firm, and indicates a company's ability to pay its short-term debts. The excess of current assets is the working capital. Different industries have different working-capital requirements; those with rapid turnover have less need than those in, say, the capital-goods industry, where turnover may be slow.

working conditions The environment in which a person works; federal and provincial labour laws and collective-bargaining agreements play a large role in defining working conditions. The concerns range from job safety and health hazards to lunch and rest breaks, hours of work, vacations with pay, and the physical environment of the workplace.

working control The ownership of sufficient voting shares of a company to exercise control over its management and policies. Working control is usually 51 per cent but, in a major corporation, with widely held ownership of its shares, working control can be much less than 51 per cent.

Working Party Three (WP3) A small but important committee of officials from central banks and finance ministries of key members of the ORGANIZATION FOR ECONOMIC CO-OPERATION AND DEVELOPMENT, that analyzes short-term BALANCE-OF-PAYMENTS problems on a regular basis. The group, which was formed in 1961 when the United States realized that it had to do something about its emerging balance-of-payments problems, reports to the Economic Policy Committee of the OECD, a committee of finance ministers from OECD countries. The members of WP3 include Canada, Britain, France, Germany, Italy, Japan, the Netherlands, Sweden, Switzerland, and the United States. See also GROUP OF TEN.

working poor People who work full-time but who do not earn enough to keep themselves above the POVERTY LINE. The 1973 federal *Working Paper on Social Security in Canada* proposed a number of measures to boost the income of the working poor. The one measure that was adopted was the boost in the family allowance, from an average of $7.21 per child to $20 per child.

workmen's compensation A form of income support for workers and their families in the event of injury or death on the job. Help is also provided in the form of medical and rehabilitation assistance. The cost of workmen's-compensation assistance is borne by employers, who are assessed according to the degree of risk in their industry.

The programs are run by the provincial governments, and date back to 1915, when Ontario became the first province to introduce legislation. Until then, injured workers and their families had had to sue employers for financial compensation for injuries or disease caused by the employer's negligence. This meant that many workers never received compensation because they could not afford the costs of going to court; if they could, they might have to wait several years for a settlement.

Under workmen's-compensation laws, workers cannot sue their employers, but are assured of compensation for themselves and their families. Benefits range from up to 75 per cent of average weekly earnings (with some adjustment for inflation) in cases of complete disability, to much less for partial disability, depending on the nature of the handicap. More than 90 per cent of Canadian workers are covered by workmen's compensation. Workmen's-compensation boards administer the funds, and determine which workers qualify for assistance and how much they shall get.

World Bank See INTERNATIONAL BANK FOR RECONSTRUCTION AND DEVELOPMENT.

World Economic Conference An international conference held in London from 12 to 27 June 1933, to try to cure the world depression and end the protectionist trade and banking policies that were only making a grave economic situation worse. The draft agenda proposed the restoration of the gold standard, along with tariff reductions and other forms of international economic co-operation. The conference followed British, French, and U.S. discussions, and was organized under the League of Nations as the International Conference on Monetary and Economic Questions. The conference attracted leaders from all over the world, including Prime Minister R. B. Bennett of Canada.

The conference was dealt a death blow by U.S. President Franklin Roosevelt, who vetoed a conference plan to stabilize major international currencies, even though all of his senior aides supported it. With the U.S. rejection of the plan for currency stabilization being read as a signal that the U.S. was not prepared to exercise international economic leadership, the conference lost its momentum. It failed to reach any agreement of importance on international trade or currency arrangements that would have ended the beggar-thy-neighbour policies of many countries, which were making the depression worse and preventing economic recovery. Following the collapse of the conference, the various trade and currency blocs reverted to their former practices.

World Food Conference A United Nations conference held in Rome, from 5 to 16 November 1974, to draft a set of policies to increase world food supplies and improve distribution systems, so as to avert future famines and end malnutrition in the less-developed countries. Canada was one of the participants. Some twenty policies were adopted, and two new bodies, the WORLD FOOD COUNCIL and the INTERNATIONAL FUND FOR AGRICULTURAL DEVELOPMENT, were created.

World Food Council A United Nations body created in 1974, following the WORLD FOOD CONFERENCE, that brings together agriculture and development ministers from thirty-six countries, including Canada, to discuss major issues in solving problems of world food production and security, and food-aid programs. It has attempted to persuade the less-developed countries to allocate more of their development resources to agriculture and to establish an International Emergency Food Reserve. It is the only U.N. ministerial body, and it has to some extent replaced the highly politicized FOOD AND AGRICULTURE ORGANIZATION as the most important forum for serious discussion between developed countries and less-developed countries on world food problems. See also INTERNATIONAL FUND FOR AGRICULTURAL DEVELOPMENT.

World Health Organization (WHO) A United Nations agency, based in Geneva, whose mandate is to improve health conditions world-wide and to raise health standards. Its specific activities include measures to prevent the spread of disease, emergency help to deal with health problems in areas struck by natural disasters, the establishment of safe and uniform standards for drugs, health research, the collection of statistics, and the improvement of health-care services in LESS-DEVELOPED COUNTRIES. Canada is an active member.

World Intellectual Property Organization (WIPO) A specialized international agency created in 1974 to protect patents, copyrights, trademarks, and other forms of INTELLECTUAL PROPERTY through international agreements and conventions. WIPO is attempting to establish uniform standards of protection for the owners of intellectual property. Canada is a member. The agency is based in Geneva.

world oil price See INTERNATIONAL OIL PRICE.

write-down The reduction in the value of an asset in a company's balance sheet, to reflect the real loss in value of the asset. For example, if a company takes over another company that ends up losing money, at some point its value will be reduced on the acquiring company's own books.

write-off The removal of an asset from a company's balance sheet, to reflect the fact that the asset is of no value.

x-efficiency A term used to describe the efficiency with which a firm is managed—in other words, how well it acquires and uses the various FACTORS OF PRODUCTION. A firm that operates at maximum x-efficiency is one that is operating at its minimum costs. But if it is protected from competition through monopoly, high tariffs, or subsidies, it is less likely to operate at maximum x-efficiency.

yardstick A standard used in making comparisons or in assessing performance. For example, a yardstick for desirable economic growth might be the average annual rate of economic growth for the previous decade. Productivity increases can be used as a yardstick against which to measure the inflation potential of wage increases.

year-end audit The annual review of a firm's or an organization's financial records—including its BALANCE SHEET and EARNINGS STATEMENT—that is conducted by outside accountants to verify their accuracy.

yield The annual return on an investment. It is expressed as a percentage of the cost or current market value of the investment. A $1,000 investment in a bond that pays $95 in annual interest has a yield of 9.5 per cent; the same $1,000 investment in a common share that pays $37.50 in dividends has an annual yield of 3.75 per cent. Fixed-interest bonds can only be sold to other investors during a period of rising interest rates if the price of the bond falls, and thus permits the yield to keep pace with rising interest rates. A $100 bond yielding 5 per cent might have to fall to, say, just under $67 if interest rates rose to 7.5 per cent; $5 is 7.5 per cent of $67. In a period of falling interest rates, bond prices will rise.

yield to maturity The total yield of a bond, including both the interest received on the bond's market value plus the amount of principal that will be received when the bond matures. This is an important concept when a bond is selling below or above its FACE VALUE.

Z

zero-base budgeting system (ZBBS) A system of budget planning that helps to evaluate the spending within government departments and to determine the relative importance of different government programs. Under this system, all spending is reviewed each time a budget is drawn up, with each department starting from a base of zero for each activity, instead of routinely assuming that every program will automatically be carried forward from one year to the next. This forces officials each year to justify all of their spending on any particular program, as well as to justify spending on a relatively unimportant, ongoing program instead of shifting the resources to a new and more important program.

zero population growth (ZPG) A population-growth rate of zero; the number of births and deaths in the population are equal. It means that each couple should have 2.11 children, since some children will die early in life or will not have children when they grow up.

zero-sum game A conflict game in which one participant can only gain at the expense of another; the sum of gains and losses adds to zero for every possible move. The situation is used in game theory to simulate conflicts between companies over markets, between nations over resources, or between Ottawa and the provinces over tax dollars.

zoning A planning tool used by municipal governments to control the type of development that takes place in different parts of the community. A community will zone some areas for industry, others for commerce, others for high-density housing, and others still for single-family housing. Zoning rules designate both the kinds of use permitted on a particular piece of land and the DENSITY of that activity. Zoning plans are usually drafted as by-laws. Since municipalities are creatures of the provinces, provincial governments have a veto over zoning decisions of municipal councils. Spot-rezoning refers to an exemption in the zoning for a particular piece of land.

The No-Homework Women's Bible Study: Group Hug Holidays

CHRISTINE TATE

This book belongs to:______________________________

The No-Homework Women's Bible Study: Group Hug Holidays

By Christine Tate

ISBN-13: 978-1497354395

DEDICATION

This book is dedicated to those we lost this year: our unborn child; Bill Tate, my husband's father; and Bebe Owen, my husband's grandmother. They went on before us this year to be with the Lord. We love you and miss you. Rest in peace and we'll see you in glory.

In Memoriam:

Bill Tate, November 11, 1937 - January 14, 2014

and

"Bebe" Owen, August 24, 1919 - March 6, 2014

and

Miscarriage, May 9, 2014

CONTENTS

GROUP CONTACT INFORMATION

NAME	PHONE	EMAIL

USING THIS STUDY GUIDE

The study group should be a safe, loving, supportive environment to explore various topics as God's guidance through the power of the Holy Spirit leads your group. Before beginning this study, please make sure all group members are aware of and follow these ground rules:

- What is shared in the group, stays in the group!
- Be a good listener and an even better Christian friend.
- Be patient, kind, loving, and respectful of other group members.
- Always give Godly advice.

Be sure to write your name in the space provided at the beginning of this book. This study involves passing books around from time to time and this will help books get back to their rightful owners.

It is helpful to choose a group leader to keep things on track and moving forward. At the first meeting, everyone should pass their book around the circle and write their contact information in each group member's book using the page provided.

Each weekly study begins with an **Ice Breaker**. The leader should coordinate the activity so that everyone has a chance to participate and share their responses. Then, moving on to the **Lesson**, take turns reading each section as you go around the circle. Next, the group leader guides the group through the **Discussion Questions**. The questions are designed to stimulate group interaction—tangents are encouraged! Be sure to write down specific prayer needs for group members and notes for personal growth in the space provided at the end of the weekly lesson. The **Weekly Challenges** are optional suggestions for group members to try during the week to extend the discussion into action. The session should end with the group leader leading everyone in the closing prayer given in the section titled **Closing Prayer.** A suggestion to encourage group bonding is for everyone to stand arm-in-arm in a circle for a "group hug" during the closing prayer.

If you enjoy this study and would like to find other studies written by Christine Tate or be notified when new studies become available, please visit my website at http://christinetate.webstarts.com. You can also follow my blog at http://christinetate.wordpress.com. Feedback is also encouraged as I always love to hear from my Christian sisters.

May God bless you, guide you and nurture you as you begin this journey!

AVAILABLE TITLES

The No-Homework Women's Bible Study: Group Hug

The No-Homework Women's Bible Study: Group Hug II

The No-Homework Women's Bible Study: Group Hug III

The No-Homework Women's Bible Study: Group Hug Holidays

COMING SOON IN 2014

The No-Homework Women's Bible Study: Group Hug IV

The No-Homework Women's Bible Study: Group Hug V

The No-Homework Women's Bible Study: Group Hug VI

HOLIDAY 1: CHRISTMAS PRIORITIZING

Ice Breaker *(15 minutes)*: Going in a circle, have the first person complete the sentence "When I get home today, I'm going to _______." Then, have the next person in the circle repeat the entire sentence adding "and _______", filling in their own add-on to the sentence making a chain of activities as you go around the circle. Continue until someone forgets the chain and ends the game. See how long your group can make the list before someone forgets the order!

Lesson *(10 minutes)*:

God's Promise: When you make God your priority, He'll take care of the everything else.

Scripture:

"Now when Jesus was born in Bethlehem of Judea in the days of Herod the king, behold, there came wise men from the east to Jerusalem, saying, Where is he that is born King of the Jews? For we have seen his star in the east, and are come to worship him." *Matthew 2:1-2*

"...and, lo, the star, which they saw in the east, went before them, till it came and stood over where the young child was. When they saw the star, they rejoiced with exceeding great joy. And when they were come into the house, they saw the young child with Mary his mother, and fell down, and worshipped him: and when they had opened their treasures, they presented to him gifts; gold, and frankincense and myrrh." *Matthew 2:9-11*

"I (Jesus) and my Father are one." *John 10:30*

"Now when Jesus heard these things, he said to him, Yet lack you one thing: sell all that you have, and distribute to the poor, and you will have treasure in heaven: and come, follow me. And when he heard this, he was very sorrowful: for he was very rich." *Luke*

18:22-23

"For the love of money is the root of all evil: which while some coveted after, they have erred from the faith, and pierced themselves through with many sorrows." *1 Timothy 6:10*

"Jesus said to him, You shall love the Lord your God with all your heart, and with all your soul, and with all your mind. This is the first and great commandment." *Matthew 22:37-38*

"You shall have no other gods before me. You shall not make any graven image, or any likeness of anything that is in heaven above, or that is in the earth beneath, or that is in the water under the earth. You shall not bow down yourself to them, nor serve them: for I the Lord your God am a jealous God..." *Exodus 20:3-5*

"Then said I to them, Cast you away every man the abominations of his eyes, and defile not yourselves with the idols of Egypt: I am the Lord your God." *Ezekiel 20:7*

"Love not the world, neither the things that are in the world. If any man love the world, the love of the Father is not in him." *1 John 2:15*

"But seek first the kingdom of God, and His righteousness; and all these things shall be added to you." *Matthew 6:33*

"And whatsoever you do in word or deed, do all in the name of the Lord Jesus, giving thanks to God and the Father by him." *Colossians 3:17*

"For where your treasure is, there will your heart be also." *Luke 12:34*

Commentary: The responsibilities of life can sometimes be overwhelming. There is not always enough time, money or energy to go around. Prioritizing is a necessary part of living an organized and successful life. Setting priorities is good for us because it leads to having achievable goals. God is clear that our first priority must always be Him. The wise men understood this well. When they saw the star in the east, they dropped everything and went to see baby Jesus in Bethlehem. Being wealthy and educated, they must have had many responsibilities at home that required their attention, but when the opportunity came to seek Jesus, all else paled by comparison. They had their priorities right and were rewarded with the opportunity to be in the presence of the Lord.

God does not approve when we put Him second. He is jealous for our hearts, minds and souls and does not share them with anyone or anything. Idols can easily become our priority and displace God as the primary focus in our lives. Simply put, an idol is an affair of the heart. Anything that takes your focus away from God is an idol. Idols can take many forms including cigarettes, food, money, possessions, goals, and other relationships. Wherever there is a distraction that causes you to put God second in your life, it needs to be removed or put in its proper place.

Idols can also become points of stress in our lives. When you put the wrong things first in your life, those things can become a detriment to your well-being. For example, when the pursuit of money occupies the primary place in your heart, you'll weary yourself trying to catch lightening in a bottle, always wanting more. The stress will eat you alive. Putting God first never causes that kind of stress. In fact, making God a priority relieves stress. When God is in His rightful place, you can rest in the comfort of knowing He has your back and is in control. So put God first, have a plan, do your best and then relax.

How we approach life says a lot about our priorities. Talk to someone for ten minutes and you'll instantly know where their heart is by what they talk about. God wants us to have full and interesting lives. As long as our interests don't become more important to us than He is, God will be content. God is the only priority that matters and nothing else is really worth the stress.

Discussion Questions *(30 minutes)*:

1. What are the main priorities in your life right now (i.e. money, time, relationships, health, school/work, family and taking care of yourself)? In what order are your current priorities? What do you want more of in your life? What could you do with less of in your life?

2. What does making God a priority mean to you? Is God a priority in your life? Where does He fit in? How do you make Him a priority?

3. What is your definition of an idol? Are there idols in your life that compete for first place with God?

4. What is the difference between setting a priority and living a priority? Why do you think people get distracted and spend time, energy and resources on things that don't matter?

5. Are you willing to break the idols in your life? How can you break the idols in your life? What concrete steps can you take to release your personal idols so God can occupy His rightful place in your life and heart? Will breaking the idols in your life cost you anything? Are you willing to pay the price?

Optional Weekly Personal Challenges:

- Meet with a professional financial planner to do some economic housekeeping.

- Get a credit card size "stress meter" card and put it in your wallet. Use it often to assess your stress level. When your stress level is high, close your eyes, take three deep breaths and mentally repeat Luke 12:34 ("For where your treasure is, there will your heart be also").

- Improve your vocabulary to improve your interpersonal communication skills by putting a Word-A-Day calendar prominently where you will see it every day. Commit to using the word of the day three times in everyday speech throughout the day.

- Swap your desk chair for a balance ball to gain core strength and balance and improve overall health. If you do not have a desk chair, sit on a balance ball while watching TV instead of using the couch.

Closing Prayer *(5 minutes)*:

Father, forgive us when we get our priorities mixed up. Teach us how to order our lives properly. Guide us as we continually strive to show You that You are the most important thing in our hearts, minds and lives. Without You, nothing else matters. In Jesus' name we pray, Amen.

Notes:

____

____

____

____

____

____

____

____

____

HOLIDAY 2: VALENTINE'S DAY
LEARNING TO LOVE

Ice Breaker *(15 minutes)*: Using only positive, loving, encouraging and nurturing words, pass your books in a circle and have each person write in the space provided below what they think makes you unique and why they love you. Be sure to check the name at the beginning of the book to confirm whose book you are working on. When all books have made a full circle, share the responses with the group.

I think you are unique because:

I love you because:

Lesson *(10 minutes)*:

God's Promise: God will always show His love for us by taking care of us and never leaving us.

Scripture:

"For God so loved the world, that He gave His only begotten Son, that whosoever believes in Him should not perish, but have everlasting life." *John 3:16*

"No, in all these things we are more than conquerors through Him that loved us. For I am persuaded, that neither death, nor life, nor angels, nor principalities, nor powers, nor things present, nor things to come, nor height, nor depth, nor any other creature, shall be able to separate us from the love of God, which is in Christ Jesus our Lord." *Romans 8:37-39*

"But God commends His love toward us, in that, while we were yet sinners, Christ died for us." *Romans 5:8*

"Beloved, let us love one another: for love is of God; and every one that loves is born of God, and knows God. He that loves not knows not God; for God is love." *I John 4:7-8*

"Know therefore that the Lord your God, He is God, the faithful God, which keeps covenant and mercy with them that love Him and keep his commandments to a thousand generations..." *Deuteronomy 7:9*

"I will never leave you, nor forsake you." *Hebrews 13:5*

"God is...a very present help in trouble. *Psalm 46:1*

"I love them that love me; and those that seek me early shall find me." *Proverbs 8:17*

"A new commandment I give to you, that you love one another; as I have loved you, that you also love one another. By this shall all men know that you are my disciples, if you have love one to another." *John 13:34-35*

"Though I speak with the tongues of men and of angels, and have not charity, I am become as sounding brass, or a tinkling cymbal. And though I have the gift of prophecy, and understand all mysteries, and all knowledge; and though I have all faith, so that I could remove mountains, and have not charity, I am nothing. And though I bestow all my goods to feed the poor, and though I give my body to be burned, and have not charity, it profits me nothing. Charity suffers long, and is kind; charity envies not; charity vaunts not itself, is not puffed up, does not behave itself unseemly, seeks not her own, is not easily provoked, thinks no evil; rejoices not in iniquity, but rejoices in the truth; bears all things, believes all things, hopes all things, endures all things. Charity never fails: but whether there be prophecies, they shall fail; whether there be tongues, they shall cease; whether there be knowledge, it shall vanish away. For we know in part, and we prophesy in part. But when that which is perfect is come, then that which is in part shall be done away. When I was a child, I spoke as a child, I understood as a child, I thought as a child: but when I became a man, I put away childish things. For now we see through a glass, darkly; but then face to face: now I know in part; but then shall I know even as also I am known. And now abides faith, hope, charity, these three; but the greatest of these is charity." *I Corinthians 13:1-13**

**Notice the use of the word "Charity" as a synonym for "Love" in the above verse.*

"For the poor shall never cease out of the land: therefore I command you, saying, you shall open your hand wide to your brother, to your poor, and to your needy, in your land." *Deuteronomy 15:11*

"Then shall the King say to them on his right hand, Come, you blessed of my Father, inherit the kingdom prepared for you from the foundation of the world: for I was hungry, and you gave me meat: I was thirsty, and you gave me drink: I was a stranger, and you took me in: naked, and you clothed me: I was sick, and you visited me: I was in prison, and you came to me. Then shall the righteous answer him, saying, Lord, when did we see you hungry, and fed you? Or thirsty, and gave you drink? When did we see you a stranger, and took you in? Or naked, and clothed you? Or when did we see you sick, or in prison, and came to you? And the King shall answer and say to them, verily I say to you, inasmuch as you have done it to one of the least of these my brothers, you have done it to me." *Matthew 25:34-40*

"But whosoever has this world's good, and sees his brother have need, and shuts up his bowels of compassion from him, how dwells the love of God in him? My little children, let us not love in word, neither in tongue; but in deed and in truth." *1 John 3:17-18*

Commentary: Scripture tells us to love our enemies (*Matthew 5:44*). But what does it really mean to love? Webster's dictionary defines "love" as:

LOVE: 1. A deep and tender feeling of affection for or attachment or devotion to a person or persons. 2. An expression of one's love or affection. 3. A feeling of brotherhood and good will toward other people. 4. A strong liking for or interest in something.

God defines "love" as:

LOVE: Greater love has no man than this, that a man lay down his life for his friends. (*John 15:13*)

Notice the contrast in definitions. Man defines love in terms of feelings and emotions. God defines love in terms of actions. Our culture would have us confuse the true nature of love with other inferior, false imitators such as warm fuzzy feelings, attraction, lust and passion. When God says He loves us, He isn't talking about any of those commonly accepted social terms representing love. He is telling us He is ready, at a moment's notice, to take action on our behalf as a sign of His commitment to us. He will be there for us and help us no matter what. He will never leave us or act in a way that is not in our best interests. Even when we are at our most unlovable, He will stay by our side with unshakable tenacity.

To God, love is honoring a commitment and fulfilling its obligations. We will not always feel like loving someone. It's in those times we must rely on doing what our head tells us is the right thing to do. If we wait until we feel like doing the loving thing, there is a good chance we may never do it. Ironically, by taking steps to commit loving actions, in turn, loving feelings usually follow. The important thing to remember is that in the kingdom of God, love is an action, not a feeling.

Discussion Questions *(30 minutes)*:

1. Why do you think society defines love as a feeling while God refers to love in terms of actions? Do you think God's actions in your life would be different if He applied the world's definition of love as a feeling instead of an action?

2. Are the loving relationships in your life based more on feelings or actions?

3. Why do you love God? Is it because of the things He can do for you? What would some of those things be? Would your feelings toward God change if His actions in your life changed?

4. What can you do to show God, through your actions, that you love Him? How can you serve others more?

5. How many biblical examples can you think of where love is represented through actions? How many biblical examples can you think of where love is represented as an emotion?

Optional Weekly Personal Challenges:

- Volunteer at a soup kitchen.
- Run an errand for someone else.
- Hug as many people as you can this week.
- Give someone a flower.

Closing Prayer *(5 minutes)*:

Father, we want to love others the way You love us. As we go through our week, reveal to us ways in which we can translate feelings of love into actions of love. In Jesus' name we pray, Amen.

Notes:

HOLIDAY 3: EASTER GROUPTHINK

Ice Breaker *(15 minutes)*: Below is a Mad Lib. Complete the passage by filling in the missing words with the type of word indicated. Then, share your unique interpretation of the passage with the group. An example is given at the back of the book if needed.

Once there was a _______________ (adjective) woman. Her name was _________________ (name of woman sitting to your left). Her ____________ (noun) was as beautiful as the _______________ (noun). When she ______________ (verb), people ________________ (verb) like _________________(noun). Everyone thought she was as _______________ (adjective) as _______________ (noun). God ____________ (verb) her very much and thought she was _______________ (adjective).

Lesson *(10 minutes)*:

God's Promise: When you find the inner strength to follow God's ways, even when it causes you to go against mainstream opinion, God will make straight your paths.

Scripture:

"When the morning was come, all the chief priests and elders of the people took counsel against Jesus to put him to death: and when they had bound him, they led him away, and delivered him to Pontius Pilate the governor. Then Judas, which had betrayed him, when he saw that he was condemned, repented himself, and brought again the thirty pieces of silver to the chief priests and elders, saying, I have sinned in that I have betrayed the innocent blood. And they said, What is that to us? See you to that. And he cast down the pieces of silver in the temple, and departed, and went and hanged himself." *Matthew 27:1-5*

"Now at that feast the governor was wont to release to the people a prisoner, whom they would. And they had then a notable prisoner, called Barabbas. Therefore when they were gathered together, Pilate said to them, Whom will you that I release to you? Barabbas, or Jesus which is called Christ? For he knew that for envy they had delivered him. When he was set down on the judgment seat, his wife sent to him, saying, Have you nothing to do with that just man: for I have suffered many things this day in a dream because of him. But the chief priests and elders persuaded the multitude that they should ask Barabbas, and destroy Jesus. The governor answered and said to them, Whether of the twain will you that I release to you? They said, Barabbas. Pilate said to them, What shall I do then with Jesus which is called Christ? They all said to him, Let him be crucified. And the governor said, Why, what evil has he done? But they cried out the more, saying, Let him be crucified. When Pilate saw that he could prevail nothing, but that rather a tumult was made, he took water, and washed his hands before the multitude, saying, I am innocent of the blood of this just person: see you to it. Then answered all the people, and said, His blood be on us, and on our children. Then released he Barabbas to them: and when he had scourged Jesus, he delivered him to be crucified." *Matthew 27:15-26*

"In all your ways acknowledge Him, and He shall direct your paths." *Proverbs 3:6*

"Ponder the path of your feet, and let all your ways be established." *Proverbs 4:26*

"And make straight paths for your feet, lest that which is lame be turned out of the way; but let it rather be healed. Follow peace with all men, and holiness, without which no man shall see the Lord: looking diligently lest any man fail of the grace of God; lest any root of bitterness springing up trouble you, and thereby many be defiled..." *Hebrews 12:13-15*

"Giving no offence in anything, that the ministry be not blamed..." *2 Corinthians 6:3*

"Finally, my brethren, be strong in the Lord, and in the power of his might. Put on the whole armor of God, that you may be able to stand against the wiles of the devil. For we wrestle not against flesh and blood, but against principalities, against powers, against the rulers of the darkness of this world, against spiritual wickedness in high places. Wherefore take to you the whole armor of God, that you may be able to withstand in the evil day, and having done all, to stand. Stand therefore, having your loins girt about with truth, and having on the breastplate of righteousness; and your feet shod with the preparation of the gospel of peace; above all, taking the shield of faith, wherewith you shall be able to quench all the fiery darts of the wicked. And take the helmet of salvation, and the sword of the Spirit, which is the word of God: praying always with all prayer and supplication in the Spirit, and watching thereto with all perseverance and supplication for all saints..." *Ephesians 6:10-18*

Commentary: Following the crowd against your better judgment never leads to good things. Judas cooperated with groupthink and eventually committed suicide over the guilt it caused him. The crowd is not always right. Might never makes right. God wants us to independently think for ourselves and form our own opinions based on biblical truths applied to the facts of the situation. When people are in groups, they tend to feel pressure to conform to the dominant opinions within the group and "go with the flow". The impulse is to go along to get along, even if that means compromising their own beliefs. This is not the plan God has for His children.

The crowd can be easily persuaded and manipulated by a few cunning people. Jesus was crucified because a few chief priests and elders manipulated the masses into thinking it was a good idea. Eloquent and persuasive leaders can make you question your own position and make the wrong position seem right. It's natural to doubt the validity of your own thoughts and beliefs when you are the one fish swimming against the stream, but we must always remember to put what God would have us do ahead of what others think we should do.

We are to give careful thought to our ways. Really look at the people you spend the most time with in your life and where your outside influences exist. When we connect ourselves with a Christian crowd, the peer pressure is likely to be for Godly things. When in the company of other Christians, if the group ever starts to head down the wrong path, the word of God can be used as a guiding force for direction. But even if the rest of the group ignores the word of God, you have a responsibility to apply what you know to be true. God holds you responsible for the decisions you make. Make sure they are the right ones and stand strong in your beliefs.

Discussion Questions *(30 minutes)*:

1. Discuss times in your life when you have experienced the urge to quietly follow the crowd. Was the crowd going in a Godly direction at the time? How did you respond to the situation?

2. What is the best way to issue your dissent when you are in a situation where you do not agree with the dominant direction of the group? Is there ever a time when silence is the appropriate answer?

3. Identify a time when you saw a leader manipulate a group of people. What techniques did that person use to persuade the crowd? Identify as many hallmarks of false leadership guidance as you can. How can we, as

Christians, protect ourselves from falling prey to false guidance?

4. How does false leadership compare and contrast to Godly leadership? What qualities should we look for and value in a leader?

5. False leadership guidance is not limited to secular situations. Drawing on your personal experiences as a Christian, discuss both good and bad examples of pastoral leadership within the church.

Optional Weekly Personal Challenges:

- Write a letter to the newspaper challenging the perspective of an opinion article with which you disagree.

- Take a "media fast" for one day this week. Avoid all external forms of information from computers, television, the radio, cell phones, iPads/android tablets, or newspapers. Spend that day meditating on the issues facing our country and/or your life and what God's word says about those issues.

- Identify something in your life you are currently working on and make a simple plan for its completion. Draw a straight line and map out the linear process you should take, being sure to mark significant milestones along the way.

- Get a "Shepherd's Guide" for your local area and support local Christian owned businesses. The "Shepherd's Guide" is a free directory of Christian businesses and can usually be found at entrances to Christian bookstores or online (http://www.shepherdsguide.com/).

Closing Prayer *(5 minutes)*:

Father, we confess our weaknesses to You and ask for Your strength to always do and say the right thing in any situation according to Your holy word. Enlighten us through the power of the Holy Spirit to clearly know that which is right and that which is wrong. In Jesus' name we pray, Amen.

Notes:

HOLIDAY 4: MEMORIAL DAY
FREE WILL

Ice Breaker *(15 minutes)*: Below are seven verses from the Bible. Choose your favorite verse from the list and share with everyone why you chose it. How does it speak to your heart? What important message do you feel it highlights?

"I can do all things through Christ who strengthens me." *Philippians 4:13*

"For God so loved the world, that he gave his only begotten Son, that whosoever believes in him should not perish, but have everlasting life." *John 3:16*

"For I know the thoughts that I think toward you, says the Lord, thoughts of peace, and not of evil, to give you an expected end." *Jeremiah 29:11*

"The Lord is near to them that are of a broken heart; and saves such as be of a contrite spirit." *Psalm 34:18*

"Yea, though I walk through the valley of the shadow of death, I will fear no evil: for you are with me; your rod and your staff they comfort me." *Psalm 23:4*

"Judge not, that you be not judged." *Matthew 7:1*

"Trust in the Lord with all your heart; and lean not to your own understanding." *Proverbs 3:5*

Lesson *(10 minutes)*:

God's Promise: Choose God and He will choose you.

Scripture:

"Behold, I stand at the door, and knock: if any man hear my voice, and open the door, I will come in to him, and will sup with him, and he with me." *Revelation 3:20*

“Seek the Lord while he may be found, call upon him while he is near: let the wicked forsake his way, and the unrighteous man his thoughts: and let him return to the Lord, and he will have mercy upon him; and to our God, for he will abundantly pardon.” *Isaiah 55:6-7*

“Behold, I set before you this day a blessing and a curse; a blessing, if you obey the commandments of the Lord your God, which I command you this day: and a curse, if you will not obey the commandments of the Lord your God, but turn aside out of the way which I command you this day, to go after other gods, which you have not known.” *Deuteronomy 11:26-28*

“...I have set before you life and death, blessing and cursing: therefore choose life...” *Deuteronomy 30:19*

“And if it seem evil to you to serve the Lord, choose you this day whom you will serve; whether the gods which your fathers served that were on the other side of the flood, or the gods of the Amorites, in whose land you dwell: but as for me and my house, we will serve the Lord.” *Joshua 24:15*

“...Repent, and turn yourselves from all your transgressions; so iniquity shall not be your ruin...For I have no pleasure in the death of him that dies, says the Lord God: wherefore turn yourselves, and live.” *Ezekiel 18:30-32*

“Now the word of the Lord came to Jonah the son of Amittai, saying, Arise, go to Nineveh, that great city, and cry against it; for their wickedness is come up before me. But Jonah rose up to flee to Tarshish from the presence of the Lord, and went down to Joppa; and he found a ship going to Tarshish: so he paid the fare thereof, and went down into it, to go with them to Tarshish from the presence of the Lord. But the Lord sent out a great wind into the sea, and there was a mighty tempest in the sea, so that the ship was like to be broken. Then the mariners were afraid...And he (Jonah) said to them, Take me up, and cast me forth into the sea; so shall the sea be calm to you: for I know that for my sake this great tempest is upon you...So they took up Jonah, and cast him forth into the sea: and the sea ceased from her raging...Now the Lord had prepared a great fish to swallow up Jonah. And Jonah was in the belly of the fish three days and three nights." *Jonah 1:1-17*

"Your kingdom come, Your will be done in earth, as it is in heaven." *Matthew 6:10*

Commentary: God calls us to Him and it is our decision to respond to His call or not. He values freedom and free will. It is not in His nature to compel anyone to worship Him. Although He wants us to make the right choice and choose Him, if someone chooses not to follow Him, He respects that choice. We all have the free will to choose to become a believer or not.

Once we make the decision to follow Christ, as believers, we are then called to voluntarily surrender our own will and allow His will to be accomplished in our lives. We pray this whenever we pray the Lord's Prayer. When we erringly exercise our free will to follow our own devices, natural consequences follow. Jonah, having first made the choice to follow God, then chose not to cooperate with God's will and reaped the unfortunate consequences of that choice.

Our forefather's understood that all men should be free to come to God in their own way when they are ready. Based on this principle, they championed the pursuit of religious freedom. Their choice wasn't free though. It came with a heavy price in terms of many lives lost over the course of many battles to create a country where people could be free to worship or not worship as they chose. Because they were following God's will though, they were ultimately victorious.

Memorial Day is more than just a time to remember those who went on before us to be with the Lord. It is a time to celebrate free will. It is a blessing to have the freedom of choice to make our own decisions. We can choose life or we can choose death. We can choose bondage or freedom. We can choose to follow God's rules or our own. We can choose His leadership for our lives or lean on our own understanding. In the end, the choice is ours.

Discussion Questions *(30 minutes)*:

1. What does free will mean to you? How much free will do you think we have? Do we have free will to choose to come to God or does God determine who will come to Him?

2. Have you chosen God? If you have, what do you think is God's will for your life? Why do you think people don't choose God? Does God have a will for non-believers? How do you think it makes God feel when people exercise their free will to not be a part of His kingdom?

3. Do you think believers relinquish their right to free will once they make the commitment to follow God? Or, put another way, do we retain our free will to sin and make choices that are contrary to His will?

4. Why do you think God asks us to submit to His will? Why do you think God allows humans to have free will? Do you think there are times when God does not allow us to exercise our free will?

5. Do you think you have a say in God's plan for your life? Does God factor your prayer requests in when He designs His will for your life? What requests have you made to God that might influence how He directs your steps?

Optional Weekly Personal Challenges:

- Read "The Book of Questions" by Gregory Stock. Form your answers based on what you believe God would have you choose to do in each situation.

- Place a statue of an angel or the Ten Commandments in a conspicuous place on your property or on your apartment door.
- Audibly, at a respectful volume, pray before your meal when you dine out in public.
- Make a long list of healthy food choices and pin it on the front of your refrigerator. Choose to eat only foods from that list when you are hungry.

Closing Prayer *(5 minutes)*:

Father, we thank You for the freedom You give us to make our own choices. Give us the strength to choose to resist temptations that would take us in a direction contrary to Your will for us. We ask that You give us the wisdom, discernment and strength of conviction to always choose Your path instead of following the desires of our own heart. In Jesus' name we pray, Amen.

Notes:

HOLIDAY 5: FOURTH OF JULY SPARKLE AND SHINE!

Ice Breaker ***(15 minutes)*****:** If you were a flower, what would you look like? Draw yourself as a flower and share it with the group along with an explanation of why you drew the flower the way you did.

Lesson ***(10 minutes)*****:**

God's Promise: God thinks you are an amazing woman and enjoys watching you sparkle and shine like fireworks on the Fourth of July.

Scripture:

"But now, O Lord, You are our Father; we are the clay, and You our potter; and we all are the work of Your hand." *Isaiah 64:8*

"I will praise You; for I am fearfully and wonderfully made:

marvelous are Your works; and that my soul knows right well." *Psalm 139:14*

"Keep me as the apple of the eye..." *Psalm 17:8*

"...for he that touches you touches the apple of His eye." *Zechariah 2:8*

"We love Him, because He first loved us." *1 John 4:19*

"Behold, what manner of love the Father has bestowed upon us, that we should be called the sons of God..." *1 John 3:1*

"The Lord has appeared of old to me, saying, Yea, I have loved you with an everlasting love: therefore with loving kindness have I drawn you." *Jeremiah 31:3*

"For you are an holy people unto the Lord your God: the Lord your God has chosen you to be a special people unto Himself, above all people that are upon the face of the earth." *Deuteronomy 7:6*

"Fear not, little flock; for it is your Father's good pleasure to give you the kingdom." *Luke 12:32*

"But God commends His love toward us, in that, while we were yet sinners, Christ died for us." *Romans 5:8*

"Wherefore you are no more a servant, but a son; and if a son, then an heir of God through Christ." *Galatians 4:7*

"Are not five sparrows sold for two farthings, and not one of them is forgotten before God? But even the very hairs of your head are all numbered. Fear not therefore: you are of more value than many sparrows." *Luke 12:6-7*

"...and as the bridegroom rejoices over the bride, so shall your God rejoice over you." *Isaiah 62:5*

"...He will rejoice over you with joy; He will rest in His love, He will joy over you with singing." *Zephaniah 3:17*

"Finally, brethren, whatsoever things are true, whatsoever things are honest, whatsoever things are just, whatsoever things are pure, whatsoever things are lovely, whatsoever things are of good report; if there be any virtue, and if there be any praise, think on these things." *Philippians 4:8*

"Wherefore come out from among them, and be separate..." *2 Corinthians 6:17*

"...but I have chosen you out of the world,..." *John 15:19*

"And be not conformed to this world: but be transformed by the renewing of your mind, that you may prove what is that good, and acceptable, and perfect will of God." *Romans 12:2*

"And it came to pass, that on the eighth day they came to circumcise the child; and they called him Zacharias, after the name of his father. And his mother answered and said, Not so; but he shall be called John." *Luke 1:59-60*

Commentary: You are special to God. Embrace and celebrate your uniqueness. Let your distinctiveness be as bold and bright as the stars. If God had wanted us to all be alike, He would have made us all alike. But He didn't. He rejoices in our individuality and we should too.

More importantly, Christians are not like others who are of this world and we should not try to be like them. Elizabeth, who was an out-of-the-box thinker, did not name her son after his father as was the custom of those days. She bucked the trend and it pleased God. He took pleasure when she found the inner personal strength to be the unique creature He created her to be.

There is a tendency for people to value things more when their cost is higher. When people have nice things they treasure, they take great care with them. Our cost was high to God. He paid for us with His son's life so we could be with Him. Since the price God paid for us was much more expensive than a brand new, fully loaded Lexus, doesn't it make sense that He would value us that much more?

See yourself through His eyes as the wondrous creation He made you to be. You are a one-of-a-kind precious jewel to Him. Guide your mind to only think positive things about yourself. Don't believe the lies Satan whispers to your heart. See yourself the way God sees you. Now go out there and sparkle and shine!

Discussion Questions *(30 minutes)*:

1. Describe yourself through God's eyes. How do you think God sees you, personally, when He looks down from His heavenly throne and gazes at you? What, specifically, about you does He take pleasure in? How did He make you unique? What strengths/skills/talents/abilities did God give you to be His special creation? Do you have any emotional scars blocking your ability to see yourself the way God sees you?

2. What are you doing in your life to prove God correct in how He sees you? How are you using your strengths/skills/talents/abilities in your life right now to God's glory?

3. What thoughts does Satan whisper to your heart to make you believe you are less than how God sees you? How do you combat those thoughts? What verse(s) do you focus on to banish the lies when those thoughts come? What else can you do to limit the impact when others express their lack of approval towards you?

4. Is your self-image based on the approval of others or the approval of God? Why do you think other people have an impact on the way people see themselves? How does the way God sees you impact your self-image?

5. Discuss the difference between love and approval.

Optional Weekly Personal Challenges:

- Come up with three adjectives for this sentence "God thinks I am _____, _____, and _____." Repeat the sentence to yourself three times a day for a week.
- Go an entire day without looking in the mirror. During that time, mindfully focus on how your actions make you feel.
- Choose a favorite photo of yourself and place it in a spot where you will be reminded of the best that you can be every time you look at it.
- Set a personal goal for you to achieve based on your own special talents and abilities (i.e. run a marathon, complete a cross-stitch project, build a birdhouse, etc.). For every day that you take a step towards achieving the goal, put $1 in a special cookie jar. After you complete the goal, use the money to treat yourself to something special (i.e. facial, manicure/pedicure, massage, lunch or movie with friends, etc.)
- Go to a paint-your-own pottery place and meditate on the first scripture verse given while you paint (*Isaiah 64:8*).

Closing Prayer *(5 minutes)*:

Father, we thank You for loving us enough to pay the ultimate price through Jesus' death on the cross. Teach us how to honor that sacrifice by fearlessly being the best that You created us to be. Show us how we can sparkle and shine for You in our lives. In Jesus' name we pray, Amen.

Notes:

HOLIDAY 6: LABOR DAY
GIVE IT YOUR BEST SHOT

Ice Breaker *(15 minutes)*: Have everyone in the group attempt to accomplish the following tasks:

1. Pat your head and rub your stomach at the same time. Switch hands and repeat the task using opposite hands from your first attempt (i.e. if your right hand was patting your head and left hand was rubbing your stomach the first time, use your left hand to pat your head and right hand to rub your stomach on your second attempt).

2. Touch your tongue to your nose.

3. Wiggle your ears.

4. Lick your elbow.

Lesson *(10 minutes)*:

God's Promise: When you commit to excellence and hard work in all that you set your hand to accomplish, God sees from His heavenly throne and rewards the intent of your heart.

Scripture:

"By the sweat of your brow you will eat your food until you return to the ground..." *Genesis 3:19*

"...if any would not work, neither should he eat." *II Thessalonians 3:10*

"Go to the ant, you sluggard; consider its ways and be wise!" *Proverbs 6:6*

"Ants are creatures of little strength, yet they store up their food in the summer..." *Proverbs 30:25*

"Laban said to him, Just because you are a relative of mine, should you work for me for nothing? Tell me what your wages should be." *Genesis 29:15*

"Do not hold back the wages of a hired worker overnight." *Leviticus 19:13*

"Be content with your wages." *Luke 3:14*

"Slaves, submit yourselves to your masters with all respect, not only to those who are good and considerate, but also to those who are harsh." *1 Peter 2:18*

"Servants, be obedient to them that are your masters according to the flesh, with fear and trembling, in singleness of your heart, as to Christ; not with eye service, as men pleasers; but as the servants of Christ, doing the will of God from the heart; with good will doing service, as to the Lord, and not to men: knowing that whatsoever good thing any man does, the same shall he receive of the Lord, whether he be bond or free." *Ephesians 6:5-8*

"Whatever you do, work at it with all your heart, as working for the Lord, not for men." *Colossians 3:23*

"Whether therefore you eat, or drink, or whatsoever you do, do all to the glory of God." *1 Corinthians 10:31*

"Commit your works to the Lord, and your thoughts shall be established." *Proverbs 16:3*

"I have glorified You on the earth. I have finished the work which You have given me to do." *John 17:4*

"I can do all things through Christ who strengthens me." *Philippians 4:13*

"His lord said to him, Well done, good and faithful servant; you have been faithful over a few things, I will make you ruler over many things. Enter into the joy of your lord." *Matthew 25:23*

"Wherefore seeing we also are compassed about with so great a cloud of witnesses, let us lay aside every weight, and the sin which does so easily beset us, and let us run with patience the race that is set before us, looking to Jesus the author and finisher of our faith; who for the joy that was set before him endured the cross, despising the shame, and is set down at the right hand of the throne of God." *Hebrews 12:1-2*

"Come to me, all you that labor and are heavy laden, and I will give you rest." *Matthew 11:28*

Commentary: W-o-r-k is not a bad, four letter word. God expects us to work while we are here passing time on earth. He admonishes us to not be lazy and work diligently at whatever He calls us to do. People think of work as being gainfully employed, but it is much more than that. Housewives don't bring home a paycheck, but they still work very hard. Work is putting effort into completing the task God has chosen for you to accomplish. It can take on many forms, but it is still work.

God tells us that work should be rewarded. Sometimes the reward is non-monetary in nature and comes in the form of praise and appreciation. Mothers don't get paid, but they deserve recognition for all they do for their families. Like a paycheck, that recognition should be issued frequently and in a timely manner. If you are a business owner, you have a responsibility to pay your employees and do so in a timely manner. All employees deserve a paycheck even when employees are family members. No one should be taken advantage of for free labor, regardless of their relationship to others or nature of their work.

Always put your best foot forward. Do everything, no matter how small the task or job, as if you were doing it for God. We are not to make excuses for failing to try our hardest. The terms of our employment or situation do not dictate the amount of effort we choose to apply. Whatever we do, God wants us to give it our very best effort. That's why we put our best clothes on to go to church on Sunday. It shows God that we respect Him enough to put our best foot forward for Him. Yes, He will still love us just as much if we show up in church in sweatpants and He would rather have us there dirty than not at all, but isn't God worth more than just your least efforts?

Discussion Questions *(30 minutes)*:

1. What task has God given you to complete at this time in your life? Are you content with that path or are you trying to change directions?

2. Do you cut corners in your life right now? Where? How often do you give something "just enough" instead of "good enough"? If God were physically standing in front of you, would that change how you go about different tasks in your life? What excuses do you tell yourself to justify less than enthusiastic efforts?

3. If today were judgment day, could your actions stand on their own in front of God and be worthy of His approval? What would you wish you had done better?

4. How many times a day do you put your best foot forward? Is it possible to put forth too much effort?

5. Is your commitment to excellence affected by the company you keep? Do you find yourself performing better when you are around certain people rather than other people? What causes you to relax your efforts?

Optional Weekly Personal Challenges:

- To strengthen your natural abilities, do some brain training exercises this week by using the opposite side of your body more than you usually do to complete simple everyday tasks. For example, if you usually brush your teeth with your right hand, brush them with your left hand every time you brush this week. Engage in "brain training" type games that can be found on websites like www.lumosity.com.

- Show up to work 5 minutes early and leave 5 minutes late. If you don't have a job outside the home, show up to church 5 minutes early and be the last one out the door when service is over. Arrive at your appointments (doctor/dental/car repair, etc.) 5 minutes early.

- Schedule your day in advance. Account for where you will be and what you will be doing at what times. Then stick to the schedule.

- Get dressed up for church this Sunday.

Closing Prayer *(5 minutes)*:

Father, forgive us for failing to please You by giving less than our best efforts in the tasks You give us. Motivate us as we go through our daily lives to always put our best foot forward and do all to Your glory. In Jesus' name we pray, Amen.

Notes:

____

____

____

____

____

____

____

____

HOLIDAY 7: HALLOWEEN
GOOD VS. EVIL

Ice Breaker *(15 minutes)*: Pick a number. It can be any number you like. Write the number in the first space provided (a), then follow the directions that follow (b-e). When everyone has completed the instructions, compare your answers.

a. Write your number:____

b. Add the next highest number to it:____ + ____ = ____ (i.e. if you chose 7, your equation would be 7 + 8 = 15)

c. Add 9 to the total you received for the answer to b:____ + 9 =

____

d. Divide the total for line c by 2:____ / 2 = ____

e. Subtract your original number from line a:____ - ____ = ____

If you completed the above steps correctly, your answer will be 5.

Lesson *(10 minutes)*:

God's Promise: You will always triumph over trials and temptations the devil throws at you when you choose God's team.

Scripture:

"There was a man in the land of Uz, whose name was Job; and that man was perfect and upright, and one that feared God, and eschewed evil...Now there was a day when the sons of God came to present themselves before the Lord, and Satan came also among them. And the Lord said to Satan, Whence come you? Then Satan answered the Lord, and said, From going to and fro in the earth, and from walking up and down in it. And the Lord said to Satan, Have you considered my servant Job, that there is none like him in the earth, a perfect and an upright man, one that fears God, and eschews evil? Then Satan answered the Lord, and said, Does Job fear God for naught? Have not You made an hedge about him, and about his house, and about all that he has on every side? You have blessed the work of his hands, and his substance is increased in the land. But put forth Your hand now, and touch all that he has, and he will curse You to Your face. And the Lord said to Satan, Behold, all that he has is in your power; only upon himself put not forth your hand. So Satan went forth from the presence of the Lord." *Job 1:1, and 6-12*

"You believe that there is one God; you do well: the devils also believe, and tremble." *James 2:19*

"For the time will come when they will not endure sound doctrine; but after their own lusts shall they heap to themselves teachers, having itching ears; and they shall turn away their ears from the truth, and shall be turned to fables." *2 Timothy 4:3-4*

"And he said to them, I beheld Satan as lightning fall from heaven." *Luke 10:18*

"...for Satan himself is transformed into an angel of light." *2 Corinthians 11:14*

"How are you fallen from heaven, O Lucifer, son of the morning! How are you cut down to the ground, which did weaken the nations!" *Isaiah 14:12*

"Be sober, be vigilant; because your adversary the devil, as a roaring lion, walks about, seeking whom he may devour..." *I Peter 5:8*

"I can do all things through Christ who strengthens me." *Philippians 4:13*

"Now may the God of hope fill you with all joy and peace in believing, that you may abound in hope, through the power of the Holy Ghost." *Romans 15:13*

"If God be for us, who can be against us?" *Romans 8:31*

"And the God of peace shall bruise Satan under your feet shortly. The grace of our Lord Jesus Christ be with you. Amen." *Romans 16:20*

Commentary: Like the Ice Breaker today, we don't always understand how everything works. But just because we don't understanding something doesn't mean it doesn't exist. While it's hard for many to comprehend the concept of true evil, make no mistake, it does exist just as surely as God exists. And the evil has a name: the devil (a.k.a. Satan, Lucifer, Beelzebub, Baal, Prince of Darkness, the Dragon, and the Old Serpent).

Yes, there is a devil. The devil and his demons are as much a part of our religion as God and His angels. Contrary to popular media presentations, the devil is not a red, hoofed and horned creature with a pointy tail and pitchfork who is holed away in a secret, fire-filled pit somewhere deep within the earth. Rather, he is a handsome deceiver who spends his time actively traveling the face of the earth interacting with humans for the purpose of causing people to fall away from God. And if he can trip up a mature Christian, that's the lottery jackpot. The devil was God's best and brightest creation and truly a force to beware.

Too often Christians blame God for the devil's work in their lives. It's easy to forget there are two sides to the classic battle between good and evil. As a Christian, God is always for you and the devil is always against you. When things go wrong, and they will, don't blame God for the devil's handiwork. People tend to immediately assume God is at fault. It is important to remember God wants only good things for us and the devil desires only bad things for us. Remember Job? If the Devil hadn't wanted to first test Job, God would not have allowed the process to proceed. Even after God allowed Job to be tested, God did not take one action to initiate any of the tests that followed. All of Job's misfortune happened at the hand of the devil. Satan tried to get God to do his dirty work. God's response was that the devil had permission to test Job, but only by the work of the devil's own hand (*Job 1:12*). Evil really does exist. It is Satan who is to blame when things go wrong. Not God.

Discussion Questions *(30 minutes)*:

1. Is it appropriate for Christian children and adults to actively participate in a holiday, Halloween, that has become synonymous with the devil and all things dark in nature? Does God approve of zombie, vampire and witch costumes? Have you ever participated in alternative Halloween events such as Harvest parties?

2. Do you think it is safe to play with Ouija boards, Runes, Tarot cards or go to psychics? Have you ever unwittingly invited the devil into your life? Is there such a thing as white witchcraft or "good" witches?

3. Do ghosts exist? Where do they come from and what is their purpose? Have you ever experienced any poltergeist type activity?

4. Explore your beliefs about the devil. Does he really exist? Where does he exist? What does he look like? What is his relationship to both God and man? What role do you think the devil has had in your life? Has he ever tempted or tested you? Have you ever blamed God for things the devil did?

5. Discuss different ways the devil tries to make Christians falter in their faith. Do you always recognize the devil's tactics? Do you think the devil pursues all Christians equally, or does he have "high value" targets of particular importance to him?

6. Discuss ways Christians can stand strong in resistance to the devil. Is there a specific prayer you pray or verse you recite when Satan comes knocking? Do you have trusted Christian counsel to guide you through obstacle courses the devil sets up for you?

Optional Weekly Personal Challenges:

- Volunteer to assist at a Harvest party through a local church. If churches in your area don't have Harvest parties, organize one.
- Apologize to God for a time when you were angry with Him and/or blamed Him for something unpleasant in Your life.
- Remove from your home any items that are pagan or ungodly in nature (i.e. images of skulls and crossbones, statues or pictures of gods from other cultures, games such as Ouija boards, Runes and Tarot cards, erotic romance novels, etc.)
- Buy yourself a cross necklace and wear it. If you don't wear jewelry, buy or make a T-shirt to wear that is Christian in nature (i.e. a shirt with the slogan "Jesus' Girl" or "I'm going to heaven. Are you?")

Closing Prayer *(5 minutes)*:

Father, we proclaim You as the one true God and seek to know Your face. We know You only have good in mind for us and ask Your forgiveness for times when we may have unfairly blamed You for the devil's actions. Grant us that we may see clearly who is truly to blame when troubles befall us in the future. In Jesus' name we pray, Amen.

Notes:

____

____

____

____

HOLIDAY 8: THANKSGIVING
HELPING OTHERS

Ice Breaker *(15 minutes)*: Which symbol below do you think best represents the Christian faith? Choose your favorite religious symbol from the pictures given and share with the group why it is your favorite.

Lesson *(10 minutes)*:

God's Promise: God will always give you discernment to handle any situation He brings into your life.

Scripture:

"Enter into His gates with thanksgiving, and into His courts with praise: be thankful to Him, and bless His name. For the Lord is good; His mercy is everlasting; and His truth endures to all generations." *Psalm 100:4-5*

"Now the end of the commandment is charity out of a pure heart, and of a good conscience, and of faith unfeigned..." *I Timothy 1:5*

"For the poor shall never cease out of the land: therefore I command you, saying, You shall open your hand wide to your brother, to your poor, and to your needy, in your land." *Deuteronomy 15:11*

"Give to him that asks you, and from him that would borrow of you turn not away." *Matthew 5:42*

"Then shall the righteous answer him, saying, Lord, when did we see you hungry, and fed you? Or thirsty, and gave you drink? When saw we you a stranger, and took you in? Or naked, and clothed you? Or when saw we you sick, or in prison, and came to you? And the King shall answer and say to them, Verily I say to you, inasmuch as you have done it to one of the least of these my brethren, you have done it to me." *Matthew 25:37-40*

"But if any provide not for his own, and especially for those of his own house, he has denied the faith, and is worse than an infidel." *I Timothy 5:8*

"Then shall the kingdom of heaven be likened to ten virgins, which took their lamps, and went forth to meet the bridegroom. And five of them were wise, and five were foolish. They that were foolish took their lamps, and took no oil with them: but the wise took oil in their vessels with their lamps. While the bridegroom tarried, they all slumbered and slept. And at midnight there was a cry made, Behold, the bridegroom comes; go out to meet him. Then all those virgins arose, and trimmed their lamps. And the foolish said to the wise, Give us of your oil; for our lamps are gone out. But the wise answered, saying, Not so; lest there be not enough for us and you: but go rather to them that sell, and buy for yourselves." *Matthew 25:1-9*

"For even when we were with you, this we commanded you, that if any would not work, neither should he eat." *2 Thessalonians 3:10*

Commentary: God wants all of His children to have thankful hearts and spirits of gratitude. But Thanksgiving isn't just about being thankful: it's about giving others a reason to be thankful by helping them. The Indians had love and compassion enough in their hearts to help the Pilgrims survive that long, first winter in America, and they weren't even Christians. How much more must we, knowing the one, true living God, help others when we have a chance to do good. God always wants us to be a blessing to as many people as possible as often as possible.

Most Christians understand the concept of helping others. What is sometimes overlooked is when to stop giving. Be open to the possibility that the day may come when it is time to change the way you help someone. Sometimes, for one reason or another, it is appropriate to walk away from a situation. If what you are doing is having a negative impact on your own family, that contradicts God requirement of us to take care of our own family first. It takes humility to admit there are times when you are not the best person to help someone or deal with a situation. In those instances, the help you give them is getting them to the right person or resources who are more appropriate to help them. There may also be times when you are the right person to help them, but they refuse to help themselves. In such circumstances, God doesn't hold us endlessly accountable to be their permanent enabler. Sometimes releasing them to experience the natural, God-given consequences of their own actions may be the healthiest thing you can do for them to motivate them to do their necessary part and step up to the plate.

There is an old saying "People come into our lives for a reason and a season". When the time comes for you to release a situation, don't feel guilty for letting go. Know that you have done your best with the resources God gave you to work with, then do the best thing you can do for the person: pray for them. Just because you are not able to help them anymore on a physical level doesn't mean you can't still be a prayer warrior for them on a spiritual level. Never underestimate the power of prayer. It's always the best help you can give anyone!

Discussion Questions *(30 minutes)*:

1. Have you ever experienced a situation where you helped someone and they weren't thankful for your assistance? Has anyone ever rejected your attempts to help them?

2. List as many ways as you can for Christians to dispense charity both at home, within the community and around the world.

3. Do you feel there is ever a time to "cut someone off"? Under what circumstances? How would you define a toxic circumstance or toxic relationship?

4. How would you feel emotionally if you had to stop helping someone? Are you comfortable walking away from a situation where you have become emotionally invested?

5. If you perceived it was time to release a particular situation, how do you think God would want you to go about extricating yourself from further involvement?

Optional Weekly Personal Challenges:

- Make 30 small, handmade crafts. Then go door to door delivering them at a local nursing home.

- Make an extra contribution to your church's Missions program and then say a special prayer over the ministry.

- Sponsor a child in a foreign country.

- Participate in a Shoebox gift giving program such as the one found at http://www.samaritanspurse.org/what-we-do/operation-christmas-child/.

Closing Prayer *(5 minutes)*:

Father, we thank You for the opportunities You give us to help others. We ask for Your wisdom to know how best to help those you bring into our lives and for Your strength, discernment and grace when it is time to release a situation and move on to Your next assignment for us. In Jesus' name we pray, Amen.

Notes:

WEEK 3 MAD LIB EXAMPLE

Once there was a **beautiful** woman. Her name was **Nancy**. Her **skin** was as beautiful as the **sun**. When she **smiled**, people **melted** like **butter**. Everyone thought she was as **sweet** as **sugar**. God **adored** her very much and thought she was **awesome**.